International Marketing

International Marketing
a cultural approach

———— ♦♦♦ ————

JEAN-CLAUDE USUNIER

Université Pierre Mendès-France

PRENTICE HALL

New York London Toronto Sydney Tokyo Singapore

First published 1993 by
Prentice Hall International (UK) Limited
Campus 400, Maylands Avenue
Hemel Hempstead
Hertfordshire, HP2 7EZ
A division of
Simon & Schuster International Group

Designed by Claire Brodmann
Typeset in 10/12pt Times
by P&R Typesetters Ltd, Salisbury, UK

**Printed in Great Britain by
Redwood Books, Trowbridge, Wiltshire**

Library of Congress Cataloging-in-Publication Data

Usunier, Jean-Claude.
    International marketing : a cultural approach / Jean-Claude
Usunier.
        p.   cm.
    Includes bibliographical references and index.
    ISBN 0–13–194580–7 (pbk)
    1. Export marketing—Social aspects.   2. International business
enterprises—Social aspects.   3. Intercultural communication.
I. Title.
HF1416.U85   1993
658.8'48—dc20   92-33999
                                                                CIP

British Library Cataloguing in Publication Data

A catalogue record for this book is available from
the British Library

ISBN 0–13–194580–7 (pbk)

3   4   5   97   96   95   94   93

Contents

Foreword   xi
Acknowledgements   xiii
Introduction   1

PART I *Scanning the environment: The cultural variable in international marketing*   9

1   Culture and marketing   11
1.1 Marketing: borrowed concepts and practices   12
1.2 Culture and consumer behaviour   15
1.3 Marketing as exchange and communication: cultural relativity   20
1.4 Customization of marketing strategies to local contexts   22
1.5 Business negotiation and sales practices   27
     Appendix 1   Teaching materials   30
     A1.1   Teaching note: Learning by self-teaching   30

2   The cultural process   38
2.1 Culture: definition(s)   39
2.2 Elements of culture   41
2.3 Culture and nationality   46
2.4 Culture and competence   50
2.5 Culture and social representations   53
     Appendix 2   Teaching materials   54
     A2.1   Critical incident: An old lady from Malaysia   54
     A2.2   Critical incident: The parable   55
     A2.3   Reading: Body ritual among the Nacirema   55

3   Cultural dynamics   63
3.1 An inventory of basic differences in cultural assumptions   63

3.2 Culture-based cognitive styles and attitudes towards action   67
3.3 National cultures and organization   73
3.4 Cultural borrowing and change in societies   81
3.5 Cultural hostility   85
      Appendix 3   Teaching materials   88
      A3.1   Critical incident: An American in Vietnam   88
      A3.2   Exercise: Seven cultures of the South Sea   89
      A3.3   Cross-cultural scenario: Inshallah   91
      A3.4   Cross-cultural interaction: Engineering a decision   91
      A3.5   Cross-cultural interaction: Opening a medical office in Saudi
             Arabia   92

4   Culture, language and communication   98
4.1 Language as a basis for culture and communication: the Whorfian
      hypothesis   99
4.2 Verbal communication: explicit versus implicit contextual messages   102
4.3 Non-verbal communication and meta-communication   105
4.4 Ethnocentrism, stereotypes and misunderstandings in intercultural
      communication   108
      Appendix 4   Teaching materials   115
      A4.1   Reading: Language and time patterns: the Bantu case   115
      A4.2   Case: Supreme Canning   117
      A4.3   Case: Doing business in China: a success in getting paid   119
      A4.4   Case: When international buyers and sellers disagree   120
      A4.5   Critical incident: Scandinavian Tools Company   121
      A4.6   Exercise: Following directions   123
      A4.7   Exercise: World picture test   125
      A4.8   Rationales for section A3.3 (cross-cultural scenario) and
             sections A3.4 and A3.5 (cross-cultural interactions)   126

5   Cross-cultural market research   131
5.1 Establishing cross-cultural equivalence   132
5.2 Research approaches: emic versus etic   135
5.3 Translation equivalence   141
5.4 Comparability of data   143
5.5 Representativeness and comparability of national/cultural samples   146
      Appendix 5   Teaching materials   149
      A5.1   Case: Eliot Greeting Card Company   149
      A5.2   Exercise: Hair shampoo questionnaire   156
      A5.3   Exercise: Slogans and colloquial speech   160

PART II *Global marketing or intercultural marketing?*   167

6   Globalization of markets?   169
6.1 Is the consumer becoming global?   170

6.2   Is there a globalization of competition?   177
6.3   International marketing strategies: are they becoming global?   179
      Appendix 6   Teaching materials   185
      A6.1   Case: Parker Pen   185
      A6.2   Case: Lakewood Forest Products   188

7   Intercultural marketing   194
7.1   Why global strategies exist, but global marketing does not   194
7.2   Intercultural marketing as an implementation framework for a global
      business strategy   205
7.3   Intercultural marketing means commerce   209
      Appendix 7   Teaching materials   213
      A7.1   Case: IKEA   213
      A7.2   Exercise: Dangerous Enchantment   217

8   Adaptation or standardization of product policy: a model for
      choice   222
8.1   A framework for the choice between adaptation and standardization
      based on product attributes   223
8.2   The physical attributes   223
8.3   The service attributes   227
8.4   The symbolic attributes   229
      Appendix 8   Teaching materials   233
      A8.1   Case: Lestra Design   233
      A8.2   Case: Irish Cream O'Darby   243

9   Management of images related to nationality and brand name   248
9.1   National images diffused by the product's origin and by its brand
      name   249
9.2   Consumer product evaluation according to country of origin   251
9.3   National, international and global brands   262
      Appendix 9   Teaching materials   270
      A9.1   Case: Soshi Sumsin Ltd   270
      A9.2   Case: Derivados de Leche SA   272

PART III   *Marketing in the intercultural environment*   281

10   The critical role of price in relational exchange   283
10.1 Bargaining   284
10.2 Price and consumer evaluations   288
10.3 International price tactics   292
      Appendix 10   Teaching materials   298
      A10.1   Case: Saito Importing Company   298
      A10.2   Case: Riva International   299
      A10.3   Critical incident: Taman SA   301

11   International distribution and sales promotion   305
11.1 The cultural dimension of distribution channels: the case of Japanese
      Keiretsus   306
11.2 Criteria for choosing foreign distribution channels   315
11.3 Incentives for sales representatives: a cross-cultural analysis   317
11.4 Sales promotion: other customs, other manners   322
      Appendix 11   Teaching materials   326
      A11.1   Case: ComputerLand in Japan   326
      A11.2   Case: Aunt Sarah's Fried Chicken   327
      A11.3   Case: Sunbeam in Italy   330
      A11.4   Critical incident: Setco of Spain   335

12   International promotion and advertising   340
12.1 Marketing communications are strongly culture-based   342
12.2 Technological advances will partially break down cultural resistance   353
12.3 Technological, economic and regulatory advances in progress open the
      door for more specific and segmented marketing   357
12.4 The globalization of advertising agencies   358
      Appendix 12   Teaching materials   362
      A12.1   Case: Levi Strauss Company: World-wide advertising strategy
              or localized campaigns?   362
      A12.2   Case: Agencia de Publicidad Aramburu SA (APA)   366
      A12.3   Case: Nove Ltd   375
      A12.4   Critical incident: Excel and the Italian advertising campaign   379
      A12.5   Critical incident: The Brenzy nouveau has arrived!   381
      A12.6   Exercise: Borovets – a Bulgarian ski resort   384

PART IV   *Intercultural marketing negotiations*   389

13   Intercultural marketing negotiations I   391
13.1 The dynamics of trust in relational marketing   392
13.2 The influence of culture on some important aspects of marketing
      negotiations   398
13.3 Who is seen as a credible partner?   400
13.4 Culture-based dispositions for being integrative in negotiations   403
13.5 Existence of a common rationality between the partners   408
13.6 Oral versus written agreements as a basis for trust between the parties   410
      Appendix 13   Teaching materials   414
      A13.1   Case: McFarlane Instruments   414
      A13.2   Negotiation game: Kumbele Power Plant   416
      A13.3   Note: Cases and teaching materials for intercultural
              negotiation simulations   420

14	Intercultural marketing negotiations II	430
14.1	The cultural relativity of business time	430
14.2	Time-based misunderstandings in international business negotiations	433
14.3	Some elements of the national style of business negotiation	435
	Appendix 14 Teaching materials	443
	A14.1 Negotiation simulation: Lump Sum	443
	A14.2 Case: Tremonti SpA	446
15	Bribery in intercultural marketing negotiations	453
15.1	Facts	·454
15.2	Methods	455
15.3	The process of illegal payments	456
15.4	Implicit economic explanations for illegal payments	458
15.5	The means of redistribution: an important aspect	462
15.6	The responsibility of the payer	463
15.7	Negative aspects of illegal payments in the recipient country	466
15.8	Reducing illegal payments	468
	Appendix 15 Teaching materials	468
	A15.1 Case: Houston Oil Supply	468
	A15.2 Case: G. H. Mulford Pharmaceutical Company	471
Postscript		477
Author index		481
Subject index		488

Foreword

Trade and war, or both together, have been the oldest reasons for contact between cultures. Trade was a primary motive for the voyages of discovery that have been made during the past three thousand years. Archaeological excavations show evidence of objects having been traded with foreign peoples hundreds of miles away as far back as 1000 BC. International marketing, therefore, should be nothing new. The book in front of you, as one of the first attempts to cover the subject more than just superficially, does not need any excuse.

Jean-Claude Usunier's book brings together two currents in the management literature. One deals with marketing and market research; the other deals with culture and organizations. Few marketing texts so far have done more than just pay lip service to the phenomenon of culture. I have an impression that many international marketing practitioners carry considerably more sophisticated notions about culture than the marketing texts did; but they were not the people who wrote the books.

The literature on culture and organization has boomed in the past twenty years, both on a popular and on a more fundamental level. Its findings have only slowly been recognized by the marketing theorists; possibly because the reward systems of university departments unfortunately often lead to intellectual inbreeding, and subdisciplines publish in their own professional journals which are rarely read by their colleagues in the next corridor of the university building.

International market research has produced interesting comparative data, but the market research profession tends to be secretive. Usually its data are only sold at consulting prices to people unlikely to use them for more fundamental research. Thus, very rarely has any secondary research been carried out on comparative market research data. In a few cases where I have managed to get – or buy – access to international market research data, I was able to point to revealing correlations with other data that were freely available in the libraries. And this could have helped the users of the market research reports to make sense out of the findings. However, few market researchers seem to be interested in these more fundamental relationships. There is an unfortunate culture of superficiality in the market research profession that has not helped the growth of its field into a science. I can understand that new data are handled in a proprietary fashion, but once the data have lost their news value – say, after six months – couldn't they be made available to bonafide researchers?

In world history, countries that developed political and economic power have always subsequently become exporters of ideas. The leading position of the United States in the post-Second World War decades has led to a dominance of US-developed management theories and techniques. Recently these have been supplemented with Japanese theories and techniques, reflecting Japan's growing importance on world markets. When it comes to the study of culture, this kind of single-sourcing of ideas is dysfunctional. By its very nature, the study of culture should be fed by ideas from all around the world.

Management and marketing are cultural artefacts, and therefore should also be studied cross-nationally. This is not obvious to everybody. In 1980 I published an article with the subtitle 'Do American theories apply abroad?' Today this is no longer a taboo question, but at the time my article raised a storm of protests from the one side, and a massive request for reprints from the other – primarily from Canada.

The fact that Jean-Claude Usunier's work was first published in French and now appears in an English translation is still unusual in the management and marketing field. It guarantees a fresh look at the problems. The author is intimately familiar with both the English-language and the French-language literature on the subject, which has enabled him to write a truly international text on International Marketing. Both he and his publisher should be congratulated on their venture.

Geert Hofstede
Maastricht, the Netherlands

Acknowledgements

I wish to acknowledge the help of various institutions which during the last ten years have provided me with the opportunity to teach international marketing and have encouraged me to put more and more emphasis on the cultural dimension: Boeki Kenshyu Centaru (International Institute for Studies and Training), Fujinomiya (Japan), Helsinki School of Economics (Finland), Ecole Supérieure de Commerce de Paris (France), Irish Continuing Education Authority (Dublin, Ireland), Universidade Federal do Rio Grande do Sul (Porto Alegre, Brazil), Universidade Federal da Paraiba (Joao Pessoa, Brazil), University of California at Los Angeles (United States), Programme Marcom (Sofia, Bulgaria), Université Laval (Quebec, Canada), Ecole des Hautes Etudes Commerciales de l'Université de Lausanne (Canton de Vaud, Switzerland).

Throughout these assignments I have had the opportunity to teach students and trainees of fifty-five different nationalities. Talking with them, during and after class sessions, enabled me to learn a lot, and I am grateful to them. Finally I would like to express my grateful thanks to some colleagues who have been instrumental in helping me with their advice and support at various stages of this book: Michael Hay (London Business School), Francis Léonard (Ecole des Hautes Etudes Commerciales de l'Université de Lausanne), Robert Locke (University of Hawaii), Reijo Luostarinen (Helsinki School of Economics), Constantin Napoléon-Biguma (Faculté Libre de Sciences Economiques, Lille), Richard Thorpe (Manchester Polytechnic), José de La Torre (University of California at Los Angeles and INSEAD), Dany Van den Bulcke (RUCA, Universiteit Antwerpen, Belgium), Gérard Verna (Université Laval, Quebec), Jyoti Gupta (Ecole Supérieure de Commerce de Paris) and Jim Corbett (Ecole Supérieure des Affaires, Grenoble).

'Parker Pen' [see pp. 185–7], 'Lakewood Forest Products' [see pp. 188–91] and 'IKEA' [see pp. 213–16] from International Marketing, second edition by Michael R. Czinkota and Illka A. Ronkainen, copyright © 1990 by The Dryden Press, reprinted by permission of the publisher.

I also wish to thank Cathy Peck, Julia Helmsley, Jill Birch and Frances Dedrick from Prentice Hall (UK) who have been instrumental in editing this book and Stuart Maslen for his insightful and patient help in translating and restyling. I remain responsible for any errors and shortcomings in the book.

Introduction

Dear reader,
You may start reading at almost any chapter, since each one is designed to be almost self-sufficient.[1] The purpose of this introduction is to explain what my goals were in writing the book, and also the ways in which you may use it. It aims to be a sort of 'travel companion' for people constantly involved in business relations with foreigners (at least to them), either as export and international marketers or because they are involved in multinational marketing. It is intended both for students (mostly MBA students) and practitioners. It attempts to provide readers with a framework for capitalizing on their own personal experiences in the field of international marketing, with particular emphasis on the development of behavioural skills in intercultural business relationships.[2]

International trade: the ignorance of national culture

One of the seminal texts on international trade is Chapter XXII of David Ricardo's *On the Principles of Political Economy and Taxation* (1817), which deals with foreign trade. The text dates back to the early nineteenth century, and explains how countries may derive benefits from developing international trade rather than simply producing and trading within their own domestic market. Ricardo considers the case of two countries, England and Portugal, and two types of goods, wine and sheets, as a model. The law of comparative or relative advantage conveys a powerful message: a country which is at a competitive disadvantage for both products still benefits from participating in international trade because it finds a better exchange ratio between the two goods than that provided by its domestic market. By concentrating efforts and resources on the product in which they have a relative advantage, rather than by exporting one product and importing the other, countries can probably increase their national welfare and certainly global welfare.

An implicit assumption underlies this model: that products and consumers' tastes, habits and preferences are identical in the two countries (and therefore in all the countries of the world).[3] However, England was producing very little wine at that time, and it is doubtful that British wine had the same physical characteristics, alcohol content or taste

1

as Portuguese wine. Furthermore, the English usually drink beer in pubs, whereas the Portuguese prefer to drink *vinho verde* or *porto* while listening to *fado*. Similarly, the preferences of the English and the Portuguese were probably distinct enough to enable them to recognize clearly their own home-produced sheets as they had different fabrics and embroideries: natives of the two countries would have been fully aware of the origin of the sheets on which they were sleeping.

All this contemplation of 'wine and sleep' probably appears rather anecdotal and naïve. But the cultural variable – mainly related to *national* culture – has been somewhat neglected in international trade, whether on theoretical grounds or for practical purposes. In international trade theory, which is almost purely economics-based, it has been ignored from the very start. Classical economists and their successors do not like 'national culture', and here one can detect an aura of inertia and resistance to change: their theories favour commonalities rather than differences, and they are based on utility maximization as opposed to identity building.

Ricardo's theory was contemporaneous with a major change in Britain's economic policy: the introduction of the Corn Laws. Ricardo demonstrated that England should reduce its customs duties and thereby open up its domestic market to foreign agricultural commodities – especially those from the Colonies which were more cost-competitive – in order to specialize in certain manufactured goods to be exported world-wide. Nevertheless the rationale behind this type of decision appears rather simplistic when real people are facing its real-world consequences: rapid deruralization, lack of self-sufficiency in food supplies for the country as a whole, changes in the landscape, the emergence of new urban social strata and so on.

From this initial assumption, it is apparent that the defence of cultural identity was inextricably linked to protectionist attitudes in international trade. This is illustrated in France by the *lois Méline*, introduced at the end of the nineteenth century out of a desire to protect French food supplies and French farmers, even though this meant higher costs for the consumer. This was also true in Germany where the writings of Friedrich List promoted a nationalistic approach to economic growth. In practice it is difficult to make a sharp distinction between the protection of national/cultural interests (people's own identity being largely enhanced by what they consume) and those of certain industries which may deprive consumers of bargains or even deprive them of the opportunity to buy particular products on the basis of questionable arguments.

Hence there is a natural tendency to ignore the cultural variable, except as a rather anecdotal and residual explanation. This tendency, which is very visible in the case of international trade theory, has been largely inherited by international business and marketing, where culture remains a weak and subsidiary element. This is exactly how partisans of market globalization – inevitably including Theodore Levitt (1983) – see the cultural variable: as a vestige of the past, in a world where we all tend to adopt a sort of 'modern' life-style.

Cultural differences are not easy to define

Practitioners as well as theoreticians do not always appreciate cultural differences, for a number of converging reasons. First, the consequences and results of such differences are obvious but they are not simple to analyze, describe or categorize. Second, even if there are many practical consequences, the precise process by which behaviour is moulded is never fully determinable. Moreover, the efforts which have been made to describe and analyze the influence of culture on various aspects of business life often appear stereotypical, anecdotal and only indirectly productive. In the fields of organization and management there have been some real breakthroughs, such as the work by Hofstede (1980) on the impact of national culture on management styles. But in the field of marketing, and more generally *business relations*, the intercultural approach has received less attention.

It is a simpler and (seemingly) more practical solution to pretend, as the supporters of globalization do, that cultural differences tend to disappear, and the world market(s) should therefore be treated as a 'global village'. They are not entirely correct, because their statements are principally normative ones, the bases of which are not fully supported by empirical evidence, as will be shown in Chapter 6. However, it is perfectly true that many universal elements do exist among national cultures. Culture is not viewed here as an all-purpose, static explanation in which people remain a fixed entity: what is described in the book is the dynamic, borrowed and reinvented nature of cultural materials. The *cultural identity factor* is also emphasized here.

Italians seem to be similar to Germans when both are compared to the Japanese. But if one is interested in observing and identifying what is original in these three national cultures, it soon becomes obvious that – at a deep level – they are incommensurable. They may be compared by some precise variables and quantified dimensions, but this gives no indication of their unity and internal coherence. A fingerprint is composed of the convolutions of the skin at the tip of a phalanx, and in this sense a fingerprint is universal. But every individual digital imprint is different for every member of humankind: in this sense they have a pure and incomparable identity.

A cultural approach to international marketing

This book is a training instrument for international marketing. It is assumed that the reader understands basic marketing concepts. There are references to a number of articles and books which relate to several aspects of marketing (market research, marketing management, sales-force management, marketing communications, etc.) and international marketing. But it is not a classical text of consumer marketing with an emphasis on world markets. It adopts a cultural approach to international marketing, which has two main dimensions:

1. A cross-cultural view. This method *compares* national marketing systems and local commercial customs in various countries. It aims to emphasise what is country-specific and what is universal. This type of analysis is essential for the preparation and implementation of marketing strategies in different national contexts.
2. An intercultural view, which is centred on the study of *interaction* between business people, buyers and sellers (and their companies) who have different national cultural backgrounds. This intercultural view also relates to the interaction between products

(and their physical and symbolic attributes) from a particular nation-culture (i.e. a country with a definite and homogeneous national culture) and the consumers from a different nation-culture, and to the interaction between messages (conveyed by brands and advertising) and consumers from a different nation-culture. To this extent it is interaction in its broad sense: not only between people, but also between people and messages, and people and products.

Companies cannot afford to spend vast resources on training people in interculturalism in marketing, even when they appreciate that it is a key element. They prefer to hire people with such skills from the labour market. In my opinion the development of such skills is mostly an individual goal. Potential demand is rapidly increasing with the multi-nationalization of businesses: the opening up of the internal market in the European Community,[4] for instance, will magnify the need for marketing/sales executives gifted with a true ability to communicate and interact with their colleagues in multicultural teams. This book is therefore primarily concerned with behavioural training for the international marketing executive, with text and learning materials included in each chapter.[5]

The word 'commerce' was used in the title of the French edition of this book, *Commerce entre cultures*, as well as the term 'marketing' in the subtitle, *Une Approche Culturelle du Marketing International*.[6] These two words have their own meaning. 'Commerce' is a nineteenth-century word relating to exchange activities, for which the *Collins Dictionary* (1990, p. 192) gives the following definitions:

> 1. the activity embracing all forms of the purchase and sale of goods and services; 2. social relations; 3. *Arch.* sexual intercourse.

Commerce has a wider sense than marketing, but in the United States the concept of marketing and marketing activities has tended to broaden over the last fifteen years. An article by Richard P. Bagozzi (1975) develops the idea of 'marketing as exchange', where marketing becomes the science of exchange. Keegan (1984, p. 3) also stresses that:

> The focus of marketing in the strategic concept has shifted from the customer or the product to the firm's external environment. It is recognized that knowing everything there is to know about the product, is not enough. To succeed, let alone survive, organizations need to *understand their customer in context*.

When the word 'commerce' is used in this text, it refers to the complex dimensions of business relationships entwined with interpersonal relations. The use of the word 'marketing' systematically encompasses a sense of its American origin. This is not done to deny its real value but to facilitate a better understanding of the way in which it was imported into and customized within various countries. Marketing techniques, methods, theories and concepts have achieved real success world-wide because they are a powerful tool in increasing markets, securing market share, satisfying customer needs and raising profits. I have tried to show the cultural relativity of marketing concepts and practices, and possibly their limits and implementation conditions, and not to question them as a whole.

In the course of trading one should make friends. I am not a firm believer in the adage that the consumer should be treated like royalty. It is widely used in books on achieving excellence, and is mostly an organizational creed which aims to strengthen the motivation of teams of employees and sales personnel in order to serve the customers better. The best aphorism would probably be: 'A client is a friend'. It sets notions of equality and shared knowledge, and a halo of positive relations which brings mutual rewards, in a faithful and confident atmosphere. These notions are more in line with the normative reality of what a good business relationship should be, where long-term reciprocity enhances trust between the parties. Similarity between people is a strong facilitator of friendly relations. When this basic condition is not met (that is, in the international context as opposed to the domestic market), friendship with the client is much more difficult to establish, maintain and develop. When one is faced with this challenge, intercultural marketing skills make sense.

The basic assumption behind this book is that culture penetrates our inner being subconsciously and at a deep level. World cultures share many common features. Nevertheless they all display a unique style when such common elements are combined: kinship patterns, education systems, valuation of the individual and the group, emphasis of economic activities, friendship patterns, time-related organization patterns, the criteria for aesthetic appreciation, and so on. The examples which are used in this book are by their very nature eclectic. I have chosen those examples which seem to be concurrently the most striking and pertinent. I have borrowed from a wide range of sources in as much detail as possible.

The first chapter presents the cultural dimension of international marketing. The following three chapters are devoted to the cultural variable, in attempting to define it, to delineate the components of culture and finally to emphasize its dynamic nature. The last chapter of Part One looks at international market research from a cross-cultural methodological perspective. The process of culture often involves borrowing, and therefore a degree of mixing and dilution; but elements borrowed from another culture are chewed, swallowed and digested in a unique manner, which ultimately makes them elements of *pure identity*. Although these chapters have been placed at the beginning of the book, there is no inherent reason why they should necessarily be read first. The choice is yours.

Part Two deals with the globalization of markets and its general impact on international marketing strategies, with special emphasis on the issues relevant to product policies: adaptation/standardization dilemmas, brand names for international markets, images of the country of origin and their possible use in supporting sales.

Part Three relates to a number of marketing decisions: pricing, distribution and communication. Emphasis has deliberately been placed on the culture-based approach to such decisions: that is why, for instance, I accentuate bargaining (with its cultural variations) in the chapter on pricing, and the Japanese *keiretsu* distribution system in the chapter on distribution decisions.

Part Four relates to international marketing negotiations, giving some attention to the questions of bribery and business ethics in international marketing.

It was a deliberate decision not to treat various aspects of the classical topics of international business and marketing, especially international market entry schemes (exporting, licensing, joint ventures), in order to keep the book as structured as possible. The book is written from a European viewpoint with a French flavour. No international marketing textbook may be considered universal, and this one is no exception. It is written by a Frenchman, certainly in a much less pragmatic and issue-orientated style than most international marketing textbooks. Statements may often be considered as value judgements, since they are not as frequently backed by facts and empirical evidence as is the case in English and American textbooks and therefore it may sometimes look unusual to native English-speaking readers. I believe they have to consider it as part of the message of the book: it is a more contextual, and therefore less explicit, relationship with the reader.

The chapters are followed by cases, exercises, critical incidents, and so on. An instructor's manual is available. Since several translated editions of this book will be published (in French, English, German, Italian and Japanese), it may be used in cross-cultural training settings where people may read approximately the same materials in their own native language.

A method for the comprehension of foreign environments

I did not choose to highlight a particular area of the world. This could have proved useful for an in-depth analysis of a particular culture, but I am not an area specialist. With a few exceptions this will also be true of the readers of this book. With the globalization of competition and the ease of travelling and telecommunication, there are opportunities for travel to many countries and for trade with a large proportion of them. Moreover, multinational companies do not favour the specialization of their international personnel in a specific cultural area, since they are supposed to have a fairly general interaction ability.

I have no wish to describe cultures exhaustively, either from an insider's point of view or objectively. What I have attempted to provide for the reader is *a method for dealing with intercultural situations in international marketing*. The underlying postulate of this book is that international business relationships have to be built on solid foundations. Transaction costs in international business are high: only a stable and firmly established link between business people will enable them to overcome disagreements and conflicts of interest. In international marketing it is advisable to be methodical and long-term orientated, to select a limited number of partners and opportunities and to develop them to their fullest extent.

Notes

1. The notes in each chapter direct the reader to further references. They also provide the reader with some additional explanations and other guidance for more in-depth analysis.
2. In order to improve the content of this book I welcome readers' comments, suggestions and reports of personal experiences which relate to any of the chapters. Please write to the author at this address: ESA, BP 47, F-38040 Grenoble cedex 9, France.
3. There are many other implicit assumptions in Ricardo's text, which is both visionary and confused: (1) gains from trading internationally must offset transportation, customs duties and

trading costs; (2) there are constant returns to scale; (3) products are identical or are at least perceived as such, by both consumers and merchants; (4) information must be available and sufficient for merchants in the two countries to be aware of the potential gains deriving from international trade; (5) no other financial or government restriction or market barrier limits international trade for these products. It is easy to see that this list largely covers the main aspects of international trade as it has developed since Ricardo's time: (1) cost and quality improvements in international transportation; (2) experience effects (related to increasing returns to scale); (3) the marketing approach to international trade; (4) the development of international tele-communications networks; (5) the domination of the free-trade model world-wide; the steady decrease of tariff barriers (at least in developed countries) under the influence of GATT; the creation of free-trade areas and customs unions; the problem of non-tariff barriers.

4. The new Maastricht Treaty (which promotes political union through European citizenship), European economic and monetary union (February 1992) and the creation of the European Economic Space (between EEC and EFTA countries, October 1991) will certainly increase the pace towards a common multicultural market in Europe.

5. Learning materials include additional readings, cross-cultural exercises and scenarios, cases, critical incidents, and teaching notes. An instructor's manual is available, with teaching aids and suggestions for additional learning materials.

6. It is planned that a German version of this book, co-authored with Björn Walliser, and a Japanese version, co-authored with Hiroshi Kosaka, will be available a few months after this edition is published.

References

Bagozzi, Richard P. (1975), 'Marketing as exchange', *Journal of Marketing*, vol. 39, no. 4, pp. 32–9.

Hofstede, Geert (1980), *Culture's Consequences: International differences in work related values*, Sage: Beverly Hills, CA.

Keegan, Warren J. (1984), *Multinational Marketing Management*, 3rd edn, Prentice Hall: Englewood Cliffs, NJ.

Levitt, Theodore (1983), 'The globalization of markets', *Harvard Business Review*, vol. 61, May–June, pp. 92–102.

Ricardo, David (1817), *On the Principles of Political Economy and Taxation*, ch. XXII, 'Bounties on exportation and prohibitions on importation', in Piero Sraffa (ed.) (1951), *The Works and Correspondence of David Ricardo*, Cambridge University Press: Cambridge.

◆◆◆

PART ONE

Scanning the environment
the cultural variable in international marketing

1

•••

Culture and marketing

This chapter takes an initial census of the impact of culture on the different aspects of market survey, strategy and marketing activities, and therefore refers to later chapters where these questions are dealt with in greater detail. It also provides definitions for the words 'trade', 'marketing' and 'sale', which will be helpful throughout this book.

The first basic link between culture and marketing, which is almost never mentioned,[1] is the initial entrenchment of marketing in one particular national culture: that of the United States. Marketing concepts and practices have been enthusiastically adopted in many other countries, even those which do not share the same cultural background. All countries have their traders and merchants, and since marketing is a powerful tool for developing and controlling existing and new businesses, they may rightfully borrow it. But in doing so, they transform it and then integrate it into their own culture. The first section of this chapter will focus on some aspects of the borrowing mechanism. There will then follow a description of some of the main variations in consumer behaviour across cultures; it is assumed that consumers are individuals influenced by their own cultural background.

Marketing is an exchange process involving communication: accordingly section 1.3 focuses on the way in which cultural background influences communication and exchange. Two examples are used to illustrate this: the role of emotions in Japanese marketing, and the role of symbolic linkage between objects and persons in the Italian style of marketing.

Section 1.4 is devoted to the reassessment of marketing strategies, where they have to be determined and implemented in different cultural contexts. These differences relate to such aspects as competition avoidance patterns, market organization, relations between distribution channels, producers and consumers, and finally the legal environment of marketing. International marketing strategies and their implementation are treated at greater length in the second and third parts of this book.

Section 1.5 of this chapter deals with a topic that is not often tackled in international marketing literature: marketing and business negotiations. Inevitably a marked cultural variance exists in the area of crucial personal skills development; the last three chapters of the book are devoted to intercultural negotiation and business management.

1.1   Marketing: borrowed concepts and practices

Marketing concepts and practices were initially and for the most part developed in the United States, and have continued to spread because of the success of large US-based multinational companies on world-wide consumer markets. They have been popularized by Philip Kotler's *Marketing Management* (1991) in its numerous translations and editions. Still, nowhere is their influence so strong as in the United States. In France, where much has been borrowed from America, about ten thousand students attend a basic course in marketing each year. This compares to three hundred thousand in the United States. Since the US population is four times that of France, the *marketing intensity* of the United States, on the figures mentioned, is still seven or eight times that of France. The same ratios hold true for most developed countries outside the United States. In addition to quantitative differences in marketing intensity across countries, there are also qualitative differences in content, style and practices.

The success of the term 'marketing' gave a new image to trade and sales activities in many countries where it had often previously been socially and intellectually devalued:[2] in Ancient Greece the god Hermes, messenger of the Olympian gods, was also the god of communication, exchange, trade and merchants (and also thieves).[3] Despite the success and the seemingly general acceptance of the term 'marketing', there have been some basic misconceptions of it in many countries, especially developing ones (Amine and Cavusgil, 1986). For instance, a survey of Egyptian business people indicates a clear lack of understanding as to what the term really means (El Haddad, 1985). Either managers do not understand what marketing is all about or, if they do, they tend to believe that it has no application to their business. In fact they see marketing as the mere fact of selling, or the promotion of sales. Although 'marketing' has been imported (as a word, and even as a sort of slogan), its cultural roots and its precise meaning have been forgotten.

In Japan, most of the books on marketing management were borrowed from the United States and then translated directly without much adaptation. Moreover market survey techniques, the underlying concepts and the wording of questions, as well as questionnaire, interview and sampling techniques, were all widely imported. As the Dutchman Van Raaij said (1978, p. 699):

> Consumer research is largely 'made in the U.S.A.' with all the risks that Western American or middle-class biases pervade this type of research in the research questions we address, the concepts and theories we use and the interpretations we give.

In fact it is more frequently only the word itself, rather than its whole sense and the social practices it involves, that has been imported. It is normal to find large gaps between the rhetoric of marketing and the actual selling practices adopted by companies. Marketing did not really replace long-established commercial practices in many countries (Allen, 1978): it superimposed itself on local selling practices and merged with them.

In French companies one often finds both a *directeur du marketing* (vice-president, marketing, in the United States) and a *directeur commercial* (sales and distribution). However, in the United States a vice-president, marketing, deals not only with marketing strategy but also with sales and the sales force. The most common form of organization in France has a *directeur commercial* who is actually responsible for a large part of what Americans call 'marketing' as a functional area. The duties of a *directeur commercial* are primarily the supervision of sales, distribution outlets and sales representatives, as well as the management of customer relations. The *directeur du marketing* will most often be responsible for marketing surveys and/or communication. The organizational relationship between the *directeur du marketing* and the *directeur commercial*, whether parallel or hierarchical (the marketing department is usually subordinate to the sales department) will not encourage them to collaborate. Managers tend to see marketing as somewhat 'intellectual', with little practical orientation, directed towards long-range targets and the strategic consideration of markets, or even as being preoccupied solely with advertising strategy, a rather 'indirect' method of influencing the market.

Marketing: American vocabulary, information sources and concepts

The imported nature of marketing concepts and practices is clearly evidenced by the vocabulary, information and reference sources, and the origin of literature on the subject, all of which demarcate it as an area of knowledge. Marketing vocabulary is now used world-wide: everybody is familiar with the words 'mailing', 'media planning' and 'merchandising'. Even though efforts have been made in some countries to localize these words,[4] they have generally failed. For instance, in France hardly anyone uses the official word *la mercatique* (it sounds ugly). It is legitimate and indeed wise to retain an imported word in its original form until its total integration as a concept has been realized. This evidence of borrowing allows the foreign origin of the concept to be kept in mind and thereby, paradoxically, improves its chances of successful localization.[5] Data and information sources (Nielsen panels, for instance) and consultancy businesses (advertising agencies, market consultants) are mostly of American origin,[6] even if they are far from being all-American. Last but not least, the marketing journals and academic reviews, such as the *Journal of Marketing*, the *Journal of Marketing Research* and *Advertising Age*, came largely from the United States.[7] In Europe (France, Germany, England, Benelux and north European countries) as well as in Canada and Japan, there are many other journals that exist. But research and new advances by practitioners as well as academics are made on the basis of imported materials.[8] As Lazer, Murata and Kosaka point out about Japan (1985, p. 71): 'what has occurred [in Japan] is the modification and adaptation of selected American constructs, ideas and practices to adjust them to the Japanese culture, that remains intact.' They stress especially the importance of economic non-functionality, which 'emphasizes that marketing actions consider individual human factors rather than merely economic efficiency and business profits'.

A progressive integration: the French and Japanese examples

Nevertheless, out of all the countries which have proceeded with a cultural borrowing of marketing, some of them do seem to have integrated it properly. But they have added a seasoning of their own.

Johansson and Nonaka (1987) show that Japanese firms use market survey techniques which are quite distinct from those used by US companies. The Japanese do survey markets, but afterwards take a decision on whether to follow the conclusions of the survey. For example, some surveys were presented to Akio Morita, founder and president of the Sony corporation, which suggested that the Walkman would not be bought by consumers: they would not buy a tape recorder that does not record, even a portable one. Following his intuition, though undoubtedly after fairly wide consultation, Akio Morita and Sony took the decision to launch the Walkman, with the success we all know. It is quite certain that an American boss would not have taken such a decision.

In fact, Japanese firms take a direct interest in the realities of the market-place and outlets. They look for information from the actual *buyers* (not the potential consumers), who are interviewed about the products they want, and how the products themselves could be better tailored to consumers' needs. Johansson and Nonaka cite the example of the chief executive officer of Canon-USA. He spent six weeks visiting Canon distribution networks, chatting to sales executives, customers and store managers, in order to find out why Canon cameras were not selling as well as the competition. This attitude is quite different from the prescriptions of traditional market research, which are as follows:

1. Market research has to be representative, therefore a representative sample must be used.
2. Market research must be scientifically objective. A questionnaire (that is, a systematic but not necessarily open-ended information retrieval instrument) should be administered by non-participating researchers (they should not be personally involved in the consequences of the responses given by interviewees).
3. Market research must study the *potential* market, not the actual market (that is, real buyers and real users).
4. As far as possible, the people who undertake market research should not be the same people who ultimately decide on the marketing strategy to be adopted. There is the potential danger that the boss of Canon-USA could be manipulated by customers and distributors, who might take the opportunity to demand lower prices or other benefits by overstating competitors' strengths. There is also the risk that, by focusing on the actual market, as yet untargeted market segments could be ignored or neglected.

As Johansson and Nonaka emphasize (1987, p. 16):

Japanese-style market research relies heavily on two kinds of information: 'soft data' obtained from visits to dealers and other channel members, and 'hard data' about shipments, inventory levels, and retail sales. Japanese managers believe that these data better reflect the behaviour and intentions of flesh-and-blood consumers. Japanese companies want information that is context specific rather than context free – that is, data directly relevant to consumer attitudes about the product, or to the way buyers have used or will use specific products, rather than research results that are too remote from actual consumer behaviour to be useful.

A similar situation is also found in France, where adaptation to the cultural context has now been broadly achieved. There are now several French textbooks – about ten on marketing management, and at least one or two on specialized areas of marketing. A continuous effort has been made to allow 'marketing' to denote the 'rationalisation of trade and sales practices'. It is seen as confronting the traditional commercial style with new concepts that are better suited to international competition (Dayan *et al.*, 1988, p. 14):

> In a [French] company, at the beginning of the industrial revolution ... selling was not considered to be an honourable activity. The essence of trading – bargaining with the client – is seen as not being codifiable; it is an *art*, based on individual talents, intuitions and experience. Consequently commercial activities do not follow the standards of the company as a whole, which are based on rationality, logic and organization. ... With the advent of *marketing*, brand image activities have been improved, and they have been better integrated into the company as a whole. A full-scale marketing campaign attracts significant areas of the human, intellectual and financial resources of a company: it often has a critical influence on strategic decisions, it uses more and more sophisticated techniques and it adopts a rational approach, which raises the marketing campaign to the level of other functional areas.

In this short passage from the introduction to a French marketing textbook, several elements typify the import process and its limits: the expression 'full-scale' suggests that there are still many marketing campaigns which perform only a reduced part of the marketing function; the *power* of marketing within the organization is an important issue *per se*; the dialectic opposition of irrationality and art versus logic and rationalization. In French society, only Cartesian logic may give legitimacy and credibility to marketing.

1.2   Culture and consumer behaviour

Although consumer behaviour has strong universal components,[9] its cultural variations cannot be ignored (Dubois, 1987). Without giving an exhaustive list, several essential points of cultural influence on consumer behaviour are worth considering in some detail:

1. Hierarchy of needs, which distorts demand across product categories.
2. Culture-based values, especially on individualistic or collectivist orientations, which influence purchasing behaviour and the decision process (individual versus family).
3. Institutions which influence consumer behaviour greatly.
4. Influence through cultural variations in the personal factors of consumer behaviour: brand loyalty, consumer involvement, perceived risk, cognitive style.

Hierarchy of needs

Culture influences the 'hierarchy of needs' (Maslow, 1954) on at least two levels:[10] first, one of the basic axioms of Maslow's theory is not true in every culture (one need must be satisfied before the next need can appear); second, similar kinds of needs may be satisfied by very different products and consumption types.

The level of economic development naturally has some influence: in a less developed economy, people usually have more basic survival needs. However, dominant values may clash with the pragmatic idea that you have to be able to buy food before buying a refrigerator to keep the food fresh. Some cultures (for example, Hindu) encourage needs of self-realization (the highest level), the satisfaction of which does not necessarily imply material consumption. The need for safety (shelter and basic personal protection) is not satisfied according to the same criteria in different cultures.

Thus one of the basic axioms of Maslow's theory – that needs must be satisfied at a particular level in order that the needs higher up the hierarchy may appear – is not true from a cross-cultural point of view. In many Third World countries one may deprive oneself of food so as to be able to buy a refrigerator, thereby replacing the satisfaction of a physical need of safety with the satisfaction of a need of social status and self-esteem (Belk, 1988).

Individualism and collectivism

Most of the available marketing literature depicts individual consumers who make their own decisions. Although industrial marketing literature deals with organizational purchase and buying centres,[11] and the effects of family decisions on consumer behaviour have been meticulously studied, the individualistic conception remains very much at the heart of the mental picture of marketing. The family is seen as an interacting group of individuals, all influencing each other. An *organic* conception of the family as a single decision-making unit is not easily grasped. Moreover research methods themselves are not totally unbiased: are the people questioned representative and can they be considered as reflecting family behaviour? Who should be questioned and in what circumstances?

However, various authors within the field of cross-cultural marketing have pointed out the role of the group as an organic entity, as opposed to a casual collection of individuals who share information and some common interests and constraints, living together within the family cell. This is especially true in Asia (Kushner, 1982; Laurent, 1982; Redding, 1982; Yau, 1988; Yang, 1989). Redding (1982, pp. 104, 112–13), for instance, emphasizes that:

> In most Asian cultures there is a particular grouping to which a person belongs, which involves him in patterns of obligation and behaviour of a special kind. ... It would, for instance, be naive to suppose that the buying power of a teenage market in a Western country would be equivalent to one in, say, Hong Kong or Singapore. The discretion over the use of income is heavily influenced, in the case of the Chinese teenager, by the expected contribution to the family. The tradition of deference to parental wishes also affects buying patterns in clothing, leisure expenditure, etc, especially as it is normal to live at home until marriage.

In addition, a Chinese individual must always take into account all the members of the family when making a purchase decision, compared to an interactive decision-making process undertaken by the husband or wife in the West where important household expenditure is concerned (Yau, 1988). In the East the model of the 'extended family' has survived apparently westernized ways of life (Laurent, 1982); it has a powerful influence on many purchase decisions. Even Chinese people, who may sometimes appear quite individualistic when outside their national context, remain strongly bound by their family ties. Yang (1989) describes the influence of what he calls 'familism' on their behaviour as individuals, as family members and as consumers (Box 1.1).

Box 1.1 *The role of familism in Chinese consumer behaviour*

The single most essential concept to characterize Chinese culture is undoubtedly familism (Ballah, 1970; Yang, 1972). Confucius himself defined five fundamental human relations, three of which relate to family relations: parent and child, husband and wife, and brother and sister. All five of them had roughly equal weight in terms of importance. Later some of his influential disciples, however, made filial piety the most important among the five (Hsieh, 1967). In any case, a Chinese individual's relationship with family members is a permanent one, which is never grown out of. The Chinese definition of family is often very broad, including various lineages and generations. The single most influential group on an individual's behaviour is family members, usually extended family members. The influence of family members on an individual's behaviour is very far-reaching; often it extends to areas definitely considered private by Western standards. In contrast to their relationships with their families, Chinese people's relationships with secondary groups beyond the family are usually ill-defined and sometimes non-existent (King, 1981). The consequences of this emphasis on familism and filial piety are many. First, a Chinese individual's behaviour often cannot be considered as an act reflecting personal preferences or will. It is often the result of a consensus or compromise between the individual and the family members, or a take-over by the family's, usually the parents', preferences or will. Second, social harmony is highly valued in a society whose basic social unit is the extended family (Chien, 1979). The maintenance of stable and peaceful co-existence is more important than anything else when there are many people who are interdependent on and interconnected with each other, constantly involved at any given time and place. Third, an individual's relationship with core family members is not only strong and spontaneous but also collective. The bonds are so natural that they are also very casual. They do not usually need deliberate cultivation by saying 'I love you' all the time or showering each other with gifts (Hsu, 1971). Finally, an individual's relationship with other non-family members is usually formalized but peripheral. The affection of strangers is not deliberately sought after but can be naturally developed. It is also possible for strangers to become a part of the 'extended' family and to be treated accordingly, but not until trust has been established (Fei, 1948). In other words, the Chinese intergroup relations are often limited to two types: family (inside) and non-family (outside). Other group memberships are not usually sought and therefore not easily established.

(Yang, 1989. Reproduced with the kind permission of the journal.)

Institutions, social conventions, habits and customs

Institutions, such as the State, the Church and trade unions, also have an influence on the marketing environment. The French Catholic hierarchy has generally been opposed to Sunday trading (Dubois, 1987). It is clear that some products have a strong dependence on culture, whatever their mode of distribution or consumption. An example would be marriage-related goods such as a wedding dress or the products featured on wedding lists.

Of all the cultural conventions that structure daily life, as far as behaviour with regard to consumption is concerned, the most important is eating. Variations exist on the following points:

◆ The number of meals consumed each day.
◆ The standard duration of a meal.
◆ The composition of each meal. The portions may differ in size, comprising various kinds of food (local ingredients or cooking style); the nutritional content may be composed so that the eater can cope with long or short time periods without further calorific input during the day.
◆ The social function: either as a communal meal where people entertain themselves by eating and chatting together, or simply as a means of feeding oneself, without any symbolic, personal or collective connotation. A meal may be considered merely as 'fuel' or as a daily 'social event'.
◆ Is the food ready-made or prepared from basic ingredients? Are there servants to help prepare the meal? What is the cultural significance of the meal being prepared by the wife for her husband (or, less frequently vice versa) or for anybody else in a particular situation?

The list is endless, because nothing is more essential, more universal and at the same time more accurately defined by culture than eating habits. Eating habits should be considered as the whole process of purchasing food and beverages, cooking, tasting and even commenting. In many countries, commercials advertising ready-made foods (canned or dried soups, for instance) faced resistance in the traditional role of the housewife, who was supposed to prepare meals from natural ingredients for her family. As a result, advertisers were obliged to include a degree of preparation by the housewife in the copy strategy.

The influence of culture on selected aspects of consumer behaviour

Consumers can be loyal, that is, they repeat their purchases on a regular basis, buying the same brand. Loyal consumers prefer to be sure of what they buy. However, by doing this they reduce their opportunity to find other, and perhaps better, choices which would provide them with more value for their money. Other classes of consumers try new brands, shift from one brand to another when a new one is promoted, take advantage of temporary price rebates: they are basically disloyal consumers.

Disloyalty is the natural counterpart of *loyalty* (to a brand, a product, a store, etc.): what is culturally meaningful is to observe which one of these two opposite attitudes is considered as the legitimate, fundamental behaviour. In the United States brand loyalty is very carefully surveyed and explanatory variables (demographics, life-styles and situational variables) are researched.[12] Standard behaviour is that of disloyalty. A consumer supposedly shifts from one brand to another (brand switching) because it is standard behaviour to test several competing products successively, thereby fostering price competition, or to respond spontaneously to the stimuli of advertising and sales promotion. Equally, it is assumed that consumers are not especially rewarded by their practice of buying the same brand and/or shopping in the same store (they can be 'brand loyal' and/or 'store loyal'). The fact that consumers may enjoy the same stable environment, of which their favourite products would form a basic constituent, is somewhat underestimated. Stated otherwise, it is assumed that consumers enjoy change more than stability. Of course, in the United States there are large groups of loyal consumers: habit and stability are a reality for many Americans. But the number of these groups is, in all probability, less than in some other countries where brand loyalty is normal behaviour.

Where consumers are more fundamentally loyal, less brand-conscious and not so used to rational price/quality cross-brand or cross-product comparisons, it may be assumed that marketing strategies have to be different from those in countries where consumers frequently shift from one brand to another. In the former case it may be necessary to build a loyal consumer base from scratch, whereas in the latter case it may be more effective to persuade disloyal customers to switch from other established brands and then to try to turn the newly developed consumer base into a loyal one.

The involvement of the consumer in product purchase or consumption varies across cultures. Yang (1989) depicts Chinese consumers as having a low involvement level when products are used for private consumption: they are likely to adopt a rather simple cognitive stance, favouring the physical functions of the product and being mostly concerned with price and quality. There is a high level of purchasing involvement when the Chinese consumer buys products for their social symbolic value. Since people greatly value social harmony and the smoothness of relationships within the extended family, the social significance of a product is highly important: it may express status, gratitude, approval or disapproval.[13]

Perceived risk, which is an important variable in consumer behaviour, differs according to its breakdown into various components: physical risk, financial risk, social risk etc. (Van Raaij, 1978). Whereas people in some cultures may be more susceptible to physical risk (because the mortality rate is low, death is feared and avoided), others may be more sensitive to social risk (because a purchase may risk the loss of status in other people's eyes). Let us take an example: when buying a car in a country where road safety is not a high priority, the perceived physical risk is low; where mileage is irrelevant because gas is so cheap, there is a low perceived financial risk; but where an engine breakdown is a disaster, due to little or no available maintenance, there is a high perceived reliability risk. The perceived risk is quite different from that experienced by the average purchaser of a car in a Western European country.

The cognitive style assumed by the classical models of consumer behaviour (Howard and Sheth, 1969; Engel and Blackwell, 1982) is that of an individual reviewing opportunities, evaluating alternatives, rationally searching for information, relying on opinion leaders and word-of-mouth communication, who is influenced by social environment and situational factors and also by the stimuli of marketing strategies (particularly advertising and sales promotion), chooses the best alternative, progressively forms the intention to purchase and finally (perhaps) actually buys the product. These models have a rather analytical and abstract style, as is the case with most consumer behaviour theory. Many authors claim that Asian consumers tend to have a quite different cognitive style: the Chinese as well as the Japanese have a more synthetic, concrete and contextual orientation in their thought patterns (Lazer *et al.*, 1985; Yau, 1988; Yang, 1989). Chapter 3 shows how intellectual approaches vary across cultural groupings to such an extent that the diversity of cognitive styles cannot be ignored.[14]

1.3   Marketing as exchange and communication: cultural relativity

Marketing may be seen primarily as a process of exchange, where communication, broadly defined, is central. As Richard Bagozzi (1975, p. 35) states:

> In order to satisfy human needs, people and organizations are compelled to engage in social and economic exchanges with other people and organizations. This is true for primitive as well as highly developed societies. Social actors obtain satisfaction of their needs by complying with, or influencing, the behaviour of other actors. They do this by communicating and controlling the media of exchange,[15] which in turn, comprise the links between one individual and another. Significantly, marketing exchanges harbour meanings for individuals that go beyond the use of media for obtaining results in interactions.

Consumers buy meanings and marketers communicate meanings through products and advertisements. Many of these meanings are culture-based: they are intersubjectively shared by a social group (D'Andrade, 1987). Intersubjective sharing of meanings implies that each person in the group knows that everyone else knows the cognitive schema. Therefore in the process of exchange through buyer–seller relations, marketing communications or product consumption, interpretations are made spontaneously as if they were obvious facts of the world, and a great deal of information in the process of marketing as exchange and communication need not be made explicit.

Culture may be considered as a sort of metalanguage (for definition, see p. 108), which is central in the marketing process when viewed as exchange and communication, as noted by Bagozzi. It works as a kind of game rule, implicitly indicating how people will interact in an exchange relationship, their constraints and their leeway in behaviour and decisions. The attitudinal differences towards market research between American and Japanese people is a good example of this: what is the 'right' (legitimate, appropriate) way to communicate with the market? Who is the market (actual buyers versus potential consumers)? In each case the objective is seemingly the same: to collect relevant information and market data in order to decide on marketing strategies.

Two examples will help us illustrate the differences in marketing metacommunication; first, the role of emotions in Japanese marketing, and second, the emphasis on the symbolic relationship between person and object in the Italian style of marketing. Chapter 4, which is devoted to language, culture and communication, develops these themes.

The role of emotions in Japanese marketing

There is a wide range of books on Japanese marketing, which are unfortunately written only in Japanese, thereby limiting access for many readers. But the Japanese provide details in English in the review of the largest Japanese advertising agency, *Dentsu Japan Marketing/Advertising*.[16] Koichi Tanouchi, professor of marketing at Hitotsubashi University, depicts the Japanese style of marketing as being fundamentally based on emotions and sensitivity. He first emphasizes, as many authors do, that Japan is orientated towards rice production and is not a nation of hunters and gatherers. This means more collective organization and interpersonal sensitivity: the cultivation of rice needs the flooding of paddy-fields, which cannot be decided by an isolated landowner; paddy-fields have to be flooded simultaneously. This involves a strong collective solidarity, serious planning and individual tenaciousness. Tanouchi states that, in his opinion, 'masculine' values are less developed in Japan than 'feminine' values, which he illustrates by the example of marital relationships in household and personal spending (1983, p. 78):

> In Japan, the husband is supposed to hand all his income over to his wife. If he doesn't, he is criticized by people around him. If she complains about this to his boss in his business company, the boss is very likely to take the wife's side, and advise him to give all his salary to his wife and add that that is the best way to keep peace at home and that everyone else is doing so. The wife has the right to decide how much money her husband can have for daily lunch and coffee. Regularly, about once in a half year, Japanese newspapers carry a research report about the average amount of the money the average husbands get from their wives. Wives decide their husbands' lunch money watching these figures.

Tanouchi, as well as other authors (Lazer *et al.*, 1985), argues that sensitivity and emotions permeate most aspects of Japanese marketing. It is evidenced by the high level of sensitivity and response to *actual* consumer needs and by the search for social harmony between producers and distributors (see section 11.1 on the *keiretsu* distribution). It is also prominent in Japanese sales force commission arrangements, where collective reward systems are often used. They foster co-operation, discourage threatening individual competition and promote social harmony in the sales team (section 11.3).

The role of the symbolic link between object and person through the medium of design in Italian marketing

It can be said that a specific Italian marketing style is emerging. This style is characterized by the heavy emphasis (and corresponding financial commitment) given to product appearance and design. The article sold is intended to act as a link between the producer-seller and the consumer-purchaser: both appreciate the aesthetic qualities of the object. The Italians concentrate on the style and functionality of an object and its integration in the environment (see page 253, 'Confession of a purchaser of Italian products'). Within this type of framework, where the symbolism of the object and the consumer's wishes are considered as points of focus, importance should be given to qualitative studies.

Box 1.2   *The functional form of the cigarette lighter*

The stylized fluidity of the 'functional forms' testifies to the connotation of mental dynamics, the semblance of a lost relationship, in an attempt to reconstruct a purpose through the accumulation of signs. For example, a lighter in the shape of a pebble was successfully launched by advertising some years ago. The oblong, elliptic and asymmetrical form is 'highly functional', not because it provides a better light than other lighters, but because it fits exactly into the palm of the hand. 'The seas have polished it into the shape of the hand': it is an accomplished form. Its function is not to give a light, but to be easy to handle. Its form is, so to speak, predetermined by Nature (the sea) to be handled by man. This new purpose is the sole rhetoric of the lighter. The connotations are here twofold: as an industrial object, the cigarette lighter is designed to recall one of the qualities of the hand-crafted object, the shape of which furthers the gesture and the body of man. Moreover the allusion to the sea brings us to the myth of Nature, itself cultured by man, which follows all his desires: the sea plays the cultural role of a polisher; it is the sublime handicraft of nature. As a stone rolled by the sea, furthered by the hand producing light, the cigarette lighter becomes a wonderful flint; a whole prehistoric and artisanate purpose comes into play in the very practical essence of an industrial object.

(Baudrillard, 1968, pp. 82–3. Reproduced with permission. Author's translation.)

Baudrillard (1968) and his 'system of objects', which was fairly successful in France, ultimately achieved real success in Italy, where he is guru of marketing semiology (Box 1.2).

Dino Buzzati, author of *The Desert of the Tartars*, has written a short story entitled *Suicide in the Park* which illustrates quite clearly this fusion between person and object through the medium of the imagination; it can lead to a fascinating and passionate relationship. It is of course unrealistic to claim that the Italians are alone in having an awareness of the symbolic consumer–object relationship, but they incorporate it at a very high level and make it an essential element of their marketing communication.

1.4   Customization of marketing strategies to local contexts

To evaluate cultural programming, it is sufficient to apply common sense from an ingenuous intellectual standpoint. For example: is it quite normal that firms engage in fierce competition? Is it not more in keeping with human nature to seek agreement, to divide territory between the parties and to sign pacts of commercial non-aggression, even though their duration may be limited? In fact it is easy to appreciate that behind the normative position which we have largely adopted through its incessant repetition – it is essential to be competitive – a more complex reality exists. To varying degrees, competition and alliances between companies will always occur as mixed realities. Even more complex is the code which delineates to newcomers to the competitive scene (a national market) how they should behave towards those who are already part of that scene. This leads to a necessary customization of marketing strategies according to the *actual* rather than the ideal competition patterns.

Market situations and competition avoidance patterns

Competition is not necessarily self-perpetuating. Despite liberal ideology, which is laudable and worthy of respect and which has produced a reasonable number of happy endings, 'the invisible hand of the market' (in the words of Adam Smith) is not always in evidence and is sometimes actually non-existent rather than merely invisible. The dynamics of competing companies may lead to the concentration of supply among a limited number of companies and therefore to an actual decrease in the sum total of competing forces. The United States, the archetype of enacted liberalism, has been much more realistic in this regard than other countries since they introduced effective institutions at an early stage (for example, anti-trust legislation and the Sherman Act) to oversee the proper functioning of competition, the discouragement of dominant positions and the establishment of monopolies through fusion or amalgamation of companies.

However, as Cateora emphasizes, perhaps to an exaggerated extent (1983, p. 128): 'Except in the United States, 20th century orientation toward competition has been to avoid it whenever possible.' Inevitably one thinks of the large German cartels: Interessen Gemeinschaft Farben for example, which prior to the Second World War brought together the three major chemical companies of Bayer, BASF (Badische Anilin und Sofa Fabrik) and Hoechst that are now at the forefront of the world chemical industry. One also thinks of the Japanese *zaibatsus* Mitsui, Mitsubishi and Sumitomo, industrial giants which, under the control of one extended family, encompass activities ranging from banking to car production, and from trading to shipbuilding. The Americans prohibited these *zaibatsus* after their victory over the Japanese in 1945. This has not stopped their continued existence on an informal basis, nor has it prevented competition from progressing extremely effectively within the Japanese market (see Chapter 11).

Abeglen and Stalk (1986) have demonstrated, using the example of the motorcycle industry, how competition between companies in Japan is often savage. Honda, which in the 1950s was far behind Tohatsu, has completely overtaken this firm to the extent that in 1964 Tohatsu went bankrupt. After entering the motor-car sector during the 1960s, Honda suffered a relative loss of competitiveness in the face of competition from Yamaha, which achieved almost the same market share in 1981. At the beginning of the 1980s, Honda decided to attack Yamaha. Whereas Honda introduced 81 new models and ceased production of 32 (113 changes in product range in all), Yamaha 'only' introduced 34 new models and withdrew 3 (37 changes). This strategy, in combination with a fierce attack on a price and distribution level, led to the collapse of Yamaha at the start of 1983. In addition to substantial losses, Yamaha announced redundancies and a restructuring programme as well as a reduction in stocks. Yamaha's chairman, Koike, was forced to acknowledge his failure publicly. This story, along with many similar ones, shows just how cut-throat the

Table 1.1   *Basic forms of markets according to Von Stackelberg.*

	Sellers		
	One	Some	Many
Buyers			
One	Bilateral monopoly	Contradicted monopsony	Monopsony
Some	Contradicted monopoly	Bilateral oligopoly	Oligopsony
Many	Monopoly	Oligopoly	Pure and perfect competition

competition in Japan has been, contrary to popular opinion. It is one of the principal sources of Japanese strength when stepping into foreign markets. This fierce competition is also underestimated by foreign companies that want to establish themselves in Japan.[17]

The simple truth is, however, that an industrialist's vocation is not to enjoy competition as an end in itself. Competition is imposed by public authorities through the opening of frontiers and ultimately by competitors themselves. If industrialists possess the legal and informal means to reduce it, they will do so, as long as the type of agreement is stable and they do not allow themselves to be taken advantage of by the competing firms with which the agreements are made. In fact a German economist, Von Stackelberg (1940), had the idea of combining situations in the field of supply and demand to construct a typology of forms of deal. He distinguishes vendor and purchaser according to whether they number one, several or many (see Table 1.1).

Every country has a few monopolies, several markets where pure and perfect competition reigns and a large number of oligopolies (large-scale consumption and durable consumer goods), oligopsonies and bilateral oligopolies (industrial input goods, such as steel, chemicals and rubber, and capital goods). What varies according to culture is social approval or disapproval – the level of agreement and implicit consensus between local decision-makers as to whether a monopoly, through the restrictions on excessive competition, may be desirable for the community or constitute a danger to it. Intruders, coming from abroad, will then be seen either positively (from the point of view of the consumer) or negatively (from the point of view of the firm in competition with the foreign company, since ultimately the consumers are also often employees and thus potentially unemployed).

Indeed the Americans are often shocked by the amount of protection afforded to their flagship national companies by certain European governments. The Airbus/Boeing saga is typical of these conceptual differences, the roots of which are partly derived from culture. The Europeans consider that the money lent by their governments, often seen as sunk costs, was used wisely in view of the success of the Airbus aircraft, the number of jobs created, the positive effects on the balance of payments and the preservation of the civil aeronautic industry in Europe which was previously under threat (a collective view, and not purely liberal). However, for the Americans the affair was a costly mess that helped no one: the hugely successful Boeing company was challenged by disloyal competition, the European taxpayer was further burdened and the standard rules governing international trade were distorted. Nevertheless, if Airbus did not exist, Boeing would be in a situation of quasi-monopoly (except for McDonnell Douglas, but its share of the market is insignificant compared to that of Boeing). Logically this ought to offend the Americans.

The role of distribution as a cultural 'filter'

Distribution forms subtle relationships with consumers by means of direct contact. People get into the habit of buying certain products which are backed by fixed services, at clearly defined times, in particular shops. The considerable differences in opening hours between northern and southern Europe clearly illustrate the influence of culture on the system of distribution. Door-to-door sales and distribution techniques are slow to catch on in many countries where they violate personal privacy.

Depending on the country, the distribution system can be the vehicle for varying degrees of relationship between the producers and the national distributors. France, which largely invented the concept of the hypermarket, benefits from a distribution set-up that is effective, powerful and independent of producers. It is so strong that products bearing the store name are able to compete with the producers' brands. The system is therefore inherently susceptible to penetration by imports.

At the other extreme, Japan (whose system of distribution is described in detail in Chapter 11) is the place where links between producers and distributors are traditionally very strong. Central to this are the *keiretsus* of distribution, true vertical relationships that mix business and emotion in typically Japanese fashion, between producers, wholesalers, semi-wholesalers and retailers. Based on a powerful sense of loyalty, with many services being rendered by one party for the other, these networks are clearly much more difficult for foreign companies to penetrate.

Legal marketing environments

The relativization of marketing strategies is often imposed by legal dispositions concerned with commercial activities which are indirectly an expression of certain national cultural characteristics. This gives rise to a number of issues:

1. The fact of incurring moral approbation or condemnation for certain practices often leads to public debate which in turn influences the regulator when introducing legislation. For example there are different levels of acceptance of the use of nudes in television or magazine advertising, which lead to moral controversies in the public domain when foreign advertisements, introduced by the means of imported magazines or satellite broadcast, are perceived as shocking by the local audience. Another example is offered by the attitudes of regulators towards advertising targeted to a children's audience. Children are easy to influence, and it is sometimes argued that excessive need creation, which parents cannot always satisfy, may destabilize family relationships. The following topic is also often debated: how should children be hired

and compensated for their taking part in a television commercial? Some countries have such stringent regulations (France for instance) that many of the local commercials, targeting children as consumers, are produced abroad (in England for instance).

2. The idea that society should protect citizens from the abuses of marketing. It is assumed that consumers are either informed and responsible people or individuals who find themselves at a disadvantage in relation to the advertiser. Many Latin countries forbid campaigns that take the form of competitions which are considered to be immoral (as a result lotteries are state monopolies, so that private interests cannot exploit the taste of the public for gambling), whereas they are permitted in Anglo-Saxon countries. Certain countries forbid promotional gifts or strictly limit their value, whereas other countries authorize them without any restriction. A possible reason for these diverging regulatory attitudes derives from the differences in response to the following question: are people capable of a rational economic evaluation of the value of the gift, capable of relating it to the full price they pay? Finally are they considered able to come to a sound buying decision, even though they may have been unduly influenced? Section 11.4 examines the relativity of regulatory approaches in the field of sales promotion.

3. Agreement with the morality of certain kinds of representation, in advertising in particular: the images of women and the representations of 'ideal' people which lead to a desire to identify with those depictions. Chapter 12 suggests an attitudinal approach towards advertising in general, advertising material in particular and the media, for different national cultures.

The role of the public: attitudes towards consumerism

To complete this description of factors that govern a relativization of marketing strategy, the role of the public, who have an influence on the exchange, must be added. For instance, the consumer movement is particularly important and is developed to a greater or lesser extent depending on certain basic premisses:

- Is it legitimate that consumers should make their dissatisfaction known? This is not the case in societies where long periods favourable to supply (when, during decades, the local supply has been systematically much lower than the demand) have implanted the contrary idea. Shopping in Eastern Europe illustrates the extent to which a customer complaint can seem an absurd step to take.
- Is it legitimate for consumer action to be capable of forcing a producer, whose product quality is dubious, to close down? In other words, may consumers legitimately cause job losses and take away the livelihood of workers who are not ultimately responsible for the situation?

I pose these questions not out of a desire to adopt any particular position, but merely to demonstrate that it is not inherently obvious that the defence of the consumer has a wholly positive social value.

1.5   Business negotiation and sales practices

Business negotiation is the job not only of the salesperson, but also of those who assist in this task: engineers, sales representatives, lawyers, for example, who share in the job of business negotiation abroad. As Jolibert and Tixier (1988, p. 11) emphasize in an attempt to distinguish between sales and business negotiation:

> During sale the business conditions are fixed by the vendor. The purchaser is not in a position to debate them. ... The job of the vendor therefore consists of convincing the purchaser of the worth of his offers, of the appropriateness of the product offered to meet the needs of the purchaser. ... Negotiation begins when there is a *possible discussion* about the terms of business between the purchaser and the vendor.

Although the transactions in which business terms are fixed (in legal jargon, a unilateral contract) extend fairly consistently to the scenario where every term is negotiable (a multilateral contract where everything can be freely determined between the parties), it can be useful to separate sales and business negotiation. There follows, first, a description of the differing culture-based representations of what constitutes a good salesperson, from a comparative point of view of selling styles within one country; second, an examination of certain aspects of the purchaser–vendor relationship which are influenced by culture.

What makes a good salesperson?

Let us begin with an apparently straightforward question: what must a salesperson do when asked to sell poor-quality products?

Fortunately the question is never framed in such radical terms. But intermediate situations exist where the vendor (if we assume that the vendor's role is to present the client's demands to the vendor's company) perceives the weaknesses of a product through reports from clients who are already users. Should the vendor inform the company, in particular the production department, or merely consider the terms of business (the offer made) as fixed and stick to the role of persuasion?

Thus the conception of what constitutes a good salesperson comes long before the corresponding value judgement. One may regard the seller's role as strictly separate from that of the business negotiator, in a hierarchical situation where sales staff are supposed to sell, obediently and efficiently, the products remitted to them and not to debate the marketing mix (product and price). On the assumption that the role of salespeople is principally that of persuasion, how should they set about achieving it? It is realistic to presume that the art of persuasion is subject to cultural variations that are highly significant. The following questions outline possible ways of differentiating the sales technique:

1. How far can one take persuasion without becoming insistent, annoying or irritating?
2. Is one persuasive merely by listening, where clients appreciate salespeople to whom they can talk, or by talking?
3. With what arguments should the seller best use the inevitably limited time to persuade the prospective purchaser?

For example, Cateora (1983, p. 115) proposes some stereotypical selling styles:

- In Asian countries, where people mind arrogance and the showing of extreme self-confidence, vendors should make modest, rational, down-to-earth points; they should avoid winning arguments against the buyer, who could suffer from a 'loss of face', and react quite negatively.
- In Italy, on the contrary, the lack of self-confidence would be perceived as a clear sign of lack of personal credibility and reliability; thus one needs to argue strongly in order to be considered as a serious partner.
- In Great Britain, it is advisable to use the *soft sell* approach (do not be pushy with your prospective buyer).
- In Germany, you should use the *hard sell* approach (make visits, offer trials, be very present).
- When selling to a Mexican buyer, one should emphasize price.
- In Venezuela, a vendor will have to emphasize the quality of the goods.

It is clear that a real variety of selling styles related to national culture exists, from the market trader to the executive selling billion-dollar contracts, from the friend to the distant acquaintance. This is true even though, objectively, the stereotypes quoted above are undeniably biased and deceptive. Every style of selling exists in every culture, but the one adopted by the majority of sellers will become a modal characteristic by virtue of its frequency.

It could be suggested that a salesperson should be able to sell anything, that the job is that of short-term persuasion at any price. Equally, however, one could put forward the idea that the seller is above all the representative of the client within the company, in which case one should have a long-term outlook, listen to the client and even be willing to lose an order once in a while. These two opposing views are culturally relative, based on communication patterns (see Chapter 4) or the organization of business time. Selling styles also depend on which type of concrete results (winning new customers, reaching a quantitative sales target) and/or more subjective achievements (getting on well with clients, maintaining a friendly atmosphere in the sales team) are considered as evidence of the seller's efficiency or inefficiency.

Is a good salesperson a negotiator? Definitely, in my opinion, and above all in the international world, where competition is of course more open and needs are more varied. One's room for manoeuvre is often greater than in a domestic context. Furthermore, in a broad sense selling involves the negotiation of representation or dealership contracts with intermediaries (agents, distributors, importers and so on) or partners (licensees, or local companies with which joint ventures are formed).[18]

Negotiate with whom? With clients of course, but also with the organization whose products or services are to be sold. The company itself, because it is far removed from the client, has to be convinced of the need to make concessions. It is fairly clear that the role of the international salesperson requires sophisticated skills of which the ability to negotiate, whether commercially or within one's own organization, is far from being the least important.

Aspects of the buyer–seller relationship dictated by culture

It is not only the selling style that will be governed by culture, but also some of the basic conditions of the buyer–seller relationship will be similarly predetermined.[19] In other words, the relationship as such is partially pre-ordained, from which the roles adopted largely follow. Three illustrations of this are given below, but they are not an exhaustive description of the influence of culture on the process and outcome of negotiations (this is studied in detail in Chapters 4, 13 and 14):

1. The position of strength. Numerous empirical studies have been undertaken to determine which role, buyer or seller, holds the *ab initio* position of strength in intracultural business negotiations. Graham (1981) suggests that one of the reasons for the American trade deficit with Japan was the difference in the representation of the buyer–seller relationship regarding the position of strength. The Japanese believe that strength lies with the purchaser whom the salesperson must do the utmost to satisfy, whereas the Americans envisage a more egalitarian position. As Graham points out in his study of cultural adaptation in intercultural business negotiation (Graham, 1981, p. 9):

   > Anthropologists tell us that power relations usually determine who adopts and adapts behavior in a cross-cultural setting. Japanese executives in an American setting are likely to be the ones to modify their behavior. ... However, if an American seller takes his normative set of bargaining behavior to Japan, then negotiations are apt to end up abruptly. The American seller expects to be treated as an equal and acts accordingly. The Japanese buyer is likely to view this rather brash behavior in a lower status seller as inappropriate and lacking in respect. The Japanese buyer is made to feel uncomfortable, and he politely shuts the door to trade, without explanation. The American seller never makes the first sale, never gets an opportunity to learn the Japanese system.

2. The medium of communication. The progress of negotiation is effected by acts of communication, either verbal (oral, written) or non-verbal. Chapter 4 describes the role of language and the intracultural systems of verbal and non-verbal communication, to enable a clearer appreciation of the risks of misunderstandings in such situations.[20] Communication is coded/decoded within a set cultural/linguistic framework. There is no universal framework, unless it is the extremely deceptive 'international English' which gives native English-speakers the false impression that they are living in a 'global village'.

3. The decision-making process. Little mention of this subject is made in this book, which is above all devoted to the influence of culture on business and not to the functioning of the organization. It is, however, a very important subject in the overall framework of business negotiation. The Japanese style of reaching decisions by committee, for example, can disorientate people of other nationalities who are used to decisions being made by a boss, which thereby concentrates a great deal of power in one person's hands.

Chapter 3 describes the approach of cross-national cultural differences which have an influence on purely operational decisions, such as at what level of the organization and with which people the salesperson must make contact to maximize the chances of doing business. There are many examples of firms which, after protracted negotiations with Japanese companies, heard nothing more for two or three months. They assumed that they had lost the deal, but to their surprise they ultimately received an agreement. The process of *ringi* had been at work in the Japanese company – a procedure of written consultation which requires the input of various interested parties, meetings and careful consideration of objections and suggestions.

APPENDIX 1

———— ❖❖❖ ————

Teaching materials

A1.1 Teaching note: Learning by self-teaching

The training method for doing business with people from different national/cultural backgrounds has often been considered self-evident: learning by experience. It is regarded as comparable to the learning process of small children beginning to speak by themselves. Any beginner, whether baby, child or adult, naturally faces a learning process which is partly self-taught. People 'learn' only because they are able to transfer knowledge into their own mental schemas. This holds true whatever the type of knowledge acquired: be it maths, geography, marketing or carpentry. Even though knowledge may appear, at first sight, to be the sole result of a rather didactic and institutionalized learning process (ranging from apprenticeship to higher education), there is always a strong dimension of what is sometimes called 'action learning', where people learn by relating their practice to their formal knowledge acquisitions. Didactic learning is mostly based on formal class-room teaching: the teacher speaks and the students listen. But, paradoxically, formal teaching in fact serves as a strong support for self-teaching. Therefore, in the learning process, it is important to assess clearly which are the respective contributions of the purely 'self-taught' aspect (no assistance at all) and of the purely 'educated' aspect (entirely assisted and guided). The combination of formal, 'educational' teaching and self-teaching results in the total process of 'learning'. The following sections address some key issues when marketing and selling to people of different cultures.

Re-reading situations and experiences

Re-reading situations and experiences occupies a central role in the self-teaching process. It is necessary to confront what has been personally experienced (accompanied by the concrete sanctions and rewards related to experience) with the precepts arising from what has been formally learnt. This can be done spontaneously, almost unwillingly and unconsciously. But it seems better to have a more systematic approach to re-reading situations to avoid any 'mental sedimentation', where deep-rooted stereotypes protect people from their differences.[21] If people simply live intercultural experiences without being aware and discerning meaningful lessons, the learning value will be quite limited. It may even be a negative learning process, whereby prejudices and stereotypes are reinforced.

Re-reading means to systematically verify one's own interpretations by asking questions of the very people who have brought the information, or with whom one is interacting: for instance, to ask about the meaning of keywords in a foreign language when they appear untranslatable, or to investigate by asking questions about the rationale of individual or collective conduct. Generally it is fairly easy to contact informants who bring reliable information. Most of us like the fact that people take some interest in us. It is advisable to re-read failures (at least, the situations which we *perceived* as having negative rather than positive outcomes) as well as successes.

Being sensitive to symbolic thinking

In 'modern' societies we have largely abandoned symbolic thinking and communication for a much more binary, precise language; explicit words supposedly depict realities which are usually assumed to be measurable. A figure one is simply a figure one, but its graphics or colour may make it completely different from another figure one, just because it is evocative. 'Suicide at the park' gives a neat illustration of symbolic thinking: the author, Dino Buzzati, describes the desire for a sports car, the symbolic aspects of the motivations for buying the car, the masculine and feminine connotations in buying and driving it, and ultimately the symbolic dimension of scrapping the car when it gets old. In this case the object defends itself by committing suicide. Although impossible in the 'real' world, the story suggests and depicts *symbolic realities*.

Some readers may be disappointed because this story does not seem to be directly applicable. The usefulness of cross-cultural marketing knowledge is clearly *indirect*: it may sometimes seem that it takes a long time to get to the point. But 'digitalized' descriptions of cultures are of little use, if not downright dangerous, because they may be misleading.[22]

Digitalized, explicit thinking and its main correlate – the strong belief in the measurable nature of reality – are good *per se* because they often lead to directly applicable knowledge. But explicit thinking must not progressively replace and finally cancel our capacity to think in a suggestive, analogic and implicit way. The skill which has to be developed is that of *re-contextualization*. When faced with situations and communications which have been impoverished in terms of perceived context, it is necessary to look for the context in order to communicate better, to make more appropriate decisions and to refine implementation.[23]

Integrating one's own stereotypes and prejudices

I use the word 'integrate' deliberately. The aim is not to eliminate our stereotypes or prejudices, but to understand how they function, and, to perceive their limits: they make sense only in the native cultural community, in relation to particular cultural values; they may become dysfunctional in other contexts.

To search for all our stereotypes and prejudices may prove self-destructive. On the contrary, the aim is to improve adaptability to foreign contexts. For example, a person may hold as true the prejudice that the individual is the real source of change in society – that the capacity to tackle issues and design projects lies with the individual rather than the group. Integrating such a 'useful' prejudice means not giving it up, since it has a strong influence on behaviour and daily relations with other people, but becoming aware of its limits (in an Asiatic context, for instance).

Reading

Nothing is more enjoyable than a good book. If you travel to Thailand, Nigeria or Japan (or almost any country), begin the preparation for your stay by reading a novel by a well-known local author (provided that there is at least one author whose work is translated into English, which is usually the case). It will tell you far more, and in a much more agreeable way, than a standardized description, which will only provide you with regurgitated information.

A second category of book proves useful: history. If you want, for instance, to negotiate with Yugoslavians (Serbs, Croats, Slovenes, Bosnians), Bulgarians, Albanians, Greeks or Turks, reading about the history of the Balkans will give you some insight about the people. It is always necessary to put real people in their historical context: it is the only way to become aware of the relative positions of various ethnic or religious groups and their fights, struggles and clashes of interest. When choosing agents, making contacts or influencing decisions, it is always relevant to know *who is who*.

Let us continue with this list of deceptively obvious remarks. You should also study a world atlas: the physical, human and economic geography of a country gives much information on how to do business there. Furthermore, the lack of such knowledge would be resented by your foreign counterparts (although they will not complain explicitly).

One cannot object that it is too much work. A three-year overseas assignment constitutes almost one-tenth of a professional career. It clearly deserves significant educational investment. If the expected flow of business when selling overseas does not justify such self-education investment, it simply means that the stake is not worth the cost of the trip. Transaction costs when dealing overseas are much more important than when dealing in the domestic market.[24] At either a company or a personal level, investments in intercultural marketing skills must be balanced with long-term return perspectives.

Some basic principles

1. Do not hesitate to 'look inside yourself'. In the modern world, introspection is no longer valued. Psychoanalysis has played a major role in this process by effectively challenging the ability of individuals to assess objectively their internal thoughts and

feelings. Nevertheless, self-education in the field of intercultural marketing assumes a state of mind where people are able to investigate their own mental programming, basically by an introspective approach.

2. One need not be angelically empathetic. There are conflicts that are entirely interest-based; rarely are conflicts in business based purely on cultural misunderstandings. The objective is not to understand in order to adapt, but more to understand how best to defend one's interest and views.

3. The very innermost part of the individual is culture-free. Although it is not easy to discover the individual persona under the 'cultural' garments, it appears to be one of the main tools for influencing other people. When one knows how to do so, it is possible to establish relationships which are no longer distorted by culture-based misunderstanding.

Notes

1. Ignorance of the imported character of marketing is both necessary and deceptive. For the transplant to be successful, it must not be considered so foreign that it is ultimately rejected. But also in this process the precautions that must be taken to 'naturalise' the transplant should not be underestimated.

2. For example, because of the Catholic lack of consideration for money and business (see Chapter 10, p. 291).

3. Greek antiquity affords interesting possibilities of comparison on several levels; marketing and sophism (Greek pre-Socratic philosophy, which developed the art of effective arguments which could be misleading if necessary) both follow a pragmatic, down-to-earth objective, based on a relativist conception of reality. 'They consider themselves multi-purpose tools, and are unconcerned with the final outcome of the actions which they render effective. Marketing and sophism, since they are techniques of efficient speech, use the art of rhetoric with the aim of seduction and persuasion' (Laufer and Paradeise, 1982, p. 27).

4. See Chapter 3, section 3.4, on cultural borrowing.

5. The transplant has all the more chance of success due to the strong fascination for what is made abroad. Although there is an enduring attraction to one's own culture, it is essential to accept that advances are also made elsewhere. In some ways it is similar to the situation that currently exists with Japan. In an interesting article entitled 'The European world seen by the Eastern Empire', Yan Chen (1991) quotes the reformer Liang Quichao who wrote in 1897 on the subject of European countries, which were considered, unlike China, as innovative:

> 'In innovative countries the sovereigns are wise, their mandarins faithful and courageous, their people intelligent and heroic, their politics successful, their business prosperous, their products excellent, etc. Travel in their country brings you such pleasure and joy that you forget to return home. Will you then pose further questions as to the prosperity of these countries?' (pp. 51–2).

6. Throughout this book the expressions 'America' and 'Americans' are used; this is a reference to the United States and its inhabitants.

7. Among the academic journals in the field of marketing and management (American unless otherwise stated), which regularly publish contributions on various aspects of international marketing is the following non-exhaustive list: *Business Horizons*; *California Management*

Review; *Columbia Journal of World Business*; *Dentsu Japan Marketing/Advertising (Japanese)*; *European Journal of Marketing (British)*; *Harvard Business Review*; *Harvard L'Expansion (French)*; *Harvard Espanzione (Italian)*; *Harvard Manager (German)*; *International Marketing Review (British)*; *International Journal of Advertising*; *International Journal of Consumer Marketing*; *International Journal of Research in Marketing (Dutch/international)*; *Irish Marketing Review (Irish)*; *Journal of Advertising Research*; *Journal of Business Research*; *Journal of Consumer Research*; *Journal of International Business Studies*; *Journal of Marketing*; *Journal of Marketing Research*; *Journal of Purchasing and Materials Management*; *Journal of the Market Research Society (British)*; *Management International Review (German)*; *Marketing Science*; *Marketing: Zeitschrift für Forschung und Praxis (German)*; *Recherche et Applications en Marketing (French)*; *Revue Française de Gestion (French)*; *Revue Française du Marketing (French)*; *Scandinavian Journal of International Business*.

8. Consider, for instance, the percentage of US references in the bibliographies of British, German and French marketing reviews: always at least 50 per cent of the references, and often as much as 90 per cent on specialized topics, are American.

9. This section does not seek to question the universality of marketing theory as a whole, of which consumer behaviour is a large part, but to emphasize the cultural relativity of some of its hypotheses and models, and to show the cross-cultural variability, even when a concept may be considered universal (brand loyalty, for instance).

10. In Maslow's hierarchy of needs, physiological needs are at the bottom because they are the most fundamental; safety needs (being sheltered and protected from dangers in the environment) emerge when physiological needs are satisfied; then come needs for friendship and love relationships, which Maslow calls social needs. The next level, esteem, is the desire for respect from others which is strongly supported by status-improving goods. The final need, when all other levels have been satisfied, is the need for self-realization, which encompasses the development of one's own personality.

11. The buying centre is a unique decision-making group, the members of which come from the various sub-units of an organization that are concerned with a procurement decision. Each of these departments is likely to have its own goals and interests which may conflict with those of other departments.

12. There are of course large groups of loyal consumers in the United States. In the stream of research on the modelling of choice/non-choice of the individual consumer, based on panel data and logit models, the brand loyalty variable always appears as highly significant. See for instance: Peter M. Guadagni and John D. C. Little (1983), 'A logit model of brand choice calibrated on scanner data', *Marketing Science*, vol. 2 (Summer), pp. 203–38; Gerard J. Tellis (1988), 'Advertising exposure, loyalty and brand purchase: a two-stage model of choice', *Journal of Marketing Research*, vol. XXV (May), pp. 133–44; Sunil Gupta (1988), 'Impact of sales promotions on when, what and how much to buy', *Journal of Marketing Research*, vol. XXV (November), pp. 342–55.

13. On consumer involvement see for instance Jean Noel Kapferer and Gilles Laurent (1986), 'Consumer involvement profiles: A new practical approach to consumer involvement', *Journal of Advertising Research*, vol. 25, pp. 48–56.

14. Chapter 3 elaborates on intellectual styles, that is cognitive styles in general. For an investigation of particular consumer cognitive style, see: C. Pinson, N. K. Malhotra and A. K. Jain (1988), 'Les styles cognitifs des consommateurs', *Recherche et Applications en Marketing*, vol. 3, no. 1, pp. 53–74; K. M. Goldstein and S. Blackman (1978), *Cognitive Style: Five approaches and relevant research*, John Wiley: New York.

15. In this quotation, the word 'media' should be interpreted broadly as referring to any means of communication and exchange.

16. Dentsu, the largest world-wide advertising agency, publishes a yearbook which presents an exhaustive set of figures on the trends of Japanese marketing and advertising, the *Dentsu Japan Marketing/Advertising* yearbook. Such compilations are also available in other large industrial countries, published by the national association of advertisers, the association of advertising agencies or by large advertising agencies themselves.

17. The Lestra Design case, at the end of Chapter 8, is that of a French exporter of eiderdowns and duvets, facing the harsh competition of the Japanese market and confronted with the high demand of Japanese distributors for quality.

18. On these types of agreement, see for example: J. B. McCall and M. B. Warrington (1990, *Marketing by Agreement*, 2nd edn, John Wiley: London; K. R. Harrigan (1985), *Strategies for Joint Venture*, Lexington Books: Lexington, MA; S. Young, James Hamill, Colin Wheeler and J. Richard Davies (1989), *International Market Entry and Development*, Harvester Wheatsheaf, Hemel Hempstead.

19. Culture differences only influence the *context* of business and marketing negotiation, then its process, and finally the outcome. But it should not be overestimated since the positions may be centred on facts that are quite independent of the cultural variables, such as the possession by one party of a specific asset, patent, trademark or distribution network, which enables this party to maintain a strong position from the start of the negotiations.

20. Three words are used to qualify a situation, according to the cultural setting:

    ♦ *Intracultural*, where participants belong to the same culture.
    ♦ *Cross-cultural*, where one compares two or more groups of people belonging to particular cultures. It is a comparative perspective; it may be also an interactionist perspective, but between people belonging to the same cultural grouping.
    ♦ *Intercultural*, where the encounter is between people, or groups of people, belonging to different cultures. The outcome of the interaction will be partly the result of what has been observed in a cross-cultural setting, as well as a totally new relationship based more on the actual interaction than on the basic intracultural behavioural norms of the people involved (Graham and Adler, 1989).

21. See section 4.4 on this topic.

22. By 'digitalized' I mean when reality has been reduced to some essential variables, implicitly measured on a simple axis where data are evaluated as plus or minus. Digitalized thinking may be entirely retrievable in a computer with binary language.

23. For Edward Hall's theory of context in communication, see Chapter 4.

24. See the introduction to Chapter 13.

References

Abegglen, James and George Stalk Jr (1986), 'The Japanese corporation as competitor', *California Management Review*, vol. xxviii, no. 3 (Spring), pp. 9–27.

Allen, David E. (1978), 'Anthropological insights into consumer behavior', *European Journal of Marketing*, no. 3, pp. 45–57.

Amine, Lyn S. and S. Tamer Cavusgil (1986), 'Demand estimation in a developing country environment: difficulties, techniques and examples', *Journal of the Market Research Society*, vol. 28, no. 5, pp. 43–65.

Bagozzi, Richard P. (1975), 'Marketing as exchange', *Journal of Marketing*, vol. 39, no. 4, pp. 32–9.

Ballah, R. N. (1970), *Tokugawa Religion*, Beacon Press: Boston.

Baudrillard, Jean (1968), *Le Système des objets*, Gallimard: Paris.

Belk, Russell W. (1988), 'Third World consumer culture', in E. Kumçu and A. Fuat Firat (eds), *Research in Marketing*, supplement 4, JAI Press: Greenwich, Connecticut.

Cateora, Philip R. (1983), *International Marketing*, 5th edn, Richard D. Irwin: Homewood, IL.

Chen, Yan (1991), 'L'Europe vue par l'Empire du Milieu', *Intercultures*, no. 12, January, pp. 45–56.

Chien, M. (1979), *Chinese National Character and Chinese Culture: A historical perspective*, The Chinese University of Hong Kong Press: Shatin, Hong Kong (in Chinese).

D'Andrade, Roy (1987), 'A folk model of the mind', in Dorothy Quinn and Naomi Holland (eds), *Cultural Models in Language and Thought*, Cambridge University Press: Cambridge, pp. 112–48.

Dayan, Armand, Jérôme Bon, Alain Cadix, Renaud de Maricourt, Christian Michon and Alain Ollivier (1988), *Marketing*, Collection PUF Fondamental, Presses Universitaires de France: Paris.

Dubois, Bernard (1987), 'Culture et marketing', *Recherche et Applications en Marketing*, vol. 2, no. 3, pp. 37–64.

El Haddad, Awad B. (1985), 'An analysis of the current status of marketing in the Middle East', in Erdener Kaynak (ed.), *International Business in the Middle East*, de Gruyter: New York, pp. 177–97.

Engel, J. F. and R. D. Blackwell (1982), *Consumer Behavior*, 4th edn, The Dryden Press: Hinsdale, Ill.

Fei, X. T. (1948), *Rural China*, Guancha She: Shanghai (in Chinese).

Graham, John L. (1981), 'A hidden cause of America's trade deficit with Japan', *Columbia Journal of World Business* (Fall), pp. 5–15.

Graham, John L. and Nancy J. Adler (1989). 'Cross-cultural interaction: The international comparison fallacy?', *Journal of International Business Studies*, vol. 20, no. 3, pp. 515–37.

Howard, J. and J. N. Sheth (1969), *The Theory of Buyer Behavior*, John Wiley: New York.

Hsieh, Y. W. (1967), *Filial piety and Chinese society'*, in C. A. Moore (ed), *The Chinese Mind*, University of Hawaii Press: Honolulu, pp. 167–87.

Hsu, F. L. K. (1971), 'Philosophical homoeostasis and jen: Conceptual tools for advancing psychological anthropology', *American Anthropologist*, vol. 73, pp. 23–44.

Johansson, Johny K. and Ikujiro Nonaka (1987), 'Market research the Japanese way', *Harvard Business Review*, May–June, pp. 16–22.

Jolibert, Alain and Maud Tixier (1988), *La Négociation Commerciale*, Editions ESF: Paris.

King, A. Y. C. (1981), 'The individual and group in Confucianism: A review', paper presented at the conference on Individualism and Holism: The Confucianist and Taoist philosophical perspective in June, York, ME.

Kotler, Philip (1991), *Marketing Management*, 7th edn, Prentice Hall: Englewood Cliffs, NJ.

Kushner, J. M. (1982), 'Market research in a non-Western context: The Asian example, *Journal of the Market Research Society*, vol. 24, no. 2, pp. 116–22.

Laufer, Romain and Catherine Paradeise (1982), *Le Prince bureaucrate: Machiavel au pays du marketing*, Flammarion: Paris.

Laurent, Clint R. (1982), 'An investigation of the family life cycle in a modern Asian society', *Journal of the Market Research Society*, vol. 24, no. 2, pp. 140–50.

Lazer, William, Shoji Murata and Hiroshi Kosaka (1985), 'Japanese marketing: Towards a better understanding', *Journal of Marketing*, vol. 49 (Spring), pp. 69–81.

Maslow, Abraham H. (1954), *Motivation and Personality*, Harper & Row: New York.

Redding, S. B. (1982). 'Cultural effects on the marketing process in Southeast Asia', *Journal of the Market Research Society*, vol. 24, no. 2, pp. 98–114.

Tanouchi, Koichi (1983), 'Japanese-style Marketing Based on Sensitivity', *Dentsu Japan Marketing/Advertising*, vol. 23 (July), 77–81.

Van Raaij, W. F. (1978), 'Cross-cultural methodology as a case of construct validity', in M. K. Hunt (ed.), *Advances in Consumer Research*, Association for Consumer Research: Ann Arbor, vol. 5, pp. 693–701.

Von Stackelberg, H. (1940), *Die Grundlagen der Nationalökonomie*, Springer Verlag: Berlin.

Yang, Chung-Fang (1989), 'Une conception du comportement du consommateur chinois', *Recherche et Applications en Marketing*, vol. IV, no. 1, pp. 17–36.

Yang, M. C. (1972), 'Familism and Chinese national character', in Y. Y. Lee and K. S. Yang (eds), *Symposium on the Character of the Chinese*, Institute of Ethnology, Academia Sinica (in Chinese), pp. 127–74.

Yau, Oliver H. M. (1988), 'Chinese cultural values: Their dimensions and marketing implications, *European Journal of Marketing*, vol. 22, no. 5, pp. 44–57.

2

The cultural process

Not everything is culture-based. It would be most dangerous to equate the behaviour of individuals entirely with that of the cultural grouping to which they belong. Furthermore we often have a rather stereotyped perception of such behaviour, which provides only a shallow, imperfect picture of the operation of a cultural group. Interpretation is often defensive and the analysis neither comprehensive nor fully explicatory.

International marketing automatically accords a prominent place to the cultural variable, despite the difficulties of isolating it for direct implementation. The principal aim is to identify, recategorize, evaluate and finally select market segments. Nation-states are an enduring reality. In many cases, though not all, national territory and the concept of a nation are united by the existence of groups that are relatively homogeneous on an ethnic, linguistic and religious level. Lack of homogeneity is often at the centre of disputes between different cultural communities. The cultural variable is complex, and the way in which it influences behaviour is difficult to analyze.

The objective of this chapter is to clear the way for the arguments that will be expounded later in the book. Initially this involves the definition of culture and its major constituents, and an examination of its relationship with nationality (i.e. the concept of national character) and individual psychology (that is, personality/individual character). Culture is not only used as a guide for communication and interaction, quite sub-consciously, with others in one's own community, but also for rather more conscious interaction with people belonging to other cultural communities. In preparing this chapter, I have borrowed largely from the field of anthropology, particularly cultural anthropology, but also from the disciplines of sociology, social psychology and cross-cultural psychology.

I would strongly urge interested readers to use the notes and bibliographical references at the end of this and the two following chapters, and to refer to the sources mentioned in their original form wherever possible.

2.1   Culture: definition(s)

In French the word culture was defined by Emile Littré, in his dictionary which appeared at the end of the nineteenth century, as 'cultivation, farming activity'. The abstract sense probably originated in Germany, where the word *Kultur* was used as early as the eighteenth century to refer to civilization. In the Anglo-Saxon world the abstract notion of culture came into widespread use at the beginning of the twentieth century.

   Many definitions have been formulated for culture: because it is a vague, abstract notion, there are many candidates for the ultimate definition. Kroeber and Kluckhohn (1952) devoted a whole article to a review of the definitions of culture and listed no less than 164! This did not prevent them from adding their own. Most of these definitions were the work of anthropologists, generally those who had studied 'primitive' societies (American Indians, Pacific Islanders, African natives and so on). But their definitions also took into account 'civilized' societies and 'modern' cultures. The use of several definitions, each one adding to the cultural jigsaw puzzle, will help to determine the main aspects of this abstract and elusive concept.

Particular solutions to universal problems

Kluckhohn and Strodtbeck (1961, p. 10) emphasize the following basic points:

1. '... there is a limited number of common human problems for which all peoples at all times must find some solution.'
2. 'While there is a variability in solutions of all the problems, it is neither limitless nor random but is definitely variable within a range of possible solutions.'
3. '... all alternatives of all solutions are present in all societies at all times, but are differentially preferred. Every society has, in addition to its dominant profile of value orientations, numerous variant or substitute profiles.'

How does culture link the individual to society?

Ralph Linton (1945, p. 21) advanced the following definition: 'A culture is the configuration of learned behaviour and results of behaviour whose component elements are shared and transmitted by the members of a particular society.' At a previous point in his book, Linton clearly indicates the limits of the cultural programming which society can impose on the individual (1945, pp. 14–15, my emphasis):

> No matter how carefully the individual has been trained or how successful his conditioning has been, he remains a distinct organism with his own needs and with capacities for independent thought, feeling and action. Moreover *he retains a considerable degree of individuality.* ... Actually, the role of the individual with respect to society is a double one. Under ordinary circumstances, the more perfect his conditioning and consequent integration into the social structure, *the more effective his contribution to the smooth functioning of the*

whole and the surer his rewards. However societies have to exist and function in an ever-changing world. The unparalleled ability of our species to adjust to changing conditions and to develop ever more effective responses to familiar ones rests upon the residue of individuality which survives in every one of us after society and culture have done their utmost. As a simple unit in the social organism, the individual perpetuates the *status quo*. As an individual he helps to change the *status quo* when the need arises.

What use is culture to the individual?

According to Goodenough (1971), culture is a set of beliefs or standards, shared by a group of people, which helps the individual decide what is, what can be, how to feel, what to do and how to go about doing it. On the basis of this definition there is no reason for culture to be equated with the whole of one particular society. It may be more related to activities which are shared by a particular group of people. Thus individuals may share different cultures with several different groups. When in a particular cultural situation, they will 'switch into' the culture that is operational. The term 'operational' describes a culture which is shared by those among whom there must be co-operation and which is suitable for the task.

Goodenough's concept of 'operational culture' assumes that the individual can choose the culture in which to interact at any given moment or in any given situation. This is of course subject to the overriding condition that the culture has been correctly internalized from past experiences. Although the concept of operational culture is somewhat debatable, it does have the advantage of highlighting the multicultural nature of many individuals in today's societies (bi-nationals, multilingual people, people who have a particular national identity and an international professional culture, employees influenced by corporate culture). It draws our attention to the important issue of the sources of the individual's acculturation.

How are the 'borders' of a culture defined?

As Child and Kieser emphasize (1977, p. 2):

> Cultures may be defined as patterns of thought and manners which are widely shared. The boundaries of the social collectivity within which this sharing takes place are problematic so that it may make as much sense to refer to a class or regional culture as to a national culture.

In colloquial language, when we talk about 'Texans', 'Parisians', 'docs', or 'showbiz people', we are referring to cultures as well as to the groups of people who share them. But it is important to consider the following issue: to what extent do the characteristics of these groups, relating to certain patterns of thought, belief or behaviour, really differentiate them from other cultural groups?

2.2 Elements of culture

Culture is much more of a process than a distinctive whole, which would be entirely identifiable by the sum of its elements. The elements are organically interrelated and work as a coherent set. Culture is not just a 'toolbox' for it also provides people with 'directions for use' in their daily life in the community. Nevertheless it may be interesting to identify some key elements of culture. Tylor (1913) describes culture as a complex and interrelated set of elements, comprising knowledge, beliefs and values, arts, law, manners and morals and all the other kinds of skills and habits acquired by a human being as a member of a particular society.

The biological foundations of culture

The anthropologist Bronislaw Malinowski has evidenced the relationship between the purely biological needs of people and the way in which they are organized and regulated within the framework of the cultural community. For Malinowski (1944, p. 75) there are clearly biological foundations of culture: 'We have to base our theory of culture on the fact that all human beings belong to an animal species. ... No culture can continue if the group is not replenished continually and normally.' He develops the example of eating habits, which must be regarded as both biological *and* cultural:

> Cultural determination is a familiar fact as regards hunger or appetite, in short the readiness to eat. Limitations of what is regarded as palatable, admissible, ethical; the magical religious, hygienic and social taboos on quality, raw materials, and preparation of food; the habitual routine establishing the time and the type of appetite – all these could be exemplified from our civilization, from the rules and principles of Judaism, or Islam, Brahmanism or Shintoism, as well as from every primitive culture.

Malinowski (1944, pp. 86–7) also evokes the cultural relativity of sexual behaviour:

> The specific form in which the sexual impulse is allowed to occur is deeply modified by anatomical inroads (circumcision, infibulation, clitoridectomy, breast, foot and face lacerations); the attractiveness of a sex object is affected by economic status and rank; and the integration of the sex impulse involves the personal desirability of a mate as an individual and as a member of the group. It would be equally easy to show that fatigue, somnolence, thirst and restlessness are determined by such cultural factors as a call to duty, the urgency of a task, the established rhythm of activities.

Language

Language has a prominent role as an element of culture. The linguist and anthropologist Benjamin Lee Whorf (Carroll, 1956, p. 65), who worked as a chemical engineer for a fire insurance company, spent his spare time tracing the origins and grammar of American-Indian languages. He is the author of a seminal, and quite controversial, hypothesis, often referred to as the Whorfian hypothesis or Whorf–Sapir hypothesis. Aspects of this theory have been incorporated, either explicitly or implicitly, at many points in this book, particularly those chapters in which language and linguistics figure strongly: market research (Chapter 5), brands (Chapter 9), advertising (Chapter 12) and negotiation (Chapter 13). Whorf defines his basic tenet as follows:

> The ethnologist engaged in studying a living primitive culture must often have wondered: 'What do these people think? How do they think? Are their intellectual and rational processes akin to ours or radically different?' But thereupon he has probably dismissed the idea as a psychological enigma and has sharply turned his attention back to more readily observable matters. And yet the problem of thought and thinking in the native community is not purely and simply a psychological problem. It is quite largely cultural. It is moreover largely a matter of one especially cohesive aggregate of cultural phenomena that we call a language.

In short, Whorf defends the idea that the language we learn in the community where we are born and raised shapes and structures our world-view and our social behaviour. It influences the way in which we address issues, select those we consider relevant, solve problems and finally act. Although the Whorfian hypothesis has been harshly criticized by many linguists, it remains a *fundamental metaphor*, though not a fully validated scientific theory. It is noted as a central issue in the discussion of the pitfalls of intercultural communication (in Chapter 4). It is also mentioned in the examination of time patterns and their influence on business attitudes (when negotiating or dealing with delivery times or appointments), using the case of the Bantu people as an illustration. Bantu do not have a specific word (like most Western culture) which clearly differentiates the 'here' and the 'now'. They have a common time-space localizer (Chapter 4, Box 4.1 and Section A4.1).

Social institutions, material and symbolic productions

Language is an essential part of culture: it is often regarded as a reflection of culture. It is the basic input of any culture-based communication process, because everyday life is mostly a matter of interaction through communication in a culturally homogeneous community. But obviously it is not the only element of the culture shared by a community: for instance, the Swiss use different languages but have shared a common culture for more than seven centuries. Accordingly, three other types of element appear to be quite significant:

1. Institutions, broadly defined, because they are the 'spine' of the cultural process, in that they link the individual to the group. This area may include family institutions as well as political institutions, or any kind of social organization within which the individual has to comply obediently with rules in exchange for various rewards (e.g. being fed, loved, paid and so on). These rules are not static and an individual may also sometimes act as a proactive agent of change.
2. Productions (again, broadly defined): not only material productions, but also productions of intellect, artistry and service in so far as they transmit, reproduce, update and continuously attempt to improve the knowledge and skills in the community.[1]

3. Symbolic and sacred elements,[2] because they are the basis of the description (and therefore management) of the relationship between the physical and the metaphysical worlds. Cultures range from those where there is complete denial of the existence of any kind of metaphysical world to those where symbolic representations of the metaphysical world are present in everyday life.[3]

There is nothing to prevent a particular cultural item from belonging to these four elements of culture simultaneously, which then appear as different layers. For instance, music is at the same time a language, an institution, an artistic production and also has a symbolic element.

Productions are diverse: tools, machines, factories, paper, books, instruments and media of communication, food, clothing, ornaments, etc. As a result, we often confuse an influential civilization (which corresponds to the German word *Kultur*) with a cultural community that succeeds in producing a large variety of goods and services in large quantities. But material consumption or wealth orientation are not definitive proof of cultural sophistication. *There is no hierarchy, apart from the purely subjective, between world cultures.* There are many very different cultural attitudes to the material world, its importance and the level of priority in the community's resource allocation given to productions and material achievements.

In *A Scientific Theory of Culture* (1944), Bronislaw Malinowski compiled a list of universal types of institutions, to which the following refers. The first type of institution is based on the integrative principle of *reproduction*: it is underpinned by blood relationships and marriage as an established contractual framework. It covers all kinds of kinship patterns – the family as the basic institution formed by parents and children. The reproduction principle also incorporates the ways in which courtship and marriage are legally organized. The extended family must also be considered: clan organization and its nature (matrilineal, patrilineal), the regulation of inter-clan relationships, etc.

The second type of institution is based on the integrative principle of *territoriality*. Common interests are dictated by neighbourhood and vicinity. Co-operation may be enhanced by the commonly perceived threat of potential foes who are located outside the common territory. This type of institution may range from a horde of nomads to a village, a small town community, a region, a province or, at the largest level, the 'mega-tribe' composed of all the people sharing the nationality of a particular nation-state. Initially territoriality is concrete, based on physical space and some kind of fencing or borders. In the modern world, it may be extended to abstract territories (associations, clubs, alumni and so on).

The third integrative principle is a *physiological* one: people in the community are basically characterized by their sex, age, physical traits or defects. This includes institutions such as the sexual division of labour, sex roles, the relationship patterns between age groups and the way in which minority members of the community are treated (asylums for the mentally ill, or special homes for the disabled).

The fourth principle deals with the *spontaneous tendency to join together* in order to pursue common goals. This gives rise to various kinds of associations: primitive secret societies, clubs, artistic societies, mutual companies, etc.

The fifth principle is that of *occupational and professional activities*: it deals with the way labour is divided and the kinds of expertise that have been developed. In modern societies, this includes all those institutions which maintain the fabric of a society: economic organization, the medical system, the legal system, the police, the army, educational institutions and religious bodies.

The sixth principle concerns the unavoidable *hierarchy* of any society: the existence of rank and status positions. This includes the following, *inter alia*: the nobility, the middle class and slaves, or more generally any kind of social class or caste system. The social hierarchy may follow a variety of criteria: ethnicity, education or the level of riches, etc.

The seventh principle proposed by Malinowski corresponds to the necessity of gathering and co-ordinating these diverse elements into a reasonably coherent whole, that is, *totality*. The political process, whatever it may be (feudal, democratic, theocratic, dictatorial, etc.), expresses the need for totality. It deals with the collective decision process at the highest level. The various strata of totality, such as the individual striving for identity and the community striving for coherence, may compete with each other: that of a minority, that of a State; more generally sub-groups of the mega-tribe of a nation-state. A minority, willing to practise its religion and mores (e.g. polygamy), may be opposed to the state which tries to maintain the global coherence by limiting social customs to the dominant solution (e.g. monogamy). More generally any sub-group of the 'mega-tribe', composed of all the nationals of a definite state may feel that their particular interests are conflicting with those of the community as a whole. These oppositions will be stronger in 'simple' states (where the nationals are not necessarily homogeneous from a cultural point of view) and a nation-state (where the nationals share a common linguistic and cultural background).

Culture as a collective fingerprint: are some cultures superior?

Culture is *the* domain of pure quality. There are no 'good' or 'bad' elements of a particular cultural group. Value judgements should be avoided as much as possible. In this respect the nature of culture is entirely qualitative. Culture is identity: a sort of collective fingerprint. To this extent it exhibits differences but it may not be judged as globally superior or inferior. It may be evaluated and indeed ranked, but only on the basis of facts and evidence according to precise criteria and for very specific segments of culture-related activities. Some people may be said to make better warriors, others to hold finer aesthetic judgement, or to be more gifted in the composition of music, and so on. But culture is a set of *coherent* elements: straightforward comparison might allow us to indulge in the rather dangerous illusion that it is possible to select the best from each culture to make an 'ideal' combination. However, as we will see later on, it is not quite that easy.

There is a joke about the Europeans which illustrates this: 'Heaven is where the cooks are French, the mechanics are German, the policemen are English, the lovers are Italian, and it is all organized by the Swiss. Hell is where the policemen are German, the mechanics are French, the cooks are British, the lovers are Swiss, and it is all organized by the Italians.' It is easy to see that not only would it be difficult to take the best traits from a culture while rejecting the worst, but also the end result of any attempt to combine the best of several cultures could be a disaster. This is because *coherence* is needed at the highest level (corresponding to *identity* at the individual level).

The importance of the symbolic dimension

Objects which are the productions of culture cannot be described only by their physical attributes: they always contain a symbolic or sacred element. This is also true of many behavioural artefacts (see the reading 'Body ritual among the Naciremas' on page 55). Mircea Eliade (1956, p. 79)[4] describes how the arts of the blacksmith and the alchemist, the forerunners of modern metallurgy and chemistry, holds a powerful symbolic dimension:

> The alchemist, like the smith, and like the potter before him, is a 'master of fire'. It is with fire that he controls the passage of matter from one state to another. The first potter who, with the aid of live embers, was successful in hardening those shapes which he had given to his clay, must have felt the intoxication of the demiurge: he had discovered a transmuting agent. That which natural heat – from the sun or the bowels of the earth – took so long to ripen, was transformed by fire at a speed hitherto undreamed of. This demiurgic enthusiasm springs from that obscure presentiment that the great secret lay in discovering how to 'perform' faster than Nature, in other words (since it is always necessary to talk in terms of the spiritual experience of the primitive man) how, without peril, to interfere in the processes of the cosmic forces. Fire turned out to be the means by which man could 'execute' faster, but it could also do something other than what already existed in Nature. It was therefore the manifestation of a magico-religious power which could modify the world and which, consequently, did not belong to this world. This is why the most primitive cultures look upon the specialist in the sacred – the shaman, the medicine-man, the magician – as a 'master of fire'.

Numerous illustrations of the strength of symbolic dimensions are given throughout the book. In marketing communication, symbolic dimension is of the utmost importance: products and their advertising communicate through the symbolism of colour, shape, label, brand name and so on. The interpretation of symbols is strongly culture-bound.

Traditional societies have always been more consciously involved in symbolic thought and behaviour than modern societies. Since less is *explained*, more must be *related*. For example: Why does the sun shine every day? Should its disappearance be considered ominous? What should be done to satisfy it so that it goes on spreading its generous rays on the fields and rivers? The bloody ritual sacrifices in the pre-Colombian civilizations were heavily charged with symbolic content.[5] Human sacrifices were dedicated to the sun, as were the blood and the heart which were pulled out of the bodies of living people. The Spanish conquerors were utterly horrified by these sacrifices because they did not understand the meaning of them. The Spaniards were helped in their conquest by a myth: Mayas and Aztecs were waiting for the return of Quetzalcoatl, a sort of man-god, who had been a benevolent ruler over his people and whose return was to herald a golden age. When the bearded Hernan Cortès landed in Mexico accompanied by strange creatures (the Indians believed that horses and their riders were a single body), they saw him as Quetzalcoatl.

Of course, symbols are not only related to religious and metaphysical matters: they also extend into everyday life. It is a common error to believe that the symbolic dimension has largely disappeared in modern life, forgotten by modern people who have progressed along the road towards science and knowledge, pushing back the boundaries of the metaphysical world, which will ultimately be eliminated. The illusion of the pre-eminence of science generated by technological breakthroughs in the nineteenth century is now largely abandoned by today's top scientists. As Stephen Hawking points out (1988, p. 13):

> ... ever since the dawn of civilization, people have not been content to see events as unconnected and inexplicable. They have craved an understanding of the underlying order in the world. Today we still yearn to know why we are here and where we came from.

2.3   Culture and nationality

Nationality is one delimitation of individuals belonging to a large group. It is related to the operational nature of culture, and is promulgated by its obvious convenience. However, the direction of causality between these two concepts of nationality and culture is not self-evident. It is likely that, historically, shared culture has been a fundamental building block in the progressive construction of modern nation-states. But as soon as these states began to emerge, they struggled against local particularisms, patois and customs, and tried to homogenize institutions. Conflicts in large countries have often had a strong cultural base: the War of Secession in the United States, the rivalry between the English and the Scots in Great Britain and the progressive elimination of local powers in the highly centralized French State, all have distinctive cultural elements at stake: language, values, religion, concepts of freedom, etc.

Nevertheless an attempt to equate culture directly with the nation-state, or country, would be misguided for a number of convergent reasons:

1. A country culture can only be defined by reference to other country cultures. India is a country culture in comparison with Italy or Germany, but the Indian subcontinent is made up of highly diversified ethnic and religious groups (Muslims, Hindus, Sikhs, etc.) and languages (there are more than twenty principal languages). India is a profoundly multicultural country.
2. Some nation-states are explicitly multicultural – Switzerland, for instance. One of the basic levels of organization is the canton (*Gau* in German), which defends local particularisms. Precise staffing levels have been established in public bodies, companies and banks, which prevent discrimination between linguistic communities whose numbers are unequal: the German-speaking Swiss make up almost three-quarters of the total population, the French-speakers a little more than 20 per cent, Italian-speakers 3–4 per cent and Romansch-speakers about 1 per cent. However, there is a common misconception that Switzerland administers its multiculturalism without encountering any difficulties.[6] The Swiss political system, which was established more than seven centuries ago, enables the people to manage successfully the complex trade-off between an exacerbated compliance with local peculiarities and a common attitude towards anything that is not Swiss.[7]
3. Political decisions, especially during the last century, have imposed the formation of new states, particularly through the processes of colonization and decolonization. The fixing of borders of these new states often showed little respect for cultural realities,

and international negotiators obviously had very little in common with the people for whom they were making decisions. Many significant national cultures, such as that of the Kurds (split between the Iraqis, the Turks and the Iranians) or the Eritreans (in Ethiopia), have never been accorded the right to a territory or a state.

Sources of culture

The national element is not always the main source of culture when regarded from an 'operational culture' perspective (Goodenough, 1971). Figure 2.1 shows some basic sources of cultural background at the level of the individual. For instance medical researchers or computer hardware specialists, whatever their nationality, share a common specialized education, common interests and largely the same professional culture. This is developed through common training, working for the same companies, reading the same publications world-wide, and contributing to research where international cross-cultural comparability of purely scientific methods and results is fundamental.

Likewise, the sense of belonging to an important ethnic group may override, and even nullify the feeling of belonging to a particular nation-state. The Tamil population in Sri Lanka, which makes up about 20 per cent of the total Sri Lankan population and is mostly centred around Jaffna in the north of the island, is strongly linked with the large Tamil community in southern India (numbering 55 million), which supports them in their claim for autonomy. The Tamils are involved in a brutal struggle with the Singalese community, which accounts for the largest part of the population. The sense of belonging to a large ethnic group is, in this case, much stronger than the feeling of belonging to a national group.

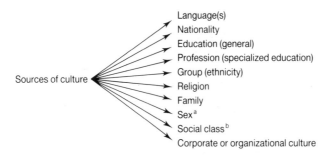

Sources of culture →
- Language(s)
- Nationality
- Education (general)
- Profession (specialized education)
- Group (ethnicity)
- Religion
- Family
- Sex[a]
- Social class[b]
- Corporate or organizational culture

[a] In 1948 the anthropologist Margaret Mead published *Male and Female* (William Morrow: New York), which draws on her in-depth knowledge of several South Pacific and Balinese cultures. It not only depicts their organization of relationships between men and women, the division of labour and roles in the community, but also explains how these patterns may be compared to those of contemporary American society. *Male and Female*, which has been a continuous best-seller, is an excellent and detailed introduction to sex cultures. Although rarely mentioned in this book, which is principally concerned with territory and national culture, the difference between masculine and feminine culture is in fact the most basic cultural distinction.

[b] Social class may be a distinctive source of culture, to a greater or lesser degree, depending on the country. For instance in France and England, where there are traditions of accepted birth inequalities and a strong historical orientation, social class is a very distinctive source of culture; the way one speaks immediately reveals one's social class. However in the United States, Japan or the Scandinavian countries, this is not so marked. But like sex, and unlike most other sources, social class is not a territory-based source of culture.

Figure 2.1   Sources of culture.

National/cultural territories with specific, recognized borders are rarely fully homogeneous. The transition from one to another is often facilitated by 'cross-border' cultures. Examples of this are numerous. In the area around the border between France and Spain, for instance, two cultures, which are almost national cultures, exist side by side and offer continuity between the two countries: the Basque country to the west, Catalonia to the east. The painter Salvador Dali, a Catalan born in Figueras (Spain) which is 20 km from the French border, was fascinated by the train station at Peripignan in France – the French part of Catalonia. In reality these two places, on either side of the border, belong to the same Catalan culture, which is sustained by the use of the Catalan language. Other examples show that some people have been able to reach a compromise: the Swedish-speaking minority on the west coast of Finland, for instance, or the Alsatians in France. Alsatians speak a mostly German-based patois, behave in the workplace like Germans and traditionally lean towards a sense of French nationality and the adoption of the French life-style outside the workplace. People who belong to these 'cross-border' cultures generally have a privileged position as 'exporters' from one country to other.

Physical and climatic conditions are also a fairly systematic source of differentiation (subtle rather than fundamental). Hence almost every apparently unified country is made up of a 'North' and a 'South'. Even in a country that is homogeneous from a linguistic, ethnic, religious and institutional point of view, such as Sweden, there is a fairly marked difference, at least for the Swedes, between the culture and life-style of a southern city (say, Malmö) and a northern town (say, Luleå). This difference may not be so strongly perceived by foreigners, who initially appreciate only their own differences from Swedes and Sweden as a whole.

Cultural homogeneity and relevant segmentation

In order to identify market segments it is important to determine the level of geographic/geopolitical division, which will provide us with the most efficient segmentation criteria in cultural terms. Should one, for instance, target a transitional ethnic segment, a national segment or a cross-border regional segment? Chapters 5 and 7 examine the issue of regional versus national segmentation, which is particularly important in large countries like the United States.

Some factors of homogeneity are clearly favourable to the emergence of a homogeneous culture in a nation-state and hence to the possible confusion of culture and country and treatment of the latter as a culturally unified and coherent segment (which could be broken down into sociodemographic microsegments):

+ Linguistic homogeneity.
+ Religious homogeneity.
+ Ethnic homogeneity.
+ Climatic homogeneity.
+ Geographic homogeneity.
+ Institutional and political homogeneity.
+ Social/income homogeneity.

The word 'homogeneity' implies one of the following:

1. The existence, throughout the whole population, of a unique modality (that is, only one religion, or one language) or a reduced standard deviation (in per capita income, for instance, across all social strata) in comparison with the mean value of the characteristic across the whole population.
2. An accepted diversity, that is, an agreement for maintaining several official languages, more or less spoken and/or understood by everybody, or several different religions (as in Germany), but all of them officially recognized and financed by the state.
3. 'Perceived homogeneity', that is, the perception of differences within a country as being acceptable within the national community. For instance, people may observe huge differences in wealth and income but consider it acceptable, for various reasons: fatalism, indifference, or metaphysical justification.

The concept of national culture

The concept of national culture may seem dangerous in many respects, because it sums up a complex and multiform reality. In short, as a variable it is too artificial to avoid the traps of cliché and stereotype. The following two questions should enable a better grasp of the concept:

1. Is this concept coherent and substantial enough to constitute an explanatory variable, not only in the scientific sense, but also from a pragmatic point of view?
2. How does it influence behaviour: can one speak of national character or national culture?

The answer to the first question is clear: the concept of national culture suffers a systematic lack of coherence. It is an 'intersection' of concepts, one being the result of the merging of culture (a mostly anthropology-based concept), and the other, more official, concept being that of the nation-state. As discussed earlier, cultures do not often correspond to nation-states but to linguistic, ethnic, religious or even organizational entities. This is due to the fact that in modern times, the most frequent mode of political organization of individuals within a particular society is that of the nation-state, hence the emergence of this 'intersection' concept of national culture.[8] Despite this, it can still be an interesting Pandora's box.

The second question merits consideration, but the two possible responses as to whether culture directly influences personality cannot be assessed on a scientific basis. Some people favour the idea that the cultural variable directly influences individual psychological characteristics, i.e. culture has a distinct imprint on personality. Personality traits exist for which the average individual in one culture scores significantly higher (or lower) than individuals belonging to another culture. This is the idea of national character, or more precisely the concept of modal personality, which has been developed in greater detail by Inkeles and Levinson (1969).[9] This approach largely grew out of enquiries which now seem to have lost some of their relevance: why are certain people more violent, more aggressive, more domineering, collectively more prone to declare war on other nations or to organize and implement genocide? These questions stemmed from the Second World War, especially the Nuremberg trials. Numerous empirical studies have been undertaken, particularly during the 1950s and 1960s, taking as a starting point the formation process of national character (where there could be a divergence between nations): rearing practices, early childhood, education systems, the socialization process of children, etc. Generally the results neither prove nor disprove the existence of national character (Inkeles and Levinson, 1969).

The second approach is that of the anthropologist Ralph Linton in his book, *The Cultural Background of Personality*. His definition of culture is quoted on page 39. According to Linton, individual psychology and therefore personality traits are largely free from the influence of culture (1945, pp. 14–15): 'His [the individual's] integration into society and culture goes no deeper than his learned responses, and although in the adult the greater part of what we call the personality, there is still a good deal of the individual left over.' The question of whether personality is modal (culture-bound) or culture-free, is not just academic. From a pragmatic perspective, it is very important to define one's own position. In Linton's view, individuals may have personalities evinced by universal traits – quite separate from their cultural background. From a 'national character' perspective, one would expect to meet people with an average personality which reflects their culture.

2.4 Culture and competence

Some environmental predispositions

Some peoples seem to be more work-orientated and more efficient when it comes to producing material goods. Among the most efficient peoples are those who lost the Second World War:[10] Germany, Japan and Italy. Climate has often been considered an environmental variable which has a strong influence on performance. Box 2.1 contains the beginning of Montesquieu's theory of climates (1748). The physiological explanations are scarcely credible now; it is nevertheless a starting point for the north/south stereotype. The question is: do some countries/climates tend to harden (or soften) people, with the result that they become more (or less) inclined towards activities of war, commerce or industry,[11] and more (or less) efficient in pursuing these activities?

It is a different assumption to say that climate has a direct influence (as Montesquieu argues) or an indirect influence on skills. The indirect influence may be combined with the direct influence because climate may have had a long-term influence on the culture, which would in turn influence skills and behaviour. If the influence is direct, air conditioning is obviously the solution (although one cannot have an air-conditioned battle); or if climate has both a direct and an indirect influence, via progressive genetic adaptation and/or cultural traits acquired through education and socialization, which reflect the adaptation to a less favourable milieu (at least from a temperature point of view), then air conditioning is still necessary but not sufficient.

National character and educational practices

An important issue in the field of national character research is the influence of education practices on the development of adult personalities as individuals with a clear cultural background. Margaret Mead for instance, in her description of American character, notes that adult personality in the United States must be seen as an adolescent peer culture. In this setting, education favours diffuse, depersonalized authority where children face a demand for strong inner moral control. In this shame-orientated society guilt is the consequence of value violation. In many European countries, the cheerful, easy-going, informal Americans are often jokingly referred to as being big children.

One of the most efficient ways to study the formation process of national character is to observe education systems and rearing practices; particularly the rearing of small children, up to the age of 5 or 6. Some of the key elements of personality development are

Box 2.1   *Of the difference of men in different climates*

A cold air* constringes the extremities of the external fibres of the body; this increases their elasticity, and favors the return of the blood from the extreme parts to the heart. It contracts[†] those very fibres; consequently, it increases also their force and elasticity. People are therefore more vigorous in cold climates. Here the action of the heart and the reaction of the extremities of the fibres are better performed, the temperature of the humors is greater, the blood moves freer towards the heart, and reciprocally, the heart has more power. This superiority of strength must produce various effects; for instance, a greater boldness, that is, more courage; a greater sense of superiority, that is, more frankness, less suspicion, policy, and cunning. In short, this must be productive of very different tempers. Put a man into a close warm place, and, for the reasons above given, he will feel a great faintness. If, under this circumstance, you propose a bold enterprize to him, I believe you will find him very little disposed towards it: his present weakness will throw him into a despondency; he will be afraid of every thing, being in a state of total incapacity. The inhabitants of warm countries are, like old men, timorous; the people in cold countries are, like young men, brave. If we reflect on the late** wars, (which are more recent in our memory, and in which we can better distinguish some particular effects, that escape us as a greater distance of time,) we shall find that the northern people, transplanted into southern regions[††], did not perform such exploits as their countrymen who, fighting in their own climate, possessed their full vigor and courage.
*This appears even in the countenance: in cold weather people look thinner.
[†]We know it shortens iron.
**Those for the succession to the Spanish monarchy.
[††]For instance in Spain.

(Montesquieu, 1748, vol. 1, book XIV, ch. 11, pp. 224–5.)

here: feeding and nourishing, weaning, personal hygiene and toilet training, the degree and modes of socialization into various parts of the community (with other children, with adults, with the opposite sex), the demands and prohibitions imposed on small children, and finally the reward/sanction systems which help to orientate their behaviour.[12]

Culture and skills

It seems that cultural background has an influence on perceptual and cognitive skills and their orientations and capacities. Segall *et al.* (1990) clearly demonstrate the existence of differences in perception of visual illusions. They base their findings on the following simple theory: if people belonging to various human groups differ in their visual inference systems,[13] this is because the physical environment at which they are used to looking may differ widely from group to group. Some people live in a constructed environment, based on straight lines and sharp angles (especially those of modern buildings and industrial objects), whereas other people live in a more rounded and curvilinear physical setting. The daily environment shapes people's visual inferences: the very same objects are seen differently (where vision is considered as a culturally built interpretation of specific retina signals).

The variations in levels of competences and skills across cultural groups is another important issue. The first research on the intellectual abilities of non-European people was been undertaken by researchers such as Lévy-Bruhl, who classified the thought patterns of primitives as 'pre-logical'. Little by little this somewhat extreme attitude, that 'primitives' could never conceive of anything in the way that we do (we being the modern, westernized people of European culture or origin), has given way to a more reasonable position. Franz Boas became interested in the idea of the psychic unity of mankind: every human group studied presents common traits such as the ability to remember, to generalize, to form concepts and to think and reflect logically on abstract concepts. In fact it seems more likely that differences in ability in specific activities should be attributed to the cultural relativity of skills and competences developed by the individuals in the specific cultural grouping where they have been raised.[14] The scores on intelligence quotient (IQ) tests will always remain relative to the type of questions asked and to the situations evoked in the verbal part of the test (reading, memorization and understanding of texts); even that part of the test which is clearly quantitatively orientated (maths, geometry, statistics, logic) demands the manipulation of abstract and mathematical signs. One cannot claim that it encompasses all the possible facets of human intelligence, nor even that it offers total objectivity in the experimental and empirical methods of evidencing them. It is therefore necessary to accept that, evidently, definitions of intelligence are culturally contingent. This does not mean that all people are equally intelligent, nor that IQ tests are of no interest or practical usefulness. It simply means that the results should be interpreted cautiously when tests are administered to people who do not originate from the culture where these tests were conceived and/or are not familiar with this culture.[15]

2.5   Culture and social representations

The notion of social representation will be valuable throughout this book, even where there is no explicit reference to it. One example will suffice as an explanation of the practicalities of this concept: the acceptance (or prohibition in some countries) of comparative advertising across countries is related to social representations of the necessity to inform consumers, to allow price competition and even to risk the denigration of one company by another through a comparative advertising campaign (see Chapter 12).

Moscovici (1961) considers social representation (SR) a 'forgotten concept'. He traces it back to Durkheim, for whom it was a class of psychic and social phenomena that relate the individual to the social aspect of collective life. Social representations are miniatures of behaviour, copies of reality and forms of operational knowledge in order to reach and implement everyday decisions. For instance, people may use a combination of social representations in order to make their health-care decisions. Moscovici gives the following example that in the south west of the United States Hispanic populations concurrently use four bases of knowledge for classifying and interpreting illnesses: the traditional popular medical knowledge, which relates mainly to pains and sufferance; the medical knowledge orally transmitted within Amerindian tribes; the modern (English) popular medical knowledge; and medical scientific knowledge (established and recognized). According to the seriousness of the illness and the availability of money for paying for the cure, Hispanic populations let themselves be guided either by collective representations or by scientific information in order to choose which one of these four sources should be pursued in search of a cure.

Social representations are collective images which are progressively formulated within a particular society. They may be surveyed by public opinion polls. Robert Farr (1988, p. 383) explains that social representations of health and sickness may have a strong influence on consumption patterns. Villagers in many European countries, for instance, tend to lament the invasion of the countryside by urban development; the entire population compares the constraints of city life to the natural pace of country life. These social representations help to explain the development of natural and organic products, direct from the farm, with no additives or industrial processing, and they are largely supported by the diffusion of ecological ideas in modern society.

Jodelet (1988, p. 360) posits social representations at the very intersection of psychological/individual and the social/collective levels. They serve as artificial reference images, as frameworks 'which enable us to interpret what happens to us, possibly even to give sense to the unexpected; categories which serve to classify circumstances, phenomena, individuals with whom we have to deal and theories which enable us to make a decision on these issues'.

The method of analysis and interpretation of daily reality through the use of this sort of preconceived reference framework could be considered in some respects as prejudice – a pejorative word. It would give but a scant idea of the dynamic, collectively verified and validated nature of social representations, which are constantly updated through social situations, individual behaviour and social activities. The media, public opinion polls, news summaries, court decisions and sentences are all sources from which people derive their opinions and stimulate debate and social information processes, which in turn continuously update dynamic social representations.

Social representations do vary across societies. They therefore have a cultural value for the individuals when they have to decide what is, what can be, how to feel, what to do, and how to go about doing it (operating culture). Social representations are less profound, as they alter within shorter time spans (ten to twenty years), than basic cultural orientations which change over centuries – the latter are reviewed in the next chapter.[16] But social representations are none the less important – they may oppose basic cultural orientations since their time-scale is short term and they are more suited to the urgent need for collective and individual adaptation to reality.[17]

APPENDIX 2

—————— ◆◆◆ ——————

Teaching materials

A2.1 Critical incident: An old lady from Malaysia

The frail, old, almost totally blind lady appeared at every clinic session and sat on the dirt floor enjoying the activity. She was dirty and dishevelled, and obviously had very little, even by Malaysian *kampong* (local village) standards.

One day the visiting nurse happened upon this woman in her kampong. She lived by herself in a rundown shack about 10 by 10 feet. When questioned how she obtained her food, she said she was often hungry, as she only received food when she worked for others – pounding rice, looking after the children, and the like.

The nurse sought to obtain help for the woman. It was finally resolved that she would receive a small pension from the Department of Welfare which would be ample for her needs.

At each weekly clinic, the woman continued to appear. She had become a center of attention, laughed and joked freely, and obviously enjoyed her increased prestige. No change was noted in her physical status, however. She continued to wear the same dirty black dress and looked no better fed.

The nurse asked one of the rural health nurses to find out if the woman needed help in getting to a shop to buy the goods she seemed so sorely in need of.

In squatting near the woman, the rural health nurse noted a wad of bills in the woman's pocket. 'Wah,' she said, 'It is all here. You have spent nothing. Why is that?'

The woman laughed and then explained: 'I am saving it all for my funeral.'

(Weeks *et al.*, 1987, pp. 24–5. Reproduced with the kind permission of the publisher.)

A2.2 Critical incident: The parable

The leader tells the following parable to the group, illustrating with rough chalkboard drawings if desired:

> Rosemary is a girl of about 21 years of age. For several months she has been engaged to a young man named – let's call him Geoffrey. The problem she faces is that between her and her betrothed there lies a river. No ordinary river mind you, but a deep, wide river infested with hungry crocodiles.
>
> Rosemary ponders how she can cross the river. She thinks of a man she knows who has a boat. We'll call him Sinbad. So she approaches Sinbad, asking him to take her across. He replies, 'Yes, I'll take you across if you'll spend the night with me.' Shocked at this offer, she turns to another acquaintance, a certain Frederick, and tells him her story. Frederick responds by saying, 'Yes, Rosemary, I understand your problem – but – it's your problem, not mine.' Rosemary decides to return to Sinbad, spends the night with him, and in the morning he takes her across the river.
>
> Her reunion with Geoffrey is warm. But on the evening before they are to be married, Rosemary feels compelled to tell Geoffrey how she succeeded in getting across the river. Geoffrey responds by saying, 'I wouldn't marry you if you were the last woman on earth.'
>
> Finally, at her wit's end, Rosemary turns to our last character, Dennis. Dennis listens to her story and says, 'Well, Rosemary, I don't love you ... but I will marry you.' And that's all we know of the story.

(Weeks *et al.*, 1987, pp. 24–26. Reproduced with the kind permission of the publisher.)

Discussion guide

1. Before any discussion, participants should be asked to write down individually on a piece of paper the characters of whose behaviour they most approve, plus a sentence or two explaining their first choice.
2. Participants may be split into small groups of four or five, to share their views and raise relevant issues.
3. The discussion should centre around the cultural relativity of values and their relation to one's own cultural background.

A2.3 Reading: Body ritual among the Nacirema

The anthropologist has become so familiar with the diversity of ways in which different peoples behave in similar situations that he is not apt to be surprised by even the most exotic customs. In fact, if all of the logically possible combinations of behavior have not been found somewhere in the world, he is apt to suspect that they must be present in some yet undescribed tribe. This point has, in fact, been expressed with respect to clan organization by Murdock (1949:71). In this light, the magical beliefs and practices of the Nacirema present such unusual aspects that it seems desirable to describe them as an example of the extremes to which human behavior can go.

Professor Linton first brought the ritual of the Nacirema to the attention of anthropologists twenty years ago (1936: 326), but the culture of this people is still very poorly understood. They are a North American group living in the territory between the Canadian Cree, the Yaqui and Tarahumare of Mexico, and the Carib and Arawak of the Antilles. Little is known of their origin. although tradition states that they came from the east. According to Nacirema mythology, their nation was originated by a culture hero, Notgnihsaw, who is otherwise known for two great feats of strength – the throwing of a piece of wampum across the river Pa-To-Mac and the chopping down of a cherry tree in which the Spirit of Truth resided.

Nacirema culture is characterized by a highly developed market economy which has evolved in a rich natural habitat. While much of the people's time is devoted to economic pursuits, a large part of the fruits of these labors and a considerable portion of the day are spent in ritual activity. The focus of this activity is the human body, the appearance and health of which loom as a dominant concern in the ethos of the people. While such a concern is certainly not unusual, its ceremonial aspects and associated philosophy are unique.

The fundamental belief underlying the whole system appears to be that the human body is ugly and that its natural tendency is to debility and disease. Incarcerated in such a body, man's only hope is to avert these characteristics through the use of the powerful influences of ritual and ceremony. Every household has one or more shrines devoted to this purpose. The more powerful individuals in the society have several shrines in their houses and, in fact, the opulence of a house is often referred to in terms of the number of such ritual centers it possesses. Most houses are of wattle and daub construction, but the shrine rooms of the more wealthy are walled with stone. Poorer families imitate the rich by applying pottery plaques to their shrine walls.

While each family has at least one such shrine, the rituals associated with it are not family ceremonies but are private and secret. The rites are normally only discussed with children, and then only during the period when they are being initiated into these mysteries. I was able, however, to establish sufficient rapport with the natives to examine these shrines and to have the rituals described to me.

The focal point of the shrine is a box or chest which is built into the wall. In this chest are kept the many charms and magical potions without which no native believes he could live. These preparations are secured from a variety of specialized practitioners. The most powerful of these are the medicine men, whose assistance must be rewarded with substantial gifts. However, the medicine men do not provide the curative potions for their clients, but decide what the ingredients should be and then write them down in an ancient and secret language. This writing is understood only by the medicine men and by the herbalists who, for another gift, provide the required charm.

The charm is not disposed of after it has served its purpose, but is placed in the charm-box of the household shrine. As these magical materials are specific for certain ills, and the real or imagined maladies of the people are many, the charm-box is usually full to overflowing. The magical packets are so numerous that people forget what their purposes were and fear to use them again. While the natives are very vague on this point, we can only assume that the idea in retaining all the old magical materials is that their presence in the charm-box, before which the body rituals are conducted, will in some way protect the worshipper.

Beneath the charm-box is a small font. Each day every member of the family, in succession, enters the shrine room, bows his head before the charm-box, mingles different sorts of holy water in the font, and proceeds with a brief rite of ablution. The holy waters are secured from the Water Temple of the community, where the priests conduct elaborate ceremonies to make the liquid ritually pure.

In the hierarchy of magical practitioners, and below the medicine men in prestige, are specialists whose designation is best translated 'holy-mouth-men.' The Nacirema have an almost pathological horror of and fascination with the mouth, the condition of which is believed to have a supernatural influence on all social relationships. Were it not for the rituals of the mouth, they believe that their teeth would fall out, their gums bleed, their jaws shrink, their friends desert them and their lovers reject them. They also believe that a strong relationship exists between oral and moral characteristics. For example, there is a ritual ablution of the mouth for children which is supposed to improve their moral fiber.

The daily body ritual performed by everyone includes a mouth-rite. Despite the fact that these people are so punctilious about care of the mouth, this rite involves a practice which strikes the uninitiated stranger as revolting. It was reported to me that the ritual consists of inserting a small bundle of hog hairs into the mouth, along with certain magical powders, and then moving the bundle in a highly formalized series of gestures.

In addition to the private mouth-rite, the people seek out a holy-mouth-man once or twice a year. These practitioners have an impressive set of paraphernalia, consisting of a variety of augers, awls, probes, and prods. The use of these objects in the exorcism of the evils of the mouth involves almost unbelievable ritual torture of the client. The holy-mouth-man opens the client's mouth and, using the above mentioned tools, enlarges any holes which decay may have created in the teeth. Magical materials are put into these holes. If there are no naturally occurring holes in the teeth, large sections of one or more teeth are gouged out so that the supernatural substance can be applied. In the client's views, the purpose of these ministrations is to arrest decay and to draw friends. The extremely sacred and traditional character of the rite is evident in the fact that the natives return to the holy-mouth-men year after year, despite the fact that their teeth continue to decay.

It is to be hoped that, when a thorough study of the Nacirema is made, there will be careful inquiry into the personality structure of these people. One has but to watch the gleam in the eye of a holy-mouth-man, as he jabs an awl into an exposed nerve, to suspect that a certain amount of sadism is involved. If this can be established, a very interesting pattern emerges, for most of the population shows definite masochistic tendencies. It was to these that Professor Linton referred in discussing a distinctive part of the daily body ritual which is performed only by men. This part of the rite involves scraping and lacerating the surface of the face with a sharp instrument. Special women's rites are performed only four times during each lunar month, but what they lack in frequency is made up in barbarity. As part of this ceremony, women bake their heads in small ovens for about an hour. The theoretically interesting point is that what seems to be a preponderantly masochistic people have developed sadistic specialists.

The medicine men have an imposing temple, or *latipso*, in every community of any size. The more elaborate ceremonies required to treat very sick patients can only be performed at this temple. These ceremonies involve not only the thaumaturge but a permanent group of vestal maidens who move sedately about the temple chambers in distinctive costume and headdress.

The *latipso* ceremonies are so harsh that it is phenomenal that a fair proportion of the really sick natives who enter the temple ever recover. Small children whose indoctrination is still incomplete have been known to resist attempts to take them to the temple because 'that is where you go to die.' Despite this fact, sick adults are not only willing but eager to undergo the protracted ritual purification, if they can afford to do so. No matter how ill the supplicant or how grave the emergency, the guardians of many temples will not admit a client if he cannot give a rich gift to the custodian. Even after one has gained admission and survived the ceremonies, the guardians will not permit the neophyte to leave until he makes still another gift.

The supplicant entering the temple is first stripped of all his or her clothes. In every-day life the Nacirema avoids exposure of his body and its natural functions. Bathing and excretory acts are performed only in the secrecy of the household shrine, where they are ritualized as part of the body-rites. Psychological shock results from the fact that body secrecy is suddenly lost upon entry into the *latipso*. A man, whose own wife has never seen him in an excretory act, suddenly finds himself naked and assisted by a vestal maiden while he performs his natural functions into a sacred vessel. This sort of ceremonial treatment is necessitated by the fact that the excreta are used by a diviner to ascertain the course and nature of the client's sickness. Female clients, on the other hand, find their naked bodies are subjected to the scrutiny, manipulation and prodding of the medicine men.

Few supplicants in the temple are well enough to do anything but lie on their hard beds. The daily ceremonies, like the rites of the holy-mouth-men, involve discomfort and torture. With ritual precision, the vestals awaken their miserable charges each dawn and roll them about on their beds of pain while performing ablutions, in the formal movements of which the maidens are highly trained. At other times they insert magic wands in the supplicant's mouth or force him to eat substances which are supposed to be healing. From time to time the medicine men come to their clients and jab magically treated needles into their flesh. The fact that these temple ceremonies may not cure, and may even kill the neophyte, in no way decreases the people's faith in the medicine men.

There remains one other kind of practitioner, known as a 'listener.' This witch-doctor has the power to exorcise the devils that lodge in the heads of people who have been bewitched. The Nacirema believe that parents bewitch their own children. Mothers are particularly suspected of putting a curse on children while teaching them the secret body rituals. The counter-magic of the witch-doctor is unusual in its lack of ritual. The patient simply tells the 'listener' all his troubles and fears, beginning with the earliest difficulties he can remember. The memory displayed by the Nacirema in these exorcism sessions is truly remarkable. It is not uncommon for the patient to bemoan the rejection he felt upon being weaned as a babe, and a few individuals even see their troubles going back to the traumatic effects of their own birth.

In conclusion, mention must be made of certain practices which have their base in native esthetics but which depend upon the pervasive aversion to the natural body and its functions. There are ritual fasts to make fat people thin and ceremonial feasts to make thin people fat. Still other rites are used to make women's breasts larger if they are small, and smaller if they are large. General dissatisfaction with breast shape is symbolized in the fact that the ideal form is virtually outside the range of human variation. A few women afflicted with almost inhuman hypermammary development are so idolized that they make a handsome living by simply going from village to village and permitting the natives to stare at them for a fee.

Reference has already been made to the fact that excretory functions are ritualized, routinized, and relegated to secrecy. Natural reproductive functions are similarly distorted. Intercourse is taboo as a topic and scheduled as an act. Efforts are made to avoid pregnancy by the use of magical materials or by limiting intercourse to certain phases of the moon. Conception is actually very infrequent. When pregnant, women dress so as to hide their condition. Parturition takes place in secret, without friends or relatives to assist, and the majority of women do not nurse their infants.

Our review of the ritual life of the Nacirema has certainly shown them to be a magic-ridden people. It is hard to understand how they have managed to exist so long under the burdens which they have imposed upon themselves. But even such exotic customs as these take on real meaning when they are viewed with the insight provided by Malinowski when he wrote (1948: 70):

> Looking from far and above, from our high places of safety in the developed civilization, it is easy to see all the crudity and irrelevance of magic. But without its power and guidance early man could not have mastered his practical difficulties as he has done, nor could man have advanced to the higher stages of civilization.

References cited

LINTON, RALPH
      1937   The Study of Man. New York, D. Appleton-Century Co.
MALINOWSKI, BRONISLAW
      1948   Magic, Science, and Religion. Glencoe, The Free Press.
MURDOCK, GEORGE P.
      1949   Social Structure. New York, The Macmillan Co.

(Miner, 1956. Reproduced with the permission of the review and Mrs Agnes Miner.)

Notes

1. One may be wary of the ethnocentric (Western/modern) bias of the author, i.e. an overemphasis on culture as striving only for the improvement of material productions; in some cultures, the dominant values may be extremely antagonistic towards material preoccupations.
2. See, for instance, 'Body ritual among the Naciremas' (page 55); 'Dangerous Enchantment' (page 217); the symbols related to colours, shapes and odours in Chapter 8; the symbolic value placed on country images in Chapter 9. The creation of symbols and the process of their interpretation are explained in Chapter 8, page 230.

3. A central preoccupation of cultural communities is to define, through religious and moral beliefs, whether there is life after death and of what kind. The scientific movement, especially at the end of the nineteenth century, has seemed close to eliminating these questions by pushing back the boundaries of the metaphysical world. Nowadays scientists recognize that the metaphysical question will never be resolved fully by scientific knowledge. What is in fact of interest to us is not the answers to these questions *per se*; it is the consequences of moral and religious assumptions, which differ widely across cultures, on individual and collective behaviours.

4. Mircea Eliade is probably the greatest twentieth-century historian of religion. A Romanian by birth, he has held the chair of religious history at the University of Chicago. His books, both academic and fictional, are extremely useful in the investigation of the symbolic and sacred aspects of mythologies and rites. One of his novels, *Maitreyi* (originally in Romanian; in French, *La nuit bengali*), tells the love story of a young European engineer and a Bengali girl, and clearly illustrates how cultural differences can sometimes cause dramatic situations.

5. The conquest of Mexico by Hernan Cortès is a fascinating example of the almost total destruction of a culture heavily loaded with symbolism (mostly that of the Aztecs and the Mayas) by only a very small group of Spanish invaders. When Cortès's army left the island of Cuba, sailing to Mexico, it numbered only 508 soldiers, 100 sailors and ten horses. At that time Mexico City had half a million inhabitants.

> The Mayas, the Totonacs and the Mexicas were deeply religious people, totally subservient to the will of their gods and the sovereignty of their priest-kings. These people waged a ritualistic war on each other which was based on magic as much as military strategy and in which the desired outcome, decided in advance by the mysterious agreements of celestial powers, was not the conquest of land or the amassing of riches, but the triumph of the Gods, who received in sacrifice the heart and the blood of the vanquished. Disturbed by the mythical return of the ancestors and of the divine feathered serpent, Quetzalcoatl-Kukulcan, the Indians were blinded, unable to see the actual intentions of those whom they had termed the *Teules*, the Gods. And when the Indians understood that the Spaniards, whom they considered as demi-gods, were involved in a massive slaughter of Mexican Indians, from which none of them would emerge unscathed, it was too late. The Spaniards had taken advantage of their hesitation to penetrate deep into the Mexican empire, to provoke dissension, and to conquer lands and take slaves. (J. M. G. Le Clézio, 1988, *Le Rêve mexicaine ou la pensée interrompue*, Gallimard: Paris, p. 19).

See also *Historia Verdadera de la conquista de la Nueva Espana*, written by a member of the Cortès troop, Bernal Diaz del Castillo (Espasa-Calpe: Madrid, 1968) and *Historia General de las cosas de la Nueva Espana*, written by Bernadino de Sahagun a few years after the conquest (which took place around 1520) and the destruction of the Aztec and Maya cultures, with the objective of preserving as far as possible the traces of this civilization which had suffered such an abrupt disappearance. For a thorough analysis of culture collisions in colonial history, see Urs Bitterli (1989), *Cultures in Conflict*, Polity Press: Oxford.

6. A famous Swiss novelist, Charles Ferdinand Ramuz, has often set the relations between communities as a background to his novels. *La Séparation des races*, for instance, is the story of the kidnapping of a young girl from Bern by her Valaisan lover and the consequent mobilization of their respective communities.

7. For the relationship between Swiss national culture and Swiss management style, see: Alexander Bergmann, François Hainard and Laurent Thévoz (1990), *La Culture d'enterprise suisse, élément constitutif et reflet de la culture nationale*, CEAT/HEC: Lausanne.

8. The vagueness of this concept probably explains why it has been systematically underestimated, especially in international trade theory. Theory-builders who generally seek to construct formally convincing theoretical explanations, tend to remove such vague variables from their models even if they are explanatory. However, the fact that a construct is not easily measurable is no justification for ignoring it.

9. The literature review carried out by Inkeles and Levinson (1969) is certainly the most exhaustive one (100 pages) available. It might appear somewhat dated, but since national character changes over decades and centuries, their review remains largely up-to-date.

10. This is coincidental; as for the 'winners', their economic performance shows a more mixed picture.

11. War is assimilated here with commerce and industry because, from a historical perspective, war was a *normal* activity. The idea that war produces the vanquished and the victorious but that they are all losers, is rather a new one. When pursuing colonial wars, commerce and industry were legitimately included in the ultimate goals. The idea of bringing civilization to the barbarians included the extirpation of 'evil' beliefs, magic and sorcery, and their substitution of Christianity.

12. An important figure in these studies of childhood and society is Erik Erikson (1950), who has developed a theory of ego development stages (in the Freudian sense) on the basis of field observations of American Indians, Sioux and Yurok, US Americans, Germans and Russians. It is clearly beyond the reach of this book to sum up, even very briefly, the richness of the empirical and theoretical research on national differences which has been published by anthropologists, sociologists and psychologists. The references at the end of this chapter suggest two reviews of such cross-national research: Inkeles and Levinson (1969) and Segall *et al.* (1990).

13. By 'visual inference' is implied the mental system which enables people to transform retinal perceptions into a 'brain image' (Segall *et al.*, 1990, ch. 4).

14. For example, the human resource management of local sales personnel or staff. If sales clerks show signs of lack of competence in managing the customer database for invoicing, sales promotions, etc., this may be attributed to one of two causes, which lead to different courses of action: individual lack of competence, in which case the clerks should be fired; such competences are not common to this culture, in which case they have to be trained specifically.

15. After using admission tests for graduate and postgraduate programmes in Grenoble, it became clear that the average scores of black African students were lower than those of European students. Nevertheless we recruited some excellent African students by accepting them at a lower threshold-score, after taking into account the cultural gap.

16. Basic cultural orientations may also be called *value* orientations (Kluckhohn and Strodtbeck, 1961) or dimensions of cultural variation (Triandis, 1983).

17. The cultural short term is probably in the range of twenty years: there is no visible change, at the deepest level, within the time period of one generation.

References

Carroll, John B. (1956), *Language, Thought and Reality: Selected writings of Benjamin Lee Whorf*, MIT: Cambridge, MA.

Child, J. and A. Kieser (1977), 'A contrast in British and West German management practices: Are recipes of success culture bound?', paper presented at the *Conference on Cross-Cultural Studies on Organizational Functioning*, Hawaii.

Eliade, Mircea (1956), *Forgerons et Alchimistes*, Flammarion: Paris. English translation (1962), *The Forge and the Crucible*, University of Chicago Press: Chicago.

Erikson, Erik (1950), *Childhood and Society*, Norton: New York.

Farr, Robert M. (1988), 'Les Représentations sociales', in Serge Moscovici (ed.), *Psychologie sociale*, PUF Fondamental: Paris.

Goodenough, Ward H. (1971), *Culture, Language and Society*, Modular Publications, 7, Addison-Wesley: Reading, MA.

Hawking, Stephen (1988), *A Brief History of Time*, Guild Publishing: London.

Inkeles, Alex and Daniel J. Levinson (1969), 'National character: The study of modal personality and sociocultural systems', in Gardner Lindzey and Elliot Aronson (eds), *Handbook of Social Psychology*, vol. IV, Addison-Wesley: Reading, MA, pp. 418–506.

Jodelet, Denise (1988) 'Représentations sociales: phénomènes, concept et théorie', in Serge Moscovici (ed.), *Psychologie sociale*, PUF Fondamental: Paris.

Kluckhohn, Florence R. and Frederick L. Strodtbeck (1961), *Variations in Value Orientations*, Greenwood Press: Westport, CT.

Kroeber, Alfred L. and Clyde Kluckhohn (1952), *Culture: A Critical Review of Concepts and Definitions*, Anthropological Papers, no. 4, Peabody Museum: Cambridge, MA.

Lévi-Strauss, Claude (1958), *Anthropologie Structurale*, Paris, Plon.

Linton, Ralph (1945), *The Cultural Background of Personality*, Appleton-Century: New York.

Malinowski, Bronislaw (1944), *A Scientific Theory of Culture and Other Essays*, The University of North Carolina Press: Chapel Hill, NC.

Miner, Horace (1956), 'Body ritual among the Nacirema', *American Anthropologist*, vol. 58, pp. 503–7.

Montesquieu, Charles de (1748), *The Spirit of Laws*, translated from the French by Thomas Nugent (1792), 6th edn, McKenzie and Moore: Dublin.

Moscovici, Serge (1961), *La Psychanalyse, son Public et son Image*, Presses Universitaires de France: Paris.

Segall, Marshall H., Pierre R. Dasen, John W. Berry and Ype H. Poortinga (1990), *Human Behavior in Global Perspective*, Pergamon: New York.

Triandis, Harry C. (1983), 'Dimensions of cultural variation as parameters of organizational theories', *International Studies of Management and Organization*, vol. XII, no. 4, pp. 139–69.

Tylor, Edward (1913), *Primitive Culture*, Murray: London.

Weeks, William H., Paul B. Pedersen and Richard W. Brislin (1987), *A Manual of Structured Experiences for Cross-cultural Learning*, Intercultural Press: Yarmouth, ME.

3

———— ◆◆◆ ————

Cultural dynamics

Culture is sometimes regarded as a somewhat vague concept. The Swedish writer Selma Lagerlöf defines culture as 'what remains when that which has been learned is entirely forgotten'.[1] Depicted thus, culture may appear to be rather a 'rubbish-bin' concept. Its main use would be as a 'synthesis variable': an explanation that serves as a last resort, that is, when all other concepts or more precise theories have been successfully validated. It would also serve as an explanatory variable for residuals, when other more interpretive explanations are unsuccessful.

However, the definition quoted above does have the important merit of identifying two basic elements of cultural dynamics (at the level of the individual):

1. It is learned.
2. It is forgotten, in the sense that we cease to be conscious of its existence as learned behaviour.

Yet culture remains present throughout our daily individual and collective activities, and is therefore entirely orientated towards our adaptation to reality (both as constraints and opportunities). To this extent it is almost unthinkable that a culture could stand perfectly still, except in the case of those primitive societies that live in quite stable natural and social environments, located in remote places and subject to no exterior interference. At the periphery of a fixed set of basic cultural orientations, other sources of culture intervene, as a result of which new solutions are borrowed for tackling existing issues or for solving entirely new problems.

3.1   An inventory of basic differences in cultural assumptions

Table 3.1 presents basic differences in cultural assumptions. They are mostly based on the 'value orientations' of the anthropologists Florence Kluckhohn and Frederick Strodtbeck (1961)[2] which are often cited – an indication of their analytical power, at least as far as it is perceived by the social scientists.

63

Table 3.1 *Principal differences in basic cultural assumptions.*

Cultural orientations	Relation to communication and action styles (in a broad sense)
1. Personalization versus depersonalization (concrete space versus abstract space):	
(a) What the 'other' *does* versus what the 'other' *is*: emphasis on family, group membership, age, religion or social status.	Necessity of being personally acquainted with other people if one is to communicate and interact with them efficiently versus ability to communicate easily with unknown persons.
(b) Who is a member of the group (family, tribe, clan, club, professional society, nation, etc.).	Belonging to the in-group (or reference group) may be a necessary condition for efficient communication on a specific range of topics, and/or to be considered as a reliable, bona fide partner.
(c) The relevant size of the in-group (reference group, membership group).	For an individual who belongs to the out-group, what are the prerequisites for assimilation (if any)?
(d) Group membership and integration conditions.	
2. Time patterns:	
(a) Economicity of time ('time is money').	Is time regarded as a scarce resource or, conversely, as plentiful and indefinitely available? See section 14.1.
(b) Monochronism versus polychronism.	Only one task is undertaken at any (preset) time, following a schedule ('agenda society'), versus dealing simultaneously with different tasks, actions and/or communications (polychronism) for convenience, pleasure and efficiency (see section 14.1).
(c) Temporal orientations. Emphasis on time orientation:	
(i) towards the past;	Do people consider that the past is important, that resources must be spent on teaching history and building museums, referring to oral and written traditions and past works? Basic assumption: our roots are implanted in the past and no plant can survive without its roots.

Table 3.1 *Continued*

Cultural orientations	Relation to communication and action styles (in a broad sense)
(ii) towards the present;	Do people consider that we basically live 'here and now'? Not only should the present be enjoyed but, since it is not *always* enjoyable, it must be accepted for what it is: the only true reality we live in (basic assumption).
(iii) towards the future.	Do people easily and precisely envisage and plan their future? Are they project-orientated, making long-term preparations, appreciating the achievements of science, and so on? Do they feel that there is a positive orientation in the passage of time, where the future is inevitably 'bigger and better'? See section 14.1.
3. Attitude towards action: (a) Mastery of nature versus subjugation to nature: existence and degree of legitimacy of a Promethean (proactive) view of human life.	People believe that it is possible to cope with any problem or any situation and that, to mankind, nothing is impossible; evil is when one does nothing ('master of destiny'); versus the belief that there are many situations where people cannot do anything; destiny binds us and we should not try to find alternatives (fatalistic orientation); evil is when one does not accept one's own destiny ('subjugation').
(b) Ideologism versus pragmatism.	Ideologism: thinking patterns, communication (style of speech) and actions should always be set within the context of broad ideological principles (religious, political, social, legal, etc.); versus pragmatism: precise issues must be addressed; a practical attitude is favoured: orientation towards problem solving and concrete results. See section 13.5.
(c) 'Uncertainty avoidance' (Hofstede).	Tendency to avoid risks ('uncertainty avoidance'), to prefer stable situations, uncertainty-reducing rules and risk-free procedures, which are seen as a necessity for efficiency. Or, conversely, a risk-prone attitude (low 'uncertainty avoidance') where people as individuals are seen as the engine of change, which is perceived as a requirement for efficiency.

Table 3.1   *Continued*

Cultural orientations	Relation to communication and action styles (in a broad sense)
(d) 'Masculine' orientation versus 'feminine' orientation (Hofstede).	See section 3.3.
4. Self-concept and concept of others:	
(a) Human nature is basically good versus evil.	Communication and general interaction patterns are based on *ab initio* confidence or, conversely, *ab initio* distrust. See section 13.6.
(b) Individualism versus collectivism.	The individual is seen as the basic resource and therefore individual-related values are strongly emphasized (personal freedom, human rights, equality between men and women); versus the group is seen as the basic resource and therefore group values favoured (loyalty, sense of belonging, sense of personal sacrifice for the community, etc.).
(c) Group cultures with close physical contact versus individualistic cultures desiring private space.	Tendency to live near to one another, and to be undisturbed by such intimacy. Conversely, tendency to feel the need for private space around one's body, and to resent intrusion into this space (low-context cultures according to Edward Hall, 1966).
(d) When evaluating others, emphasis placed on: (i) age; (ii) sex; (iii) social class (power distance).	Who are the persons to be considered trustworthy and reliable, with whom it is possible to do business? See section 13.3.
(e) Emphasis placed on the self-concept perceived as culturally appropriate: (i) self-esteem – low/high; (ii) exercise of power: low/high; (iii) level of activity: strong/weak.	How should one behave (the question is usually unconscious) to give the correct appearance: shy/extrovert, arrogant/humble, busy/idle?

Cultural assumptions are basic responses, expressed in a rather dichotomous manner, to fundamental human problems. They provide the members of a particular cultural community with a basic framework for the evaluation of solutions to these problems, combining a cognitive dimension (people think it works that way), an affective dimension (people like it that way) and a directive dimension (people will do it that way). Kluckhohn and Strodtbeck (1961, pp. 11, 12) have collected these common human problems under five main categories:

1. What is the character of innate human nature (*human-nature* orientation): good or evil, neutral, or a mix of good and evil? Is this state of human nature mutable or immutable?
2. What is the relation of humans to nature and supernature (*nature* orientation): subjugation to nature, harmony with nature or mastery over nature?
3. What is the temporal focus of human life (*time* orientation): past, present or future?
4. What is the modality of human activity (*activity* orientation): should people be (*being*) should people do (*doing*) or should they do in order to be (*being-in-becoming*)?
5. What is the modality of the relationship between humans (*relational* orientation): lineality, collaterality or pure individuality?

Naturally these modalities are to be found in every society: people *are* and *do*, and they are always the children of parents, in the sense that some kind of family nucleus exists everywhere. But different assumptions result in variations as to the kind of response which is dominant in a particular society. We have combined this approach with those adopted by Hall (1959, 1966, 1976, 1983), Hofstede (1980a) and Triandis (1983) to depict differences in basic cultural assumptions in Table 3.1.

3.2 Culture-based cognitive styles and attitudes towards action

Basic cultural assumptions, and their combinations, have an influence on the way we cognitively evaluate real-world situations and the issues that face us. Some examples will demonstrate that we do know how to construct our reality but only within our native cultural community.

Why act?

Not everyone is preoccupied with doing, acting, being efficient and achieving tangible results which can be appraised by others. From an existential point of view this preoccupation with 'doing' is not really justified: in the long term we will all be dead, as Keynes said. Moreover, assuming that we do all care about efficiency, there are many different ways of achieving it.

Montesquieu illustrates the spontaneous irritation of people who are 'doing'-oriented towards those who are more 'being'-oriented when, in *The Spirit of Laws*, he comments on what he calls *indolent nations*:

> The Indians believe that repose and non-existence are the foundations of all things, and the end in which they terminate. Hence they consider entire inaction as the most perfect of all states, and the object of their desires. To the supreme Being they give the title of immoveable. The inhabitants of Siam believe that their utmost happiness consists in not being obliged to animate a machine or to give motion to a body.[3]

Not only are the Indians and Siamese[4] more 'being'-orientated, they also have a quite
different view of the relationship with nature than Westerners (subjugation to nature rather
than mastery over nature). Ultimately their religions include belief in reincarnation: on the
death of the body, the soul transmigrates or is born again in another body. Life therefore
is not seen as 'one shot', but more as a cyclical phenomenon.[5] This puts less pressure on
people to be 'doing'-orientated but also means more inducement to *be* blameless and
virtuous since that will influence the status of further reincarnations; inaction is one of the
surest ways to lead a blameless life.

Another important distinction to be made is whether a culture tends to classify words,
speeches and, more generally, acts of communication, in the 'deeds' category. In many
cultures there are popular sayings which effectively condemns speech on the basis that it
is not real action ('do, not talk'). In the real world, life is more complicated:
communications are a category of act, and their potential influence on others is beyond
doubt. But whether communication (in what particular form?) is considered as
significantly related to action, differs across cultures.

Let us take the example of poetry, which in Islam is highly esteemed. One can be
fascinated by poetry, by the beauty of words and songs (and the fact of being fascinated
can lead to *being acted on*), as this commentary on the life of the Prophet illustrates:

> Thus, Mohammed was sitting in the great courtyard of the Caaba, surrounded by the
> faithful, foreigners and Qureichits. The melodious music of the verses of the Koran was
> playing while the Prophet was gazing at the audience; the sparkle in His eyes and the beauty
> of the songs held the people spellbound. The people kept on repeating: 'If You are a prophet,
> perform a miracle for us, so that we may believe in You.' And the messenger of God
> invariably answered: 'O Arab People, is not the miracle powerful enough, that your everyday
> language has been chosen for the Book, in which a single verse makes us forget about all your
> poems and all your songs?' It is said that, on hearing this response, non-believers committed
> themselves to convene all the poets of Arabia, so that they might create at least one verse, a
> few words, the beauty of which would match that of the Koran. The poets arrived at Caaba
> and began to perspire under the torrid sun. They toiled, they spared themselves no anguish in
> seeking to perform what had been requested of them. But as soon as they began to recite their
> works, even the fiercest opponents to the Prophet themselves were compelled to admit that
> none of their words could rival the verses of the Koran. Poetic spirit is so greatly esteemed
> among Arabs that many of those who were in the Caaba at that moment knelt down and were
> converted to Islam. The unrivalled beauty of the language had convinced them of its heavenly
> origin. (Mohammed Essad Bey, 1934, pp. 98–9, my translation)

The word 'poetry' comes from the Greek word 'to do' (*poïo*).[6] Such an etymology, which
is at first sight surprising, sheds some light on the opposing value judgements of the
usefulness of poetry, which are made according to different basic cultural assumptions. On
the one hand it may be seen as rather distanced from action in the real world, on the other
as a direct source of inspiration for action. Indeed if a 'classical' model of action is
assumed, i.e. one that is culturally European/Western-based, the following sequence
occurs:

1. Analysis of the problem and the issues at stake.
2. Gathering of relevant information.

3. Listing and evaluating possible solutions.
4. Selecting the 'best' decision.
5. Implementation: that is, mainly articulating individual and collective action since the implementation process is generally scattered among numerous diverse agents, whereas the decision itself tends to be more individualized, or at least taken by a limited number of people.
6. Appraisal of the outcome, control of the difference between target and actual outcomes, and possibly feedback to a previous step in the sequence.

This sequence may be easily criticized for being culturally non-universal: Japanese people have no word for decision-making (Lazer *et al.*, 1985), and action/decision/control processes are viewed mainly as *implementation issues*. This is why they first insist on consulting each one of a large group of people at various levels in the organization, who will comment on *how* to do something (not necessarily on *why*). But even if we were to accept that this sequence is true, it would still involve a great deal of cultural relativity.

What information is relevant for action? How should it be used?

The dimensions of ideologism and pragmatism are, to varying degrees, combined.[7] It would be a mistake to consider Americans as pure pragmatists with no leaning for ideology. In fact they identify problems clearly and precisely as 'issues'. They collect evidence systematically and their attitude is matter-of-fact.[8] To be 'down to earth' is a positive expression in English, whereas its French equivalent may often be pejorative (*être terre à terre*).[9]

But it is also true that free-market/individual-oriented ideology has a strong presence in the United States, enshrined in the Constitution, in anti-trust legislation, in corporate law and so on. However it is rarely present on a *daily* basis, when information directly relevant to action is gathered or discussed. Ideology is generally accepted unquestionably. It is therefore somewhat irrelevant to debate practical matters as an ideologist would.

Conversely, one may well be conscious of pragmatic considerations when ideology and ideas are the object of debate. In international business negotiations there is often discussion of principles, which may seem inconsequential due to the inevitable generality of such discussion. However, it may lead to a substantive outcome later on. The fundamental skill of diplomats (who are, in many respects, culture experts) is to occasion the acceptance and underwriting of basic principles by their counterparts, the effectiveness of which is only apparent at a later date.

How are individual and collective action to be combined?

Japanese people are often depicted as collectivist, in contrast to the Americans who are deemed more individualistic.[10] There is undoubtedly an element of truth in this distinction, but it is necessary to outline its limits. For the word 'individual', let us substitute three words which encompass most of its various facets: *human being*, *person* and *individual*; and for 'collectivity' let us substitute the words *group*, *community* and *society*. Who is more humane, more personal and more sensitive in interpersonal relations, more attentive and understanding than the average Japanese person? Who cares more about the community than the average American, whose objective is to 'socialize in the community'? In the United States the word 'community' is used extensively.

Indeed Americans and Japanese share a common problem (as defined by Kluckhohn and Strodtbeck, 1961): that of combining individual actions and collective undertakings. This problem may be solved only by a process which is essentially dialectic. In any society there exists a dominant cultural assumption about what the *first* (but not the *sole*) priority should be: either the individual is the most important (as in the United States); or else the group is the basic survival unit to which the individual must be subordinate (as in Japan). Then comes the reverse cultural assumption, which dialectically complements the basic assumption: that the community is where people integrate to build a common society, and their reciprocal links should be strictly and explicitly codified (United States); or (Japan) that the utmost level of sensitivity must be developed in interpersonal relations so that the working of the group is kept as smooth as possible.

Actual (empirical) reality versus potential reality: which should be preferred?

It is a frequent mistake to believe that reality is simple, in the sense that it is directly related to our perceptions and the ways in which we act on it and try to change it.[11] It is what we call 'common sense', that is, shared meaning which makes sense in the cultural community *simply because we share it*,[12] even though it may appear nonsense to people belonging to other cultural communities. Indeed our relation to the real world is heavily filtered by a series of convergent factors:

1. Our perceptual apparatus is partly culturally formed (see sections 2.4 and 8.4).
2. We implicitly choose to privilege the search for certain categories of fact and represent them in a particular way.[13]
3. We admit the truthfulness of these facts according to criteria which are determined in part by our cultural background. When and how they are established as true (meaning that there is a consensus about their being a part of the real world) is also culture-based.[14]
4. Even when these facts have been established as true, there still remain different readings and interpretations of them, depending on culture-based values and social representations.[15]

We may favour either *actual/empirical reality*, that is, the ways in which we experience reality here and now (or the way it is revealed by empirical science), or *potential reality*, that is, the reality we imagine and dream about but which also motivates us to achieve. Potential reality is in a sense the *possible* future of actual reality. Our sense of potential reality relies much more on imagination than on actual perceptions. Since it is beyond the reach of our perceptions and we cannot experience it, we have to envisage potential reality. Potential reality is a rich ground for action, because it directly supports our Promethean desires to exert mastery over nature. It helps us to achieve objects and projects which can make us feel equal to gods ('space conquest' projects, for instance).

Galtung (1981) uses this distinction between actual reality and potential reality in order to contrast what he calls the 'intellectual styles' of four important cultural groups:[16] the 'Gallic' (prototype: the French), the 'Teutonic' (prototype: the Germans), the 'Saxonic' (prototype: the English and the Americans) and the 'Nipponic' intellectual style (prototype: the Japanese).

Saxons prefer to look for facts and evidence, which results in factual accuracy and abundance. As Galtung states (1981, pp. 827–8) when he describes the intellectual style of Anglo-Americans:

> ... *data unite, theories divide*. There are clear, relatively explicit canons for establishing what constitutes a valid fact and what does not; the corresponding canons in connection with theories are more vague. ... One might now complete the picture of the Saxonic intellectual style by emphasizing its weak points: not very strong on theory formation, and not on paradigm awareness.

Galtung contrasts the Saxonic style with the Teutonic and Gallic styles, which place theoretical arguments at the centre of their intellectual process. Data and facts are there to illustrate what is said rather than to demonstrate it.

> Discrepancy between theory and data would be handled at the expense of data: they may either be seen as atypical or wholly erroneous, or more significantly as not really pertinent to the theory. And here the distinction between empirical and potential reality comes in: to the Teutonic and Gallic intellectual, potential reality may be not so much the reality to be even more avoided or even more pursued than the empirical one but rather a *more real reality*, reality free from the noise and impurities of empirical reality. (p. 828)

However, Teutonic and Gallic intellectual styles do differ in the role that is assigned to words and discourse. The Teutonic ideal is that of the ineluctability of true reasoning, *Gedankennotwendigkeit*,[17] that is, perfection of concepts and the indisputability of their mental articulation. The Gallic style is less preoccupied with deduction and intellectual construction. It is directed more towards the use of the persuasive strength of words and speeches in an aesthetically perfect way (*élégance*). Words have an inherent power to convince.[18] They may create *potential reality*.

Finally the Nipponic intellectual style, imbued with Hindu, Buddhist and Taoist philosophies, favours a more modest, global and provisional approach. Thinking and knowledge are conceived of as being in a temporary state, open to alteration. The Japanese 'rarely pronounce absolute, categorical statements in daily discourse; they prefer vagueness even about trivial matters ... because clear statements have a ring of immodesty, of being judgements of reality' (Galtung, 1981, p. 833).

Of course, every culture has a mixed use of actual/empirical reality and potential reality. But they differ in the places granted to each of these, and in the degree of distrust of potential reality. Obviously potential reality is more dangerous to deal with: it is easier to speak about it than to act on it. Facts are not 'stubborn' if they are remote and vague. This leads on to the last point to be made about cultural action styles: the problematical link between what one says and what one does.

Box 3.1   *Wishful Thinking in international delivery dates*[19] .

When selling industrial equipment or turnkey projects on world-wide markets, it is always necessary to stipulate one delivery date or more.[20] The effects of such an announcement may be severe: the buyer may cancel the order because the date is too late. However, this date rarely depends exclusively on the person who sets it. One may spontaneously leave some time between the announced date (an actual reality) and the real delivery date (a potential reality), surmised from the previous performance of the seller's organization.

Wishful Thinking (WT) is a necessary input in this process: it explains why the initially announced delivery date may be very different from the ultimate one. Wishful Thinking is a true 'art of communication' which is preferred more in Latin cultures than in Anglo-Saxon cultures.[21] The negative consequences of WT, such as deceitful behaviour, are much less emphasized in Latin than in Anglo-Saxon cultures. Naturally, in addition to the cultural background there are also some personalities and psychological profiles which are more prone to Wishful Thinking.[22]

WT consists in first thinking, then saying, how *one wants things to be*, not how they are. Since nobody knows exactly how things will be in the future, a non-WT orientated person will try to say how he or she thinks quite realistically they will be, not as he or she wants them to be. WT deals with the future: when a culture is weakly future-orientated,[23] its use is easier. People do not worry about periods which they do not clearly envisage. The use of WT is made easier when the level of uncertainty is high, and where people do not strive to avoid uncertainty (Hofstede's low uncertainty avoidance).[23] If a culture clearly divides words from deeds (*do what you say, say what you do*), the use of WT is inhibited. When, on the other hand, speech is considered as a prominent modality of action, WT may possibly become a necessity (to galvanize people while at the same time evoking an improbable future). WT is closely related to present orientation: it is a convenient way to escape from the constraints of longer-term realities by focusing on the here and now. It dodges problems to be solved, and hides divergences and possible conflicts. But this is only in the short term.

A seller with a strong WT communication has the tendency to tell a client spontaneously that the delivery date requested is entirely feasible. The seller also manoeuvres verbally around past realities which may not be wholly reassuring: a six-week delay in the last shipment, for instance. The buyer may also have a WT communication framework, and is in fact 'buying' friendly relations rather than hard data, preferring to be 'happy now'. On the other hand, if the buyer is not WT-prone, the seller is judged negatively and the order is not placed, unless there is some compelling rational argument such as a shortage of this type of supply, particularly high quality or exclusive technology.

(Adapted from Usunier; 1989, pp. 89–90.)

Words and deeds: misadventures

Words and deeds may be classified either in two separate categories or combined. They may be set opposite each other on the basis that words are empty or hollow, or joined on the basis of the action of words on others: speech implies influencing and often, consequently, causing someone to act. Most acts of authority are only words. To illustrate some culture-based misadventures in the word/deeds relation, Box 3.1 offers the example of the international negotiation of a delivery date.

3.3 National cultures and organization

A large number of publications are devoted to the impact of cultural differences on management and organization (that is, *inside* companies). The impact of national cultures has been assessed on various issues such as structure, hierarchical relationships, management of expatriates, variation in motivation patterns across cultures (see for instance: Hofstede, 1980b; Laurent, 1983; Adler, 1986). These issues are clearly outside the principal remit of this book, which is to consider the interaction of companies with their environment (their *outside*), that is, with markets, customers, distribution channels or various influential groups (consumer movements, regulatory authorities, etc.). Nevertheless a summary of the advances made in cultural differences and organization studies is worthwhile for the following two reasons at least. Firstly, national cultures have been described in a rather technical manner (compared, measured) as they relate to business in general: most of the dimensions outlined for management and organization practices also make sense for marketing and sales. Second, many issues in this book are on the fringes of marketing and management: sales force stimulation, business negotiation or the organization of marketing activities.

National cultures and management practices

The cover story of an issue of *Fortune* magazine accurately features the difficult question of the transposability of management styles: it shows an American with slanting eyes eating (or, more probably, trying to eat) a hamburger with chopsticks. Geert Hofstede, of Dutch nationality, was one of the first researchers to question the adaptability of US management theories and practices to other cultural contexts.

Empirical studies for Hofstede's work were undertaken between 1967 and 1973 within a large multinational company, in 66 of its national subsidiaries.[24] The database contains more than 116,000 questionnaires: all categories of personnel were interviewed, from ordinary workers to general managers. Out of 150 questions, 60 questions deal with the values and beliefs of the respondents on issues related to motivation, hierarchy, leadership, well-being in the organization, etc. The questionnaire was administered in two successive stages (1967–9 and 1971–3) so as to verify validity by replication. Versions of the questionnaire were drafted in 20 different languages. The results drawn from this data were further validated by a systematic comparison with the results of 13 other cross-cultural studies (Hofstede, 1980b, 1983).

Interviewees all belonged to the same multinational corporation. This company had a very strong corporate culture which was shared by its employees. Consequently there was no variance on this dimension across the sample. Each national sample allowed for a similar representation of age groups, sex and categories of personnel, thereby avoiding a potential source of variance across national subsidiaries' results. Finally the only source of variance was the difference in national cultures and mentalities.[25]

Hofstede, by means of factor analysis of the respondents' scores, was able to derive four main dimensions on which national cultures exhibit significant differences (for management-related issues):

1. *Power distance*. This measures to what extent a society and its individual members tolerate an unequal distribution of power in organizations and in society as a whole (see Box 3.2). It is evidenced as much by the behavioural values of superiors (who display their power and exercise it) as by the behavioural values of subordinates (who wait for their superiors to show their status and power, and are uncomfortable if they do not personally experience it). In low power-distance societies, members of the organization tend to feel equal, close to each other in their daily work relationships; when the real hierarchical distance is high, power may be delegated. In high power-distance societies, superiors and subordinates feel separated from each other; it is not easy to meet and talk with higher ranking people, and the real power tends to be very much concentrated at the top.

2. *Uncertainty avoidance*. This measures the extent to which people in a society tend to feel threatened by uncertain, ambiguous, risky or undefined situations. Where uncertainty avoidance is high, organizations promote stable careers, produce rules and procedures, etc. 'Nevertheless societies in which uncertainty avoidance is strong are also characterized by a higher level of anxiety and aggressiveness that creates, among other things, a strong inner urge to work hard.' (Hofstede, 1980a).

3. The third dimension is *individualism/collectivism*. In collectivist countries there is a close-knit social structure, where people neatly distinguish between members of the in-group and members of the out-group. They expect their group to care for them in exchange for unwavering loyalty. In individualistic societies, social fabric is much looser: people are basically supposed to care for themselves and their immediate family. Exchange takes place on the base of reciprocity: if an individual gives something to another, some sort of return is expected within a reasonable time lag.[26]

4. The fourth dimension is *masculinity/femininity*. A society is masculine when dominant values favour assertiveness, earning money, showing off possessions and caring little for others. Conversely, feminine societies favour nurturing roles, interdependence between people and caring for others (who are seen as worth caring for, because they are *temporarily* weak). This dimension has been so called because, on average, men tended to score high on one extreme and women on the other, whatever the society.

Table 3.2 shows the value of these dimensions for the fifty-three countries/regions. Figure 3.1 presents a diagrammatical map of countries when individualism and power distance are combined.

Hofstede's main tenet concerns the *cultural relativity of management theories*. These theories are rooted in the cultural context where they were developed, therefore any simple direct transposition is difficult. For motivation, Hofstede shows the linkage which exists between US-based motivation theories and American culture. For instance, Abraham Maslow's 'hierarchy of needs' and McClelland's theory of the achievement motive are directly related to two dimensions of US culture: its strong masculinity and its individualism. People are seen as being motivated in an overtly conscious manner by the expectancy of some kind of results from their acts: they are basically motivated by extrinsic reasons and rewards. In contrast Freudian theory, which has not been greatly applied by US management theorists, represents the individual as being pushed by internal forces, often unconsciously, the id and the super-ego interacting with the ego. According to Hofstede, Austria, where Freud was born and where he drafted his theories, scores significantly higher than the United States on uncertainty avoidance and lower on individualism. This may explain why motivation is more related to interiorized social

Box 3.2   *More equal than others*

> In a peaceful revolution – the last revolution in Swedish history – the nobles of Sweden in 1809 deposed King Gustav IV whom they considered incompetent, and surprisingly invited Jean Baptiste Bernadotte, a French general who served under their enemy Napoleon, to become King of Sweden. Bernadotte accepted and he became King Charles XIV; his descendants occupy the Swedish throne to this day. When the new King was installed he addressed the Swedish parliament in their language. His broken Swedish amused the Swedes and they roared with laughter. The Frenchman who had become King was so upset that he never tried to speak Swedish again.
>
> In this incident Bernadotte was a victim of culture shock: never in his French upbringing and military career had he experienced subordinates who laughed at the mistakes of their superior. Historians tell us he had more problems adapting to the egalitarian Swedish and Norwegian mentality (he later became King of Norway as well) and to his subordinates' constitutional rights. He was a good learner, however (except for language), and he ruled the country as a highly respected constitutional monarch until 1844.
>
> One of the aspects in which Sweden differs from France is the way its society handles *inequality*. There is inequality in any society. Even in the most simple hunter-gatherer band, some people are bigger, stronger or smarter than others. The next thing is that some people have more power than others: they are more able to determine the behaviour of others than vice-versa. Some people are given more status and respect than others.

(Geert Hofstede, 1991, *Cultures and Organizations: The software of the mind*, McGraw-Hill: Maidenhead. Reproduced with the publisher's permission.)

Scanning the environment

Table 3.2   *Values of Hofstede's cultural dimensions for 53 countries or regions.*

Country/region	Dimensions			
	Power distance	Uncertainty avoidance	Individualism	Masculinity
East African region[a]	64	52	27	41
West African region[b]	77	54	20	46
Arabic countries	80	68	38	53
Argentina	49	86	46	56
Australia	36	51	90	61
Austria	11	70	55	79
Belgium	65	94	75	54
Brazil	69	76	38	49
Canada	39	48	80	52
Chile	63	86	23	28
Colombia	67	80	13	64
Costa Rica	35	86	15	21
Denmark	18	23	74	16
Ecuador	78	67	8	63
Finland	33	59	63	26
France	68	86	71	43
West Germany	35	65	67	66
Great Britain	35	35	89	66
Greece	60	112	35	57
Guatamala	96	101	6	37
Hong Kong	68	29	25	57
India	77	40	48	56
Indonesia	78	48	14	46
Iran	58	59	41	43
Ireland	28	35	70	68
Israel	13	81	54	47
Italy	50	75	76	70
Jamaica	45	13	39	68
Japan	54	92	46	95
South Korea	60	85	18	39
Malaysia	104	36	26	50
Mexico	81	82	30	69
New Zealand	22	49	79	58
Netherlands	38	53	80	14
Norway	31	50	69	8
Pakistan	55	70	14	50
Panama	95	86	11	44
Peru	64	87	16	42
Philippines	94	44	32	64
Portugal	63	104	27	31
Salvador	66	94	19	40
Singapore	74	8	20	48

Table 3.2   *Continued*

Country/region	Dimensions			
	Power distance	Uncertainty avoidance	Individualism	Masculinity
South Africa	49	49	65	63
Spain	57	86	51	42
Sweden	31	29	71	5
Switzerland	34	58	68	70
Taiwan	58	69	17	45
Thailand	64	64	20	34
Turkey	66	85	37	45
United States	40	46	91	62
Uruguay	61	100	36	38
Venezuela	81	76	12	73
Yugoslavia	76	88	27	21
Overall mean	57	65	43	49
Standard deviation	22	24	25	18

[a]Ethiopia, Kenya, Tanzania and Zambia.
[b]Ghana, Nigeria and Sierra Leone.
[c]Saudi Arabia, Egypt, United Arab Emirates, Iraq, Kuwait, Lebanon and Libya.

values. 'Freud's superego acts naturally as an inner uncertainty-absorbing device, an internalized boss' (Hofstede, 1980a).

Generally speaking, these differences have to be taken into account when designing sales force stimulation systems across national subsidiaries which have different cultural contexts. In masculine, individualistic countries, where there is also lower uncertainty avoidance, extrinsic rewards should be preferred (bonuses, gifts, holidays, monetary incentives). In societies which are more feminine, and/or more collectivist, and/or with higher uncertainty avoidance, intrinsic rewards should be chosen because they fit with profound inner values.[27]

Hofstede also takes the example of the direct transposition of the American MBO (Management By Objectives) in France, where it became the DPPO (*Direction Participative Par Objectifs*). MBO stems from a society where:

• Subordinates are independent and feel sufficiently at ease with their bosses to negotiate meaningfully with them (low power distance).
• Subordinates as well as superiors are willing to take risks (low uncertainty avoidance).
• The outcome is considered important by superiors and subordinates (high level of masculinity).

DPPO, the French version of MBO, enjoyed brief success at the end of the 1960s but had become a flop by the mid-1970s. Indeed in the French cultural context DPPO created anxiety, in a country where hierarchy is traditionally strong (high power distance) and where that structure protects people against uncertainty. MBO assumes a depersonalized authority (role authority) whereas, according to Hofstede, from their childhood French people are used to high power distance and strongly personalized authority. Despite efforts to introduce Anglo-Saxon management methods, French bosses do not easily decentralize management and delegate authority.

In a study at Insead, reported by Hofstede, O. J. Stevens asked students of various nationalities to write their own diagnosis of and solution to a small case study about a conflict between the sales department and the product development department. The French saw the problem basically as one that the hierarchy should solve, a solution being sought from the chairperson. The Germans blamed the absence of formal rules and written procedures. The English saw the problem as resulting basically from a lack of interpersonal communication. Stevens concluded that 'the *implicit model* of the organization for most French was a pyramid (both centralized and formal); for Germans

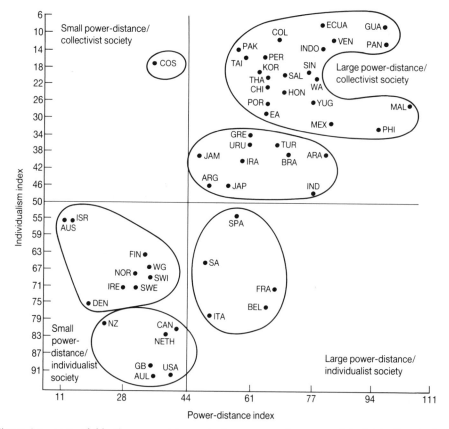

Figure 3.1 Map of fifty-three countries ranked on power-distance and individualism indices. (Source: Hofstede, 1980b.)

a well-oiled machine (formalized, but not centralized); and for most British a village market (neither formalized, nor centralized) (Hofstede, 1980a, p. 60).

Organization types may be more adapted to some cultures than to others. In matrix organization, for instance, there is a double hierarchical linkage (with a product division at the European level and a subsidiary general manager at the country level): this is not very well accepted either by the French or by the Germans. For the French, it violates the principle of unity of commandment; for the Germans, it thwarts their need for organizational clarity and will not be deemed acceptable unless individual roles inside the organization are unambiguously defined.

Cultural assumptions and actual behaviour

The basic cultural assumptions described in section 3.1 (and listed in Table 3.1) are in fact deep-rooted beliefs which generate basic values. Indirectly they guide our daily behaviour, but they may also clash with it. By their very nature they are unconscious, as is the process by which they shape our conduct. There is some leeway for other sources of influence: for instance, we use social representations to make decisions. We are influenced by other values and other standards of demeanour, which work closer to the surface than basic cultural assumptions (e.g. sex roles, family values, friendship patterns). These standards of demeanour help people to manage adjustments in the short term; they change over shorter periods of time (ten or twenty years) than basic cultural assumptions (probably formed over centuries). This leads to two questions:

1. To what extent do less profound levels of culture, e.g. corporate culture or educational culture, influence people?
2. To what extent do people, more or less consciously, feel a contradiction between these different sources of prescriptive behaviour?

Taking their views from Schein's (1981) culture model, Derr and Laurent (1989) present what they call the 'levels of culture triangle' (see Figure 3.2). Basic cultural

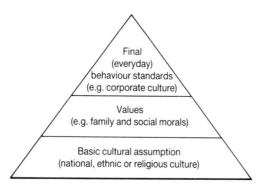

Figure 3.2 Basic cultural assumptions and actual behaviour. (Source: André Laurent, 1989. Reproduced with permission.)

assumptions are at the bottom of the triangle: values and behavioural norms which derive from the society in its present state. At the top of the triangle are behavioural standards, which are prescribed in a much more direct and explicit way, which Derr and Laurent call 'artifacts': for instance, company procedures, business ethics codes[28] and generally all those standards which unashamedly seek to shape employees' behaviour (inside the company). Whereas cultural assumptions are based on national culture, 'artifacts', values and norms are based on organizational culture.

Multinational companies (MNCs) offer their employees the most fruitful opportunities for intercultural exchange. One might believe that, despite differences in national culture, the values shared by executives in MNCs do converge, as they spend years working with different people. In order to grasp differences in cognitive styles, Laurent (1983) asked managers of different nationalities to indicate their agreement or disagreement with the following statement (item 24 of Laurent's questionnaire on management styles): 'It is important for a manager to have at hand precise answers to most of the questions that his subordinates may raise about their work.'

Figure 3.3 reproduces the results (the percentage of respondents replying in the affirmative) for various national groups. Obviously Swedes do not need omniscient managers (10 per cent). Among Westerners at the other extreme, the Italians (66 per cent) and the French (53 per cent) believe that managers should have precise answers to most of their subordinates' questions. It seems that most Anglo-Saxon and northern European people tend to see managers as *problem solvers*, whereas Latin and Asian people see them more as *experts*.

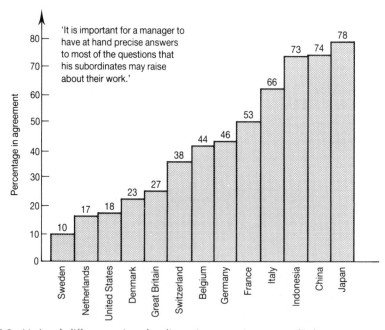

Figure 3.3 National differences in subordinates' expectations towards their superiors. (Source: Laurent, 1983. Reproduced with permission.)

These differences were observed in people working in their home country. Laurent (1989) asked the same question of executives who had been working for a long time in MNCs where teams had been built up from a large number of different nationalities. One would expect to observe a decrease in the differences between national groups of managers. Surprisingly, the situation is exactly the opposite. Laurent has observed in MNCs an increase of differences across national groups. This suggests that, behind superficial agreements, people's basic cultural assumptions are reinforced. When a corporate culture tries to shape a manager's (or more generally an employee's) daily behaviour, it succeeds from the outside (because people are concerned about their job and career). But it only scratches the surface of people and does not significantly affect the two bottom levels of Figure 3.2. Moreover, since values are forced upon them, not only do they fail to impinge on basic cultural assumptions, but they even reinforce them.

3.4 Cultural borrowing and change in societies

Isolated cultures, united cultures

Cultures are rarely pure, except in a few areas where people have been almost untouched by foreign influences. An example of such cultural isolation might be Japan which, during the era of Tokugawa shoguns, withdrew from all contact with outside people and cultures. The Tokugawa period lasted for more than two centuries before the Meiji era, which started after 1868 and initiated a period of increased accessibility of foreign influences to Japan. Reischauer, a specialist in Japanese history, explains in his book *Japan: Past and present* (1946, 1990) that two centuries of complete peace were enforced by the Tokugawa regime with extreme vigour. The Tokugawa shoguns have left their mark on the behaviour of Japanese citizens. In the sixteenth century the Japanese were keen, adventurous and somewhat bellicose. By the nineteenth century they had become docile and humble subjects, awaiting orders from their hierarchical superiors, which they resignedly implemented. Reischauer hypothesizes that the collective regimentation under the Tokugawa shoguns led to an inward-looking people who indulged in conformism, which served as consensus. He further notes that, at the beginning of the nineteenth century, antagonism in Japanese society was almost non-existent: the rules of propriety were strictly observed, and violence was extremely rare. Reischauer argues that when the Japanese were confronted with an unknown situation, they displayed very little ability to adapt, much less than other peoples.[29] The Tokugawa period appears good in many ways, especially as regards the general level of education and the development of the arts. However, it largely interrupted the natural evolution of economic and social change. The Tokugawa shoguns crystallized an outdated political and social order. Only after the beginning of the Meiji era in 1868 did the Japanese begin to interact with the Europeans, who had achieved an enormous breakthrough in the field of scientific knowledge during the previous two centuries. The succession of these two periods, one of great isolation and one of openness towards foreign cultures, probably explains the paradoxical relationship of the Japanese with international trade and international marketing. In one sense they are very ethnocentric, but simultaneously they are quite capable of overcoming their ethnocentrism to become, ultimately, highly successful international marketers.

In many other cases, cultures do mix. Contact may inevitably be bellicose, due to the conflicting interests of countries and their cultures (religion, language, social and political systems) over borders. The perennial conflicts between the region south of the Mediterranean Sea (mostly Arab and Muslim) and the northern region (mostly Christian) are an example of this pattern of conflict/co-operation. Cultural encounters occur even in wartime. When besieged by the Turks in the fifteenth century, the Viennese were introduced by their opponents to a new, tasty and stimulating beverage: coffee. It is through the Viennese as intermediaries that coffee was introduced into the West. Even during the Crusades (tenth to twelfth centuries), warriors on both sides had quiet moments when, for instance, they enjoyed each other's food. In *The Crusades through Arab Eyes* (1985), Amine Maalouf describes how the Templars grew accustomed to understanding and accepting the customs and beliefs of the Muslims.[30] In the following extract, Templars, although themselves Christians, side with a Muslim in defending Islamic religious practices:[31]

> When I was visiting Jerusalem, I used to go to Al-Aqsa mosque, where my Templar friends were staying. Along one side of the building was a small oratory in which the *Franj* had set up a church.[32] The Templars placed this spot at my disposal so that I might say my prayers. One day I entered, said *Allahu Akbar*, and was about to begin my prayer, when a man, a *Franj*, threw himself upon me, and turned to the east, saying, 'Thus do we pray.' The Templars rushed forward and led him away. I then set myself to prayer once more, but this man, seizing upon a moment of inattention, threw himself upon me yet again, turned my face to the east, and repeated once more, 'Thus do we pray.' Once again the Templars intervened, led him away, and apologized to me, saying, 'He is a foreigner. He has just arrived from the land of the *Franj* and he has never seen anyone pray without turning his face to the east.' I answered that I had prayed enough and left, stunned by the behaviour of this demon who had been so enraged at seeing me pray while facing the direction of Mecca.

Cultural borrowing is general . . . and disguised

Culture is identity, but not pure identity:[33] the basic requirement for the introduction of a new cultural item (a product, a life-style, a word, a dance, a song) is that it looks (and in fact is) *coherent* with the culture which adopts it. That is why cultural borrowing is often disguised, by a change of name or by means of 'reinvention', whereby a local inventor/ discoverer is found. It is fascinating to see how many countries seek to claim credit for particular inventions (the Xerox machine, for instance) at the same time.

As indicated by Cateora (1983), one view of culture is that of the accumulation of a series of the best solutions to the common problems faced by the members of a particular society. This definition, very Anglo-Saxon in its problem-solving orientation, does have an advantage: it emphasizes the 'shopping' aspect of cultural dynamics. There have always been different kinds of travellers (explorers, warriors, merchants, colonials, etc.) who have brought back foreign innovations to their native country. Usually by accident, or sometimes by an almost systematic process (like the Japanese, because they are overly conscious of their insularity and cultural isolation), societies may find good imported solutions. Jeans, as informal trousers for casual wear, have made their way through all cultures. The fabric originally came from France (*de Nîmes* – denim) and the name from Italy – short for Jean Fustian from Gênes (Genoa). Afterwards this 'American' invention made its way back to Italy and most of the countries of the world.

Although cultural opportunism is understandable, it is often hidden by the need to maintain cultural identity. Few societies are prepared to accept that a large part of their culture is really foreign: cultural borrowing is therefore somewhat hypocritical. Marketing concepts and theories, largely US-based, have been imported into a large number of countries.[34] However, in a somewhat linguistically defensive country like France it was considered necessary to create a new word and rename the concept *la mercatique*, despite the fact that the original word, 'marketing', contains no letter outside the French alphabet and is more easily pronunciated in French.

The word *mercatique*, a neologism, was created in 1973 by the Commission de Terminologie Française, established by the French Ministry of Economics and Finance.[35] Despite this centrally inspired procedure, people in everyday life still use the original word, 'marketing'. The argument in favour of *la mercatique* was as follows:

> Not only did *mercatique* have a clear etymology (from the Latin *mercatus*, the market) but also its definition, by its strictness, allowed for a more profound understanding of the concept and avoided the deviations, misinterpretations and misconceptions that the blurredness of the English expression entailed. These misconceptions were frequent: thus, for Pierre Hazebroucq, secretary of the Académie des Science Commerciales, the word 'marketing' designated 'everything related to influencing markets'; similarly P. Kotler wrote, in *Management Direction* in June 1974, that marketing management was the set of actions which aims at regulating the level, the pace and the nature of demand for one or several products of a company – this dragged up memories of the 1900–50 period, where the supply side was given higher priority, that is demand had to adapt to those products which were actually offered. How, under these conditions, was it possible to get young people interested in commercial action and entrepreneurship?
>
> Whereas, with the French concept of *mercatique*, young people passionately fond of trade action discovered an outlet for their enthusiasm; 'manipulative' commercial activities were rejected, as well as activities which were limited exclusively to the act of buying or solely to the act of selling, often with contempt for customers, or at least a definite lack of attention to their needs. (Darbelet and Lauginié, 1988, pp. 133–4)

People who speak the common language have not adopted the word *mercatique*. Other French words created to replace a foreign word or concept have, however, been completely successful. For instance, *ordinateur* has replaced 'computer', which has been borrowed by many other languages from the United States, where computers were invented. Some words and concepts are borrowed easily in their original form when they are obviously related to some well-established stereotype of a particular country: ersatz (high reputation of German chemistry), leitmotiv (German music), showbiz (US dominance), élégance (French reputation for style), kamikaze or hara-kiri (Japanese capacity for self-sacrifice), mamma (Italian sense of the motherly role in the family).

But, generally speaking, cultural borrowings are disguised and finally they disappear. Numerous words, goods and even life-styles (the 'weekend', for instance) have been largely borrowed. Such words as 'magazine' and 'assassin' have been directly imported from Arabic. During the Crusades, the Crusaders played endless games of dice, which Arabs call *az-zahar*: a word that the *Franj* adopted to designate not the game itself but the concept of chance (Maalouf, 1985).

The example of the Japanese borrowing of Chinese writing more than fifteen centuries ago is a true example of imitation, but also of reinterpretation, which makes this appropriation a genuine element of Japanese culture (see Box 3.3). The Japanese, when they first read ideograms (which they later called kanji) did not immediately recognize

Box 3.3   *The origins of Japanese writing*

The Japanese write their language with ideograms they borrowed from China nearly two thousand years ago. Some two thousand years before that, the ancient Chinese had formed these ideograms, or characters, from pictures of things they knew. To them the sun had looked like this ☼, so this became their written word for **sun**. This form was gradually squared off and simplified to make it easier to write, changing its shape to 日. This is still the way the word sun is written in both China and Japan today.

The ancient Chinese first drew a tree like this 𣎼. This was also gradually simplified and squared, to 木, which became the written word for **tree**. To form the word for **root** or **origin** the Chinese just drew in more roots at the bottom of the tree to emphasize this portion of the picture, 夲, then squared and simplified the character to 本. This became the written word for **root** or **origin**.

When the characters for **sun** 日 and **origin** 本 are put together in a compound they form the written word 日本 **Japan**, which means literally origin-of-the-sun.

A picture of the sun in the east at sunrise coming up behind a tree forms the written word for **east** 東. A picture of the stone lantern that guarded each ancient Chinese capital squared off and simplified to abstract form 京 forms the written word for **capital**. These two characters put together in a compound form the written word 東京 Eastern-capital, TŌKYŌ.

The characters may look mysterious and impenetrable at first approach, but as these examples show, they are not difficult at all to understand. The characters are not just random strokes: each one is a picture, and has a meaning based on the content of the picture.

The Japanese written language contains a number of these characters, but fortunately not as many as Westerners often assume. To graduate from grammar school a student must know 881 characters. At this point he is considered literate. A high school graduate must know 1,850. To read college textbooks, about three thousand characters are necessary.

All these thousands of characters, however, are built up from less than 300 elements, or pictures, many of which are seldom used.

(Len Walsh, 1969, *Read Japanese Today*, Charles E. Tuttle: Rutland, VT, and Tokyo. Reproduced with permission.)

them as representing *ideas*, but experienced them more directly as *sounds*. Therefore the kanji system works as a pictogram system representing both ideas and sounds. It is further completed by two syllabaries, which represent only sounds: hiragana for native words and katakana for imported words. The katakana syllabary is typical of the Japanese attitude towards cultural imports: they do not object (as the French do, for instance), but at the same time it is a necessity to signal clearly the foreign origin of some words and concepts by writing such words in katakana, which represents the same syllables as hiragana (an apparent waste of effort).

Other examples of cultural borrowing are numerous: music, clothes, architecture, building techniques, food, recipes, etc. Borrowing sometimes goes as far as pure and simple copying, and possibly product counterfeiting.[36] The Japanese have been remarkably skilful at borrowing European music culture, becoming the most important producers of musical instruments world-wide. Even castanets – an ethnically Spanish product – are made in Japan for sale in Spain.

3.5 Cultural hostility

Limits to borrowing clearly appear when it is seen as a threat to cultural coherence. This is especially true of religious practices, social morals and even daily customs.[37] For instance, it is not easy to import polygamy or clitoral excision for babies into cultures where monogamy and child protection are strongly established practices. As previously stated, there must be a minimum level of coherence and homogeneity in cultural assumptions and behaviour in the cultural community if people are to synchronize themselves and live peacefully together.

Racism

Racism is often confused with cultural hostility, whereas in fact it precedes cultural hostility. But cultural hostility does not necessarily imply racism: one may be hostile to people of (some) other cultures, without being a racist. Behind racism there is a *theory*: that, because of their race (i.e. physiology), some human beings are inferior at various levels (intelligence, creative abilities, moral sense, etc.). The theories of Gobineau and Hitler's *Mein Kampf* are writings which clearly developed and propagated racist views.

The following passage on slavery, written by Montesquieu in 1748 (*The Spirit of Laws*, book XV, ch. 5, p. 242, my emphasis), exemplifies racism:

> Were I to vindicate our right to make slaves of the Negroes, there should be my arguments. The Europeans, having extirpated the Americans, were obliged to make slaves of the Africans, for clearing such vast tracts of land. Sugar would be too dear, if the plants which produce it were cultivated by any other than slaves.
>
> These creatures are all over black, and with such a flat nose, that they can scarcely be pitied. *It is hardly to be believed that God, who is a wise being, should place a soul, especially a good soul, in such a black ugly body.*[38]

Racist theses and opinions have been progressively abandoned (as scientific theories, at least) over the last two centuries. An issue which is still discussed is that of differing intellectual capacity among people of different races or ethnic groups. It is always measured by IQ tests, which are of western/US origin. Although observed differences across ethnic groups are undisputable, their explanation is debated: some people argue about genetic differences being the explanatory variable, others (Segall *et al.*, 1990) attribute these differences to a series of non-genetic factors. Environmental factors, for instance, such as the absence of a formal education system, on average tend to diminish IQ scores. Such detrimental factors are to be found, significantly, more among groups with low and median IQ scores.

The IQ test itself is biased in as much as it penalizes, by its very construction, those who have been designated from the start as 'culturally inferior'. The IQ test does not take into account many skills and competences, which were unknown to the authors of the test. Moreover, recent studies show that the *inter-individual* variability of genetic character-istics is much larger than the *inter-racial groups* variability (Segall *et al.*, 1990, p. 102). In other words, genetic differences among Europeans, or genetic differences among South African Zulus, are *automatically* significantly higher than the genetic differences between the average European and the average Zulu – a strong anti-racist argument.[39]

Cultural hostility

In contrast to racism, cultural hostility does not imply prior prejudices as to who is inferior or superior according to race or culture. Culture is part of one's own patrimony as a person. There is a strong affective dimension, when one feels that one's proper cultural values are threatened. This feeling may result from either of the following:

1. Simple interactions with people whose cultural values are quite different. One does not feel at ease, communication is experienced as burdensome and there is little empathy. A defensive response may then develop, frequently the case of unconscious (and minor) cultural hostility.
2. Collective reactions. Cases are so numerous world-wide that it would need many pages to quote them exhaustively: Transylvanian Hungarians and Romanians, Armenians of High Karabakh and Azeris of the Azerbaijan enclave in Soviet Armenia; Walloons and Flemings in Belgium; Protestant and Catholic communities in Ulster; etc. *Identity is a matter of culture rather than race*.

It is not only territorial conflicts but also economic competition that may cause cultural hostility. The Japanese are sometimes considered negatively in the United States, which has a large trade imbalance with Japan. In his controversial best-selling book, *The Japan that Can Say No*, Shintaro Ishihara (1991) argues that anti-Japanese racial prejudice is the main cause of 'Japan-bashing' in the United States. Ishihara, a member of the Japanese diet, quotes what he said to politicians in Washington:

> I admit that Caucasians created modern civilization, but what bothers me is you seem to think that heritage makes you superior. In the thirteenth century, however, the Mongols under Genghis Khan and his successors overran Russia and Eastern Europe ... Caucasians adopted

Mongol-style haircuts and shaved eyebrows. ... Just as Orientals of today are crazy about the clothing and hairstyle of the Beatles, Michael Jackson and Sting, Occidentals of Genghis Khan times copied Mongolian ways. (p. 27)

Cultural hostility, when directed at successful nations, is often a fairly ambiguous feeling, whereby admiration and envy for the other's achievements go along with contempt for many traits of the envied people and obvious unwillingness to understand the root causes of the other's success. This also results in naive copies of selected cultural artifacts as magical ways of becoming stronger – in *Robinson Crusoe* savages were about to eat Man Friday in order to gain his qualities.

In the case of immigrants, Mauviel (1991, p. 73, my translation) comments on the frequent confusion between racism and cultural hostility:[40]

... the dominant ideology has been so interiorized that a new, very subtle rhetoric enables us to avoid any direct, frank response to the problems concerning immigrants – the most important issue is not to be accused of 'racism'. And one places under this word the most dissimilar elements, which often have nothing to do with race, in its biological acceptance. ... The media especially like the meaningless expression 'everyday racism'. As for the phrase 'ethnic group', which has replaced the word 'race', those who use the expression would have a hard time trying to define it.

Box 3.4 *Nigerian women of Chambave*

Hundreds, if not thousands, of Nigerian women – graduates in chemistry, law and other subjects, nurses, etc. – came to Italy in search of a better life. Most of them end up walking the streets, or are love traders on the *tangenziali*, the freeways round cities, and even on country roads. The most striking example to me, because of its symbolic meaning, is that of the 'train of sin', from Turin to Aosta, which brings thirty to forty Nigerian women every summer evening on the 9.15 p.m. bus to Chambave, which is located between Aosta and San Vincenzo; they are joining their 'shift' on highway 26. These *pendolari del amore* (commuters) have lost the dream that they previously held, namely that of being salespeople for Italian shoes. One should not be astonished that the mayor [of Chambave], surrounded by the local council and the population of the valley, has organized a silent protest march. However, there is clearly a flourishing market, if one just looks at the evidence of the numerous cars with roaring engines that wait for the women. One may guess what the relations are between this village of nine hundred people and the African women, who are no longer prepared to accept being kept out of sight. In these matters, the most shocking hypocrisy is the rule; only conspicuous incidents that attract people's attention, like those at Chambave, help us to become aware of these new forms of shameful exploitation, a direct consequence of the under-development of the countries of the South.

(Maurice Mauviel (1991), La grande misère de l'antiracisme français', *Intercultures*, no. 12, pp. 81–2. Reproduced with permission.)

There are differences across countries: Mauviel shows that the Italians are not so reluctant to speak openly on cultural hostility problems. The Italian press 'lets reality be seen, it does not cover it with an embarrassed veil, it allows the publication of the most diverse opinions'. He describes, for instance, the case of the Nigerian women at Chambave (near Torino) which, 'as revealed by the press, demonstrates the irresponsibility of those who vow to have multiracial or multi-ethnic societies' (Box 3.4).

The next chapter further examines the mechanism of cultural hostility, which is sometimes increased by language and communication problems. Intercultural mis-understandings may stem from a lack of competency in the other's language, or from the natural tendency to adopt defensive stereotypes. It often results in a snowballing cultural hostility.

APPENDIX 3

———— ◆◆◆ ————

Teaching materials

A3.1 Critical incident: An American in Vietnam

An American in Vietnam recalls an illuminating story told him by a Vietnamese who complained about a lack of understanding between the two allies. They were discussing the fate of a province chief named Vong, once hailed by the Americans as the best province chief in Vietnam. Vong was accused of embezzling some 300,000 American dollars earmarked for an airstrip, and was tried and sentenced to be executed. It seemed a harsh sentence, considering the corruption prevalent at the time, and the American asked the Vietnamese if he agreed.

'No,' the Vietnamese said, 'Vong should be executed because he's a stupid man.'

'Stupid? Because he got caught?' the American asked.

The Vietnamese impatiently shook his head. 'No, no, not because he took the money,' he said. 'That is not important. But you know what this stupid man did? He pacified six more hamlets than his quota. This caused the general who gave him the quota to lose face, and that is stupid.'

The perplexed American said, 'In America, he'd get a medal for exceeding his quota.' The Vietnamese shook his head and said, 'You Americans will never understand the Vietnamese.'

What aspects of the incident are significant in describing the difference in opinion between these two persons?

(Weeks *et al.*, p. 22. Reproduced with the kind permission of the publisher.)

A3.2 Exercise: Seven cultures of the South Sea

You will find below a short excerpt from Margaret Mead's book *Male and Female*. She introduces briefly each of the seven South Sea peoples, who live in fairly diverse natural settings and have different kinds of activities and social organization.

For you, this is an exercise in imagination. You are asked to perform the following task, which is both easy and complicated: starting from Margaret Mead's basic cultural descriptions, try to characterize the selling styles of these seven peoples. For instance, consider the following questions for each of these societies:

1. Is selling considered a socially respectable activity?
2. Who is the more powerful: buyer or seller?
3. What is the communication style (hard/soft)?
4. Are people long-term transaction-orientated (buyer and seller tending to be loyal to each other in the long run)?
5. What kinds of sales argument (seduction, force, blackmail, etc.) would be used?
6. Does selling exist at all? Is selling meaningful? Why?

The Samoans

The Samoans are a tall, light-brown-skinned Polynesian people living on a small group of islands, part of which belong to the United States. Their way of life is formal and stately. Chiefs and orators, village princes and village princesses, patterned groups of young and old, combined together to plant and reap, fish and build, feast and dance, in a world where no one is hurried, where food is plentiful, nature is generous, and life is harmonious and unintense. They have been Christian for over a hundred years, and have fitted the tenets of Christianity into their own traditions, wearing beautifully starched cottons on Sunday, but still barefoot, and proud of their own way of life.

The Manus of the Admiralty Islands

The Manus people are a small, energetic tribe of fishermen and traders who build their houses on piles in the salt lagoons, near to their fishing-grounds. Tall, brown-skinned, lean and active, with nothing but their wits, their skill, and an ethics which says that the ghosts of the dead will penalize the unindustrious, they have built a high standard of living, which they maintain by continuous hard work. Puritan to the core, committed to effort and work, disallowing love and the pleasures of the senses, they take quickly to the ways of the Western world, to machinery, to money.

The Mountain Arapesh

The Mountain Arapesh are a mild, undernourished people who live in the steep, unproductive Torricelli Mountains of New Guinea, poor themselves, and always struggling to save enough to buy music and dance-steps and new fashions from the trading peoples of the sea-coast, and to buy off the sorcerers among the fiercer people of the interior plains. Responsive and co-operative, they have developed a society in which, while there is never enough to eat, each man spends most of his time helping his neighbour, and committed to his neighbour's purposes. The greatest interest of both men and women is in growing things – children, pigs, coconut-trees – and their greatest fear that each generation will reach maturity shorter in stature than their forebears, until finally there will be no people under the palm-trees.

The cannibal Mundugumor of the Yuat River

These robust, restive people live on the banks of a swiftly flowing river, but with no river lore. They trade with and prey upon the miserable, underfed bush-peoples who live on poorer land, devote their time to quarrelling and head-hunting, and have developed a form of social organization in which every man's hand is against every other man. The women are as assertive and vigorous as the men; they detest bearing and rearing children, and provide most of the food, leaving the men free to plot and fight.

The lake-dwelling Tchambuli

The Tchambuli people, who number only six hundred in all, have built their houses along the edge of one of the loveliest of New Guinea lakes, which gleams like polished ebony, with a back-drop of the distant hills behind which the Arapesh live. In the lake are purple lotus and great pink and white water lilies, white osprey and blue heron. Here the Tchambuli women, brisk, unadorned, managing and industrious, fish and go to market; the men, decorative and adorned, carve and paint and practise dance-steps, their head-hunting tradition replaced by the simpler practice of buying victims to validate their manhood.

The Iatmul head-hunters of the Great Sepik River

On the big, slow-moving river into which the Yuat River drains, for which the mountains where the Arapesh live is one watershed, to which the Tchambuli lake is connected by canals, are the swagger villages of the Iatmul people, head-hunters, carvers, orators, tall and fiercely, brittlely masculine, where women serve as spectators to the endless theatricality of the men's behaviour. Rich in sago swamps that provide them with a steady food-supply, well fed on fish that the steady industry of the women provides, they have built magnificent ceremonial houses, and beautifully carved war-canoes, and accumulate in their big villages the art-styles, the dance-steps, the myths, of all the lesser peoples about them, outstanding among their neighbours, and vulnerable in the intensity of their pride.

The Balinese

The Balinese, who can be numbered in hundreds of thousands, not in a few thousands like the Samoans or a few hundreds like the New Guinea peoples, are not a primitive people, but a people whose culture is linked through Asia with our own historical past. Light, graceful, wavy-haired, with bodies every segment of which moves separately in the dance, they have a highly complex and ordered way of life that in its guilds and Hindu rituals, its written records and temple organizations, its markets and its arts, is reminiscent of the Middle Ages in Europe. Crowded on a tiny island with a beautiful, highly diversified, changing landscape, they have turned all life into an art. The air is filled with music day and night, and the people, whose relations to each other are light, without enduring warmth, are tireless in rehearsal for a play where those disallowed feelings will be given graceful stylized expression.
(Margaret Mead, 1948, The seven South Sea peoples', in *Male and Female*, William Morrow: New York, pp. 52–5. Reproduced with permission.)

A3.3 Cross-cultural scenario: Inshallah

Stefan Phillips, a manager for a large U.S. airline, was transferred to Dhahran, Saudi Arabia, to set up a new office. Although Stefan had had several other extended overseas assignments in Paris and Brussels, he was not well prepared for working in the Arab world. At the end of his first week Stefan came home in a state of near total frustration. As he sat at the dinner table that night he told his wife how exasperating it had been to work with the local employees, who, he claimed, seemed to take no responsibility for anything. Whenever something went wrong they would simply say '*Inshallah*' ('If God wills it'). Coming from a culture which sees no problem as insoluble, Stefan could not understand how the local employees could be so passive about job-related problems. 'If I hear one more *inshallah*,' he told his wife, 'I'll go crazy.'

What might you tell Stefan to help him better understand the cultural realities of Saudi Arabia?
(Gary P. Ferraro, 1990, *The Cultural Dimension of International Business*, Prentice Hall: Englewood Cliffs, NJ, p. 118. Reproduced with permission.)

A3.4 Cross-cultural interaction: Engineering a decision

M. Legrand is a French engineer who works for a Japanese company in France. One day the general manager, Mr Tanaka, calls him into his office to discuss a new project in the Middle East. He tells M. Legrand that the company is very pleased with his dedicated work and would like him to act as chief engineer for the project. It would mean two to three years away from home, but his family would be able to accompany him and there would be considerable personal financial benefits to the position – and, of course, he would be performing a valuable service to the company. M. Legrand thanks Mr. Tanaka for the confidence he has in him but says he will have to discuss it with his wife before deciding. Two days later he returns and tells Mr. Tanaka that both he and his wife do not like the thought of leaving France and so he does not want to accept the position. Mr. Tanaka says nothing but is somewhat dumbfounded by his decision.

Why is Mr. Tanaka so bewildered by M. Legrand's decision?[41]

1. He believes it is foolish for M. Legrand to refuse all the financial benefits that go with the position.
2. He cannot accept that M. Legrand should take any notice of his wife's opinion in the matter.
3. He believes M. Legrand is possibly trying to bluff him into offering greater incentives to accept the offer.
4. He feels it is not appropriate for M. Legrand to place his personal inclinations above those of his role as an employee of the company.

(Richard W. Brislin, Kenneth Cushner, Craig Cherrie, Mahealani Yong (1986), *Intercultural Interactions: A practical guide*, Sage: Newbury Park, CA, pp. 158–9. Reproduced with permission.)

A3.5 Cross-cultural interaction: Opening a medical office in Saudi Arabia[42]

Dr. Tom McDivern, a physician from New York City, was offered a two-year assignment to practice medicine in a growing urban center in Saudi Arabia. Many of the residents in the area he was assigned to were recent immigrants from the much smaller outlying rural areas.

Because Western medicine was relatively unknown to many of these people, one of Dr. McDivern's main responsibilities was to introduce himself and his services to those in the community. A meeting at a local school was organized for that specific purpose. Many people turned out. Tom's presentation went well. Some local residents also presented their experiences with Western medicine so others could hear the value of using his services. Some of Tom's office staff were also present to make appointments for those interested in seeing him when his doors opened one week later. The meeting was an obvious success. His opening day was booked solid.

When that day finally arrived, Tom was anxious to greet his first patients. Thirty minutes had passed, however, and neither of his first two patients had arrived. He was beginning to worry about the future of his practice while wondering where his patients were.

What is the major cause of Tom's worries?

1. Although in Tom's mind and by his standards his presentation was a success, people actually only made appointments so as not to hurt his feelings. They really had no intention of using his services as modern medicine is so foreign to their past experiences.
2. Given the time lag between sign up and the actual day of the appointment, people had time to rethink their decision. They had just changed their minds.

3. Units of time differ between Arabs and Americans. Whereas to Tom his patients were very late, the Arab patient could still arrive and be on time.
4. Tom's patients were seeing their own traditional healers from their own culture; after that, they could go on to see this new doctor, Tom.

(Richard W. Brislin, Kenneth Cushner, Craig Cherrie, Mahealani Yong (1986), *Intercultural Interactions: A practical guide*, Sage: Newbury Park, CA, pp. 160–1. Reproduced with permission.)

Notes

1. This aphorism (my translation) is attributed to the Swedish writer Selma Lagerlöf by Karl Petit (1960), *Dictionnaire des citations*, Marabout p. 100. Selma Lagerlöf is the author of, among other works, *Gösta Berling* (1957), Editions Je sers: Paris, a unique account of the Swedish soul.
2. Kluckhohn and Strodtbeck (1961, p.49) have tested their value orientation theory across five very distinct cultural communities, each one comprised of American citizens living in close proximity to each other in the south-western part of the United States, in similar natural environments.

   > Two of the populations are American Indian; one an off-reservation settlement of Navaho Indians ... the other the Pueblo Indian community of Zuni. The third is a Spanish American village which we have named Atrisco. A Mormon village and a recently established farming village of Texan and Oklahoman homesteaders ... are the two other communities.

3. Excerpt from Charles de Montesquieu (1748), *The Spirit of Laws*, translated from the French by Thomas Nugent (1792), 6th edn, McKenzie and Moore: Dublin, vol. 1, book XIV, ch. V, pp. 228–9.
4. Siam is the name originally given by the French to the present Thailand; Siamese are therefore Thai people.
5. *Metempsychosis* (the migration of the soul from one body to another) is a very strong belief which arises as a response to an important common human problem: do we have a soul? What is the relation between the physical world and the metaphysical world? Believers (people raised in the cultures where this belief is prevalent) are more patient, seemingly less 'doing'-orientated, simply because achieving position in lives to come is more important than what is achieved in one's present life.
6. This verb means to 'make', to 'produce', to 'build'; it may refer to objects, buildings, works of art (Pierre Chantraine, 1974, *Dictionnaire étymologique de la langue grecque*, Editions Klincksieck: Paris, p. 992).
7. The dimensions of ideologism and pragmatism are described in Chapters 13 and 14, with regard to their influence on international negotiation styles.
8. This means implicitly: compared to Latins, such as myself. We are generally much less cautious in taking such steps, if indeed we ever stop to identify them clearly. Even the style of this book reveals that I come from an ideologist-orientated society (French).
9. The expressions 'matter-of-fact'; and 'down to earth', which are both positive in English, may be translated by *être terre à terre*. The French language also has two expressions, but one is pejorative and the other is positive – *avoir les pieds sur terre* (*Harrap's Concise French–English Dictionary*, 1984, Harrap: London, p. 369).

10. The opposition of individualism to collectivism is a complex topic: there is more to it than meets the eye. For the influence of the individualist/collectivist dimension on sales force reward, see Chapter 11. See also the case of National Offices Machines in Cateora (1983, pp. 544–50).

11. A direct and univocal relation to reality simply means that people are sincerely *convinced* that what they perceive is the *only possible* reality. Chapter 8 presents the example of colours – how they are perceived and named, and what symbolic values are put on them.

12. The English language is more realistic than the French language here: *common sense* (shared) as opposed to the French *bon sens*, that is *good* sense – a value judgement which is sometimes wrong.

13. To illustrate this I will use the example of the painting *La Pipe* by the Belgian René Magritte, which may be seen at the Los Angeles County Museum of Art. It simply shows a pipe with a thin trail of smoke rising from it – that is (almost) all. But there is also a short subtitle at the bottom of the painting that reads *ceci n'est pas une pipe* ('this is not a pipe'): a very 'down-to-earth' way of reminding us that *images of reality should not be confused with reality itself*. We may create images of reality, especially through the media (for example, a war reported on television), but we may also ignore large chunks of reality simply because we cannot bring it within the field of our limited perceptual apparatus. At the Mount Wilson observatory in California, for example, photographs of the stars are taken with a special film and with a shutter exposure of four hours: but the stars in the skies are far more numerous than we will ever see with our poor eyes.

14. Those who wish to enlarge their world-view by freeing themselves, at least partially, from the mental programmes brought to them by culture, risk being misunderstood. This is in fact a legitimate reaction on the part of other members of the group. By trying to escape a single cultural programming, such people exhibit a definite lack of humility in setting themselves apart from the community. Furthermore any homogeneous human group feels fairly threatened when members of the group overstep the threshold of non-conformism. They may finally be understood (because the message is useful as an instrument of change that is needed in the society), or live alone, or be beheaded (e.g. Thomas Moore).

15. Clifford Geertz in *Local Knowledge* (1983) quotes a long passage from a Danish traveller and trader, L. V. Helms, who when travelling in India accurately reports the ritual of the cremation of a dead man and his three (living) widows. Helms describes very carefully the background to the incident, which takes place around 1850. He is horrified by the ritual, amazed by the absence of reaction of the crowd attending the event and stunned by the lack of fear of the three women who throw themselves alive into the flames. Geertz emphasizes the relations of culture to *moral imagination*: what is seen as mere barbary by one culture is experienced as wholly normal by another.

    Another more recent example of cross-cultural differences in the interpretation of facts is given by the totally diverging views during the Gulf War about Saddam Hussein (whose biography and acts are well known): bloodthirsty dictator for some, hero of the Arab world for others. When Saddam Hussein fired Scud missiles at Saudi Arabia and Israel, interpretations of this simple act were also totally diverging. For an interpretation of the Gulf War reportage as advertising for weapons, see: Rune Ottosen (1992), 'The Media and the Gulf War reporting: Advertising for the arms industry?', *Bulletin of Peace Proposals*, vol. 23, no. 1, pp. 71–83.

16. The article by Johan Galtung which we quote deals with the intellectual style of academicians. Since it describes 'intellectual styles' in general (not only the style of the intellectuals), this framework is used as 'ideal types'. Johan Galtung, a Norwegian, is a reputed scholar in peace research. His numerous articles and books are an important source of reflection on national culture and the conflicts between cultural communities.

17. The concept of *Gedankennotwendigkeit* is typical of German thinking patterns, where abstraction is taken to its limits. It is not by chance that German philosophers have a world-wide reach. The German language is probably the richest in the world for abstract words. It favours pure conceptual thinking. The construction of *Gedankennotwendigkeit* is itself proof (sorry: an illustration...) of this: *denken* means 'to think', *Gedanken* are 'thoughts'; *Not* means 'necessity', *wenden* is 'to turn', *-keit* is a suffix which abstracts the whole as 'the state of being...'. As a result of this rebus, *Gedankennotwendigkeit* is something like 'the state of being turned into necessary (unavoidable, pure) thoughts'. (*Langenscheidt German–English Dictionary*, 1970, used for the translation of component words, Basic Books: New York).

18. People on the French television channels often quote or argue about figures and facts which are never really checked. To an Anglo-Saxon eye this would appear as a lack of seriousness regarding data. But French people *know* that figures and facts should be treated with some scepticism.

19. There is no expression in French for Wishful Thinking (except perhaps *des vœux pieux*), so the English expression was used in the original French text.

20. A more detailed presentation of cultural differences related to time and their impact on marketing and management may be found in J. C. Usunier (1991), 'Business time perceptions and national cultures: A comparative survey', *Management International Review*, vol. 31, no. 3, pp. 197–217.

21. The fact that the phrase 'wishful thinking' is rather pejorative, shows that, normatively, in Anglo-Saxon cultures, it should be avoided. In Latin cultures it appears more natural.

22. To use a (very elementary) Freudian distinction: the denial of WT responds to the *anal* principle of tightening oneself up and controlling one's behaviour, when strongly integrating reality as a constraint; conversely, the use of WT denotes an *oral* behaviour, favourable words (*paroles*), which describe the reality in a much more pleasant way than it actually is, provide wishful thinkers (and above all, wishful *speakers*) with a pleasure of mouth. This oral denial thwarts the frustrations of reality, like the little child that sucks its thumb, when something has made it unhappy.

23. See Table 3.1 and page 74 for explanation of concept.

24. Not all subsidiaries are included in the final analysis; depending on the data under review, 40–55 countries are finally comparable.

25. One of the most difficult issues, at the empirical level, is to identify clearly the variance related to national differences from other sources of variance which are related to individual differences (e.g. age, sex, social class, education). For a discussion of this point, see Hofstede (1980a).

26. The difference between loyalty and reciprocity is very important, especially in terms of friendship models. See Chapter 14 on the differences between the American and the Chinese models of friendship and their consequences on attitudes taken during business negotiations.

27. Chapter 11 develops in greater detail the cultural relativity of sales force stimulation systems.

28. See for instance section A12.5.

29. Reischauer's book is now published under the title *Japan: The story of a nation*. The text has been updated since it was first published as *Japan: Past and present*, and the ideas about the consequences of the Tokugawa period on Japanese behaviour are no longer to be found in the new version, perhaps because they were resented by Japanese readers. Even distant historical events and periods may still be controversial nowadays, when different interpretations are at stake.

30. Amine Maalouf is a Lebanese journalist, who served as the editor of the weekly magazine *An-Nahar International* and as the editor-in-chief of *Jeune Afrique*. He has published three books

which show how Muslims see Westerners. Cultural knowledge is somewhat dissymetric: Muslims know European culture much better than Europeans know Muslim cultures. Apart from *The Crusades seen through Arab Eyes* Amine Maalouf has published two novels, which are interesting from an intercultural perspective: *Léon l'africain* and *Samarcande*. Reading such books help us to avoid misconceptions which arise from our sparse knowledge of Arabs and the Muslim world.

31. Writings of the Damascene emir Usamah, quoted by Amine Maalouf (1985, pp. 128–9).
32. *Franj* is (the transcription of) an Arab word designating the French, or more generally European, Crusaders.
33. Let us be very clear about this: I am not at all an advocate of 'cultural purity'. But in all societies there is a need for some coherence, which will slow up the pace of what can be digested by them.
34. See Chapters 1 and 5.
35. See for instance: 'L'Enrichissement du vocabulaire économique et financier', *Les Notes bleues* Ministère de l'Economie des Finances et du Budget, no. 425, 27 February to 5 March 1989. It is curious to note that changes in the language are centrally decided (the French Jacobin tradition).
36. To counterfeit a product is not to counterfeit the culture where it originated: if people are able to copy the know-how they no longer need to copy the products themselves. For more about counterfeiting, see Czinkota and Ronkainen (1990, pp. 548–52).
37. It may be true also of goods or services; see section 6.1.
38. The French text is even worse (in term of racism) than the translation from the French.
39. See ch. 5 of Segall *et al.* (1990, pp. 93–112), which asks 'Are there racial differences in cognition?' and which offers an in-depth review of the empirical studies of the difference in intellectual performance across ethnic groups.
40. Mauviel remarks that numerous studies have been dedicated to immigrant populations as such, but little research is concerned with the relations between the native lower-class population and the immigrant communities (this is true of France, and probably many other countries). This explains why we know little about cultural hostility, which has been more or less taboo as a research topic, probably due to the fear that unveiling somewhat negative attitudes could encourage their expression. This taboo is especially strong in countries with a significant colonial history (England, France, the Netherlands), which explains a certain feeling of guilt.
41. The rationales behind the alternative explanations for A3.3, A3.4 and A3.5 can be found in section A4.8.
42. Information about cultural time patterns may be found in chapter 4 (Box 4.1 and section A4.1) and in section 14.1.

References

Adler, Nancy J. (1986), *International Dimensions of Organizational Behavior*, PWS-Kent: Belmont, CA.

Cateora, Philip R. (1983), *International Marketing*, 5th edn, Richard D. Irwin: Homewood, IL.

Czinkota, Michael R. and Illka A. Ronkainen (1990), *International Marketing*, 2nd edn, Dryden Press: Hinsdale, IL.

Darbelet, Michel and Jean-Marcel Lauginié (1988), *Economie d'Entreprise*, vol. I, Editions Foucher: Paris.

Derr, C. B. and A. Laurent (1989), 'The internal and external career: A theoretical and cross-cultural perspective', in M. B. Arthur, D. T. Hall and B. S. Lawrence (eds), *Handbook of Career Theory*, Cambridge University Press: Cambridge.

Essad Bey, Mohammed (1934), *Mahomet*, Payot: Paris.

Galtung, Johan (1981), 'Structure, culture and intellectual style: An essay comparing Saxonic, Teutonic, Gallic and Nipponic approaches', Social Science Information, vol. 20, no. 6, pp. 817–56.

Geertz, Clifford (1983), *Local Knowledge*, Basic Books: New York.

Hall, Edward T. (1959), *The Silent Language*, Doubleday: New York.

Hall, Edward T. (1966), *The Hidden Dimension*, Doubleday: New York.

Hall, Edward T. (1976), *Beyond Culture*, Doubleday: New York.

Hall, Edward T. (1983), *The Dance of Life*, Anchor Press/Doubleday: New York.

Hofstede, Geert (1980a), *Culture's Consequences: International differences in work-related values*, Sage: Beverly Hills, CA.

Hofstede, Geert (1980b), 'Motivation, leadership and organization: Do American theories apply abroad?', *Organizational Dynamics*, Summer, pp. 42–63.

Hofstede, Geert (1983), 'National cultures in four dimensions: A research-based theory of cultural differences among nations', *International Studies of Management and Organization*, vol. XII, nos 1–2, pp. 46–74.

Ishihara, Shintaro (1991), *The Japan that Can Say No*, Simon & Schuster: New York.

Kluckhohn, Florence R. and Frederick L. Strodtbeck (1961), *Variations in Value Orientations*, Greenwood Press: Westport, CT.

Laurent, André (1983), 'The cultural diversity of Western conceptions of management', *International Studies of Management and Organization*, vol. XII, 1–2, nos 1–2, pp. 75–96. In Nancy J. Adler, Nigel Campbell and André Laurent (1989), 'In search of appropriate methodology: from outside the People's Republic of China looking in', *Journal of International Business Studies*, vol. XX, no. 1, p. 69.

Laurent, André (1989), presentation to the European Foundation for Management Development Seminar 'Cultural shock', *EFMD Annual Conference* in March, Marseille.

Lazer, William, Shoji Murata and Hiroshi Kosaka (1985), 'Japanese marketing: Towards a better understanding', *Journal of Marketing*, vol. 49 (Spring), pp. 69–81.

Maalouf, Amine (1985), *The Crusades through Arab Eyes*, Schocken Books: New York.

Mauviel, Maurice (1991), 'La Grande Misère de l'antiracisme français', *Intercultures*, no. 12, January, pp. 69–82.

Montesquieu, Charles de (1748), *The Spirit of Laws*, translated from the French by Thomas Nugent (1792), 6th edn, McKenzie and Moore: Dublin.

Reischauer, Edwin O. (1946), *Japan: Past and present*, Alfred A. Knopf: New York.

Reischauer, Edwin O. (1990), *Japan: The story of a nation*, 4th edn, McGraw-Hill: New York.

Schein, Edgar H. (1981), 'Does Japanese management style have a message for American managers?', *Sloan Management Review* (Fall).

Segall, Marshall H., Pierre R. Dasen, John W. Berry and Ype H. Poortinga (1990), *Human Behavior in Global Perspective*, Pergamon: New York.

Triandis, Harry C. (1983), 'Dimensions of cultural variation as parameters of organizational theories', *International Studies of Management and Organization*, vol. XII, no. 4, pp. 139–69.

Usunier, Jean-Claude (1989), 'Interculturel: La parole et l'action', *Harvard-L'Expansion*, no. 52 (Spring), pp. 84–92.

Weeks, William H., Paul B. Pedersen and Richard W. Brislin (1987), *A Manual of Structured Experiences for Cross-cultural Learning*, Intercultural Press: Yarmouth, ME.

4

———— ◆◆◆ ————

Culture, language and communication

When marketing and selling internationally, there is a large number of issues and contracts which are subject to negotiation:[1] sales contracts, agency agreements, joint ventures, exclusive distributor or dealership agreements, management contracts, etc. These transactions often take place between people who do not share the same cultural background, the same language or the same ways of communicating. It might be argued that business people who rationally discuss clauses of written contracts in situations where substantive interests are at stake will always quickly surmount the relatively minor communication misunderstandings which will unavoidably arise as a result of their different cultural backgrounds. The assumption underlying such frequent and implicit arguments is that 'homo economicus' will prevail over a person's cultural background: *utility takes precedence over identity.* The rational appreciation of their own interests will instil in each party not only the will, but also the capacity to negotiate on the basis on common interests.[2] The same questions arise among multicultural teams in large multinational companies: for instance, when managing sales teams in foreign subsidiaries.

However, in the real world, cultural differences do not only entail behavioural customs and manners, such as politeness, the way to speak to someone or, more generally, the ways and means of addressing other people. Language has a prominent place in communication, hence linguistic differences are one of the main causes (but not the only one) of inter-cultural communication misunderstandings. The anthropologist and linguist Benjamin Lee Whorf went further, arguing that language shapes our world-view, our behaviour towards others and our manner of acting. The first section of this chapter is devoted to an examination of the strengths, limits and operational value of what is called the Whorfian (or Whorf-Sapir) hypothesis.[3]

Intercultural communication involves as many verbal elements as non-verbal ones (sections 4.2 and 4.3). Differences in the coding/decoding process, whenever they are ignored by the communicators, may continue to exist throughout the whole negotiation process; instead of disappearing, they may become more marked, even when people seem to be better acquainted with each other. The fourth section of the chapter seeks to explain the source of misunderstandings in intercultural communication and to provide the reader with some basic clues for their avoidance. It deals with the simplified images of other people (stereotypes), their operational value and their limitations. It offers a list of suggestions which facilitate an improvement in intercultural communication as a means of rendering business transactions more effective.

4.1 Language as a basis for culture and communication: the Whorfian hypothesis

The influence of language on culture

The first proponent of the idea that language has a decisive influence on culture was the linguist Edward Sapir. Language creates categories in our minds, which in their turn directly influence the things we judge to be similar and those which *deserve* to be differentiated. It is our *Weltanschauung* that is determined: our way of observing, of describing, of interacting and finally the way in which we construct our reality. Sapir (1929, p. 214) writes:

> The fact of the matter is that the real world is to a large extent unconsciously built up on the language habits of the group. No two languages are ever sufficiently similar as to be considered as representing the same social reality. The worlds in which different societies live are distinct worlds, not merely the same world with different labels attached.

The linguist and anthropologist Benjamin Lee Whorf developed and extended Sapir's hypothesis. The Whorf-Sapir hypothesis contends that the structure of language has a significant influence on perception and categorization. But although the empirical testing of this hypothesis seems to have been fairly thorough,[4] it is not considered valid by many linguists. For example, the gender given to words is not necessarily indicative of a particular cultural meaning (for example, the gender of the earth, the sun and the moon, of vices and virtues, etc.) for it often seems to reflect an arbitrary choice. It may, however, be the case that this gender had a certain meaning at the genesis of the language but that this meaning has since been lost (Box 4.1).

Another example of the language–culture link may be given by the way – linguistic as well as cultural – Anglo-Saxons deal with action. They may use a rich vocabulary, which is often difficult to translate into other languages if real meaning equivalence is sought; for example: 'problem solving', 'issue', 'matter of fact', 'down to earth', '(empirical) evidence', 'completed', 'feed-back', 'to perform', 'achievement', 'individual', 'data', 'to check', 'to plan', 'deadline', 'cognitive', 'emotional', 'successful', etc. Even such an elementary word as 'fact' has a rather demanding content: in English it must be an *established* piece of reality. Its French equivalent, *fait*, is less demanding in terms of unanimously agreed reality (*les faits peuvent être discutés*; facts may be discussed). In German, a fact may be translated by *Tatsache*, *Wirklichkeit*, *Wahrheit* or *Tat*: it refers as much to a piece of *reality* as to a piece of *truth* or a piece of *action*.

The following passage caricatures the Anglo-Saxon way of acting:

> This man is achievement and deadline oriented. He first reviews the issues at stake. Then he tries hard to gather data, to verify, measure. As much as possible he will bring hard facts, empirical evidence, not simple opinions. If and when his thoughts and his emotions are conflicting, he will choose to behave as a matter-of-fact and down-to-earth guy. Being individually rewarded, he is therefore eager to perform the task and complete the job. He (almost) always meets his schedule.

When trying to translate this short passage into other languages, the difficulties extend far beyond the purely lexical and grammatical.[5] They are *cultural translation* difficulties. These problems correspond to what is often called the spirit of a language: far from being merely a chain of words, a language contains a series of stands taken on the nature of our relationship to reality. The following is a simple example: try to translate the English word 'upset' used in the expression 'to be upset'. It may be translated in French as *être bouleversé*, *préoccupé*, *ému*, *impressionné*, etc. But French has no word which gives a

---

Box 4.1   *Time patterns revealed by language*[6]

Time representations are conveyed through the medium of language, as a means of communication and therefore collective action. Whorf comments on the Hopi language in the following terms (Carroll, 1956, pp. 57–8):

> After long and careful study and analysis, the Hopi language is seen to contain no words, grammatical forms, constructions or expressions, that refer directly to what we call 'time', or to past, present, and future, or to motion as kinematic rather than dynamic (i.e. as a continuous translation in space and time rather than as an exhibition of a dynamic effort in a certain process), or that even refer to space in such a way as to exclude that element of extension or existence that we call 'time', and so by implication leave a residue that could be referred to as 'time'. Hence, the Hopi language contains no reference to 'time', either implicit or explicit.

For those who have doubts about the existence of differences in cultural representations of time, which are revealed, conveyed and reproduced by language, the example of the English/American word 'deadline' is illustrative. A quick translation into French would give *échéance* (temporal) or *délai de rigueur* (Langenscheidt, 1989) but would not render the intensity of this word. It seems to suggest something like 'Beyond this (temporal) line, you will (there is a danger of) die (dying)'. It therefore bestows a genuine notion of urgency to what was originally a very abstract notion (a point which has been agreed upon on the time line). The 'procedural–traditional' time of American Indians (Graham, 1981) is hardly a 'time' in the sense that we give to this word. This point is developed later (see the reading in section A4.1 and section 14.1) by looking at the set of Bantu languages, which are spoken by tens of millions of people in the southern part of Africa.

truly equivalent meaning for the simple reason that the French, on one side, and the English and the Americans on the other, do not express their emotions in the same manner. 'Upset' expresses some sort of violation of an inner personal order, modesty and self-restraint in relation to the exterior world which could observe this disorder negatively. 'Upset' emphasizes the strong prescription, integrated throughout the whole education process, of a high demand for 'self-control' (an English word which also exists unchanged in French). French people cannot be 'upset', simply because they generally do not feel scared to manifest their feelings and emotions.

The influence of culture on language

The most obvious influence is that of a vocabulary with its own particular capacities and limits. A specific example of this is the new technological vocabularies (computer science, nuclear technology, audiovisual communication, aerospace technology, etc.) which are largely borrowed and exchanged between linguistic and national cultures, the benefit being the creation of a nearly universal technical culture. There are also vocabularies which have been enriched because of physical occurrences that demand a precise description, as in the huge number of terms for different types of snow that exists in the language of Eskimos and all peoples who live near the Arctic Circle. Another case in point is the rich culinary vocabulary of France, where a preoccupation with good food is an element of society that strongly influences daily life.

However, without taking up a debate on the causality of language and culture, which is scientifically very complex and which also risks turning into a 'chicken-and-egg' argument, common-sense reasoning reveals several major limitations to the Whorfian hypothesis: what of those who speak many languages, or who were raised in diverse linguistic and cultural environments?[7]

In a static scenario, i.e. where an individual or a particular group has been educated in a totally homogeneous cultural environment, language can have an influence on world-view and on one's actions when confronted with reality. But the theory is much less valid in a dynamic scenario, i.e. where language changes from generation to generation or where people travel abroad. Then they will encounter opportunities to borrow language and culture. Interaction between language and culture is reciprocal, particularly in the light of the cultural borrowing mechanisms described in the preceding chapter.

A 'reasonable' version of the use of the Whorfian hypothesis

The first consequence of the Whorf-Sapir hypothesis, as far as one chooses to adhere to it, is that business people from different cultures not only communicate in different ways, but also perceive, categorize and construct their realities differently. This therefore presupposes a 'state of alert' in communication: a readiness to accept that words, even those that are translated with no apparent difficulty, only offer an illusion of sharing the same vision of reality. It is necessary to retain as many foreign words as possible in their original form, in the following manner:

1. By forcing oneself to recognize their unique nature.
2. By questioning the interpreters, or even one's foreign business partners, about the inner meaning within the context of a particular culture.
3. By clearly identifying areas of genuine common identity.

Then, in the examination of events, it is necessary to try to extricate the true meaning of each clause, starting from the perspective that they are never exactly equivalent. This is true even in the case where a dictionary seems to indicate (falsely) that an Anglo-Saxon term such as 'act of God' is the strict equivalent of a French term (here, *force majeure*).[8]

4.2   Verbal communication: explicit versus implicit contextual messages

The use of the word 'context' and the emphasis on the role of context in communication are due to Edward T. Hall, an American anthropologist (Hall, 1960, 1976, 1983). Having studied during the 1940s the culture and social integration of Hopi and Navajo Indians, he advised first diplomats and then business people in their dealings with other cultures. This naturally led him to an interest in intercultural communication, a field to which he has been a major contributor over the last forty years.

Instinctively, the mode of communication that first springs to mind is the verbal mode. Languages and words have a (more or less) precise meaning; in any case, we live with the necessary fiction that words and their combinations have a particular meaning, and that the listener receives a clear message from the speaker. The acceptance of this fiction allows us to avoid the time-consuming task of constantly verifying that the message received is the same message that was sent. However, the communication mechanism incorporates many elements:

1. Even in an exchange that is primarily verbal, part of the message is non-verbal: gestures, gesticulations, attitudes, etc.
2. A single unit of communication can integrate feedback mechanisms to verify or improve the clarity of the message.
3. In most cases, communication is not independent of its context.

Although Edward Hall does not define context precisely, the following components can reasonably be presumed: location, people involved (age, sex, dress, social stature, etc.) and the context of the conversation itself (work, a show, social negotiations, the sale of something).

Context will often influence communication without the participants being aware of it. For example, cultural prejudices may interpose: does a young speaker deserve trust? Is the age-credibility relationship positive, negative, or neutral? Is it necessary to know one's conversation partner relatively well to be able to talk seriously about business (intensity of the personalization, or conversely the depersonalization, of the conversation)? Context brings together the sum of interpretation mechanisms that originate within culture and which allow the explanation of a message.

High context and low context

In certain cultures communication uses low context and explicit messages (see Figure 4.1). These messages are almost 'digital' and could be translated into simple computer units (bits). Figure 4.1, in the style of Edward Hall, places the Swiss at the intersection of the axes. This signifies a great deal of precision in the verbal aspect of communication and with regard to temporal factors. Therefore in Switzerland a speed limit must surely be interpreted literally. The speed limit on motorways is 120 km per hr. For a driver who is caught speeding by the police, a speedometer error of 6 per cent is allowed, and the fine is then given in proportion to the speed violation. When arriving late for a doctor's appointment, the Swiss have to pay a penalty of 15 Swiss francs and reschedule the appointment if the doctor is unavailable.[9]

These two examples should be taken for what they are: not illustrative of an unhealthy preoccupation with punctuality, exactness and respect for rules, but as evidence of a strong social order which is costly but also greatly beneficial for all. In this manner Swiss doctors, having made a preliminary evaluation on the telephone with their patients, will schedule their time and that of their patients very precisely. If each party makes an effort

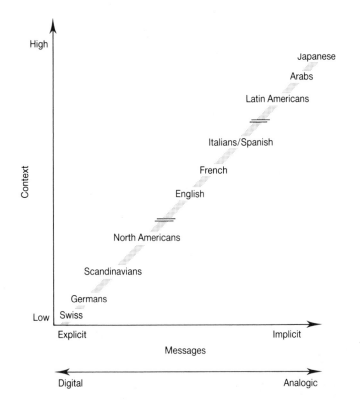

Figure 4.1 Messages and context (adapted from Edward T. Hall).

to keep the appointment, the result is a genuine timesaving. Patients also avoid a long stay in the waiting room where they would be exposed to the germs of the other patients.

The following are further examples of explicit messages which, in low context, must be taken literally:

- 'The appointment is at 5.15 p.m.' (probably with a maximum of five minutes leeway).
- 'I can offer you a price of 140 dollars per package of 12, to be delivered in cases of 144 within 5 weeks' (an example of a seller's explicit message to a potential buyer).

The North American cultures (United States and Canada) as well as the Germanic (Germany and Austria) and the Scandinavian cultures also feature among those with explicit communication and low context.[10] At the other end of the axes we find the Japanese. Here context plays a significant role. One example is the rules of politeness: the manner of speaking perceptibly shifts in register between more than twenty subtly different forms according to the age, sex and social position of the conversation partner, and the relative position of the speaker in the social hierarchy to the listener (e.g. pupil/ teacher, buyer/seller, employee/employer). The word 'no' practically does not exist in the Japanese vocabulary – a 'yes' in certain circumstances can actually mean 'no' (see Box 4.2).

No one belonging to cultures that use implicit messages and high context (Middle Eastern, Latin American, Japanese) can communicate without a fairly good understanding of their

Box 4.2   *Sixteen ways to avoid saying 'no' in Japanese*

1. Vague 'no'.
2. Vague and ambiguous 'yes' or 'no'.
3. Silence.
4. Counter question.
5. Tangential responses.
6. Exiting (leaving).
7. Lying equivocation or making an excuse – sickness, previous obligation, etc.).
8. Criticizing the question itself.
9. Refusing the question.
10. Conditional 'no'.
11. 'Yes, but …'
12. Delaying answers (e.g. 'We will write you a letter').
13. Internally 'yes', externally 'no'.
14. Internally 'no', externally 'yes'.
15. Apology.
16. The equivalent of the English 'no' – primarily used in filling out forms, *not* in conversation.

(Keiko Ueda 1974. Reproduced with permission.)

conversation partner. Impersonal dealings (such as when American business people come for a day to discuss a contract, get rapidly to the heart of the matter and use the limited time to discuss, insisting upon concentrating on crucial matters) will make people from those cultures ill at ease and impede their conversation.

A misunderstanding between the two communicators may arise over their differences of opinion as to what is truly important. The person from a high-context culture will prefer to spend some time chatting about life in general with the very purpose of getting to know the negotiating partner. The person from a low-context culture, on the other hand, will prefer to get straight down to business, to avoid wasting time on chatting and to proceed directly to a rational discussion of the project.

We can place Latin-European cultures as well as the British culture midway between these two extremes. It is important to note that this study, which is of a global nature, leaves two questions unanswered that would allow a more subtle understanding: what elements of context are important, and what is their effect on the interpretation of messages? This leads us to examine cultural differences and their links with communication.

4.3 Non-verbal communication and meta-communication

When two business people from different cultures communicate, in addition to their verbal communication they exchange elements of non-verbal communication. This constitutes a part of the context that Edward Hall speaks about (1959, 1960, 1976), which must be used in the decoding of implicit messages. The elements of context can be separated into four levels:

1. The analogical component of verbal messages: a 'yes' which is said in such a way that it means 'no' (see Box 4.2), profuse thanks which contain a meaning other than their 'digital' content precisely because of their excess, etc.
2. Non-verbal communication: gestures, gesticulations, etc.
3. Messages that the speakers often emit unknowingly according to their personal characteristics: size, age, weight, sex, dress, etc. All of these characteristics are culturally encoded in the culture of the speaker, and decoded by the listener's own cultural programming.
4. The elements of interpretation which are dictated by the framework of the conversation: place, time, etc.

Communication through gestures: body language

Body language is an infinite source of differences and misunderstandings. Condon and Youssef (1975) recount the following story. A professor of English origin, who taught at the University of Cairo, was sitting in his chair with his feet in front of him, the soles of his shoes turned towards his Egyptian students. A Muslim considers this to be one of the worst possible insults. A student demonstration followed, which was echoed by the newspapers who denounced British arrogance and demanded that the English professor be sent back to his home country.

Ways of greeting people differ greatly between cultures. While the French have a habit of shaking hands the first time they meet a person each day, the Anglo-Saxon cultures use this custom much less extensively. They are surprised at the (for them) excessive use that the French make of the handshake. In Japan a bow is the appropriate manner of greeting. In certain large department stores, there are hostesses whose sole job is to bow to each customer who comes into the store. Anyone who has observed bowing rituals at Japanese train stations or airports cannot help but be struck by the complexity of these bowing ceremonies, where the number, depth and synchronization is accurately codified. As Ferraro (1990, p. 73) emphasizes:

> In fact it is possible to tell the relative social status of the two communicators by the depth of their bows (the deeper the bow, the lower the status).... The person of lower status is supposed to initiate the bow, and the person of higher status determines when the bow is completed.

The meaning of hand gestures is also a point of great cultural difference. Moving the head back and forth means 'yes' in most western European countries, but it means 'no' in Greece and Bulgaria; moving the head from left to right is a sign of negation for some, and affirmation for others. In many Western countries it is considered a gesture of affection to pat a child on the head, but in Malaysia and many Islamic countries the head is considered to be the source of all spiritual and intellectual activity and is therefore sacred (Harris and Moran, 1987).

One area of non-verbal communication of which the importance and cultural variation cannot be denied is that of physical contact. Ferraro (1990) offers a complete description of the forms of non-verbal communication involving a physical contact:[11] various peoples kiss (cheek, lips, hand, foot), take a person by the arm or shoulders, pinch the cheek, shake hands, tickle, stroke, pat, etc. These gestures, which run into the realm of familiarity and sexual conduct, are subject to extremely varied codes of use. Russian men kissing and Arab men holding hands in the street are shocking to Anglo-Saxons.

Ferraro (1990, pp. 85–6) recounts his own experience while conducting anthropological field research in Kenya:

> After several months of living and working with Kikuyu, I was walking through a village in Kiambu district with a local headman who had become a key informant and a close personal acquaintance. As we walked side by side my friend took my hand in his. Within less than 30 seconds my palm was perspiring all over his. Despite the fact that I knew cognitively that it was a perfectly legitimate Kikuyu gesture of friendship, my own cultural values (that is, that 'real men' don't hold hands) were so ingrained that it was impossible for me not to communicate to my friend that I was very uncomfortable.

The significance of communication codes is complex, and it would be wrong to contrast peoples who are reserved in their physical contact (including Anglo-Saxons) with those who are more liberal. Nowhere does there exist true freedom from mores. The way in which American and European men and women show their feelings for each other by kissing in public may seem, to other peoples, to be a shocking demonstration of something that should be kept private. Dancing, which is a large part of social gatherings, may seem indecent to some and perfectly innocent to others. Everyone has the tendency to adopt an ambiguous position. We simultaneously envy and reject those customs which are forbidden in our own culture but permitted in others. Montesquieu, in his *Persian Letters* (1721), gives a good illustration of these ambiguities and phantasms (Letter LXXIX, 'The Chief Black Eunuch writes to Usbek, in Paris'):

> Yesterday some Armenians brought a young Circassian slave to the serail, wanting to sell her. I took her into the secret apartments, undressed her and examined her critically. The more I examined her, the more attractions I found; with virginal modesty she seemed to want to conceal them from my sight. I could see what it cost her to obey: she reddened at finding herself naked even in front of me, who am exempt from any passion which might be alarming to chaste women, am indifferent to the power of the sex, and, being an agent of modesty, can be completely free in my actions while having nothing but chastity in my eyes, and inspiring nothing but innocence. As soon as I judged her worthy of you I lowered my eyes, put a scarlet gown around her and a golden ring on her finger, and prostrated myself at her feet; I worshipped her as the queen of your heart. I paid the Armenians and hid her from all eyes. Happy Usbek! you possess more beauties than there are in all the palaces of the Orient. What a pleasure it will be for you to find the most ravishing things in Persia on your return, and to see beauty reborn in your serail while time and habit combine to destroy it!

Facial expressions and communication with the eyes

Laughing, smiling, frowning and knitting one's brow express communication. A smile can be a sign of satisfaction, agreement, embarrassment, or nothing at all. Certain cultures consider the spontaneous facial expression of attitudes and emotions to be normal. The reverse is true in other cultures, particularly in Asia where it is considered desirable not to show emotion; from this comes the impression of Asians as inscrutable and stoic. According to Morsbach (1982, p. 308):

> Self control, thought of as highly desirable in Japan, demands that a man of virtue will not show a negative emotion in his face when shocked or upset by sudden bad news; and, if successful, is lauded as *taizen jijaku to shite* (perfectly calm and collected) or *mayu hitotsu ugokasazu ni* (without even moving an eyebrow).... The idea of an expressionless face in situations of great anxiety was strongly emphasized in the *bushido* (way of the warrior) which was the guideline for samurai and the ideal for many others.

Visual contacts (looking someone straight in the eyes or looking away, lowering the eyes, or turning them away when they meet someone else's eyes, who will also do the same) are all given different meanings in different cultures. This is proof that the same conduct (as innocent as it may be) can be arbitrarily given totally opposite meanings. As remarked by Harris and Moran (1987), Arabs often look each other straight in the eyes, because they believe that the eyes are the windows of the soul and that it is important to know the heart and soul of those with whom one works. On the contrary, Japanese children are taught in school not to look their teacher in the eyes, but to rest their gaze at the level of the neck. When they become adults, it is considered a gesture of respect to lower their eyes in front of their superiors. The French have a tendency to look people straight in the eyes – like the Americans and other Europeans, they tend to associate a lack of honesty with someone who looks away. This could potentially signal an unfriendly, defiant, impersonal or inattentive attitude.

Meta-communication

Communication presupposes that 'game rules' exist between speaker and listener in the positions they adopt as they send messages to each other, like two tennis players hitting the ball back and forth to each other. These rules, as noted above, have to a large extent a culture-specific coding.

Paul Watzlawick and the communication theorists of the school of Palo Alto (Watzlawick, Helmick Beavin and Jackson, 1967) have emphasized what they call 'meta-communication', that is, communication about the *rules* of communication itself. The Greek prefix *meta* means 'above' (i.e. of a higher order). When implicitly and often unconsciously meta-communicating, people not only exchange messages, that is, basic units of communication, but they also define at the same time the 'what, how and why' of the ways in which they communicate. Any interaction may be defined by analogy with game playing, that is 'as sequences of moves strictly governed by rules of which it is immaterial whether they are within or outside the awareness of the communicants, but about which meaningful *metacommunicational* statements can be made' (Watzlawick *et al.*, 1967, p. 42). The interest of this concept in the area of intercultural communication is obvious: a large part of meta-communication follows culture-based rules, which are homogeneous between communicators belonging to the same group.

The rules of good communication are largely cultural. The element that creates the feeling that messages are passing well between two conversation partners is their ability to avoid an unsuccessful conversation (the messages pass badly, are distorted, or the conversation is interrupted) while allowing themselves to discuss and establish the rules of their communication. In an intercultural situation, meta-communication is in itself more difficult, although here it is even more necessary to meta-communicate adequately. Box 4.3 presents the substantive difficulties involved in arriving at a discussion and clarification of the rules of communication (about what friendship means and involves).

4.4 Ethnocentrism, stereotypes and misunderstandings in intercultural communication

One may add that the cultural mechanism (living according to one's culture in daily life) is almost an unconscious action. The cost of adopting the cultural demeanour of the environment in which one lives is minimal. Along with the fact that they are eventually rejected, the identification and adoption of the traits of another culture are generally associated with a high cost. This is clearly shown by the difficulties encountered by immigrants in integrating, even those who have immigrated voluntarily.

Ethnocentrism

Owing to the high cost of changing one's culture, most people live without even envisioning such a possibility. This causes what James Lee (1966) calls the SRC (Self Reference Criterion): we all have an automatic and unconscious tendency to refer to our own thought framework, which is mainly tied to our national culture (which in general we did not choose), to interpret situations, evaluate people, communicate, negotiate, or decide which attitude to take. This framework is generally modelled by ethnocentrism. The concept of ethnocentrism was first introduced by G. A. Sumner (1906) more than eighty

Box 4.3   *Language of friendship*

The American finds his friends next door and among those with whom he works. It has been noted that we take people up quickly and drop them just as quickly. Occasionally a friendship formed during schooldays will persist, but this is rare. For us [Americans] there are few well-defined rules governing the obligations of friendship. It is difficult to say at which point our friendship gives way to business opportunism or pressure from above. In this we differ from many other people in the world. As a general rule, in foreign countries friendships are not formed as quickly as in the United States, but go much deeper, last longer and involve real obligations. For example:

It is important to stress that in the Middle East and Latin America your 'friends' will not let you down. The fact that they personally are feeling the pinch is never an excuse for failing their friends. They are supposed to look out for your interests.

Friends and family around the world represent a sort of social insurance that would be difficult to find in the United States. We do not use friends to help us out in disaster as much as we do as a means of getting ahead – or at least, of getting the job done. The United States systems work by means of a series of closely tabulated favors and obligations carefully doled out where they will do the most good. And the least that we expect in exchange for a favor is gratitude.

The opposite is the case in India, where the friend's role is to 'sense' a person's need and to do something about it. The idea of reciprocity as we know it is unheard of. An American in India will have difficulty if he attempts to follow American friendship patterns. He gains nothing by extending himself on behalf of others, least of all gratitude, because the Indian assumes that what he does for others he does for the good of his own psyche. He will find it impossible to make friends quickly and is unlikely to allow sufficient time for friendships to ripen. He will also note that as he gets to know people better, they may become more critical of him, a fact that he finds hard to take. What he does not know is that one sign of friendship in India is speaking one's mind.

(Edward T. Hall, 1960. Reproduced with permission.)

years ago, to distinguish between *in-groups* (those groups with which an individual identifies) and *out-groups* (those regarded as antithetical to the *in-group*). Ethnocentrism has been extended by psychologists at the level of the individual, where it relates to the natural tendency of people to refer themselves spontaneously to the symbols, values and ways of thinking of their own ethnic or national group (their in-group). Ethnocentrism may lead to disinterest and even contempt for the culture of other groups (Levine and Campbell, 1972).

Lee (1966) suggests the following steps in order to try to eliminate the decisional bias, related to SRC when dealing with international operations:

1. Define the problem or the objectives, as would be done according to the customs, behavioural standards, and ways of thinking of the decision maker's country.
2. Define the problem or the objectives, as would be done according to the customs, behavioural standards, and ways of thinking of the foreign country (where the decision will be *implemented*).
3. Isolate the influence of the self reference criterion on the problem, and identify the extent to which it complicates the decision-making problem.
4. Redefine the problem (and often the objectives), without the bias related to the SRC, and then find the solutions and make decisions which fit with the cultural context of the foreign market.

In this way one can imagine the following situation. People are standing in line at an amusement park, such as Disneyland, where there are some very popular attractions. In the original context in the United States, discipline with respect to queues is strong, they are usually well organized and there are even tangible precautions for this (yellow lines on the ground indicating to people where to stop for queueing, visible corridors for queuing in line, etc.). In the foreign context of France, where there is a developed sense of 'free-for-all' and less of a habit of organized queues combined with a reluctance towards anything that seems too socially structured, the problem will not present itself in the same terms.

Although it constitutes the first practical framework that allows us to attribute an operational value to cultural representation, the SRC also comprises a degree of naivety and insufficiency. It presupposes that it is possible to penetrate easily the mysteries of a culture without being a native. Cultural expertise is a complex reality. Sometimes neither marketing experts from the original country (in total ignorance) nor foreigners (through lack of consciousness of their own culture) are capable of diagnosis in the second and third phases. The effect of the effort of bias removal and the results achieved by the use of the SRC are not immediate.

Stereotypes

As emphasized by Gauthey and Xardel (1990, p. 20), if the French perceive Americans as being tough in business and arrogant, and see the British as insincere, it is for the most part due to stereotypes which give a distorted view. American arrogance is, in fact, related to a hierarchy of different values: professional relations are centred on the task in hand, the object of discussion, to the exclusion of personal relations with the other party.

Stereotypes, although sometimes representing a simplification which is intellectually useful, none the less have the function of reducing and conserving our differences, which can make them dangerous. Gauthey (1989, p. 63) notes the personal aspect: 'It seems a thousand times easier to stay attached to our own values and to transfer onto the foreigner the responsibility to change his point of view than to decenter ourselves, that is to leave our system of reference and put ourselves in the place of the other.' Characteristic of stereotypes is a cognitive function (wherein they work as a simplified intellectual representation of other people) and also an emotional function (self-defence against a difference that provokes anxiety). Michel Droit, in his book *Chez les Mangeurs d'hommes* ('With the Man-Eaters'), exposes the stereotype of the sorcerer in primitive societies. He describes the people of Papua New Guinea as seen by civilized observers who are necessarily their ideological enemies (1952, p. 124, my translation):[12]

> Armed with tamed snakes which they use to execute their victims, with poisons, enchanted prayers and medicinal herbs known only to them, sorcerers, through well-organized propaganda and strong co-operative solidarity, let entire populations live in fear and sometimes in terror of their 'nepou', that is their evil powers.

Stereotypes are often used to capture the salient traits of a 'foreign' national character. Box 4.4 shows how French people are viewed (at least stereotypically) by people of other nations.

Self shock

It is necessary to acknowledge that the problem of cultural representation is more complex than simply 'getting to know the other'. As shown by Zaharna (1989) in a review article on the culture shock experienced by people of different cultures, the problematic representation of the 'other' may evolve into a confrontation (equally problematic) with oneself. Zaharna calls this process 'self shock'. Experiencing how others actually are may be somewhat destabilizing: identity confusion is a typical feature of culture shock (Oberg, 1960). Self shock is probably one of the principal causes of stereotyping. Stereotypes often protect 'the self', much more than they really provide information on 'the other'.

When meeting people from other cultures, such as expatriates meeting local executives or international sellers meeting local buyers, the encounter is an intercultural one where the absence of previous knowledge of the other's culture makes for uncertainty. At first, one might think that the basic problem is 'getting to know the other'. But in the intercultural encounter, there is in fact a 'progressive unfolding of the self' which can be attributed to 'a set of intensive and evocative situations in which the individual perceives and experiences other people in a distinctly new manner and, as a consequence, experiences new facets and dimensions of existence' (Adler, 1975, p. 18). In intercultural encounters, the necessary introduction of the 'other' risks disturbing one's personal identity, which is placed in question by the 'mirror effect'.

Within our own cultural context, we have unconsciously built our 'self image'. We necessarily construct an image of ourselves from the observations that we make, based on the responses of others to our conduct. This is emphasized by Erikson (1950, p. 135): 'Identity is the confidence gathered from the fact that our own ability to maintain interior resemblance and continuity equals the resemblance and continuity of the image and the sense that others have of us.' But the process of the creation and maintenance of personal identity has two characteristics that make it problematic in the intercultural encounter:

1. It happens for the most part outside our consciousness.
2. It requires a good capacity for interpersonal communication.

According to Zaharna 'self shock', contrary to culture shock which is seen as a reaction to difference between oneself and the other, is a concept that extends to differences with and inside the self. The root of 'self shock' is in the intimate workings of the relationship

Box 4.4   *Some stereotypes of the French (undeserved?)*

How various nationalities perceive the French:

The Germans: Pretentious and offhand. Fashionable, womanizing, frivolous, fickle, well-mannered, resourceful.

The British: Nationalistic, chauvinistic, intransigent, centralist, dependent on the state, polite but not open-minded, humourless, short-tempered.

The Dutch: Cultured, fond of good living, fidgety, talkative, not very serious, feelings of superiority.

The Spanish: Pretentious, early sleepers, cold and distant, hypocritical, impolite, patronizing, hard working.

The Swedish: In-built superiority complex, scornful, boastful, talkative, immoral, dirty, neo-colonialists, disorganized, cultured. Gastronomy, suffocating hierarchy.

The Finns: Xenophobic, superficial, scornful, chauvinistic, courteous, romantic, enjoying life, patriotic, chaotic.

The Americans: Chauvinistic, well-mannered. Combination of good food and good conversation, Paris. Curious about foreign people, pretentious, talkative, pleasant, intelligent.

The Russians: Talkative, self-satisfied, lazy. Luxury, inequality, culture. Pleasant, intelligent, resourceful.

The North Africans: Fairly racist, a little stingy, reasonably honest. Good education and good food. Selfish.

The Asians: Exhibitionist, indiscreet. Reticent in making friends. Bureaucracy and red tape.

The Black Africans: Racist, honest, lacking respect for elders and betters. At odds with themselves and nature. Not spontaneously hospitable.

(Jean-Pierre Gruère and Pierre Morel, 1991, *Cadres français et communications interculturelles*, Eyrolles: Paris, p. 51. Reproduced with permission.)

between the ego (that is, personal identity), our behaviour and the 'other' (as the 'other' *actually* is, and as *perceived* by us, and also as forcing us to reflect upon ourselves). Self shock emerges as a deep imbalance between our need to confirm our identity and our ability to do so. In one way, this situation places the individual in a position of 'double-bind' (Bateson, 1971). The self-shock situation increases our need for the reinforcement of our personal identity, while at the same time resulting in a loss of ability to satisfy this need. Thus, one can understand more easily that certain stereotypes or abrupt judgements about foreigners result almost directly from our attempts to defend ourselves by avoiding the painful double constraint of self shock.

Gauthey (1989, p. 64) cites the case of the general manager of a software company, a subsidiary of a French advertising and communications group, who says: 'I can't stand the English, and when I go to London, I never leave the airport.' This attitude is clearly defensive: in refusing to leave the airport, he stays on neutral international ground, with no risk of being confronted by the image of himself that he will be shown by the English.

International empathy: a naive concept

Here we can catch a glimpse of the immense naivety of those who well-meaningly argue in favour of cultural empathy (being open-minded, sincerely interested in the other, ready to listen, etc.). This communication tactic, although well-meant, may only last for a brief period – the time during which the personal identity of the 'empathizer' has not yet come into play. There are a series of concrete issues at stake, which are discussed in various chapters of this book:[13]

1. Which personality types and/or personal backgrounds are best suited to intercultural communication?
2. Correlative questions: are we able to communicate better with particular countries and cultures? How can we increase our abilities?
3. A question rarely dealt with: if an adjustment must be made during the intercultural encounter, who should be the one to adapt? Beyond personal capacities, empathy or the position of strength, can the intercultural learning situation be led other than bilaterally? In other words, why learn if the other does not learn too? Why not learn simultaneously, rather than in two parallel learning situations that may never meet?

How to improve communication ·effectiveness and decrease the risk of misunderstandings

1. Begin with a thorough knowledge of the intercultural obstacles that exist, such as language and problems of communication in general. Business people often underestimate or even completely overlook this point, since they often share a technical

culture with their conversation partner. They are also deceived by the almost international atmosphere, which can be quite misleading. As Glenn Fisher emphasizes (1980, p. 8):

> Obviously, the modern intensity of international interaction, especially in business and in technological, communication and educational fields, has produced something of an internationalized 'culture' which reduces the clash of cultural backgrounds and stereotyped images. Happily for us this *modus vivendi* is largely based on Western practices and even on the English language, so many otherwise 'foreign' counterparts are accommodating to the American style of negotiation.

Unfortunately in the real world, people who do not feel the need to adapt, especially as far as language is concerned, may be considered indolent. The result of such indolence is the mistaken impression that their partners are just like them: often similarities are illusions, especially when foreigners seem to share the same 'international culture' with oneself. Those who adapt are aware of differences, whereas those to whom others adapt remain unaware.

2. The use of interpreters. In many cases interpreters serve the crucial purpose of 'transposing'. They do not work like a dictionary, translating literally. They may translate better from one language into another than in the opposite direction, depending not only on which their native language happens to be but also on any personal leaning towards one party. It is also necessary to make sure that they are truly loyal to the party who has hired them. It may be advisable to hire several interpreters when the business at stake justifies it.

3. It must be clearly appreciated that there is always a part of any language which cannot be translated. Culture-specific meaning is conveyed by language as it reflects the culture. Always keep in mind the Italian adage *traduttore/traditore* (translator/traitor).

4. Develop a 'defusing' ability when conflicts of negative stereotypes arise. Subjective misunderstandings in intercultural communication often snowball and mix with purely interest-based, objective conflicts, resulting in confrontations that may not be 'productive'. Some conflicts are necessary and even beneficial, where confrontation should not be avoided. But in many other cases, cultural misunderstandings may have a purely negative influence on the dealings that follow, possibly even leading to the cessation of negotiations.

5. Keep in mind that all this must be prepared in advance, and unfortunately cannot be improvised. An effort to help the other, intelligently and agreeably, to understand one's own culture is a prerequisite, which may often be part of 'wining and dining'. When formal business negotiations or even preliminary business talks begin and one side lacks even minimal knowledge of the partner's culture, the relations will often turn sour. It will quickly be too late to approach basic issues related to common understanding and cultural differences. The only way to resolve the problem is to discuss on the substantive ground that 'business is business'. Thus training in intercultural commerce seems more like a preliminary investment to improve the effectiveness of business deals than a way of resolving urgent problems. In medical terms, intercultural understanding in business is the prevention rather than the cure.

Teaching materials

A4.1 Reading: Language and time patterns: the Bantu case

Cultural and linguistic unity of the Bantu area

The Bantu area spreads along the southern side of a line which starts from Douala, Cameroon, by the Atlantic Ocean, and finishes at the mouth of the Tana river in the Indian Ocean. It divides northern and southern Africa. The Bantu area covers most of the southern cone of this continent.

These wide territories (several million square kilometres) are occupied by Bantu people, with the limited exceptions of some other small ethnic groups. The cultural unity of this people has been established on the basis of common linguistic features. As early as the middle of the nineteenth century, W. Bleek (quoted by Kadima and Lumwanu, 1989) had recognized that Bantu languages shared common lexical elements and many grammatical forms. In taking Bleek's work one stage further, anthropologists, historians and linguists have tried to identify the common social and cultural traits which allow a particular area to be classified as Bantu.

Alexis Kagame (1975), for instance, has studied Bantu linguistic systems, especially their underlying structures. He has collated what he terms 'compared Bantu philosophy'. The convergence of authors when describing the conception of time in Bantu cultures is quite marked.

The unification of time and space

At the heart of the Bantu's intuition of time lies the postulate of a very close relation between time and space. Within this postulate none of these basic dimensions of reality exist without the others. Alexis Kagame reveals this conceptual link.:

> Ontologically, Bantu culture puts into one of four categories whatever may be conceived or said.
> 1. The being – of intelligence (man).
> 2. The being – without intelligence (thing).
> 3. The being – as localizer (be it place or date).
> 4. The being – modal (incidentality, or modification of the being).

The major assumption made by Kagame is that translation of Bantu words in metaphysical categories is possible. He therefore translates *ha-ntu* by the being-localizer. This common word expresses the unity of space (place) and time (date). In the Bantu language this term means both the 'there' of locus and the 'now' of time. It is an indivisible localizer, both spatial and temporal.

The localizing prefix *ha-*, which forms *ha-ntu*, and its variants *pa-ntu* and *ka-ntu* are found in the eastern zone of the Bantu territory. Its equivalent in the western zone is *va*, whereas it is *go* in the southeastern part of the Bantu area.

The idea of unification between space and time in Bantu languages is shared by Emil Pearson, who has lived in the southeast of Angola since the 1920s. He writes in his book *People of the Aurora* (1977, p. 75):

> In the Ngangela language there is no word, as far as I know, for 'time' as a continuous, flowing passage of events or the lack of same. Time is experiential or subjective, that is, it is that which is meaningful to the person or thing which experiences it. *Time and space are cognate incidents of eternity.* The same word is used for both 'time' and 'space' (the latter in the sense of 'distance').
>
> 'Ntunda' can either express meaningful time or meaningful space. For example: 'Ntunda kua i li' – 'There is some distance'; and 'Ntunda i na hiti' – 'Time has passed'. The related verb 'Simbula', means 'delay', the thought being of awaiting 'meaningful time'. To the European the African may seem to be idling away useful time, whereas the latter, according to his philosophy, is awaiting experiential time, the time that is right for accomplishing his objective. 'Time' is locative, something that is virtually concrete, not something abstract.
>
> The locatives 'Ha', 'Ku' and 'Mu' are used for expressing 'time' as well as 'place'. Example: 'Ha Katete' – 'In the beginning' (as to either time or place); 'Ku lutue' can mean either 'in front' or 'in the future'. 'Mu nima' can mean 'behind' as to place, or 'after' as to time.

Bantu time experience

Two significant points sharply contrast the way Bantus experience time with the western way of experiencing it within a technological environment. First, Bantus have no theoretical substantive to designate time as an entity *per se*, which can be quantified and measured. Second, for Bantus, the temporal dimension is intrinsic to the event itself. It is not an abstraction as in most Occidental developed cultures. To these cultures it appears as a content which flows regularly from the past to the future, through the present; a flow in which everything moves at the same speed, being 'in time'.

For Bantu peoples time has no real value, no meaning, without the occurrence of an event which will serve as a 'marker'. The intuition of time only becomes effective when an action or an event happens: warriors' expedition, arrival of the train, rainfall, starvation on the increase. Time then becomes individualized. It is drawn out of anonymity. It is not anybody's time which would be abstractedly defined. It is concrete time concerning people I know. Instead of considering time as a straight railway track, where events may happen successively, it will only be spoken of as 'the time of this …' or 'the time of that …', or time which is favourable for this and that.

That is why, on many occasions, there is no point in giving dates, that is to refer oneself to ideal time co-ordinates. History is not a series of dates, but a link between various events. Everything possesses its own internal time. Each event occurs at its own time.

(Jean-Claude Usunier and Constantin Napoléon Biguma (1991), 'Gestion culturelle du temps: le cas bantou', in Franck Gauthey and Dominique Xardel, eds, *Management interculturel: modes et modèles*, Economica: Paris, pp. 95–114. Reproduced with the kind permission of the publisher and the co-author.)

A4.2 Case: Supreme Canning

The Supreme Canning Company (the true name of the company is disguised) is an independent United States packer of tomato products (whole peeled tomatoes, chopped tomatoes, katsup, paste, pizza and other sauces, and tomatoes and zucchini). The company is located in the State of California. Although it produces some cans with its own brand label, much of its output is canned for others and their brand names and labels put on the cans. It produces shelf-size cans for eventual sale at retail, gallon-size cans for use by restaurants and industrial users, and 55 gallon drums for use by others for repacking or further processing. Its annual processing capacity is in excess of 100,000 tons of tomatoes (processed during an operating season of approximately three months in length).

During the decade before 1987, the California canning industry had suffered from heavy competition from abroad and inadequate local demand. A somewhat increasing domestic demand for specialty tomato products, especially pizza and other sauces, was not adequate to absorb increasing imports. The high value of the US dollar, through 1985, had made it difficult for United States companies to sell abroad. Excess capacity and the resulting depressed prices had led to bankruptcy for a number of Californian canners.

With the decline of the value of the dollar during 1986 and 1987, and the efforts of Japan to reduce its trade barriers and increase imports, it appeared that Supreme Canning Company might be able to get into the Japanese market. An inquiry received from a food packer and distributor in Japan indicated interest from that side. The Japanese firm produced and distributed a large number of products, was well known in Japan, and was much larger than the US company.

Since Supreme Canning Company did not have well-known brand names of its own, the company was interested in acting as a large-scale supplier of products made to customer specifications for use by the customer or distribution under the customer's label. Thus, the inquiry from Japan was most welcome.

The Japanese company invited senior executives of the American firm to visit their production facilities and offices in Japan. Both the president and chairman of the board of Supreme Canning Company had a four-day visit with the executives of the company in Japan. The president of the US company, who had some knowledge of Japanese business practice from studies at Stanford University and from his widespread reading, attempted to act as a guide to Japanese business practice. The chairman of the board had little knowledge of Japan, and viewed himself as a decisive man of action. Although there were a few minor misunderstandings, the visit was concluded successfully and the Americans invited the Japanese to visit their plant in California for four days.

The Japanese indicated their interest in the signing of a mutual letter of cooperation. The American chairman of the board was not interested in this, but rather wanted some specific agreements and contracts. As the time for the Japanese visit to the United States drew near, the Japanese indicated that their president would not be able to come. Some senior executives would be able to meet, but they would only be able to spend two days instead of four. The vice-chairman of the board of the California company wrote asking why the Japanese were not going to send their president, and inquiring why they could not spend four days instead of two, 'as we did in Japan.' The letter was frank and direct. The tone was that of a person talking to an equal, but not with any great deal of politeness.

The Japanese company decided to cancel the visit, and no further negotiations or serious contacts were made.

Some months later, a local businessman of Japanese extraction asked the president of Supreme Canning Company if some representatives of another (and even larger) Japanese food products producer and distributor could visit the plant. Four Japanese showed up along with the local businessman, who acted as interpreter and go-between. The three middle-aged Japanese produced their meishi (business cards) and introduced themselves. Each spoke some English. The older man did not present a card and was not introduced. When the president of the American company asked who he was, the go-between said, 'He's just one of the company's directors.' The visit concluded without discussion of any business possibilities, but this was to be expected in an initial visit from Japanese businessmen.

Supreme's president later found out the family name of the unknown visitor, and immediately recognized it as being that of the president of the Japanese company. He assumed that the president of the Japanese company had come but had hidden the fact. He felt that he had been taken advantage of. He telephoned the go-between and told him that he never wanted anyone from that company in his plant again.

From a description of the unknown visitor, a consultant to the company realized that the visitor was not the president of the Japanese company. Rather, it was the semi-retired father of the president. The father retained a position on the board of directors and maintained an active interest in company activities, but was not active in day-to-day affairs. Unlike his son who was fluent in English, he spoke only Japanese. The consultant suddenly realized that the chairman of the board of the American company apparently did not understand:

1. about the Japanese preference for getting to know people well before doing business;
2. the significance of a letter of cooperation (which could be expected to be a first step in concluding a long-term business agreement);
3. the status relationship in Japan of little companies to big ones (larger companies have greater status, and their managers are shown greater respect);
4. the status relationship in Japan of sellers to buyers (buyers have greater status, and their managers are shown greater respect).

(Mitsuko Saito Duerr, of San Francisco State University, in Gerald Albaum, Jesper Strandskov, Edwin Duerr and Laurence Dowd (1989), *International Marketing and Export Management*, Addison-Wesley: Reading, MA, pp. 85–7. Reproduced with permission.)

Questions

1. Was the chairman of the American company wrong for not having found out in advance about Japanese business practices? Why did he not do so? (Same questions for the Japanese companies and US business practices.)
2. What are the principal cultural mistakes made (a) by the Americans from the Japanese perspective, and, (b) by the Japanese from the American perspective?
3. What should the president of the American company do now?

A4.3 Case: Doing business in China: a success in getting paid

In recent years, the People's Republic of China (PRC) has become much more open to trade with the West, and has also made substantial internal economic reforms. Companies in Japan, the Western European countries, the United States, and elsewhere have viewed the Chinese market as having enormous potential. With a population of a billion, and a growing economy, it has appeared to many to be worthwhile to make a major effort to gain a foothold in the market. Both direct exports and joint ventures have been used.

In spite of the economic reforms, however, the PRC remains a tightly controlled, centrally directed economy. Most commercial enterprises and almost all production facilities are state owned and state run. Only a small number of designated organizations are allowed to engage in international trade, and all of these are state owned.

All contracts for trade must receive several government approvals. Larger contracts must receive more approvals than smaller ones. It is not always apparent to the outsider, or perhaps even to some of the Chinese, what specific approvals will be required in particular cases.

While letters of credit may be issued to companies exporting to China, these do not provide the same level of assurance that a letter of credit issued by, say, a London bank would. The Chinese bank will simply not release foreign exchange, regardless of the existence of a letter of credit, without the approval of appropriate government agencies. Foreign companies selling to the government may not receive a letter of credit, but may feel that they can rely on the good faith of the government.

A major United States exporter recently called upon the US Embassy in Beijing requesting assistance in solving a problem. About one year earlier they had sold approximately US$8.0 million worth of equipment to the China National Technology Import Company for use by the Chinese Ministry of Petroleum Industries (MOPI). To date, no payment had been received, and the company did not seem to be getting anywhere in its attempts to collect.

The commercial attaché at the embassy called the Technology Import and Export Department of the Ministry of Foreign Economic Relations and Trade (MOFERT), the Chinese department which would appear to be in charge of the transaction. MOFERT agreed to a meeting at 10.00 a.m. the next day. After the commercial attaché had briefed MOFERT representatives on the problem, they indicated that they were not in charge of the transaction; it came under the jurisdiction of the Import and Export Department, not the Technology Import and Export Department. Nevertheless, they agreed to see what they could do to help. The commercial attaché expressed hope that the problem could be resolved as expeditiously as possible since the payment was already a year overdue.

At 2.00 p.m. the same afternoon, MOFERT officials called and informed the commercial attaché that the problem had been resolved and that payment would be forthcoming. They explained that MOPI had delayed submitting the request for initial contract approval and had sent that along with the request for payment. This had caused a delay. The rules had been changed so that, in addition to the approvals required when a contract is to be signed, an additional set of approvals is required from the same organizations when the goods are delivered. In the case of this contract, two separate sets of approvals were required from each of the following:

1. MOPI;
2. MOFERT;
3. the State Planning Commission;
4. the State Administration for Foreign Exchange Control.

Questions

1. Why does the People's Republic of China have a State Administration for Foreign Exchange Control, and so many approvals required for a purchase of goods from overseas?
2. Is the additional difficulty in trying to sell to the People's Republic of China, compared with trying to sell to France or Taiwan, worth the trouble? Why or why not?
3. If you wanted to export to the People's Republic of China, would you go to your own government or embassy in China for assistance? Why or why not?
4. If the United States company had a similar problem in France, is it likely they would have contacted their embassy for assistance? Why or why not?

(George Lee, of San Francisco State University and formerly Commercial Attaché, US Embassy, Beijing, People's Republic of China. Reproduced with the kind permission of the author.)

A4.4 Case: When international buyers and sellers disagree

No matter what line of business you're in, you can't escape sex. That may have been one conclusion drawn by an American exporter of meat products after a dispute with a West German customer over a shipment of pork livers. Here's how the disagreement came about:

The American exporter was contracted to ship '30,000 lbs. of freshly frozen U.S. pork livers, customary merchandisable quality, first rate brands.' As the shipment that was prepared met the exacting standards of the American market, the exporter expected the transaction to be completed without any problem.

But when the livers arrived in West Germany, the purchaser raised an objection: 'We ordered pork livers of customary merchantable quality – what you sent us consisted of 40 percent sow livers.'

'Who cares about the sex of the pig the liver came from?' the exporter asked.

'We do,' the German replied. 'Here in Germany we don't pass off spongy sow livers as the firmer livers of male pigs. This shipment wasn't merchantable at the price we expected to charge. The only way we were able to dispose of the meat without a total loss was to reduce the price. You owe us a price allowance of $1,000.'

The American refused to reduce the price. The determined resistance may have been partly in reaction to the implied insult to the taste of the American consumer. 'If pork livers, whatever the sex of the animal, are palatable to Americans, they ought to be good enough for anyone,' the American thought.

It looked as if the buyer and seller could never agree on eating habits.

(Reproduced with the kind permission of the Dun and Bradstreet Corporation.)

Questions

1. What does 'customary merchandisable quality' mean? Where? In which language and cultural context?
2. Discuss how ethnocentrism and SRC (Self Reference Criterion) are at work in this case.
3. In this dispute, which country's law would apply, that of the United States or of West Germany?
4. If the case were tried in US courts, who do you think would win? And if tried in German courts? Why?
5. Is formal litigation justified in such a case? How can one solve this problem? How can one avoid this type of conflict in the future?

A4.5 Critical incident: Scandinavian Tools Company

A major Swedish company that specialized in metal tools and factory equipment had created a few years ago a French subsidiary, based in Lyons, France. This plant was at first supplied with inputs (specialty steels, high-speed steels for blades and saws, etc.) from Sweden. It mostly produced and sold for the French markets and for exports to the other southern European markets, namely Italy, Spain and Portugal. The drive and energy for creating this new venture had been brought by a young Swedish executive, Bo Svensson. Svensson had spent part of his curriculum as a student and then as a young engineer in France. Thereafter he had been in a position to convince the top management of this large Swedish multinational company to launch a new subsidiary in France.

Svensson was very enthusiastic about France. He liked the country very much and had learned the language, which he spoke fluently with a slight northern European accent. In the rush of starting the new company everything went smoothly. Svensson, who was chief executive officer of the French venture, knew how to secure customers and make them loyal; he also knew how to deal with the headquarters in Sweden. The market was quickly growing and competition was not particularly harsh. At the beginning, products were made in Sweden and then exported to France, where Svensson and the subsidiary dealt with marketing and distribution.

After a few years demand began to swell, so the parent company in Sweden decided to build a production plant in France. Machines and factory equipment for the new plant came from Sweden, and the factory was quickly operating at normal capacity. Svensson then hired a vice-president for administration, André Ribaud, an ambitious young executive, also in his thirties, with a law background. The two men got on well together, although their backgrounds and personal profiles were quite different. They shared the work and responsibilities: Svensson was in charge of relations with headquarters, marketing and the monitoring of financial performance; as plant manager, Ribaud was in charge of production operations, human resource management, cost accounting, monitoring cost prices and delivery delays.

After a few years it appeared that Svensson felt more and more relaxed in his job. Autonomous in his profitable subsidiary of (at that time) 200 employees located in a place remote from Sweden, he was very free with his timetable. He was also very free with personal expenses, which he was entitled to have reimbursed by the subsidiary: he simply had to sign his own expenses receipts. Svensson did not hesitate to use this facility: he did not make a clear distinction between his own money and the company's money. Svensson gradually got into the habit of abusing company-paid personal expenses. Ribaud was shocked. Svensson even went so far as to have the expenses of his mistress paid by the subsidiary.

Meanwhile Ribaud was still working as efficiently as during the initial years. Growth had been impressive. Starting with a few employees in an office of two rooms in Lyons, the subsidiary had grown to a dynamic medium-sized company with more than 500 people on the payroll; Scandinavian Tools France had bought out two plants from competitors. Following these changes, Ribaud's responsibilities quickly increased. He had involved himself completely and passionately with the company. He knew each member of staff personally and was respected by them.

Over time the relationship between the two men had considerably worsened. Svensson saw that Ribaud was winning more and more influence and power inside the company, and was well known by the customers. He felt jealous of him and tried his best to make Ribaud's life in the company difficult. Ribaud, on the other hand, increasingly resented the excessive expenses and the catty remarks of his boss, for whom he no longer felt any esteem. Svensson was a complex, energetic and whimsical character. His charisma and stamina had enabled him to seduce the French clients as well as the management staff at the headquarters in Sweden. The excellent financial performance of the French subsidiary had been feeding a confidence relationship with his superiors, who were also Swedish compatriots. They had trust in his management talents and therefore they allowed him a large degree of freedom. He had also established friendships with some of the senior directors at the headquarters, especially with the director in charge of public relations. Svensson was well known at headquarters level, and he understood company 'politics' quite well.

After fifteen years of almost steady growth, the market was reaching the stage of maturity. Competitors were aiming at the horizon of 1992, with its concomitant cancelling of borders within the EC, and there were many acquisitions by large European and American competitors. The French subsidiary had lost part of its profitability. The middle management was complaining to Ribaud about Svensson's lack of interest in the subsidiary and his mismanagement. Everybody believed that emergency decisions had to be made before the situation got even worse. But Svensson tuned a deaf ear to their complaints and remained unwilling to enter into discussion with either Ribaud or the other executives. The French were also amazed, and somewhat shocked, to see that there was no reaction from headquarters. It looked as if headquarters had little interest in the destiny of the French subsidiary. People at headquarters still seemed to have confidence in Svensson, who knew how to make them feel secure.

Ribaud did not feel comfortable in this situation. He felt that the financial balance of the subsidiary was threatened and that one factory would probably have to close in the near future. It also seemed to him that the interests of Swedish shareholders were not being adequately taken into account. Relations between Svensson and Ribaud were so damaged that Svensson was convinced that Ribaud was plotting against him. Svensson therefore systematically took a contradictory stance to Ribaud, at the risk of making inappropriate decisions which could possibly lead the subsidiary almost to the brink of bankruptcy.

Each time Ribaud brought up these problems during meetings with people from headquarters, Svensson abruptly interrupted him, shifting from English to Swedish in order to keep him out of the conversation. Under heavy pressure from some of the executives of the subsidiary who were about to resign and leave the company, Ribaud felt obliged to react. He had tried, during visits from members of the Swedish headquarters, to give them an idea of the situation in a very allusive manner. But he got the impression that he was not being heard. They had their own image of the chief executive officer, which was clearly different.

In desperation, Ribaud decided to send an official note to the top management in Stockholm, in which he told them that he would be obliged to resign if nothing was done to put an end to the present disorder. He tried to write it as objectively as possible, in a matter-of-fact style, citing evidence and hard facts. This was not an easy task since objectivity may prove difficult in such circumstances and, moreover, he was denouncing his boss, which is never very pleasant. He called one of the members of the top management in Stockholm whom he knew a little better than the others, explained about the letter and sent him a copy.

What answer could he expect?

A4.6 Exercise: Following directions

Objective

To clarify for participants the formats of their communication and the difficulties and inaccuracies encountered when implementing those formats.

Participants

Any number of dyads, each individual in a given dyad representing a different culture. Facilitator.

Materials

1. One or more index cards for each participant (see Figure 4.2).
2. Answer sheets and pencils for each participant.

Setting

Dyads should be seated around a table. If there are several dyads, each should be seated at a different table.

Time

Variable, depending on participant characteristics, number of cards per participant and processing phase; anywhere from ten minutes to an hour or more.

Procedure

1. Participants are divided into culturally mixed dyads and seated around tables.
2. At each table, one participant sits on one side of the table and is designated as 'source', the other is seated on the other side and is designated as 'respondent'.
3. Each participant is given an answer sheet and one or more index cards. The index card, as shown in Figure 4.2, contain eight matrices of twenty-five dots each. The cards contain one matrix of twenty-five dots, on which five of the dots are connected by five lines. Each card design is unique.

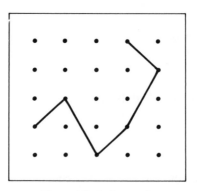

Figure 4.2 Index card.

4. Each source must verbally communicate the design on one of his cards to the respondent seated across from him who must reproduce it on one of the blank matrices on his answer sheet within a recommended time limit of ten to fifteen seconds.
5. Participants alternate being sources and respondents and may change their partners with each new round of activity.
6. Facilitator leads discussion tying in participants' experience with the exercise objective, emphasizing the role cultural difference may play in confounding communication.
7. Suggestions variations of this exercise are:
   (a) Ask participants to draw their own designs and then communicate them to each other.
   (b) Draw and communicate more complex designs (eight dots and eight lines) in the same amount of time.
   (c) Communicate designs drawn on irregular matrices.
   (d) If several dyads take part in the exercise, make each correct communication worth one point. Besides the element of inter-dyad competition, the success of each dyad member becomes contingent upon the success of the other. Some interesting effective data may be generated for discussion.

(Royal Freuhling, of the University of Hawaii, 1975, in William H. Weeks, Paul B. Pedersen and Richard W. Brislin (1987), *A Manual of Structured Experiences for Cross-Cultural Learning*, Intercultural Press: Yarmouth, ME, pp. 10–13. Reproduced with the kind permission of the publisher.)

A4.7 Exercise: World picture test

Objective

To clarify participants' understanding of countries and cultures of the world through their knowledge of geography.

Participants

Three or more persons. Facilitator.

Materials

Paper and pens.

Setting

No special requirements.

Time

At least thirty minutes to one hour.

Procedure

1. Each participant is given a sheet of paper and a pen and asked to:
   (a) draw a map of the world as best they can within a five minute time period
   (b) name as many of the countries as they can
   (c) checkmark any country they have visited for a week or longer
   (d) exchange papers with other members of the group and discuss what differences are evidenced in what the other person put into their drawing and/or left out of the drawing.
2. Discuss the following points:
   (a) Does a person's awareness of the shape of a country reveal that person's awareness of the shape of the culture?
   (b) When a person leaves out a country, what does this mean?
   (c) When a person leaves out a continent, what does this mean?
   (d) What country did the person place in the center of the map and what does that mean?
   (e) When a person draws a country out of place in relation to other countries, what does this mean?
   (f) Were they better acquainted with countries they had visited?
   (g) When the person objects violently to doing the drawing, what does that mean?
   (h) How well did persons draw home countries of other group members?
   (i) What do the persons plan to do as a result of what they learned in this exercise?

(William H. Weeks, Paul B. Pedersen and Richard W. Brislin (1987), *A Manual of Structured Experiences for Cross-Cultural Learning*, Intercultural Press: Yarmouth, ME, pp. 107–8.

A4.8   Rationales for section A3.3 (cross-cultural scenario) and sections A3.4 and A3.5 (cross-cultural interactions)

A3.3 Scenario: Inshallah

This scenario can best be understood by first appreciating the very different views in U.S. culture and Saudi culture concerning 'locus of control.' In the United States it is believed that ultimately people are responsible for their own destiny. If something goes wrong, it is believed, it is frequently possible for the individual to *do* something (that is, to change certain behavior) to bring about the desired outcome. In Saudi Arabia, and indeed throughout the Arab world, people are taught from an early age that all things are subject to the direct will of Allah. All plans for the future (including, of course, business plans) are viewed with a sense of inevitability and will be realized only if God wills it. This is not to say that people in the Arab world would not work hard to help bring about the desired results. Rather, they believe that despite the effort, the desired ends will not happen unless God is willing. Perhaps Stefan would have been less frustrated if he had translated *inshallah* to mean 'if possible' or 'God willing' rather than as a knee-jerk response used to absolve oneself of all responsibility for one's actions.

(Ferraro, 1990, p. 162. Reproduced with permission.)

A3.4 Interaction: Engineering a decision

1. There is little evidence for this in the story. While the financial benefits are relevant, to Mr. Tanaka they are probably a minor consideration in the situation. Please choose another response.
2. It is quite probable that coming from a male-dominant Japanese society he does think it odd that M. Legrand should mention his wife's opinion. However, the decision not to go to the Middle East also appears to be M. Legrand's personal inclination so this does not fully account for Mr. Tanaka's bewilderment. There is another explanation. Please choose again.
3. It is unlikely that Mr. Tanaka would consider this. There are factors far removed from personal gain dominating his concern. Please choose again.
4. This is the most likely explanation. In Japanese and many other collectivist societies a person is defined much more as a collection of roles (parent, employee, servant, official) than by his or her individual identity. As such, fulfilling these roles to the best of one's ability is regarded as more important than one's personal inclinations. Thus Mr. Tanaka would see that M. Legrand's responsibility as a company employee would be to accept the position whether or not he is personally happy about the idea. M. Legrand's refusal is thus bewildering and makes him think that his belief in M. Legrand's dedication has been completely misplaced. M. Legrand however comes from a culture where individual freedoms are highly valued and so exercises his right to refuse the offer with little compunction. The cultural conflict thus resides in different strengths of values applied to the roles occupied by a person in the culture.

(Richard W. Brislin, Kenneth Cushner, Craig Cherrie and Mahealani Yong, 1986, *Intercultural Interactions: A practical guide*, Sage: Newbury Park, CA, pp. 177–8. Reproduced with permission.)

A3.5 Interaction: Opening a medical office in Saudi Arabia

1. It is unlikely that people would sign up solely to satisfy a newcomer's feelings. There is a better explanation. Please select again.

2. If there is a considerable time lag between when a person makes a decision and the action upon it, it is possible that they may change their mind. However, there is no indication in the incident to support this. Please select another response.
3. Units of time reference differ markedly between Arab and American cultures. To an American, the major unit of time is five minutes. Fifteen minutes is a significant period of time. To an urban Arab, the unit of time that corresponds to our five-minute block is fifteen. Thus, when the Arab is thirty minutes late (by the clock), he is not even ten minutes late by his standards. This is the best answer. Tom's patients may still arrive.
4. While the patients may be seeing their own traditional healers, they would not necessarily do so in the strict sequence suggested by this alternative. There is a more precise explanation. Please choose again.

(Richard W. Brislin, Kenneth Cushner, Craig Cherrie and Mahealani Yong, 1986, *Intercultural Interactions: A practical guide*, Sage: Newbury Park, CA, p. 179. Reproduced with permission.)

Notes

1. Here, *international trade* means the relations of exchange between economic agents from different countries; *international management* means the activities involving the management of an international company, be it an exporting firm or a multinational company; *international marketing* means the design and implementation of marketing strategies across different national markets.
2. The existence of common interests, outside the perception of those negotiating, is an illusion. As shown by many authors, it is the *perceived* common ground which is important (Pruitt, 1983). For more information see Chapters 13 and 14, which complement this chapter directly, in that negotiation and communication are two sides of the same coin.
3. Depending on your own linguistic background, in reading this chapter you may be wondering how the linguistic mix (original French text, English translation) has influenced the kind of arguments put forward and the way in which they have been expounded. The Whorfian hypothesis is presented in detail in the writings of Benjamin Whorf, collected after his death by John B. Carroll (1956). The next chapter presents certain corollaries to this hypothesis as they relate to market research.
4. The verifications of the Whorf-Sapir hypothesis seem to have been fairly conclusive, in particular those related to the comparative experiments based on Navajo and Anglo-American children. They both shared all principal sociocultural characteristics (education, family income, religion, etc.) except language (experiences reported by Ferraro, 1990, pp. 54–5).
5. I wrote this short English text myself, therefore it is not a 'valid' text but a caricature or exercise in reflection. Native anglophones will notice the Gallic style with respect to idioms.
6. See also in Chapter 14 the cross-cultural differences in the concepts of time and their influences on international business negotiations.
7. In Japan I had a student who was the son of the Turkish ambassador to the United Nations. Having been raised in France, Belgium, Italy and Brazil, he was studying for a Master's degree in international management at the American Graduate School of International Management in Phoenix, Arizona. Already a fluent speaker of Turkish, French, English, Italian and Portuguese,

he was learning Japanese. But really he was incapable of passing from one of these languages into another. When in the middle of a conversation I asked him for the English translation of a French word (I taught in English), he could never do this without a considerable delay. In fact *he thought separately in each one of these languages*, which is fairly consistent with the Whorfian hypothesis.

8. As a practical example of the research in equivalence/non-equivalence of terms, take two dictionaries and look in them at the translations in both directions. The Langenscheidt *Compact Dictionary* translates 'act of God' as *force majeure*, but it translates *force majeure* as 'overpowering circumstances'; *Harrap's Concise* does not include the expression 'act of God' in the English section and translates *force majeure* as 'circumstances outside one's control'. The only solution is to consult a lawyer about the meaning of these two expressions and their respective legal consequences.

9. This is true only in certain cantons in Switzerland; the example reported here (by a Portuguese friend originating from Madeira island) took place in Geneva.

10. I do not argue that these national cultures have much in common. The concept of low context/ explicit messages only relates to communication. In other respects they may differ widely (masculinity/femininity, uncertainty avoidance, etc. – see section 3.3).

11. Ferraro (1990, ch. 4) presents a complete description of non-verbal modes of communication in different cultures. The teaching of non-verbal communication is, however, very difficult. It is better to aim for a state of alert so that one does not decode non-verbal messages erroneously, rather than try to gain full command of different types of non-verbal communication. Deep cultural learning is very hard after childhood.

Special attention has not been paid to the 'language of spaces': for instance, the codes concerning social distance – how far should one stand from other people in order to respect their area of private space (if such an area even exists)? A complete approach to these relations with space was proposed by Edward T. Hall (1966) in *The Hidden Dimension*, Doubleday: New York. In this book he developed the concept of 'proxemics' – the term he has coined for the interrelated observations and theories of man's use of space as a specialized elaboration of culture.

12. The point is not to pretend that Michel Droit's description of the sorcerer is false. His reading partially reveals reality but also ignores how the sorcerer is integrated into the Papuan community.

13. See the teaching notes at the end of Chapter 1. It is intended to facilitate further learning by trial and error in the field of intercultural communication in marketing-related activities.

References

Adler, Peter S. (1975), 'The transitional experience: An alternative view of culture shock', *Journal of Humanistic Psychology*, vol. 15, pp. 13–23.

Bateson (1971), introduction to *The Natural History of an Interview*, University of Chicago Library Microfilm Collection of Manuscripts in ·Cultural Anthropology, series 15, nos 95–8.

Carroll, John B. (1956), *Language, Thought and Reality: Selected Writings of Benjamin Lee Whorf*, MIT: Cambridge, MA.

Condon, John C. and Fahti Youssef (1975), *Introduction to Intercultural Communication*, Bobbs Merrill: Indianapolis.

Droit, Michel (1952), *Chez les Mangeurs d'hommes*, La Table Ronde: Paris.

Erikson, Erik (1950), *Childhood and Society*, Norton: New York.

Ferraro, Gary P. (1990), *The Cultural Dimension of International Business*, Prentice Hall: Englewood Cliffs, NJ.

Fisher, Glenn (1980), *International Negotiation: A cross-cultural perspective*, Intercultural Press: Yarmouth, ME.

Gauthey, Franck (1989), 'Gérer les différences dans l'entreprise internationale', *Intercultures*, no. 6, April, pp. 59–66.

Gauthey, Franck and Dominique Xardel (1990), *Le Management Interculturel*, PUF, Collection 'Que sais-je?': Paris.

Graham, Robert J. (1981), 'The role of perception of time in consumer research', *Journal of Consumer Research*, vol. 7, March, pp. 335–42.

Hall, Edward T. (1959), *The Silent Language*, Doubleday: New York.

Hall, Edward T. (1960), 'The silent language in overseas business', *Harvard Business Review*, May–June, pp. 87–96.

Hall, Edward T. (1966), *The Hidden Dimension*, Doubleday: New York.

Hall, Edward T. (1976), *Beyond Culture*, Doubleday: New York.

Hall, Edward T. (1983), *The Dance of Life*,. Anchor Press/Doubleday: New York.

Harris, Philip R. and Robert T. Moran (1987), *Managing Cultural Differences*, 2nd edn, Gulf Publishing Company: Houston, TX.

Kadima, K. and F. Lumwanu (1989), 'Aires linguistiques à l'intérieur du monde Bantu: Aspects généraux et innovations, dialectologie et classifications', in Théophile Obenga (ed.), *Les Peuples Bantu, migrations, expansion et identité culturelle*, Editions L'Harmattan: Paris, pp. 63–75.

Kagame, Alexis (1975), 'Aperception empirique du temps et conception de l'histoire dans la pensée Bantu', in *Les Cultures et le temps*, Payot/Unesco: Paris, pp. 103–33.

Langenscheidt (1989), *Compact Dictionary French–English/English–French*, by Kenneth Urwin.

Lee, James A. (1966), 'Cultural analysis in overseas operations', *Harvard Business Review*, March–April, pp. 106–11.

Levine, Robert A. and Donald T. Campbell (1972), *Ethnocentrism: Theories of conflicts, ethnic attitudes, and group behavior*, John Wiley: New York.

Montesquieu, Charles de (1721), *Persian Letters*, Penguin Classics edn 1973, Penguin: London.

Morsbach, Helmut (1982), 'Aspects of non-verbal communication in Japan', in Larry Samovar and R.E. Porter (eds), *Intercultural Communication: A reader*, 3rd edn, Wadsworth: Belmont, CA.

Oberg, Kalvero (1960), 'Culture shock: Adjustment to new cultural environments', *Practical Anthropology*, vol. 7, pp. 177–82.

Pearson, Emil (1977), *People of the Aurora*, Beta Books: San Diego.

Sapir, Edward (1929), 'The status of linguistics as a science', *Language*, vol. 5, pp. 207–14.

Sumner, G.A. (1906), *Folk Ways*, Ginn Custom Publishing: New York.

Ueda, Keiko (1974), 'Sixteen ways to avoid saying "no" in Japan', in J.C. Condon and M. Saito (eds), *Intercultural Encounters in Japan*, Simul Press: Tokyo, pp. 185–92.

Watzlawick, Paul, Janet Helmick Beavin and Don D. Jackson (1967), *Pragmatics of Human Communication: A study of interactional patterns, pathologies and paradoxes*, W. W. Norton: New York.

Zaharna, R.S. (1989), 'Self shock: The double-binding challenge of identity', *International Journal of Intercultural Relations*, vol. 13, no. 4, pp. 501–26.

5

—— ◆◆◆ ——

Cross-cultural market research

Some brief introductory examples will serve to explain the topic of this chapter, that is, the problems which are met when undertaking market research across national/cultural environments and their solutions. This chapter aims to provide the reader with some basic insights, drawn mostly from cross-cultural methodology in the social sciences, on how to solve these problems. Typical research questions may be similar to the following:

- How should one undertake a market survey for instant coffee in a traditionally tea-drinking country (i.e. Great Britain or Japan); what information and data must be sought? How should this data be collected?
- Which information-gathering technique should one use in a country where, for instance, potential respondents resent interviews as an intrusion into their privacy?
- Where the starting point is a questionnaire which was originally designed for a specific country/culture, how should it be translated and adapted to the cultural specificities of other countries in which it is to be administered?

The simultaneous launch of new products on several different national markets is becoming more and more frequent, therefore research of these markets has to be undertaken simultaneously. Cultural differences are the main characteristic when contrasting national contexts, as non-tariff barriers are eased. In cross-cultural marketing research, the way in which a problem is stated in each country can affect the results (Mayer, 1978). Taking once more the instant-coffee example, there is a marked difference in the research perspective according to which research questions are addressed:

- How does one recover the market share lost by instant coffee to ground coffee in a traditionally coffee-drinking country? This requires the investigation of consumption patterns in certain social and family situations, when people are drinking specific coffee-based beverages.[1]
- How does one increase the market share for instant coffee (out of the total hot beverages market) in a traditionally tea-drinking country?

According to Berent (1975), the formulation of research objectives when developed through differing cultural contexts cannot be the same as the formulation for domestic market research. An understanding of the cross-cultural environment is a basic requirement of research objective formulation. Given the growth in the multi-nationalization of business (Levitt, 1983), establishing the psychometric quality of research instruments, the consistency of behavioural/attitudinal constructs[2] and the equivalence of samples are of paramount concern to the multinational marketer (Green and Langeard, 1979; Douglas and Craig, 1983, 1984). This chapter presents the main limits to equivalence across national/cultural contexts when one undertakes cross-cultural market research and the solutions, at various levels: basic concepts under review, equivalence of research instruments, translation problems, culture-based attitudes of surveyed people and sampling issues.[3]

5.1   Establishing cross-cultural equivalence

If the type of data sought and the research procedures implemented are considered to be of general application (i.e. no differences such as those described in Chapter 1),[4] the main difference between domestic and cross-cultural market research lies in the likely difficulties in establishing equivalence at the various stages of the research process. Problems generally arise from the diversity and complexity of marketing operations in the international environment.

♦ The complexity of the research design is greatly increased when working in an international, multicultural and multilinguistic environment (Douglas and Craig, 1983), not to mention the difficulties in establishing comparability and equivalence of data.
♦ Even larger problems may arise when differences in sociocultural or psychographic variables imply different attitudes and behaviour when using particular types of product.

For instance, Plummer (1977) compared the attitudes of women from the United States, Canada, Europe and several Commonwealth countries regarding housework, childcare and the use of deodorants, and demonstrated a wide range of results due to cultural differences. He showed, for example, that the US housewife does not consider house cleaning as important as her Italian counterpart. The benefits expected from cleaning products are probably more functional for Americans and more symbolic for the Italians, since Italian housewives regard their role in a more traditional way. Therefore the list of benefits shown on cards to potential interviewees should be changed according to each country (see the hair shampoo exercise in section A5.2).

Levels of cross-cultural equivalence

Douglas and Craig (1983, p. 4) have defined international marketing research as 'research conducted to aid making decisions in more than one country'. Management must provide

Table 5.1 *Categories of cross-cultural equivalence (Source: Douglas and Craig, 1984, p. 95. Reproduced with permission.)*

A. Construct equivalence	B. Measure equivalence
1. Functional equivalence	1. Calibration equivalence
2. Conceptual equivalence	2. Translation equivalence
3. Category equivalence	3. Metric equivalence
C. Sample equivalence	D. Instrument administration equivalence
1. Respondent equivalence	1. Data collection procedures
2. Composition of sample	2. Contextual equivalence
3. Frame equivalence	3. Temporal equivalence
4. Sample selection equivalence	

Note: The various levels of cross-cultural equivalence displayed in this table are explained in the text of the chapter; however, two are not mentioned because they overlap with other levels. *Contextual equivalence* relates to elements in the context of the data collection process that have an influence on responses. As Douglas and Craig explain (1984, p. 109): 'In the Scandinavian countries, for example, respondents are considerably more willing to admit overdrinking than in Latin America. In India, sex tends to be a taboo topic.' *Temporal equivalence* is near to calibration equivalence (in terms of calibrating dates and time periods). It relates to the problem of the differential of the ageing of information across countries: in a country with a 1 per cent annual inflation rate, income and price data are comparable across years; whereas in a Latin American country with 2000 per cent annual inflation rate, it is necessary to indicate on which exact day the data were collected and what the price indexes and exchange rates were at that time.

guidelines for data collection. Consequently the systematic collection of data is vital, either domestic or international. It is important to follow a precise plan which outlines the various steps of the research process (Green, Tull and Albaum, 1988), starting with a clear and concise statement of the research problem.

The relevant literature comprises several studies which explore the issue of cross-cultural equivalence (Green and White, 1976; Green and Langeard, 1979; Douglas and Craig, 1983; Adler, 1983; Sekaran, 1983; Poortinga, 1989). In one of the most exhaustive reviews of equivalence levels, Douglas and Craig (1984) identify the various levels where non-equivalence, causing non-comparability, may arise in comparative consumer research. They present thirteen areas of data equivalence (see Table 5.1).

The number of equivalence levels reviewed has dramatically increased in recent years (for earlier assessments of cross-cultural equivalence levels, see: Frijda and Jahoda, 1966; Prezworski and Teune, 1967; Whiting, 1968; Strauss, 1969; Berry, 1969; Brislin *et al.*, 1973; Van Raaij, 1978; Eckensberger, 1979; Leung, 1989; Poortinga, 1989). Douglas and Craig's list could be increased as some equivalence levels can be further broken down. For instance, translation equivalence may be divided into the following subcategories: lexical equivalence, idiomatic equivalence, grammatical–syntactical equivalence and experiential equivalence (Sechrest *et al.*, 1972).

Variations in the reliability of research instruments

Variation in cross-cultural reliability of underlying instruments has already been assessed, and Davis *et al.* (1981) claim that measurement unreliability is a threat to cross-national comparability. They investigated the problem of measurement reliability in cross-cultural marketing research for three types of consumer behaviour measures (demographics, household decision involvement and psychographics) across five country-markets, utilizing three different reliability assessment methods. Their findings show that it is easier to obtain measurement equivalence between demographic variables than between psychographic variables such as life-styles. Assessment method and the nature of the construct may be two causes of measurement unreliability across countries.

What is the relevant geographic segmentation: national versus regional differences?

National differences are of course not the only source of variance in consumer behaviour across different geographic locations. Any geographic division may be taken as a base for segmenting marketing variables, for instance psychographics, and looking at their generality across different geographic locations (Lesser and Hughes, 1986). As emphasized by Garreau (1981), who describes the 'nine nations of North America', regional differences in large countries with multi-ethnic and multicultural backgrounds can explain differences in consumer behaviour. Kahle (1986) shows that geographic segmentation is a basis for finding differences in values, whereas Gentry *et al.* (1987) show that geographic subcultures in the United States vary culturally. In administering a questionnaire in four regions of the United States – west (Washington), north central (Wisconsin), southwest (Oklahoma) and northeast (Massachusetts) – Gentry *et al.* (1987, p. 415) show that

> geographic regions vary in terms of innovativeness and perceived risk. Further differences exist across regions in terms of cultural adherence, religious commitment, and fate-orientation. . . . Residents in those areas with more adherence to traditional values are less likely to try new products.

But regional differences within countries, even if perceived more clearly by nationals than by foreigners, are not very strong compared to international differences. For instance, Saegaert *et al.* (1978) do not find significant differences in 'fad food' use among Anglo- and Mexican Americans. Calantone *et al.* (1985) find English Québecois women to be more similar to French Québecois women than to Ontario English women (all of these people being Canadians) in the benefits they seek from a brassière. Their findings support the idea of the assimilation model, where the cultural values of the immigrants tend to merge with those of the locally dominant cultural group.

Variations in knowledge and familiarity with products, concepts or attitudes

Comparison of results across countries should be made while simultaneously analyzing and checking for the reliability measures of the rating scales. Parameswaran and Yaprak (1987) compare the attitudes of respondents in two countries (the United States and Turkey) towards the people and products from three countries of origin (West Germany, Japan and Italy) using three products (cars, cameras and electronic calculators). They demonstrate that the same scale may have differing reliabilities when used by the same individual in evaluating products from differing cultures. The cars reviewed are the Volkswagen Golf (VW Rabbit, West Germany), the Honda Civic (Japan) and the Fiat 128 (Italy). Cameras considered are Leica (West Germany), Canon (Japan) and Ferrania (Italy). The brands of electronic calculators used are Royal (West Germany), Canon (Japan) and Olivetti (Italy).

> ... differing levels of awareness, knowledge, familiarity and affect with the peoples, products in general, and specific brands from a chosen country-of-origin may result in differentials in the reliability of similar scales when used in multiple national markets.... Two alternative courses of action may alleviate this problem. Measures to be used in cross-national market comparisons may be pre-tested in each of the markets of interest until they elicit similar (and high) levels of reliability.... Alternatively, one might devise a method to develop a confidence interval (akin to statistical spreads based on sample sizes) around the values of the measure based on its reliability (Parameswaran and Yaprak, 1987, pp. 45–6).

In the following text, the main problems encountered in achieving these levels of equivalence are defined and illustrated.

5.2   Research approaches: emic versus etic

In general, market research measurement instruments adapted to each national culture (the *emic* approach) offer more reliability and provide data with greater internal validity than tests applicable to several cultures (the *etic* approach, or 'culture-free tests').

The origin of the emic/etic distinction

This classic distinction in cross-cultural research was originated by Sapir (1929) and further developed by Pike (1966). The emic approach holds that attitudinal or behavioural phenomena are expressed in a unique way in each culture. Taken to its extreme, this approach states that no comparisons are possible. The etic approach, on the other hand, is primarily concerned with identifying universals. The difference arises from linguistics, where phon*etic* is universal and depicts universal sounds which are common to several languages, and phon*emic* stresses unique sound patterns in languages.

Conceptual equivalence

A basic issue in cross-cultural research is the determination of whether the concepts used have similar meaning across the social units studied. Problems of conceptual equivalence are more frequent when testing the influence of certain constructs on consumer behaviour, for example, when a uniform cognitive theory is used in several countries (Green and White, 1976). The hypothesis of the cognitive theory that people do not willingly behave contradictorily may hold true in the United States while not being applicable to some other countries (conceptual equivalence).

The following statement from the anthropologist Clifford Geertz (1983, p. 59) gives a slight feeling of how difficult it may be to reach true conceptual equivalence between cultures:

> The Western conception of a person as a bounded, unique, more or less integrated, motivational and cognitive universe, a dynamic center of awareness, emotions, judgement and action, organized in a distinctive whole ... is, however incorrigible it may seem, a rather peculiar idea, within the context of world's cultures.

Such basic concepts as beauty, youth, friendliness, wealth, well-being, sex appeal and so on are often used in market research questionnaires where motivation for buying many products is related to self-image, interaction with other people in a particular society and social values. They are *seemingly* universal. However, it is always advisable to question the conceptual equivalence of all these *basic words* when designing a cross-cultural questionnaire survey.

The example of consumer dissatisfaction

Constructs such as consumer dissatisfaction have been used for assessing cross-cultural differences in consumer attitudes. Richins and Verhage (1985) have studied differences between US and Dutch consumers relating to their dissatisfaction and complaining behaviour, for which they had their questionnaire reviewed by a panel of Dutch experts and made some minor changes to the wording of the questions. They look for conceptual equivalence of the dissatisfaction concept: does it have the same meaning, socially and individually, for the US and the Dutch people to be 'dissatisfied with a product or a service'? Richins and Verhage find 29 per cent of the variance to be attributable to national differences, the most salient ones being as follows:

> Dutch consumers perceive more inconvenience and unpleasantness in making complaints than do American consumers.... Dutch consumers were less likely than Americans to feel a social responsibility to make complaints.... Seemingly contradicting this finding, however, Dutch consumers are more likely than Americans to feel bothered if they don't make a complaint when they believe they should, a sort of guilt. Perhaps this seeming contradiction indicates that Dutch respondents tend to feel a personal rather than social obligation to make complaints (Richins and Verhage, 1985, p. 203).

Cavusgil and Kaynak (1984) propose an interesting enlargement of the consumer dissatisfaction concept to the case of developing countries. They distinguish between micro-level sources (e.g. excessive prices, misleading advertising, lack of performance, etc.) and macro-level sources of consumer dissatisfaction (e.g. low income, inflation, etc.) with the possibility of interaction between the two levels. They state:

> In general micro-level sources appear to lead, over time, to a diffuse, latent discontent with the state of the marketplace; that is to a macro-level dissatisfaction. Unsatisfactory experiences with specific products and services seem to be reflected in a disillusionment with all institutions in the society (Cavusgil and Kaynak, 1984, p. 118).

Moreover the complaining behaviour does not have the same meaning at all, in the case where buyer and seller know each other personally, either as acquaintances or relatives: 'Personal relationships with vendors often prove advantageous. Usually food shoppers get to know how far they can trust a food retailer, and can negotiate prices and other terms' (Cavusgil and Kaynak, 1984, p. 122).

These studies illustrate the practical difficulties in dealing with the conceptual equivalence of constructs used in a survey. When looking at the underlying dimensions across countries, one often realizes that they are not equivalently weighted or articulated in the total construct. For instance, in the construct 'waiting in line (to be served)', the dimension 'losing one's time' may be emphasized in a time-conscious culture whereas it may be almost non-existent in one which is not economically time-minded. When 'waiting in line', the dimension of 'guilt for pushing in' is more developed in guilt-orientated societies.

Often the conceptual equivalence of several basic interrelated constructs has to be questioned, in as much as they relate to consumer behaviour idiosyncrasies for the specific type of product or service surveyed. Box 5.1 shows some construct equivalence problems in the case of life assurance policies.

Many popular marketing constructs have been used in cross-cultural research settings (perceived risk, brand loyalty, Rokeach value survey, life-styles, etc.). Generally speaking, conceptual equivalence is an obstacle to the direct use of constructs which have been uniquely designed for US culture. The perceived risk construct, for instance, may differ in its components across cultures. It may be broken down into several subdimensions: social risk, physical risk, financial risk (Van Raaij, 1978). The emphasis placed on these subdimensions may vary across cultures: when buying cars, for example, people in some cultures may give more value to social risk (because their purchase and use of cars is mostly status-orientated) whereas in other cultures people may be more concerned with physical safety (because death in accidents is greatly feared).

Therefore it is necessary to investigate, far more frequently than is actually done, the construct validity in each culture where a cross-cultural consumer behaviour study is undertaken. This should be done by following recognized procedures to assess the validity[5] of the underlying constructs at the conceptual level and reliability at the empirical/measurement instrument level (Campbell and Fiske, 1959; Churchill, 1979; Churchill and Peter, 1986).

Box 5.1 *A multinational survey on life assurance: conceptual equivalence problems in Islamic countries*

In Islam it is considered evil to talk about death. Nevertheless Muslim people do not fear death. On the contrary, they are probably much less frightened by the prospect of death than most people in Western/Christian countries. But the notion of *destiny* is of the utmost importance: humans may not decide about their own death, nor are they entitled to control the process of it. One is not allowed to challenge the course of destiny, and therefore one should not speculate on one's own life and death. A verse of the Koran says approximately this: 'Behave each day as if your life will be very long, and for your afterlife, behave as if you will die tomorrow.' In Saudi Arabia, life assurance is forbidden. But some high-risk industries, such as oil production, bypass this prohibition by insuring their local employees through foreign life-assurance companies, with policies located abroad.

In the Islamic world people do not like to invest and bet on the long term. Effort must be rewarded quickly if it is to be maintained. The concept of a financial product such as life assurance needs a long-term orientation and a strong individual capacity to imagine the future. Projection towards the future is a culture-related trait (see section 3.1 and Chapter 14). In Islam, you may certainly imagine how you will be tomorrow, but not at a particular place or moment. The future tense exists, but it is surely not as accurate or meticulous as that of the American or European languages. Moreover, protection of the family and solidarity within the extended family are highly valued and work effectively. If a man dies, his brother will care for his wife and children.

The concept of life assurance is related to culture in at least the following four aspects: protection of the family and/or the individual; future orientation; betting on one's own life and death; the degree of solidarity in the family and extended family group. In Islamic countries it is important not to offend interviewees at first contact. It is better to rely on in-depth non-directive interviews and focus groups carried out principally by briefed local researchers who have a thorough personal knowledge of Islam and the local culture (the Islamic world spreads from black Africa to China). Some research questions will have to be addressed in order to prepare an adequate marketing strategy. Which is the appropriate mix, for the design of the life assurance policies offered to potential consumers, in terms of death benefit (amount of money to be paid when a person under a life assurance policy dies) and annuities (a series of payments made at regular intervals on the basis of the premiums previously paid)? Which term(s) should be proposed for people before they receive the benefits of their life assurance policy? How should the beneficiaries be designated? How to communicate this offer to potential consumers through advertisement: which brand name to adopt and which themes and advertising style should be favoured in the advertising campaign?

Similar activities performing different functions: functional equivalence

By the same token, if similar activities perform different functions in different societies, their measures cannot be used for the purpose of comparison (Frijda and Jahoda, 1966). Some variables frequently used in market surveys are not functionally equivalent across countries. A similar product may perform different functions (Green and White, 1976): for example, a bicycle in one country may be considered a transportation vehicle while in another country it may be a leisure item. Stanton, Chandran and Hernandez (1982) illustrate this functional equivalence problem by taking the example of hot milk-based drinks. Whereas in the United States and England they are considered an evening drink, best before going to sleep, in much of Latin America a 'Chocolate Caliente' is a morning drink (no functional equivalence).

A watch may be used as wrist-jewellery or an instrument for handling time and daily schedules. The same holds true for a fountain pen. In some countries its function may be as a simple general-purpose writing instrument; in others it may be regarded mostly as an instrument for signing documents. Elsewhere it may be considered purely non-functional since it needs time and care to refill it, and often leaks over one's fingers

Measurement equivalence and calibration equivalence

The validity of a rating scale in a cross-cultural study is affected by the metric equivalence of the scales and by the homogeneity of meanings. Pras and Angelmar (1978) did a comparison of verbal rating scales (semantic differentials) in French and English. They show that difficulties can occur in determining lexical equivalents in different languages of verbal descriptions for the scale (see Table 5.2). It is also difficult to ensure that the distances between scale points (adjectives, for instance) are equivalent in the two languages (metric equivalence). In this case the standard deviation for French respondents was significantly smaller than for US respondents, this being due to a greater cultural homogeneity in France.

The method suggested by Pras and Angelmar leads to the rejection of definitional equivalence of concepts with source language measurement instruments: in other words, it is naive to use a differential semantic scale originally written in English, French or any other language and translate it lexically (simply with dictionary-equivalent words) into other languages. Pras and Angelmar favour decentred measurement (Campbell and Werner, 1970), which means constructing reliable and valid scales for all the countries under survey. In this case the original wording of the scale may be changed if it provides better measurement equivalence across countries/cultures.

Calibration equivalence relates to differences in monetary units; especially in high-inflation contexts where daily prices over a year cannot be directly compared with those of a low-inflation country. Naturally, exchange rates and units of weight, distance and volume cause calibration equivalence problems. Apart from objective calibration equivalence, there is also a perceptual calibration equivalence: for instance, how many colour classes are recognized by people from a particular country? This might prove

Table 5.2 Adjectives which have the same level of meaning in two languages and provide similar distances between the points of the scale.
(Source: Pras and Angelmar, 1978, p. 76.)

Colloquial rating scale			Formal rating scale		
US adjectives		French adjectives	US adjectives		French adjectives
Fantastic	20	20 Extraordinaire	Remarkably good	17	17 Très bon
Delightful	17	17 Superbe	Good	14	14 Bon
Pleasant	14	14 Très correcte	Neutral	10	10 Moyen
Neutral	10	10 Moyen	Reasonably poor	6	6 Faible
Moderately poor	7	7 Assez faible	Extremely poor	3	3 Très mauvais
Bad	4	4 Remarquablement faible			
Horrible	2	2 Terriblement mauvais			

useful for a packaging test or a product test.

> Western subjects, for example, have more colour classes than African subjects, and some primitive people only have a two-term colour language. The Bantu of South Africa, for example, do not distinguish between blue and green. Consequently they do not discriminate between objects or symbols in these colours. (Douglas and Craig, 1984, p. 100)

Encouraging feedback from the informant on cultural adequacy

For all these reasons, it seems necessary to design research procedures where feedback from the informant is possible: for instance focus groups, in-depth interviews and open-ended questions (Goodyear, 1982). Unique features of cultural behaviour cause non-equivalence. It is impossible to unveil these levels of non-equivalence if the instrument and methodology prevent them from appearing. A pragmatic solution is to ask interviewees their opinion of the relevance of questions, words and concepts used in the questionnaire, at the end of the normal interview process.

A questionnaire forced upon interviewees does not elicit information (see the hair shampoo exercise in section A5.2). If emic feedback is to be introduced, both interviewers (if they have not personally prepared the questionnaire) and interviewees must be in a situation here they may comment on the questions themselves and explain what is culturally adequate in their context and what is not. Interviewees should be given the opportunity at the end of their basic answering process to elaborate freely on what they think of the questions, the situations described and so on. This orientation is slightly different from the traditional one where interviewed people are simply required to answer, not 'criticize', the questions. Emic feedback allows an improvement in the adequacy of the source culture's constructs and instruments.

A hybrid emic/etic approach

Wind and Douglas (1982) propose a new hybrid approach which they define in the following way:

> The proposed approach develops country, culture or sub-culture specific concepts and measures. These are compared, combined or modified, and wherever possible common 'pan-cultural' concepts, which do not have a specific cultural bias, and which reflect the idiosyncratic characteristics of each country, culture or sub-culture are identified. Country-specific measures of the 'pan-cultural' and country idiosyncratic concepts are developed and compared. To the extent possible they are combined and country-specific measures are administered, generating the secondary data for the comparison.

5.3   Translation equivalence

For many reasons which are outlined principally in Chapter 4, translation techniques, even sophisticated ones, might prove incapable of achieving full comparability of data.

Back-translation and related techniques

The back-translation technique (Campbell and Werner, 1970) is the most widely employed method of reaching translation equivalence (mainly lexical and idiomatic) in cross-cultural research. This procedure helps to identify probable translation errors. One translator translates from the source language into a target language. Then another translator, ignorant of the source-language text, translates the first translator's target language text *back* into the source language. Then the two source-language versions are compared.

For instance, when translating *un repas d'affaires* ('a business meal' in English) from French to Portuguese in the preparation of a questionnaire for Brazil, it is translated as *jantar de negocios*. When back-translated, it becomes a *dîner d'affaires* ('business dinner'). In Brazilian Portuguese, there is no specific expression for *un repas d'affaires*. It is either a 'business lunch' (*almoço de negocios*) or a 'business dinner'. One has to choose which situation to elicit in the Brazilian questionnaire (as would be the case in English): the 'business meal' has to be either at noon or in the evening in the Portuguese version. When back-translating, discrepancies may arise from translation mistakes in either of the two directions or they may derive from real translation equivalence problems which are then uncovered. Then a final target-language questionnaire is discussed and prepared by the researcher (who speaks the source language) and the two translators. Practically it is advisable to have one translator who is a native speaker of the target language and the other one a native speaker of the source language. It means that they are translating *into* their native language rather than *from* it, which is always more difficult and less reliable.

However, back-translation can also instil a false sense of security in the investigator by demonstrating a spurious lexical equivalence (Deutscher, 1973). Simply knowing that words are equivalent is not enough. It is necessary to know to what extent those literally equivalent words and phrases convey equivalent meanings in the two languages or cultures (Mayer, 1978).

Sechrest, Fay and Zaidi (1972) identify four types of translation problems: vocabulary equivalence, idiomatic equivalence, grammatical–syntactical equivalence and experiential equivalence. The latter means that translated terms must refer to real items and real experiences, which are familiar in both cultures. An expression such as 'dish-washing machine' may face experiential equivalence problems when people, even if they know what it is, have never actually seen this type of household appliance nor experienced it.

Another technique, blind parallel translation (Mayer, 1978), consists of having several translators translate simultaneously and independently, from the source language into the target language. Then, the different versions are compared and a final version is written.

Combined translation techniques, limits of translation

Parallel and back-translation can be merged, as shown in Figure 5.1. When two languages and cultures present wide variations, such as Korean and French, combining parallel and back-translation provides a higher level of equivalence (Marchetti and Usunier, 1990).

For example (Usunier, 1991), two Koreans translate the same French questionnaire F into two Korean versions, K1 and K2. A third Korean translator, who is unfamiliar with the original French text F, translates K1 and K2 into F1 and F2. A final Korean questionnaire, K3, is then prepared by comparing the two back-translated French versions F1 and F2. English is used to help compare them as it is widely used and more precise than either French or Korean. This example could be refined: the number of parallel translations may be increased, or back-translation processes may be independently performed.

A more sophisticated solution to the problem of translation has been suggested by Campbell and Werner (1970). Research instruments should be developed by collaborators in the two cultures, and items, questions or other survey materials should be generated jointly in the two cultures. After back-translation, or after any initial translation process has been performed, there is an opportunity to change the source-language wording. This technique, called *decentring*, not only changes the target language, as in the previous techniques, but also allows the words in the source language to be changed, if this provides enhanced accuracy. The ultimate words and phrases employed will depend on which common/similar meaning is sought in both languages simultaneously, without regard to whether words and phrases originate in the source or the target languages. In the above example of the business meal, choosing the decentring method would imply changing the words in the source questionnaire to 'business lunch'.

5.4 Comparability of data

When secondary data – especially published statistical data – are sought, there may be some difficulties in comparing these data across countries:

- Differences in categories: for instance, for age brackets, income brackets or professions.
- Difference in base-years, when some countries have no recent data.

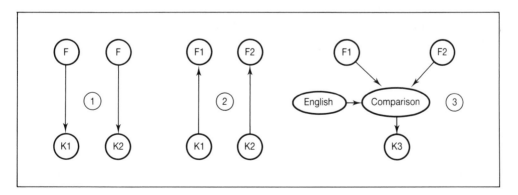

Figure 5.1 Examples of translation techniques. (Source: Marchetti and Usunier, 1990.)

+ Unavailable or unreliable data, the data collection procedure by the local census bureau being biased for certain reasons (non-exhaustive census, inadequate sampling procedure).

When primary data are concerned, discrepancies in response patterns across countries may cause data unreliability and so limit direct comparison. Let us assume that through any of these translation procedures we are able to develop equivalent national versions of a common questionnaire for a cross-cultural market research study. Response equivalence problems will appear, such as the following:

+ Sampling unit (who should the respondent be?).
+ Secrecy/unwillingness to answer.
+ Response biases.
+ Yea-saying pattern (and also nay-saying pattern).
+ Item non-response pattern.
+ Extreme response style.

Error measurement sources related to response styles are multiple and may directly create discrepancies between observed measurement and true measurement. Some basic precautions may help to avoid the generation of data with a great deal of measurement error.

Choice of respondents

An important criterion is the choice of respondents. Selecting a unit of analysis is a key issue in the conceptualization of comparative research design. The role of respondents in the buying decision process (organizational buying, family buying, information and influence patterns, etc.) may vary across countries. This statement is as relevant for industrial markets as for consumer goods markets (Hempel, 1974; Wind and Douglas, 1982; Douglas, 1976; Green *et al.*, 1983). In the United States, for instance, it is not uncommon that children have a strong influence when buying cereals, desserts, toys or other items, whereas in countries that are less child-orientated, children's influence on the buying decision will be much smaller (Douglas and Craig, 1984). The same holds true for the extended-family pattern in Southeast Asia (Laurent, 1982; Redding, 1982), which heavily influences individual buying decisions. It is therefore of primary interest to assess, first, the basic equivalent sampling units: for instance, when researching for industrial products, comparing the position, role and responsibility of industrial buyers throughout different countries.

Reluctance to answer

Respondents sometimes feel that the interviewer is intruding into their privacy. They prefer not to answer, or they consciously bias their answers, fearing that their opinion could later be used against them (Stanton *et al.*, 1982). Many countries have strong privacy/intimacy patterns, where the family group is protected from external, impersonal interference. Tuncalp (1988) explains that the very private and reserved nature of Saudis is not conducive to personal interviews. Being independent, Saudis do not want to be possibly exposed to justifying or explaining their actions when answering a barrage of questions.

Biased answers

Sexual biases between interviewer and respondent are also an important source of the reluctance to grant interviews (Kracmar, 1971). In many traditional countries housewives are reluctant to grant interviews to male interviewers. Ethnic bias may also exist between the interviewer and the respondent: a Chinese person may feel uncomfortable when interviewed by a Malay (Kushner, 1982).

Much response bias may result from the interviewees not understanding that the process of interviewing them is in order to generate objective data. Informants may perceive the

Box 5.2   *The weaknesses and strengths of the 'local researcher'*

1. Weaknesses.
   (a) Often of lower intellectual ability and research experience than his or her equivalent in developed countries.
   (b) Often finds it difficult to adopt neutral, objective stance with reference to informants or clients. May want to be didactic in groups and may well prefer to distort findings to reflect a more educated picture of his countrymen than exists in reality. Alternatively, may seek to distance himself from the 'average consumer' by exaggerating their foibles and lack of sophistication. He himself, especially if he is from an educated family, may be out of touch with his countrymen.
   (c) He may be unwilling or unable, even for business reasons, to cross traditional barriers of class, religion or tribe.
   (d) He rarely has the Puritan work ethic and does not always see the value of objective truth. Delays, shortcuts and distortion are likely.
2. Strengths.
   (a) He knows the country and its people. He can usually establish rapport easily and understands what is said. If he knows the Western country he can also interpret the significance of what is said, to explain differences.
   (b) He knows the *language*. Language can be an enormous barrier, as anyone who has tried to interview through interpreters must recognise.
   (c) He is immune to local ailments and is physically comfortable in the (research) environment. He can cope, through familiarity, with common problems.

(Goodyear, 1982, pp. 90–1. Reproduced with the kind permission of the publisher.)

purpose of research as a very long-winded form of selling, especially in developing countries (Goodyear, 1982). The objective and the process of the interview must often be explained at the beginning. When briefing native interviewers (management students) in Mauritania, I was asked the following question: 'What do you want us to tell the interviewee to answer?' It was necessary to explain to the interviewers that interviewing was a distanced and objective process, where interviewees had complete freedom of response. The idea of objective truth, external to personal relations, is unfamiliar to Mauritanians (Box 5.2).

Some respondents, especially in Latin-American countries (Stanton *et al.*, 1982) tend to present a 'courtesy bias' by answering in order to please the interviewer. Respondents tend to tell the interviewer what they think the interviewer would like to hear. This response pattern probably takes place in countries where people tend to have difficulty in answering opinion surveys and market research questionnaires. When they accept, it can be through some kind of personal favourable sentiment towards the interviewer. Douglas and Craig (1983) describe this response style as introducing a 'yea-saying' pattern. Response scores tend to be inflated and the mean score of the respondents are biased towards the positive end of the scale.

Item non-response is an important source of bias in cross-national surveys. Respondents may be unwilling to respond to some questions, such as those relating to income or age. Douglas and Shoemaker (1981), studying non-response of different items in a public opinion survey in eight European countries, found evidence of non-response being higher for income in the United Kingdom and Ireland, whereas the willingness to respond to political questions was highest in Germany and Italy.

Response styles

Another potential bias may also be introduced by significant differences in extreme response style patterns across countries. US people tend to respond with more enthusiasm, and therefore present a more extreme response style in answering, than the Japanese (Zax and Takashi, 1967), or Koreans (Chun *et al.*, 1974). This could produce a bias in the standard deviation of data, increasing it artificially in cultures where people tend to over-react to questions, compared to other cultures where people may tend to suppress their opinions.

5.5 Representativeness and comparability of national/cultural samples

Sampling is a basic step in most market surveys. A complete census, where the whole population of interest is researched, generally proves too costly. Therefore it is advisable to infer the characteristics of the whole population from a limited sample. In this process, the following tasks must be carried out:

1. Finding a sampling frame, the basic characteristics of which are known (a telephone directory, an electoral list, etc.).

2. Drawing a sample from this frame, by a method which may be either probabilistic or non-probabilistic.
3. Checking that the selected sample is representative of the population under study.

The main problem in the cross-cultural sampling process is the selection of samples that can be considered comparable across countries. According to Green and White (1976), reaching perfect comparability is very difficult – in fact almost impossible. These limitations should be considered when interpreting research findings.

An initial issue to be addressed is the two-level type of sampling:

- First level: sample of countries or cultures.
- Second level: samples of individuals within these countries or cultures, i.e. within each national sample.

At the first level, the research question is directly comparative.[6] For instance, what are the main sociodemographic and economic variables which, across countries, determine the per capita consumption of a particular product or service: motor insurance, wallpaper, milk powder, etc.?[7] Strategic marketing decision-making often needs such research for selecting target national markets and markets with low actual demand but high growth potential, and for deciding where to locate efforts for the future. A comparative design may also be useful when one tries to derive an estimated market demand figure in a country where statistical sources are scarce and unreliable. Amine and Cavusgil (1986) give examples of methods for estimating the Moroccan demand for wallpaper and bandages.[8]

A second issue is the representativeness of each sample in each country or culture (Douglas, 1980). In cross-cultural research it seems a priori relevant to follow a systematic procedure, the same in every country, to achieve reliability and comparability of data. Unfortunately demographic definitions do not correspond exactly from one country to another, age does, of course, as long as people know their birth dates, but occupation, education and socioeconomic status usually do not. If data are presented in categories, say for income or age bracket, these categories will most likely not correspond exactly across countries (category equivalence). Religion and tribal membership will also have to be added to traditional demographics as they are of the utmost importance in some less developed countries (Goodyear, 1982).

A representative sample?

The researcher then constructs a sample which represents the population of interest. However, a sample split into 50 per cent men and 50 per cent women conveys a different meaning in a country where women's rights are recognized to that in more traditional countries where women's status is lower. As such, the expression 'representative sample' makes little sense if one does not clarify which traits and characteristics this sample actually represents. For instance, shopping behaviour is very different world-wide: in some places men tend to do most of the shopping, in other countries mostly women; this also depends on various other factors (income level, type of product, etc.). In this case the samples must represent actual shoppers rather than men and women as they are in the general population of potential shoppers.

In order to define a sampling procedure for cross-cultural research, one must select a method which is based on several national samples, each of them being fully representative of the population of the country which it attempts to represent, and which furthermore provides comparable data across countries. Douglas and Craig (1983) stress the limited availability of an exhaustive sampling framework which corresponds exactly to the characteristics of the population at a global (multi-country) level.

Sampling frames are often biased. A sample drawn from the electoral list in Bolivia may over-represent men since women are not as likely to vote (Stanton *et al.*, 1982). Tuncalp (1988) states that most sampling frames in Saudi Arabia are inadequate: there is no official census of the population, no elections and therefore no voter registration records, and telephone directories tend to be incomplete. Tuncalp suggests further that non-probability sampling is a necessary evil.

Douglas and Craig (1983) also suggest that an empirical method (non-probability sampling procedures) may prove as efficient as probability sampling, when researching cross-culturally. Data can be collected at a reasonable cost, compatible with the objectives of the survey. Therefore the basic criterion for selecting the sampling procedure(s) will remain the comparability of results across countries. Sentell and Philpot (1984) propose a method for evaluating the representativeness of samples taken from imperfectly known parent populations. Their method is based on the comparison of proportions estimated from two independent samples, focusing on situations where the larger sample size is unknown. Their method is implemented by testing two sets of sample statistics of Thai households.

Estimating sample size also appears as a critical step. The use of traditional statistical procedures, such as constructing confidence intervals around sample means, or hypothesis testing, is difficult to implement in as much as they require precise estimates of the variance of the population. This variance estimate is often unavailable in countries which have poor census data. The most frequently used procedure is therefore the selection of sample size, country by country, taking into account their respective peculiarities (Douglas and Craig, 1983).

If research starts from a domestic survey, where the home country representativeness has been emphasized, and is then extended to other countries, it may be difficult to achieve comparability. Brislin and Baumgardner (1971) state that although true random sampling is necessary for the successful completion of research projects, studies using non-random samples can also be valuable, if they include all the characteristics of the subjects and environment that could potentially influence the results or their interpretation.

Finally one may conclude that representativeness and comparability of cross-cultural samples can be better achieved by using different samples and sampling techniques which produce equivalent levels of reliability rather than by using the same procedure with all samples. The main problem (before any statistical procedure is implemented) is to secure equivalence in meaning: does it make sense to represent the same populations across various countries? Do the samples actually represent these populations in the same way?

Conclusion

Propositions in this chapter may be summed up as follows:

♦ It is dangerous to prepare a foreign or international market survey as a pure transposition of domestic research. The nature and scope of researched market information, the ways to collect it, the accuracy of the data as well as the criteria of reliability of the data present a cross-cultural variance. This holds true even when they are perceived as normatively quite universal. International market researchers have to unveil their own ethnocentric biases, by giving feedback opportunities to their informants or to local collaborators.

♦ From this point on, a systematic search for *formal* equivalence may appear dangerous. Equivalence of constructs and instruments has to be established first. As stated by Van Raaij (1978, p. 699), 'We should encourage researchers in other cultures to study their own reality rather than to replicate American studies.' In this sense the recommendation would be simply to look for the meaning.

APPENDIX 5

———— ♦♦♦ ————

Teaching materials

A5.1 Case: Eliot Greeting Card Company

The Eliot Company was established by Gregory Eliot in the early 1950s in St. Louis, Missouri. Although the company only had about 4 percent of the U.S. greeting card market, it had been profitable since its beginnings, and had shown modest growth in a market environment dominated by Hallmark Company (which maintained over 40 percent of the market), American Greetings (about 30 percent market share), and several smaller companies that had market shares of 5 to 15 percent. Eliot had been successful largely by carving itself a niche, marketing lines of specialty cards for which the other firms seemed to have little interest.

Recently, however, the greeting card market had been experiencing a period of (at least temporary) flat sales. This was seen to be the result of both the relatively weak economy and a dramatic increase in telephone advertising, urging consumers to 'reach out and touch someone' at the expense of sending greeting cards. This has led to rather intense marketing efforts by the larger greeting card companies to gain percentage points of the relatively sluggish market. It was becoming obvious that the competition was turning its attention to the specialty lines that Eliot had been able to use to its advantage for so long. (See Exhibit 1.)

Exhibit 1   'Greetings, One and All!' Cardmakers Gear up for Mother's Day, and Every Day

Just in case anyone forgot, the greeting card industry is busy reminding people that Sunday is Mother's Day. Of course, everyone will want to pick up cards for Mom, wife, and Grandma. But what about sisters and favorite aunts? Sure. There are Mother's Day cards for them too, and a host of greetings for a mother-in-law. How about someone expecting a baby in July? No problem. Any number of companies make Mother's Day cards for mothers-to-be. And why should Pop feel left out and have to wait until June for his special day? Hallmark puts out a card that says 'You're a terrific parent, too, Dad!' Why in fact should Mother's Day be restricted to parents? It is not. A card by Recycled Paper Products of Chicago has this touching message: 'Although you're not my mother, your little motherlies mean a lot to me. Happy Motherish Day.'

No business is better than greeting cards at finding imaginative ways to package and promote an old product. The leading companies, Hallmark of Kansas City and American Greetings of Cleveland, have roots that go back almost to the turn of the century, but they strive to be as innovative as fledgling Silicon Valley computer firms. The cardmakers are experimenting with different styles, coming up with novel reasons for people to buy their wares and using new technology that enables cards to play tunes or talk. Hallmark offers 1,200 varieties of cards for Mother's Day, the year's fourth biggest card day (after Christmas, Valentine's Day, and Easter), while American Greetings boasts of 1,300. The products range from a traditional card with a picture of flowers and syrupy poetry for $1 or less to a $7 electronic version that plays the tune of 'You Are the Sunshine of My Life.'

Hallmark holds about 42 percent of the $3.2 billion-a-year greeting card business, followed by American Greetings' 30 percent. The two leaders are now being challenged by Cincinnati-based Gibson Greetings, which has captured an estimated 10 percent share, up from 5 percent in 1978. Gibson scored a coup in February by striking a deal with Walt Disney Productions for the rights to use Mickey Mouse and his friends, who had previously been featured on Hallmark cards. Gibson had also signed up Garfield the Cat and the Sesame Street characters, but Hallmark's line of Peanuts cards is still one of the industry's most successful. American Greetings got a boost last year by reaching an agreement with Sears to be the exclusive card seller in all its department stores. That more than matched a similar arrangement that Hallmark has with J. C. Penney.

As the top three cardmakers battle among themselves, they also keep an eye on about 300 smaller manufacturers, which are often daring and inventive. Says Hallmark Chairman Donald Hall, 'Industries that aren't competitive get stagnant after a while. Ours is very competitive, and the fever of creativity is at a high point.'

One sign of the industry's brainstorming is the burgeoning number of occasions for which greetings are available. Card buyers can now congratulate a friend on getting a driver's license, buying a new car, or completing a successful diet. Customers can use cards to announce a divorce, propose a tryst, or console a pal whose pet dog has died. Carrying that marketing strategy to an extreme, California Dreamers, a Chicago company, has put out an all-purpose generic greeting card. The message: 'Whatever.'

The card manufacturers have been alert to changes in the American family. Says Richard Connor, executive vice-president of American Greetings, 'The divorce rate has brought about new families, single fathers, and working mothers. These new relationships open up new avenues for card sending.' One of Hallmark's Mother's Day cards shows Mom at her office. Both American Greetings and Hallmark have cards with messages to 'Mom and Her Husband' or 'Dad and His Wife.'

Paper Moon Graphics, a small, fast-growing Los Angeles firm, has won over customers with a combination of quirky humor and striking visual images. One of its cards shows a bride perched on the shoulders of her groom, who is standing precariously on a high wire. Inside, it says, 'So Far ... So Good. Happy Anniversary!' Maine Line of Rockport, Maine, has found a profitable niche by specializing in cards that appeal to women. A sample message: 'A woman in the White House would feel right at home ... She already knows how to clean up the mess men have made.' Maine Line even has a few cards that could be used by homosexuals. One says, 'Hip hip hooray, I'm glad you're gay.'

The industry leaders have responded to the competition by introducing their own yuppie-style cards. Hallmark has a new line called Modern Woman, with messages that might often seem risqué for the venerable 75-year-old firm. Example: 'You're such a totally together man. You're sensitive, kind, understanding and a good listener ... Nice buns, too! Happy Birthday.'

One of the newest frontiers in the industry is talking cards. The voice comes from a minute speaker connected to a microchip, where the message is stored. One card by American Greetings has the words 'Open this birthday card fast' printed on the outside. When the card is opened, a relieved voice says, 'Thanks, it was really getting stuffy in here. Happy Birthday!' Priced as high as $10, the electronic cards are still a novelty item. But since the cost of microchips is coming down, the industry hopes that tuneful and talking cards may eventually become a mainstay of Mother's Day, and every other conceivable occasion. (Source: 'Greetings, One and All,' *Time*, May 13, 1985, p. 54.)

◆◆◆

For the first time in its history, Eliot Greeting was faced with a decline in its modest share, each point of which was worth several millions of dollars in sales. At a brainstorming session by the firm's board of directors, President Tom Eliot suggested that one possible solution to the problem would be to develop an export market for its products to avoid the high costs of head-to-head competition for U.S. customers. He reasoned that it would be easier for the company to design and make cards for English-speaking consumers in countries like England and Australia than to continue to slug it out with the market leaders at home.

Bill Yates, vice president of Sales, had an alternative suggestion. He had recently returned from a vacation in the U.S. Southwest where he had become aware of the large number of Hispanic Americans, who were, according to his sales representatives, beginning to improve their traditionally low economic status. Yates's idea was to create and market a line of greeting cards for this largely Spanish-speaking group of Americans for whom greeting card sending was at a relatively low level, compared to the general population. He argued that, rather than expanding its efforts to approach foreign customers, the firm would be better able to take advantage of its existing production and distribution system to develop this relatively untapped market at home. An argument developed between Tom Eliot and Bill Yates as to which avenue would be the best source of growth for Eliot Greeting Card Company. Tom had recently seen an article in the local paper (see Exhibit 2) describing his competitor's moves in the U.S. Hispanic market. He certainly did not want another slugfest with competition. Bill argued that the potential of the U.S. Hispanic market was large enough for all greeting card firms and that they would either have to develop skills now or later in marketing cards to this significant segment in the U.S. market. They agreed to postpone a decision until they could get more information on each option.

Exhibit 2   'Greeting Card Firms Expand Hispanic Line'

Two major U.S. greeting card companies are expanding their lines of Spanish language cards and gift items in response to growing demand from the Hispanic market.

Hallmark Cards, Inc., and American Greetings Corp. have announced plans to publish more greeting cards written in standard, dialect-free Spanish incorporating new designs that eschew old-fashioned stereotypes in favor of popular characters such as Strawberry Shortcake.

Old views knocked

The U.S. Census Bureau says that Hispanics comprised 6.4 percent of the total population in 1980 and increased in number by 61 percent during the 1970s.

The U.S. Hispanic Chamber of Commerce, which meets in San Antonio later this week, has reported that the nation's 20 million Hispanics now have purchasing power worth $70 billion – a figure the chamber expects to more than double by the year 2000.

Recent marketing studies have knocked down some old views about Hispanic consumers and provided new data on buyers seeking high-quality goods and services.

Hallmark Cards, the industry leader with $1.5 billion in annual sales, expects to double its Spanish language line of everyday and seasonal cards by next May, said Nancy Matheny, manager of marketing and communications.

American Greetings has launched a new line of Spanish language cards, posters, and calendars featuring popular characters such as Ziggy and Strawberry Shortcake, and the 'classical romantic' expressions of its 'Soft Touch' series.

The 95 new designs, now available in San Antonio stores, will expand the company's current line of approximately 300 everyday and seasonal greeting cards, invitations, and gift tags in Spanish, said product manager Ross Bennett.

American Greetings, the largest publicly held greeting card publisher with $1 billion in annual sales, based its latest expansion on the results of focus group interviews with Hispanic women in Los Angeles and New York City, Bennett said.

Women predominate in both the Hispanic and Anglo card markets, accounting for 90 percent of all card buyers and 85 percent of all dollars spent on greeting cards, Bennett said from his Cleveland office.

Bennett said the Hispanic women interviewed told American Greetings:

- Spanish language greeting cards are difficult to find, even in mostly Hispanic neighborhoods in large cities.
- Cards in Spanish are sent most frequently to older relatives and friends, especially those who still speak mostly Spanish, and to those living in Mexico, Puerto Rico, Cuba, and other foreign countries. Cards in English usually are preferred for young relatives, such as brothers and sisters, and for children, co-workers, and non-Hispanic friends. Exceptions to these general rules are religious observances, such as baptisms, weddings, name days, and fifteenth birthday days, when Spanish-language greetings are preferred.
- The industry's offerings in Spanish had been inferior to their English language

counterparts. Among the criticisms: limited variety of designs, poor quality of photographs and paper, and overuse of loud, garish colors.

Bennett said the U.S. Hispanic population's growing affluence during the past ten years has created a need for Spanish cards of improved quality and variety. The old stereotypes of sombreros and burros do not work anymore, he added.

But simply translating an English language sentiment into Spanish and slapping on a new cover will not sell more cards to Hispanic customers, industry leaders say.

Both Hallmark and American Greetings employ linguistic consultants and bilingual editors to develop pithy verses in traditional, or Castillian, Spanish.

'We don't regurgitate English words or sentiments straight into Spanish,' Matheny said from Hallmark's Kansas City, Missouri, headquarters, Cultural and linguistic idiosyncrasies are incorporated in the company's line of Spanish cards, which was begun in 1982 with 100 designs.

Matheny predicted the firm will produce 500 to 600 everyday and seasonal designs in Spanish by May 1985. Hallmark and its Ambassador subsidiary publish cards and other items in 20 languages for sales in 100 countries, with 11 million cards produced daily.

Differences blur

Bennett pointed out that Spanish greeting cards should be written in a standard, grammatically correct version of the language that does not reflect any regional dialect, just as English cards are written.

American Greetings' research showed that card senders preferred to write their own personal message on the card to incorporate any regionally distinct dialect, he said.

A recent survey of the U.S. Hispanic market by Yankelovich, Skelly & White, Inc., revealed a 'blurring of differences' among Spanish-speaking nationalities, leading the researchers to propose that all Hispanics be considered as one population segment for marketing purposes. 'Localized patterns of speech, slang, etc., are felt to be a lessening barrier between Hispanics of different national origins,' the report states.

Rousana Cards, a Hillside, N.J., company specializing in greeting cards aimed at Hispanics, blacks, and other ethnic groups, has been publishing cards in Spanish since 1947.

Rousana President Ira F. Rubin said although his firm's cards generally use vernacular Spanish, some idioms also are included. He cited one example: *yerno*, the standard Spanish word for son-in-law, becomes the feminine *yerna*, daughter-in-law, only in a Puerto Rico dialect. Rubin's company publishes cards for *yernas* and markets them in appropriate neighborhoods.

'We feel very bullish regarding greeting cards in Spanish,' Rubin said. 'People have told us that as Latins become more Anglicized, we would lose our market, but that just doesn't happen.' (*Source:* 'Greeting Card Firms Expand Hispanic Line', *Express-News* (San Antonio, Texas), September 18, 1984.)

◆◆◆

English-speaking export markets

The English-speaking export market was a potentially large one. Its major components were the United Kingdom (England, Scotland, Wales, and Northern Ireland), Canada, Australia, and New Zealand. These four countries comprised a total population of 46.2

million, broken down as follows:

United Kingdom	55,226,400
Canada	24,343,200
Australia	13,548,500
New Zealand	3,125,100
	96,243,200

In addition, the Republic of South Africa had a population speaking English as a first language of nearly 1 million. Several other former British colonies, such as Kenya, Hong Kong, and Singapore, had English-speaking minorities, but the major English-speaking countries offered a greater immediate potential. All four of the English-speaking nations were economically developed. Canada had been classified by most experts as belonging to the small group of affluent nations even though it had been experiencing serious economic problems in the mid-1980s. The other three countries were clearly in the category of developed nations, having predominantly middle-class populations with considerable disposable income.

Culturally, the four nations share a common heritage with the United States, but each culture has evolved somewhat differently over the years. Although they all speak the English language, they exhibit varying degrees of difference in word usage. Since the Eliot Company's product is written communication, it would be dangerous for its management to assume that identically worded messages would have identical meaning in each country. Much of the charm and appeal of greeting cards comes from subtle plays on words, and such messages might not be perceived in the same way in the other countries. Canada would present the least difficulty in this matter. Because Canada shares a long border with the United States and Canadians are exposed to large amounts of American media (television and magazines), word usage is very similar in the two nations – similar enough that identical messages would usually be successful. However, in the United Kingdom, where a 'cupboard' is a 'closet' and 'to chat' is 'to schmooze', the danger of miscommunication is very real. This is equally true of Australia and New Zealand. Eliot would have to test all messages with local experts and, in many instances, work out entirely different messages for each country.

A second major cultural difference between the United States and these other English-speaking countries may lie in the use and perception of greeting cards. Historically, in English-speaking cultures, a personally written note or letter has been considered the polite and proper method of communicating with a friend. Standardized, preprinted messages, such as are found on greeting cards, were considered to be less polite, less caring substitutes. Greeting cards may have complete acceptance in the United States, but before the Eliot Company decides to launch its products in any of these other countries, it must learn how their residents perceive greeting cards today.

The U.S. Hispanic market

Some preliminary demographic data were gathered to support the feasibility of Yates's proposal to sell Spanish language cards to the Hispanic market in the United States. The

1980 census estimated conservatively that Hispanics numbered nearly 15 million in the United States and that their growth rate was much higher than that of the population at large. It was speculated both because of immigration and high fertility rates that by the year 2000, Hispanics would surpass blacks in numbers in the United States and hence become the largest minority group. Yates was placed in charge of conducting secondary research into the idea and he hired the consulting firm of Lorca and Associates, specialists in the U.S. Hispanic market. Yates requested that the firm provide recommendations concerning general customer behavior of the Hispanic population so that decisions could be made about what the company would need to do to design and market greeting cards to the Spanish-speaking market in the United States.

The consultant's report

José Lorca, president of the consulting firm, presented Bill Yates with a review of the literature pertaining to the consumer behavior characteristics of U.S. Hispanics. He took some pains to point out that empirical data about this subpopulation were very meager and that much of the information came from articles in trade periodicals. These sources reflect experience by firms who have been interested in the Hispanic market, but do not report much of the hard data which would normally be expected to support conclusions made about Hispanics. He expressed a desire for more extensive consumer research to verify the speculations used to characterize the Hispanic market. With this caution in mind, Lorca reported his interpretations. He extracted seven themes from these studies which to him summarized the traits attributed to Hispanic consumers:

1. A preference for locally owned, Spanish-speaking businesses as well as a preference for Spanish ethnic products.
2. A high degree of brand loyalty and susceptibility to brand influences.
3. A tendency for purchases to be influenced by pride in Hispanic heritage.
4. A high degree of price consciousness and careful shopping characteristics.
5. A high degree of influence from 'family' in making purchase decisions.
6. Preference for Spanish language media, especially radio and television.
7. A tendency to become 'acculturated' with rising affluence.

Thus, Eliot Greeting was confronted with the prospect of developing the use of greeting cards among a relatively provincial and traditional group of potential customers who appeared to be heavily dependent upon their cultural background for purchase decisions. Moreover, as these individuals become more economically secure, they become more like typical American consumers.

Lorca pointed out several other problems with developing the Hispanic market. First, it could not be said that the consumers in the overall Hispanic market were homogeneous. In addition to the acculturation characteristic (Hispanics were not alike at different economic levels), U.S. Hispanics represent a number of different ethnic subgroups, depending on their national origins. These include Mexican Americans (59 percent), Puerto Ricans (15 percent), and Cubans (6 percent) as well as Hispanics with origins in other Central and South American countries and Europe (20 percent). These groups differ widely in cultural traits, especially in the particular dialects of Spanish spoken. He also noted that nearly all these people speak a kind of Spanish that is considerably different from the classical Castillian Spanish typically taught in Spanish courses offered at U.S. high schools and universities. This fact seemed particularly important to the creation of Spanish verses for greeting cards, especially in light of the uniquely personal nature of messages used.

Questions

1. Isolate the probable impact of culture on Hispanic preferences and purchasing patterns for greeting cards. Investigate the symbolic meaning of sending a greeting card (to whom, on which occasions, in which language?).
2. Assuming that Eliot Greeting Card Company has decided to undertake an in-depth market survey in order to decide whether to develop the Hispanic market, how would you design such a survey? What information is needed? How would you collect it?
3. What issues will have to be addressed prior to the development of the English-speaking export market?
4. What are the benefits of each strategy: Hispanic market in the United States versus English-speaking export market?

(Adapted from a case prepared by Joel Saegaert, University of Texas at San Antonio, in Edward Cundiff and Marye Tharp Hilger, 1988, *Marketing in the International Environment*, 2nd edn, Prentice Hall: Englewood Cliffs, NJ, pp. 156–63. Reproduced with permission.)

A5.2 Exercise: Hair shampoo questionnaire

You will find below a market survey questionnaire, administered by interviewers to women interviewees between the ages of 18 and 30. It was originally designed for the US market.

   You are asked to suggest cross-cultural adaptations to this instrument: a similar market survey, as far as the objectives are concerned, will be undertaken in other countries. More precisely, you are asked to do the following:

1. Review the possible problems related to the translation of the questionnaire, suggest solutions and translate it into . . . .[9]
2. Review the data collection procedure, from the point of view of the interviewer as well as from that of the interviewee.
3. Suggest changes in the questionnaire design and/or wording, and/or modifications in survey methods, if:
   (a) the information sought is meaningless in the local context;
   (b) the required information is meaningful but the data collection procedures are

inadequate; either they will not enable you to collect the information, or else this information will be biased.

- You must do this for each of the following countries: Algeria, Brazil, France, Germany, Thailand.
- You should then propose a 'central' version of the questionnaire, that is, a survey instrument which enables you to collect the maximum amount of information, which could be retrieved in a reliable manner, in the largest possible number of countries. This questionnaire would then help the meaningful comparison of countries.

Questionnaire used in hair shampoo study

Time Interview Started _____
Ended _____

Respondent Name _____ Respondent No. _____

Address _____

City _____ State _____

Telephone No. _____

Interviewer Name _____

Interview Date _____

Screening Questions (Part S)

Hello, I'm _____ of the Wharton School, University of Pennyslvania. We're conducting a survey on women's attitudes and opinions about hair care products.

1. On the average, how often do you shampoo your hair at home?

More than twice a week	_____
Once or twice a week	_____
Once or twice every two weeks	_____
Once or twice every three weeks	_____
Twice a month	_____
Less than twice a month	_____

IF LESS THAN TWICE A
MONTH, TERMINATE

2. What is your age? _____
   (IF UNDER 18 OR OVER 30 TERMINATE)

PART A

First I'm going to show you a set of 16 cards. Each card contains the name of a benefit that a hair shampoo might provide. (PLACE SET OF WHITE CARDS ON TABLE IN FRONT OF RESPONDENT.) Please take a few moments to look over these benefits. (ALLOW TIME FOR RESPONDENT TO STUDY THE CARDS.)

Now, thinking about various brands of hair shampoo that you have tried or heard about, pick out those benefits that you think are most likely to be found in almost any hair shampoo that one could buy today. (RECORD CARD NUMBERS IN FIRST COLUMN OF RESPONSE FORM A AND TURN SELECTED CARDS FACE DOWN.)

Next, select all of those remaining benefits that you think are available in at least some hair shampoo – but not necessarily all in a single brand – that's currently on the market. (RECORD CARD NUMBERS IN SECOND COLUMN OF RESPONSE FORM A. RECORD REMAINING CARD NUMBERS IN THIRD COLUMN. THEN RETURN ALL CARDS TO TABLE.)

Next, imagine that you could make up an ideal type of shampoo – one that might not be available on today's market. Suppose, however, that you were restricted to only four of the sixteen benefits shown on the cards in front of you. Which four of the sixteen benefits would you most like to have? (RECORD CARD NUMBERS IN FOURTH COLUMN OF RESPONSE FORM A.)

RESPONSE FORM A

(1)	(2)	(3)	(4)
Benefits Most Likely to be Found in Almost Any Hair Shampoo – Card Numbers	Benefits Available in Some Shampoo – Card Numbers	Remaining Benefits – Card Numbers	Four-Benefit Ideal Set – Card Numbers

PART B

Now, let's again return to some of the shampoo benefits you have already dealt with. (SELECT WHITE CARD NUMBERS 1 THROUGH 10; PULL OUT CARD 4 AND PLACE IT IN FRONT OF RESPONDENT.)

Suppose a shampoo were on the market that primarily stressed this benefit – 'Produces Hair that Has Body.' If you could get a shampoo that made good on this claim, which one of the remaining nine benefits would you most like to have as well? (RECORD NUMBER IN RESPONSE FORM B.) Which next most? (RECORD.) Please continue until all of the 9 benefits have been ranked.

RESPONSE FORM B

(Enter Card Numbers 1 Through 10 Excluding Card #4)

( ) Most Like to Have   ( )

( ) Next Most   ( )

( )   ( )

( )   ( ) Least Most

( )

PART C

Now, I am going to read to you some short phrases about hair. Listen to each phrase carefully and then tell me what single words first come to your mind when you hear each phrase? (RECORD UP TO THE FIRST THREE 'ASSOCIATIVE-TYPE' WORDS THE RESPONDENT SAYS AFTER EACH PHRASE IN RESPONSE FORM C.)

RESPONSE FORM C

(a)   Hair that has body

_____ _____ _____

(b)   Hair with fullness

_____ _____ _____

(c)   Hair that holds a set

_____ _____ _____

(d)   Bouncy hair

_____ _____ _____

(e)   Hair that's not limp

_____ _____ _____

(f)   Manageable hair

_____ _____ _____

(g)   Zesty hair

_____ _____ _____

(h)   Natural hair

_____ _____ _____

PART D

At this point I would like to ask you a few questions about your hair.

1. Does your hair have enough body?

Yes _____ No _____

2. Do you have any special problems with your hair?

Yes _____ No _____

If yes, what types of problems?

_____

_____

How would you describe your hair?

3. My hair type is:

Dry _____ Normal _____ Oily _____

4. The texture of my hair is:
   Fine _____   Normal _____   Coarse _____
5. My hair style (the way I wear my hair) is:
   Straight _____
   Slightly wavy or curly _____
   Very wavy or curly _____
6. The length of my hair is:
   Short (to ear lobes) _____
   Medium (ear lobes to shoulder) _____
   Long (below shoulder) _____
7. How would you describe the thickness of your hair?
   Thick _____   Medium _____   Thin _____

PART E
   Now I would like to ask you a few background questions.
1. Are you working (at least twenty hours per week, for compensation)?
   Yes _____   No _____
2. Are you married?
   Yes _____   No _____
3. What is your level of education?
   Some high school _____
   Completed high school _____
   Some college _____
   Completed college _____
4. (HAND RESPONDENT INCOME CARD.) Which letter on this card comes closest to
   describing your total annual *family* income before taxes? (CIRCLE APPROPRIATE
   LETTER.)

A. Under $9,000	E. $30,001–45,000
B. $9,001–15,000	F. $45,001–60,000
C. $15,001–20,000	G. Over $60,000
D. $20,001–30,000	

(THANKS VERY MUCH FOR YOUR HELP)

(Green, Tull and Albaum, 1988. Reproduced with permission.)

A5.3 Exercise: Slogans and colloquial speech

Marketing communications (advertising copy, slogans, promotional offers, text on
coupons, etc.) are language based. The quality of reception of the marketing messages by
the target audience is very sensitive to the accuracy of the wording. Marketing
communication is based on everyday – colloquial – speech, often very idiomatic.

The basic purpose of this exercise is fairly simple; it may be implemented with a group composed of people who have different linguistic backgrounds, but yet have a capacity to communicate with each other since some of them speak several languages. It does not imply that total fluency is necessary. Participants should simply take care to translate *into* the language(s) which they speak fluently (not *from*).

The exercise consists of the following:

1. Collecting slogans (and, more generally, short marketing communication texts) from magazines, billboards, posters, television commercials, sponsor announcements or short texts such as those found in greeting cards; translating them into other languages, with the objective of finding the equivalent meaning and local wording. The translation techniques explained in section 5.3 (back-translation, parallel translation and a combination of the two) should be used.
2. Collecting 'identical' slogans (again, generally any short marketing communication text) that are pushing the same international brand in different countries, then analyzing and comparing how similar propositions and concepts are conveyed in the different languages. Bookshops that sell foreign newspapers and magazines will be useful places to find the basic data.

Notes

1. The simple word 'coffee' covers a whole range of beverages, which are enjoyed in very different social settings (at home, at the workplace, during leisure time, in the morning, or at particular times during the day), in quite different forms (in terms of quantity, concentration, with or without milk, cold or hot), prepared from different forms of coffee base (beans, ground beans, instant).
2. The word 'construct' relates to a concept which has several underlying dimensions, and may be measured quantitatively by identifying these various dimensions. The construct 'consumer dissatisfaction and complaint behaviour' (Richins, 1983, reported in Richins and Verhage, 1985, p. 198) identifies five domains of attitude towards complaining:

   (1) beliefs about the effect experienced when one complains;
   (2) perceptions of the objective cost or trouble involved in making a complaint;
   (3) perception of retailer responsiveness to consumer complaints;
   (4) the extent to which consumer complaints are expected to benefit society at large; and
   (5) the perceived social appropriateness of making consumer complaints.

3. This chapter assumes that the reader has prior knowledge of marketing research techniques. It is advisable for non-informed readers to refer to a textbook of market research, for instance Green, Tull and Albaum (1988).
4. It is not self-evident (as shown in section 1.1, which relates to the Japanese style of market research) that research procedures and the type of data sought are completely independent of the cultural context of the research*er*. But this chapter emphasizes dependence on the research*ed* context.
5. Green, Tull and Albaum (1988) give the following definitions of validity and reliability of measurement: 'By validity the behavioural scientist means that the data must be unbiased and relevant to the characteristic being measured . . . . By reliability [the behavioural scientist] means the extent to which scaling results are free from experimental error' (pp. 249 and 253). Validity

is then broken down into content, criterion and construct validation: see Green *et al.* (1988, ch. 7, 'Measurement in marketing research', pp. 240–79).

6. Geert Hofstede (1991), in his new book *Culture and Organizations: Software of the mind*, has added an appendix entitled 'Reading mental programs'. He clearly explains that samples of cultures should not be confused with samples of individuals. He draws attention to the risk of abusive stereotyping, whereby country characteristics are considered as individual characteristics: 'Mean values are calculated from the scores on each question for the respondents from each country. We do not compare individuals, but we compare what is called central tendencies in the answers from each country' (Hofstede, 1991, p. 253).

7. There is some discussion on the issue of whether two-nation studies constitute a cross-cultural design. Nath (1968), in a review of cross-cultural management research, reported that 54 per cent of the fifty-seven studies he reviewed involved only two nations. Researchers favouring the etic approach consider that only studies of several cultures give a deeper understanding of the effects of culture on behaviour. That is what Hofstede (1980) calls 'ecological correlations' – correlations related to observed mean scores of different national or cultural groups.

8. For instance, it is possible to estimate a regression equation explaining per capita annual wallpaper consumption with explanatory variables such as income per capita, percentage of home ownership, frequency of use of other wall-covering materials, etc. To estimate the parameters it is possible to use a cross-section sample (data for a sample of countries, for the same year), or a pooled cross-section/time series sample, when the countries' data are available for several years. For a country where wallpaper consumption is unknown, it is then possible to compute it with the values of the explanatory variables. ('Bandages' is the US word for 'plasters'.)

9. This is *optional*. Instructors will define this according to their teaching objectives and to the existing language competencies. Cultural and linguistic contexts may be varied *ad libitum*. This is related to the participants themselves (nationalities, language skills, personal experiences in various countries, etc.) who are one of the main resources as far as cultural and language expertise are concerned. Students may also try to find information on foreign cultural contexts, either by using secondary data, or by interviewing natives.

References

Adler, Nancy J. (1983), 'A typology of management studies involving culture', *Journal of International Business Studies*, Fall, pp. 29–47.

Amine, Lyn S. and S. Tamer Cavusgil (1986), 'Demand estimation in a developing country environment: difficulties and examples', *Journal of the Market Research Society*, vol. 28, no. 5, pp. 43–65.

Berent, P. H. (1975), 'International research is different', in Edward M. Mazze (ed.), *Marketing in Turbulent Times, and Marketing: The Challenges and the Opportunities*, Proceedings of the American Marketing Association: Chicago, pp. 293–7.

Berry, John W. (1969), 'On cross-cultural comparability', *International Journal of Psychology*, vol. 4, no. 2, pp. 119–28.

Brislin, R. W. and S. Baumgardner (1971), 'Non-random sampling of individuals in cross-cultural research', *Journal of Cross-Cultural Psychology*, December, pp. 397–400.

Brislin, R.W., W.J. Lonner and R.M. Thorndike (1973), *Cross-Cultural Research Methods*, John Wiley: New York.

Calantone, R., M. Morris and J. Johar (1985), 'A cross-cultural benefit segmentation analysis to evaluate the traditional assimilation model', *International Journal of Research in Marketing*, vol. 2, pp. 207–17.

Campbell, D. and D. Fiske. (1959), 'Convergent and discriminant validation by the multitrait-multimethod matrix', *Psychology Bulletin*, vol. LVI, pp. 81–105.

Campbell, D.T. and O. Werner (1970), 'Translating, working through interpreters and the problem of decentering', in R. Naroll and R. Cohen (eds), *A Handbook of Method in Cultural Anthropology*, The Natural History Press: New York, pp. 398–420.

Cavusgil, S. Tamer and Erdener Kaynak (1984), 'Critical issues in the cross-cultural measurement of consumer dissatisfaction: Developed versus LDC practices', in Erdener Kaynak and Ronald Savitt (eds), *Comparative Marketing Systems*, Praeger: New York, pp. 114–30.

Chun, K.T., J.B. Campbell and J. Hao (1974), 'Extreme response style in cross-cultural research: A reminder', *Journal of Cross-Cultural Psychology*, vol. 5, pp. 464–80.

Churchill, G.A. (1979), 'A paradigm for developing better measures of marketing constructs', *Journal of Marketing Research*, vol. XVI (February), pp. 64–73.

Churchill, G.A., Jr and J.P. Peter (1986), 'Relationships among research design choices and psychometric properties of rating scales: A meta-analysis', *Journal of Marketing Research*, vol. XXIII (February), pp. 1–10.

Davis, H.L., S.P. Douglas and A.J. Silk (1981), 'Measure unreliability: A hidden threat to cross-national research?', *American Marketing Association Attitude Research Conference* in March, Carlsbad, CA, pp. 1–40.

Deutscher, I. (1973), 'Asking questions cross culturally: Some problems of linguistic comparability' in Donald P. Warwick and Samuel Osherson (eds), *Comparative Research Methods*, Prentice Hall: Englewood Cliffs, NJ, pp. 163–86.

Douglas, Susan P. (1976), 'Cross-national comparisons and consumer stereotypes: a case study of working and non-working wives in the US and France', *Journal of Consumer Research*, vol. 3 (June), pp. 12–20.

Douglas, Susan P. (1980), 'Examining the Impact of Sampling Characteristics in Multi-Country Survey Research', proceedings of the 9th annual meeting of the European Academy for Advanced Research in Marketing, Edinburgh.

Douglas, Susan P. and C.S. Craig (1983), *International Marketing Research*, Prentice Hall: Englewood Cliffs, NJ.

Douglas, Susan P. and C.S. Craig (1984), 'Establishing equivalence in comparative consumer research', in Erdener Kaynak and Ronald Savitt (eds), *Comparative Marketing Systems*, Praeger: New York, pp. 93–113.

Douglas, Susan P. and Robert Shoemaker (1981), 'Item non-response in cross-national surveys', *European Research*, vol. 9 (July), pp. 124–32.

Eckensberger, L.H. (1979), 'A metamethodological evaluation of psychological theories from a cross-cultural perspective', in Lutz H. Eckensberger (ed.), *Cross-Cultural Contributions to Psychology*, Swets and Zeitlinger: Amsterdam, pp. 255–75.

Frijda, N. and G. Jahoda (1966), 'On the scope and methods of cross-cultural research', *International Journal of Psychology*, vol. 1, no. 2, pp. 109–27.

Garreau, J. (1981), *The Nine Nations of North America*, Houghton Mifflin: Boston, MA.

Geertz, Clifford (1983), *Local Knowledge*, Basic Books: New York.

Gentry, J.W., P. Tansujah, L. Lee Manzer and J. John (1987), 'Do geographic subcultures vary culturally?' in Michael J. Houston (ed.), *Advances in Consumer Research*, vol. 15, Association for Consumer Research: Provo, UT.

Goodyear, Mary (1982), 'Qualitative research in developing countries', *Journal of the Market Research Society*, vol. 24, no. 2, pp. 86–96.

Green, R.T. and P.D. White (1976), 'Methodological considerations in cross-national consumer research', *Journal of International Business Studies*. Fall–Winter, pp. 81–7.

Green, Robert T. and Eric Langeard (1979), 'Comments and recommendations on the practice of cross-cultural marketing research', paper presented at the International Marketing Workshop, *EIASM*, Brussels, November, pp. 1–16.

Green, R.T., J.P. Leonardi, I.C.M. Cunningham, B. Verhage and A. Strazzieri (1983), 'Societal development and family purchasing roles: A cross-national study', *Journal of Consumer Research*, vol. 9 (March), pp. 436–42.

Green, Paul E., Donald S. Tull and Gerald Albaum (1988), *Research for Marketing Decisions*, 5th edn, Prentice Hall: Englewood Cliffs, NJ.

Hempel, D.J. (1974), 'Family buying decisions: A cross-cultural perspective', *Journal of Marketing Research*, vol. 11 (August), pp. 295–302.

Hofstede, Geert (1980) *Culture's Consequences: International differences in work-related values*, Sage: Beverly Hills, CA.

Hofstede, Geert (1991), *Culture and Organizations: Software of the mind*, McGraw-Hill: Maidenhead, Berkshire.

Kahle, L.R. (1986), 'The nine nations of North America and the value basis of geographic segmentation', *Journal of Marketing*, vol. 50 (April), pp. 37–47.

Kracmar, J.Z. (1971), *Marketing Research in Developing Countries: A handbook*, Praeger: New York.

Kushner, J.M. (1982), 'Market research in a non-Western context: The Asian example', *Journal of the Market Research Society*, vol. 24, no. 2, pp. 116–22.

Laurent, C.R. (1982), 'An investigation of the family life cycle in a modern Asian society', *Journal of the Market Research Sociey*, vol. 24, no. 2, pp. 140–50.

Lesser, J.A. and M.A. Hughes (1986), 'The generalizability of psychographic market segments across geographic locations', *Journal of Marketing*, vol. 50 (January), pp. 18–27.

Leung, K. (1989), 'Cross-cultural differences: Individual level vs culture-level analysis', *International Journal of Psychology*, vol. 24, pp. 703–19.

Levitt, T. (1983), 'The globalization of markets', *Harvard Business Review*, May–June, pp. 92–102.

Marchetti, R. and J.C. Usunier (1990), 'Les problèmes de l'étude de marché dans un contexte interculturel', *Revue française du marketing*, no. 13 (May), pp. 167–84.

Mayer, C.S. (1978), 'Multinational marketing research: The magnifying glass of methodological problems', *European Research*, March, pp. 77–84.

Nath, R. (1968), 'A methodological review of cross-cultural management research', *International Social Science Journal*, vol. 20, no. 1, pp. 37–61.

Parameswaran, R. and A. Yaprak (1987), 'A cross-national comparison of consumer research measures', *Journal of International Business Studies*, Spring, pp. 35–49.

Pike, K. (1966), *Language in Relation to a Unified Theory of the Structure of Human Behavior*, Mouton: The Hague.

Plummer, J. (1977), 'Consumer focus in cross-national research', *Journal of Advertising Research*, vol. 6, Spring, pp. 5–15.

Poortinga, Ype H. (1989), 'Equivalence in cross-cultural data: An overview of basic issues', *International Journal of Psychology*, vol. 24, pp. 737–56.

Pras, B. and R. Angelmar (1978), 'Verbal rating scales for multinational research', *European Research*, March, pp. 62–7.

Prezworski, A. and H. Teune (1967), 'Equivalence in cross-national research', *Public Opinion Quarterly*, vol. 30, pp. 551–68.

Redding, S.G. (1982), 'Cultural effects on the marketing process in Southeast Asia', *Journal of the Market Research Society*, vol. 24, no. 2, pp. 98–114.

Richins, M. (1983), 'Negative word-of-mouth by dissatisfied consumers: A pilot study', *Journal of*

Marketing, vol. 47 (Winter), pp. 68–78.

Richins, M. and B. Verhage (1985), 'Cross-cultural differences in consumer attitudes and their implications for complaint management', *International Journal of Research in Marketing*, vol. 2, pp. 197–205.

Saegaert, J., E. Young and M. Wayne Saegaert (1978), 'Fad food consumption among Anglo and Mexican consumers: An example of research in consumer behavior and home economics', in H. Keith Hunt (ed.), *Advances in Consumer Research*, proceedings of the 8th annual conference, Association for Consumer Research, Ann Arbor, Michigan, USA, pp. 730–3.

Sapir, Edward (1929), 'The status of linguistics as a science', *Language*, vol. 5, pp. 207–14.

Sechrest, L., T. Fay and S.M. Zaidi (1972), 'Problems of translation in cross-cultural research', *Journal of Cross-Cultural Psychology*, vol. 3, no. 1, pp. 41–56.

Sekaran, U. (1983), 'Methodological and theoretical issues and advancements in cross-cultural research', *Journal of International Business Studies*, Fall, pp. 61–73.

Sentell, G.D. and J.W. Philpot (1984), 'A note on evaluating the representativity of samples taken in less developed countries', *International Journal of Research in Marketing*, vol. 1, pp. 81–4.

Stanton, J.L., R. Chandran and S. Hernandez (1982), 'Marketing research problems in Latin America', *Journal of the Market Research Society*, vol. 24, no. 2, pp. 124–39.

Strauss, M.A. (1969), 'Phenomenal identity and conceptual equivalence of measurement in cross-national comparative research', *Journal of Marriage and the Family*, May, pp. 223–9.

Tuncalp, S. (1988), 'The marketing research scene in Saudi Arabia', *European Journal of Marketing*, vol. 22, no. 5, pp. 15–22.

Usunier, J.C. (1991), 'Business time perceptions and national cultures: A comparative survey', *Management International Review*, vol. 31, no. 3, pp. 197–217.

Van Raaij, F.W. (1978), 'Cross-cultural research methodology as a case of construct validity', in H.K. Hunt (ed.), *Advances in Consumer Research*, vol. 5, Association for Consumer Research, Ann Arbor, pp. 693–701.

Whiting, J.W.M. (1968), 'Methods and problems in cross-cultural research', in G. Lindzey and E. Aronson (eds), *The Handbook of Social Psychology*, Addison-Wesley: Reading, MA, pp. 693–728.

Wind, Y. and S.P. Douglas (1982), 'Comparative consumer research: The next frontier', *Management Decision*, vol. 20, no. 4, pp. 24–35.

Zax, M. and S. Takashi (1967), 'Cultural influences on response style: Comparison of Japanese and American college students', *Journal of Social Psychology*, vol. 71, pp. 3–10.

PART II

Global marketing
or intercultural marketing?

6

••◆••

Globalization of markets?

'Globalization' is a simple word which has achieved great success. 'Globalization of markets' (Levitt, 1983) is an expression which relates first to demand: tastes, preferences and price-mindedness are becoming increasingly universal. Second, it relates to the supply side: products and services tend to become more standardized and competition within industries reaches a world-wide scale. Third, it relates to the way firms, mainly MNCs, try to design their marketing policies and control systems appropriately so as to remain winners in the global competition of global products for global consumers.

Globalizing means homogenizing on a world-wide scale. The implicit assumption behind the globalization process is that all the elements will globalize simultaneously. There seems to be a lot of propaganda (not in a disparaging sense) involved. As Ghoshal points out (1987, p. 425): ' "Manage globally" appears to be the latest battlecry in the world of international business.' A central assumption of globalization is that the mostly artificial trade barriers (non-tariff, regulations, industrial standards, etc.) have kept many markets at the multidomestic stage. If these barriers are removed, which is the aim of Europe 1992, 'insiders' who hold a large market share just in their home market may only be protected from new entrants by natural culture-related entry barriers.

From an international marketing point of view, which favours looking at consumers and marketing policies across countries, the idea of globalization has been strongly challenged. It has even been renamed 'the myth of globalisation' (Wind, 1986; Wind and Douglas, 1986). Little empirical evidence has been found for the world-wide homogenization of tastes and the preferences of a 'world' consumer (Dichter, 1962) for standardized, low-priced, quality goods. Those interested in the influence of culture on consumer behaviour and the implementation of marketing policies (Usunier and Sissmann, 1986; Dubois, 1987) have found arguments in favour of cultural resistance to the globalization process. Natural entry barriers related to culture seem to remain important in particular industries (food, beverages, advertising, printing and publishing, to name but a few).

The purpose of this chapter is to show that there are neither reasons nor evidence that

This chapter is largely drawn from Jean-Claude Usunier (1991), pp. 57–78. Reproduced with the kind permission of the publisher.

the globalization process occurs on the consumer's side. Paradoxically, Levitt's article remains propaganda even though McDonald's has opened a store in Moscow.

But competition is globalizing (Porter, 1986) and therefore companies tend to standardize their product mix. Globalization is an agenda for action, described in this way by several authors ('a new paradigm for international marketing', Hampton and Buske, 1987) and practised as such by many MNCs. It is a normative message rather than a clear movement towards a 'world consumer', for which empirical evidence and positive knowledge would have gathered general agreement. It may even become an over-simplified strategic message intended at clear organizational communication in a very centralized decision and implementation framework.

This chapter reviews the globalization process, conceptual literature and also empirical support at each of the following four levels:

1. Consumer behaviour: do tastes tend to homogenize? Do cross-cultural differences in consumer behaviour tend to diminish?
2. Competition: is there a clear move towards global rather than regional or local competition between companies?
3. Are company policies globalizing as international marketing programmes (standardization of product policies)?
4. Are company policies globalizing as control systems of implementation (centralization versus decentralization, organizational issues)?

6.1 Is the consumer becoming global?

There are at least three main issues under this heading:

1. What is more culture-free and what more culture-bound in terms of product categories on the one hand, and consumer behaviour on the other?
2. Is there any empirical evidence which shows that consumption patterns, tastes and preferences homogenize at world level?
3. What is the degree of autonomy of consumers in pushing or limiting the movement towards globalization? Naturally, they may or may not buy globalized products and services – to this extent they 'vote with their feet'. But they also buy what is available in stores, astutely brought to them by sophisticated merchants. In this respect there could be some resistance to change, not at the level of individual buying decisions, but at more of a macro-level: people asking to have their 'way of life' protected, especially through some kind of protectionist measures.

Culture-bound versus culture-free

It is likely that we will see greater natural entry barriers related to culture in industries that market culture-bound products or services. Consumption is tightly connected to life-styles and culture. Much evidence, even if anecdotal in nature, clearly shows that, especially in consumer goods, culture bonds are strong. For instance, symbolic associations linked to objects or colours may vary considerably across countries and cultures (Usunier, 1985).

Carlsberg had to add a third elephant to its label in Africa, since two elephants seen together are considered an ominous sign (McCornell, 1971).

On the other hand, culture bonds should not be systematically overestimated. Universal appeal for quality and low-priced products does exist. Culture bonds arise under the following conditions:

♦ A rich cultural context surrounds the product: shopping for, buying and/or consuming it (e.g. flowers, local ethnic products).
♦ There is an investment of consumers' cultural and often national background and identity in the consumption act. Consuming then becomes, consciously or unconsciously, more than simply buying for utilitarian purposes (preference for products made in one's own country, for instance, or eating habits).

The nature of the product naturally has some influence on the level of universality of needs. Non-durables appeal more to tastes, habits and customs, therefore they are more culture-bound (Douglas and Urban, 1977; Hovell and Walters, 1972). Empirical evidence (Peterson, Blyth, Cato Associates Inc. and Cheskin Masten, 1985) shows that industrial and high-technology products (for instance, computer hardware, machine tools and heavy equipment) are considered the most appropriate for global strategies, whereas clothing, confectionery, food or household cleaners are considered less appropriate.

Last but not least, language, which is a major constituent of culture, remains a strong element of culture bonds (Carroll, 1956), whether for genuinely cultural products (records, television series, newspapers, magazines, books, etc.) or for that part of all products which displays written language (packaging, brand name). In a recent empirical survey of US brands as global brands, Rosen, Boddewyn and Louis (1987) studied 650 US brands and their international scope (how many countries, the age of the brand, etc.). Their general conclusion states that:

> ... despite all the talk about the internationalisation of marketing efforts, the international diffusion of US brands is actually rather limited.... Moreover, based on the telephone follow-up responses, one suspects that if the daunting task of doing a census of all brands were to be achieved, the finding might be that most US brands are not marketed abroad. (p. 17)

Empirical evidence of consumers' globalization

Eshghi and Sheth (1985) have investigated the globalization of consumption patterns with data provided by Leo Burnett Advertising Agency. They compared life-style variables across four countries (France, Brazil, Japan and the United States). Modern life-style and traditional life-style groups were contrasted in each country. Their hypothesis was that life-style contrast (within countries) would account for more variance in consumption behaviour than the national contrast (across countries). The dependent variables were six consumption variables in dichotomous form: users versus non-users and owners versus non-owners of stereo equipment, soft drinks, fruit juices, alcoholic beverages, cars and deodorants.

Their general conclusion is as follows:

> The results ... indicated that life style influences are significant in explaining consumption behaviour, but the effect is not very strong. The data suggest that national and cultural influences continue to determine the consumption patterns across the four countries examined. But it must be emphasized that the inclusion of national identity as an independent variable in the analysis does not eliminate the effect of modern life style ... but it is not strong enough to influence consumption behaviour at this time. (Eshghi and Sheth, 1985, p. 144)

Zaichkowsky and Sood (1988) have looked at consumer involvement in fifteen countries (Argentina, Barbados, Canada, the United States, Finland, Yugoslavia, Sweden, China, Austria, Colombia, Australia, Chile, England, Mexico, France) with eight 'potentially global' products/services (air travel, beer, jeans, eating at a restaurant, hair shampoo, going to the cinema, soft drinks and stereo sets). The same questionnaire, back-translated in each language was administered to groups of approximately 50 students for each country.

The independent variables were the fifteen countries, whereas the dependent variables were, first, a PII (personal involvement inventory), intended to measure the respondents' involvement level with the goods and services, and, second, the frequency of use of each product or service over a suitable time frame (self-reported).

Results indicate that the greatest variation in use due to country effect was to be found in restaurants (22 per cent), air travel (31 per cent) and hair shampoo (45 per cent). The greatest variation in involvement levels due to country effect (i.e. as a variance source) was found in soft drinks (20 per cent) and going to the cinema (12 per cent). Stereo sets product use is weakly influenced by country effect (10 per cent) and involvement level is not related to country (1 per cent). It is difficult to draw simple conclusions about globalization as a whole from Zaichkowsky and Sood's findings. They nevertheless show clearly that the level of consumer globalization is fairly different according to which product/service category is considered.

Huszagh, Fox and Day (1986) have approached the consumption globalization process empirically by addressing three questions:

1. Which foreign markets are similar?
2. Which products exhibit potential for a global strategy by exhibiting similar acceptance rates?
3. Are there fundamental product characteristics which can explain acceptance rates?

They first clustered twenty-one countries, choosing sixteen variables such as urbanization, consumer price index, life expectancy and average working week. A subcluster of five countries (Belgium, the Netherlands, France, the United Kingdom and West Germany) was finally selected as a 'more homogeneous grouping in order to develop a more favourable empirical setting for a global marketing approach' (p. 35).

Penetration/consumption rates for twenty-seven products were collected for the five countries, and a coefficient of variation was computed for each product's penetration rate across countries. The divergence in acceptance rates (coefficients of variation) was then plotted against three product perception scales: durable/non-durable, household/personal and sensory/functional.

A rather counterintuitive result is drawn from this experimental design:

> In summary, the three plots indicate that the more nondurable/sensory/personal a product is, the more consistent the acceptance rate . . . . However the relationships are not clearly defined . . . . Nevertheless, to some extent, these patterns do support Levitt's promise that 'high touch' products are the most amenable to global marketing. (Huszagh *et al.*, 1986, p. 41)

Woods, Chéron and Kim (1985) have looked at differences in consumer purpose for purchasing in what they term 'three global markets', i.e. the United States, Canada and South Korea. The consumer purposes considered are maintenance (basic necessities, convenience), enjoyment, enhancement (satisfied self-image, improves appearance) and defence (protects health, avoids offending). Convenience samples of female shoppers in shopping centres in the United States and Canada and female workers at the workplace in Korea were chosen. Respondents were asked to indicate, for sixteen products, one or more purposes out of fourteen associated with the four major purposes indicated above.

There seems to be a larger use of products for maintenance purposes in Korea than in the United States or in Quebec, whereas US consumers are more hedonistically orientated. Both the Korean and the Québecois female consumers are more defence-orientated. Different patterns of use of products for enhancement purposes appear across the three national groups.

Woods *et al.* (1985, p. 168) conclude:

> Taken as a whole, the findings reported here indicate that the age of universal marketing is not yet upon us. The findings do reveal that Koreans, who are members of a developing economy, are thinking about products in some of the same terms as are those in the United States and Quebec. Yet important differences are found in the reasons why they purchase products familiar to all three cultures. Women in Quebec also differ from those in the United States in the reasons they purchase products. Thus, aside from the economic differences and differences in purchasing power, cultural and psychological differences are pervasive enough to call for differences in marketing strategies.

Some arguments against the existence of a global consumer

It will not be so easy to globalize consumers' motivations. Account managers working in large international advertising agencies face the complex task of managing a brand's images across several countries; they accumulate in-depth experience of consumers' response to global product offers. Harold Clark (1987) of J. Walter Thompson argues, with many practical cases at hand, the following:

1. Consumers are not 'global' themselves (national and cultural variance remains quite significant).
2. Consumers do not generally buy 'global' brands or products. They do not really care whether the brand is or is not available elsewhere in the world.
3. Since what consumers value is personal and individual, they will naturally let their individuality affect the values they place on the brands they buy. They contribute actively in this way to the *persona* of the brand in their own situation. (Clark, 1987, p. 35).

These last two arguments are very important ones. Consumers always 'construct' the identity of brands, even for 'global products', and they do so on a local culture and identity base. 'Global brands' might well be portfolios of local marketing assets, federated under a common, lexically identical name (see Box 6.1).

From this review of literature we may conclude that the globalization process is pushed on consumers rather than pulled by them, and therefore one of the main obstacles to globalization (cultural differences) tends to be neglected, despite the fact that it remains significant. These natural entry barriers related to culture are influential both in consumer behaviour and in the marketing environment where strategies are implemented. This explains many of the failures of over-globalizing marketing strategies. Many indicators of existing cultural differences do not seem to be about to vanish in the near future, for example languages, eating habits, political institutions, cultural conflicts between communities in politically homogeneous countries, etc.[1]

Evidence is at least inconclusive about globalization of consumption patterns. The issue of finding convincing positivistic-orientated proof of this process is a difficult one. A research agenda for testing consumer globalization would include such issues as the pace and process of it, the market segments involved and the geographically significant cultural areas (building on other research agendas such as Jain, 1989). There are severe methodological problems involved in such a research design. Some of these are listed under the following:

1. Which aspect of consumer behaviour is studied?: buying behaviour, shopping behaviour, life-style, values, psychometrics and underlying attitudes, influence processes (in the family, word-of-mouth communication), and so on.

Box 6.1   *'European' beers*

Typical of the diversity of the European brewing industry is how different brands in their segments are viewed from country to country. Brands, which do not have their origin in a country, which are 'foreign', are invariably viewed as premium segment products. A good example of this is BSN's Kronenbourg 1664, which is sold in France as an ordinary segment beer, but is viewed in almost all other (European) markets as a premium product. As an Italian brewer puts it: 'Foreign brands command a premium price for their image of higher quality.' However, potential hazards exist for brewers in pursing this policy: 'In Great Britain, (Belgian) Stella Artois is a premium beer, one of the most expensive beers you can get there, and people buy it because it is expensive. It is marketed and promoted that way. The British are travelling people, so now when they come to Belgium, they discover that Stella Artois is a cheap beer. So they ask themselves if it is justified to pay so much for it in Great Britain' (French brewing manager).

(Murray Steele, 1991, 'European brewing industry', in Roland Calori and Peter Lawrence (eds), *The Business of Europe*, Sage Publications: London, p. 58. Reproduced with the kind permission of the author.)

2. The use of culturally unique research concepts squeezes differences, even when the toughest cross-cultural precautions have been taken. The concepts and theories of marketing are mostly US-culture based. Their complete ability to capture consumer behaviour aspects which are absolutely specific to other cultures is questionable (Van Raaij, 1978).

3. The assimilation (often implicit) between 'national' and 'cultural' variables (country = culture) conceals the complex processes behind world-wide cultural homogenization. This relates to the problems of
   (a) clustering cultures;
   (b) treating subcultural variables within countries (Hispanics in the United States, for instance); and
   (c) questioning the relevance of geographic borders as a proxy variable for cultural borders (if any).

4. Which is the relevant sample of relevant countries and relevant products, that may help prove a trend towards globalization of consumption patterns?

5. Most of the studies are synchronic in design, because globalization is only recently being studied. In fact they should be diachronic, and look at the pace of the homogenization process by using at least two time periods. The best would be an annual survey, which could be regularly monitored in order to check whether the process is really en route on the consumer's side.

The most disputable and debatable aspect of globalization is the implicit assumption that we are all converging towards a 'modern life-style'; this controversial claim implies that the 'American way of life' would have universal appeal. The true globalization of consumption patterns will occur when the 'globalization route' ceases to be one way. Let us imagine an improbable example: some US consumers of pasteurised *foie gras* (made in the United States by French producers) ask the FDA (US Food and Drug Administration) to remove its regulation prohibiting the import of traditionally prepared French *foie gras*. FDA inspectors visit French *foie gras* laboratories and refuse most of them the right to export to the United States since hygiene standards are not met (too much antiseptic would kill the taste). If US consumers really want to become global, they will have to be able to import genuine, not pasteurised, French *foie gras*, which contains some innocent bacteria but also has real taste and consistency.

Will consumers resist the globalization process?

Another implicit assumption behind consumption-patterns globalization literature is that consumers are pleased with it (low-price, good-quality products) and therefore do not resist the process. They might, nonetheless, be self-contradicting individuals – for instance, buying P & G's Pampers for their baby, and at the same time complaining about the Americanization of society. They might resist at several levels: as citizens voting for protectionist governments, or as consumer lobbyists supporting public action (against fast food, for instance). Therefore they could lobby in order to recreate some kind of artificial entry barriers which had previously been removed.

Global marketing can be presented as a very powerful tool to promote economic development (Cundiff and Hilger, 1982). It would enhance the needs and desires of badly treated consumers who live in sellers' economies. Marketing would then favour the creation of local industries to produce consumer goods and meet their demands.

However, Belk (1988) describes a Third World consumer culture and emphasizes the hedonistic attraction for conspicuous consumption, even when basic utilitarian needs have not been met.

> One 'solution' under such circumstances is to sacrifice consumption expenditure in other areas ... in order to afford payments on such luxury items as refrigerators, televisions, and automobiles.... A reduction in food consumption in order to afford a refrigerator is more than a little ironic. (Belk, 1988, p. 118)

Thus a growing body of literature, relating to marketing and economic development, emphasizes a marketing system which 'must design, deliver, and legitimate products and services that increase the material welfare of the population by promoting equity, justice, and self reliance without causing injury to tradition' (Dholakia *et al.*, 1988, pp. 141–2). This means clearly resisting some of the uglier consequences of globalization, such as the Nestlé infant formula problem in developing countries (Sethi and Post, 1978).

There is increasing interest in marketing literature concerning 'culture' as a variable. This has long been disfavoured compared to psychological and psychosociological explanations, where the implicit model was that of a universal individual (fully in line with the globalization assumptions). This is the objective of the cognitive anthropology approach (Roth and Moorman, 1988), which tries to understand and explain the patterns in cognitive views of cultural phenomena, and to help discover why members of various cultures appear to respond to marketplace phenomena differently. This view clearly recognizes the importance of cultural group members' knowledge and beliefs in consumption patterns.

The culture of consumption is encouraging individuals to interpret their needs exclusively as needs for commodities and people may well have a need to consume culture, which is more tailored and localized (Sherry, 1987); this means consuming both local cultural products and those products whose consumption process is part of the genuine local culture. Sherry (1987, p. 189) states:

> ... the guiding rule of such a marketing strategy, as in any ethically invasive procedure, is *primum non nocere*: first do not harm. In the rush to globalization, the preservation of local culture has been considered primarily as an opportunity cost. If cultural integrity is epiphenomenal to business practice, splendid; if not, social disorganization is frequently the cost of progress.

There are of course two different (but complementary) issues here:

1. Knowing whether there are intellectual, ethical and practical reasons for protecting local cultures and consumers from the globalization of consumption patterns.
2. Identifying whether resistance mechanisms to globalization actually occur at the individual and/or social level.

This echoes Clark's (1987) arguments about false 'global' consumers, buying false 'global' products, with their own culture-bound motivations and purposes. It suggests that most of the resistance will be hidden from global marketers. One example will serve to illustrate this point: McDonald's in France, where there is great cultural resistance against fast food and hamburgers, especially as a matter of national pride. But McDonald's has achieved great success with a limited number of successful 'luxury' (high end of the market) fast-food stores located in the centre of major towns in France. Nevertheless an anti-fast-food consumer association has been established to resist the fast-food movement, and nutrition specialists have clearly shown that traditional French meals (of diverse foods, lasting one hour) is much better for digestion and prevents cancer of the digestive tract. McDonald's is quite popular with the young generation, and today's children will be tomorrow's adults and parents. At the same time, McDonald's is trying to establish some outlets at motorway crossings in the suburbs. But these outlets do not offer breakfast service: how would French people react to 'Eggs McMuffin'?[2]

If a definitive lead of globalized consumption patterns over local ones is predicted in the very long term, the process of mixing both types of consumption patterns, localized and globalized ones, will be complex. It would be worthwhile to survey some of these processes, at a micro-level and over a long period of time, in order to capture the real globalization process at work.

6.2   Is there a globalization of competition?

Evidence from macroeconomic data

There is little doubt about the globalization of competition. Market areas do not depend mainly on consumer's preferences. Their reach is influenced much more by trade barriers, whether tariff or non-tariff (that is, artificial entry barriers), and also, positively, by opportunities of economies of scale and experience effects (that is, natural entry barriers unrelated to culture). Clear evidence from macroeconomic figures shows that competition is globalizing, both at a world-wide level and at a regional level.

Over the last forty years, international trade has expanded steadily and significantly quicker than the sum of the gross national product (GNP) of the nations involved in international trade. On a common 100 basis in 1970, the index volume of world exports was 180 in 1984 against only 154 for total world output. Even more significantly, the index of total world exports of manufactured goods was 238 in 1984 and only 167 for the total world output of manufacturing industries (GATT, 1986). This relates to a long-term trend: the increase of production scales. Industrial productivity goes along with the freeing of international markets and the growth of international trade. Thus in a simple regression equation, the average world-wide industrial productivity is a very good explanatory variable of the ratio of world exports to world total output over a long period (1955–76) (Usunier, 1980).

This rule also holds true in very recent times (Ludlow, 1990): in the six years from 1983 to 1988 (inclusive) trade growth exceeded the increase in world output, generally by two or three percentage points in annual growth rate. Economic linkage between countries and therefore competition between companies continue to grow. A comparable evolution may be observed, at an even greater pace, at the regional level. Distances are less important and the move to world-wide globalization has its roots at regional level. This is part of the message of Ohmae (1985). In Europe the growth of intra-regional international trade has been much faster than the overall world trade growth during the 1960s and 1970s (Usunier, 1980). But also intra-West-Pacific trade has grown significantly more (32 per cent p.a.) from 1980 to 1988, compared to 14 per cent p.a. for the intra-western-European trade and 16 per cent p.a. for the intra-North-American trade, for the same period (Ludlow, 1990). This evidences a relative slow-down of the globalization of competition in Europe at the beginning of the 1980s. This is, however, going to change with the implementation of the EC 1992 programme and the removal of physical borders on 1 January 1993 (see Box 6.2).

Globalization of competition: evidence from business and industries

Many companies have been compelled to globalize their business, for example Black & Decker, because of fierce competition with the Japanese power-tool maker Makita. Reasons for this are stated by *Fortune* magazine, reporting the strategic move of Black & Decker towards globalization:

> Makita is Black & Decker's first competitor with a global strategy. It doesn't care that Germans prefer high powered, heavy-duty drills, and that Yanks want everything lighter. make a good drill at a low price, the company reasons, and it will sell from Baden-Baden to Brooklyn. (Saporito, 1984, p. 24)

This trend towards globalization of competition has been clearly noted, almost advertised, in business journals ('Your new global market: how to win the world war for profits and sales', cover page of *Fortune*, 14 March 1988). In most of these articles, which generally relate to competition dynamics in a specific industry, the vocabulary is often borrowed from the military: war, battlecries, strategic weapons, etc.

Naturally this is not seen so clearly in company brochures, where companies promote an image of themselves as dedicated more to customer service and to product/service integrity. Sumitomo Trading Company (Sumitomo Corporation, 1988) emphasizes that:

> the survival of the Sumitomo name for almost four centuries is testimony to the soundness of [our] business philosophy.... That is why we have the confidence to call ourselves Global Market Makers. Being global implies the worldwide, long term perspective from which we build relationships and undertake business.

Michael Porter (1986) has clearly analyzed the change in patterns of international competition. At the industry level, where competitive advantage is won or lost, there is a shift from multidomestic industries to global ones. Porter does not consider a consumer-led globalization but a strategic move of companies trying to integrate activities on a world-wide basis, to gain competitive advantage over their competitors at various levels of the value chain. Nevertheless *this process remains conditional on the maintenance of the freeing of trade barriers*, e.g. discussions in the GATT framework between nation-states. Companies, even large MNCs, are not parties to GATT multilateral trade talks. De Bettignies (1989) shows that the globalization of the Japanese economy is posing some real threats to both the United States and Europe. Therefore free trade can be maintained and expanded (to services, for instance) only if a certain equilibrium of the balance of trade of nation-states permits the maintenance of the low trade-barriers environment which favours globalization at the industry level.

6.3   International marketing strategies: are they becoming global?

Competition is becoming global, artificial entry barriers are tending to disappear. But global markets remain more apparent than real when one looks at consumption patterns (Sheth, 1986). So how can products and marketing strategies be globalized under the fierce pressure of the globalization of competition and also under the constraint of consumers who tend to resist, at least partly, the globalization movement? Here there are two major issues:

1. Standardization of marketing programmes: what should be the degree of similarity between countries in marketing activities and policies?
2. Organizational questions related to the successful implementation of the standardized marketing strategy.

Box 6.2   *Europe 1992 agenda: globalizing competition*

From the Treaty of Rome to the Single European Act, the main European treaties have always had one main focus: to increase the size of fragmented national European Markets. Custom duties have been abolished between the six founding member-states in July 1968. But the pace of integration has slowed down with the entry of new members.

Increased worldwide competition, especially coming from the Japanese and South-East Asian nations, resulted in an enhancement of awareness about the necessity to really build a large internal market (EC's White Paper, completing the internal market, 1985).

The logic which lies behind the 1992 agenda, which is an appendix of EC's 1985 White Paper, is clearly presented by the authors of the survey on the cost of non-Europe (Cecchini, 1988, p. xx, our italics):

> For business and government, *the two main actors*, the road to market integration will be paved with tough adjustments, and the need for new strategies. For business, removing protective barriers creates a permanent opportunity, but signals a *definitive end to national soft options* ... profits which derive from cashing in on monopoly or protected positions will tend to be squeezed. The situation will be one of *constant competitive renewal*.

(Usunier, 1991, p. 73. Reproduced with the kind permission of the publisher.)

Standardization of international marketing programmes

Before Buzzell's (1968) seminal article 'Can you standardize multinational market-ing?', natural entry barriers related to culture were seen as very high, commanding adaptation to national markets and offsetting the potential advantages of scale economies. Buzzell clearly showed that with the decrease of purely artificial trade barriers, large international companies could create natural entry barriers unrelated to culture through economies of scale. Since then there have been numerous texts which have sought to advise business people how to make the best choices between standardization and adaptation of marketing policies to foreign markets (for instance: Keegan, 1969; Hovell and Walters, 1972; Hout *et al.*, 1982; Hamel and Prahalad, 1985; Quelch and Hoff, 1986; Ghoshal, 1987; Hampton and Buske, 1987). This literature is normative in aim, categorizing and descriptive in nature, and oscillates between two extremes:

- On the one hand, globalization is seen as the new 'paradigm' for international marketing (Hampton and Buske, 1987). 'Consumers in increasing numbers demonstrate that they are willing to sacrifice specific preferences in product features, function and design for a globally standardized product that carries a lower price' (p. 263). According to Hampton and Buske there is a shift to the global marketing paradigm since the process of adapting products to national wants and needs contradicts their global convergence.
- On the other hand, globalization is seen as a necessary trend, but with the constraints of the environment. The physical conditions of a country as well as the laws relating to product standards, sales promotion, taxes or other aspects may affect standardization of marketing programmes, especially in developing countries (Hill and Still, 1984a).

In both cases, what consumers actually want in various national markets is not really considered: differences are either denied or treated as an external constraint. This constraint should be taken into account only when ignoring critical differences in consumer behaviour and marketing environment could lead to market failures (Ricks, 1983).

Behind the globalization debate there is a quite practical issue in terms of the everyday life of companies: the traditional dilemma between production flexibility and marketing's tendency to customize products to diversified needs. Factory managers prefer to be inflexible, for low-cost purposes, whereas marketing managers favour as much tailoring to customers' needs as possible.

Developments in factory automation nowadays allow product customization without major cost implications (Wind, 1986). New strategies have been found to serve diversified needs, customize products and at the same time maintain low costs due to economies of scale and experience effects. Modular conception of products permits shared economies of scale at the components level, whereas lagged differentiation maintains a high scale of production as long as possible in the production process and organizes cheap final customization either in the factory or in the distribution network (Stobaugh and Telesio, 1983; Deher, 1986; see Box 6.3).

So why maintain such a strong 'paradigm for action' emphasis on globalization if consumption patterns are not clearly globalizing and if adjusting to global competition is reconcilable with tailoring products and marketing strategies to national markets?

Box 6.3   *Increasing standardization of intermediary components*

In the same way as the modular design of products, the greatest possible use of standardized components in the production process enables the manufacturer to postpone final product differentiation. This involves the sharing of identical components for diverse end-consumer products: for example the same plug will fit various different appliances. These standardized components are therefore modules, which are designed to be suitable for a wide variety of possible usages. This approach allows a significant reduction in the numbers of components.

The following examples clearly illustrate the advantages of this lagged differentiation.

The crystal glassworks at Saint-Louis only have a limited number of basic moulds which they use to produce all their glassware. The many possible finishes (size, engraving, decoration, etc.) are applied at the end of the line to plain glasses. These unfinished glasses of different sizes and shapes are mass produced.

The same basic cream cheese Tartare is packaged in different ways, right at the end of the production line: packed in aluminium foil in individual servings, in a plastic tub, canned or wrapped. In other cases, a basic cheese will be flavoured differently (cherry, walnut, port wine, rose or other flower perfumes, etc.). Some packaging is standardized and can be used for different products. For example small plastic containers can be used for melted cheese as well as various types of fresh cheese.

Canson & Montgolfier manufacture papers of different weights on rolls 2.20 metres wide and several hundred metres long. This 'upstream' operation requires large-scale investment and a high level of technology, and has limited flexibility. As far as possible, each type of roll is manufactured in batches (several times a year) and stored before its final processing. Cutting, shaping and finishing is carried out on standard rolls, which are then customized to the required formats and styles of each country. At Petit-Bateau, which manufactures traditional knitwear, the knitting is done on unbleached yarn. Dying is applied to the yarn subsequently. Likewise, standardized patterns permit the creation of a large number of different clothes. At Dim, a lingerie manufacturer, tights are produced undyed. The dye, which is subcontracted, is applied at the last possible opportunity on untreated standard tights. This allows flexible tailoring to the different shades sought by consumers. Irons by SEB-Calor are all manufactured on the same moulding, which gives rise to 100 different models, according to function, colour, casing, voltage and brand name. Christofle's Arab cafetières, designed exclusively for the Middle East, are manufactured with the same stamping moulds as other cafetières.

(Deher, 1986, p. 66. Reproduced with the kind permission of the publisher.)

Globalization as a way to change the organizational design of international marketing activities

The reasons for this are mostly organizational ones. MNCs which grew fast world-wide in the 1960s and 1970s did so by granting a large degree of decisional autonomy to the subsidiaries in their home market. Subsidiaries were asked to replicate the corporate values and organizational practices of the parent company but also encouraged to adjust completely to the local market.

Later on, subsidiary managers used the message of 'our market is unique' to defend specific, nationally designed marketing policies. Hence they defended their autonomy even at the expense of sometimes rather fallacious arguments. MNCs probably needed at the beginning of the 1980s to shift their organizational design towards more centralization. Parent companies wanted to have a more united implementation scheme of new, more centrally designed international marketing strategies, responding to the globalization of competition (see Box 6.4).

Box 6.4 *Some reactions from European managers of Procter & Gamble to the Eurobrands issue*

'We have to listen to the consumer. In blind tests in my market that perfume cannot even achieve breakeven.'

'The whole detergent market is in 2-kilo packs in Holland. To go to a European standard of 3 kg. and 5 kg. sizes would be a disaster for us.'

'We have low phosphate in Italy that constrain our product formula. And we just don't have hypermarkets like France and Germany where you can drop off pallet loads.'

(*Comments of some managers in national subsidiaries*)

'There is no such thing as a Eurocustomer so it makes no sense to talk about Eurobrands. We have an English housewife whose needs are different from a German Hausfrau. If we move to a system that allows us to blur our thinking we will have big problems.

Product standardisation sets up pressures to try to meet everybody's needs (in which case you build a Rolls-Royce that nobody can afford) and countervailing pressures to find the lowest common denominator product (in which case you make a product that satisfies nobody and which cannot compete in any market). These decisions probably result in the foul middle compromise that is so often the outcome of committee decision.'

(*Comments of a general manager to P & G European headquarters*)

(Bartlett, 1983. Reproduced with permission.)

As an illustration it is worth quoting what *Fortune* magazine (Saporito, 1984, p. 26) called Black and Decker's gamble on globalization:

> Globalization did not go down well in Europe for one good reason: Black & Decker owned half the market on the continent, and an astounding 80% in the U.K. European managers asked: 'why tamper with success?'. But Farley (B & D new chairman) believed that the company was treading water in Europe – sales failed to grow last year – and that Makita's strategy made globalization inevitable.... Those who don't share Farley's vision usually don't stay around long. Last year he fired all of his European managers.

A plausible hypothesis is that the direction of causality does not go from consumption pattern globalization (as an explanatory variable) to international marketing programmes of companies (as a variable to be explained), but from real and perceived patterns of globalization of competition (exogenous) to desired changes in organizational design (recentralization, endogenous), under the constraint of hard-to-globalize-if-not-impossible consumption patterns and still diverging national environments (legal, distribution networks, sales promotion methods and so on).

Most top executives probably feel intuitively that the second model is true, but for the purpose of action it is, also probably, better to verbalize the first one. If the globalization of consumption patterns and national marketing environments is presented as an unquestionable postulate, it is much easier to 'sell' the recentralization policy within the organization than to present consumption pattern differences as a constraint on the globalization policy. In the latter case, managers of subsidiaries would be much more justified in advocating their local specificities in order to resist implicitly the recentralization policy.

If this holds true we would see some inconclusive and shallow empirical evidence when researchers look at the issue of whether international marketing programmes have experienced a trend towards greater standardization.

Picard, Boddewyn and Soehl (1989) replicated a 1973 survey by Hansen and Boddewyn (1976) of the level of standardization of European marketing policies of US multinational companies operating in Europe (fifty usable answers in 1973, seventy-one in 1983). This diachronic approach reveals mixed evolution:

- In consumer durables there was a decrease across the board in the degree of standardization of marketing policies, apart from product policy.
- In consumer non-durables, with the exception of branding, the percentage of respondents with standardized marketing policies in all EEC countries was much higher in 1983 than 1973.
- Counterintuitively, there is a significant trend away from standardization of products for industrial goods. This trend towards adaptation to national contexts is also true for other elements of the marketing mix (advertising, branding, after-sales service).

Hill and Still (1984a) examined the international marketing policies of 19 MNCs that sell to LDC (less developed countries) markets. Out of 2,200 products sold by the 61 subsidiaries in the sample, 1,200 had originated in either the United States or the United Kingdom. Their findings show that 'nearly seven changes (product adaptation) out of ten (69.4%) are marketing oriented ... for most products, the process of managing product adaptation is critical' (p. 94). They also found that greater product adaptation was required from MNCs in rural areas than in urban areas in the LDCs (Hill and Still, 1984b).

With the purpose of examining the level of advertising standardization, Ryans and Ratz (1987) exploited thirty-four usable responses from international advertising/marketing managers who were delegates at an international advertising conference. They self-reported on their company's practices, in the framework of a questionnaire survey. Ryans and Ratz's findings indicate relatively high levels of advertising standardization for campaign themes, creative execution and media execution. Only parent company managers were interviewed and their quantitative report (based on levels of agreement or disagreement on a rating scale) may be rather distanced from actual local decisions as advocated by Clark (1987). An interpretive key to their findings is offered by Ryans and Ratz themselves (1987, p. 157):

> It is interesting to observe, however, that the majority of respondents thought that usage situations for their products were very similar worldwide ... [an] explanation is that international advertising managers have adopted the position of the globalists and assume it holds true for their products.

Conclusion

At this point it is quite clear that our demonstration tends to show that globalization is a process which occurs at the competition level (where artificial entry barriers are progressively replaced by natural entry barriers related to scale and experience, especially culture-related experience) rather than at the consumer-behaviour and marketing-environments levels where natural entry barriers related to culture diminish progressively and only in the long term.

At the micro-level, companies should be very cautious about globalizing marketing strategies in Europe, for instance. Competition is globalizing, but not so much the consumers and the marketing environments. Therefore, for large companies willing to create scale advantages across European markets in culture-bound industries, it is advisable to proceed through acquisition of local companies which have culture-related national business experience. Instead of a simple global marketing strategy it is possible, as Chapter 7 emphasizes, to adopt an intercultural marketing strategy which basically follows the same goals but is more respectful of local culture and attempts to serve purely national as well as transnational market segments.

——————— ♦♦♦ ———————

Teaching materials

A6.1 Case: Parker Pen

Parker Pen Company

Parker Pen Company, the manufacturer of writing instruments based in Janesville, Wisconsin, is one of the world's best known companies in its field. It sold its products in 154 countries and considered itself number one in 'quality writing instruments,' a market that consists of pens selling for $3 or more.

In early 1984, the company launched a global marketing campaign in which everything was to have 'one look, one voice,' and with all planning to take place at headquarters. Everything connected with the selling effort was to be standardized. This was a grand experiment of a widely debated concept. A number of international companies were eager to learn from Parker's experiences.

Results became evident quickly. In February 1985, the globalization experiment was ended, and most of the masterminds of the strategy either left the company or were fired. In January 1986, the writing division of Parker Pen was sold for $100 million to a group of Parker's international managers and a London venture-capital company. The US division was given a year to fix its operation or close.

Globalization

Globalization is a business initiative based on the conviction that the world is becoming more homogeneous and that distinctions between national markets are not only fading but, for some products, they will eventually disappear. Some products, such as Coca-Cola and Levi's, have already proven the existence of universal appeal. Coke's 'one sight, one sound, one sell' approach is a legend in the world of global marketers. Other companies have some products that can be 'world products,' and some that cannot and should not be. For example, if cultural and competitive differences are less important than their similarities, a single advertising approach can exploit these similarities to stimulate sales everywhere, and at far lower cost than if campaigns were developed for each individual market.

Compared to the multidomestic approach, globalization differs in these three basic ways:

1. The global approach looks for similarities between markets. The multidomestic approach ignores similarities.
2. The global approach actively seeks homogeneity in products, image, marketing, and advertising message. The multidomestic approach produces unnecessary differences from market to market.

3. The global approach asks, 'Should this product or process be for world consumption?' The multidomestic approach, relying solely on local autonomy, never asks the question.

Globalization requires many internal modifications as well. Changes in philosophy concerning local autonomy, concern for local operating results rather than corporate performance, local strategies designed for local – rather than global – competitors, are all delicate issues to be solved. By design, globalization calls for centralized decision making; therefore, the 'not invented here' syndrome becomes a problem. This can be solved by involving those having to implement the globalization strategy at every possible stage as well as keeping lines of communication open.[3]

Globalization at Parker Pen Company

In January 1982, James R. Peterson became the president and CEO of Parker Pen. At that time, the company was struggling, and global marketing was one of the key measures to be used to revive the company. While at R.J. Reynolds, Peterson had been impressed with the industry's success with globalization. He wanted for Parker Pen nothing less than the writing-instrument equivalent of the Marlboro man.

For most of the 1960s and 1970s, a weak dollar had lulled Parker Pen into a false sense of security. About 80 percent of the company's sales were abroad, which meant that when local-currency profits were translated into dollars, big profits were recorded.

The market was changing, however. The Japanese had started marketing inexpensive disposable pens with considerable success through mass marketers. Brands such as Paper Mate, Bic, Pilot and Pentel each had greater sales, causing Parker's overall market share to plummet to 6 percent. Parker Pen, meanwhile, stayed with its previous strategy and continued marketing its top-of-the-line pens through department stores and stationery stores. Even in this segment Parker Pen's market share was eroding because of the efforts of A.T. Cross Company and Montblanc of West Germany.

Subsidiaries enjoyed a high degree of autonomy in marketing operations, which resulted in broad and diverse product lines and 40 different advertising agencies handling the Parker Pen account worldwide.

When the dollar's value skyrocketed in the 1980s, Parker's profits plunged and the loss of market share became painfully evident.

Peterson moved quickly upon his arrival. He trimmed the payroll, chopped the product line to 100 (from 500), consolidated manufacturing operations, and ordered an overhaul of the main plant to make it a state-of-the-art facility. Ogilvy & Mather was hired to take sole control of Parker Pen advertising worldwide. (Among the many agencies terminated was Lowe Howard-Spink in London, which had produced some of the best advertising for Parker Pen's most profitable subsidiary.)

A decision was also made to go aggressively after the low end of the market. The company would sell an upscale line called Premier, mainly as a positioning device. The biggest profits were to come from a rollerball pen called Vector, selling for $2.98. Plans were drawn to sell an even cheaper pen called Itala – a disposable pen never thought possible at Parker.

Three new managers, to be known as Group Marketing, were brought in. All three had extensive marketing experience, most of it in international markets. Richard Swart, who became marketing vice president for writing instruments, had handled 3M's image advertising worldwide and taught company managers the ins and outs of marketing planning. Jack Marks became head of writing instruments advertising. At Gillette he had orchestrated the worldwide marketing of Silkience hair-care products. Carlos Del Nero, brought in to be Parker's manager of global-marketing planning, had broad international experience at Fisher-Price. The concept of marketing by *centralized* direction was approved.

The idea of selling pens the same way everywhere did not sit well with many Parker subsidiaries and distributors. Pens were indeed the same, but markets, they believed, were different: France and Italy fancied expensive fountain pens; Scandinavia was a ballpoint market. In some markets, Parker could assume an above-the-fray stance; in others it had to get into the trenches and compete on price. Nonetheless, headquarters communicated to them all:

> Advertising for Parkers Pens (no matter model or mode) will be based on a common creative strategy and positioning. The worldwide advertising theme, 'Make Your Mark with Parker,' has been adopted. It will utilize similar graphic layout and photography. It will utilize an agreed-upon typeface. It will utilize the approved Parker logo/design. It will be adapted from centrally supplied materials.

Swart insisted that the directives were to be used only as 'starting points,' and that they allowed for ample local flexibility. The subsidiaries perceived them differently. The U.K. subsidiary, especially, fought the scheme all the way. Ogilvy & Mather London strongly opposed the 'one world, one brand, one advertisement' dictum. Conflict arose, with Swart allegedly shouting at one of the meetings: 'Yours is not to reason why; yours is to implement.' Local flexibility in advertising was out of the question.

The London-created 'Make Your Mark' campaign was launched in October 1984. Except for language, it was essentially the same: long copy, horizontal layout, illustrations in precisely the same place, the Parker logo at the bottom, and the tag line or local equivalent in the lower right-hand corner. Swart once went to the extreme of suggesting that Parker ads avoid long copy and use just one big picture.

Problems arose on the manufacturing side. The new $15 million plant broke down repeatedly. Costs soared and the factory turned out defective products in unacceptable numbers. In addition, the new marketing approach started causing problems as well. Although Parker never abandoned its high-end position in foreign markets, its concentration on low-price, mass-distribution products in the United States caused dilution of its image and ultimately losses of $22 million in 1985. Conflict was evident internally and the board of directors began to turn against the concept of globalization.

In January 1985, Peterson resigned. Del Nero left the company in April. Swart was fired in May, Marks in June.

(This case was prepared for discussion purposes and not to exemplify correct or incorrect decision making, in Michael R. Czinkota and Illka A. Ronkainen, 1990, pp. 778–82. Reproduced with permission.)

Questions

1. What marketing miscalculations were made by the advocates of the globalization effort at Parker Pen? (You should think in terms of product policy, target segments and competitive forces.)
2. Was the globalization strategy sound for writing instruments? If yes, what was wrong in the implementation? If not, why not?
3. Should the merits of global marketing be judged by what happened at Parker Pen Company?

A6.2 Case: Lakewood Forest Products

Since the 1970s the United States has had a merchandise trade deficit with the rest of the world. Up to 1982, this deficit mattered little because it was relatively small. As of 1983, however, the trade deficit increased rapidly and became, due to its size and future implications, an issue of major national concern. Suddenly, trade moved to the forefront of national debate. Concurrently, a debate ensued on the issue of the international competitiveness of U.S. firms. The onerous question here was whether U.S. firms could and would achieve sufficient improvements in areas such as productivity, quality, and price to remain long-term successful international marketing players.

   The U.S.–Japanese trade relation took on particular significance, because it was between those two countries that the largest bilateral trade deficit existed. In spite of trade negotiations, market-opening measures, trade legislation, and other governmental efforts, it was clear that the impetus for a reversal of the deficit through more U.S. exports to Japan had to come from the private sector. Therefore, the activities of any U.S. firm that appeared successful in penetrating the Japanese market were widely hailed. One company whose effort to market in Japan aroused particular interest was Lakewood Forest Products, in Hibbing, Minnesota.

Company background

In 1983, Ian J. Ward was an export merchant in difficulty. Throughout the 1970s his company, Ward, Bedas Canadian Ltd., had successfully sold Canadian lumber and salmon to countries in the Persian Gulf. Over time, the company had opened four offices worldwide. However, when the Iran–Iraq war erupted, most of Ward's long-term trading relationships disappeared within a matter of months. In addition, the international lumber market began to collapse. As a result, Ward, Bedas Canadian Ltd. went into a survivalist mode and sent employees all over the world to look for new markets and business opportunities. Late that year, the company received an interesting order. A firm in Korea urgently needed to purchase lumber for the production of chopsticks.

Learning about the chopstick market

In discussing the wood deal with the Koreans, Ward learned that in order to produce good chopsticks more than 60 percent of the wood fiber would be wasted. Given the high transportation cost involved, the large degree of wasted materials, and his need for new business, Ward decided to explore the Korean and Japanese chopstick industry in more detail.

He quickly determined that chopstick making in the Far East is a fragmented industry, working with old technology and suffering from a lack of natural resources. In Asia, chopsticks are produced in very small quantities, often by family organizations. Even the largest of the 450 chopstick factories in Japan turns out only 5,000,000 chopsticks a month. This compares to an overall market size of 130 million pairs of disposable chopsticks a day. In addition, chopsticks represent a growing market. With increased wealth in Asia, people eat out more often and therefore have a greater demand for disposable chopsticks. The fear of communicable diseases has greatly reduced the utilization of reusable chopsticks. Renewable plastic chopsticks have been attacked by many groups as too new fangled and as causing future ecological problems.

From his research, Ward concluded that a competitive niche existed in the world chopstick market. He believed that, if he could use low-cost raw materials and assure that the labor cost component would remain small, he could successfully compete in the world market.

The founding of Lakewood Forest Products

In exploring opportunities afforded by the newly identified international marketing niche for chopsticks, Ward set four criteria for plant location:

1. Access to raw materials.
2. Proximity of other wood product users who could make use of the 60 percent waste for their production purposes.
3. Proximity to a port that would facilitate shipment to the Far East.
4. Availability of labor.

In addition, Ward was aware of the importance of product quality. Because people use chopsticks on a daily basis and are accustomed to products that are visually inspected one by one, he would have to live up to high quality expectations in order to compete successfully. Chopsticks could not be bowed or misshapen, have blemishes in the wood, or splinter.

In order to implement his plan, Ward needed financing. Private lenders were skeptical and slow to provide funds. This skepticism resulted from the unusual direction of Ward's proposal. Far Eastern companies have generally held the cost advantage in a variety of industries, especially those as labor-intensive as chopstick manufacturing. U.S. companies rarely have an advantage in producing low-cost items. Further, only a very small domestic market exists for chopsticks.

However, Ward found that the state of Minnesota was willing to participate in his new venture. Since the decline of the mining industry, regional unemployment had been rising rapidly in the state. In 1983, unemployment in Minnesota's Iron Range peaked at 22 percent. Therefore, state and local officials were anxious to attract new industries that would be independent of mining activities. They were excited about Ward's plans, which called for the creation of over 100 new jobs within a year.

Hibbing, Minnesota, turned out to be an ideal location for Ward's project. The area had an abundance of supply of aspen wood, which, because it grows in clay soil, tends to be unmarred. In addition, Hibbing boasted an excellent labor pool, and both the city and the state were willing to make loans totaling $500,000. Further, the Iron Range Resources Rehabilitation Board was willing to sell $3.4 million in industrial revenue bonds for the project. Together with jobs and training wage subsidies, enterprise zone credits, and tax increment financing benefits, the initial public support of the project added up to about 30 percent of its start-up costs. The potential benefit of the new venture to the region was quite clear. When Lakewood Forest Products advertised its first 30 jobs, more than 3,000 people showed up to apply.

The production and sale of chopsticks

Ward insisted that in order to truly penetrate the international market, he would need to keep his labor cost low. As a result, he decided to automate as much of the production as possible. However, no equipment was readily available to produce chopsticks, because no one had automated the process before.

After much searching, Ward identified a European equipment manufacturer who produced machinery for making popsicle sticks. He purchased equipment from this Danish firm in order to better carry out the sorting and finishing processes. However, because aspen wood was quite different from the wood the machine was designed for, as was the final product, substantial design adjustments had to be made. Sophisticated equipment was also purchased to strip the bark from the wood and peel it into long thin sheets. Finally, a computer vision system was acquired to detect defects in the chopsticks. The system rejected over 20 percent of the production, and yet some of the chopsticks that passed inspection were splintering. However, Ward firmly believed that further fine-tuning of the equipment and training of the new work force would gradually take care of the problem.

Given this fully automated process, Lakewood Forest Products was able to develop capacity for up to 7,000,000 chopsticks a day. With unit manufacturing cost of $0.03 and an anticipated unit selling price of $0.057, Ward expected to earn a pretax profit of $4.7 million in 1988.

Due to intense marketing efforts in Japan and the fact that Japanese customers were struggling to obtain sufficient supplies of disposable chopsticks, Ward was able to presell the first five years of production quite quickly. By late 1987, Lakewood Forest Products was ready to enter the international market. With an ample supply of raw materials and an almost totally automated plant, Lakewood was positioned as the world's largest and least labor-intensive manufacturer of chopsticks. The first shipment of six containers with a load of 12,000,000 pairs of chopsticks to Japan was made in October 1987.

(Michael R. Czinkota, in Michael R. Czinkota and Illka A. Ronkainen, 1990, pp. 472–5. Reproduced with permission.)

Questions

1. Why haven't Japanese firms thought of automating the chopstick production process?
2. What are the important variables for the international marketing success of chopsticks?
3. Rank, in order, the variables in Question 2 according to the priority you believe they have for foreign customers, especially Japanese and Korean consumers.
4. How long will Lakewood Forest Products be able to maintain its competitive advantage?

Notes

1. The IKEA case at the end of chapter 7 and Lakewood Forest Products case at the end of this chapter will help the reader reflect on those cases where consumers accept product standardization.
2. I would like not like to be understood: this example should not be interpreted as anti-McDonald's. I have been a loyal consumer of McDonald's in many places of the world. But one cannot pretend that McDonald's has no cultural influence in foreign (non-US) countries.
3. Laurence Farley (1985), 'Going Global: Choices and challenges', presented at the American Management Association Conference, 10 June, Chicago, IL.

References

Bartlett, Christopher (1983), 'Procter & Gamble Europe: Vizir launch', *Harvard Business School Case* 9-384-139.
Belk, Russell W. (1988), 'Third World consumer culture', in E. Kumçu and A. Fuat Firat (eds), *Marketing and Development: Toward broader dimensions*, JAI Press: Greenwich, CT, pp. 103–27.
Buzzell, Robert D. (1968), 'Can you standardize multinational marketing?', *Harvard Business Review*, November–December, pp. 102–13.
Carroll, John B. (1956), *Language, Thought and Reality: Selected writings of Benjamin Lee Whorf*, MIT Press: Cambridge, MA.
Cecchini, Paolo (1988), *The European Challenge 1992*, Wildwood House: Aldershot.
Clark, Harold F., Jr (1987), 'Consumer and corporate values: Yet another view on global marketing', *International Journal of Advertising*, vol. 6, pp. 29–42.
Cundiff, Edward W. and Marye Tharp Hilger (1982), 'The consumption function: Marketing's role in economic development', *Management Decision*, vol. 20, no. 4, pp. 36–45.
Czinkota, Michael R. and Illka A. Ronkainen (1990), *International Marketing*, 2nd edn, Dryden Press: Hinsdale, IL.
De Bettignies, Henri (1989), 'The globalization of the Japanese economy: Implications for Europe and the United States', *IBEAR*, University of Southern California, 1989/5.

Deher, Odile (1986), 'Quelques facteurs de succès pour la politique de produits de l'entreprise exportatrice: les liens entre marketing et production', *Recherche et applications en marketing*, vol. 1, no. 3, pp. 55–74.

Dholakia, Ruby Roy, Mohammed Sharif and Labdhi Bhandari (1988), 'Consumption in the Third World: Challenges for marketing and economic development', in E. Kumçu and A. Fuat Firat (eds), *Marketing and Development: Toward Broader Dimensions*, JAI Press: Greenwich, CT, pp. 129–47.

Dichter, Ernest (1962), 'The world consumer', *Harvard Business Review*, vol. 40, no. 4, pp. 113–22.

Douglas, Susan P. and Christine D. Urban (1977), 'Life-style analysis to profile women in international markets', *Journal of Marketing*, vol. 41 (July).

Eshghi, Abdolezra and Jagdish N. Sheth (1985), 'The globalization of consumption patterns: An empirical investigation', in Erdener Kaynak (ed.), *Global Perspectives in Marketing*, Praeger: New York, pp. 133–48.

GATT (1986), *Le Commerce International en 1985–1986*, GATT: Geneva.

Ghoshal, Sumantra (1987), 'Global strategy: An organizing framework', *Strategic Management Journal*, vol. 8, pp. 425–40.

Hamel, Gary and C. K. Prahalad (1985), 'Do you really have a global strategy?', *Harvard Business Review*, vol. 63, July–August, pp. 139–48.

Hampton, Gerald M. and Erwin Buske (1987), 'The global marketing perspective', in S. Tamer Cavugsil (ed.), *Advances in International Marketing*, JAI Press: Greenwich, CT, vol. 2, pp. 259–77.

Hansen, D. M. and J.J. Boddewyn (1976), *American Marketing in the European Common Market, 1963–1973*, Marketing Science Institute: Cambridge, MA, report no. 76-107.

Hill, John S. and Richard R. Still (1984a), 'Adapting products to L.D.C. tastes', *Harvard Business Review*, March–April, pp. 92–101.

Hill, John S. and Richard R. Still (1984b), 'Effects of urbanization on multinational product planning: Markets in L.D.C.s', *Columbia Journal of World Business*, vol. 19 (Summer), pp. 62–7.

Hout, Thomas, Michael E. Porter and Eileen Rudden (1982), 'How global companies win out', *Harvard Business Review*, vol. 60, September–October, pp. 98–105.

Hovell, P.J. and P.G.P. Walters (1972), 'International marketing presentations: Some options', *European Journal of Marketing*, vol. 6, no. 2, pp. 69–79.

Huszagh, Sandra M., Richard J. Fox and Ellen Day (1986), 'Global marketing: An empirical investigation', *Columbia Journal of World Business*, vol. xx, no. 4, pp. 31–43.

Jain, Subhash C. (1989), 'Standardization of international marketing strategy: Some research hypotheses', *Journal of Marketing*, vol. 53, January, pp. 70–9.

Keegan, Warren J. (1969), 'Multinational product planning: Strategic alternatives', *Journal of Marketing*, vol. 33, January, pp. 58–62.

Levitt, Theodore (1983), 'The globalization of markets', *Harvard Business Review*, vol. 61 (May–June), pp. 92–102.

Ludlow, Peter W. (1990), 'Global challenges of the 1990s: Future of the international trading system', *Economic Impact*, 1990/1, pp. 4–10.

McCornell, J.D. (1971), 'The economics of behavioral factors in the multinational corporation', in Fred E. Allvine (ed.), *Combined Proceedings of the American Marketing Association*, p. 260.

Ohmae, Kenichi (1985), *Triad Power: The coming shape of global competition*, The Free Press: New York.

Peterson, Blyth, Cato Associates Inc. and Cheskin Masten (1985), 'Survey on global brands and global marketing', Empirical Report, New York.

Picard Jacques, J.J. Boddewyn and Robin Soehl (1989). 'U.S. marketing policies in the European

Economic Community: A longitudinal study, 1973–1983', in Reijo Luostarinen (ed.), *Dynamics of International Business*, proceedings of the 15th annual conference of the EIBA, Helsinki, vol. 1, pp. 551–79.

Porter, Michael E. (1986), 'Changing patterns of international competition', *California Management Review*, vol. xxviii, no. 2, pp. 9–39.

Quelch, John A. and Edward J. Hoff (1986), 'Customizing global marketing', *Harvard Business Review*, vol. 64, May–June, pp. 59–68.

Ricks, David A. (1983), *Big Business Blunders: Mistakes in multinational marketing*, Dow Jones-Irwin: Homewood, IL.

Rosen, Barry-Nathan, Jean J. Boddewyn and Ernst A. Louis (1987), 'US brands abroad: An empirical study of global branding', *International Marketing Review*, vol. 6, no. 1, pp. 7–19.

Roth, M.S. and C. Moorman (1988), 'The cultural content of cognition and the cognitive content of culture: Implications for consumer research', in M.J. Houston (ed.), *Advances in Consumer Resarch*, Association for Consumer Research: Provo, UT, vol. 15, pp. 403–10.

Ryans, John K. and David G. Ratz (1987), 'Advertising standardization: A re-examination', *International Journal of Advertising*, vol. 6, pp. 145–58.

Saporito, Bill (1984), 'Black & Decker's gamble on globalization', *Fortune*, 14 May, pp. 24–32.

Sethi, S.P. and J.E. Post (1978), 'Infant formula marketing in less developed countries: An analysis of secondary effect', in S.C. Jain (ed.), *AMA Educators Proceedings*, American Marketing Association: Chicago, pp. 271–5.

Sherry, John F. (1987), 'Cultural propriety in a global marketplace', in A. Fuat Firat, Nikhilesh Dholakhia and Richard P. Bagozzi (eds), *Philosophical and Radical Thought in Marketing*, Lexington Books: Lexington, MA.

Sheth, Jagdish N. (1986), 'Global markets or global competition?', *Journal of Consumer Marketing*, vol. 3 (Spring), pp. 9–11.

Stobaugh, Robert and Piero Telesio (1983), 'Assortir la politique de fabrication à la stratégie des produits', *Harvard-L'Expansion* (Summer), pp. 77–85.

Sumitomo Corporation (1988), *Global Market Makers*, Sumitomo Shoji Kaisha: Tokyo.

Usunier, Jean-Claude (1980), 'Les Lois de déformation des réseaux du commerce international', unpublished doctoral thesis, University of Paris II.

Usunier, Jean-Claude (1985), 'Adaptation ou standardisation internationale des produits: une tentative de synthèse', proceedings of the annual conference of the French Association of Marketing, Le Touquet.

Usunier, Jean-Claude (1991), 'The "European consumer": Globalizer or globalized?', in Alan Rugman and Alain Verbeke (eds), *Research in Global Strategic Management*, vol. 2, JAI Press: Greenwich, CT, pp. 57–78.

Usunier, Jean-Claude and Pierre Sissmann (1986), 'L'Interculturel au service du marketing', *Harvard-L'Expansion*, no. 40 (Spring), pp. 80–92.

Van Raaij, F.W. (1978), 'Cross-cultural research methodology as a case of construct validity', in H.K. Hunt (ed.), *Advances in Consumer Research*, vol. 5, Association for Consumer Research: Ann Arbor, pp. 693–701.

Wind, Yoram (1986), 'The myth of globalization', *Journal of Consumer Marketing*, vol. 3, (Spring) pp. 23–6.

Wind, Yoram and Susan P. Douglas (1986), 'Le Mythe de la globalisation', *Recherche et applications en marketing*, vol. 1, no. 3.

Woods, Walter A., Emmanuel J. Chéron and Dong Han Kim (1985), 'Strategic implications of differences in consumer purposes in three global markets', in Erdener Kaynak (ed.), *Global Perspectives in Marketing*, Praeger: New York, pp. 155–70.

Zaichkowsky, Judith L. and James H. Sood (1988), 'A global look at consumer involvement and use of products', *International Marketing Review*, vol. 6, no. 1, pp. 20–33.

7

───── ◆◆◆ ─────

Intercultural marketing

Clearly then, globalization is really a process that occurs at the competition level. Artificial entry barriers, mostly tariff and non-tariff, are progressively replaced by natural entry barriers related to scale and experience. As far as consumer behaviour and marketing environments are concerned, natural entry barriers related to culture will diminish progressively and only in the long run. Global marketing is often said to be the only possible solution for marketing in 'the global village'. This book supports the opposite viewpoint, since there are still many very different (marketing) 'villages'. In this chapter the following ideas are defended:

1. Strategic management has to be 'global', whereas marketing management needs to be tailored to local contexts.
2. An intercultural orientation to international marketing best serves a global strategic view.[1]

7.1 Why global strategies exist, but global marketing does not

Multidomestic and global markets

This distinction, evidenced by Michael Porter, has been widely applied since the beginning of the 1980s. At the industry level, there is a shift from multidomestic competition patterns to global ones. According to Porter, competition becomes global when 'a firm's competitive position is significantly affected by its position in other countries and vice-versa' (1986, p. 18). When an industry is multidomestic, separate strategies are pursued in different national markets, and the competitive scene remains basically a domestic one. There are some fundamental reasons for industries to remain multidomestic:

- Wide differences in consumer needs and attitudes across markets.
- Legal barriers resulting from domestic regulations (which has long been the case of banking and insurance).

♦ Non-tariff barriers which artificially maintain competition between purely national competitors (food and drug health regulations, for instance).

Accordingly, the basic preoccupation of a global strategy is (very briefly defined) the configuration and co-ordination of activities, including marketing, across national markets.

Trends towards global (competitive) markets

There are clear trends towards the globalization of competition which have been detailed in section 6.2. Nevertheless the trends towards global markets differ fairly widely depending on the industry. The causes are multiple:

1. The influence of national regulations and non-tariff barriers varies to a large degree across product categories.
2. The potential for experience effects also varies across product categories: for example, there is less potential for cost reduction due to volume increase in the case of cheeses compared to microchips.
3. International 'transportability', in other words, to what extent do transportation costs impinge on the degree and patterns of globalization of an industry? Exporting may be the dominant pattern for easily transportable products. Direct foreign investment may be the prevailing one for industries whose products are expensive to transport long distance.
4. The degree of culture bonding to a product: once again, the trend towards globalization in the cheese industry is slower (although clearly existent) than the trend towards globalization in the microchip industry.

Experience effects

The *ab initio* experience effects potential differs widely across product categories. The Boston Consulting Group has isolated one of the main reasons for this through research into the success of various companies, Japanese included, in global markets. Experience effects provide companies with the ability to reduce units costs dramatically through an increase in product quantity. The experience effects determine the relationship of unit cost to cumulated production volume according to the following formula:

$C_n = C_1 n^{-\lambda}$

where

C_n is the cost of the nth unit;
C_1 is the cost of the first unit;
n is the cumulated number of units produced;
λ is the elasticity of the unit cost with respect to the cumulated production volume.

The form of the function reflects a constant elasticity. Let us call k the effect of elasticity. When production is doubled, the cost (therefore to a certain extent the price)[2] will decrease by $1 - k = 1 - 2^{-\lambda}$ per cent each time the experience doubles.

If, for example, *k* equals 70 per cent, the cost will decrease by 30 per cent on a doubling of the cumulated production (1–70% = 30%). Experience effects theory has been supported by empirical verification (Day and Montgomery, 1983).[3] Experience effects have been estimated for such diverse products and services as long-distance telephone calls in the United States, bottle tops in West Germany, refrigerators in Great Britain and Japanese motorcycles.

The source of experience effects is fourfold:

1. The effects of *learning by doing*. The more times one carries out a task or manufactures a component or a product, the more efficiently it is done or, alternatively, the less time is taken to do so.
2. *Scale effects*. By increasing the scale of production, the average cost can be reduced. Many industrial products require a large amount of research and development for product design, yet only a small quantity of raw materials for their manufacture (e.g. pocket calculators).
3. *Technological advances*. The increase in cumulated production offers a dual possibility of technological improvements. On one hand, production equipment may be refined; on the other hand, the product itself can be simplified and rendered cheaper to produce. These product simplifications usually result from a decrease in the number of parts, and not from a reduction in the number of functions and the degree of sophistication, which would adversely affect the consumer.
4. *Economies of scope*: component parts may be shared by different products. For instance, the same basic diesel engine may be used for a fork-lift elevator, a small truck, a van, a car, or as an on-board motor for a boat, at the expense of slight final adaptations. The increase in the production scale of shared components (or shared overhead costs, or any kind of shared common inputs) results in economies of scope.

Not every product has the same potential for experience effects. The potential is clearly smaller for cheese or books than for hi-fi systems or microcomputers. An examination of Japanese successes in world markets demonstrates that they have concentrated on goods that have very high experience effects, such as motorcycles, motor cars, photocopiers, video equipment, hi-fi systems, television sets, outboard motors, musical instruments and cameras. Right from the start, Japanese companies opted for global markets, even though their domestic market for such products was itself very substantial. Competitors have struggled to resist the competitive pressure of Japanese companies. The motorcycle industry is typical of the lack of experience effects amongst European manufacturers.

In an attempt to compete with the Japanese (Honda, Yamaha, Suzuki, Kawazaki) Motobécane, a French manufacturer,[4] launched a 125cc motorcycle several years ago. This model had a two-stroke engine that operated on a mixture of petrol and oil, since Motobécane was unable to make a four-stroke engine,[5] like Honda, or an 'oil lube' (a device for mixing oil and petrol automatically). This motorcycle emitted a thick cloud of white smoke through its exhaust. The range of models offered has remained very limited, as with other French motorcycles. The 350cc Motobécane, which could have enjoyed a lucrative market by supplying the French police, was not fast or reliable enough. The 125cc as well as the 350cc were complete flops. Motobécane remained a company operating mainly in the French domestic market and as a result the company was undersized. The lack of experience effects in the company was a barrier to technological improvements.

International transportability

The unit weight, that is, dollar price per kilogram or per pound, differs widely across category of goods, and therefore across the industries that manufacture them. Cement or basic ordinary steel products range from 50 cents per kilogram to several dollars per kilogram, whereas cars range from 10 dollars per kilogram (for example, a small family car at the bottom end of the market) to 60 or 70 dollars per kilogram for luxury cars at the top end of the market (large Mercedes, BMWs or Jaguars). A portable computer may reach a price of 750 dollars per kilogram (or even more), not to mention its component chips which may climb to several thousand dollars per kilogram.

In the international transportation system, shipping charges do not follow a simple tariff, which would be directly proportional to weight. They are calculated on the basis of a mix of criteria, depending on the nature of goods to be shipped and on the shipping line. Shipping lines are also subject to economies of scale. Transportation cost factors are influenced by the forces of competition between transportation companies, and also by the method of transportation (ship, aeroplane, truck or train). The mix of criteria includes weight, volume, dimensions, ease of loading and unloading, perishability, packaging, and speed of delivery. However, weight, volume and perishability are clearly the most detrimental factors to the ease of international transportation.

Some markets will remain almost exclusively multidomestic, because some goods and services cannot be transported – hairdressing services, for instance.[6] Although transportability may have a negative influence on the cross-border transactions of goods and services, it does not hamper the globalization of an industry where cross-border investments are possible. In the cement industry, markets are regionally segmented within countries because of the high cost of transportation in proportion to basic unit price. The cement industry still competes on a global basis through international investments and also the sale and licensing of technology.

Transportability concerns not only the product, but sometimes also the consumer. This leads to the question of whether consumers are transportable, rather than the products or services which are offered to them. Ski resorts are a good example: ski slopes, buildings and equipment are not transportable, nor is snow. But potential skiers may be transported at low cost on charter flights, from countries without mountains, snow or ski resorts (but with some purchasing power). Thus we may observe in the international ski-resort industry a twofold pattern of globalization. On the one hand, some world-famous ski resorts, such as Val d'Isère in France, Kitzbühel in Austria or Zermatt in Switzerland, enjoy a global market. People arrive from many parts of the world, often on package holidays sold by tour operators or travel agencies. On the other hand, there remains in most ski-orientated countries a large number of purely local ski resorts ('ski villages') which compete on a more domestic basis. This part of the industry is multidomestic. Between these two segments, one globalized, one multidomestic, there are in fact many intermediate ski resorts which compete on a regionally globalized basis. This is the case with most medium-size ski resorts in the European Alps: in Austria, France, Germany, Italy, Switzerland and some East European countries,[7] which compete for European skiers.

The disconnection between sourcing and marketing

The countries where sourcing and marketing take place may be highly disconnected in industries which compete on a global basis. The sites of most cost-efficient production are often export processing zones in newly industrialized countries. Consumer markets may be located in very remote places. In Chapter 8, the case of 'multinational production' is reviewed. The same brand may be 'made in' various countries which generate different country-of-origin images. Consumers, who use country of origin as an information cue for comparing brands, are now becoming more and more aware of the actual disconnection between sourcing and marketing. It re-emphasizes how strongly marketing globalization (that is, demand-side globalization) is disconnected from competition globalization (that is, supply-side).

Culture-bound versus culture-free: the European case

The distinction between culture-bound and culture-free products or services may also exert an influence on the degree and pace of the globalization of competition, as the example of competition in Western (EEC) Europe demonstrates.

In 1962 Fournis remarked that there cannot be such an individual as a 'European consumer' since customs and traditions tend to persist. European countries, and cultures, are deeply rooted in the past. Furthermore a long history of wars and conflicts has maintained strong feelings of national identity. Diverging economic performance between northern and southern Europe has fed sharp income-per-capita differences which, added to behaviour differences between European consumers, have been found to discourage globalization (Boddewyn, 1981). Naturally, European cultures share some common cultural values: the majority of them, regarding the events of life (birth, marriage and death), share a set of values which differentiates Occidental culture from Oriental. The showing of emotions, for instance, differs widely between Europeans and Asians; and where Orientals tend to favour group harmony, Europeans choose self-esteem and respect of individuals (Valette-Florence, 1990).

Nevertheless this apparent cultural homogeneity of Europe, when compared to Asia, ceases to be so clear when we look at cultural variance within Europe. Stoetzel (1983), who observed public opinion polls in Europe over a period of years ('Eurobarometer'), shows that there are more 'European cultures' than a 'European culture' as such. Family relation patterns, morals and elements of everyday life such as meals and social, family and business life tend to be somewhat heterogeneous (see Box 7.1).

There still exist huge differences in the pattern of household expenditure across EC countries. For instance in 1982, UK households spent 14.7 per cent of their budget on food, West Germany 14.6 per cent, Portugal 37 per cent and Greece 35.6 per cent. The average EC figure at the same time was 20.5 per cent. Italian people consumed 152 kilograms per year of vegetables, the French 108 kilograms, and the Germans only 81 kilograms. French people consume 20.9 kilograms per year of cheese compared to 4.7 kilograms for the Spanish and 6.3 kilograms for the British (source: OECD, year 1985). Many other examples could be cited, such as beverages and newspapers.

Box 7.1   *Does the European consumer need a European culture?*

An implicit assumption underlying the treaties building the European Community is the respect of national cultures and identities. This assumption is extremely strong and time-resistant. A very basic element of this is language. The original six countries had four different languages, the current twelve have ten languages. One of them, Gaelic, the original national language of Ireland is almost no longer in use in its very home country. As a result of the 'Babel Tower' aspect of this incredible situation and the communication difficulties which arise from it, an army of more than 3,000 full time translators are employed by the EEC.

The issue of a common language for Europe has never been addressed, at least publicly. It is a taboo, even an absolute taboo. In the Single European Act of 1987, the article 34 states that: 'This act [is] drawn up in a single original in the Danish, Dutch, English, French, German, Greek, Irish, Italian, Portuguese and Spanish languages, the texts in each of these languages being equally authentic...' (European Communities, 1987, p. 574).

One of the main proponents of the tabooing of the common European language issue is France. There is great pride in France about the French language. It is recognized as one of the two official languages of the United Nations, on a par-basis with English. French people adopt a rather defensive attitude in the face of English. The French authorities have regularly issued during the last fifteen years official decrees prohibiting the use of English words, especially business words, in French texts (Usunier, 1990). French fears are very typical of resistance to globalization, since it is believed that through consumption patterns the whole French society and culture could be 'Americanized'. We are fascinated by the American Way of Life as an exotic item. But many French people, including politicians, would be horrified to have it 'at home'. Although the fears are perhaps justified, the defensive measures are certainly inadequate.

Northern European countries show that it is quite feasible to have a twin-language culture. The 'local' culture corresponds to ethnic ways of life and consumption patterns, which are not to be globalized. The other half is English language based. it corresponds to international life-style and globalized consumption patterns. Television channels in English like Sky Channel and Super Channel can be seen in any Northern European country. This is not the case in France where the development of cable-television has been restricted. A few years ago the number of householders with cable television in France was half that of Ireland, a country with 15 times less population, and a much lower per capita purchasing power.

Most people believe that satellite TV in Europe, and other new communication technology will encourage standardization of the profile of the European Consumer (Valette-Florence, 1991; Usunier and Sissmann, 1986). A common European language would greatly facilitate the construction of a common European culture, and thereby lead to the emergence of new European consumption patterns.

(Jean-Claude Usunier, 1991, 'The "European consumer": Globalizer or globalized?', in Alan Rugman and Alain Verbeke (eds), *Research in Global Strategic Management*, vol. 2, JAI Press: Greenwich, CT, pp. 73–75. Reproduced with the kind permission of the publisher.)

Marketing strategies for culture-bound products will still need a great deal of tailoring to each national market, or to groups of countries, even after 1992. Beer, for instance, is subject to differences in national tastes, in terms of being more or less bitter, foamy, bubbly, sugary, alcoholic, etc. Even companies such as Heineken, which is the leading European beer producer, will continue to tailor their products and marketing policies even after 1992 (distribution systems for beer also differ widely in Europe). Whitelock (1987) shows that standard sizes for pillowcases vary in the various European national markets: 60×75 centimetres in Great Britain, 65×65 in France, 60×70 in the Netherlands and 80×80 in West Germany. He interviewed various textile companies which all agreed on the necessity to adapt sizes, even after 1992. Nivea skin care cream, produced by the German multinational company Beiersdorf (BDF), has a large share in each national market in Europe. Nevertheless its consistency has to be changed and its formula adapted according to whether it is sold in northern Europe or in southern Europe, and 1992 will not change this adaptation requirement (Mourier and Burgaud, 1989).

What is a global strategy?

A world view versus a local view

A 'global strategy' clearly implies a world view of competition and competitive advantage, not simply a belief that consumers and markets are themselves global. The issue of global strategies has been extensively documented in the strategic management literature;[8] it is clearly outside the scope of this book, which emphasizes the cultural dimensions of international marketing, to discuss in full detail the specific issues related to global strategies.

In cultural terms, the ethnocentrism of the managing team of any company is evidenced by the way in which it treats the domestic/national market on one hand and 'foreign' markets on the other. This issue is not purely academic; it permeates the ways in which a company organizes its international activities and the nationalities of its top executives, as well as other more practical considerations such as the choice of the language(s) to be spoken between subsidiaries and head office.

Once the company has achieved a certain level of development in foreign markets, the 'export' view and the 'international development' view can no longer co-exist effectively. They are dependent on four different perspectives: ethnocentrism, polycentrism, regiocentrism and geocentrism, two of these (ethno- and geocentrism) being somewhat irreconcilable. This is illustrated by Figure 7.1.

In terms of sets theory, the domestic market is perceived as disjointed from foreign markets, whereas in the geocentric view, the domestic market is seen as belonging to the world market in the same way as any other domestic market. Ethnocentric companies view international operations as secondary to their domestic operations. A company that considers its national base as a top priority will impose its own language on its foreign subsidiaries. It will supply the domestic market first when production capacity is overstretched. It will never invite a non-national onto the board of directors unless this person shares the company's native language and culture. Conversely the firm that considers its national base as just one of many, a geocentric company, will make the opposite choices. This is in line with the distinction made by Wind, Douglas and Perlmutter (1973) in the ERPG model (ethnocentric, polycentric, regiocentric, geocentric) of behaviour of international companies. Polycentrism results from the recognition of differences that occur in overseas markets. Each country is accepted as one of many ethnocentric places which may have their own marketing policies and programmes. Regiocentrism reflects the change of a company towards a more open understanding of world marketing, where regional marketing strategies are designed (see Figure 7.1).

When companies distance themselves from an ethnocentric attitude by virtue of their management style and corporate culture, they develop genuinely offensive and defensive

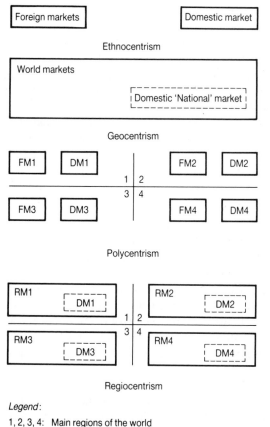

Figure 7.1 Four different views of how a company's domestic market is related to world markets.

marketing strategies in foreign markets. Such a strategy manifests itself in flexible reallocation of resources from one market to another. For instance, a company will relocate into market Y, where it holds a solid position, as a reaction to one large competitor launching a price offensive in country X. This type of situation is conceivable in strongly oligopolistic markets where several (five to ten) large multinationals control the world market, as happens in the food industry or the liquified gases industry.

Nevertheless it seems that stiff competition gives way to forms of co-operation between large companies from developed countries. The theory developed by Kenichi Ohmae, head of the Tokyo office of McKinsey Consultants, in his book *Triad Power: The coming shape of global competition* (1985), emphasizes the need for companies who want to survive international competition to have a solid base in each of the three major industrialized regions' market areas: North America, Japan and Europe. Ohmae further suggests that in each of these regions, companies should establish links of international division of labour with neighbouring developing countries. Companies in Latin-American countries are natural subcontractors for North American companies. Southeast Asian countries subcontract for Japanese firms. The same co-operation pattern should occur between African countries and European companies. To ensure this necessary tripolar presence (called the 'triad'), Ohmae advocates that alliances should be built between companies belonging to one of the developed market areas. Most of these companies, even large ones, cannot afford individually to make the necessary investment that would ensure full presence in the three regions of the triad.

Prioritized market(s) often remain undiscussed. To avoid this kind of 'collective unconsciousness', companies must reflect on how prioritized markets relate to corporate culture, to the search for market and business opportunities and to the decision-making process. Some European companies still supply their domestic market as a priority, on the basis that this market is the 'home base'. This attitude has two dangerous consequences:

1. It leads to a bias in product design The modest sales records of certain European cars, mainly French and Italian, in the North American, principally the US market, is, at least partly, attributable to local French and Italian motor regulations which bias the design of cars, and make them inappropriate for use in America. In France, the speed restrictions on motorways and a high-cost road tax, largely progressive with the size of the engine, has discouraged the production of large bourgeois cars and sports cars. The same holds true in Italy, where the high cost of petrol has encouraged the production of small cars, too small in fact for US consumers. This has dissuaded car manufacturers in those countries from building high-speed luxury saloons, a gap in the market which was mostly filled by the Germans and the Swedes, before the Japanese came with their Lexus and Acuras.

2. Home-base-orientated companies often suffer the unfortunate reputation abroad of unreliability with respect to delivery dates. This is due to a 'marginal' conception of foreign markets, which are considered as a provisional outlet when the home market is depressed. It leads to a consistent preference for supplying a domestic customer in preference to a foreign customer. Even though such foreign customers may have ordered earlier, they will be forced to wait and will only receive delivery after domestic

customers have been satisfied. A genuine respect for delivery dates should have led to a different outcome.

As soon as domestic demand increases, such prioritization of national markets implies that production capacity will cease to be used for supplying foreign customers. As a consequence, there is a general risk that attempts to set up stable business relationships with customers and intermediaries in foreign markets will be hampered. Typically, foreign agents will only be visited when business at home is slack, and will be let down (as will foreign customers) as soon as the home market situation improves. This attitude fails to satisfy the essential precondition for effective international development.

The world market share concept: global size and the diagnosis of economic market share

The main usefulness of the world market share concept is to prevent a company from being ethnocentric when defining its position *vis-à-vis* the competition. Competition is seen from the outset as being global. The following example illustrates the dangers of not using the world market share concept.

Fenwick, the leading company for fork-lift trucks in France, is also a word used in everyday speech as a synonym for fork-lift trucks. A few years ago the company controlled 40–50 per cent of the French market and nearly went bankrupt because it lacked international size. This company only produced 4,000 fork-lift trucks per year, whereas its Western competitor, Toyota, produced 35,000 and its main East European competitor, Balkankar (a Bulgarian company), 70,000. This had a negative effect on Fenwick's unit costs. Fenwick should have adapted its marketing strategy, by reducing the depth of its product range, thereby increasing production size within a narrower product range. Toyota was in a position to offer a very wide product range (diesel or electric, with varying loading capacities, etc.). Fenwick, on the other hand, should have restricted its range albeit at the consequent risk of losing customers who expect to find a single supplier capable of dealing with all their requirements.

A diagnosis of a particular company's situation within world markets requires the following evaluations (even though estimates may only be approximate):

1. What is the size of the world market (volume, units, sales figure)?
2. What is the company's production size?
3. What is the company's share of the world market?
4. What is the *minimum* world market share necessary to remain competitive, considering potential experience effects?

The world market for fork-lift trucks was roughly 200,000 units per year. Fenwick held only 2 per cent of this market. 'Competitive' market share could be estimated to have been 10 per cent, or 20,000 trucks a year. Fenwick was therefore well below required global size. In view of this, it should have reduced its range to either diesel or electric fork-lifts and to a limited range of sizes so that the production could have been much greater on the more specialized world market.

There is no precise rule for estimating the 'competitive' world market share. This figure depends on the optimum size of production, which in turn depends on the potential for experience effects for a specific product or service. They are, though, much stronger under the following conditions:

- When the product/service is mass produced.
- When the product/service involves a production process with large initial fixed costs (in R & D, and/or in production facilities investment, and/or in initial marketing costs).
- When the added value of the product/service is high, when the whole production cycle is considered.
- When the product/service is in a fairly open international market; any producer may sell throughout the world without suffering prohibitive transport costs, customs barriers, statutory restrictions or market barriers (e.g. differences in taste).

Limitations on international size arise in various areas; for example cement (very high transport costs/product price), pharmaceuticals (statutory restrictions), foodstuffs (taste differences), etc. As far as services are concerned, the potential for experience effects is much smaller, since in many cases services must be performed in a direct relationship with the consumer, are often intangible and therefore cannot be held in stock. In addition their market area is often fairly localized and they are subject to local customs and ways of life, such as the type of food and service found in a restaurant or the kind of treat offered by hotels.

The easiest empirical solution for the evaluation of 'competitive' market share is to examine the size of competitors, and to determine the size of those competitors who operate most effectively.

Global markets as a set of coherent opportunities

Global markets work as a set of coherent opportunities, through markets being at different product life-cycle (PLC) stages and through learning opportunities. According to product life-cycle theory (Vernon, 1966), national markets at different development stages offer different kinds of opportunities. If, for instance, the market for wallpaper is saturated in developed economies, it may be opening up in newly industrialized countries. PLC theory clearly indicates the way in which sourcing and marketing activities should be disconnected. PLC theory, in conjunction with the world market share concept, assists in the identification of what to supply and from where, and in which countries to market.

Global markets are also full of *learning opportunities*; the internationalization process has been presented mostly as a learning and experiencing process (Johanson and Vahlne, 1977). Since the cultural variable is fundamental to this learning process, some markets may be used almost purely as learning opportunities. When Procter & Gamble attacked the Japanese market for baby diapers it initially achieved great success. Its market share subsequently dropped sharply against the main Japanese competitor Kao. P & G did its best to survive in the face of harsh competition from Kao and other Japanese producers, to satisfy the exigent Japanese consumers and to make its way through the Japanese *keiretsu* distribution system (see Chapter 11). P & G's experience in Japan has made it aware of the competitive threat of the Japanese producers. P & G realized that it would face harsh competition if Japanese producers were to decide to expand in world markets. This has already helped P & G resist the internationalization of Kao which, up to now, has never succeeded in becoming a global competitor to P & G.

Global markets may also be seen as partnership opportunities: with the local consumers, with the distributors and (why not?) with competitors. A Danish chewing-gum company, Dandy A/S, which produces Stimorol, encountered difficulties in selling its products in France. Dandy was particularly successful at producing chewing gum dragé. Hollywood France (owned by the US company General Foods/Kraft) was less successful in the production of this type of product, but had better access to the major distribution outlets (hypermarkets). In fact, only large companies are able to have their products referenced, that is, registered as products accepted for sale by the channel. Referencing requires the payment of large 'entry fees' to the hypermarkets, which are only semi-legitimate. Dandy of Denmark and Hollywood ended up forging a cross-competence alliance whereby Dandy produces Hollywood dragé products and markets Hollywood products through Dandy's international sales organization, and Hollywood markets Dandy's Stimorol brand in France and produces the Dandy stick products.[9]

7.2 Intercultural marketing as an implementation framework for a global business strategy

As argued above, marketing cannot be global *per se*. Marketing is localizing as much as globalizing. It aims to customize product and marketing strategies to customer needs, to diversified distribution channels and to local media and communication styles, within the framework of a global strategy. Intercultural marketing tries to balance cross-national differences, in so far as they require mandatory adaptation, and cross-national commonalities which should be exploited in the building of size and experience effects.

The highest common cultural denominator (HCCD)

When issues related to cultural difference are addressed for designing international marketing strategies, they should refer to precise products or product categories. The relationship of dairy products to Japanese culture is manifestly much weaker than it is to most European cultures. Conversely, in the case of hi-fi systems or televisions it is much stronger. Furthermore, the closer one comes to elements of the *physical* environment which influence the local culture (climate, density of population, housing, flora and fauna, etc.), the more the HCCD tends to lower. The absence of visible cattle rearing on most Japanese islands, except Hokkaido, distances Japanese people from dairy products to an exceptional degree, particularly when compared to Holland or France, where cows can be seen grazing on any trip to the countryside. Japanese people find cheese, the most sophisticated dairy product, quite a strange kind of food and only a very few of them like it.

Cultural consumption (music, literature, cinema, etc.) is inherently more strongly suffused with cultural particularism. Music and literature in their industrial form, i.e. the book and the record, are two products where global marketing has been employed. Success has sometimes been remarkable, but instances remain limited. The amazing success of Harlequin novels or Michael Jackson records, for example, has several characteristics which make them genuine exceptions.[10] Their success is based on cross-culturally equivalent factors of profound attraction. These factors have sometimes bypassed the filter of national cultures. The romantic and melodramatic adventures of Harlequin heroes have found a lonely female public eager for tenderness in the majority of urban centres. Likewise, the meanings conveyed by the music of Michael Jackson extend far beyond US culture, even though it evokes images of the American way of life, and is thereby at the forefront of modern music. The character of Michael Jackson touches deep layers of individual character (sexual ambiguity) in his admirers. This process is largely individually based and independent of culture.

Cultural products which build on fairly universal feelings and ways of being are the ones to which standardized marketing policy can be applied. For the remainder of cultural products the situation is quite different. There is a fairly wide gulf between marketing techniques which tend towards standardization and the cultural dimension which tends to curb internationalization. In the case of the record industry, and more particularly for the collections of popular music, marketing techniques have generally evolved in the same direction over the last ten years in every industrialized nation. This evolution is characterized by an increased importance in large-scale distribution or specialized chains, an equivalent price level for everyone in relation to average household expenditure, promotion channels and relatively identical advertising with the predominant role taken by traditional media (press, radio, television) and a global standardization of product presentation.

The inherent cultural dimension of the popular song has, however, curbed internationalization and therefore the intercultural marketing of certain kinds of music. American country music has failed, up to now, in its attempt to achieve major success in Europe. Its only real international development occurred in Australia, despite achieving a critical success in the United Kingdom. A reason for this is the absence of a significant segment of the European population which can identity itself with the images evoked by the music of the American West, the symbol of a tradition of pioneers. The Australian bush, on the other hand, similar in many respects to the American Midwest, has given birth to an Australian musical tradition whose roots are in country music. This facilitated the marketing of American products in Australia and vice versa.

Cultural identification

Intercultural marketing is greatly facilitated when the conditions for product identification are already present in the market to be conquered. Consumers buy the meanings that they find in products for the purpose of cultural identification.

This identification can be traced to factors of change in a society. Identification may also result from the desire for assimilation to a particular type of civilization. The first alternative is illustrated by the attempt made by record companies to commercialize classical music on a large scale in the forms of collections. Market surveys have shown that in the West, the acquisition of classical records combined with a superficial knowledge of the most famous pieces promotes a personal image of stability and respectability for people between the ages of 25 and 40. These aspirations are further reinforced by a desire for personal achievement in professional life and successful integration into social life.

As a result, certain record companies have launched mass-market collections of classical music, the marketing strategy for which has been a strict implementation of the rules of global marketing: same product, same packaging, same price and same type of communication. The marketing concept behind these collections has, however, been less successful when classical music has ceased to be a major element in the acquisition of respectability for this specific segment of the population. This has occurred particularly in developing countries where the average level of education among the middle class lags somewhat in comparison to Western countries. Such has been the case in Latin America.

International marketing can take advantage of the desire for assimilation into a different society

McDonald's Big Mac and Coca-Cola are the sources of meanings that provide their buyers with the possibility of cultural adaptation to a desired way of life. Rock music represents, for many young Europeans, even non-Anglo-Saxons, a more tolerant and leisurely way of life. Identification with these symbols is one of the necessary conditions for being *trendy*. The international marketing of rock music achieves even greater success where certain values (e.g. individualism, strong desire for equality) are already present in the market segment to be conquered, in this case young people between the ages of 10 and 25.

The process of cultural identification functions in two ways: that of *identity* (the reproduction of national culture as it used to be, the desire to be 'at home'), and that of *exoticism* (the desire to escape from one's own culture, to experience different values and ways of life). These two ways are intermingled in a quite ambiguous fashion in the process of cultural identification. This ambivalence prohibits any simplistic approach to the process of cultural identification. For marketing implementation, however, it is often necessary to cluster countries or consumers who share certain meaningful cultural characteristics. Such clusters form *cultural affinity zones* and *cultural affinity classes*.

Cultural affinity zones

Attempts to market records on a global level have led to the pinpointing of cultural affinity zones in which the same marketing strategy with the same type of products can be successfully implemented. In Europe, for example, two of these zones are quite separate (Figure 7.2) – Scandinavia and the Mediterranean countries. A third zone encompasses Central European countries and Great Britain which serve as a bridge between northern and southern Europe, while retaining their own distinct personality. Despite the traditional isolation of the United Kingdom, there are less differences between Great Britain and Denmark or Sweden than Italy or Spain. Accordingly a song that is successful in Britain is more likely to repeat this success in Holland or Denmark than in southern Europe. The long-established differences between Saxon and Latin culture are reinforced by the religious divide between Protestants and Catholics. Cultural affinity zones display similar characteristics for easily identifiable criteria such as language, religion, family life patterns, work relations and consumption patterns. Intercultural marketing can effectively begin by choosing one of the main countries from a cultural affinity zone. This 'lead country' will subsequently be used as a base for market entry into other countries throughout the zone. A hierarchy of cultural affinity zones can be established. The marketing teams can interact with each other across zones, especially in countries which lie at the border of two zones. As an example, Figure 7.2 offers a *hypothetical map* of the zones of cultural affinities for Western Europe.

The operational mapping of these zones is based on criteria at the interface of culture and marketing. They must also have a strong relationship to the category of products studied: for example, opening hours in distribution outlets, attitude towards prices (strong or weak inflation, orientation towards bargaining), attitude towards innovation, etc.

For instance, when launching a compilation album internationally, a simultaneous promotion of the same record with a strong product image is possible throughout Europe. There is simultaneous commercialization in every country. But success is certain when a new product is launched initially in lead countries and only subsequently commercialized in the other countries of the zones. Success in Latin countries during the summer, when waves of migrant holiday-makers come from all over Europe, will have a greater chance of spreading into Nordic countries once the holiday-makers return home and go into record shops to buy the songs they have heard on holiday. Equally, a band may be so successful in a single country such as Germany that its music spreads into neighbouring countries. It spreads particularly rapidly in the border regions because of media overlap. In many places radio and television broadcasts are received on both sides of the border. Belgium, which is located between three other countries, Germany, France and Holland,

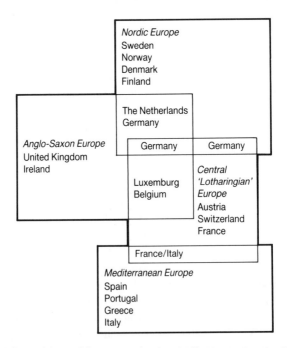

Figure 7.2 A hypothetical map of the zones of cultural affinities in Europe. (Source: Usunier and Sissmann, 1986, p. 85. Reproduced with permission.)

receives up to sixteen television channels. The Brussels agglomeration is an audience for the French media, and the Flemish area for Dutch and German media. The launch of a new product through cultural affinity zones can take from eighteen months to two years. This is a relatively long period of time, since the normal life span of a song is generally in the order of three months.

Cultural affinity classes

A further step in the intercultural marketing approach is to concentrate not only on nationality-based cultural criteria. One should also take account of consumer attitudes, preferences and life-styles that are *linked to age, class and ethnic- or profession-based cultures*. This does not, however, exclude other possible criteria for segmentation. Cultural affinity zones correspond to a large extent to national cultural groups. Cultural affinity classes exist in terms of age brackets or, more generally, across sociodemographic categories, for example people between the ages of 15 and 20 in Japan, Europe and the United States. People within a cultural affinity class share common values, behaviour and interests, and tend to present common traits as a consumer segment.

Which cultural affinity classes demonstrate the highest variance in terms of cultural affinity zones?: are consumption behaviour, values and life-styles among the 15- to 20-year-olds more homogeneous across Europe than among the 30- to 40-year-olds? Cultural affinity classes, in as far as they create a sense of belonging to a common group across different countries, are probably an ideal means of defining an international target for standardized products. Furthermore the development of new media such as satellite television channels will help the international launch of products targeted at the same cultural affinity classes across different countries. Accordingly, market research should survey consumer segments, each one corresponding to a box in the matrix (see Table 7.1). This matrix displays countries in columns and cultural affinity classes in rows.

If similar behaviour is observed by market researchers across the different boxes of the matrix with regard to key consumer behaviour figures (e.g. consumption of soft drinks, organization of personal time, time spent listening to the radio or watching television, etc.), the emergence of a common consumption culture can be detected for several countries.[11] If, on the other hand, different cultural affinity classes at the national level adopt similar behaviour at the international level, marketing communication will have to be modified to facilitate the process of diffusion from one country to another. If a drink (white wine, for example) that is popular among 25- to 30-year-olds in one country is also popular among 50- to 60-year-olds in another country, this is an indication of a weak affinity of national cultures.

7.3 Intercultural marketing means commerce

In this short, and final section of the chapter, let us normatively, that is, offering prescriptions rather than facts, recall that intercultural marketing implies commerce. As previously cited, commerce is defined (*Collins Dictionary*) as follows:

> 1. the activity embracing all forms of the purchase and sale of goods and services; 2. social relationships; 3. *Arch.* sexual intercourse.

Table 7.1   *Matrix of country/classes of cultural affinity.*

Country	1, 2, 3, ... i . . . . N
Classes of cultural affinity according to sociodemographics, psychographics, or other criteria	
1	
2	
3	
4	
.	
.	
.	
.	
.	
i	
.	
.	
.	
n	

Excerpt from: Jean-Claude Usunier and Pierre Sissmann (1986), 'L'Interculturel au Service du Marketing', *Harvard L'Expansion*, no. 40, Spring, page 87. Reproduced with permission.

An argument in favour of the rehabilitation of commerce is that it favours the social interaction between vendor (producer and/or distributor) and consumer.[12] The quality of this social interaction, including marketing strategies which respect cultural integrity, guarantees the effective implementation of global strategies.

Continuity in commercial relationships

The preoccupation with *marketing continuity* is a directly operative one. There are many reasons why the relationship and the lines of communication between a producer and the ultimate consumer may be broken.[13] Here are some examples:

♦ Distribution acts as a filter; consumers complain (about product reliability, for instance), but for some reason (there is no form, no specific communication channel with the producer) these complaints are not taken seriously or indeed are simply ignored.
♦ A product is refused by the distribution, for substantive reasons which nevertheless remain ignored. For instance, packets of biscuits are delivered to stores in cardboard boxes. Store employees experience difficulties in opening these boxes, which are stapled in such a way that employees are injured when they try to open them in order to put the biscuits on the shelves.

◆ A class of potential consumers is neglected by marketing communications, since only actual buyers are targeted.

The example of Japanese *keiretsus* (Chapter 11) demonstrates the value of building communication channels which help in the design and implementation of marketing strategies. Where opportunities for the return of products are liberal, distributors may warn producers about products which are defective or with which consumers are simply not happy. When, conversely, producers or retailers reject consumer complaints and therefore the return of products, they will often shift responsibility for the failure onto the consumers. They will, for instance, tell them that they have not read the instructions, or have misused the product, or fixed it incorrectly. Let us once again take an example – Box 7.2.

Commerce is non-technocratic marketing

The four-'P's model (McCarthy, 1964) of the marketing mix (product, price, place and promotion) is certainly a good one. It has helped in the past and continues to assist greatly

Box 7.2 *'Tubeless tyres,' you said . . .*

A consumer bought a leading European make of tyre for his car. He asked his garage to fit the tyres. In fact they fitted tubeless tyres since they were supposed to be cheaper (as they did not need air chambers). These tyres, however, kept deflating. When complaining for the first time, the consumer was told by the garage to be slightly more careful in inflating the tyres. They had to be reinflated roughly twice a week. The customer contacted his garage again but was merely told that it 'didn't usually happen'. The customer asked if the tyre company would take back the defective tyres but the garage told him that that was impossible and that in any case the tyres did at least stay inflated for a couple of days.

Finally, after going backwards and forwards several times, the customer had air chambers put into the tyres. The problem immediately ceased. When he spoke to his garage, they informed him that the wheel rims had warped slightly owing to the 30,000 miles that the car had done. Other cars (the garage mentioned a German make) had rims made out of a thicker steel which was more resistant and therefore did not warp. Such a car could have tubeless tyres fitted successfully, whatever its age.

The customer asked the garage to pass on this information to the tyre manufacturer so that it could inform tyre centres which cars were not suitable for tubeless tyres after a certain mileage had been covered. The garage said that this was impossible.

The information was not passed on. Tubeless tyres continue to deflate in a fairly large number of cases. Customers either fit air chambers or buy a different car . . . or they change their make of tyre.

in the design of marketing strategies. It also serves to question their coherence and soundness. It is a paradigm which has been extremely useful in the development of marketing plans. But it may be somewhat technocratic. Little by little, it has led to rather ritualized marketing practices where functions and their content are rigidly defined: market research specialists are not product managers, nor are they advertising managers or sales promoters. Each of these specialists has defined tasks and functions. Whenever an issue does not fall clearly within their explicit responsibility, it will not even be considered. When questions arise as to consumer complaints management, it is not clear who should be in charge of it. The correct answer should be that everybody is in charge of consumer complaints. Great care should be taken to avoid *nobody* being in charge of consumer complaints.

Technocratically orientated market research treats the customer too impersonally, as an abstract unit in a sample (see Chapter 1 for market research Japanese-style). All the messages coming from consumers are strictly filtered by close-ended questions, which pre-shape what people actually say. A large part of what they *would be willing to say* is in fact often ignored. The four-'P's paradigm of marketing theory has led to practices which are overly ignorant of company environment (Zeithaml and Zeithaml, 1984). Various segments of the public (consumers, actual buyers, competitors, etc.) are often ignored simply because there is no established communication channel to hear their voice.

A negotiation and human resource emphasis

A commerce orientation means that not only personnel but also clients should be seen by a company as its human resources. The frontiers of the organization should be less clear-cut. Most companies are very dichotomous, that is, they have their 'inside' and their 'outside'. Insiders are generally people listed on the payroll. Consumers, even when it is claimed that they are 'kings'[14] (slogans emanating from within the company), are in fact treated as pure *outsiders*. There is little personal knowledge of who the consumers are. A consumer who wants to meet a top executive (just to explain something about the product or the service, with a positive view towards its improvement) will generally not even be received. Very often distribution channels will be used as shock-absorbing mattresses. As distribution channels are in direct contact with the customer, if something goes wrong, it is *their* job to deal with it. Splendid isolation of manufacturers is too often the rule of non-commerce-orientated organizations, whenever they claim to be marketing-orientated. To avoid this bias, consumers must be viewed as one of the key human resources of the company. They are not kings, but suitable people with whom to negotiate reasonable changes to the buyer/seller relationship.

——————— ♦♦♦ ———————

Teaching materials

A7.1 Case: IKEA

IKEA in the USA

IKEA, the world's largest home furnishings retail chain, was founded in Sweden in 1943 as a mail-order company and opened its first showroom ten years later. From its headquarters in Almhult, IKEA has since expanded to world-wide sales of $2.6 billion from 83 outlets in 20 countries (see Table 7.2). In fact, the second store that IKEA built was in Oslo, Norway. Today, IKEA operates large warehouse showrooms in Sweden, Norway, Denmark, Holland, France, Belgium, West Germany, Switzerland, Austria, Canada, the United States, Saudi Arabia, and the United Kingdom. It has smaller stores in Kuwait, Australia, Hong Kong, Singapore, the Canary Islands, and Iceland. A store near Budapest was expected to open by 1990, with others to follow in Poland and Yugoslavia. Even the Soviet Union is not considered out of bounds.

The international expansion of IKEA has progressed in three phases, all of them continuing at the present time: Scandinavian expansion, begun in 1963; West European expansion, begun in 1973; and North American expansion, begun in 1974. Of the individual markets, West Germany is the largest, accounting for 30 percent of company sales. The phases of expansion are detectable in the world-wide sales shares depicted in Figure 7.3. 'We want to bring the IKEA concept to as many people as possible,' IKEA officials have said.

The IKEA concept

Ingvar Kamprad, the founder, formulated as IKEA's mission to 'offer a wide variety of home furnishings of good design and function at prices so low that the majority of people

Table 7.2 *IKEA's international expansion.* (Source: *IKEA Facts, 88/89.*)

Year	Outlets	Countries	Coworkers	Catalog circulation	Turnover in Swedish crowns
1954	1	1	15	285,000	3,000,000
1964	2	2	250	1,200,000	79,000,000
1974	10	5	1,500	13,000,000	616,000,000
1984	66	17	8,300	45,000,000	6,770,000,000
1988	75(83[a])	19(20[a])	13,400[b]	50,535,000[c]	14,500,000,000[d]

[a]Stores/countries being opened by the end of 1990.
[b]13,400 coworkers are equivalent to 10,700 full-time workers.
[c]14 languages, 27 editions.
[d]Corresponding to net sales of the IKEA group of companies.

can afford to buy them.' The principal target market of IKEA, which is similar across countries and regions in which IKEA has a presence, is composed of people who are young, highly educated, liberal in their cultural values, white-collar workers, and not especially concerned with status symbols.

IKEA follows a standardized product strategy with an identical assortment around the world. Today, IKEA carries an assortment of 12,000 different home furnishing that range from plants to pots, sofas to soup spoons, and wine glasses to wallpaper. The smaller items are carried to complement the bigger ones. IKEA does not have its own manufacturing facilities but designs all of its furniture. The network of subcontracted manufacturers numbers nearly 1,500 in 50 different countries. IKEA shoppers have to become 'prosumers' – half producers, half consumers – because most products must be assembled.

Manufacturers are responsible for shipping the components to large warehouses, for example, to the central one in Almhult. These warehouses then supply the various stores, which are in effect miniwarehouses. The final distribution is the customer's responsibility. IKEA does cooperate with car-rental companies to offer vans and small trucks at reasonable rates for customers needing delivery service.

Although IKEA has concentrated on company-owned, larger scale outlets, franchising has been used in areas in which the market is relatively small or where uncertainty may exist as to the response to the IKEA concept. IKEA uses mail order in Europe and Canada but has resisted expansion into it in the United States, mainly because of capacity constraints.

IKEA offers prices that are 30 to 50 percent lower than fully assembled competing products. This is a result of large-quantity purchasing, low-cost logistics, store location in suburban areas, and the do-it-yourself approach to marketing. IKEA's prices do vary from market to market, largely because of fluctuations in exchange rates and differences in taxation regimes, but price positioning is kept as standardized as possible.

IKEA's promotion is centered on the catalog. The IKEA catalog is printed in 14 languages and has a world-wide circulation of over 50 million copies (see Table 7.2). The catalogs are uniform in layout except for minor regional differences. The company's advertising goal is to generate word-of-mouth publicity through innovative approaches.

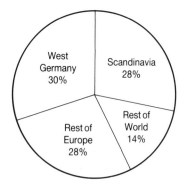

Figure 7.3   IKEA world-wide sales expressed as percentages of turnover.

Table 7.3   *The IKEA concept.*

Target market:	'Young people of all ages'
Product:	IKEA offers the same products world-wide. The countries of origin of these products are: Scandinavia (52 percent), Western Europe (21 percent), Eastern Europe (20 percent), and others (7 percent). Most items have to be assembled by the customer. The furniture design is modern and light. Textiles and pastels.
Distribution:	IKEA has built its own distribution network. Outlets are outside the city limits of major metropolitan areas. Products are not delivered but IKEA cooperates with car rental companies that offer small trucks. IKEA offers mail order in Europe and Canada.
Pricing:	The IKEA concept is based on low price. The firm tries to keep its price image constant.
Promotion:	IKEA's promotional efforts are mainly through its catalogs. IKEA has developed a prototype communications model that must be followed by all stores. Its advertising is attention getting and provocative. Media choices vary by market.

Local store managers have substantial leeway in promotional decision making (for example, in choosing an advertising agency) but have to adhere to certain guidelines to ensure a universal image.

The IKEA concept is summarized in Table 7.3.

IKEA in the competitive environment

IKEA's strategic positioning is unique. As Figure 7.4 illustrates, few furniture retailers anywhere have engaged in long-term planning or achieved scale economies in production. European furniture retailers, especially those in Sweden, Switzerland, West Germany, and Austria, are much smaller than IKEA. Even when companies have joined forces as buying groups, their heterogeneous operations have made it difficult for them to achieve the same degree of coordination and concentration as IKEA. Because customers are usually content to wait for the delivery of furniture, retailers have not been forced to take purchasing risks.

The value-added dimension differentiates IKEA from its competition. IKEA offers no customer assistance but creates opportunities for consumers to choose, transport, and assemble units of furniture. The best summary of the competitive situation was provided by a manager at another firm: 'We can't do what IKEA does, and IKEA doesn't want to do what we do.'

IKEA in the United States

After careful study and assessment of its Canadian experience, IKEA decided to enter the U.S. market in 1985 by establishing outlets on the East Coast. IKEA's three stores

(Philadelphia, Woodbridge near Washington, D.C., and Baltimore) generated $93 million in 1988. The overwhelming level of success in 1987 led the company to invest in a warehousing facility near Philadelphia that receives goods from Sweden. Plans call for 60 additional stores over the next 25 years with only gradual expansion to the West Coast.

(Illka A. Ronkainen, in Michael R. Czinkota and Illka A. Ronkainen, 1990, *International Marketing*, 2nd edn, The Dryden Press: Hinsdale, IL, pp. 203–7. Reproduced with permission.)

Questions

1. Which features of the 'young people of all ages' are universal and can be exploited by a global/regional marketing strategy? How would you analyze them in terms of cultural affinity classes?
2. What accounts for IKEA's success with a standardized product and marketing strategy in a business which is usually described as having some of the strongest cultural influences (styles of furniture, household items and, more generally, life-styles at home are culture-bound)? Consider, for instance, that an American buying IKEA beds will also have to buy IKEA sheets because the beds are in European sizes.
3. Is IKEA destined to succeed everywhere it cares to establish itself? What are the possible limitations of the IKEA concept?

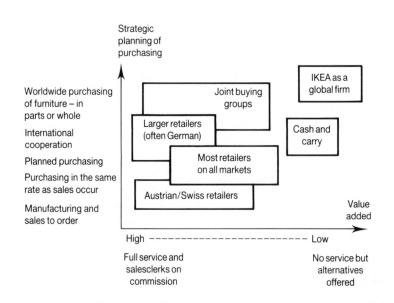

Figure 7.4 Competition in furniture retailing. (Source: Rita Martenson, 1987, 'Is standardization of marketing feasible in culture-bound industries? A European case study', *International Marketing Review*, vol. 4, Autumn, p. 14.)

A7.2 Exercise: Dangerous Enchantment

You will first read the short extract from *Dangerous Enchantment*, the evocative title of the novel by Anne Mather (1966). Harlequin books are a world-wide success. They are translated into fifteen languages and read in many countries. Therefore they can be considered as a truly 'global' cultural product.

The next day Julie had collected herself. She was glad in a way that she had seen the woman with Manuel. At least it brought it home to her more strongly than any words could have done the completely amoral attitude he possessed.

Marilyn had seen the television as well, however, and said:

'I say, Julie, did you see that Manuel Cortez is back in England?'

Julie managed a casual shrug. 'So what?'

'Darling, really!' Marilyn gave her an old-fashioned look. 'Surely you aren't as indifferent as all that! I know you refused a date with him, but I'm sure that was more because of Paul Bannister than anything else.'

Julie tossed her head. 'I really can't see what all the fuss is about. Paul would make four of him!'

'You must be joking!' Marilyn giggled. 'Get you! I didn't know Paul was becoming such a dish all of a sudden. Why? What's changed him?'

Julie refrained from replying. She had no desire to get involved in an argument about Paul when it meant her stating things that in actual fact were not true. It was no use pretending about Paul's attractions; he was handsome, yes, and tall, yes, and young; but there was nothing particularly exciting about him and Julie could never understand girls who thought men's looks were enough. She had known many men, and in her small experience personality mattered far more than mere good looks.

However, during her lunch break she did borrow a newspaper from Miss Fatherstone in the hope that there might be more particulars about the woman with Manuel, but there was not. There was a picture of him at the airport, and a small article, and that was all.

When they left the building that evening it was snowing, and an icy wind was blowing, chilling them to the bone. Julie, wrapped in a loose dark blue mohair coat, hugged her handbag to her as she started along towards the main thoroughfare accompanied by Donna and Marilyn. She wore knee-length white boots, but between the place where her boots ended and the place where her skirt began she felt frozen, and she wondered whether for the winter at least she should go back to normal-length skirts.

Her hair was blowing about her face, for she was wearing no hat, and she walked straight into the man who stood purposely in her way.

'I'm sorry. . . .' she began hastily, a smile lightening her face, and then: 'You!'

Manuel smiled, and her heart leapt treacherously into her throat. She had let go of Donna's arm in her confusion, but both Marilyn and Donna were staring open-mouthed. Manuel took Julie's arm, and said smoothly:

'You will excuse me, ladies,' in a mocking tone, and drew Julie across the pavement to the familiar green Ferrari.

'No, wait!' began Julie, but it was no use. Manuel had the car door open, and was propelling her inside, his hard fingers biting cruelly into her arm.

'Don't argue,' he said, for all the world as though it was a natural occurrence that he should meet her from work.

Julie did not want to create a scene in the street, so she climbed into the luxurious warmth of the car, and sliding across out of the driver's seat, she allowed him to slide in beside her.

He slammed the door, flicked the ignition, and the car moved silently forward, purring like a sated panther.

She stole a glance at him as they turned into the main thoroughfare, and saw, with a sense of inevitability, that far from changing he was much more attractive than she remembered. He turned for a moment to look at her as they stopped at some traffic lights, and said:

'How have you been?'

Julie contemplated her fingernails. 'Fine. And you?'

He shrugged, and did not reply, and she felt like hitting him. How dared he sit there knowing that she must have seen him with that girl yesterday! She looked out of the car window, suddenly realizing that she was allowing him to drive her heaven knows where, and she was making no comment.

'Where are you taking me?' she asked in a tight little voice.

'Home,' he said lazily. 'Where do you think? I thought I would save you the journey on such a ghastly night. Tell me, how do you stand this climate? It's terrible. Me, I like the sun, and the sea, and warm water to swim in.'

'Don't we all?' remarked Julie dryly. 'This will do.' They had reached the end of Faulkner Road.

Manuel shook his head. 'What number?'

'Forty-seven. But please, I'd rather you didn't drive along there. It would only cause speculation, and if you should be recognized....' Her voice trailed away.

'That's hardly likely tonight,' remarked Manuel cooly, and drove smoothly to her gate where he halted the car.

'Thank you, señor.' Julie gave a slight bow of her head, and made to get out, but Manuel stopped her, his fingers biting into her arm.

'Aren't you pleased to see me?' he asked mockingly.

Julie looked at him fully. 'No, not really.'

'Why?'

'Surely that's obvious. We have nothing to say to one another.'

'No?'

'No.' Julie brushed back her hair as it fell in waves over her eyes. It glistened with tiny drops of melted snow and she was unaware of how lovely she was looking.

Manuel shrugged, and lay back in his seat. 'Go, then.'

Julie felt furious. It always ended this way, with herself feeling the guilty one. Well, he wasn't going to get away with it! She swung round on him.

'Don't imagine for one moment that I've been brought home believing your little tales!' she cried angrily. 'I know perfectly well that the reason you *have* brought me home is because you could hardly take me to the apartment when you already have one female in residence!'

Manuel stared at her, a dull flush just visible in the muted light of the car rising up his cheeks.

(Anne Mather, 1966, *Dangerous Enchantment*, Harlequin: London, pp. 89–92. Reproduced with permission.)

Questions

1. Identify the main sociodemographic characteristics of the target audience of such books.[15]

2. Identify from the text (situations, characters and the relations between them) how, and to what extent, this text moves people in such a way as to touch feelings and emotions that are widely shared in the world population.
3. Define the target audience of Harlequin books, in terms of cultural affinity class(es).

Notes

1. This chapter is partly based on Usunier and Sissmann (1986). Pierre Sissmann was at that time European marketing manager of CBS International, in charge of co-ordinating marketing strategies for the seventeen national European markets of CBS records. This explains why so many examples in this chapter relate to the record industry. Reproduced with the kind permission of the co-author, Pierre Sissmann, and the publisher, *Harvard-L'Expansion*.
2. Price decrease will only result if the market situation, especially the competition, is strong enough to ensure that consumers share in the cost decrease.
3. The supporting evidence, as emphasized by Montgomery and Day, is mostly graphical in nature but there are also some econometric studies in various industries, which clearly support the experience curve doctrine: Arrow (1961), Rapping (1965), Barkhai and Levhari (1973), Stobaugh and Townsend (1975) and Liebermann (1981). The experience curve doctrine has been rebutted (Alberts, 1989) by the argument that the first cause of unit cost decrease with increased volume of production is *innovation*. In fact innovation is a continuous process (in most cases) which is possible only in as much as large volumes have already been, and will be, produced and sold.
4. Now renamed MBK (a subsidiary of Yamaha).
5. A four-stroke engine does not need a mix of oil and petrol, whereas a two-stroke engine either uses pre-mixed petrol and oil or has a special mixing device ('oil lube') which pumps oils and petrol from two separate tanks.
6. Except for some *haute coiffure* services, which may expand by means of international franchising.
7. See the exercise in section A12.6
8. For those keen to pursue this avenue further, see: Hout *et al.* (1982); Christopher Bartlett (1983), 'MNC's get off the reorganization merry-go-round', *Harvard Business Review*, March–April; Hamel and Prahalad (1985); Quelch and Hoff (1986); Ghoshal (1987); Michael E. Porter (ed.) (1986), *Competition in Global Industries*, Harvard Business School Press: Boston, MA; Christopher Bartlett and Sumantra Ghoshal (1987), 'Managing across borders: New strategic requirements', *Sloan Management Review* (Summer); Yves Doz and C.K. Prahalad (1987), *The Multinational Mission*, The Free Press: New York; and Frank Bradley (1991), *International Marketing Strategy*, Prentice Hall: Hemel Hempstead.
9. Example from Svend Hollensen (1991), 'Shift of market servicing organization in international markets: A Danish case study', in Harald Vestergaard (ed.), *An Enlarged Europe in the Global Economy*, proceedings of the 17th annual conference of the European International Business Association, Copenhagen Business School: Copenhagen, p. 736.
10. Harlequin books have succeeded by using a consistent formula such as that employed by the British publishers Mills and Boon.
11. Marieke K. De Mooij and Warren J. Keegan (1991, pp. 110–30) review comparative life-style research in Europe and in Asia. The changes in life-styles across European countries are monitored through extensive surveys, such as the ACE (Anticipating Change in Europe) study, CCA Eurostyles and Sinus Gmbh 'Social milieus'. A similar attempt has been made in Asia by

the Survey Research Group (SRG), which conducts life-style surveys in Hong Kong, Malaysia, the Philippines, Singapore, Thailand and Taiwan.

12. Commerce, being related to money (negatively valued by certain religions), has often been negatively perceived in Catholic societies as well as others – Hindu, for instance. Commerce traditionally enjoys a much better image as an acceptable social standard activity in some other societies (religions), e.g. Muslim, Protestant and Jewish.

13. A good introduction to this new style of marketing (more consumer- and relation-orientated, less strategy-orientated) is *Hearing the Voice of the Market* by Vincent P. Barabba and Gerald Zaltman (1991), Harvard Business School Press: Cambridge, MA. Another reference for new insights into this interactionist style of marketing is Robert Prus (1989), *Making Sales* and *Pursuing Customers*, Sage Publications: Newbury Park, CA.

14. *The customer is king, le client est roi, der Kunde ist König,* etc.

15. The short extract has been chosen for its capacity to illustrate the style of Harlequin books.

References

Alberts, William L. (1989), 'The experience curve doctrine reconsidered', *Journal of Marketing*, vol. 53, July, pp. 36–49.

Arrow, Kenneth J. (1961), 'The economic implications of learning by doing', *Review of Economic Studies*, pp. 155–73.

Barkai, Haim and David Levhari (1973), 'The impact of experience in kibbutz farming', *Review of Economics and Statistics*, vol. 55, February, pp. 56–63.

Boddewyn, J.J. (1981), 'Comparative marketing: The first twenty-five years', *Journal of International Business Studies*, vol. 12 (Spring–Summer), pp. 61–79.

Day, G.S. and D.B. Montgomery (1983), 'Diagnosing the experience curve', *Journal of Marketing* (Spring), pp. 44–58.

De Mooij, Marieke K. and Warren J. Keegan (1991), *Advertising Worldwide*, Prentice Hall: Hemel Hempstead.

European Communities (1987), *Treaties Establishing the European Communities*, Office for Official Publications of the European Communities: Luxemburg.

Fournis, Y. (1962), 'The markets of Europe or the European market?' *Business Horizons*, vol. 5 (Winter), pp. 77–83.

Ghoshal, Sumantra (1987), 'Global strategy: An organizing framework', *Strategic Management Journal*, vol. 8, pp. 425–40.

Hamel, Gary and C. K. Prahalad (1985), 'Do you really have a global strategy?', *Harvard Business Review*, vol. 63, July–August, pp. 139–48.

Hout, Thomas, Michael E. Porter and Eileen Rudden (1982), 'How global companies win out', *Harvard Business Review*, vol. 60, September–October, pp. 98–105.

Johanson, J. and J.E. Vahlne (1977), 'The internationalisation process of the firm: A model of knowledge development and increased market commitments', *Journal of International Business Studies* (Spring/Summer).

Liebermann, Marvin B. (1981), 'The experience curve, pricing and market structure in the chemical processing industries', unpublished working paper, Harvard University.

McCarthy, E. Jerome (1964), *Basic Marketing: A managerial approach*, Prentice Hall: Englewood Cliffs, NJ.

Mourier, Pascal and Didier Burgaud (1989), *Euromarketing*, Les Editions d'Organisation: Paris.

Ohmae, Kenichi (1985), *Triad Power: The coming shape of global competition*, The Free Press: New York.

Porter, Michael E. (1986), 'Changing patterns of international competition', *California Management Review*, vol. xxviii, no. 2, pp. 9–39.

Quelch, John A. and Edward J. Hoff (1986), 'Customizing global marketing', *Harvard Business Review*, vol. 64, May–June, pp. 59–68.

Rapping, Leonard (1965), 'Learning and World War II production functions', *Review of Economics and Statistics*, vol. 47 (February), pp. 81–6.

Stobaugh, Robert B. and Philip L. Townsend (1975), 'Price forecasting and strategic planning: The case of petrochemicals', *Journal of Marketing Research*, vol. 12, February, pp. 19–29.

Stoetzel, J. (1983), *Les Valeurs du temps présent: une enquête européenne*, PUF: Paris.

Usunier, Jean-Claude (1990), 'Some contextual aspects of the French international business education system: A pessimistic view', *European Management Journal*, vol. 8, no. 3, pp. 388–93.

Usunier, J.C. and P. Sissmann (1986), 'L'interculturel au service du marketing', *Harvard L'Expansion*, No. 40 (Spring), pp. 80–92.

Valette-Florence, Pierre (1991) 'Understanding the European consumer: myths and realities', in Spyros G. Makridakis (ed.), *Single Market Europe: Opportunities and Challenges for Business*, Jossey Bass: San Francisco, pp. 236–53.

Vernon, Raymond P. (1966), 'International investment and international trade in the product life cycle', *Quarterly Journal of Economics*, vol. lxxx, no. 2, pp. 191–207.

Whitelock, J.M. (1987), 'Global marketing and the case for international product standardization', *European Journal of Marketing*, vol. 12, no. 9.

Wind, Yoram, Susan P. Douglas and Howard V. Perlmutter (1973), 'Guidelines for developing inernational marketing strategies', *Journal of Marketing*, vol. 37, April, pp. 14–23.

Zeithaml, Carl P. and Valarie Zeithaml (1984), 'Environmental management: Revising the perspective', *Journal of Marketing*, vol. 48 (Spring), pp. 46–53.

8

♦♦♦

Adaptation or standardization of product policy: a model for choice

A central issue in international marketing strategy is the decision whether to adapt products for foreign markets after the consumer, the national markets and their particular characteristics have been surveyed, or to standardize products, which is a simplified strategy based on experience effects which result in cost reduction.

This chapter and the following one (which is devoted to the product's brand name and national image) propose a decision-making framework for the adaptation/standardization of various product attributes: physical characteristics, design, form, colour, functions, packaging, brand name and 'made-in' label. An assessment will be made of the adaptation and international standardization of different levels of product attributes: physical attributes, service attributes and symbolic attributes. The product conveys symbolic meanings through its colour, shape, country of origin, brand name and so on.

The first section of the chapter sets out a systematic model for the choice between adaptation and standardization of product policy. It can be applied successively to each existing national market as well as to markets where a company intends to set up new business. The second section is devoted to the physical attributes of the product. The third section deals with the standardization/adaptation of service attributes. The fourth section relates to symbolic attributes.

The etymology of the word 'symbol' comes from Ancient Greece, where the symbol was originally an object cut into two. The two halves were retained by the host and the guest and later passed on to their children. When these two halves were reunited, this enabled recognition of the owners and served as proof of the bonds of hospitality previously created.[1] The symbol therefore replaces, represents and denotes some other entity by means of a conventional relationship or a suggestion, the evidence of which has usually been lost. The meanings that symbols diffuse are of course culture-based. They are interpreted differently across countries.

Other important symbolic attributes are brand names and national images linked to the product, its country of manufacture and its brand name. The conversion of a national brand into an international one, and the linguistic problems that may occur, are dealt with in Chapter 9. The issue of 'global' brands, either world-wide or at a regional level, are also considered in Chapter 9.

8.1 A framework for the choice between adaptation and standardization based on product attributes

One may provocatively state that the public are not buying the product itself, but the benefits they hope to derive from the product. A product can be defined as a set of attributes which provide the purchaser/user with actual benefits. There are three layers of attributes:

1. The physical attributes (size, weight, colour, etc.). Standardization of these attributes affords the greatest potential for cost benefits since economies of scale are made principally at the manufacturing stage.
2. Service attributes (maintenance, after-sales service, spare parts availability, etc.). These attributes are fairly difficult to standardize, as circumstances for service delivery differ widely from one country to another. It should further be emphasized that most services are performed in direct relation to *local* customers. Service attributes are more dependent on culture.
3. Symbolic attributes are often the interpretive element of the physical attributes. A colour is simultaneously a chemical formula for a painting or a coat, and also the symbolic meaning conveyed by the material. Symbolic attributes affect the choice between adaptation and standardization in a fairly ambiguous manner. Consumers have confused attitudes: a liking for domestic goods based on nationalism will co-exist with a penchant and even fascination for foreign cultures and their goods. Therefore, when adapting or standardizing symbolic attributes, the requirements for nationalist symbols will intermingle with symbols of exoticism.

Figure 8.1 proposes a systematic description of the arguments in favour of adaptation on the one hand and standardization on the other. Distinctions can be made according to the different levels of attributes: physical, service and symbolic. Some arguments (originating from the company) or constraints (imposed by external influences) may affect supply (a benefit that the company can derive from changing its way of operating) or demand (which necessitates the company's adaptation to diverse aspects of demand).

8.2 The physical attributes

The experience effects, and accordingly the cost reductions related to cumulated production, clearly weigh in favour of standardization (box 1).[2] However, one should investigate the opportunity of supplying an adapted product, corresponding to the local demand, in which the adaptation would lead to a sufficient reduction in costs to compensate for the loss in cumulated volume (box 2). This situation is rare.[3] There are some examples of 'simplified' cars or 'simplified' computers designed for developing countries' environment. The advantages resulting from 'simplifications' are not at all offset by either a decrease in economies of scale (increased unit costs) or a loss in functionality.

Compulsory adaptation for the physical attributes is often related to national regulations and standards.[4] Thus (box 3):

1. The industrial standards for the electricity supply, for example: the voltage, the frequency of the alternating current (50 v. 60 Hz), the shape of plugs, etc. Certain countries use standards which seem to operate as non-tariff trade barriers. Germany is known for its use of an exhaustive system of over 30,000 industrial standards (DIN) which are determined by standard-setting committees. On the boards of these committees German manufacturers are strongly represented. Nevertheless DIN standards are far from being intended as non-tariff barriers; for instance, German bicycles use drum brakes on the rear wheels which are operated by pedalling

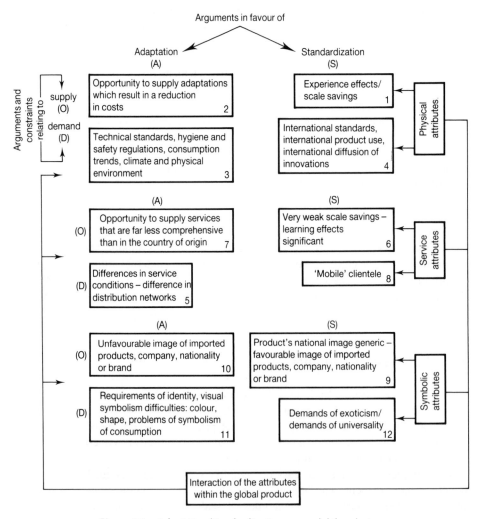

Figure 8.1 Adaptation/standardization: a model for choice.

backwards, whereas British and French bicycles use brake pads. The German standard, which may at first sight appear safer, is in fact dangerous for other European cyclists because of the risk of skidding on corners by spurious back-pedalling.

2. Safety standards: in the motor industry for example, in relation to lighting, brake systems and vehicle safety. A few years ago Peugeot had to use more than 500 national versions of its 505 range, corresponding to the different engine types available (GR, SRT, TI, STI, diesel, etc.), adapted for various countries targeted for export. This obviously had an adverse effect on costs. In addition to increased production costs, there was an inflation in required documentation and country-specific spare parts. Control of the marketing management of the 505 around the world was adversely affected.

3. Hygiene regulations: the food processing, chemicals and pharmaceutical industries must carry out adaptations in accordance with hygiene legislation. The producers of *foie gras* which is exported to the United States have to obtain an FDA (Food and Drug Administration) hygiene certification. For this they have to allow the FDA to inspect their laboratories for bacteria as well as their methods of production. FDA inspectors often require *foie gras* to be pasteurized and the laboratories disinfected with an antiseptic detergent. This inevitably affects the taste and conflicts with the traditional image of a home-made quality product.

A huge variety of regulations influences the need for adaptation (marking, labelling, locally permitted standard sizes, sales promotion laws, etc.).[5] Often newcomers to export business are only concerned with obligatory adaptation (see Box 8.1) and do not consider the loss of standardization.[6] In fact, obligatory adaptations are often minor in comparison to the required adaptations to differences in consumer behaviour and national marketing environment. Two main issues should be considered:

1. Consumption patterns: consumer tastes, frequency of consumption, the amount consumed per helping, etc. The required size of a cereal box and the ability of the packaging to preserve the product will not necessarily be the same for a country in which the average consumer eats 50 grams of cereal daily for breakfast and for a different country where the quantity of consumption is higher but the frequency lower.

2. Climate and the physical environment in general are important, and sometimes neglected, factors behind further obligatory adaptation. Motor vehicles must be specifically designed to withstand the harsh Scandinavian winters or the warmth and humidity of the Ivory Coast. The possible range of physical environments where the product will be used must be taken into account: for example, the quality of road surfaces and the existence of tracks suitable for vehicles. The diversity of physical environments is often the source of later shocks and the cause of unexpected failures. One should take into account in advance the range of elements that constitute potential demands for adaptation. This is not always such an obvious step to take. Ethnocentrism is often the rule in product design. In the case of a sheet-glass factory, the high temperature in the workshops proved to be intolerable for Saudi workers when it was set up in Saudi Arabia on the basis of European parameters (Tiano, 1981).

Yet national requirements sometimes lean towards international standardization (box 4). This may occur in four situations:

1. Although technical standards largely originate in individual countries[7] there are industries where international standards tend to develop. They can even become the dominant national standard.[8] Thus in the field of oil drilling, the API (American Petroleum Institute) standards are in force world-wide. Every oil company, whether American or not, must follow the API standards. Oil-drilling equipment manufacturers are also obliged to standardize their products in accordance with these standards. However, the number of industries with world-wide standards remains limited. The adoption of foreign/international standards can even prove to be problematic for selling in the country of origin. For instance, a European iron and steel company obtained certification from ASME (American Society of Mechanical Engineers) for the very thick steel plates used in nuclear and petrochemical plants. In this small industry, they had a quite substantial world market share. ASME certification was recognized world-wide since most nuclear plants use licensed American technology. When they

Box 8.1   *Obligatory adaptations*

A European drinks manufacturer decided to widen the range of one of its product lines with a giant-size version, with the purpose of its active promotion in several markets, the United States in particular. After completion of production facilities, the new model was launched. The company then realized to its horror that it had forgotten one small detail: the giant-size bottle was a couple of inches too tall for the shelves in the vast majority of the American stores. You can imagine the result: the sales promotion activities that were planned had to be cancelled, there was discontent among the distributors and the sales force lost a great deal of motivation while a new mould was hastily manufactured.*

Quaker Oats has an established share of the Cameroon market: it has been carefully adapted in line with consumption habits. It is easily made into the gruel that the Cameroons call *paf* or *pap*. It is usually eaten with maize or tapioca. In addition, Quaker uses metallic packaging which is perfectly suited to the preservation of the product in the Cameroon climate. The shelf life of the box is about ten years, even in a tropical country. Cameroon itself is not a wholly typical tropical country since in Douala, for instance, there is an annual rainfall of 7 metres. The metallic box ensures the product's preservation despite the humidity. It does, however, rust, and even though the product itself is not affected, certain retailers refuse to repurchase Quaker Oats because of their previous stock having rusted.**

*(Adapted from Alain Eric Giordan, 1988, *Exporter Plus 2*, Editions Economica: Paris, p. 110. Reproduced with permission.)
(Adapted from Pierre-Arnold Camphuis, 1984, 'Launching a product on the Cameroon market', Internship Report, Ecole Supérieure de Commerce de Paris. Reproduced with permission.)

subsequently came to sell their heavy steel plates for plants intended for German and French electricity utilities, US standards were not considered acceptable and they were forced to adopt German and French standards.

2. Some products achieve 'international usage': aircraft suitcases (Samsonite from Belgium, and Delsey from France), portable computers, duty-free articles, etc.

3. Innovative products often experience an international diffusion process (Rogers and Shoemaker, 1971; Ryan and Murray, 1977). Large R & D expenses are initially incurred for many innovative products, and such products are not greatly affected by culture (VCR, Laserdisc). The pace of the diffusion of innovations is largely enhanced by the strength of the groups of 'early adopters' (Rogers, 1962). Presumably, these groups correspond to people who have a high level of exposure to international travel and new products in the countries where they are first launched. By word-of-mouth communication, they transfer knowledge of the product to their non-travelling compatriots. These international travellers eventually introduce such products into their native country. They facilitate positive reactions from other consumers without exposure to these new products, in the first phases of the adoption process: awareness, interest, evaluation, testing. More generally, international travel accelerates the process of diffusion of standardized innovations.

4. The final point in box 4 encompasses the basis of Levitt's assertions about the globalization of markets (1983). According to Levitt, certain aspects of ways of life tend towards uniformity: differences in cultural preferences, national taste, standards and institutional business environment are remnants of the past. Some inheritances die off slowly, others flourish and spread out as the general preferences of the largest number. Levitt argues that the so-called ethnic markets are a good example: Chinese food, country music, pizzas and jazz now tend to be found world-wide. Although Levitt claims that he is not advocating systematic disregard for local or national differences, he probably overestimates the reality of this common sharing of world products.[9]

Whatever value judgements are made on the all-inclusive (that is, across countries, consumer segments and product categories) tendency towards homogenization of world cultures[10], this issue must be raised for each company, on the basis of its product and markets.

8.3 The service attributes

These may include the following (the list is not exhaustive):

- Repair and maintenance, after-sales service.
- Installation.
- Instruction manuals.
- Other related services (demonstrations, technical assistance).
- Delivery and delivery dates (and respect for them).
- Guarantees.
- Spare parts availability.
- Return of goods, whether defective or not.

The extent of service attributes differs according to the type of good to be serviced. Service attributes are essential for industrial equipment and many consumer durables. Although it might not seem so, they also have a significant role to play in the field of consumer non-durables. Service requirements differ widely from country to country (box 5) because they are related to environmental factors such as the following:

- The level of technical expertise.
- The level of labour costs, which is decisive in the balance between durability and reparability. Africans are experts are repairing and even revamping totally clapped-out cars. Anywhere else, these cars would be scrapped.
- The level of literacy (this may render instruction manuals useless).[11]
- Climatic differences: certain climates increase the difficulty of performing certain technical operations because of temperature, air hygrometry, etc.
- The remoteness of locations which can render services difficult and costly to perform (e.g. servicing a gas turbine in the middle of the Amazonian forest).
- Different ways of performing a service (see Box 8.2).

Box 8.2   *Who's afraid of injections?*

What is more standard in appearance than a syringe and an injection? There are, however, significant differences in the methods used to avoid causing pain to the patient. For intra-muscular syringes, there are two different ways of administering an injection. They correspond to two basic service attributes (correct injection of the substance, avoidance of pain), but are performed in two different ways:

1. Only the needle itself is stuck in, then the body of the syringe (the cylinder containing the substance and the plunger driving it) is fixed into the base of the needle, in accordance with a technique known as *luerslip* (this method is used in America). The first question asked by an American nurse is: does it unscrew? (Service attribute.)
2. French, Italian and Spanish doctors and nurses prefer (and are used to) using the fully assembled syringe. The American method would probably involve the risk of 'slashing' their patient when connecting the two parts of the syringe once the needle has been implanted (an operation they are not used to doing). The service attribute required of the syringe is therefore based on its lightness and being in one piece, which is provided by a bolt system (*luerlock*). The first question asked by a French, Italian or Spanish nurse is: does it hold tight?

Further service attributes relate to who is legally permitted and professionally qualified to administer an injection and where it is possible to buy syringes. In Italy – in contrast to other European countries – syringes are on general sale, even in corner shops. They are available in blister packaging at the supermarket. Traditionally, many housewives actually give injections to members of their family.

(Excerpt from a discussion with Beckton Dickinson, world leader in single-use medical items – consumables.)

Services are generally performed by delegation to distribution channels. The shortage of available and/or adequate channels and the small size of the distribution outlets are an obstacle to services, particularly in developing countries (Wadinambiaratchi, 1965). Actual services in developing countries are traditional ones and are of a limited technical ability: carpenters, goldsmiths and blacksmiths (Verma, 1980). Long-term development planning places very little emphasis on investment in the distribution channels (Oritt and Hagen, 1977).

Even across developed countries, differences in distribution systems are much greater than one might expect. Daily and weekly shop opening hours vary widely between northern and southern Europe. This may range from less than 60 hours per week total opening time in northern Europe to more than 100 hours per week in southern Europe. This affects the quantities purchased and the type of purchaser (for example, where the husband and wife are at work during shop opening hours, an elderly parent with different tastes may have to do the shopping for them).

The decision to adapt services to diversified international requirements implies little cost in terms of economies of scale (box 6), since increasing returns to scale are far easier to reach for the physical attributes than for the service attributes of a product. On the other hand, there can be substantial learning effects with service attributes. For example, various management procedures such as the stocking of spare parts or hotel laundering may be standardized.

In certain cases (box 7) the adaptation of service attributes will lead to cost savings because locally supplied services will be far less comprehensive than in the country of origin. This is feasible either when local service requirements are less demanding or when the product has been expressly constructed to be almost maintenance-free. In this case it will also be designed to stand up to 'untrained' users. Physical attributes will then interact with service attributes within the product as a whole (bottom of Figure 8.1).

However, service standardization (box 8) will be required when the clientele is internationally 'mobile'. Customers move with their service requirements. The global success of truck manufacturers from northern Europe (DAF, Volvo, Scania, Mercedes) is due in part to their ability to offer a standardized service in a range of countries and on sites along the routes that are most commonly taken by international lorry drivers. For instance, an engine or a gearbox can be completely overhauled within a specified period of time at any location on the route.

8.4   The symbolic attributes

National differences in the interpretation of symbols

The *symbol* can be defined linguistically as the sign that operates a relationship which is non-causal (as opposed to the *indicator*) and non-analogous (as opposed to the *icon*).[12] It works as a powerful means of suggestion and evocation. For our adaptation/ standardization framework, two different issues shall be addressed:

1. The relationship between symbolic attitudes and national product images, with respect to the product category, the name of the company, the brand name and the country of manufacture (see Chapter 9).

2. Cultural differences entail sometimes divergent symbolic interpretations. Meanings are principally conveyed by the packaging and product presentation. If a symbolic attribute which was ethnocentrically conceived has a very different and highly negative interpretation in the target culture, adaptation is required.

The link between symbols and culture

This link comprises seven successive steps. The starting point is a conceptual one: colours, for example, are wavelengths of light reflected by objects; a set of waves of different frequencies produces a colour spectrum. If it is stated that an object is red, this means the following:

1. It soaks up all received light except red.
2, The language has the term called 'red', which designates a certain part of the spectrum that reflects the object (which has no colour as such).
3. Our perceptual apparatus – eyes, retinas, optical nerves, brains – are capable of identifying the wavelengths.
4. Through a learning mechanism, both linguistic and visual, we have learned to recognize this colour as 'red' since early childhood; that is, to qualify it by imitation of all the other people who also designate this colour as 'red'.

Perception results from a culture-based adaptive process (points 2 and 4 above). Numerous experimental studies have shown that certain peoples have a less discriminating perception of colour (their vocabulary and identification is more restricted). They 'mix up' certain 'colours' that other peoples can distinguish. It has also been shown that sensitivity to visual illusions varies according to culture, particularly as a result of the effects of syncretism. Suggestive visual associations result from our daily environment. Our native physical environment shapes our perceptual universe (see section 2.4). In order to move on from the *percept* (i.e. the subjects are able to formulate verbally what has been shown to them) to the *symbolic image*, three steps must be added to the four previously set out. The cultural process intervenes at each of these three final steps:

5. An association has been established between a certain colour, form, smell, etc.[13] and a suggested meaning, as in the two parts of the Greek symbol (see the etymological definition of the symbol given on p. 222). Initially there can be a highly tangible link: for example, the colour brown may be tainted by a negative sense in the connotation of waste, since it may be concretely associated with excrement.
6. This link is ignored:[14] why in most Western countries is blue the colour for little boys and pink for little girls (important choices on baby-related markets)?
7. Then there is social overspill through education, advertising, the mass media, literature, magazines – in short, throughout society and indeed even to packaging and marketing communication in general. The symbol shares the characteristics of a language. It conveys rich and diversified meanings, full of nuances, and its messages are often implicit. It conjures up a set of evocations, suggestions and interpretations which are almost subconscious yet still very real in the minds of consumers. Indeed this set of

interpretations is to a large extent specific to each national cultures. For example: does orange juice have to be yellow, orange or slightly red, full of pulp or clear, thick or very fluid, in order to evoke different product attributes: the sense of its being a nature-based/non-artificial drink, dietary qualities, an image of refreshment, healthy for children as opposed to intended for adults?

Images diffused by symbolic attributes

Symbols, in their capacity as signs with suggestive power that is non-causal and non-analogous, rely on natural elements: colours, shapes, locations, materials, everyday objects, countryside and elements of nature, etc. In certain cultures the lake is a symbol of love, the blue of virginity. Most commonly the 'natural' backgrounds of symbols appear fairly arbitrary, in so far as the original link has been lost or transformed, as and when the symbol became widely used.

Ethnocentrism is instinctive in all symbolic thought. It is therefore quite inevitable. The inappropriate (or even just poor) use of backgrounds that diffuse symbolic images which are not adapted to the local consumer is a danger for international marketers. Lee strongly insisted on this point when he emphasized the ethnocentric bias in international decision-making, which results from the Self Reference Criterion (Lee, 1966).

Symbolism of colours, shapes, numbers, etc.

White is the colour of birth and in the West usually celebrates a life's happy events, whereas in China it symbolises mourning. Conversely black, which symbolizes death in the West (because of darkness and fears that the sun will not return?), is an everyday colour in China.

Hidden behind each symbol lies one or more material supports. Red, for example, is the colour of blood: it can evoke and suggest meanings that differ widely depending on the culture (see Figure 8.2).

Every culture has an image of blood, which feeds part of the symbolic content of the colour red (see Box 8.3). Naturally, the colour red can be linked to substances other than blood – certain flowers, for instance. Use of red as the dominant colour on a product or its packaging must therefore be very carefully considered beforehand (box 11 in Figure 8.1).

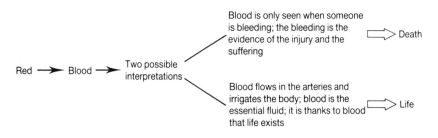

Figure 8.2 An example of diverging symbolic interpretations.

Associating symbols

The following two examples illustrate symbolic associations. Symbols which are diffused by the design of a product or its packaging may be associated with the intrinsic qualities of the product itself.

The Italian company Olivetti produced a typewriter which was such a beautiful object that a New York museum displayed it in its modern art collection. This typewriter proved to be a commercial failure in the United States even though the Americans liked its appearance. Potential purchasers found that its design did not inspire an image of robustness. Furthermore, in Anglo-Saxon societies there is often a puritanical attitude that work is an activity required by duty, which is sometimes arduous and should be more painful than enjoyable. This beautiful and enjoyable object was incompatible with such an attitude.

A French company exported to West Germany a cheese from the Pyrenees. On the packaging was a shepherd in the midst of his sheep. This picture was directly related to what was shown in the television commercial. In France this image conveyed the idea of natural fabrication and home-made qualities. A consumer test carried out in Germany, after the initial failure of the product, showed that the shepherd was associated by the

Box 8.3 *Colours, things, numbers and even smells have symbolic meanings ... often not the ones you think!*

Green, America's favorite color for suggesting freshness and good health is often associated with disease in countries with dense green jungles; it is a favorite color among Arabs but forbidden in portions of Indonesia. In Japan green is a good high-tech color, but Americans would shy away from green electronic equipment. Black is not universal for mourning: in many Asian countries it is white; in Brazil it is purple, yellow in Mexico, and dark red in the Ivory Coast. Americans think of blue as the most masculine color, but red is more manly in the United Kingdom or France. While pink is the most feminine color in America, yellow is more feminine in most of the world. Red suggests good fortune in China but death in Turkey. In America, a candy wrapped in blue or green is probably a mint; in Africa the same candy would be wrapped in red, our color for cinnamon ... in every culture, things, numbers and even smells have meanings. Lemon scent in the United States suggests freshness; in the Philippines lemon scent is associated with illness. In Japan the number 4 is like our 13; and 7 is unlucky in Ghana, Kenya and Singapore. The owl in India is bad luck, like our black cat. In Japan a fox is associated with witches. In China a green hat is like a dunce cap; specifically it marks a man with an unfaithful wife. The stork symbolizes maternal death in Singapore, not the kind of message you want to send to a new mother.

(Lennie Copeland and Lewis Griggs, 1986, *Going International*, Plume Books/New American Library: New York, p. 63. Reproduced with permission.)

Germans with dirt. The shepherd was withdrawn and subsequently replaced with a picture of mountain scenery. The product was then able to undergo a successful relaunch. For the Germans, the mountain evokes the image of clean nature. In this example the problem stems from the association of symbolic opposites: country/mountain – dirty/clean – natural/artificial. Clearly in this case the symbolic associations of the French and the Germans are very different.

Colours may also be associated with particular product categories or product attributes. Purple, for instance, is perceived as expensive in the Asian cultures, but inexpensive in the United States. Black is perceived as demonstrating trustworthiness and high quality in China (Jacobs *et al.*, 1991). Colours may also be associated with countries, the products of which are supposed to be the most likely to have this colour dominant on their packaging. By gathering data in four countries (China, South Korea, Japan and the United States), Jacobs *et al.* (1991) show that Asian nations associate red with the United States, but US people do not associate their country with red; purple is associated with France, and the four cultures reviewed associate both France and Italy with the colour green.

For those willing to design product attributes which convey appropriate symbolic meanings, the following recommendations can be made:

• When researching possible standardization, before any product launch, symbols that have a universal value (as far as they exist) should be chosen as a preference.
• Since there is a very great diversity in the interpretations and associations of symbols, any policy of standardization of product presentation or packaging must be systematically preceded by a product and packaging test carried out in each national market with local groups of consumers.

APPENDIX 8
◆◆◆

Teaching materials

A8.1 Case: Lestra Design

In May 1985 Mr. Claude Léopold, President of Lestra Design, was wondering what action he should take regarding the Japanese market. For several years, Lestra Design had been trying to enter the Japanese market for duvets and eiderdowns. The Japanese market for these products was certainly the largest in the world, but Lestra Design had faced a number of obstacles that had cooled Claude Léopold's enthusiasm. Then recently, he had met again with Daniel Legrand, a French consultant in Tokyo who had been supervising Lestra Design activities in Japan for the last two years. Daniel Legrand had explained that despite the earlier difficulties experienced by Lestra Design, the company had several alternatives which could enable it to be successful in Japan.

Lestra Design was a subsidiary of Léopold & Fils, a family business established in Amboise, a medium-sized town about 250 kilometers southwest of Paris (France). Claude Léopold's father had established the parent company in the early 1930s as a feather and down company. At first the company was mainly trading in down and feathers, but Léopold & Fils soon became a major French manufacturer of feather and down-filled cushions, pillows, bolsters and eiderdowns. In 1971, when Claude Léopold took over the business from his father, he decided to establish two new companies: Lestra Design to produce and distribute feather and down duvets; and Lestra Sport to manufacture and distribute feather and down sleeping bags. By using more aggressive sales management and the talents of his wife Josette, a renowned French fashion designer, Lestra Design rapidly became the leading duvet company in France. Josette Léopold's creative ideas for using innovative fabric designs with attractive prints helped Lestra Design and Lestra Sports quickly establish an international reputation for high class, fashionable products. Although in 1985 Léopold & Fils, together with its two subsidiaries (Lestra Sports and Lestra Design), had only 128 employees for revenues of FF72 million,[15] Claude Léopold believed that the prospect of growth in international markets was extremely promising.

Sales over the past five years had experienced double digit growth, and exports to England, West Germany and other European countries had recently started to boom, representing 20 per cent of Lestra Design sales. A few years earlier, Lestra Design had also placed an order in Japan through Kanematsu-Gosho Ltd., a 'sogo shosha' (large trading company) affiliated with the Bank of Tokyo and traditionally strong in textiles. However, the Japanese trading company had not reordered any product from Lestra Design since 1979.

Lestra Design in Japan

In 1978 Georges Mekiès, General Manager, and Claude Léopold, President of Lestra Design, had met with Daniel Legrand, a French consultant established in Tokyo. That same year, Legrand had conducted a market survey for C. Léopold which clearly indicated that a major opportunity for growth existed in Japan. With close to 120 million inhabitants and half of the population using duvets, Japan was clearly the largest market for duvets in the world.

In 1978 and 1979 Claude Léopold had been preoccupied with developing Lestra Design sales in Europe. As a result, he had not taken any immediate action to investigate further the potential of the Japanese market for Lestra Design products. C. Léopold first wanted to provide the French and other European markets with good service before addressing any other market in either the US or Japan. In autumn 1979, during the ISPO exhibition in Frankfurt (West Germany), Claude Léopold and Georges Mekiès were approached by a manager from Ogitani Corporation, a Japanese trading company based in Nagoya. Mr. Hiroshi Nakayama, the representative of Ogitani Corporation, wanted to import and distribute Lestra Design products in Japan. He especially liked the unique designs of Lestra Design's duvets and eiderdowns. He told Messrs. Léopold and Mekiès that the innovative designs as well as the French image with the 'Made in France' label would be the two strongest selling points in Japan.

The trademark issue

In December 1979 Ogitani ordered 200 duvets to be delivered to Nagoya. However, after the goods were shipped, Georges Mekiès did not hear anything from his Japanese distributor. By chance, G. Mekiès discovered on a trip to Japan in April 1980 that Ogitani had registered the two trademarks, Lestra Sport and Lestra Design, under the Ogitani name. Mr. Mekiès decided to call Mr. H. Nakayama and request a meeting in Nagoya to discuss the trademark issue. Mr. Nakayama responded that he was too busy. G. Mekiès then insisted that another executive from the trading company talk with him, but he received only a rebuff.

That same day, a furious Georges Mekiès called Yves Gasquères, the representative of the French Textile Manufacturers Association in Tokyo, for advice. Yves Gasquères, who also represented the well-known Lacoste shirts in Japan, explained that Lestra Design was not the only such case. The best advice he could give G. Mekiès was to contact Koichi Sato, a Japanese lawyer specializing in trademark disputes.

Georges Mekiès also saw Daniel Legrand, who confirmed Y. Gasquères' advice. D. Legrand said that, although trademark disputes were rapidly disappearing in Japan, there were still some recent disputes between Western and Japanese firms, especially with several big French fashion houses like Cartier, Chanel, Dior, etc. D. Legrand also mentioned the recent example of Yoplait, a major French yoghurt producer. A few years ago, Yoplait had signed a licensing agreement with a major Japanese food company, to manufacture and distribute yoghurt in Japan. While negotiating the contract, executives at Yoplait discovered that the Yoplait name had been registered by another Japanese food company under various Japanese writing transcriptions.[16] Although the French company decided to fight the case in court, Yoplait finally decided to use another name ('Yopuleito' using the Katagana transcription) for its products in Japan.

Before going back to France, Georges Mekiès arranged for Daniel Legrand to supervise the trademark dispute with Ogitani. A few weeks later, D. Legrand learned from Mr. Nakayama at Ogitani that the Japanese firm had registered the Lestra Design and Lestra Sports brands under its own name only to prevent other Japanese competitors from doing so. Mr G. Mekiès was not fully convinced, however, about the sincerity of this answer. One month later, he learned from D. Legrand that the legal department of the French Embassy in Tokyo was going to intervene in Lestra Design's favour. Finally, at the end of 1982, D. Legrand informed Léopold & Fils that Ogitani had agreed to give up the two trademarks in exchange for full reimbursement of the registration fees paid by Ogitani to the Tokyo Patent Office.

Looking for a new distributor

During his short stay in Japan, Georges Mekiès was able to size up the many business possibilities offered by the Japanese market. Despite the bad experience with Ogitani, Claude Léopold and Georges Mekiès felt that Lestra Design had a major opportunity for business development in Japan. The Lestra Design trademark was now fully protected by Japanese law. In April 1983 Claude Léopold commissioned D. Legrand to search for and select a new Japanese partner. To shorten the traditional distribution chain and reduce costs, Daniel Legrand decided to use his personal contacts at some of the major Japanese department stores. Department stores such as Mitsukoshi, Takashimaya and Seibu, which sold luxurious products, enjoyed a reputation of considerable prestige in Japan. Moreover, department stores had branches all over Japan, which would enable Lestra Design to cover the whole Japanese market. Most of these department stores were already carrying competitive duvets from West Germany and France, including prestigious brands like Yves Saint Laurent and Pierre Cardin. D. Legrand thought that department stores would be the right outlet for Lestra Design to position its products in the upper segment of the Japanese duvet and eiderdown market. D. Legrand also went to various Japanese companies in the bed and furniture industry as well as to several large trading companies such as Mitsui & Co., Mitsubishi Corporation, and C. Itoh. He also visited Mr. Inagawa, in charge of the Home and Interior Section of Kanematsu-Gosho, which used to import from Léopold & Fils. But Mr. Inagawa said that his company did not intend to import any more duvets from Lestra Design because its products were too highly priced.

The general reaction from potential Japanese buyers was that Lestra Design's colours (red, green, white) were not appropriate for the Japanese market. However, most of these buyers agreed that, with some modifications to accommodate the Japanese market, the 'Made in France' image was a great asset for selling Lestra Design products in Japan. Duvets and eiderdowns under names like Yves Saint Laurent, Courrèges or Pierre Cardin were being manufactured in Japan under license. They were being sold successfully because Japanese distributors and potential customers tended to view French interior textiles as another fashion product for which France was so famous.

To attract distributors, D. Legrand had advised Léopold & Fils to participate in the yearly Home Fashion Show held in Tokyo. However, C. Léopold and G. Mekiès had not responded to this suggestion. By June 1983, some potential distributors had already been identified, but most of them wanted to license the design and then manufacture in Japan rather than import the final products from France. However, C. Léopold clearly preferred to export directly from France and thus create more jobs for his own employees.

Akira Arai

In July 1983 D. Legrand met with Akira Arai, President of Trans-Ec Co. Ltd., Japan, a firm specializing in importing and exporting down and feathers. A. Arai, 41 years old, had started his own company six years earlier, after working for a large trading company since his graduation from Keio University.

Akira Arai was enthusiastic about French duvets and quilts and the Lestra Design products mainly because of the 'Made in France' label and the prestige attached to French textiles. Like most of the potential distributors D. Legrand had talked to, A. Arai also perceived Lestra Design products as French fashion products similar to the duvets and quilts sold in Japan under prestigious names like Yves Saint Laurent, Cardin or Courrèges. Some French fashion designers almost unknown in France had built a very strong reputation in Japan. Both A. Arai and D. Legrand felt that there was room in Japan for

Lestra Design to achieve a strong brand recognition. Akira Arai had had some experience working with other French firms. In the past, he had imported down and feathers from Topiol, a French company which was an indirect competitor of Léopold & Fils. D. Legrand thought that Mr. Arai, who had already heard about Lestra Design, could be a potential partner for the French company. Arai knew the down and feather industry thoroughly, and he had good connections in the complex distribution system of the Japanese duvet industry. A. Arai had also been highly recommended by Mrs. Eiko Gunjima, in charge of fashion items at the Commercial Section of the French Embassy in Tokyo.

Meeting Japanese tastes

In July 1983 Messrs. Legrand and Arai met again in Roppongi, a fashionable district of Tokyo where Mr Arai's office was located. Akira Arai explained that it would be difficult to sell Lestra Design duvets in Japan as they appeared in the current Lestra Design catalogue. In his opinion, Lestra Design would have to adapt its products for the Japanese market. A. Arai proposed that Lestra Design send him a sample that would meet the market requirements (i.e., sizes, colours, fillings, etc.). In particular, he felt that the choice of colours was very important. Although A. Arai liked the innovative motifs and the colours of Lestra Design products, he told D. Legrand that Japanese customers would rarely buy a red, pink or black duvet. Most duvets sold in Japan were in soft colours with many flowers in the design. D. Legrand emphasized that Lestra Design was introducing something really new to the Japanese market, but A. Arai insisted that most Japanese customers would prefer floral motifs on their duvets. Indeed, Daniel Legrand had noticed that almost all the Japanese duvets displayed in Tokyo stores had designs with floral motifs.

Secondly, A. Arai recommended that Lestra Design duvets be smaller than French duvets and should be paving blocked (quilted) to prevent the down from moving too freely inside the duvet. A. Arai noted all these requirements, including all the technical details needed to manufacture the duvet, so that Lestra Design could meet the Japanese trade expectations. A. Arai's product was quite different from those manufactured by Lestra Design, but D. Legrand was confident that the French company had the flexibility to adapt its products to the Japanese market. A. Arai also requested that Lestra Design deliver the sample within a month. D. Legrand had trouble explaining that Lestra Design, like most French firms, would be closed during the whole month of August for its summer holidays. A. Arai joked about the French taking so much holiday in summer, but he agreed to wait until the beginning of September.

The dust problem

At the beginning of October 1983, D. Legrand went to Arai's office with the sample that he had just received from France. With almost no hesitation, Georges Mekiès had agreed to completely redesign a duvet to meet the Japanese customer's expectations. The fabric was printed with floral motifs, paving blocked and exactly the requested size. Mr. Arai seemed pleased when he first saw the product. Then, as D. Legrand watched, A. Arai picked up the sample, carried it to the window, folded it under his arm and then slapped it vigorously with his hands. Both men were surprised to see a small cloud of white dust come from the duvet. Mr. Arai placed the sample on his desk, shook his head in disappointment and stated, 'This is not a good product. If Lestra Design wants to compete against the big Japanese, German and other French brands, the product must be perfect.'

D. Legrand immediately telexed Mr. Arai's reaction to Georges Mekiès. In A. Arai's opinion, the problem had to do with washing the duvet. Although Mr. Mekiès was surprised by the result of Mr. Arai's test, he agreed to send a new sample very soon.

Just after New Year's Day D. Legrand arrived at Mr. Arai's office with a new sample. Mr. Naoto Morimoto, in charge of the Bedding and Interior section of Katakura Kogyo,[17] a major textile trading company, had also been invited by Mr. Arai to examine the new sample. Naoto Morimoto was an old friend of A. Arai as well as a potential customer for Lestra Design products. After the ritual exchange of business cards between Messrs Legrand and Morimoto, A. Arai proceeded with the same test. Again, some dust came out although less than last time. Messrs. Arai and Morimoto decided to open the duvet and look inside for an explanation to the problem. In their opinion, the feathers had not been washed in the same way as in Japan. Mr. Morimoto suspected that the chemicals used to wash the duvet were very different from those traditionally used in Japan. Moreover, Mr. Arai found that the duvet was filled with both grey and white down. He asked D. Legrand to recommend that Lestra Design use only new white down and no feathers at all, even very small ones. In front of Legrand, Akira Arai also demonstrated the same test with several Japanese and German duvets. No dust came out. As a result, D. Legrand and A. Arai decided to send Mr. Mekiès samples of both a Japanese and a German duvet so that he could test the dust problem himself. With the two samples, Arai attached a note emphasizing that 'to compete successfully in Japan, Lestra Design products must be perfect, especially since the Japanese customer generally believes that textiles and fashion products from France are of high quality.'

At the end of March 1984 a third sample arrived in Tokyo. Mr. Mekiès had phoned D. Legrand beforehand emphasizing that the utmost care had been given to this sample. But again this time, the sample failed Mr. Arai's test. D. Legrand immediately phoned G. Mekiès to inform him of the situation. Mr. Arai was frustrated and, as he listened to Mr. Mekiès' voice on the telephone, it sounded as if Léopold & Fils were about to give up on the Japanese market. Georges Mekiès could not fully understand Mr. Arai's problem, because in his whole career at Lestra Design he had never heard any complaint about dust coming out of Lestra Design duvets.

D. Legrand thought that the only way to save the Japanese business would be for Georges Mekiès to visit Tokyo. D. Legrand emphasized again the considerable opportunities offered by the Japanese market and thus convinced Mr. Mekiès and Jacques Papillault, Lestra Design's Technical Director, to board the next flight for Tokyo. Mr. Mekiès said they would only be able to stay 48 hours in order to meet with Mr. Arai.

Mr. Mekiès' trip to Tokyo

A few days later Messrs. Mekiès and Papillault were in Tokyo. Mr. Arai claimed that he was genuinely interested in selling Lestra Design products in Japan, but he explained that in order to compete with existing Japanese duvets, Lestra Design products had to meet the local standards of quality. Messrs. Arai and Morimoto insisted that, since French textile products carried such a high image in Japan, they should be of the finest quality. Mr. Arai also stressed that only new white goose down should be used to fill the duvet. In an aside conversation with Daniel Legrand, Georges Mekiès asked if this requirement came directly from the final customer. D. Legrand replied that it did not seem to be the case. He himself had interviewed Japanese customers in down and duvet shops and had found that the average customer did not know about the different qualities of down nor did customers seem to care whether the down was grey or white. Mr. Mekiès was therefore a bit surprised by Mr. Arai's requirement. In France, as in most European countries, the customer was usually only concerned about price and design. D. Legrand explained that A. Arai meant to use 'new white goose down only' as a major selling point to market Lestra Design duvets as a high quality product to the distributors and retailers. From previous conversations with both wholesalers and retailers, D. Legrand explained that 'new white goose down only' was indeed a reasonable expectation, consistent with the upper positioning of European products in Japan as well as with the high quality associated with French fashion items.

According to the trade, the 'new white goose down only' argument would also justify the premium price charged by the retailers for Lestra Design products. Retail prices for Lestra Design products in Japan were expected to range from ¥60,000 to ¥110,000[18] and to be comparable with competitive high quality products imported from West Germany. However, prices varied greatly, from a retail price index of 100 to 300, depending on the quality of the down and feathers and their mixture inside the duvet. In fact, some stores, both in Japan and Europe, allowed customers to choose the filling for their duvets and eiderdowns, a policy which gave the customer a lot of pricing flexibility.

Retail prices for Lestra Design in Japan were more than two times higher than in France. Such a difference could be explained by the typically lengthy distribution system in Japan, which contributed to inflating the price of imported goods. For an ex-factory price index of 100, cost, insurance and freight would add 4 per cent, and duties an additional 6 per cent. Then, Mr. Arai would price the goods so that he could gain a 12 per cent markup on his selling price to Mr. Morimoto, who would receive a 10 per cent commission from the smaller wholesalers. In turn, the small wholesalers would put a 20 per cent markup on their selling price to the retailers, who would finally sell Lestra Design products at a price which would allow them a 40–60 per cent markup. On a retail price basis, Lestra Design products in Japan would be about 30–50 per cent more expensive than most local products of similar quality. Cheap models (either made locally or imported from China) would sell for ¥40,000. On the other hand, Nishikawa, the market leader, offered many models in Lestra Design's price range as well as a few prestigious models over ¥1,000,000. In selling competitive products from West Germany in Japan, the German tradition in making duvets was strongly emphasized. Advertising for these products would often carry the German flag, feature the 'Made in Germany' label and include a commercial slogan in German.

The washing formula

The conversation between Messrs. Arai and Mekiès then moved to the dust problem. Mr. Arai explained that, in his view, the problem lay with the composition of the chemical formula used to wash the down. Mr. Arai had already made arrangements to visit a Japanese duvet and eiderdown manufacturer in the afternoon. To get this Japanese company to open their doors, he had simply told the plant manager that a group of French importers was interested in buying the company's products. As a result, the Japanese manufacturer was quite willing to let the French group visit the factory. Georges Mekiès and Daniel Legrand were impressed by the state-of-the-art equipment used by the Japanese firm. Jacques Papillault noticed that the Japanese were using microscopes and some very expensive machines that he had never seen in Europe to determine, for example, the greasiness of the down. Georges Mekiès was also amazed to observe three Japanese employees in white smocks separating down from small feathers with small tweezers. According to Jacques Papillault, not a single Western manufacturer was as meticulous as this Japanese company. During the visit, Georges Mekiès also picked up some useful information about the chemical formula used by the Japanese manufacturer to wash the down and feathers.

The next day, George Mekiès and Jacques Papillault flew back to France fully aware that much remained to be done to crack the Japanese market. Before leaving, G. Mekiès told Mr. Arai that this trip had been extremely useful, and that Léopold & Fils would work hard to make a new sample that would meet the Japanese quality standards. Mr. Arai also promised Georges Mekiès that he would try to get more information about the chemical formula used by the Japanese company they had visited.

New challenges

Two weeks later, Mr. Arai sent Léopold & Fils some additional information on the chemical formula. Georges Mekiès then contacted a large French chemical company that immediately produced an identical formulation for Lestra Design. At the end of April, Mr. Arai told D. Legrand that Lestra Design should hurry with its new samples. Most wholesalers would be placing orders in May for late October delivery to the retail shops. Mr. Arai also indicated that Mr. Morimoto from Katakura Kogyo had already selected some designs and had basically agreed to order 200 duvets at the FOB price of FF1,200 each, provided that Lestra Design solved the dust problem.

In late May 1984 three new duvet samples arrived in Japan. Mr. Arai found them much better than the previous ones. However, he still felt that the dust problem was not completely solved. Messrs. Arai and Morimoto decided to have the fabric inspected in the laboratories of the Japanese Textile Association in Osaka. They both explained to Daniel Legrand that the fabric used by Lestra Design did not have the same density of threads per square inch as most Japanese duvet fabrics had. D. Legrand reported this latest development to Georges Mekiès, who was obviously upset by this new complaint from the Japanese. D. Legrand was also worried that the time required to have the fabric inspected would further delay the manufacturing of the 200 duvets that Mr. Morimoto was planning to order. In the meantime, Lestra Design had been obliged to order the fabric with the printed design selected by Mr. Morimoto in order to get exclusivity with its French supplier.

'Gokai' (misunderstandings)

At the end of June 1984 Mr. Takeshi Kuroda, an executive from Katakura Kogyo who was on a business trip in the southern part of France, visited Messrs. Mekiès and Léopold in Amboise. Mr. Mekiès had trouble communicating with the Japanese executive because of Mr. Kuroda's limited ability in English. However, Mr. Mekiès understood from Mr. Kuroda that Lestra Design had the green light to manufacture 200 duvets using the fabric selected by Mr. Morimoto. Mr. Mekiès communicated the good news to D. Legrand who phoned N. Morimoto to thank him for the order. Mr. Morimoto was surprised by D. Legrand's call because he personally had not taken any steps to confirm the order. Mr. Morimoto had first wanted to have the results of the test being conducted in Osaka. Finally, in early July, the report from the Japanese Textile Association brought bad news for Lestra Design. The Japanese laboratories found that the density of Lestra Design's fabric was far below that of most Japanese duvet fabrics.

The test results confirmed the fears of Messrs. Arai and Morimoto that the fabric problem created a major obstacle for selling Lestra Design duvets in Japan. Although the test could not legally prevent Lestra Design from selling on the Japanese market, A. Arai and N. Morimoto insisted that the French products had to be perfect to be sold in Japan. Thus, Naoto Morimoto told Daniel Legrand that he would not be able to proceed with importing the 200 duvets into Japan. Daniel Legrand tried to counter with the argument that the test was merely a non-tariff barrier for Lestra Design products in Japan. However, N. Morimoto answered that Lestra Design had to meet the market requirements to succeed in Japan.

When Daniel Legrand phoned the Lestra Design office in Amboise, Georges Mekiès was very upset. As far as he knew, the Japanese were the only ones in the world to conduct this kind of investigation, which he believed was a non-tariff barrier to prevent non-Japanese products from entering the Japanese market. Georges Mekiès' exasperation was increased because, following Mr. Kuroda's visit, the 200 duvets for Katakura Kogyo had already been manufactured. Because the duvets had been made to fit Japanese specifications, they could only be sold in Japan. Daniel Legrand replied that he would explain the situation to Mr. Morimoto and that he would try to convince him to do something about it. During the following days, D. Legrand tried hard to persuade Naoto Morimoto to accept the order. It seemed to him that Mr. Kuroda was directly responsible for the misunderstanding. But Mr. Morimoto remained inflexible and said that he could not buy products inferior in quality to those sold by Japanese competitors.

During the latter half of 1984 little communication took place between the French and the Japanese. Claude Léopold and Georges Mekiès were upset by the attitude of the Japanese. On the Japanese side, Messrs. Arai and Morimoto said that it was too late to meet with the distributors as most of their orders had already been placed in late July for the winter season. However, Daniel Legrand and Akira Arai had remained loosely in touch. At the end of February 1985 A. Arai said that he was still interested in importing Lestra Design's products. Both Daniel Legrand and Akira Arai were also convinced that, despite all the setbacks, there was still hope for Lestra Design to grasp a share of the huge Japanese market for duvets. Daniel Legrand had learned that Lestra Design's major French competitor had faced similar problems in Japan and had decided to give up the Japanese market. On the other hand, he knew that several German competitors were operating successfully in Japan.

In April 1985, Daniel Legrand took advantage of a business trip to France to visit Messrs. Léopold and Mekiès in Amboise. He was aware that Lestra Design was making a successful start in the US. In fact, Mr. Léopold was just back from an exhibition in New York where a major order had been placed. Daniel Legrand emphasized again the great potential of the Japanese market and the need to take a long-term view of this market. Daniel Legrand recognized that, although Japan was a tough market to crack, persistence would eventually pay off. Claude Léopold said that he had already tried hard and confessed that he was still quite disappointed by the Japanese market. However, at the end of the meeting, Claude Léopold said that he would consider one last try.

The alternatives

In early May 1985 Daniel Legrand again met with Akira Arai and Naoto Morimoto. Mr. Morimoto also mentioned that he would be interested in buying the original designs from Josette Léopold and then have the duvets manufactured in Japan under license. Claude Léopold was not keen on this idea. He knew that Yves Saint Laurent, Lanvin, and Courrèges duvets were manufactured this way in Japan. C. Léopold also knew that Lacoste shirts, although considered a universal product, had been completely adapted to suit the Japanese market. The colours, shape and even the cotton material of Lacoste shirts sold in Japan were different from the Lacoste products sold in the rest of the world. Bernard Lacoste, the son of the famous tennis player and a personal friend of Claude Léopold, ran the Lacoste business around the world. A few months earlier, Mr. Léopold had heard from B. Lacoste himself that in the previous year, the Lacoste company had had trouble with its Japanese licensee. Yves Gasquères, the French consultant in Tokyo who was monitoring Lacoste's operations in Japan, had discovered that the licensee had at one point in time 'forgotten' to pay the full amount of royalties due to Lacoste in France. Claude Léopold was therefore wondering if licensing would be the best solution.

Mr. Arai had also proposed that Lestra Design buy some Japanese fabric and manufacture the duvets in France. He argued that this would definitively solve the dust problem. Moreover, then Lestra Design products could still carry the 'Made in France' label which was so appealing to Japanese customers.

Another alternative recommended to Mr. Mekiès was buying fabric for the duvets from West Germany where textile standards were similar to the ones in Japan. Lestra Design could then print Josette Léopold's designs on the German cloth and still manufacture the duvets in France. Because the Japanese insisted on floral motifs, Lestra Design could even buy fabric with floral prints in West Germany. Mr. Arai had found that many Japanese companies like Nishikawa (the leading duvet manufacturer in Japan) were already buying a lot of German fabric for duvets. However, in order to be granted the design exclusivity, Mr. Mekiès needed to buy a minimum amount of fabric, the equivalent of 300 duvets.

As he was reviewing these different alternatives for Lestra Design, Claude Léopold wondered if he should continue trying to gain a foothold in the Japanese market, or should he simply forget about Japan and focus more on Europe and the United States?

(This case was written by Assistant Professor Dominique Turpin, IMD, Lausanne, Switzerland. Reproduced with his kind permission. Some names have been disguised.)

Questions

1. Is the French concept of quality the same as the Japanese concept of quality? If no, how would you relate it to the differences between the French culture and the Japanese culture? If yes, why is quality a culturally universal concept?
2. How would you interpret the attitude of Lestra Design's Japanese partners?
3. What are the difficulties encountered by Lestra Design in the business relationships with its Japanese partners?
4. What reasons could push Lestra Design to continue to try to penetrate the Japanese market for duvets and eiderdowns? What financial results may be expected, and when?
5. Suggest to Messieurs Léopold and Mekiès a strategic response concerning the Japanese market (go/no go, entry mode, producing locally or not, etc.).

A8.2 Case: Irish Cream O'Darby

Irish Cream is a typically Irish liqueur, prepared from a mix of whisky and cream, with a dash of chocolate. Irish Cream is very popular in Ireland. It conquered the US market in the 1960s and 1970s. Its success abroad has been so great that it is now no longer a negligible portion of total Irish exports.

The most famous brand is Bailey's. It holds a dominating market share, and the brand name tends to be used as a noun. People speak of drinking Bailey's rather than Irish Cream. O'Darby is a challenger to Bailey's, and it competes for the second market share with Carolan's. A fourth brand, Royal Tara, and two small competitors Waterford Cream and Emmets, share the rest of the market.

O'Darby, whose factory and headquarters are located in Cork, in the southern part of Ireland, was taken over at the beginning of the 1980s by Bacardi Rum, a leading multinational company in the spirits industry. Just a few months after the take-over, Bacardi undertook a large market survey, in the whole of the United States, to investigate how consumers perceived the generic product Irish Cream, and especially the O'Darby brand. It appeared that the green-coloured bottle was largely rejected by potential customers. A new packaging was designed, where brown colour dominated, for the bottle as well as the label. It led to an astonishing growth of sales, not only in the United States, but also in other national markets.

At the beginning of 1985, the director for the marketing of O'Darby hired a young junior marketing executive, Peter Finch, to be in charge of promoting Irish Cream O'Darby in France. Peter Finch, who had just graduated from a continuing education programme for training young export executives, travelled to France to see what could be done to increase sales. The exclusive distributor of Irish Cream O'Darby was the Bénédictine Group, a large liquor producer, which sold on the French market through a network of non-exclusive sales agents.

O'Darby was not the first company producing Irish Cream to try to penetrate the French market. In 1976 and 1977, Bailey's had spent a lot of money, especially on advertising, to launch the Irish Cream. The results had been disappointing and sales margins had not been large enough to cover the marketing expenses. Bailey's had not withdrawn, but it had discontinued its costly marketing expenses. Bailey's had concentrated its sales coverage on Paris, the northern part of France, Normandy and Brittany. It appeared that Bailey's was unsuccessful in selling to customers in the southern part of France. When trying to explain this relative failure, sales agents had mainly questioned the price level which, according to them, was too high.

During his first stay in France from March to May 1984, Peter Finch had been involved in sales promotion operations, with the help of the Bénédictine network. Shoppers in hypermarkets were asked to taste Irish Cream by giving them miniature bottles of O'Darby. It seemed to be difficult even to induce people to try the liquor.

However, this product was very popular in other developed markets under a variety of uses. For instance, in the United States consumers mixed it with Coca-Cola or orange juice, in cocktails. O'Darby was well placed for use in cocktails, compared to its competitors, because of a special formula that made it easy to mix with other beverages. In many markets, consumers used Irish Cream to coat ice-creams, cakes or strawberries. In Spain, where Irish Cream has achieved a good deal of product knowledge, Spanish consumers tend to call it Bailey's O'Darby.

In September 1985 the situation for Irish Cream O'Darby was as follows:

- It was sold almost exclusively in very large food stores (hypermarkets); it achieved a low penetration rate as a bar drink; it was rarely to be found in restaurants.
- The retail price was in the range of 45–50 francs for a bottle of 75 centilitres, compared to Bailey's which was priced in the bracket of 55–60 francs for a bottle of 70 centilitres.
- The annual sales for 1984 were 24,000 boxes of 12 bottles.
- Sales coverage was limited to Paris, the northern part of France, Normandy and Brittany. The best-selling area was the *département*[19] of Finistère (Brest, Quimper), which is located in the most western part of France; it is linked by ferries to Ireland. There, per capita consumption was three times as much as in the Paris region.
- There was no advertising. Sales promotion was done mostly by means of free sampling, in hypermarkets, disco bars or night clubs ('O'Darby party nights').
- The promotional budget, which was 300,000 francs in 1983, was more than doubled in 1984 to 700,000 francs.

Questions

1. Discuss and, possibly, criticize the marketing strategy which was adopted by Irish Cream O'Darby in order to enter the French market. In doing this you should, in particular, take care to examine what kind of market research should have been undertaken (a) prior to entering the market, and (b) after results had been achieved, and to question the coherence of the marketing mix.[20]
2. Irish Cream O'Darby has to decide on the allocation of its total marketing budget to its various national markets. You are asked to outline the criteria and design of such an allocation method.[21]

Notes

1. A.M. Bailly (1935), *Dictionnaire Grec-Français*, Hachette: Paris.
2. The numbering of boxes refers to Figure 8.1
3. The success of Japanese pick-up trucks in developing countries is to a certain extent a suitable illustration of this situation. Through adaptation involving product simplification (suspension, engine, gearbox, etc.), the Japanese have achieved an extremely low cost level.
4. In most of the literature on the adaptation of products for foreign markets, this point is often emphasized to an exaggerated degree. In Figure 8.1 it takes up only a part of one box out of twelve.
5. In many countries, public or mutual bodies offer to assist companies by examining the problems of conforming to the technical aspects of foreign standards, right from the very conception of the product.
6. A good number of companies, through a wholly understandable ethnocentrism, fail to consider the problem of adaptation of products for foreign markets. When they do consider the problem, often it is only from the perspective of adaptation to technical standards. But, even in this case, they fail to compromise with the loss of standardization.
7. There is a definite trend towards common European technical standardization. It is based on the EEC Treaty, especially Article 30, which prohibits quantitative restrictions on imports from other member states and measures having equivalent effects (that is, mainly protectionist standardization). The 'Cassis de Dijon' ruling has firmly established the 'home country rule', according to which a product should not be barred from import into an EEC country when it conforms to the standards of the EEC country in which it is produced. EEC countries, in conjunction with the six EFTA countries, are engaged in a European standardization process, through two Brussels-based organizations: CEN (Comité Européen de Normalisation), and CENELEC. This largely stems from the 1985 EEC White Paper, which identified technical barriers as one of the main obstacles to the achievement of the large internal market in Europe.
8. Product standards are in fact a very complex strategic issue (much more so than depicted here), since they have a definite influence on the competitive strategy of the firm. In high-tech industries, for instance computers, consumer electronics or telecommunications, the issue of compatibility of standards over time (multi-vintage compatibility) and across competitors, is a very important one. There are examples where promoting a standard and licensing it to the competitors (the VHS of Matsushita) proved a better strategy than keeping a monopoly on one's own standard (the Betamax VCR of Sony). Other examples show that it was more efficient to keep the technology under total control, as Xerox did for its proprietary electrostatic

photocopying technology for many years before the patent expired. For a detailed analysis of these questions, see: H. Landis Gabel (1989), 'Products standards and competitive strategy: An analysis of the principles, INSEAD Working Paper, Fontainebleau.

9. There is, in the real world, a lot of 'pizza relativity'. During in-depth interviews at Hewlett-Packard in France, some American expatriates told me that they had travelled to Geneva, Switzerland, 100 miles from the site where they were located, in order to have a meal at Pizza Hut. Although in Grenoble there are a large number of 'authentic' pizzerias (the town has a very large Italian presence), some Hewlett-Packard American expatriates preferred the taste, crustiness, toppings and cooking style of the American pizza. In September 1990, I was attending a congress in Milan and discovered that the Italian pizza (at least at the restaurant where I ate it) was not at all like those I am used to eating in Grenoble (made by cooks of Italian origin): the crust was much thicker and there was less topping. My last memory is of the oily Brazilian pizzas (which I tried only twice). Conclusion: pizzas, like 'Chinese' food, are largely localized, often because of the lack of genuine ingredients, but also because taste is localized. Local views of what is 'genuine' are mostly based on phantasms about the 'true' pizza or the 'genuine' Peking duck.

10. A very interesting description of the amalgamation of an immigrant culture's eating and consumption habits with those of the host country-culture is given by Herbert Gans in his classic book *The Urban Villagers* (1962), The Free Press: New York), about the life of Italian-Americans in a New York neighbourhood, which he calls 'West End' (ch. 9, pp. 181–95).

> Their actual diet, however bears little resemblance to that of their Italian ancestors, for they have adopted American items that can be integrated into the overall tradition. For example although their ancestors could not afford to eat meat, West Enders can, and thus spend considerable amounts for it. Typically American meats such as hot dogs, hamburger and steak are very popular indeed, but they are usually prepared with Italian spices, and accompanied by Italian side-dishes. The role of American culture is perhaps best illustrated by holiday fare. Turkey is eaten on Thanksgiving, but is preceded by a host of Italian antipastos, accompanied by Italian side-dishes, and followed by Italian desserts. This amalgamation of ethnic and American food is of course not distinctive to the West Enders, but can be found among all groups of foreign origin. (p. 184)

11. See, for instance, the role of written materials in African society (Chapter 13) and the case G.H. Mulford (section A15.2), which deals with instructions for drugs in Latin America.

12. *Dictionnaire alphabétique et analogique de la langue Française* (*Le Robert*, page 1903, our translation); The *Collins Dictionary and Thesaurus* (1987, p. 1018) defines the symbol as 'something that represents or stands for something else, usually by convention or association, especially a material object used to represent something abstract.'

13. Any animate or inanimate object may be a basis for building symbolic association. A fox may be a symbol of cunning, whereas an oak may be a symbol of strength. The use of the words 'may be' recognizes the fact that not every culture builds such associations. Either there are no foxes or oaks, or other interpretative meanings are applied.

14. Just like culture in general, there are two complementary parts but the way they are related has been forgotten (see the introduction to Chapter 3, p. 63).

15. FF7.10=US$1 in 1985.

16. The Japanese use three different types of transcription together with the occasional use of the Roman alphabet. In addition to Chinese ideograms ('kanji'), 'katagana' is used for the exclusive transcription of foreign words and names. 'Hiragana' is used for all other words not written in 'kanji'.

17. In 1983, Katakura Kogyo had profits of US$5.5 million on sales of US$2.8 billion and employed 1,852 people.
18. ¥240 = US$1 in 1985.
19. A French territorial unit, where there are generally between half a million and one million inhabitants.
20. You are not asked to prepare a marketing strategy as a whole, since the information available in this short case is not sufficient.
21. The problem is allocation between national markets (the United States, Canada, France, Spain, etc.), not between regional markets within a specific country.

References

Jacobs, Laurence, Charles Keown, Reginald Worthley and Ghymn Kyung-Il (1991), 'Cross-cultural colour comparisons: Global marketers beware!', *International Marketing Review*, vol. 8, no. 3.

Lee, J.A. (1966) 'Cultural analysis in overseas operations', *Harvard Business Review*, March–April, pp. 106–14.

Levitt, Theodore (1983), 'The globalization of markets', *Harvard Business Review*, vol. 61, no. 3, May–June, pp. 92–102.

Oritt, P.L. and A.J. Hagen (1977), 'Channels of distribution and economic development', *Atlanta Economic Review*, July–August.

Rogers, E.M. (1962), *Diffusion of Innovations*, The Free Press: New York.

Rogers, E.M. and F.F. Shoemaker (1971), *Communication of Innovations*, The Free Press: New York.

Ryan, J.F. and J.A. Murray (1977), 'The diffusion of pharmaceutical innovation in Ireland', *European Journal of Marketing*, vol. 11, no. 1 (October), pp. 3–13.

Tiano, A. (1981), *Transfert de Technologie Industrielle*, Editions Economica: Paris.

Verma, Y.S. (1980), 'Marketing in rural India', *Management International Review*, vol. 20, no. 4.

Wadinambiaratchi, G. (1965), 'Channels of distribution in developing economies', *The Business Quarterly*, University of Western Ontario, pp. 74–82.

9
——— ◆◆◆ ———

Management of images related to nationality and brand name

This chapter complements the preceding one directly: it deals with the symbolic attributes that are linked to brands and national images. These issues are particularly significant for a company which does not as yet have an established brand(s) on the international market. It is easy to avoid basic errors in relation to the choice of a brand name when starting from scratch. However, correcting mistakes once brand goodwill has been created can prove a costly and tricky operation. A brand, even one that has a poor impact, may be an asset because marketing communication investment has been made. Consumers are often confused by changes in a brand name. Brand name changes, if they are possible, risk wasting time and incurring expenditure.

First, the play of images between the images of the product's country of origin, the company name and/or the brand name of its products is discussed. This complex play of images warrants closer analysis. Once again, when starting without an established brand, there is the potential for intentional diffusion of favourable images, suitable for the product category and the targeted national segments.

The evaluation of product quality by consumers has been documented by a great number of empirical studies. The perception of certain product attributes, according to their national origin, has been experimentally assessed. The second section reviews the sixty-odd studies dealing with the country-of-origin paradigm. Consumers in different countries were questioned about their perceptions of their domestic products compared to foreign-made products of various national origins. These studies suggest consistent answers to such questions as the following: Are 'Buy British' or 'Buy American' advertising campaigns successful? Do consumers have strong preferences for their national products? Which countries are best perceived, and on which attributes? Do countries' images change over time?

The third section addresses the issue of the conversion of national brands into international brands. The linguistic obstacles that are met in this conversion are examined. The question of the so-called 'global' brands is also documented since this is becoming a significant issue in international marketing.

9.1   National images diffused by the product's origin and by its brand name

The complexity of national images diffused by the product

The purchasers of Swedish cars, who pay twice as much as for Spanish cars with comparable performance, acquire, at least to a certain extent, the symbolic label 'Made in Sweden' which, for them, suggests reliability and long life, thereby removing any fears of mechanical failure. There exists an important relation between images of products and the symbols diffused by their nationality. Relationships between product and nationality, in consumers' evaluations, were first studied with respect to the 'made in' label (Nagashima, 1970, 1977; Cattin *et al.*, 1982). But the 'made in' label is not the only element that contributes to consumer perception of product nationality (Schieb, 1977; Graby, 1980a). The following elements can be distinguished (Figure 9.1 (Usunier, 1985)):

• The image of imported products in opposition to national products, or the image of national versus international products.

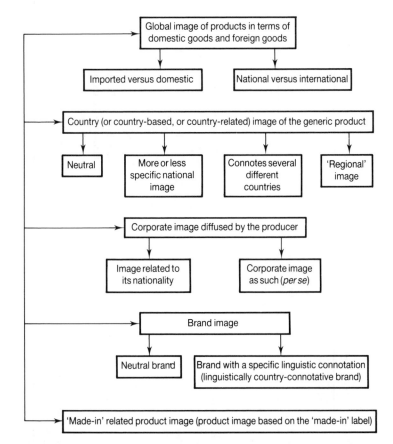

Figure 9.1   Several layers of country-, company- and brand-related product image.

Table 9.1 *Some examples of brand names and country-of-origin combined influences on product image.*

Product	National image of the generic product	National image of the manufacturer	Country evoked by the brand name label	Country image diffused by the 'Made in' label
Shalimar (perfume by Guerlain)	French	French	India/Orient	French
Kinder (milk chocolate bars of Ferrero)	Swiss and other countries	Italian (but the manufacturer's name, Ferrero, rarely appears)	German (means 'children' in German)	'Made in' weakly visible – often Italy
National (vacuum cleaner of Matsushita)	Neutral	The manufacturer's name (Matsushita) does not appear	The National brand makes people believe that it is a local production	'Made in' label weakly visible – different national origins
Coca-Cola	International	American	America	Neutral
Kremly (yoghurt by Chambourcy of Nestlé)	Balkan/Bulgarian Slav	Looks French, but is a world-wide brand from the Swiss Nestlé	Kremly (name and graphics) evokes the Kremlin, a Slav image	The 'Made in' label is a local one
Brother (typewriters by Brother)	Neutral	English/American (in fact a Japanese company)	International	The 'Made in' label indicates the origin

- National images of generic products: yoghurt calls to mind the Balkans, perfume evokes France, a pair of jeans the United States, etc.
- The national image of the manufacturing company.
- The image diffused by the brand name.
- The image of the 'made in' label in the sense of the manufacturing origin legally appended to the product; origin labelling is mandatory in international trade.

Some examples will illustrate the levels on which national images can operate (see Table 9.1). The set of normative recommendations for management of a product's national image includes the following elements:

- One should diffuse an image which corresponds in each country to what is locally valued (imported or national) in the category of the product concerned. This can lead to the adoption of a name from the target country, imposed by prevailing nationalistic feelings.
- If the generic product is generally associated with a specific country of origin, one should not hesitate to change the brand name. For example, a French manufacturer of machine tools should not be reluctant to adopt a German name.
- It is often advisable to reduce the physical size of the 'made in' label if the perception of the country of origin proves negative for local consumers (provided it is permitted, or ignored, by locally prevailing regulations). On the other hand, one should magnify it in the contrary case.
- The visibility of the company name, the brand name and the 'made in' label should be adjusted depending on their respective ability to convey the desired symbolic meanings.

9.2   Consumer product evaluation according to country of origin

The use of the 'country of origin' attribute

Consumers use the manufacturer's country of origin on a symbolic level. In other words, they use it as an associative link: Germany – robustness, France – luxury, Italy – beauty, etc. The cognitive processes that lead to these evaluations are therefore worth examination. Numerous studies have been devoted the country-of-origin paradigm.[1] The simplistic approach which directly assimilates a country image with the image of the product originating from that country is gradually being disregarded. Studies now try to analyze the complex consumer evaluation processes that relate the image of the country of origin to product attributes perception. There follows as accurate a picture as possible of the outcome of this research.

As Bilkey and Nes (1982) point out, the basic objective of this research was to demonstrate that the country-of-origin cue actually influenced consumers' evaluations. Attempting to determine in which direction and why, was only a secondary objective in the first studies (Schooler, 1965; Reierson, 1966, Schooler and Sunoo, 1969; Schooler, 1971; Etzel and Walker, 1974; Wang and Lamb, 1980). For instance, Schooler and Wildt (1968) showed their subjects totally identical products (drinking glasses). Some drinking glasses were supposed to have been 'Made in USA' whereas the others claimed to be 'Made in Japan'. They clearly evidenced an evaluation bias due to the effect of the country of origin. But price discounts may lead the consumer to purchase the 'worst' product – the Japanese one in this case. However, considering the *country of origin* as the only criterion in consumer evaluation of quality leads to an exaggeration in the importance of the 'made in' label.

A set of core standard images

Throughout country-of-origin studies one finds a limited number of certain stereotyped images. These fairly resistant stereotypes are consistent across consumers' nationalities: the image of robustness of German products, the image of France as associated with luxury goods, the image of Korean products of being cheap. However, shared perceptual elements are restricted and unstable: for instance, the Italians do not have the same image of their products as consumers from other countries, and the Korean image has changed over time.

Generally speaking, many elements of country of origin are not shared by consumers of different national cultures. Often, minimal differences in relationships between countries (similarity of culture and language, past colonial links, etc.) lead to differences in the perception of the same country across other countries (for example Yaprak, 1978). Krishnakumar (1974) has, for instance, shown that Indian students evaluate British products more positively than do students from Taiwan, a difference attributable to the past colonial links between Great Britain and India. Yavas and Alpay (1986) have demonstrated that in two proximate countries, Saudi Arabia and Bahrain, consumers hold the same views of products originating from abroad.

Use by consumers of the image of the country of origin of goods for their evaluation

Country of origin is only one attribute among many that characterize a product. A product possesses intrinsic attributes (size, colour and quality, for example) as well as extrinsic attributes (such as price). Country of origin is therefore only one criterion of evaluation (Erickson *et al.*, 1984). The influence of the country-of-origin evaluation cue is strongest where the consumer is unfamiliar with a product category. In this situation, the country of origin serves as a sort of proxy variable that facilitates evaluation in the absence of other criteria. It also serves to sum up diversified evaluation criteria within a sort of global evaluation (Morello, 1984). In the absence of other information cues, the consumer will use the country-of-origin to evaluate the product. Ultimately, positive evaluations of certain products of specific national origin may have a favourable influence on rather different products originating from the same country.

Various studies have insisted on the mediation of stereotypes concerning the country itself, by means of an association product to country or country to attribute, in the effect of the country-of-origin on the evaluation of the product. For example, for the Iranians 'The Germans are well-ordered and hard working, the French inventive and DIYers even in business matters, the Japanese copiers...' (Bon and Ollivier, 1979, p. 106).

The mediation of perceived risk

A sound hypothesis which has been proposed by several studies is the mediation of perceived risk to explain the influence of the country of origin on consumer evaluations. Either consumers perceive a lesser risk for national products, which would explain the preference for national products, or they perceive a lesser risk for the products of certain countries with a favourable image (see Box 9.1). Accordingly consumers would tend to prefer certain sources because they perceive a reduced risk in purchasing that country's products (Lumpkin *et al.*, 1985).

Hampton (1977) considered the situation where American goods are manufactured either in the United States or abroad in selected countries. In the sample were some strong perceived-risk countries (Algeria, Pakistan, Turkey), some moderate perceived-risk countries (Philippines, Hong Kong) and some weak perceived-risk countries (Canada, Japan, West Germany). In the questionnaire these origins were combined with a sample of products that offered diverse levels of perceived risk. Overall the results confirmed that consumers perceived less risk for goods manufactured in the United States than for the same foreign-made products, whatever the level of perceived risk of the foreign country of manufacture. In several instances, product-country connections were clearly established

Box 9.1   *Confession of a purchaser of Italian products*

When I consider the origins of my purchases I am fascinated by the number of Italian-made goods I have acquired. My Fiat Uno is the seventh Fiat I have bought. One of these Fiats (a 127) saved my life when I was in Paris. I was waiting at a red light when a Mercedes failed to brake and went into the back of me, sending me 30 yards forward. My Fiat had to be scrapped, but I was unharmed. At home, the washing machine and dryer are Zanussi, and the deep-freeze is a Hiberna. When I go trekking, my mountain shoes are from Trezetta. Like many Europeans, I like Barilla pasta and cakes. In fact, I am a price-minded consumer: Italian products are often the cheapest. Being somewhat price-averse (but not stingy), I believe that 'quality' and 'durability' will never match the price advantage. But price is not the only merit of Italian products. Italian products are much more reliable than stereotyped images would sometimes have you believe. Having successfully tried Italian products, my perceived risk is low when buying 'Made in Italy'. Italian goods are probably slightly less solid than German goods, but I very much like their *design* and function. Even though it is a small car, I like the style of the body and the interior of the Fiat Uno, as well as its sporty-looking engine. If well maintained, the durability of Italian products is excellent. Their price–quality ratio is fairly reasonable in the long run. Paradoxically, Italian products often do not reach their ideal purchasers: many purchasers of Italian products belong to the price-minded segment; they tend not to spend the required time in maintenance. Mercedes buyers, on the other hand, are much more likely to do so. The 'Made in Italy' deserves, in my opinion, better appreciation.

in consumers' minds, such as the colour television and Japan, the calculator and Hong Kong, or even instant coffee and Brazil, thereby reducing the level of perceived risk of a country as a general place of manufacture. For these specific products, these countries were considered favourable for their manufacture.

In their study of the risk perceived by Americans for clothing purposes – clothes and shoes made abroad versus those made in the United States – Lumpkin, Crawford and Kim (1985) confirm that the perceived risk is weaker for a product of national origin. They showed that perceived risk only has a strong influence when consumers are aware of the foreign origin of the clothes. They also detected differences according to the categories of products: certain countries (China, Korea) presented the same perceived risk whatever the product whereas Italy offered a weak perceived risk for shoe purchases and France offered a high perceived risk when buying jeans.

Also using clothing purposes in their experimental setting, Baumgartner and Jolibert (1977) have proved that certain traits of a foreign country may reduce the perceived risk· if the consumers (French, in this case) hold the belief that a foreign country, by virtue of its physical, climatic or social environment, is particularly suitable for the manufacture of a particular product: for instance, an English overcoat for the winter. Generally, the overall level of perceived risk for a specific national origin is reduced for its *ethnic* products.

Preference for national products

It has persistently been demonstrated that in most developed countries domestic products generally enjoy a more favourable evaluation than foreign-made products. This has been clearly evidenced for US as well as Japanese consumers (Reierson, 1966; Nagashima, 1970; Gaedeke, 1973; Lillis and Narayana, 1974; Morello, 1984; Heslop *et al.*, 1987). In the case of French consumers, Baumgartner and Jolibert (1977) also showed that there is a strong preference for domestic products. In the case of Finland, Finnish consumers deemed their products to be better in almost every attribute than seven other countries: United Kingdom, France, West Germany, Japan, Sweden, the Soviet Union and the United States (Darling and Kraft, 1977). This preference for nationally made products has been corroborated by several other studies (Bannister and Saunders, 1978, in the case of England, Graby, 1980a and 1980b, in the case of France; Cattin *et al.*, 1982, in the case of France and the United States). Conversely, in the case of developing countries, national products are not preferred to imported goods. Iranian producers, for instance, were shown to prefer imported products (Bon and Ollivier, 1979). In Iran, a product was favourably rated when it had a foreign/imported label. Bon and Ollivier did, however, observe the emergence of a deep-rooted nationalistic feeling in purchasing situations. They noted that there was at the time no 'Buy Iranian' campaign in the style of state-sponsored advertising campaigns for the purchase of national products, such as occur regularly in European countries and the United States, or as are permanently undertaken in India. Despite that, some Iranian buyers had a nationalistic tendency which consisted of buying primarily local products. They perceived imported products as unfair competition to Iranian products and considered the success of foreign-made products a potential brake on the social and economic development of Iran. This attitude, however, did not seem to be very widespread (Bon and Ollivier, 1979, p. 104). In Eastern European countries similar attitudes exist: for instance, the Hungarians generally evaluate foreign products more positively, although their image of domestic products is not particularly unfavourable (Papadopoulos *et al.*, 1990).

Consumer ethnocentrism and patriotism

Different explanations have been proposed to explain this preference for national products, observed mostly in developed countries. Graby (1980b, p. 37) suggests the following explanation for the preference for French-origin purchases by French customers:

> Unemployment appears as a prime argument; however, one should consider that high scores of agreement (on buying French as a way to maintain employment) pertain more to the unemployment problem because of its current prominence, than to a true purchasing motive.

In the same vein, an attempt has been made in the United States to measure 'consumer ethnocentrism'. Customers may consider the purchase of foreign goods to be immoral, since it puts the national economy at risk and leads to job losses (Shimp and Sharma, 1987). Shimp and Sharma studied the level of consumer ethnocentrism in different regions within the United States which were affected to a greater or lesser extent by foreign competition: Detroit, Denver, Los Angeles, North and South Carolina. They observed that consumer ethnocentrism was much stronger where the threat was perceived by individuals whose quality of life was affected by foreign competition, for instance in Detroit where unemployment in the motor industry is adversely affected by Japanese and Korean competition.

A related idea is that of 'consumer patriotism' (Min Han, 1988) which largely influences the outcome of 'Buy American', 'Buy British', 'Achetez français' or even 'Buy Canadian' campaigns (Kaynak and Cavusgil, 1983). Min Han claims that not only do patriotic consumers prefer to buy domestic products on the basis of strictly nationalistic feelings, but they also consider their quality and the service which accompanies them to be better. Min Han shows that for two different products/services, 'consumer patriotism' has contrasting effects: whereas it significantly influences the quality perception for motor cars, it does not affect the quality perception of vehicle maintenance and repair. In the case of television sets and their maintenance, the effect of consumer patriotism is non-existent.

'Buy national' campaigns should therefore be very cautious. The best approach to adopt would be to play clearly on nationalistic feelings as such, and not to attempt to influence consumers in their product evaluation. Consumers will probably remain fairly rational in their product evaluations, therefore an attempt to reinforce the quality perception of locally made products artificially could prove ineffective. The following section addresses this issue.

Are 'Buy national' campaigns effective?

The issue addressed is the assessment of the effectiveness of 'Buy national' advertising campaigns by empirical testing. Ettenson, Wagner and Gaeth (1988) investigated the case of a 'Made in the USA' campaign carried out for American clothing manufacturers. It was forecast that in 1995, 65 per cent of clothing sold in the United States would be cheap imported products. The CWPC (Crafted with Pride in the USA Council) provided a $40 million budget which initially funded a series of television commercials showing American stars boasting the superiority of American clothing. Consumers were subsequently questioned to determine the audience and the effect of the campaign. They proved reluctant to reveal themselves to be unpatriotic. Furthermore, their attitudes towards domestic products failed to correspond with their purchasing behaviour. The results of the campaign were unconvincing: 'retailers who have adopted the ''Made in the USA'' theme are promoting their merchandise in terms of an attribute that may have relatively little effect on consumers' decision making ... patriotic promotion campaigns should be considered circumspectly by retailers' (Ettenson *et al.*, 1988, p. 96). Johansson and Nebenzahl (1987) confirmed this result by showing that a campaign appealing to people to 'Buy American' had to be based on a normative influence (social norm favouring patriotic behaviour) as opposed to a cognitive influence (trying to convince the consumer that the national product is objectively superior).

Country-of-origin and brand perceptions: the effect of multinational production

As a result of the expansion of multinational firms, companies sell the same products under identical brand names in different countries throughout the world. These products actually have widely differing national origins, not necessarily that of the country of origin of the parent company. Sony products, for example, can be just as easily 'Made in France', 'Made in Germany' or 'Made in Britain' as 'Made in Japan'. An attempt must therefore be made to distinguish consumer evaluations purely related to the brand (and its country of origin, when it is identifiable) from the particular effect of the country of production. Several recent studies have been devoted to multinational production (Johansson and Nebenzahl, 1986, Min Han and Terpstra, 1988, Nebenzahl and Jaffé, 1989, Jaffé, Nebenzahl and Usunier, 1992).

Johansson and Nebenzahl (1986) were the first to consider this question. They demonstrated that a change in the place of car production (Chevrolet, Buick, Honda or Mazda) to West Germany is always positively perceived by American consumers. On the other hand, the status and quality images of these makes have suffered when a change has been envisioned in the place of their production to a country where low salaries are paid (Mexico, South Korea or the Philippines). This change clearly resulted in a loss of image in terms of social status and quality–price ratio.

Min Han and Terpstra (1988, p. 244) sought to determine which of the two effects had more influence, and their conclusion was unequivocal: 'the sourcing country has greater effects on consumer evaluations of product quality than does the brand name'. As for Eroglu and Machleit (1989), they concluded from their empirical study that consumers accord a similar influence to brand and country of manufacture respectively. The correlative question deserves consideration: what price reduction do consumers require to 'accept' a less favourable origin, in relation to a specific brand?

Johansson and Nebenzahl (1986, p. 120) have succeeded in determining the levels of monetary discounts (dollar values) at which consumers were prepared to purchase products from a 'less favourable' origin. They were, for example, willing to buy a Buick manufactured in the United States for $10,258 rather than pay $7351 for the same car if it were to be made in the Philippines. Jaffé and Nebenzahl (1989) have measured such elasticity of demand in the country of production with Israeli consumers, for three possible countries of production (South Korea, Japan and West Germany) and for three brands (Sanyo, Grundig and Sony). A discount of 30–40 per cent was necessary to sell Japanese or German brand products when they had been manufactured in South Korea.

Country image differences across product categories

Various studies have evidenced perceptual linkage between country-of-origin and product types. Certain products are considered more 'ethnic', more typical of certain countries; consumers tend to associate countries and products: Italy and pizza, Germany and machine tools, Britain and puddings (for example, Schieb, 1977; Niffenegger, White and Marmet, 1980; Kaynak and Cavusgil, 1983). Gaedeke (1973), for example, found that tinned meat made in Brazil is much more highly regarded than televisions made there, and that video recorders that are 'Made in South Korea' were more highly regarded than shoes from the same country.

Different studies have been devoted to industrial purchasing (White and Cundiff, 1978; Jolibert, 1979; White, 1979; Perrin *et al.*, 1981; Cattin *et al.*, 1982). Industrial purchasers were asked about their perception of relevant attributes of the product: price, perceived quality and technological advance. This leads to a better appreciation of the image of the country of origin of industrial goods. Germany consistently appears to have a substantial lead in product quality and reliability images, and also appears to be the most capable producer of heavy industrial equipment (Jolibert, 1979; Cattin *et al.*, 1982). This favourable image of German industrial products is to be found even in the United States, where American purchasers regard German industrial products as being of higher quality than their own. French and British industrial products are regarded as being of equivalent quality to US ones, and Italian industrial products as being of inferior quality to American products (White, 1979).

Perrin *et al.* (1981) showed in a study of the International Marketing and Purchasing European group that different national markets across Europe are not equally demanding as a whole and furthermore do not emphasize the same requirements. German and Swedish industrial purchasers prove to be more demanding, whereas the Italian and British purchasers are less so. German and Swedish suppliers have the same image of good technical quality and punctual delivery across all European markets. In the case of France, it appears that the unique trait of the achievements of French industrial companies is the exceptional quality of the relationships they construct over time with their French clients: 'actually, in no other country do purchasers accord such an advantage on this point to their national suppliers' (Perrin *et al.*, 1981, p. 102).

Influence of demographic variables on consumer attitudes towards the country of origin

The degree of consumer awareness and sensitivity to the country-of-origin attribute varies depending on the following:

◆ The effect of gender: some studies have suggested a more favourable evaluation of foreign products by women than by men (Schooler, 1971; Dornoff *et al.*, 1974; Galapakrishna *et al.*, 1989). Men are generally more influenced by 'Buy national' campaigns (Ettenson *et al.*, 1988). Nevertheless several other studies have shown that gender is not a discriminating factor (Anderson and Cunningham, 1972; Tongberg, 1972; Graby, 1982).

◆ Age groups: generally it would seem that the readiness to purchase foreign products decreases with age (Schooler, 1971; Tongberg, 1972; Dornoff *et al.*, 1974; Graby, 1982).[2] Dogmatism, greater nationalism and stabilized consumption habits are probably the result of ageing, and explain the reluctance to buy foreign goods.

◆ 'Social classes': generally a more favourable evaluation of foreign products is made by consumers when they have a higher level of education (Anderson and Cunningham, 1972; Dornoff *et al.*, 1974; Wang, 1978) or a higher income level (Wang, 1978), or when they have travelled abroad and are therefore more familiar with the products of these foreign countries (Graby, 1982).

Country image and product image[3]

Country images may become divorced from the image of their products. Imagine, for instance, the case of a country under a bloody dictatorship that nevertheless produces some excellent goods which are exported to democratic countries. The following issue therefore deserves investigation: does the image of a country (in political, economic, cultural and social terms), independently of the perceived quality of its products, have an influence on the willingness of foreign consumers to purchase that country's products? In other words, will consumers remain willing to purchase products originating from a country under a dictatorship or one which acts in contravention of certain internationally recognized rules, even if these products fit their needs? Or alternatively, does the overall level of industrial development influence the evaluations of a particular country of origin and of its products by foreign consumers?

Wang and Lamb (1983) asked ninety-four people, US nationals, about their readiness to purchase products from different countries (thirty-six in all). They also asked them to identify the political, cultural and economic environment of each country. In this way they were able to demonstrate that variables of the sociopolitical image of a country partially explained consumers' readiness to purchase products that come from there. The American consumers were more prepared to buy products coming from politically democratic countries such as those in Europe, Australia or New Zealand.

These results confirm those of Crawford and Lamb (1981), who sought to determine whether purchasers of industrial products were prepared to purchase foreign products and what their preferred sources were in terms of nationality. According to them, 'willingness to buy foreign products is influenced not only by the individual country, but also by the existing levels of economic development and political freedom' (Crawford and Lamb, 1981, pp. 30–1). A study undertaken for industrial goods from eight South American countries (Crawford, 1985) showed that American industrial purchasers preferred national sources on the basis of their political freedom and stability: at the top they put Mexico and then Brazil, and at the bottom El Salvador and Cuba. The degree of industrial development (not only based on objective data, but also perceived by partially uninformed consumers) has an influence on the image of the products. Khanna (1986) demonstrates that among the products of four countries from Asia (India, Japan, Taiwan and South Korea), evaluated by the consumers of the same four countries, the Indian products had the poorest image in terms of quality, creativity, design and technological level. Nevertheless it remains clear that vendors located in less favourable foreign environments may be cheap and reliable suppliers, in so far as they are carefully evaluated and given a fair opportunity to perform. That is the cost of their *learning* should be shared with their customer, and afterwards both will benefit.

How does the image of products from certain countries change over time?

Another important issue in country-of-origin images is whether there are changes in these images over time and, if there are, at what rate they occur. The response to this question seems to be yes, and the rate seems to be fairly rapid (Schieb, 1977). This is particularly true for products originating from Japan and the new industrial countries of Asia, such as Korea and Taiwan (Jaffé and Nebenzahl, 1989). Dornoff, Tankersley and White (1974) did observe a change in American consumer perception of imports from Asian countries over the last few years towards a more favourable attitude.

By replicating a 1967 study eight years later, Nagashima (1970, 1977) showed that Japanese businessmen's perceptions of their own products had become more favourable and that their image of the Japanese 'made in' label had significantly improved over the previous years. The Japanese stopped seeing their products modestly as simply 'cheap' and 'unreliable'.

According to Darling and Kraft (1977), the image that the Finnish consumers held of Japanese products was right in the middle of changing in 1977. At the beginning of the 1970s, Japanese products were seen as being of dubious quality; they were backed by rather restricted guarantees and poor after-sales service. At the end of the 1970s they were seen by Finnish consumers as having improved significantly as far as quality was concerned. 'Thus penetration into the Finnish market with an exceptional effort to win over the confidence of the consumer by extensive guarantees based on a local network of approved retailers, could prove to be a real success' (Darling and Kraft, 1977, p. 528).

Thee has also been a very clear improvement in the acceptance of South Korean products in the United States in the space of just over two years. Khera (1986) has demonstrated this by comparing the results of a May 1982 study (Khera, Anderson and Kim, 1983) with those of a November 1984 replication (Khera, Karns and Kim, 1985). Whereas in the first study only a third of consumers declared themselves satisfied with

Korean products, in the second they numbered almost two-thirds (65.3 per cent). The perception of the general level of Korea's industrial development (specifically in comparison with Taiwan and Brazil) improved similarly.

Issues related to the measurement of country-of-origin images

Many studies (though not all) have used samples of students to represent the overall population of consumers–evaluators, who were interviewed on products of different origins. It has often been claimed that using student samples may lead to major limitations in the external validity of these studies. Students are not definitely representative of the whole range of consumers. Furthermore the measurement instruments, such as questionnaires, psychometric scales, and the chosen categories of products or mentioned brands create problems of cross-cultural equivalence (Bamossy and Papadopoulos, 1987; Parameswaran and Yaprak, 1987).[4]

Jaffé and Nebenzahl (1984) tested the validity and the accuracy of alternative questionnaire formats. They tested two formats of questionnaire, which basically contained the same retrieved information but which were presented in two different ways. The two formats, although they had practically the same measurement accuracy, were nevertheless not wholly equivalent. Although they measured accurately, they were not measuring the same thing. In the research design a first questionnaire format (Q1) was presented to a group of respondents, who compared a set of attributes across countries; the scales in Q1 were therefore listed according to attribute. Questionnaire format Q2 was presented to a second group of respondents, who similarly compared attributes across countries; the scales in Q2 were listed according to country. Q2 is therefore more comparative across the countries, whereas Q1 is more comparative across attributes. The images of country of origin are therefore not completely comparable across studies, depending on the way in which the questionnaires are presented.

Most empirical evaluations of consumer attitudes towards countries of origin are based on likert-type interval scales. These scales present discontinuous levels of agreement/disagreement, whereas there is probably more continuity in consumer ratings. Ofir and Lehmann (1986) have tried to offer a continuous measurement of consumers' attitudes towards the countries of origin. By studying the differences in image of Austrian, Swiss and French ski resorts as perceived by American skiers, Ofir and Lehmann (1986) did not assume that there is such an ordinal evaluation as the scale on which responses are sought in most studies. They showed that it was possible to use a method which assumed a continuous underlying evaluation of the different attributes.

Combined effect of the image of the country of origin and evaluations as to the 'true' attributes of the product

Country-of-origin should not be considered as the only criterion consumers use when evaluating foreign products (Yaprak, 1987). It is often combined with other product attributes in the minds of the consumers. Some research has attempted to measure the relative impact of country-of-origin attribute, with respect to intrinsic attributes such as quality, or extrinsic attributes such as price. Accordingly, two studies dealt with the relative effect of price and perceived quality in interaction with the country of mnanufacture (Peterson and Jolibert, 1976; White and Cundiff, 1978), without being able in either of these two cases to find truly meaningful links. There was no significant influence of the country of manufacture on the perceived quality.

Thorelli, Lim and Suk (1989), by studying the interaction between store image, level of guarantee and country of origin, concluded that the effect of the country of origin on the perceived quality and the general attitude of the consumer is significantly less when the product is sold in an exclusive store with effective guarantees. This seems to concur with Reierson's conclusions (1967) that the image of a product of a specific national origin can be improved (with respect to its previous image) by association with a prestigious distributor, in this case Neiman-Marcus.[5]

Erickson *et al.* (1984) and Johansson *et al.* (1985) began to introduce more complex consumer evaluation models, where they use the country of manufacture as an informative cue. They introduced other choice attributes and examined whether the true effects of the country-of-origin attribute were operating on attitudes or beliefs. Consumer beliefs are located at a much deeper level in consumer minds than attitudes, and are far more remote from actual buying behaviour. According to Erickson *et al.* (1984), the country-of-origin effect has an influence on the formation of *beliefs*, but not directly on the *attitudes* towards the product (cars, in this case). The country-of-origin cue contributed just as much as the 'true' attributes themselves (objective ones such as price or gas mileage) to the formation of beliefs. Beliefs in turn had an influence on attitudes.

How the country of manufacture behaves on a cognitive level: as a halo effect or as (summary) global evaluation effect

Johansson *et al.* (1985) hypothesize that the country-of-origin cue works as a 'halo effect' when it influences consumer beliefs and attitudes. Johansson (1989) suggests two different interpretations of the cognitive effect of the country of origin:

1. It would be used by consumers in order to simplify the decision-making process. Consumers use this choice attribute as a summary criterion, which provides them with a 'ready-made' global evaluation. It will ease their choice, particularly when time is limited.
2. Consumers use the country of origin as a salient choice attribute when they have feelings towards and knowledge of a particular country.

According to Johansson, increased familiarity with product category reinforces the use of the country of origin as a choice attribute, contrary to what had been previously claimed.

Min Han (1990) has tested the 'halo effect' which affects consumers' beliefs and, only indirectly, their evaluations against the 'summary effect', where the country-of-origin cue directly influences consumers under the form of a global evaluation. By testing these two different models on two products (television sets and cars), he has shown that the 'halo effect' is used more when consumers are unfamiliar with the product category, whereas the 'summary effect' is used once they have achieved familiarity.

Conclusion

Taken together, the results of these studies suggest some major guidelines which should be followed when trying to construct a 'national image' strategy for its products:

* Consumers from developed countries have a general preference for their national products, but campaigns in favour of buying national goods do not reinforce this preference as such.
* Consumers do not use the country of origin as an isolated choice attribute but within the overall purchasing context (product category, perceived risk, knowledge of the brand, knowledge of and beliefs about the manufacturing country, etc.). Furthermore, country of origin is used as an evaluation criterion in conjunction with actual attributes. Attempts to dissociate the image from the reality are therefore unlikely to be successful. There is no advantage to be gained from selling poor-quality products in combination with a good 'made in' label. Such choices could be very deceptive for consumers.
* Images change fairly quickly over time. This is probably not the result of effective 'Buy national' advertising campaigns, because they had a poor impact on product image as such. Country-of-origin images change over time because products of a particular national origin are of better quality, the industrial expertise of local producers has improved and the guarantees offered to consumers are more extensive.

9.3   National, international and global brands

The majority of brands were originally conceived on a national level. Even among American brands, only a very limited number (Rosen *et al.*, 1989, see Chapter 6) have achieved international recognition. Most national brands are related to a specific linguistic context. Their evocative power is dependent on the language of the country and markets where they were originally launched.

However, certain brands were launched right from the start for their capacity to convey meaning internationally. The oil refining and distribution brand name ELF was created at the time of the merger of the petroleum groups ERAP and SNPA. Another example is that of Toyota: this name was chosen at the beginning of the 1960s by a Japanese car manufacturer which previously had a completely different name. The name was unsuitable for foreign markets and the company deemed that in the future, with increasing export sales, it would be necessary to have a name suitable for international markets. Toyota, with its three syllables, which can be pronounced in any language, was the name finally selected.

National brand names are sometimes inappropriate when they are used directly as international brand names . . .

Often, companies that start export and international businesses use their existing brand names which have particular sounds, spelling and pronunciation. The brand name should not have an unfortunate meaning in a different linguistic/cultural context. However, the reflex of questioning the translinguistic ability of a brand name is a long way from being instinctive. There is no shortage of examples: the German hair spray Caby-Net launched on the French market (*cabinet* is a toilet in French); the Japanese guns Miroku, whose name has several meanings including 'look at your arse' in French, although ultimately the name was not changed (de Bodinat *et al.*, 1984). The examples of certain American cars in South American markets are also famous. The Chevrolet (Chevy) Nova (the intended meaning was 'new') translates into Spanish as 'does not work', which gave a poor image of the car's reliability. The American Motors Matador meant 'killer' in spanish, in as far as it relates to the man who kills the bull in traditional Spanish *corridas*. The type of research that must be carried out is straightforward: it is necessary to interview a group of consumers from the target country about the perceptual effects of the intended names.

Often the brand name of products is the name of the company which manufactures them. This is a result of the history of the company. Consequently, there is no question as to whether this brand name is a good one in the minds of consumers. Since the brand name is historically related to the founders of the company, symbolically it would be difficult to change it. Such companies as Procter & Gamble, a name which is difficult to pronounce in many languages, have followed a twofold brand strategy:

1. Product brand names, such as Ivory, Camay, Pampers, Vizir and Tide, have been promoted almost independently from the Procter & Gamble company name (look at the respective sizes of the names on the packaging).
2. The Procter & Gamble name has been colloquially simplified so that it can be more easily memorized and verbalized, either to simply Procter or to P & G.

An example of lack of adaptation is offered by the leading French company for iron and steel and heavy mechanical equipment during the 1970s and 1980s, Creusot-Loire. It branded and sold its products under the company's name in many countries in the world, including the United States. Unfortunately this name was difficult to pronounce for American customers:

- The hard 'CR' sound hardly exists in English.
- 'EU' is a typically French diphthong, unpronounceable for Americans.
- 'S' must be pronounced 'Z' because it is located between two vowels (French rule!).
- 'O' is a very open sound.
- 'T' is, here, a mute consonant and must therefore be ignored in pronunciation.
- 'OI': once again a typically French diphthong (unknown in English).
- 'R' is a hard 'r', almost unused in English.
- 'E' is, at the end of the word, a mute vowel, and therefore must be ignored in pronunciation.

Naturally such a brand name is difficult to memorize for most customers in many countries. Moreover, such difficult brand names can be a serious obstacle to clear communication between buyer and seller; they may create confusion when discussing business on the phone.

It is therefore necessary to be prepared to carry out the necessary modifications.

Examples of changes of inappropriate brand names are suggested by Giordan (1988, p. 198):

> Kellog's renamed its *Frosted Flakes* to *Sucrilhos* for Brazil, as well as its *Cocoa Krispies* to *Crokinhos*; similarly Kellog's had to change its *Bran Buds* brand name in Sweden, so that Swedish people did not read that they were to be served 'grilled farmer' in their breakfast bowls.

Linguistic aspects of the brands' connotations

Table 9.2 (adapted from Vandenbergh, Adler and Oliver, 1987) shows various linguistic devices which can be used in creating brand names. Whether by accident or design, advertisers and marketers strive to give some punch and evocative capacity to their brand names. Of course this is done, as much as possible, in line with the symbolic connotations that they intend to communicate to product attributes.

There are four main categories of linguistic devices: phonetic devices (sound, perceived by the ears), orthographic devices (funny writing, perceived by the eyes), morphological devices (adding morphemes to brand name root) and semantic devices (the figure produces meaning, perceived through culture-based interpretations).

Linguistic devices in Table 9.2 help reflection on the following:

1. That which constitutes the pure linguistic capacity of a brand, independently of the established goodwill (brand recognition may be high for linguistically unadapted but long-standing brand names).
2. Are these advantages transposable into other linguistic contexts? The alliteration of Coca-Cola is, but the composition of the words Janitor-in-a-Drum or even the juxtaposition of opposites (Easy-Off) are not. This is because Coca-Cola does not require a basic comprehension of the words that make up the brand name. Required understanding of complex linguistic figures makes brand names difficult to translate and, more generally, to transpose. As a rule, the linguistic devices in categories I and II are more 'translinguistic'. A good number of the devices in category IV are not at all, especially 1, 4, 5, 6 and 7.

    It is not only the purely linguistic content of a brand name that has an influence on its verbal, auditive and intellectual meaning. The brand name is usually associated with a copyrighted design: the graphic composition of the logo conveys meaning as much as the letters of the brand name. Accordingly Cabat (1989, p. 344) emphasizes that the IBM trademark is inseparable from its graphics in its evocative ability to communicate with the consumer:

> The letters of the IBM logo are actually obtained by the superimposition of characters known as 'Mecanes' and of a 'blind' (alternate slats of coloured bands). The blind is in this case the informative image of the letters IBM, their morphological determinant.... It thereby becomes the sign of computer language, binary-based. The 'Mecanes' are typesetting characters whose square serif evokes industrial production and rooting in the mechanical world.

The imagery of the IBM brand-logo is translinguistic, and therefore offers a truly international ability to convey meaning.[6]

Table 9.2 *Linguistic characteristics, definitions and/or examples. (Source: adapted from Vanden-bergh, Adler and Oliver, 1987. Reproduced with the kind permission of the publisher.)*

Characteristics	Definitions and/or examples
I *Phonetic devices*	
1. Alliteration	Consolant repetition (*Co*ca *Co*la, *Co*coon)
2. Assonance	Vowel repetition (K*a*l K*a*n, V*i*z*i*r, *O*m*o*)
3. Consonance	Consonant repetition with intervening vowel changes (*Weight Wat*chers)
4. Masculine rhyme	Rhyme with end of syllable stress (M*ax* P*ax*)
5. Feminine rhyme	Unaccented syllable followed by accented syllable (Americ*an Air*lines)
6. Weak/imperfect/slant rhyme	Vowels differ or consonants similar, not identical (Bl*ack* & De*cker*)
7. Onomatopoeia	Use of syllable phonetics to resemble the object itself (Wisk, Cif, Wizzard)
8. Clipping	Product names attenuated (Chevy for a Chevrolet, *Deuche* for a Citroen Deux Chevaux, *Rabbit* for a Volkswagen)
9. Blending	Morphemic combination, usually with elision (Aspergum, Duracell)
10. Initial plosives[a]	/b/, /c-hard/, /d/, /g-hard/, /k/, /q/, /t/, (Bic, Dash, Pliz, Pim's)
II *Orthographic devices*	
1. Unusual or incorrect spellings	Kool-Aid, Decap'Four
2. Abbreviations	7-Up for Seven-Up
3. Acronyms	Amoco, Amro, DB, Cofinoga, Lu, BSN
III *Morphological devices*	
1. Affixation	Jell-O, Tipp-Ex
2. Compounding	Janitor-in-a-Drum, Vache-qui-rit
IV *Semantic devices*	
1. Metaphor	Representing something as if it were something else (Arrid); simile was included with metaphor when a name described a likeness and not an equality (Aqua-Fresh, Longeurs et Pointes, Head and Shoulders, Tendres Promesses)
2. Metonymy	Application of one object or quality for another (Midas, Ajax, Uncle Ben's)
3. Synecdoche	Substitution of a part for the whole (Red Lobster)
4. Personification/pathetic fallacy	Humanizing the nonhuman or ascription of human emotions to the inanimate (Betty Crocker, Clio, Kinder)
5. Oxymoron	Conjunction of opposite (Easy-Off, Crème de Peinture)
6. Paranomasia	Pun and word plays (Hawaiian Punch, Raid – insecticide, Fédor – orange juice)
7. Semantic appositeness	Fit of name with object (Bufferin, Nutella)

[a]An initial is said to be plosive if, to produce this sound, one needs first to stop the flow of air completely, then audibly release the air previously compressed.

Transposition of a national brand name to an international level

As advocated by Onkvisit and Shaw (1989), standardized international branding offers more market efficiency, by reducing advertising and inventory costs and providing convenient identification for people travelling internationally. However, the diversity of national regulations and the rarity of brands with similar spelling in some national markets sometimes make it difficult to register a standardized brand across a large number of countries.

Czinkota and Ronkainen (1990) have distinguished different possibilities for the transposition of a brand name originally created for a specific national context.

- *Translation*, pure and simple.
- *Transliteration* attempts to reconstitute in the target language the connotative meaning that exists in the source language (i.e. the language of the country where the brand is to be launched). In this way, the American hair care product *Silkience* (Gillette) is sold under the same brand name in West Germany, under the brand name *Soyance* in France and under the brand name *Sientel* in Italy.
- *Transparency*: a brand like Sony, for example, is suitable everywhere without translation problems occurring. The name Sony arose from a real 'shooting down' of the company name by the brand name of its products (Yoshimori, 1989). The original name of the firm (Tokyo Tsuhin Kogyo – Tokyo Industrial Telecommunication Company) was changed to Sony as soon as its products' brand name proved to be successful.

Functions of the brand according to national contexts

Lambin (1989) distinguishes the following functions of the trade name for the consumer:

- *Identity function*: the brand name guides consumers when making their choice.
- *Practicality*: the brand name works as a summary of information; it permits the retention of information about the characteristics of the products by the association of a trade name with them.
- *Guarantee*: as the 'signature of the manufacturer'.
- *Personalization*: the brand name allows consumers to express their individuality and originality through their purchases.
- *Entertainment function*: the brand allows the exercise of free individual choice, and therefore permits consumers to satisfy their needs for freshness, arousal, surprise, etc.

For the producer, the brand fulfils two essential functions: the *positioning* within the competitive scene and the *capitalization* of image and advertising expenditure over the long term.

These functions are very diversely valued across different countries, to the extent that some functions of the brand can be almost non-existent in certain national contexts.

Accordingly, Contensou (1989) notes that in France there is a certain social mistrust of brands, especially by public authorities: they supposedly increase prices, constituting entry barriers against possible competitors and thereby limiting competition. Furthermore, being set up on the basis of large cumulated advertising expenditure, it is claimed that they increase the price of the product to the detriment of the consumer. Contensou shows that in fact these fears are groundless and further emphasizes that (1989, p. 246) 'inflationary tendencies have no connection to brand development and the multiplication of products sold under brand names'. Kapferer (1989), taking the same defensive attitude towards brand names, has shown that they support the actual intentions of the manufacturers, their achievements in favour of consumers and that without effective attempts to foster product quality, brand images cannot be sustained.

In contrast to France, Japan seems to be a country where the brand is very highly valued. Yoshimori (1989, pp. 277–8) explains this:

> In feudal Japan, the brand was not distinct from the name of the ancestral house itself. This name had great importance, to the extent that everything was done to protect its good image, and above all to perpetuate it. Anyone who tarnished that reputation even through mere carelessness was obliged to rectify the damage through dying ... [Yoshimori then gives examples of Japanese executives who have recently committed suicide because they believed that through their actions or negligence they had tarnished the reputation of their company] ... a trading company, or any such firm, was not merely an economic entity; it also constituted a religious community which transcended the physical life of the family that controlled it. Ancestors occupied an almost divine place: it was therefore believed that the preservation and advancement of *kamei*, the name of the ancestral house, was an almost religious obligation since it (*kamei*) was the concrete translation of the presence of ancestors.

The brand in Japan is a real figurehead of competitive struggle. Abbeglen and Stalk (1986) show how, during the 1950s, the Honda brand name destroyed the Tohatsu brand (which today is completely unknown). They also describe in great deal the episodes of the Homeric quarrel between Honda and Yamaha at the start of the 1980s, which ended with a victory for Honda (see section 1.3).

In America, as in Japan, brands are central to competition. Brand marketing occupies a stable position in the strategies of American companies, but also one which is constantly changing, as are market shares. The vigour of the brand can only be built on 'tidal waves' of sales promotion and advertising as well as on consistent endeavours towards improvement of product quality. Dupuy and Thoenig (1989) compared brand status in America, France and Japan. They noted that brands in France have a much weaker status compared to the strong status in Japan and the even stronger status in the United States. By 'weak status' they mean that brands are the stakes of an unstable and conflicting appropriation process by economic agents. Large-scale retailers in France (hypermarkets) have created their own distributors' brands over the last twenty years (*produits libres*). Distributors' brands do not need any product-related advertising expenditure and tend to compete with manufacturers' brands. Therefore brand competition between distributors and manufacturers constitutes a major stake at the retail level.

Differences in national distribution systems explain to a large extent the degree of brand-related competition. In Japan, the *Keiretsu* distribution (see Chapter 11) enables the producer to control the distribution channel and therefore to direct the brand name principally towards the relationship with the consumer. In France, where large-scale distribution is involved in conflicts with producers, the channels develop their own brands. This leads to an inflation of brands which must therefore struggle to become established; this leads to a price war.

What is an international brand?

International brands share some common characteristics:

♦ *Long-term orientation*: the main objective of the brand is gradually to establish brand goodwill through consumer brand awareness and recognition. When products share very similar attributes and performance, a well-known brand may have the edge by virtue of its reputation and the consumer loyalty it has created. Accordingly, Procter & Gamble has retained brands for more than a century: Ivory soap, for example, is more than 100 years old. Camay soap is claimed to be nearly 70 years old (the brand name that is, not the formula of the product which has been regularly updated).
♦ International brands are therefore usually names whose public recognition has been based on *considerable cumulative advertising expenditure*. They are often supported by the history of prestigious companies (for cars – Mercedes, Jaguar, Ferrari, Cadillac, etc.). This brand goodwill was not 'built in a day'. These world-famous brands are obviously exceptions since, cognitively, there can only be a limited number of brands known by consumers in several countries throughout the world simultaneously (a few dozen, perhaps one or two hundred at most).
♦ Many of these international brands (Shalofsky, 1987) have a *basic credibility which is based on a national image*. Accordingly, Coca-Cola is a typical American drink; Marlboro cigarettes is in fact an American brand because of the Marlboro cowboy. Chanel No. 5 is based on the image of French *luxe* and *haute couture*, conveyed by the character of Gabrielle Chanel (Coco). Buitoni is understood as Italian pasta and Johnny Walker is a synonym for whisky from Scotland. Furthermore, as Clark (1987) argues, in each country, consumers 'repaint' the supposed international brand image with their own local images (see Chapter 6).

Brands and national images: a game of complex meanings

It is therefore advisable to be cautious before saying that a brand is universal. Even Coca-Cola is not known by this name in China since the original name would have a negative connotation. Low-calorie sugar-free Coke is called Diet Coke in the United States as well as in many other countries, but in some countries it is called Coca Light, because the word *diète* conjures up the image of a strict diet of bread and water.

Table 9.1 (page 250) shows for various brands the level of national images on which they rely, in combination with the product's origin and the manufacturer's name (also a brand). A name like Brother, for instance, offers a fairly good combination of interpretive meanings:

♦ There is no need to evoke any national image which would be related to the national image of the generic product. Brother manufactures typewriters, which are items with no 'ethnic' relation to a specific country.
♦ The Brother name diffuses an English/international image which partially hides the Japanese origin of the manufacturer. This may help when targeting nationalistic anti-Japanese consumers.
♦ The concept of brotherhood is a good one to support the image of reliability, faithfulness and loyalty of an object with which people may work closely (typing on the keyboard).

Global brands: a blurred concept

Although some people try to defend the concept (Peebles, 1989), global brands are a blurred concept and probably even a deceptive one. As emphasized in Chapter 6, global brands could only be portfolios of basically localized marketing assets (consumer franchise and goodwill based on images which are in fact heterogeneous). However, global brands may be seen as the simple collection of local brands, federated under a *lexically equivalent single name*. It is not even certain that this name, when pronounced, produces equivalent sounds and is heard in the same way. The way in which it is said and heard can be critical for television advertising, for example.

The management of global brands is a complex one. In his overview of the topic, Peebles (1989, p. 76) notes the idea of Marcio Moreira, New Products Director for McCann Erickson Worldwide, according to whom an advertiser should not pursue a global strategy to save money. The global brand, like the global campaign, requires a large amount of creative time and investment. A brand is a *sensitive asset of symbols*, suggested and maintained by diversified marketing communications: sponsoring, advertising communication, public relations, communication through the product itself or even the style of outlets. This mix of marketing communications must be carefully managed, so that the public never feels betrayed in those beliefs that have been invested in the brand.

Alain Etchegoyen (1990, p. 55, my emphasis) describes in the following way the brand image of Louis Vuitton:

> There is no mythology without gods or demi-gods. That is why one must not expect gods to collapse into the melting pot of the market. Some products have to keep at a distance so that other products appear to come from *somewhere else*. *The brand can only remain influential at the expense of maintaining a sacred fire*. The imaginary Eden of carefully tended (brand) images will not withstand the boorish hell of bar codes (products).

Furthermore, the complexity of trademark law must be considered on an international level. Although there are several international conventions, copyright and trademark regulations are still essentially based on national decrees. The 'Paris Union', an agreement which has been revised several times (the last in 1967 in Stockholm), provides that after a preliminary registration within a country of the Union, the beneficiaries have six months available for full registration. During this period they have priority (de Chantérac, 1989). But the full registrations are usually done by country, in accordance with locally prevailing regulations.

The World Industrial Property Organization (WIPO), located in Geneva, centralizes the registration formalities for the more than twenty countries that have signed the Madrid Agreement. This does not constitute neglect of the principle of registration, but a simplification of the procedure across a limited number of countries. As for the EC draft convention on European, community-wide trademarks, this draft directive has been gathering moss since 1964. In 1989 it seemed to be on the verge of being finalized (de Chantérac, 1989, p. 84), thus giving the member-states of the European Economic Community a common framework for commercial trademarks.[7]

In short, the costs and the legal complexity of managing a global brand remain extremely high. When starting from scratch, the creation of an international brand is an undertaking that should be considered as a long-term target. In this respect Yoshimori (1989, p. 279) quotes the reply of Sony's chairman, Akio Morita, in 1955 to an American client who was requesting Sony to subcontract. Morita refused to manufacture 100,000 transistor radios in OEM (Original Equipment Manufacturing) and, allegedly, said:

> Fifty years ago your brand name was probably as unknown as ours is today.... Today I decide the first stage for the next fifty years of my company. In fifty years I can promise that our name [Sony] will be just as famous as your company's is today.

APPENDIX 9

Teaching materials

A9.1 Case: Soshi Sumsin Ltd

Sammy Soshi's first assignment for his new job with Soshi Sumshin Ltd. was to recommend a new name for the firm's line of electronic products. Sammy had completed his M.B.A. at Emory University in May 1985 and had returned to Seoul, Korea, to work in his father's firm. Soshi Sumsin manufactured a line of electronic products, which included VCRs, stereos, and televisions. The senior Mr. Soshi got involved in electronics manufacturing when he agreed in 1975 to manufacture television components for an American manufacturer. Eventually, he was producing a full line of television sets, as well as VCRs and stereo equipment for three American firms. In addition, since 1982, he had been marketing his own line of products in the Korean market under the Sumsin brand name.

Mr. Soshi felt that his firm was now ready, both in terms of manufacturing know-how and capital to enter international markets under his own brand name. The American market was chosen as the first target because of its size and buying power, and an introduction date of April 1986 had been tentatively set. Having little familiarity with the American market, Mr. Soshi was relying heavily on his son, Sammy, to help with marketing decisions.

The first problem to which Sammy addressed himself was the selection of a brand name for the line. His father had planned to use the Sumsin name in the American market. Sammy pointed out that a failure to give careful consideration to the effect of a brand name in a different culture could cause major marketing difficulties later. He cited the experience of Tatung as a case in point. Tatung was a Taiwanese maker of televisions, fans, and computer terminals. When the company entered the American market, it didn't even consider changing its brand name. The Tatung company had favorable connotations in Chinese and was known in the company's oriental markets. However, in the United States, the name was not only meaningless, but it was difficult to know how to pronounce. Because of these difficulties, Tatung's American advertising agency finally decided to emphasize the strangeness of the name, and it launched a campaign based on a play on words which might help customers to pronounce Tatung. Each ad carried the query, 'Cat Got Your Tatung?' Sammy believed that a lot of effort that should have been placed on the product itself had been expended to overcome a bad trade name.

Sammy cited a second example of problems resulting from a poorly chosen brand name. Another Taiwanese company, Kunnan Lo, introduced its own brand of tennis rackets in the American market in 1977. Recognizing that their own name would present problems in the American market, they decided to select an American name. Ultimately, they decided on the name Kennedy; it was quite similar to their company name, and it was certainly familiar in the United States. However, after initial promotional efforts, it quickly became apparent that Kennedy was not a neutral name. Many tennis players were Republicans, and for them the Kennedy name had negative connotations. As a result, the name was changed to Kennex, a neutral, artificial word that was still similar to the company name. However, Kennex also quickly proved to be unsatisfactory, because of some confusion with the name Kleenex. To eliminate this confusion, the name was finally changed to Pro-Kennex, which provided both a tennis tie-in and retention of a root similar to Kunnan Lo. The waste of resources in the series of name changes would have been better avoided.

Determined to avoid the mistakes of these other companies entering the American market, Sammy Soshi carefully evaluated the alternatives available to his company. The first alternative was his father's preference – to use a company family name. However, Sumsin was somewhat difficult for English-speaking people to pronounce and seemed meaningless and foreign. Soshi was equally unfamiliar and meaningless, but he was also afraid that Americans would confuse it with the Japanese raw fish, Sushi.

A second alternative was to acquire ownership of an existing American brand name, preferably one with market recognition. After considerable research, he chose the name Monarch. The Monarch company had started manufacturing radios in Chicago in 1932, and Monarch radios had been nationally known in the 1940s. The company was badly hurt by television in the 1950s, which reduced the size of the radio market appreciably. The company was finally wiped out by the invasion of inexpensive transistor radios from Asia in the 1960s. The company filed for bankruptcy in 1972. Sammy found that he could buy the rights to the Monarch name for $50,000. The name was tied in with electronics products in the public's mind, but he wondered how many people still remembered or recognized the Monarch name. He also wondered whether this recognition might be more negative than positive because of the company's failure in the market.

A third alternative would be to select a new name and build market recognition through promotion. Such a name would need to be politically and socially neutral in the American market and ultimately in other foreign markets. It should be easy to pronounce and remember and have neutral meaning or favourable meaning to the public. The possibilities might be considered.

The first was Proteus, the name of an ancient Greek sea god. This name would be easy to pronounce in most European languages, but was almost too neutral to help sell the product. The other alternative was Blue Streak, again, an easy name in English, but not necessarily in other European languages. Sammy felt that the favorable connotation of speed and progress might provide a boost for the products to which it was applied.

Questions

1. Evaluate the alternative names being considered by Sammy Soshi. Which name would you recommend?
2. Whatever new name is chosen, should Soshi Sumsin adopt the same name in the Korean market?
3. What are the advantages of selecting different brand names, as appropriate, in each foreign market?
4. Enumerate the characteristics that should be possessed by a good international brand name.

(Adapted from Cundiff and Hilger, 1988, pp. 440–2. Reproduced with permission.)

A9.2 Case: Derivados de Leche SA

Derivados de Leche SA, founded in 1968, was the first firm to market yogurt in Mexico. It distributed yogurt under the brand name Delsa only in Mexico City, primarily in a limited number of upper-income areas. The company was family owned, and the capital was all local. For the first five years, Delsa was sold in food stores, particularly in the newly developing supermarkets, without any advertising or other promotion. Yogurt was a new, unfamiliar food product in the Mexican market, but Delsa depended primarily on word of mouth to provide product recognition.

During the next four years, the structure of the yogurt market changed dramatically with the entrance of three large multinational firms. In 1973, a number of laws regulating foreign investment in Mexico were modified under a single new 'regulation of foreign investment' law. According to this law foreign investors were welcome in Mexico on a joint labour basis so long as the foreign ownership share did not exceed 49 percent. Labor-intensive industries that helped to decentralize population were particularly welcome. All three of the multinationals entering the yogurt market operated on this joint venture basis.

The first new brand, Chambourcy, was introduced by a joint venture subsidiary of Nestlé which had operated in Mexico since 1935. This company, Industrias Alimentacias Club SA, was a major Mexican food producer with 7,000 employees. Chambourcy was launched with a strong promotional campaign and wide distribution. The following year, in 1974, a subsidiary of the French food firm, BSN-Gervais, launched their Danone yogurt in the Mexican market. Danone was also heavily supported with promotion. Finally, in 1976, a third multinational entered the market. Productos de Leche SA, was 51 percent owned by Mexican capital and 49 percent by the Borden Company of the United States; it entered the Mexican market with two brands of yogurt, Darel and Bonafina.

By 1977, the management of Derivados de Leche SA was becoming concerned about its future position on the yogurt market. All three of the multinational competitors were aggressive marketers and promoters and were strong financially. Although the foreign ownership was a minority (49 percent), management was dominated in each case by the minority ownership, so that management was competent and professional. In the short term, Delsa benefited from the primary demand creation activities of the multinationals. In 1974, Delsa sales almost doubled to 800 tons, and by 1977, it was 1,900 tons. But Delsa's market share had dropped from over 95 percent in 1972 (there were some other very small Mexican-owned competitors) to only 21 percent in 1977.

The three multinationals divided 77.5 percent of the market among them. If the trend continued, it was feared that Delsa's share of the market might drop so low that it would provide very little product recognition. And it was possible that ultimately sales volume would stabilize and perhaps even decline.

By 1978, Delsa management was faced with the grim reality of competition from financially strong and aggressive, professionally managed multinationals as shown in Table 9.3. Delsa managers felt that pricing could be blamed for this loss in market share; in 1977, the sales price of Delsa was slightly below that of its competitors. A major handicap for Delsa was its failure to promote recognition of its brand name. Although Delsa had been pulled along in the market by the initial marketing efforts which were designed to create a primary demand for yogurt, marketing efforts of the competitors were now focused almost entirely on selective brand-name promotion. Delsa management had concentrated its efforts on getting the product in retail outlets and maintaining good relationships with dealers; no effort had been made to create consumer recognition and franchise through advertising and other promotion. Management was made up of the family members who owned the company; they brought little professional training to the job.

Owner-managers of small and medium-sized firms in Mexico, tended to run their businesses for quick, short-term profit rather than long-term development. New capital investment was needed to enlarge production capacity, and serious consideration needed to be given to investing in a promotional campaign to build and maintain Delsa brand recognition.

Delsa was considering applying for a government-subsidized loan to double its production capacity from 2,000 tons per year to 4,000 tons. These loans were available only to 100 percent Mexican-owned manufacturers, but were limited to financing of manufacturing facilities. Delsa's marketing manager wanted to emphasize the local Mexican ownership of Delsa and to increase the firm's advertising budget from $20,000

Table 9.3 *The yogurt market in Mexico, 1974–77. Production and shares of different competitors (in tons and percentages). (Source: Cundiff and Hilger, 1988.)*

	1974		1975		1976		1977	
	tons	% of total	tons	% of total	tons	% of total	tons	% of total
Danone	163	6	990	31	2,420	40	2,940	32.5
Chambourcy	1,640	62	1,250	39	1,400	23.5	1,800	20
Darel and Bonafina	–	–	–	–	900	15	2,280	25
Delsa	810	30.5	936	29	1,240	20.5	1,900	21
Cremo and others	37	1.5	34	1	60	1	130	1.5
Total	2,650	100	3,210	100	6,020	100	9,050	100
100% Mexican-owned firms	·847	32	970	30	1,300	22	2,030	22
Foreign firms and joint ventures	1,803	68	2,240	70	4,720	78	7,020	78

to about $100,000. He also wanted to redesign the package so as to include some statement that indicated the brand was of pure Mexican origin. Delsa's owners wanted to put pressure on the Mexican government to limit the food processing industry to 100 percent Mexican-owned firms. It was not known what the possibilities were to get such legislation passed.

Questions

1. What are Delsa's strengths and weaknesses in competing with multinationals?
2. What is the impact of 'country of origin' on demand for yogurt?
3. What recommendations can you make to strengthen Delsa's market position?

(Adapted from Cundiff and Hilger, 1988, pp. 335–6. Reproduced with permission.)

Notes

1. See, for example, the literature review by Bilkey and Nes (1982); there have been various studies since, most of which are mentioned in this review.
2. 'Generally' means that the majority of research has concluded in that direction.
3. In this section only *products* are considered as far as their country of manufacture is concerned. Origin image for *services* has hardly been studied. However, Ofir and Lehmann (1986) have investigated the image that American tourists travelling abroad have of European resorts. The service quality image of French ski resorts appears significantly lower than that of the Swiss and Austrian ski resorts, particularly as concerns honesty and friendliness.
4. Cross-cultural equivalence issues for measurement of country-of-origin effects are subject to the same solutions as detailed in Chapter 5.
5. For the US market Morganosky and Lazarde (1987) have investigated the link between store image and the national origin of the products they offer (imported versus 'Made in the USA'). It appears that the quality rating of department stores and fashion boutiques was slightly enhanced by their association with American-made clothing, whereas it was negatively affected when their image was associated with that of foreign-made clothing. The quality image of discount stores was significantly improved when associated with American-made clothing, but not significantly hurt by association with foreign-made garments.
6. The link between brand and drawing is an intimate one. How, for instance, is the Coca-Cola brand name stored in consumers' minds? As eight letters, as the traditional design of the Coca-Cola words, or as a combination of both? Trademark legislation around the world varies a great deal according to the coverage: in France trademarks can only be composed of alphabetic letters and their design must be separately registered under the design and pattern laws if they are to be effectively protected; in the United States a trademark may be bereft of any linguistic content and can be registered solely under the trademark laws; there is no systematic need, in the United States and many other countries, for the additional registration of a trademark's design.
7. See also Thomas J. Maronick (1988), 'European patent laws: Implications for international marketing', *International Marketing Review*, vol. 5, no. 2, pp. 31–40.

References

Abegglen, James C. and George Stalk Jr (1986), 'The Japanese corporation as competitor', *California Management Review*, vol. xxviii, no. 3, pp. 9–27.

Anderson, W.T. and William H. Cunningham (1972), 'Gauging foreign product promotion', *Journal of Advertising Research*, vol. 12, no. 1, pp. 29–34.

Bamossy, G.J. and N.G. Papadopoulos (1987), 'An assessment of reliability for product evaluations scales used in country-of-origin research', in Kenneth D. Bahn and M. Joseph Sirgy (eds), *World Marketing Congress*, Academy of Marketing Science: Blacksburg, VA.

Bannister, J.P. and J.A. Saunders (1978), 'UK consumers' attitudes toward imports: The measurement of national stereotype image', *European Journal of Marketing*, vol. 12, no. 8, pp. 562–70.

Baumgartner, Gary and Alain Jolibert (1977), 'The perception of foreign products in France', *Advances in Consumer Resarch*, vol. 16, pp. 103–5.

Bilkey, Warren J. and Erik Nes (1982), 'Country-of-origin effects on product evaluations', *Journal of International Business Studies* (Spring/Summer), pp. 89–99.

Bon, Jérôme and Alain Ollivier (1979), 'L'Influence de l'origine d'un produit sur son image à l'étranger', *Revue Française du Marketing*, 1979/2, Cahier 77, pp. 101–14.

Cabat, Odilon (1989), 'Archéologie de la marque moderne', in Jean-Noel Kapferer and Jean-Claude Thoenig (eds), *La Marque*, McGraw-Hill: Paris, pp. 307–53.

Cattin, Phillipe, Alain Jolibert and Coleen Lohnes (1982), 'A cross-cultural study of "made-in" concepts', *Journal of International Business Studies* (Winter), pp. 131–41.

Clark, Harold F., Jr (1987), 'Consumer and corporate values: Yet another view on global marketing', *International Journal of Advertising*, vol. 6, pp. 29–42.

Contensou, François (1989), 'La Marque, l'efficience économique et la formation des prix', in Jean-Noel Kapferer and Jean-Claude Thoenig (eds), *La Marque*, McGraw-Hill: Paris, pp. 231–73.

Crawford, John C. (1985), 'Attitudes toward Latin American products', in Erdener Kaynak (ed.), *Global Perspectives in Marketing*, Praeger: New York, pp. 149–54.

Crawford, John C. and C.W. Lamb Jr (1981), 'Source preferences for imported products', *Journal of Purchasing and Materials Management* (Winter), pp. 28–33.

Cundiff, Edward W. and Marye Tharp Hilger (1988), *Marketing in the International Environment*, 2nd edn, Prentice Hall: Englewood Cliffs, NJ.

Czinkota, Michael R. and Illka A. Ronkainen (1990), *International Marketing*, 2nd edn, Dryden Press: Hinsdale, IL.

Darling, John B. and F. Kraft (1977), 'A competitive profile of products and associated marketing practices of selected European and non-European countries', *European Journal of Marketing*, vol. 11, no. 7, pp. 519–37.

De Bodinat, Henri, Jean-Marc de Leersnyder, Michel Ghertman, Jean Klein and Bernard Marois (1984), *Gestion Internationale de l'Entreprise*, 2nd edn, Dalloz: Paris.

de Chantérac, Véronique (1989), 'La Marque à travers le droit', in Jean-Noel Kapferer and Jean-Claude Thoenig (eds), *La Marque*, McGraw-Hill: Paris, pp. 45–90.

Dornoff, Ronald J., Clint B. Tankersley and Gregory P. White (1974), 'Consumers' perceptions of imports', *Akron Business and Economic Review*, vol. 5 (Summer), pp. 26–9.

Dupuy, François and Jean-Claude Thoenig (1989), 'La Marque et l'échange', in Jean-Noel Kapferer and Jean-Claude Thoenig (eds), *La Marque*, McGraw-Hill: Paris, pp. 159–89.

Erickson, Gary M., Johny K. Johansson and Paul Chao (1984), 'Images variables in multi-attribute product evaluations: Country of origin effects', *Journal of Consumer Research*, vol. 11, September, pp. 694–9.

Eroglu, S.A. and K.A. Machleit (1989), 'Effects of individual and product specific variables on utilizing country of origin as a product quality cue', *International Marketing Review*, vol. 6, no. 6, pp. 27–41.

Etchegoyen, Alain (1990), *Les Entreprises ont-elles une âme?* Editions François Bourin: Paris.

Ettenson, R., J. Wagner and G. Gaeth (1988), 'Evaluating the effect of country-of-origin and the ''Made in the USA'' campaign: A conjoint approach', *Journal of Retailing*, vol. 64, no. 1, pp. 85–100.

Etzel, Michael J. and Bruce J. Walker (1974), 'Advertising strategy for foreign products', *Journal of Advertising Research*, vol. 14, (June), pp. 41–4.

Gaedeke, Ralph (1973), 'Consumer attitudes towards products ''made in'' developing countries', *Journal of Retailing*, vol. 49 (Summer), pp. 13–24.

Galapakrishna, P., B.L. Garland and J.C. Crawford (1989), 'Consumer satisfaction with foreign and domestic products: A cross-cultural comparison', proceedings of the annual conference of the American Marketing Association.

Giordan, Alain Eric (1988), *Exporter plus 2*, Economica: Paris.

Graby, Françoise (1980a), 'Consumérisme et produits étrangers', *Coopération–Distribution–Consommation*, no. 5, pp. 17–23.

Graby, Françoise (1980b), 'Le Consommateur français et les produits étrangers', *Coopération–Distribution–Consommation*, no. 5, pp. 31–40.

Graby, Françoise (1982), 'Les Consommateurs et les produit étrangers: application au marché français', proceedings of the 7th international seminar on research in marketing, IAE: Aix en Provence, Lalonde des Maures.

Hampton, Gerald M. (1977), 'Perceived risk in buying products made abroad by American firms', *Baylor Business Studies*, October, pp. 53–64.

Heslop, L., N. Papadopoulos, G. Avionitis, G. Bamossy, J. Beracs, F. Bliemel, F. Graby, G. Hampton and P. Malliaris (1987), Leeflang and Rice (eds), 'A cross-national study of consumer views about domestic versus imported products', proceedings, *European Marketing Academy Conference*, Toronto.

Jaffé, Eugene D. and Israel D. Nebenzahl (1984), 'Alternative questionnaire formats for country image studies', *Journal of Marketing Research*, vol. 21, pp. 463–71.

Jaffé, Eugene D. and Israel D. Nebenzahl (1989), 'Global promotion of country image: the case of the 1988 Korean Olympic Games', in Reijo Luostarinen (ed.), *Dynamics of International Business*, vol. 1, proceedings of the xvth annual conference of the European International Business Association, Helsinki, Finland, pp. 358–85.

Jaffé, Eugene D., Israel D. Nebenzahl and Jean-Claude Usunier (1992), 'L'élasticité-prix en fonction du pays d'origine: une approche méthodologique', proceedings of the 8th conference of the Association Française du Marketing, Lyon, May.

Johansson, Johny K. (1989), 'Determinants and effects of the use of ''made in'' labels', *International Marketing Review*, vol. 6, no. 1, pp. 47–58.

Johansson, Johny K., Susan P. Douglas and Ikujiro Nonaka (1985), 'Assessing the impact of country of origin on product evaluations: a new methodological perspective', *Journal of Marketing Research*, vol. xxii (November), pp. 388–96.

Johansson, Johny K. and Israel D. Nebenzahl (1986), 'Multinational production: Effect on brand value', *Journal of International Business Studies*, vol. 17, no. 3, pp. 101–26.

Johansson, Johny K. and Israel D. Nebenzahl (1987), 'Country-of-origin, social norms and behavioral intentions', in S. Tamer Cavusgil (ed.), *Advances in International Marketing*, vol. 2, JAI Press: Greenwich, CT, pp. 65–79.

Jolibert, Alain (1979), 'Quand les directeurs d'approvisionnement français et américains évaluent l'image des produits fabriqués dans cinq pays industriels', *Revue Française de Gestion*, January–February, pp. 94–101.

Kapferer, Jean-Noel (1989), 'La Face cachée des marques', in Jean-Noel Kapferer and Jean-Claude Thoenig (eds), *La Marque*, McGraw-Hill: Paris, pp. 9–44.

Kaynak, Erdener and S. Tamer Cavusgil (1983), 'Consumer attitudes toward products of foreign origin: Do they vary across product classes?', *International Journal of Advertising*, vol 2 (April–June), pp. 147–57.

Khanna, Sri Ram (1986), 'Asian companies and the country stereotype paradox: An empirical study', *Columbia Journal of World Business* (Summer), pp. 29–38.

Khera, Inder (1987), 'A broadening base of US consumer acceptance of Korean products', in Kenneth D. Bahn and M. Joseph Sirgy (eds), *World Marketing Congress*, Academy of Marketing Science, Blacksburg, VA, pp. 136–41.

Khera, I., B. Anderson and C.Y. Kim (1983), 'Made in India versus Hong Kong/Korea/Taiwan', *Foreign Trade Review*, January–March, pp. 362–81.

Khera, Inder, David Karns and C.Y. Kim (1985), 'U.S. consumers' perceptions of Korean products and brands', Pan-Pacific Conference II, Seoul, Korea, 12–18 May.

Krishnakumar, Parameswar (1974), 'An exploratory study of the influence of country of origin on the product images of persons from selected countries', Ph.D. dissertation, The University of Florida.

Lambin, Jean-Jacques (1989), 'La Marque et le comportement de choix de l'acheteur', in Jean-Noel Kapferer and Jean-Claude Thoenig (eds), *La Marque*, McGraw-Hill: Paris, pp. 125–58.

Lillis, Charles M. and Chem. L. Narayana (1974), 'Analysis of ''made in'' product images: An exploratory study', *Journal of International Business Studies* (Spring), pp. 119–27.

Lumpkin, J.R., J.C. Crawford and G. Kim (1985), 'Perceived risk as a factor in buying foreign clothes', *International Journal of Advertising*, vol. 4, pp. 157–71.

Min Han, C. (1988), 'The role of consumer patriotism in the choice of domestic versus foreign products', *Journal of Advertising Research*, June–July, pp. 25–32.

Min Han, C. (1990), 'Country image: Halo or summary construct?', *Journal of Marketing Research*, vol. XXVI, May, pp. 222–9.

Min Han, C. and Vern Terpstra (1988), 'Country of origin effects for uni-national and bi-national products', *Journal of International Business Studies*, vol. 19, no. 2, pp. 235–55.

Morello, G. (1984), 'The made-in issue: A comparative research on the image of domestic and foreign products', *European Research*, vol. 5, no. 21, pp. 68–74.

Morganosky, Michelle A. and Michelle M. Lazarde (1987), 'Foreign made apparel: Influences on consumers' perceptions of brand and store quality', *International Journal of Advertising*, vol. 6, pp. 339–46.

Nagashima, Akira (1970), 'A comparison of Japanese and U.S. attitudes toward foreign products', *Journal of Marketing*, vol. 34 (January), pp. 68–74.

Nagashima, Akira (1977), 'A comparative ''made in'' produce image survey among Japanese businessmen', *Journal of Marketing*, (July), pp. 95–100.

Nebenzahl, Israel D. and Eugene D. Jaffé (1989), 'A methodological approach to the estimation of demand functions from country-of-origin effects', in Reijo Luostarinen (ed.), *Dynamics of International Business*, vol. 1, proceedings of the xvth annual conference of the European International Business Association, Helsinki, Finland, pp. 386–414.

Niffenegger, Phillip, John White and Guy Marmet (1980), 'How British retail managers view French and American products', *European Journal of Marketing*, vol. 14, no. 8, pp. 493–8.

Ofir, Chezy and Donald R. Lehmann (1986), 'Measuring images of foreign products', *Columbia Journal of World Business* (Summer), pp. 105–8.

Onkvisit, Sak and John J. Shaw (1989), 'The international dimension of branding: Strategic considerations and decisions', *International Marketing Review*, vol. 6, no. 2, pp. 22–34.

Papadopoulos, Nicolas, Louise A. Heslop and Jozsef Beracs (1990), 'National stereotypes and product evaluations in a socialist country', *International Marketing Review*, vol. 7, no. 1, pp. 32–47.

Parameswaran, Ravi and Attila Yaprak (1987), 'A cross-national investigation of consumers' research measures', *Journal of International Business Studies* (Winter), pp. 35–49.

Peebles, Dean M. (1989), 'Don't write off global advertising: A commentary', *International Marketing Review*, vol. 6, no. 1, pp. 73–8.

Perrin, Michel, Claude Marcel, Robert Salles and Jean-Paul Valla (1981), 'L'image des biens industriels français en Europe', *Revue Française de Gestion*, January–February, pp. 97–107.

Peterson, Robert A. and Alain Jolibert (1976), 'A cross-national investigation of price and brand as determinants of perceived product quality', *Journal of Applied Psychology*, vol. 61, pp. 533–6.

Reierson, Curtis (1966), 'Are foreign products seen as national stereotypes?', *Journal of Retailing* (Fall), pp. 33–40.

Reierson, Curtis (1967), 'Attitude changes toward foreign products', *Journal of Marketing Research*, November, pp. 385–7.

Rosen, Barry Nathan, Jean J. Boddewyn and Ernst A. Louis (1989), 'US brands abroad: An empirical study of global branding', *International Marketing Review*, vol. 6, no. 1, pp. 7–19.

Schieb, Pierre-Alain (1977), 'Le consommateur face à la multinationalité des marques et des produits', *Revue française de gestion*, vol. 11 (September–October), pp. 59–62.

Schooler, Robert D. (1965), 'Product bias in the Central American common market', *Journal of Marketing Research*, vol. 2, November, pp. 394–7.

Schooler, Robert D. (1971), 'Bias phenomena attendant to the marketing of foreign goods in the US', *Journal of International Business Studies* (Spring), pp. 71–80.

Schooler, Robert D. and D.H. Sunoo (1969), 'Consumer perceptions of international products: Regional versus national labeling', *Social Science Quarterly*, March, vol. 49, no. 4, pp. 886–90.

Schooler, Robert D. and A.R. Wildt (1968), 'Elasticity of product bias', *Journal of Marketing Research*, vol. 5, February, pp. 78–81.

Shalofsky, Ivor (1987), 'Research for global brands', *European Research*, May, pp. 88–93.

Shimp, T.A. and S. Sharma (1987), 'Consumer ethnocentrism: Construction and validation of the CETSCALE', *Journal of Marketing Research*, vol. 26, August, pp. 280–9.

Thorelli, Hans, B., Jee-Su Lim and Jong Suk (1989), 'Relative importance of origin, warranty and retail store image on product evaluations', *International Marketing Review*, vol. 6, no. 1, pp. 35–46.

Tongberg, R.C. (1972), 'An empirical study of relationships between dogmatism and consumer attitudes toward foreign products', PH.D. dissertation, Pennsylvania State University.

Usunier, Jean-Claude (1985), 'Adaptation ou standardisation internationale des produits: une tentative de synthèse', *Actes de la 1ère Conférence Annuelle de l'Association Française de Marketing*, Le Touquet.

Vandenbergh, Bruce, Keith Adler and Lauren Oliver (1987), 'Linguistic distinctions among top brand names', *Journal of Advertising Research*, August–September, p. 42.

Wang, Chih-Kang (1978), 'The effect of foreign economic, political and cultural environment on consumer's willingness to buy foreign products', Ph.D. dissertation, Texas A&M University.

Wang, Chih-Kang and Charles W. Lamb Jr (1980), 'Foreign environmental factors influencing American consumers' predispositions toward European products', *Journal of the Academy of Marketing Science*, vol. 8 (Fall), pp. 345–56.

Wang, Chih-Kang and Charles W. Lamb Jr (1983), 'The impact of selected environmental forces upon consumers' willingness to buy foreign products', *Journal of the Academy of Marketing Science*, vol. 11 (Winter), pp. 71–84.

White, Phillip D. (1979), 'Attitudes of U.S. purchasing managers toward industrial products manufactured in selected Western European nations', *Journal of International Business Studies*, Spring/Summer, pp. 81–90.

White, Phillip D. and Edward W. Cundiff (1978), 'Assessing the quality of industrial products', *Journal of Marketing*, January, pp. 80–6.

Yaprak, Attila (1978), 'Formulating a multinational strategy: A deductive cross-national consumer behavior model', Ph.D. dissertation, Georgia State University, College of Business Administration.

Yaprak, Attila (1987), 'The country of origin paradigm in cross-national consumer behavior: the state of the art', in Kenneth D. Bahn and M. Joseph Sirgy (eds), *World Marketing Congress*, Academy of Marketing Science: Blacksburg, VA, pp. 142–5.

Yavas, Ugur and Guvenc Alpay (1986), 'Does an exporting nation enjoy the same cross-national image?', *International Journal of Advertising*, vol. 5, pp. 109–19.

Yoshimori, Masaru (1989), 'Concepts et stratégies de marques au Japon', in Jean-Noel Kapferer and Jean-Claude Thoenig (eds), *La Marque*, McGraw-Hill: Paris, pp. 275–304.

PART III

Marketing in the intercultural environment

10

$\bullet\bullet\bullet$

The critical role of price in relational exchange

Price is, at first sight, anything but 'cultural'.[1] That must be conceded. In fact it resembles an intrinsically objective element of exchange. It is usually a figure, a number, a unit – at least in appearance. It is therefore assumed that price determination is, in general, an issue reserved for rational economic factors.

And yet price is still a significant element of communication between buyer and seller, a short-term and/or long-term bond between them, and, for customers, a means of evaluating products in terms of social representations (Prus, 1989a) strongly akin to culture. Price is a decisive element in the social interaction between buyer and seller. It endorses their agreement. It shapes their immediate relationship and in the long term.

The strictly economic aspects of price in international marketing are not considered in great detail: for instance, the relationship between price and costs in international marketing, the law of one price,[2] the incidence of exchange rate variance and price strategies in international marketing. However, so that readers are not left to fend for themselves in the subjects that complement those discussed in this chapter, there are references on page 303 to relevant books and articles.[3]

Bargaining is examined first: a form of relationship between buyer and seller which is classical, primitive and normal, particularly in the absence of compulsory price labelling. The importance of bargaining is often underestimated because we have become accustomed to being informed about prices because, as a rule, they are displayed. If we do not find them satisfactory we will not buy the product. The influence of customers on prices fixed by sellers usually takes the form of a 'take it or leave it' bargain. In the long run, this results in a reduction in price if sellers observe that their products are not selling well. This dichotomic attitude (choice/no choice) is contrary to the purpose of bargaining and relational exchange, where price is always supposed to be a 'friendly price', even a 'friend's price'. Each party wants to make a good deal: *human relations are practically inseparable from economic transactions.*

The second section of this chapter deals with the use of price in those situations where it is clearly marked (in contrast to a bargaining situation) and hence known by the customers so that they are in a position to appraise the price–quality ratio. Price conveys meaning. This meaning may be attributed to the product by consumers,[4] in which case the

283

seller may wish to control these attributes. The meaning conveyed by price may also be intended by the vendor in an endeavour to draw attention to other attributes of the product. Alternatively, this meaning could serve as a focal point in a commercial message. All this takes place largely in terms of social representations,[5] which derive their origins from national cultures as well as religious and social class cultures.

In the third section, company attitudes in pricing policy decisions in international markets are considered. This is a somewhat anthropomorphic approach since a company and its markets are considered as interacting parties to exchange. A company faces competition issues specific to each national market. Price is a good tactical weapon in competition. Companies are therefore forced to distort and manipulate prices between domestic markets, either to increase consumer 'brand loyalty' in certain markets through offensive strategic pricing, or to avoid parallel imports which undermine their local distribution system. Sometimes, they may even resort to over- or under-invoicing in order to make deals that otherwise would not be concluded, despite the fact that over- and under-invoicing are prohibited by most national tax regulations.

Price is treated in this chapter in terms of its *relational dimension* as the central stake in a transaction. *It is not examined in its exclusively economic role in price formation.* That dimension is not the central issue of this book, although its importance is not denied. As a result, price is considered as an object of interaction between people (or organizations); through bargaining, between a consumer and a product; as an instrument for comparisons; and finally as an object of interaction between a company and its various (national) markets.

10.1 Bargaining

The limits of price as an element of social relation: bargaining versus no-bargaining

In many countries today, people no longer bargain; at least in appearance. Bargaining is either legally prohibited or strictly controlled in most developed countries. Most sales of consumer products take place within oligopolistic distribution channels which offer merchandise for sale from producers who are themselves organized in oligopolies. In direct relations with customers, prices are unilaterally set by vendors and are therefore non-negotiable. This price is either taken or left. Bargaining at the checkout in a supermarket is unheard of and, to be blunt, rather boorish. (This is without any consideration of the various epithets that could be applied from impatient customers behind in the queue.)

Yet, once the price of a product attains a substantial level, people return to bargaining because of one of its irreplaceable functions: splitting a surplus between buyer and seller. In many markets exchange still takes place through bargaining, either legally or from necessity: for example, consumer durables and equipment for firms and households such as new cars, furniture, second-hand cars, property and industrial machinery.

In most developing countries, on the other hand, bargaining is still the rule, even for items of low value and products of little vital interest. A weak purchasing power increases considerably the importance of bargaining.In certain African markets, where sugar is sold by lump and carrots by slice (seen at the Nouakchott market in Mauritania in 1988), bargaining becomes essential for survival. Moreover, people are not pressed for time: the dividends from bargaining in relation to its cost are fundamentally different between developing and industrialized nations. Finally, bargaining has a fun dimension as well as a human one. The fun dimension exists because, in some ways, it is similar to a role play. The human dimension exists because the friendly/unfriendly aspects of commerce and bargaining are contemplated with more seriousness in developing countries than in industrialized ones where commercial intercourse has been largely 'depersonalized' (at least for consumer goods – much less so for producer goods).

This is in fact one of the major reasons that bargaining is either legally prohibited or socially restricted in developing countries. As stated by Allen (1978, p. 49):

> ... it has conventionally been supposed that bargaining is socially disadvantageous, on the grounds that it breeds hostility, rivalry and distrust . . . . While it is true that there is always an element of suspicion as to the real value of the commodity (and subsequently of the price), this suspicion never turns into an open conflict if the bargainers intend to conclude the sale. Any bargainer, whether seller or buyer, is careful not to offend his partner, for fear of putting an end to the transaction. Thus, though initiated by suspicion, bargaining tends rather to eliminate it, instituting instead an atmosphere of common interest and trust, which often leads to a lasting client relationship. In this way it cements community relations, rather than subverts them.

Ritual aspects of bargaining

Brand marketing is, by definition, unconducive to bargaining. Self-service and other non-personalized services do not allow people living in modern societies with advanced distribution systems to experience the rituals involved in bargaining. These rituals are a challenge in themselves. They are independent of the price negotiation, yet at the same time complementary. People who bargain more are no less rational; they are rational in a different way.

A Lebanese anthropologist (Khuri, 1968) describes the rituals involved in bargaining in the Middle East by emphasizing that such intercourse always begins with standard signs of respect, affection, common interest and trust. Words pertaining to parental relations are used in such circumstances to evoke affection and create an impression of friendliness and fraternity. As soon as a potential buyer shows interest in an item and requests information on the product, the seller replies vaguely:

> Between us there is no difference; we share the same interest, price is not what pleases me, what pleases me is to find out what pleases you; pay as much as you want; brothers do not disagree on price; for you it is free; it is a gift.

Nothing in this speech should be taken literally. No single potential customer would consider it as such. The opening incantation is a way of expressing a social bond of mutual interest and trust through allusions to a probable family tie in a metaphorical sense.

The potential customer then insists that a price be indicated. The vendor hesitates and, perhaps, proposes a price after having presented and lauded the merits of his product at great length. In fact, a potential customer must never pretend to doubt the qualities of the proposed item, because that could make him seem ignorant and, as such, more vulnerable. The discussion continues, each party maintaining its price (a maximum price for the seller and a minimum price for the customer) below or above which no transaction can take place. The potential buyer suggests a price, but is not necessarily willing to pay it. After an agreement has been reached, the transaction then takes place, i.e. the buyer decides to purchase the item for cash. The bargaining operation could have been primarily just to seek information on the price. This is one instance where the bargaining activity is partly, but only partly, disconnected from the sales activity. It could be disconcerting for people who are used to displayed prices and who, as a result, *do not envisage entering into any sort of pleasant economic intercourse* merely to obtain information.[6]

It is understandable that people who do not bargain every day, and who have thereby lost the habit of personalized commercial relations (if indeed they ever had it), should be rather embarrassed in these situations of implicit communication, where affection and economics, friendship and self-interest are seemingly intermingled. The novice bargainer also risks provoking the seller's hostility if the seller gets the impression (or wishes to give the impression) of being 'taken for a ride' by the buyer. In fact, what remains of bargaining in Western societies is disguised behind 'rational' arguments such as quantity discounts, stock liquidation operations and auctions on deleted items, etc. Moreover, bargaining could smear the image of the distribution channel as well as that of the goods it sells. Prus (1989b, p. 146) quotes certain remarks made by Canadian vendors:

> We're flexible, where if they're getting a larger order and they suggest it, we'll give a little .... Some customers feel that they have to have a discount to buy it. (Sales manageress, luggage)

> You can dicker[7] in furniture, appliances, carpeting, something like that, here. But not on the smaller things, like clothing, giftware, shoes. (Department store salesman)

> Normally I try not to dicker. I am quite firm on the prices. I've found that dickering can be rather awkward. It is awkward for the merchant and the customer. And it is especially awkward if other people are around. If you can stay away from dickering, you can also avoid an image as someone who will go down. I have been known to dicker, but it is something I try to avoid. (Women's clothing)

Declaring prices

As has been seen above, proposing a price is a tug-of-war exercise. Who will give way, the seller or the customer? Who should be the first to make concessions, by virtue of the position of strength that is internalized within a particular society?[8] Two items play a major role in answering these questions:

1. The initial power situation of each party.
2. The importance of the negotiation margin from the start: whatever price is initially suggested, it must leave a margin for further discussion. It could be in the vendor's

Box 10.1   *Price indication and different representations of the buyer/seller relationship*

Scenario 1 The vendor wishes to offer a fair price from the start, believing it to be more practical. The vendor further expects that it will win the customer's loyalty. The vendor therefore offers a price close to the final price. This should convince the customer of the vendor's honesty, openness and genuine desire to do business. It so happens that the customer shares these (European and American) values and decides to co-operate. An agreement is quickly reached, and each party is satisfied both with the transaction and with prospects for future business.

Scenario 2 The same vendor suggests the same price, again close to the final price, as a sign of goodwill towards the potential customer. The customer, who comes from a different culture (India or Pakistan, for instance) does not take this offer as an honest one, and is surprised and embarrassed. Instead of obtaining a low price, the customer's superior expects the greatest discount from a particularly high level. The customer cannot in these circumstances realize this objective in terms of representations framed both in the customer's own mind and in that of the superior. In fact, the vendor leaves the customer no choice; the customer must manage, in the role of price reducer, to ask for more than the vendor is willing to concede since the latter began with a price close to the final price. With no grounds to negotiate, buyer and seller will separate, dissatisfied and resolved never to do business with each other again.

Scenario 3 The vendor leaves room for negotiation right from the start so as to allow the buyer to demonstrate skill in a mutually beneficial bargaining exercise and to enable the two parties to increase the long-term value of their social relationship by means of a bargain that 'brings the parties together'. The ultimate agreed price will be close to that of Scenario 1, even though the initial positions are very different. An outcome can even be envisioned where the vendor obtains an even greater advantage in the transaction than that achieved in Scenario 1 above, in terms of price.

The representations relating to the following two aspects are central to the bargaining process:

1. What is the status of price in the process? Is price an *objective equilibrium point* of a contract between the two parties or is it the instrument of a social relationship? Is it a *subjective equilibrium point*, which results naturally from a social and individual interaction between buyer and seller?
2. To what extent can we really implement 'optimal' procedures of pricing, in order to make exchange less subjective either by substituting Adam Smith's 'invisible hand' or by establishing competitive bidding procedures (as in tender offers)?[9]

interest to exaggerate the first price in order to leave the customer some room for manoeuvre or to provide a price to take back to a superior (see Box 10.1), except, of course, where the transaction concerns a tender offer or a similar procedure where an excessively high price would eliminate that vendor from the list of pre-selected candidates. For instance, when the vendor is dealing with a buyer whose performance is subject to confirmation by superiors, that buyer is supposed to obtain a discount. The buyer's job is to reduce the price: ironically, in such a case, the vendor would be doing the favour by opening the negotiations with an exaggerated price.

10.2   Price and consumer evaluations

Culture-based appraisal of quality and price

It is common knowledge that consumers use price as a surrogate indicator of quality, especially when other criteria are absent. Subjectivity plays a major role in such instances (Zeithaml, 1988) for various reasons:

- It is very difficult to measure quality objectively. There is no generally accepted method of measuring the objective quality of a product (much less so a service).
- Even more difficult to measure is the *perceived quality* of a product. This concept of quality is subjective but not irrational, in the sense that it is based on an evaluation of intrinsic product attributes (e.g. taste, physical characteristics) and extrinsic product attributes (e.g. advertisement, brand, price).
- Perceived quality combines with other evaluation criteria (perceived monetary and non-monetary prices) to form a perceived value which shapes and determines the consumer's decision to buy or not to buy.

Perceived monetary price means that consumers may not recall the exact price, but may have framed in their minds a simplified, general impression ('it is expensive' or 'it is not so expensive after all'). This price impression should be sufficiently close to consumer expectations if they are to buy (Jacoby and Olson, 1977). With regard to perceived non-monetary price, consumer reactions could be better understood in terms of Becker's (1965) conclusions that an objective price is not the only sacrifice accepted by consumers when they buy a product. Other 'sacrifices', such as the time spent in shopping, cooking and sitting at table, should be included in the consented price (perceived non-monetary price) before enjoying any satisfaction from the product.

Some elements of Becker's model, which has firm roots in American society and culture, are not cross-culturally equivalent: what is a costly 'sacrifice' in one country may be true enjoyment in another. Consumers do not build these subjective evaluations (of quality, monetary and non-monetary price) through irrational individual idiosyncrasies but through unconscious submission, in their everyday lives, to social representations dictated by their cultural upbringing. To cite a few examples of common aphorisms (the reverse of each aphorism is also defensible):

♦ 'It is important to measure time, time is money' (see Chapter 14); therefore, perceived non-monetary price will be higher.
♦ 'Home-made food is the best': this maxim could, for instance, influence the perceived quality of frozen foods, even though there is no reason that the objective qualities (taste, dietary, conservation) should not be better.
♦ 'Where there's pleasure, time doesn't count.'

Certain representations directly influence the perceived non-monetary price of a product, particularly the desirability/non-desirability or the convenience/inconvenience of an activity forming a part of perceived non-monetary price. To put this in a simpler way, the price of a nail, for example, is not easily separable from the non-monetary price involved in driving it in (i.e. the risk of hitting one's finger in the process).[10] The idea has been developed (Usunier, 1986) that the rapid expansion of the 'do-it-yourself' market in France (in comparison to other neighbouring countries) is due to a marked preference for doing small jobs oneself instead of hiring the services of a tradesman. This behaviour can be traded to a social representation which undervalues domestics through the French concepts of equality which despises servitude and humiliation. The fiscal system corroborates this representation by offering rebates to people engaging in DIY, while restricting the opportunity to hire domestics to the very upper classes.

The weak relationship between objective quality and price, and the necessity of recourse to choice strategies

The weakness of the price–quality relationship has been examined in many studies (mostly objective quality, as in Curry and Riesz, 1988). Objective measures of the price–quality relation have been proposed: in his comparative study of the relations between objective tests of product evaluations and their price, carried out by consumer magazines (mainly consumer reports), Sproles (1977) found a positive correlation for 51 per cent of the 135 products retained in the study; in other words a high price objectively corresponded to higher quality. However, for 35 per cent of the products he found no correlation and for 14 per cent a negative correlation (lower quality products were priced higher). Similarly, Riesz (1978) found a positive rank correlation of only 0.26 per cent between price and objective quality among 685 categories of product. All subsequent studies exploring the same issue have reached similar conclusions (Zeithaml, 1988): there exists a positive but weak correlation between objective price and objective quality. This, in a way, is reassuring; a negative correlation would have been decidedly disturbing. Indeed it is not possible to state with any certainty that, for example, the Miele washing machine, three times more expensive than the Zanussi, lasts three times longer and is a considerably better performer in washing linen.

Consumers experience difficulties in establishing a clear price–quality relationship. This can be explained by the presence of a subjective, perceptual evaluation of total price (monetary as well as non-monetary price); consumers need a better understanding of these relationships to guide them in a rational decision process. Often, however, they are forced to resort to simple formulae to guide strategic choice.

Tellis and Gaeth (1990) depict three basic choice strategies when the consumer has a better knowledge of price than quality, information on the latter tending to be sparser and more difficult to assess:

1. *Best value*: people, from a rational standpoint, choose the brand with the least overall cost in terms of price and expected quality (utility maximizing).
2. *Price seeking*: price is used as a proxy for the unknown quality (inference); the consumer chooses the highest-price brand.
3. *Price aversion*: people choose the lowest-price brand, in order to minimize immediate costs (risk aversion).

The significance of these three models varies according to the situation of the consumers – the amount of information they have, their capacity to establish price–quality relations and experience; Tellis and Gaeth evidence such relations for the United States. But we could also expect different attitudes in making a strategic choice, according to the consumer's national culture.

Cultural dimensions of price–quality evaluation and consumer choice strategies

That consumers are rational and attempt to evaluate, as objectively as they can, price–quality relations is a generally accepted idea. Yet this idea of the best price–quality relationship could be contested in various ways, for example by the introduction of the concept of minimum levels of quality and maximum levels of price, below or above which consumers will eliminate a product from their list of products to consider.

• North European consumers: one may be surprised at the level of prices in northern European shops but also by the robustness and durability of products. A possible explanation is that these countries are Lutheran: this religion favours a certain austerity (in terms of material well-being) as a general way of life. Goods should be expensive in order to limit their consumption (see Box 10.2). On the other hand, people prefer lasting goods, in line with an austere, thrifty and utilitarian outlook in life. As a result, to furnish homes, for instance, they prefer sturdy, long-lasting furniture. This means looking for the best price–quality relation where the minimal level of quality is relatively high, thus eliminating a range of possibilities (even where the price is low enough to enhance the price–quality relationship). IKEA's strategy corresponds to this type of choice (see the case study at the end of Chapter 7).

• South European consumers: purchasing power in southern Europe is somewhat lower compared to the north European average. People stay outdoors for longer because the climate is warmer; social life often takes place outdoors and is much less materially austere, hence the more pronounced taste for seasonal fashions and for appearance and show. In addition, the Catholic doctrine is rather ambiguous about money, and has little to say about the price–quality ratio. Moreover, the Catholic Church has never been preoccupied, either explicitly or implicitly, with the price and quality of material possessions. The Catholic religion is not a 'lover of money' and could therefore be said to support spending implicitly. Like all idealistic systems with a worldly dimension, the Catholic doctrine manages to sustain the paradox of being anti-money but not anti-expenditure. This is the complete opposite of the Protestant paradox of thrift which considers expenditure as a catalyst for poor morality while still favouring the accumulation of wealth. The difference exists in where the shame lies: for the Catholic, spending is not *really* shameful, but money is, and the religion rejects money while accepting its pleasures. For the Protestant, (excessive) spending is shameful.

Max Weber (1958, p. 31) emphasizes the relative goodheartedness of the Catholic Church, 'punishing the heretic, but being lenient with the sinner', in contrast to the Reform Church which imposes stricter rules and regulations. Catholic influence lacks the austerity and rigour of Protestants. In a way, it accords free will to material choice, as in the famous 'Give unto Caesar what belongs to Caesar.' Consequently, the Latin (Catholic) consumer is more diverse, particularly in relation to displaying social class. Social classes are more distinct and buying has the function of reinforcing one's social image. With marked differences in buying power, one would expect diversified choice strategies among consumers:

- Snobbish consumers who, by definition, buy the most expensive foods (the Veblen effect of preferring high prices).
- Consumers who are more concerned by price and who would automatically buy the least expensive items (price-averse consumers).
- Consumers who use price–quality relations, in line with the Latin temperament which includes a propensity for intellectual logic and rationality.

Box 10.2   *The Puritan paradox*

I fear, wherever riches have increased, the essence of religion has decreased in the same proportion. Therefore I do not see how it is possible, in the nature of things, for any revival of true religion to continue long. For religion must necessarily produce both industry and frugality, and these cannot but produce riches. But as riches increase, so will pride, anger, and love of the world in all its branches. How then is it possible that Methodism, that is, a religion of the heart, though it flourishes now as a green bay tree, should continue in this state? For the Methodists in every place grow diligent and frugal; consequently they increase in goods. Hence they proportionately increase in pride, in anger, in the desire of the flesh, the desire of the eyes, and the pride of life. So, although the form of religion remains, the spirit is swiftly vanishing away. Is there no way to prevent this – this continual decay of pure religion? We ought not to prevent people from being diligent and frugal; *we must exhort all Christians to gain all they can, and to save all they can; that is, in effect, to grow rich.*

(Citation of the Methodist minister John Wesley at the end of the eighteenth century, a few years before the beginning of the Industrial Revolution in England. Quoted by Max Weber, 1958, last sentence italicized by Max Weber.)

10.3   International price tactics

Price manipulation

Vendors may interact with the customers in the markets by using price with diversified objectives. Pricing may serve such purposes as the following (Lynn, 1976):

- To achieve maximum company profits.
- To reach a target level of profits (profit objective).
- To reach a profit level that may be considered 'satisfactory'.
- To increase unit volume of sales.
- To increase cash flows.
- To set a price parity with competitors.
- To promote the image of the company and/or its products and/or brands.
- To achieve greater market stability.
- To develop new markets.
- To maintain customer loyalty.
- To eliminate competitors.

Price is a tactical variable in marketing and, quite often, a policy variable against competitors. Prices can also be manipulated and distorted between (domestic) markets as long as customer arbitrage can be avoided.[11] There follows an examination of some of these cases of tactical use of price in international markets.

Domestic markets, export markets and dumping

Who gets the lowest prices? This question requires consideration when a company operates on different national markets, in which the opportunity exists to increase profits through price discrimination. It naturally presupposes that buyers or distributors do not have the possibility of arbitrage, buying where cheapest, either for themselves or for resale at a higher price in another national market. Other reasons for price discrimination across national markets may also be found among the eleven pricing objectives cited above.

A basic issue in international pricing is the price discrimination between the domestic market and the foreign markets. It depends on the situation of the domestic market *vis-à-vis* the export market on the company's cost curve. Basic micro-economic theory teaches that for a firm to maximize its profit, it must sell its products at a price greater or equal to marginal cost. In practice, people refer to the cost price (cost price based on total costs) and rarely discard it in favour of direct costing.[12]

When a completely new model of aircraft is launched onto the market with initial fixed expenses of $5 billion, or a new model of car with overhead costs of $1 billion, is the domestic market or export market supposed to 'pay' for the depreciation of these sunk costs? This is a substantive question. Nevertheless it calls for a number of subjective considerations. Should the domestic market (or other exclusive markets) pay for their loyalty or, on the contrary, should they benefit from price cuts as compensation and encouragement for their loyalty? If British, French and Italian potential car purchasers were aware of the surcharge they pay (between 10 and 15 per cent) in comparison to, say, Belgian purchasers, perhaps they would show less loyalty.[13]

Figure 10.1 addresses the problem of where to situate the domestic and export markets respectively on the horizontal axis of the cost curve. Since sales (whether domestic or export) usually take place simultaneously, the problem is one of subjective (but stable) conceptualization of the base of the cost curve as corresponding to exported quantities. It is this concept that leads directly to the practice of *dumping*.

Dumping is based on the following assumptions:

◆ The role of the domestic market (or other exclusive markets) is to contribute to the recovery of sunk costs. These markets should therefore be situated on the ascending part of the cost curve in relation to the *x*-axis (quantities).
◆ In placing the home market on this zone, the remaining zone where marginal costs decrease would be reserved for foreign markets where competition is supposed to be more open or where more attractive prices are offered. It should, however, be remembered that one company's home market is its competitors' foreign market.
◆ Dumping assumes that foreign markets are considered as rubbish bins. This is true except in the situation where the aim is to assume the role of a predator, momentarily *flooding* the market with the deliberate intention of raising prices after a sizeable market share has been secured.[14]

Gaining market share through pricing

Slashing prices in the short term may appear an attractive strategy for obtaining new clients, building customer loyalty and finally increasing market share. This could even result in the consumer being trapped if prices are subsequently raised and if competitors,

Figure 10.1 Dumping and the relationship between unit costs and cumulated production.

who have lost market share, are not prepared to engage in a price war to regain their previous share. Competitors will therefore accept the new status quo and products will be priced high.

Slashing prices is a price tactic when viewed from the perspective of a single market. Across markets, however, it is the implementation of a global strategy.[15] The Japanese are unsurpassed in the art of initially penetrating a market through price rebates in order to obtain a sizeable share in it. Thus, in many African countries, Japanese car manufacturers entered the market twenty years ago offering cheap, reliable, air-conditioned cars (in comparison to the European cars available). Since their objective was not to eliminate competitors, the Japanese left room for European cars after having acquired the lion's share of the market. They did this by raising prices. The benefits of this were threefold: they calmed hard-pressed rivals, raised their profit margins and finally avoided the risk that their relatively low pricing would lead to a lasting unfavourable image of their products.

Avoiding parallel imports

Parallel imports may hamper the effectiveness of a marketing strategy across various national markets. For instance, if a company sells at a discount to a distributor in a Central American country because the local consumers cannot afford European or US price levels, there is a risk that the goods will be shipped back from this country to the United States and sold there through unofficial channels (Weigand, 1991). Fragmented national markets are geographically proximate, not only in Europe but also in West Africa, Latin America or Southeast Asia. Once different price levels are set between two neighbouring countries, consumers, and probably distributors, seek supplies from the cheapest sources, making the manufacturer compete with its own products. If the price differential is large enough to offset transaction costs, unauthorized intermediaries may compete with sole agents or exclusive dealers on national markets where a specific marketing strategy has been defined (see the case of Riva International in section A10.2).

Many companies that manufacture home appliances and consumer durables struggle to control the ultimate destinations of their products. For instance, Belgian, Dutch or French agents in cities close to the German border sometimes buy from German wholesalers instead of their domestic distributor, who may sell at a higher price. When price policies implement country-specific prices, they should consider all opportunities for consumer and/or distributor arbitrage. As emphasized by Weigand (1991, p. 53), consumer arbitrage is often effected through holiday travelling: 'An English tourist taking a holiday in Miami bought a place setting of bone Chinaware made in Britain. She didn't pay Britain's substantial value added tax. Further the dollar was cheaper that day...'. Weigand notes that British manufacturers recognize that these personal imports affect their domestic sales. However, they have not found a way to stop them.

The same problem applies to products whose novelty is their major commercial argument. For example, a new music album is marketed in Britain before being put on sale in Italy. In such cases it is difficult to avoid a grey market flourishing,[16] since a segment of well-informed Italian fans receive the news as soon as the album is on the market and will happily pay a premium to be among the first to have the album. The inflated profit margin is pocketed by the 'smart' people who organize the parallel market but who, in doing so, show that they understand the mechanics of urgent demand. Sales by the record company suffer as a result because the company may run out of stock in Britain and, a short time later, may be unable to sell its surplus Italian stock.

Exclusive distribution agreements in home markets would appear to be a plausible solution to the problems of the grey market. But the implementation of such clauses of exclusivity is somewhat difficult. In the United States, there is some reluctance to limit competition by granting enforceable exclusivity rights to dealers. In the United States parallel importers, competing with authorized dealers of leading brands were accorded an almost complete victory by the K Mart ruling handed down by the US Supreme Court. Large companies with well-known brands such as Cartier and Seiko were struggling against parallel importers, but the Supreme Court judged that they cannot prevent unauthorized importation of products under their brand name, since their right to control the trademark is exhausted by the sale.

European Community legislation also restricts exclusive distribution agreements.[17] It is therefore difficult to prevent distributors from seeking arbitrage opportunities. Hence grey markets have developed in Europe and other areas, seeking to overcome the many non-tariff barriers whenever price differentials offset the costs of parallel importing.

Possible solutions to the problems of grey markets, i.e. solutions which may counter parallel imports, are as follows:

1. Lower the price in a national market where it is too high and/or inflate it where it is too low, in order to offset not all, but enough, of the price differential, so that there is no more profit in parallel importing. This, however, may be at the expense of the global coherence of the marketing strategy in either one or both countries.

2. Change the product so that the official product is favourably differentiated against the parallel imported product. If changes are only superficial ones, importers and consumers will not be fooled. If changes are more significant, economies of scale are lost. Other possibilities entail changing minor product attributes: extended warranties can be granted only to authorized dealers, so that parallel importers will offer products with little or no after-sales service and guarantee. A label 'not for export' or 'for domestic sale only' may be attached to the packaging (which also clearly identifies the national origin). This may prevent some dealers from re-exporting. The effectiveness of these labels is very limited, since in most countries it is not legal for a manufacturer to prohibit the export sales of its own products.

3. Terminate the dealer agreement (or threaten to do so) when the dealer buys from unauthorized parallel sources. Weigand cites the case of Apple, which prints the following statement: 'Any Apple dealer or VAR (Value Added Retailer) found to be in violation of the mail-order or transshipping prohibitions will be stripped of its authorized status.'

4. A provisional solution to stop the flow of unauthorized parallel imports is to buy back the grey-market goods. This is positively perceived by authorized dealers, who feel actively protected by the brand owner. Generally, this solution is possible only when

a permanent solution to parallel imports has been found and is quickly implemented.

Finally it is important to emphasize the risk that consumer perceptions of the product positioning may be adversely affected by discrepancies in price for the same good across markets.[18] For example, a Toyota Celica (1990 model coupé with a 16-valve engine) cost US$17,000 in October 1990 (that is about 85,000 French francs or £8,500). The American market is a competitive one in which indirect taxes are about 10 per cent lower in comparison to the French market. The same car was sold (without options, like a compact-disc player, as in the United States) for 150,000 French francs (approximately £15,000) in France where Japanese cars are limited by agreement to 3 per cent of the market. It is in the interests of the Japanese car manufacturers to position their cars in the luxury bracket by setting higher prices. Taking into consideration the differences in indirect taxation in order to make a fair comparison, the same car was being sold at a 60 per cent premium in France compared to the United States.

For informed consumers (currently a rather rare species), buying in the home market is no longer attractive when they become aware that home-market prices are artificially inflated. Today, it is generally accepted that consumers are poorly informed as to international price differentials, and even when they are informed, they resign themselves to the idea that tariff and non-tariff barriers are set so that customers remain 'prisoners' of their home market prices. In the future both these assumptions may not still hold. Regional integration, either in South America, Europe or Southeast Asia, is speeding up. Consumers are slowly becoming aware of the price levels for similar goods and services in neighbouring countries. They are also being offered increased opportunities for buying abroad, with no customs duties or clearance formalities.

Over- and under-invoicing

Many countries have legislation which aims to control prices. The control may be effected either at retail, wholesale or production level, or at several levels simultaneously. Price increases may be curbed or limited, or even frozen. Trade profit margins may be monitored. The rationale for price control is usually a basic mistrust of free-market mechanisms, often augmented by a long-established tradition of state intervention in the economy.

The foreign exchange regulations also influence the practice of over- and under-invoicing.[19] When countries experience balance-of-trade (and, more generally, balance-of-payments) problems, they often use administrative decrees which aim to stop outright the flow of foreign currency out of the country. Local exporters are controlled: they are forced to repatriate their earnings in foreign currencies as soon as possible and to change them for local currency at sometimes derisory exchange rates. Local importers are also under close scrutiny: the absolute necessity of their purchases abroad must be assessed before they are allowed to receive foreign currency for paying their imports. Furthermore, they are often obliged to deposit a guarantee which may be more than the equivalent of their foreign purchase; this sum is deposited at the central bank in the months before payment, with little or even no interest. Where strict foreign exchange controls are enforced, there is no convertibility of the local currency into foreign 'hard' currencies.

A number of reasons clearly induce firms to practice under- or over-invoicing: they would not be willing to do this otherwise.

◆ When a country involves a high level of political risk, which is the case with many developing countries, local business people seek to transfer funds to foreign banks as fears of political upheaval increase.
◆ Local business people may wish to expatriate money through under-invoicing, simply because they need cash to buy a prohibited (or scarce) product or equipment for their production facilities and particularly for the manufacture of products for export.

Verna (1989a) describes various cases of over- and under-invoicing in international trade, relating to differences in currency convertibility. Total convertibility of a currency implies the possibility of its use in all international commercial and financial operations, whatever the object, place or sum concerned. Only a limited number of countries enjoy total convertibility of their currencies. The non-convertibility of local currencies (even more than quantitative restrictions which lead to smuggling) is responsible for over- and under-invoicing (Verna, 1989a). Local business people ask their foreign customers to under-invoice, their foreign suppliers to over-invoice, and wait for the extra money to be paid into their bank account abroad. Currency black markets exist only in countries where the national currency is totally inconvertible. As a result, huge discrepancies may be found between the black-market exchange rate and the official (central bank) exchange rate. Exporters, obliged to go through official channels, lose major benefits from their transactions. Either they have to sell foreign currency at the official rate, which is abnormally low, or buy local currency for their purchases at a rate which, conversely, is abnormally high. Local exporters are therefore tempted to under-invoice; the foreign customer will transfer to a foreign account the extra money in a fully convertible currency.[20] The local exporter should have complete confidence, or a forceful means of pressurizing the foreign customer.

Over-invoicing works in a symmetrical way for imports. When local importers ask for an import licence from their national authorities, the face value should be as high as possible, since the allowance for buying foreign currency will be increased accordingly. They will ask their suppliers to over-invoice and to transfer the extra money into a convertible foreign account to maximize their overall profits. As Verna states (1989a, p. 115):

> An import licence will authorize the importer to order goods from a foreign supplier; a specified amount in foreign currency is paid by the local authorities in the name of the importer. In return, the importer should refund the authorities in local currency, at the official rate, and also pay customs duties on arrival of the goods. To obtain such an import licence may be a sort of 'windfall' because it allows the importer to buy foreign goods at a better price than is offered on the free market, mainly through the (favourable) exchange rate differential between the official and black markets ... import licenses can sometimes be transferable. They then become objects of exchange and even the subject of an auction ... to the extent that some governments, which have become aware of this trade, sell import licences to the highest bidder.

APPENDIX 10
——————— ◆◆◆ ———————

Teaching materials

A10.1 Case: Saito Importing Company

Some years ago, Saito Importing Company, located in California in the United States, brought in a shipment of wood carving from Bali in Indonesia. At the time, the official exchange rate was 78 Indonesian rupias per US dollar. The 'black market' rate (as it was viewed by the Indonesian government), or 'free market' rate (as it was viewed by most of the rest of the world), was approximately 1300 Indonesian rupias per US dollar.

The seller requested a letter of credit for one-half the value of the shipment, to be provided by a US bank and confirmed by an Indonesian bank. A request was made that the other half of the money be deposited in an account in a bank in New York.

Obviously, the 'half' that was received in New York had a value of many times that of the 'half' received in Indonesia. The money in the bank account in New York was available for the seller to invest, to purchase goods for shipment to Indonesia or elsewhere, or to use if leaving Indonesia. Money which was held in Indonesia could, at that time, be used for such purposes only with the express approval of the Indonesian government. What the Indonesian exporter did was, of course, illegal under Indonesian law.

Saito Importing Company did not receive the goods until over a year later. Since Bali does not have a port which will accommodate ocean-going vessels, the letter of credit specified that transshipment was allowed. In the process of transshipment, the goods traveled around much of the world and were delayed while waiting for on-going vessels at points of transshipment.

When the wood carvings finally arrived in the US, Saito Importing Company declared the actual price paid for the goods, and indicated to customs why there was a discrepancy between purchase price and the value shown on the documents. The American company did not do anything illegal under US law.

Questions

1. Should the US company have refused to agree to make the payments as requested by the Indonesian exporter? What would have been the expected effect on the price the Indonesian exporter demanded?
2. What effects would you expect the unrealistic official exchange rates to have had on Indonesian exports?

(Mitsuko Saito Duerr, San Francisco State University, in Gerald Albaum, Jesper Strandskov, Edwin Duerr and Lawrence Dowd, 1989, *International Marketing and Export Management*, Addison-Wesley: Reading, MA, p. 310. Reproduced with permission.)

A10.2 Case: Riva International

Françoise Gain, the *directrice du marketing* at Riva in Brussels, Belgium, received astonishing results from the consumer panels and distributor panels for September and October 1992. It appeared that sales in Belgium and France of one of its main products, the *crème base* Riva, were 20 per cent lower than the production level in the Belgian factory, which supplied both markets. No signs of excess inventories in the distribution in France or Belgium were noticed by the sales force during visits to the distributors.

Riva Belgium was the subsidiary of Riva Products Corporation, a large US-based multinational, whose main business lines were related to the cosmetics and beauty care industry. The Belgian subsidiary was in charge of both the French and the Belgian markets. In 1988 a scientific breakthrough by the corporate R&D laboratories had led to the development of a new skin care cream. Several patents had been filed and registered to protect the property.

In Europe, the industrial use of these patents had been licensed to Riva Belgium, which began producing and selling the new skin care cream in February 1989. Sales increased quickly and the new product was received favourably by Belgian and French consumers, who liked both its efficiency and good price–quality ratio. Following instructions from international headquarters, the output of Riva Belgium was intended exclusively for supplying the Belgian and French markets as well as the markets of French-speaking Africa.

In January 1992 the English subsidiary of Riva, UK Riva Ltd, started producing the same *crème base* product. Hefty investments had been made in the English factory to ensure the best quality and a large production capacity. This product had been launched at the high end of the market for skin care cream. It was priced high and supported by heavy advertising and promotional expenses. After a promising start, deliveries had been falling off since August 1992. Actual deliveries to English distributors steadily diverged from target sales.

Françoise Gain knew about this situation as she had been engaged as an internal consultant in the launching of *crème base* Riva in the United Kingdom. However, what worried her most in November 1992 was the gap between sales .to consumers in France and Belgium and ex-works shipments. She informed Jacques Graff, chief executive of Riva Belgium and a member of the international board.

At first he did not seem to be bothered by such a gap, and showed little interest in this 'problem': 'Françoise, you know: panel data, what does it mean really? Our product sells well and that is all that matters! Tell your panel company to reconsider their samples and their data collection procedures, and you will see that everything is in fact normal.'

Françoise Gain nevertheless made the decision to undertake an audit by an external consultant. His findings exactly confirmed those of the panels and brought evidence of no sizeable excess inventory at the distribution level. Furthermore it followed from the auditor's investigations that deviations had to be ascribed mostly to deliveries to two large wholesalers, who ranked among the five largest customers of Riva Belgium.

One month after his talks with Françoise Gain, Graff received a confidential note, issued by the chief executive of UK Riva Ltd. It stated that a member of his sales force had accidentally seen, at an English wholesaler, a carton containing *crème base* Riva with country-of-origin label 'Made in Belgium'. The wholesaler had been evasive if not reluctant to tell the sales representative where it came from. Jacques Graff asked Françoise Gain to come to his room, and handed her the note without comment.

'I am not surprised by this note,' answered Françoise. 'On the contrary, it is evidence for my suspicions about parallel imports of our Belgian products to England. I have noticed that our sales which vanished from Belgium and France were precisely equal to the drop in the deliveries of UK Riva Ltd. It is now quite clear that some of our wholesalers export to English distributors and that, before doing this, they did not warn our sales and marketing group. I examined the cost structure of UK Riva production and found that our product made in Belgium could be sold by Belgian wholesalers to English distributors at a profit. Belgian distributors may price it at 15 per cent below the English price list, even though there are transport costs.'

'How is that possible?' asked Graff, amazed.

'The English *crème base* Riva was launched with heavy production and promotion costs,' explained Françoise Gain. 'It is positioned at the high end of the market. Its price is higher than any of the competing products. I told them, before launching it, that this retail price level was too high. But I faced disapproval. The finance department at UK Riva Ltd wanted a quick return on investment, taking into account the large cash outflows at the start. The marketing people, backed by the advertising agency, claimed the opportunity to seize a segment which was at the very top end of the market and which had been, up to then, neglected by competitors. Consequently my opinion was put aside.'

Jacques Graff started to walk back and forth. 'As a chief executive of the Belgian subsidiary, I am delighted. Our plant works at full capacity. But, as a member of the international board, I cannot let the English subsidiary plunge. What can we do?'

'One thing is certain,' answered Françoise Gain. 'We cannot prevent our customers, namely independent wholesalers, from exporting to England, if they wish to do so.[21] As for the English distributors, one cannot blame them for seizing a better-priced offer and simultaneously taking advantage of the promotional effort of UK Riva! I know it is more easily said than done, but you should have defined, a long time ago, an international pricing strategy at the international board level.'

'It is never too late to do the right thing! Françoise, please prepare a report on your suggestions to cope with this problem of parallel imports of the *crème base* Riva,' said Graff in conclusion.

Questions

1. Why are there problems of parallel imports? Where do they come from?
2. What can be done to stop wholesalers exporting to England?
3. Is it necessary to change the marketing strategy of *crème base* Riva, and especially its price? Where and how?
4. How should one organize for co-ordinating international marketing strategy across national markets? Please prepare the suggestions Françoise Gain is supposed to present to Graff and to the international board.

(Adapted from a case written by Alain Ollivier, Ecole Supérieure de Commerce de Paris. Reproduced with the kind permission of the author.)

A10.3 Critical incident: Taman SA

At Taman SA, a Spanish company, sales systematically exceed production. Is it a fortunate circumstance due to the know-how and energetic efficiency of the marketing and sales department? Or is it an unfortunate circumstance due to the lack of production capacity, or to the inability of the production department to plan demand peaks effectively? Nobody knows the exact answer.

To tell the truth, one should excuse both the production department and the sales department. In fact the market for high-technology products, in which Taman has built a strong European share, is growing rapidly, at about 50 per cent p.a. Not only is Taman experiencing difficulties in trying to supply its clients, but its competitors also face the same problems.

Costs, be they direct or total costs, are somewhat uncertain and fuzzy. In spite of a rather elaborate cost accounting system, accountants may endlessly argue about the real cost price of a given order. Diverse and changing factors tend to blur the calculation of costs, such as the allocation of R&D expenses, the cost of components, shared expenses between different orders, price–volume relation, etc.

The director of marketing and sales and the director of production and operations are constantly in conflict. Conflicts focus on such cases as that of Magnusson AB. Magnusson AB is a new customer from whom Taman has never, up to now, received an order. Following technical tests of Taman products by Magnusson people at their factory, and after a successful certification procedure, Magnusson is ready to place a fairly large order.

The marketing and sales director argues that getting a new client is something you have to pay for. The director of production and operations considers that the largely positive margin that this order brings is smaller than that of other orders. Besides, he fears that it could disturb the production schedule for the coming weeks and consequently that it could result in numerous delivery delays.

Write in thirty lines how you would describe this problem. What ways and means would you suggest to these two directors to solve their conflict and/or serve their customer base better?

Notes

1. At this point in the book you are probably asking yourself what further evidence I have for insisting that everything is marked by culture. I have three remarks on this issue: (a) I am not denying (as I am myself an economist) that price is above all an objective element of exchange; (b) I am therefore insisting on human and subjective aspects of relational exchange where price is examined from a sociological and interactive point of view; (c) all authors, by definition, are the promoters of the ideas they choose to defend.

2. The law of one price states that, in the absence of transport- and transaction-related costs and when there is no price discrimination, trade takes place in only one market, and not in separate markets. Then only one price prevails. Whereas market separation is a basic reality of international trade, international markets tend to become more integrated, through advances in GATT negotiations and reductions in transport costs.

3. On the issue of international pricing policy, see Czinkota and Ronkainen (1990, chs 10 and 17). On countertrade (barter, compensation, buy-back) see, for an introduction: Czinkota and Ronkainen (1990, ch. 22); for a more thorough approach: Dick Francis (1987), *The Countertrade Handbook*, Quorum Books: Westport, CT; P. Verzariu (1985), *Countertrade, Barter and Offsets: New strategies for profits in international trade*, McGraw-Hill: New York; L.G.B. Welt (1985), *Countertrade*, Longwood: Wolfeboro, NH.

4. This issue was examined in the previous chapter through the consumer's attribution of meaning to products of different brands and nationalities.

5. For explanations on social representations, see section 2.5.

6. The relationship between bargaining and price display is obvious. Wherever the law forces the vendor to display prices clearly, bargaining practices will diminish.

7. Canadian English for bargain/haggle.

8. Chapters 1 and 13 evoke national differences in representations of a priori power in sales negotiations depending on role (buyer or seller).

9. Do not be fooled by the tendency of producers and agents to make agreements readily and corner the market, etc. It is debatable whether human nature tends more to ally or to fight. Both form part of human nature. The 'invisible hand' of the market puts in a 'black box' (a unit whose precisely internal processes need not be known to enable the understanding of its function) the real behaviour of competitors, as if their innate tendency is to battle it out to bankruptcy.

10. Non-monetary price is related to time costs, search costs and the psychic costs; these costs all enter into the consumer's perception of the sacrifice involved in the consumption experience in exchange for the satisfaction which is derived. Non-monetary price varies a great deal across cultures: a trip to buy a product, or the preparation of meals, may be perceived as enjoyable in certain cultures (no sacrifice; low non-monetary price) and as an inevitable and tedious task in other cultures.

11. In fact, if consumers cannot always arbitrate (because of transaction costs, complexities of international trade operations for private people, customs regulations and technical standards), agents are often tempted to do it for them. Agents can reduce the transaction costs and rapidly gain experience in such practice. For example, certain agents specialise in re-importing into France French cars sold at lower prices in neighbouring Belgium.

12. A direct cost could become (to a certain extent) an operational version of marginal costing, corresponding to variable costs directly engaged in production. More precisely, marginal costs are expenses incurred in the production of the last unit, that is, the direct cost of this supplementary unit. For elements of cost theory see Stigler (1972).

13. This is true in mid-1992; it will not necessarily be so after the removal of physical borders in Europe in 1993.

14. Dumping is prohibited by Article VI of the General Agreement on Trade and Tariffs (GATT) where it prejudices the production of one of the contracting parties. It allows certain countries to impose anti-dumping taxes on dumping prices. The United States has exercised this clause, especially on European and Japanese steel exports.

15. The distinction between the use of price as a tactical or strategic tool is rather artificial. In reality, the integration of price tactics on domestic markets takes place within a global strategy of cost domination or differentiation. The search for economies of scale and experience effects is, in all cases, a central strategic question (see Chapter 7). Firms' international strategic pricing is described by Keegan (1984, pp. 359–60) as resulting from three possible positions:

    1. The extension/ethnocentric position: a single global price based on the factory price of the goods, the customer being charged for insurance, freight and customs costs.
    2. The polycentric adaptation position: local subsidiaries fix their own prices according to local market conditions.

3. The intermediate geocentric inventive position: the subsidiary takes into account local competition and seeks to maximize the firm's total income through international co-ordination of tactical pricing.

16. Grey market occurs when 'an exporter knowingly or unknowing sells to an unauthorized agent who competes directly with the sole agent appointed by the exporter within the same territory' (Palia and Keown, 1991, p. 47).

17. The objective of monitoring product price positioning across markets is a difficult issue. Indeed, in certain countries, agents may be forced to sell at prices lawfully dictated by producers. In other countries, however, legislation may consider such practices contrary to effective competition. *Resale price maintenance laws* prohibit the imposition of prices by the producer on an agent, even though this may be required by marketing strategy. Firms then manoeuvre around these laws through recommended retail price labelling, thus controlling agents' discretionary margin. The agent could, for example, try to sell the product at an offer price (e.g. to promote the agent's store) and conflict with the producer's pricing strategy.

18. On questions of exclusivity in agent and distributor contracts (in major areas of the world), see McCall and Warrington (1990), *Marketing by Agreement*, 2nd edn, John Wiley: Chichester; distribution arrangements in Europe and the more general issue of commercial representation contracts are clearly presented in their book.

19. A description of a typical foreign exchange control system, as well as the administrative processes and constraints it involves, is to be found in Jean-Claude Usunier (1992), *Management International*, 5th edn, Presses Universitaires de France: Paris, pp. 100–6.

20. For political risk and cover against political risk, see John D. Daniels and Lee H. Radebaugh (1992), *International Business Environments and Operations*, Addison-Wesley: Reading, MA. For an in-depth approach to political risk management, see W. Ting (1988), *Multinational Risk Assessment and Management*, Quorum Books: Westport, CT. Verna (1989b) suggests alternative ways of dealing with *hostile environments*, which result from various factors, including political risk.

21. EC competition rules (Article 85 of the Treaty of Rome) prohibit any kind of market-sharing agreement by which a company could limit the sales of its distributors exclusively to their domestic market. In order to increase competition across EC countries, Article 85 and several jurisdictional decisions of the European Court of Justice have legitimized parallel imports. A company cannot prevent its 'exclusive' German distributor from selling to Italian customers, even if this company has also appointed an 'exclusive' distributor in Italy.

References

Allen, David Elliston (1978), 'Anthropological insights into customer behavior', *European Journal of Marketing*, vol. 3, pp. 45–57.

Becker, Gary (1965), 'A theory of the allocation of time', *Economic Journal*, September.

Curry, David J. and Peter C. Riesz (1988), 'Price and price–quality relationships: A longitudinal analysis', *Journal of Marketing*, vol. 52, January, pp. 36–51.

Czinkota, Michael R. and Illka A. Ronkainen (1990), *International Marketing*, 2nd edition, Dryden Press: Hinsdale, IL.

Jacoby, Jacob R. and Jerry C. Olson (1977), 'Consumer response to price: An attitudinal, information processing perspective', in Y. Wind and P. Greenberg (eds), *Moving Ahead with Attitude Research*, American Marketing Association: Chicago, pp. 73–86.

Keegan, Warren J. (1984), *Multinational Marketing Management*, Prentice Hall: Englewood Cliffs, NJ.

Khuri, Fuad I. (1968), 'The etiquette of bargaining in the Middle East', *American Anthropologist*, vol. 70, pp. 693–706.

Lynn, Robert A. (1976), *Pricing Policies and Market Management*, Richard D. Irwin: Homewood, IL.

Palia, Aspy P. and Charles F. Keown (1991), 'Combating parallel importing: Views of US exporters to the Asia-Pacific region', *International Marketing Review*, vol. 8, no. 1, pp. 47–56.

Prus, Robert C. (1989a), *Pursuing Customers: An ethnography of marketing activities*, Sage Publications: Newbury Park, CA.

Prus, Robert C. (1989b), *Making Sales: Influence as interpersonal accomplishment*, Sage Publications: Newbury Park, CA.

Riesz, P. (1978), 'Price versus quality in the marketplace', *Journal of Retailing*, vol. 54, no. 4, pp. 15–28.

Sproles, George B. (1977), 'New evidence on price and quality', *Journal of Consumer Affairs*, vol. 11 (Summer), pp. 63–77.

Stigler, Georges J. (1972), *La Théorie des Prix*, Dunod: Paris.

Tellis, Gerard J. and Gary J. Gaeth (1990), 'Best value, price-seeking, and price aversion: The impact of information and learning on consumer choices', *Journal of Marketing*, vol. 54, April, pp. 34–45.

Usunier, Jean-Claude (1986), 'Promouvoir la qualité dans les services, pour développer l'emploi', *Cahier de Recherche ESCP*, no. 61.

Verna, Gérard (1989a), 'Fausses facturations et commerce international', *Harvard L'Expansion*, no. 52 (Spring), pp. 110–20.

Verna, Gérard (1989b), *Exporter et Réaliser des Projets*, Fischer Presses: Québec.

Weber, Max (1958), *The Protestant Ethic and the Spirit of Capitalism*, Charles Scribner's Sons: New York.

Weigand, Robert E. (1991), 'Parallel import channels: Options for preserving territorial integrity', *Columbia Journal of World Business*, vol. xxvi, no. 1, pp. 53–60.

Zeithaml, Valarie A. (1988), 'Consumer perceptions of price, quality and value: A means-end model and synthesis of evidence', *Journal of Marketing*, vol. 52, July, pp. 2–22.

11

◆◆◆

International distribution and sales promotion

This chapter considers, from a cross-cultural perspective, those elements of the marketing mix which are key in 'pushing' the product towards the customer. This does not mean, however, that no elements of channel and sales force management are of universal applicability across countries and cultures. Accordingly, the bibliographical sources at the end of the chapter refer the reader to general books on the topic.

The elements that help to 'push' the product to the customer are as follows:

◆ The distribution channels.
◆ The sales force.
◆ Sales promotion.

Once again an eclectic approach has been chosen, as exhaustiveness was not possible. Distribution channels merit specialized textbooks.[1] It was therefore decided that a distribution system be presented since it has often been claimed a complex and difficult subject. The Japanese *Keiretsu* distribution is, in some ways, very different to the Western 'modern' style of distribution channels (i.e. depersonalized, simplified, efficient). The first section is devoted to the analysis of the Japanese distribution system. A description of how the distribution system is rooted in the Japanese landscape (physically) precedes an explanation of how it also depends on the Japanese national character. These channels have been under attack from non-Japanese companies, for they supposedly favour Japanese goods and producers and they are reputed to act as a barrier to the entry of imported goods. Then it is argued that at least some of these disparaging comments (which have been voiced at the GATT international negotiations) may be partly explained by the ignorance of the fact that these channels are deeply rooted in the Japanese culture. This leads, in the second section of the chapter, to a generalization of the criteria for selecting foreign distribution channels.

The sales force is also one of the 'push' elements of the marketing mix which varies cross-culturally, simply because salespeople are *cultural* human beings working for *cultural* sales organizations. Cross-cultural aspects of selling are studied in other parts of this book: selling styles (Chapter 1); assumptions about the equality of buyer and seller, or the respective a priori power situation of buyer and seller (Chapters 1 and 13), or the degree and style of bargaining (Chapter 10). In addition, Part Four of this book is devoted to marketing negotiation in an intercultural context.

This chapter focuses on the management of the sales force by considering national differences in motivating salespeople, related to their basic cultural orientations such as a society's individualism versus collectivism, masculinity versus femininity and the degree of uncertainty avoidance. The third section of this chapter centres on the sales force compensation systems: how to motivate the sales force to achieve specific goals across different countries/cultures. This topic lies at the intersection of marketing, organization and human resource management. These last two topics have received the greatest attention and are the subject of the largest part of the literature on culture-based management.[2]

Sales promotion (section 11.4) has some universal objectives: to let potential consumers try the product, to facilitate the repurchasing, to increase the frequency of purchases, to reach a new segment of consumers, to reinforce brand loyalty, and so on. Sales promotion has developed a number of techniques, which have been well documented.[3] These techniques combine the sales proposal with the following:

♦ Competitions: games, contests, lotteries, sweepstakes, etc.
♦ Gifts: 'in-pack' gifts, purchase with purchase, free samples, reusable packagings, product bonus, etc.
♦ Collection devices of various kinds.
♦ Discounts or rebates of various kinds: coupons, 'in-pack' money-off, reimbursement offers, etc.
♦ Some kind of cross-product offer, for the purpose of consumer trial especially.

Although this whole range of techniques is known in most countries, the legitimate and legal acceptance of them varies widely. Different societies tend to make different judgements as to what is appropriate and what is not: sweepstakes and lotteries tend to be rejected where gambling is considered immoral and/or not to be associated with essential purchases (e.g. basic food), and/or where there is a state monopoly. When promoting sales, consumers may be considered either as informed and rational decision makers or, conversely, potential victims of slick salespeople.

11.1 The cultural dimension of distribution channels: the case of Japanese *Keiretsus*

Distribution and Japan

Japan is an insular, heavily populated country, where only a small proportion of the land is inhabitable. A population of approximately 120 million people is effectively concentrated into an area of roughly 60,000 square kilometres, in other words a little under 20 per cent of the total area of Germany. As a result, for every 100 square kilometres of usable space, there are 18.95 retail businesses in Japan in contrast to 1.68 in France and 0.28 in America (1985). Their distribution is highly fragmented: numerous retail firms with numerous levels of wholesale and semi-wholesale form a complex and confused network which seems illogical. Indeed, in 1971 Yoshino calculated that almost 45 per cent of wholesalers had no more than 4 employees, and that three-quarters of them had less than 10. In 1968 there were 1,389,000 retail outlets, or one for every 70 people. The situation apparently continued to evolve in the direction of fragmentation as, in 1985, almost 20 years on, there were still 1,628,000 retailers, or 1,544,700 if garages and petrol stations are deducted (Dupuis and de Maricourt, 1989).

The wholesalers and semi-wholesalers play a central role in the system. Yoshino (1971) attributes this to a historical reason: in the past, the manufacturing sector was made up of small businesses (a situation that predictably no longer wholly exists today), which lacked sufficient marketing and management capabilities. The gap was filled by distributors who provided outlets, funding, raw materials and working capital. Similarly, at the other end of the chain, the wholesalers and semi-wholesalers added their expertise to a retail business that was very fragmented.[4]

The retail trade has a close relationship with the customer. Because of the traffic problems (in town centres the speed limit is usually 20 kilometres per hour) and the lack of car parks due to shortage of space, many consumers go shopping on foot or by bicycle (Dupuis and de Maricourt, 1989). As a result, the relationship between the consumer and the retailer is a proximate one and they get to know each other well.

The high level of purchasing power in Japan contrasts with the relative difficulty of consumption on a strictly quantitative basis. The area available actually restricts many forms of consumption: it is possible neither to drive such long distances as in Europe or America simply because the roads would become completely jammed, nor to buy so much furniture or household goods since there would be no more inhabitable space. However, as a means of reinforcing this restriction in a positive way, the Japanese are extremely keen on detail, aesthetics, quality and service (Turcq and Usunier, 1985). They therefore demand extensive services from their retailers even if they have to pay for them. Accordingly, they will have the benefit of a wide range of services which, although straightforward, do make life easier for the Japanese consumer:

- Daily opening times of up to twelve or thirteen hours.
- Very restricted periods of closure during the year, for both weekly and annual holidays.
- Availability of free home delivery.
- Easy acceptance of returned goods, even though the goods may not be defective.
- Credit accounts with monthly payments for regular customers.

The compensation for the retailer is in higher gross profit margins which are about 30 per cent higher than the European average (Dupuis and de Maricourt, 1989, p. 129).

Description of the system

This strong relationship – service and loyalty, willingness to pay for the retailers' commitment to their customers – is passed on to the entire distribution structure right through the wholesalers and semi-wholesalers to the producers. Shimaguchi (1978) describes the principal characteristics of the relationships within the Japanese system of distribution by distinguishing both the practice of and the philosophy behind the system of vertical control in the distribution system that the Japanese call *Keiretsuka ryutsu*, or *Keiretsus*. This may be approximately translated into English as 'distribution channelling arrangements' or 'integrated marketing networks' (Czinkota and Woronoff, 1991, p. 57). First the practical aspects will be considered; then, after a description of the negative reactions they provoke from the non-Japanese (*gaijin*), there follows an attempt to show how Japanese business customs and the social representations behind them render these criticisms largely invalid.

The practical aspects revolve around a system of discounts, which is widespread and extremely complicated. These rebates operate on three levels: to encourage sales promotion (new consumers, support for products that are selling badly, clearing expensive stocks, etc.); as rewards (for the favourable placing of a product in the shop window or on the shop counter, in an attempt to increase sales); and finally as a means of control (limitation of turnover of competing products, reductions in the rate of return of sold goods, payments in cash or within a short period of time, respect for 'recommended' prices, etc.). These rebates are calculated either on a percentage basis or on a flat rate based on different kinds of sales calculations. Rebates are often confidential to encourage retailers to believe that they are receiving more than the others. However, to avoid frustration and jealousy, many producers have encouraged more explicit systems of rebate.

The system of *tegata* is the second aspect of these sales practices. *Tegatas* are deferred payment systems, based on promissory notes which allow the offer of extended credit periods to the operator at the next stage of the channel.[5] Trade credit is largely and liberally extended throughout the whole distribution system, rather like in Italy and France, but unlike the United States and Germany where payment times are much shorter. Payment periods range from 60 to 120 days and sometimes to 180 days. Glazer (1968, p. 20) remarks that 'everybody uses them [promissory notes] and some are referred to as ''pregnancy'' notes, in that they may not become due for nine months and more'. The practice of deferred payments has a snowball effect, where everybody in the network, financially strong or not, is threatened by notes which become uncollectable. Accounts receivable are made heavier by the *tegata* practices. Financial reliance becomes not only an individual, but also a collective issue: if one member fails, it may lead to a chain reaction of bankruptcies.

Strong links within the system of distribution to give the best possible service to the ultimate consumer

The right to return unsold products is extremely liberal. It inevitably begins with the consumers at the end of the chain. The retailers cannot afford to hold in stock those products that have been returned by customers. This requires a system similar to that prevailing in some European countries in the publishing industry. Without any explicit order from the distributor, the producer will send a *mihakarai-okuri*, which is a delivery based on the producer's estimate of the level of stock held by the intermediary. The wholesalers accept these deliveries, although sometimes grudgingly. They then have to try to sell these extra consignments further on down the line within the network. This presupposes the fairly liberal opportunity accorded to the intermediary or to consumers to return goods even when they may not be defective.

A further aspect of the Japanese method of distribution is centred on the high frequency of deliveries. Shimaguchi (1978) explains this high frequency (retailers and wholesalers are in contact daily) in terms of limited financial resources, powerful competition and *a tradition of wide personal contact between those who trade with each other*. As a result, the wholesalers are obliged to sell to retailers in small quantities and at short and regular intervals. Although wholesalers have a tendency to regard the system as inefficient, they accept it because, on a global level, it achieves an economic compromise between increased delivery costs and decreased inventory costs. It is worth noticing the similarities with the *kanban* system of just-in-time deliveries in the field of industrial procurement and subcontracting. One might expect these quasi-affective relationships between channel members to translate into non-aggressive price negotiations and ultimately non-competitive pricing. Nothing of the kind: the whole distribution system is very much concerned with price levels. Distributors enforce competition, without the need to shift frequently from one supplier to another in order to compel them to keep product prices low. Thus Weigand (1970, p. 24) notes:

> As a consequence of the Japanese commitment toward their employees, Japanese sellers must view prices as a highly flexible marketing instrument. The notion of marginal pricing and the importance of selling at prices that contribute to costs is well understood both by businessmen and by academicians.... Prices may be cut at any level in the marketing channel by firms that must have sufficient immediate income to meet their unavoidable costs, but the move ultimately will affect the retailers' cost of goods.

Furthermore, initial price setting in Japan is a key decision. Raising the price afterwards may be as difficult as reducing it. The Japanese place a high symbolic meaning on prices; a price reduction may spoil the image of the product, especially when it is intended as a gift (Montgomery, 1991). In fact, Japanese traders in the distribution system fight over price a great deal, in spite of their loyalty to each other; this, in turns, stimulates demand.

'Traders ... try to resolve their disputes flexibly not necessarily based on formal contacts but on their mutual trust and confidence which has been built up by human relationships and a long, stable continuity of transaction' (Kuribayashi, 1991, p. 55). The personal relationship and human association between the members of the system clearly introduce an emotive element. It is further supported by the practice of gifts. Twice a year, in the middle of the year at *ochugen* and at the end of the year at *oseibo*, the companies sent out an enormous number of presents (Shimaguchi, 1978) whose cost, importance and nature conform to a complex code. This practice is further reinforced by business lunches and trips with clients, which are intended to win their friendship rather than to discuss directly any business. This would be considered the height of bad manners.
manners.

In addition to the practices cited above, producers often give support to the distribution channels in the areas of sales promotion, for example by sending out extra demonstrators and salespeople to supermarkets, or 'kits' for product presentation within the department. There are incentive schemes for retailers whereby they are offered bonuses such as a *kabuki* show, a weekend in Hong Kong or even a week in Hawaii (Weigand, 1970). Although the majority of these practices do exist in other countries to varying degrees (see Box 11.1), sources agree that in Japan they exist in the strongest and most systematic form

Box 11.1   *'Master's' retailers at Dunlop France (a subsidiary of Sumitomo Rubber):* keiretsu *distribution in France*

The sports division of Dunlop France (a subsidiary of the Japanese Sumitomo Rubber) manufactures and markets tennis balls. It has developed a system of privileged relationships with its dealers, which is very much like the *keiretsu* system.

The object is to select a limited number of retail shops that procure their articles from Dunlop France. In exchange for certain commitments, retailers receive advantages from Dunlop France. Dunlop aims to improve its brand image and to increase consumer brand awareness. Which retailers may apply for the 'Master's' label? They must be independent retail stores; this excludes large specialized sport shops and hypermarkets. They should have a good reputation with potential buyers and be recognized as experts in tennis equipment; they must also offer product lines for golf and squash. Moreover, they must enjoy total freedom of procurement.

'Master's' retailers enjoy beneficial trading conditions, as in *keiretsu* distribution. Dunlop France is committed to informing them of new products before other retail stores, and supplying them with the new products first. Finally, Dunlop France publishes a complete list of the 'Master's' points of sale in the specialized tennis press (*Tennis de France* and *Tennis Magazine*).

These benefits naturally imply some obligations for retail stores. Retail stores commit themselves to maintaining a defined level of inventory and products on display, both tennis rackets and tennis balls as well as lines for golf and squash. They also commit themselves to sell at least 70 per cent of their tennis balls annually under the Dunlop brand name.

Moreover the retailer must report to Dunlop France *any remarks made by consumers that may lead to improvements in the quality of new products*. Ultimately, the retail store manager provides a sponsor (usually a well-known tennis professional) with Dunlop France rackets and balls. Presently about 150 stores bear the 'Master's' label. Dunlop France carefully ensures that the selected stores fulfil their obligations. The outcome, as far as brand awareness and brand image is concerned, proves quite satisfactory, especially for tennis rackets.

(Adapted from Eric Zeller, 1989, *Thèse professionnelle*, Masters thesis, Ecole Supérieure de Commerce de Paris, pp. 33–4. Reproduced with kind permission.)

(Weigand, 1970; Shimaguchi, 1978; Turcq and Usunier, 1985; Dupuis and de Maricourt, 1989; Kuribayashi, 1991).

Traditional gaijin *criticisms of the Japanese system of distribution*

Numerous converging criticisms of the Japanese distribution networks are made by foreign firms:

- There are complains about the distribution system being in collusion with Japanese public authorities trying to protect local business. Cateora, for instance, explains the case of the Coca-Cola company when it introduced Fresca in Japan: 'The Japan Soft Drink Bottlers Association staged an anti *Coca-Cola* campaign in which they charged unfair marketing practices. Then, when the Coca-Cola company applied to introduce Fresca, the association put so much pressure on various Japanese ministries that the company withdrew the application' (Cateora, 1983, p. 622).
- The *keiretsu* distribution creates such a chain of affective relationships operating vertically between producers, wholesalers and retailers, enacted by all the practices cited above, that foreign producers find the systems impenetrable. One of the most heavily criticized aspects is the *itten itchoai* system ('single outlet, single account') which requires retailers to order only from specified wholesalers and prohibits these same wholesalers from selling to other retailers, thus restricting competition to the wholesale stage. In the same way, numerous territorial restrictions (exclusive distribution) are reinforced by the setting up of dealerships for specified areas, which co-operate amongst themselves and increase the producers' ability to impose their marketing strategies (Ishida, 1983).
- Japanese channels are supposed to be inefficient: long, costly, complex, and imposing an ultimate surcharge on the consumer. The main reason for their continued existence, despite their inefficiency, must be the Japanese wish to exclude foreign competition, to protect 'Japan Inc.' For this reason, the Japanese system of distribution has become a major target of criticism from abroad (Haley, 1983).
- Japanese distribution systems are apparently one of the main problems encountered by foreign firms seeking to penetrate the Japanese market and are an actual cause of their failure (Ross, 1983).

Is the Japanese system of distribution impenetrable?

Hidden behind this question are further questions, as follows:

- What is the philosophy of the *keiretsu* system in Japanese distribution?
- Is there really a practical intention (implicit or explicit) to eliminate foreign rivals?
- Do real-life examples indicate that foreign companies have achieved original and efficient market entry?
- What are the stages that must be followed to permit successful entry into Japanese channels, while respecting the uniqueness of Japanese culture?

Czinkota and Woronoff (1991) emphasize that the *keiretsus*, which also exist in the production system, aim to 'keep it all in the family': subcontracting networks are institutionalized, whereas elsewhere they would be fluid and informal. Shimaguchi (1978) has described the main factors, deeply ingrained in the Japanese mentality, which underlie the *keiretsu* distribution system:

◆ A well-known Japanese psychoanalyst, Doi, wrote a famous book in 1974, entitled *Amae-no-kozo*, that is 'the anatomy of dependence'. Apparently *amae* is a unique feature of Japanese society, which is diffused throughout society, including the distribution channels. *Amae* is 'the indulgent, passive love which surrounds and supports the individual in a group, whether family, neighbourhood, or the world at large. Close dependency and high expectancy of others in a group seems to be the way of life in Japan' (Shimaguchi, 1978, p. 58). Nakane (1973) has also emphasized the role of *amae* in the building and the maintenance of group bonds in Japanese society. It means that relationships between channel members are not *depersonalized* ones, even when members belong to different companies. Frequent visits of suppliers (producers and/or wholesalers) to retailers are required for maintaining close human relationships in the channels and fostering the quality of the services rendered to the ultimate consumers.

◆ A vertical structure is virtually inevitable in view of the Japanese mentality. The notion of social status is central to Japanese culture. In the field of interpersonal relationships there are three distinct levels: the *sempai* are people of advanced years, very respected, addressed by their name and the suffix *san*; younger, less experienced people (the *kohai*) are addressed by their name with the suffix *kun*; colleagues on the same level in the hierarchy (same age, experience and seniority) are the *doryo* and should be addressed without a suffix. The determination of social status is extremely important and is one of the major reasons behind the widespread practice of exchanging business cards. Vertical relationships exist between organizations in much the same way as between individuals.

◆ Japanese business is much more turnover- than profit-orientated. Japanese companies tend, as far as possible, to accept business as soon as the sale price covers direct costs and begins to cover fixed costs. This fact is illustrated by Hanawa (quoted by Shimaguchi, 1978): '*Kami yori usui Kosen* (margins thinner than paper) is a common saying in Japanese business circles. In certain cases, with a complete disregard for producers' price lists, Japanese distributors end up bargaining machines after harsh negotiations at a price lower than list. Why such low margins? There is a Japanese business philosophy which believes that ''A deal done is better than none''.'

◆ The Japanese themselves (Yoshino, 1971; Shimaguchi, 1978; Ishida, 1983; Kuribayashi, 1991) admit that the *keiretsu* system is infused with a sense of conservatism, and that it does not lead to innovation. They probably appreciate in the distribution system (a very relational and human sector, everywhere in the world) the warm, sensitive and emotional tradition which permeates marketing and business in Japan.

The question of whether or not *keiretsu* distribution is intentionally a barrier to the entry of foreign goods on the Japanese market is a difficult one. It seems to be an accusation against the Japanese for what is essentially their way of being. As stated above, they are themselves quite critical of their distribution system. According to Ishida (1983, p. 322):

> ... the formation of distribution *keiretsu* in oligopolistic markets for highly differentiated products has the following consequences:
>
> 1. Elimination or reduction of interbrand and intrabrand price competition.
> 2. Strengthening of barriers against new entrants to the market.
> 3. Restriction of dealer independence with a consequent loss of business enthusiasm, innovation, and rationalisation.
> 4. Preservation and strengthening of oligopolies.

It may be argued that the above aims to accord tokens of goodwill to the American negotiators (in the Americans' relations with their Japanese counterparts, and in the GATT arena in general), greatly irritated by the Japanese distribution channels which Americans clearly do not understand. This does not prevent the Japanese from recognizing the way in which they may be seen by the *gaijin*. But they are not really prepared to change that part of the system which is authentically Japanese, and which constitutes the major barrier resented by non-Japanese business people.

Japanese distribution: an insurmountable barrier?

Many instances tend to show that the barriers imposed by Japanese distribution channels may be overcome. Ohmae (1985) quotes the case of the US pharmaceutical company Shaklee, which has directly transferred its door-to-door sales system from the United States to Japan. Shaklee had noticed that no legal rule obliged the sale of vitamins and nutritive pills through medical doctors or pharmacists. It was only a habit: no regulation had formally imposed it. The Japanese pharmaceutical companies observed the phenomenal growth of Shaklee sales but were unable to react. They were afraid of damaging relations with their traditional intermediaries, especially wholesalers and retail pharmacists. They were still obliged to rely on them for the sales of their drugs. Another US-based pharmaceutical company, Bristol-Meyers, also implemented such a door-to-door sales programme, with their Japanese joint-venture partner (Cateora, 1983). The product was sold in a box which contained toothpaste, analgesics and other home remedies, and was offered to households on the basis of consignment sale: every six months a salesperson visited the household, replenished the collection and collected the payment for the products that had been used.

Such cases as Rosenthal (see Box 11.2) or ComputerLand (section A11.1) clearly prove that Japanese distribution channels are penetrable by foreign companies. Montgomery (1991) also provides evidence of US companies, such as Williams Sonoma, successfully circumventing the *keiretsu* distribution system, via catalogue sales and limited retail stores of their own. Moreover, the Japanese distribution system does change, especially under the harsh competitive forces of the Japanese market. As stated by Ohmae (1985), it is not a 'stone statue', nor are there written rules which prohibit its change.

How to deal with the Japanese distribution system

Shimaguchi and Rosenberg (1979) recommend a five-stage approach for the successful introduction of a foreign product into Japanese distribution channels:

1. Find a Japanese partner; it is a key to securing adaptability to the unique cultural environment. The *sogoshosha* (trading companies) are potential partners, provided that they do not represent a competing Japanese producer or export the products of a Japanese competitor, and are not related to a larger group (*zaibatsu*) which has competing lines of products. An important choice is to decide whether to ally with a company in the same industry or in a non-related industry. Whereas one may tend naturally to the former in order to ensure a smooth start (the two partners share the same business culture), it may prove much more dangerous in the long run. The Japanese local partner may become a competitor on world markets through new products which were originally designed by the joint venture and then transferred to the Japanese partner's main operations (Czinkota and Woronoff, 1991).
2. Find an original positioning on the market, either by offering a significantly higher level of quality or a significant price advantage, or by emphasizing the exoticism of the product as being foreign and imported.
3. Identify alternative opportunities for distribution channels. Philips, for instance, has succeeded in splitting its sales of electric shavers and small household appliances between two different types of channels: large department stores and chains on the one hand, small retailers on the other.

Box 11.2   *Rosenthal in Japan*

Rosenthal, a German company, exports porcelain items, fine glassware and trinkets, which sell quite well on the Japanese market, more as gifts than for the buyer's use. The range of products offered in Japan is somewhat different to that in other countries: emphasis is put more on tea-drinking items, which may be offered as presents, than on dishes. Rosenthal constantly surveys the Japanese market, in order to adapt its product range to Japanese tastes and to find those items which could best be sold in Japan. Over the last twenty years, Rosenthal has established close relations with its Japanese distributors. They are frequently invited to visit Rosenthal's production facilities in Germany. Rosenthal assists them a great deal in the display of its products on the shelves and maintains a full-time team of window dressers in Japan. The main dealers, that is large department stores, are visited at least once a week. Moreover Rosenthal has initiated a special training session for Japanese retailers: each year a group of Japanese retailers is invited to a ten-day session in Germany, with all expenses paid by Rosenthal, in order to learn how to advise customers. Retailers greatly appreciate this support, and they willingly push Rosenthal's products, especially since margins are hefty.

(Dupuis and de Maricourt, 1989, p. 152. Reproduced with kind permission.)

4. Be patient, target for the long term and be prepared to wait for a long pay-back period (five to ten years probably).[6]
5. Be aware that it is necessary to adopt the mentality of Japanese distribution channels. Build a network of personal relationships, develop loyalty, spend time and resources building relationships of trust.

11.2 Criteria for choosing foreign distribution channels

The method for selecting channels abroad that is advocated by Cateora (1983) is entitled the 6-Cs method. It has been further developed by Czinkota and Ronkainen (1990) to become the 11-Cs method. It presents a checklist of issues that have to be dealt with in the choice of foreign distribution channels. The 9-Cs criteria, which seemed most significant, are as follows:

1. *Consumers and their characteristics*. Some geographical segments in a foreign market may be, for instance, more import-orientated. Channels serving these segments should therefore be preferred. The French beer Kronenbourg, for example, entered America and was initially available only in the centre of New York, before reaching the whole metropolis including the suburbs. The reason for this is that people within this area consume large quantities of imported as well as American beer. It was not until five years later that Kronenbourg became available throughout the whole of the United States.
2. *Culture*. This point has already been considered in the example of the Japanese distribution networks. Distribution is *the* element of the marketing mix which is most deeply rooted in culture: because it is tightly related to everyday life and human relationships (even in large-scale, self-service, apparently depersonalized stores).
3. *Character*. It is important that the image projected by the channel, its sales' methods, shop locations and clientele as well as appearance, should correspond to the image and character that the product is intended to convey. An important reason behind the success of Louis Vuitton-Malletier relates to the large scale of investment in a global network of exclusive retail outlets, located in high profile areas in major cities throughout the world.
4. Necessary *capital* relates to the issue of what financial resources are necessary to start and maintain the channel (fixed capital, working capital, possible initial losses which will need to be financed).
5. *Cost*. This criteria is strongly linked to the previous one, but relates more to trade margins than to overhead costs. It depends largely on the respective positions of strength of producers and distributors. Czinkota and Ronkainen (1990) cite the example of the United Kingdom, where distribution is in the hands of a very limited number of large chain stores such as Tesco, Sainsbury or Asda. These giants exert pressure on major manufacturers to make them bear part of the costs, in particular those relating to storage; they also request smaller, more frequent deliveries with mixed

items. A similar situation exists in France where the powerful hypermarkets impose numerous constraints on the producers which increase their overheads: payments of fixed commissions in return for the right to carry the reference number, lay-out of the counter displays by the producer's own staff, direct help in sales promotion, etc.

6. *Competition* arises in channels either through competing products being placed side by side on shelves, or through competitors refusing other producers access to the distribution channels. Czinkota and Ronkainen (1990) cite the case of the American manufacturers of caustic soda, which is used in the manufacture of glass, steel and chemical products, who have proved incapable of successful entry into the Japanese market despite their price advantage. The Japanese union of manufacturers of caustic soda formed a cartel which apparently set the level of imports, specified which trading company was to work with which American supplier and bought up the cheap American imports in order to sell them through the intermediary of its members. The success of the operation was twofold since they received the profit in place of the American exporter and still managed to keep control of their market. The American exporters were equally unsuccessful in their attempts to deal directly through small distributors, since the industrial users of the product were concerned about the risk of cutting themselves off from their main source of supply (the Japanese) if they placed orders directly with the American exporters.

7. *Coverage* is another important element. It is important to cover markets that are widely scattered. Furthermore, markets that are very concentrated tend also to concentrate maximum competition, since demand attracts supply. The coverage in terms of product range, sizes and options, must also be considered, especially when channel members look for complementary products, spare parts and so on.

8. *Continuity.* It is vital that the channel in which investment is to be made does not turn out to be unusable for some reason (e.g. bankruptcy or financial difficulties, recapture of market share by more aggressive competition, the introduction of legal prohibitions on the sale of products through the channel, etc.). Continuity may be hampered by slick competitors. Cateora (1983) cites the example of an American firm which lost roughly half its local sales in South America. Two of its European competitors had unofficially agreed to force the American company out of the market. One of the two, which was selling a wide range of products, forced the distributors to stop representing the even wider range marketed by the American. The other competitor purchased shares in the company that distributed the American company's products.

9. *Control.* The ideal situation is of course where the company creates its own distribution network, which ensures maximum control. It appears that the decision to integrate the company's own distribution abroad should be considered particularly when the product differentiation is large (i.e. where there are few substitutes) or where the network assets are transaction-specific (e.g. a product which requires lengthy training for the consumer as well as the seller) (Anderson and Coughlan, 1987). The alternative to control by equity is control set up by carefully drafted contract (the written base), or more preferably through long-established trustful relationships with the local distributor (personal verbal base). For example, Caterpillar company sells world-wide without sales subsidiary companies, by using a system of dealers (approximately 250). Some Caterpillar dealers have been in business for more than half a century.

11.3   Incentives for sales representatives: a cross-cultural analysis

Several authors in the field of international marketing have stressed the influence of culture differences on the sales force compensation systems (Cateora, 1983; Keegan, 1989; Still, 1981; Hill *et al.*, 1991). The idea that the promotion of sales personnel is made on merit and that decisions are made on an objective basis is very strong in the United States. This is linked with a 'master of destiny' philosophy (Cateora, 1983) which underlies much of US management thinking. People are in control of their own destiny and therefore responsible for the effective use of their own resources.

In many cultures which have a more fatalistic approach to life, controlling individual performance does not seem to make sense. Uncontrollable higher-order forces largely shape our acts and future. Ali and Schwiercz (1985), for instance, report that Saudi Arabian performance and evaluation control systems work informally, without systematic controls, established criteria or definite procedures.

The question of management of the sales force is not considered exhaustively here, nor the question of what type of sales rep to employ (local versus international sales reps), nor the problems of expatriation of sales and marketing personnel. The bibliographical sources at the end of the chapter refer to sales force management as a whole. These issues are in fact much more diverse than the issue addressed here, that of the cross-cultural equivalence of sales force compensation systems.

This problem occurs frequently in practice, especially when multinational companies try to unify the remuneration systems of sales staff or when they attempt to apply incentive systems that are linked to the parent company's culture to local sales reps.[7]

The case of the company that sells to international customers is not dealt with here. Such companies have international sellers, highly qualified and often multilingual, who move around the world. Such is the case with equipment goods, advanced technology or turnkey projects or services. The situation described here is more related to companies that sell durable or non-durable consumer goods, equipment goods for small businesses or intermediary industrial goods. In each country where they are established, they have a local consumer base and local sales reps, and therefore the influence of culture on sales force compensation systems is much stronger.

Incentives for sales representatives and national divergencies

Hofstede's (1980) parameters can be used (Chapter 3) as well as Hall's theory of communication (1960, 1976) to clarify this issue, which is an organizational one. The organization must encourage its sales reps and/or the sales team to attain specified objectives (turnover target, profit target, promotion of certain products, gaining market share at the expense of competitors, etc.). There are therefore several steps which are influenced by cultural differences:

1. Setting objectives.
2. Evaluation, i.e. setting up a system to calculate target-to-actual-sales deviations followed by feedback to the salespeople.

3. Compensating the sales force achievements: designing the incentive system and attempting to standardize it across countries.
4. Implementing the sales force compensation system.

Two incentive systems for monitoring the sales force (models 1 and 2) are described below. They are Weberian 'ideal types', not necessarily to be found in their pure form in the real world. The first model is appropriate for a firm belonging to an individualistic society where communication is fairly explicit (weak context, see section 4.2), power distance is small and uncertainty avoidance is weak (e.g. the United States). Model 2 is appropriate for a company originating from a society where communication is implicit (high context), power distance is high and uncertainty avoidance is strong. The masculinity/femininity cultural dimension also influences the practical implementation of these two models of sales force compensation:[8] assertive (masculine) and nurturing (feminine) feedback to low-performing salespeople and corrective actions are carried out differently.

Attitudes towards the setting of objectives and their use in performance measurement

The first step is the setting of sales objectives. Here, differences in the preciseness and contextuality of communication style across societies (Hall, 1960, 1976) affect the setting of objectives. Objectives that are precisely set, quantified and openly negotiated correspond to societies where people communicate fairly explicitly with a weak context. On the other hand, the stronger the tendency to communicate with a high context, the more a system based solely on numbers will seem poor. 'Number crunching' is not in favour of high-context societies: figures are not assumed to depict correctly the complexities of the real world. In high-context societies, numbers are considered as efficient, but oversimplified. Despite that, some kind of quantified objectives are needed, but they are not considered as accurate and do not serve the same purpose. According to the model (1, or 2), objectives may have different roles:

♦ A role of *formal and realistic evaluation* (model 1), where the sellers must deserve their salary. In societies where relations have been relatively depersonalized, people can be evaluated by figures: the bottom line is related to what an 'average seller' is expected to attain. Target levels of sales are negotiated with the salesperson. Only results are relevant. The deviation from target to actual sales is measured precisely. Corrective actions, sanctions and rewards result from the monitoring of the salesperson's performance carried out by the boss.

♦ A role of *internal incentive* (model 2), if the seller cannot easily be dismissed (societies with lifetime employment and strong uncertainty avoidance, emphasizing a high level of job security). The staff turnover is low and closer personal ties exist within a stable personnel. The risk is that sellers may seek security and lack personal initiative and drive. The objective is not openly and truly negotiated, as in model 1, since high power distance clashes with the idea that task objectives should ideally be set by oneself. It is assumed that the boss knows what the sales staff should achieve, not the salespeople themselves. The objective then is not necessarily as realistic as in model 1. The boss may manipulate by setting instrumental objectives (not true, representative ones): excessively high target levels may be set, which will serve as an ultimate level of attainment. Although everybody 'knows' that a lower performance level will be achieved, this will still be a better performance than if such an ambitious objective had not been set.

Accuracy of performance measurement

After setting objectives, deviation from the target must be measured. The accuracy (model 1) of systems of performance evaluation and incentive calculation is always higher in a situation of explicit communication. This orientation rewards individual merits, even more so when the company emphasizes individuals rather than teams. In other words, the individual is seen as the very source of the performance.

Where a high-context/implicit-communication case (model 2) is considered, the evaluation phase is not necessarily precisely and formally implemented since the objective is sometimes appreciably higher than that which the sellers can realistically attain. In failing to attain the set objectives they will, nonetheless, have employed their very best efforts. If model 1 were applied at this step only, they would be considered as underperforming. However, owing to the implicit system of evaluation, they are not considered so. There is unspoken awareness in the organization that sales objectives are not wholly realistic. No formal and quantified evaluation is implemented. Furthermore, what constitutes a good sales performance is implicitly clear within the company, making it relatively useless to assess performance very precisely.

Individualism/collectivism, uncertainty avoidance and goal setting

The individualist or collectivist orientation in a society is a meaningful axis of cultural differentiation (Hofstede, 1980). In the United States, where individualism is very strong, the cultural emphasis is put on individual achievements. It implies precise and individualized sales targets, fostering competition *within* the sales force. Competition between the salespeople, within the sales team, is considered legitimate, even though it may undermine the coherence of collective action when this is needed (exchange of information on customers and accounts, training other salespeople in sales practices, transfer of experience from senior salespeople to junior ones, etc.).

More traditional societies tend not to engage in individual goal setting and variable commission rewarding. Still (1981) argues that, in Thailand, family background largely determines social position, much more than money which confers only limited status. Therefore fixed salaries, which demonstrate social status, stability and group belonging, are more respectable and desirable than a larger income that includes a substantial but variable commission component, which emphasizes individualism and instability.

Hill *et al.* (1991, p. 23) emphasize that:

> Tradition is also an important determinant of Japanese compensation plans. Because their social system is based on hereditary and seniority criteria, salary raises, even for sales forces, are based on longevity with the company. Similarly commission systems are tied to the combined efforts of the entire sales force, fostering the Japanese team ethic and downplaying the economic aspirations of individuals.

Precise measurement of salespeople's performance may even be considered almost evil in some countries. In Southeast Asia, the ethics of non-confrontation clearly clashes with an objective review of performance. It could bring the subordinate to 'lose face' and would infringe a societal norm (Redding, 1982). Adler (1986) argues that motivation theories, which in fact underlie sales force compensation systems, are culturally bound. They were developed in the United States by Americans and for Americans. They put strong emphasis on individualism and rationalism as bases for human behaviour. According to Hofstede's empirical description of work-related values, collectivist societies, such as Japan tend to favour a global stimulation of the sales force as a team. Intrinsic rewards are favoured. Conversely, more individualistic societies such as the United States will favour individual performance variables (individual sales, profits per area, etc.) and extrinsic rewards. As a consequence the marketing information systems needed to run these stimulation methods are rather different.

The same retrieved information may serve different functional purposes according to the country. In Germany, very detailed market information will be sought in an attempt to reduce uncertainty in decision making, since Germans fear uncertainty and try to avoid it (Hofstede, 1980). In the United States, where a high value is put on assertiveness and personal achievement (masculine society, with low uncertainty avoidance) the same detailed information will be used for the precise control of salespeople.

Femininity/masculinity and ways of remedying underperformance

When sellers are clearly underperforming, there are different methods to deal with the problem, particularly from the point of view of the immediate superiors. In a masculine society, the absence of results will be emphasized in a fairly crude manner. In a company where the individual is supposed to be efficient and perform well, unsatisfactory achievements will probably lead first to a clear warning that performance must be improved. Then, if the salesperson fails to come up with arguments relating to factors outside his or her control and if underperformance continues, the employee will be dismissed. This hardline method does not, on balance, lead to better sales performance than the methods employed by companies based in feminine-orientated countries.

In countries that are more femininity-orientated (Sweden, northern European countries, France), values are placed more strongly on quality of life. There is a protective and maternal attitude on the part of the organization towards its members. This does not mean, however, that these societies strive less for efficiency than masculine societies. Sellers who underperform will simply be entitled to much more understanding. Checks are initially made to see if there are any explanations, apart from their abilities as salespeople, which may excuse their weak performance, such as poor definition of a sales area with too small a potential, or particularly strong competition within the sector, etc. When the reasons for their underperformance have been assessed with them (formally or informally), they receive assistance from colleagues and from the organization (especially in the form of additional training). It is only after the organization has done everything within its power to help the salesperson to increase his or her performance that a final decision is taken.

Compensation systems based on Hofstede's cultural values

Table 11.1 describes some basic sales force compensation systems according not only to the cultural values involved but also to the type of goods sold. Fixed salaries, for instance, are preferred where uncertainty avoidance is high. Employees who enjoy job security have a preference for a fixed salary, possibly with a limited part of it related to variable commissions. Salespeople accept pure commission payments, with no fixed salary at all, only in model 1. Table 11.1 presents basic cultural dimensions together with the type of industry, which also has a strong influence on the compensation system: sellers are not rewarded in the same way for the sale of nuclear plants, batteries and photocopiers. Large individual sales, requiring lengthy sales efforts and sales force teamwork, tend to be in line with straight salary compensation, as do the cultural values of model 2. Smaller individual sales, requiring individually identifiable sales efforts, tend to correspond with commission payments and the cultural values of model 1.

The rewards can be intrinsic or extrinsic. Intrinsic rewards are related to the satisfaction of inner needs. They are rewards which individuals give to themselves (Anderson and Chambers, 1985). They involve no pecuniary element and have no influence on material life. People may be intrinsically motivated by a job well done, the esteem of their colleagues or even the securing of a contract *per se*.

On the other hand, extrinsic rewards are material and are generally made in cash or in kind. They involve different forms of bonuses and commissions. Extrinsic rewards can be linear (in direct proportion to sales exceeding the objective), progressive or degressive, or can be triggered once a single objective has been attained; the criteria and formulae for calculating variable extrinsic rewards are very varied (Fournis, 1968; Hill *et al.*, 1991; Chonko *et al.*, 1992). Purely extrinsic rewards, such as variable commissions on sales, are motivators which work 'from the outside'. Some rewards are on the fringe of intrinsic and extrinsic rewards: for example, medals or titles (best salesperson for the period). Rewards can be centred on the individual, on the group (e.g. a leisure trip for the whole sales team) or on a mix of both (e.g. awards for the best sales teams). As is frequently the case in Japan, group rewards may take the form of a joint holiday for the sales team which is both an individual and a group reward simultaneously, contributing to the consolidation of the intra-group relationship. Various forms can be considered for rewarding individuals: short breaks or long holidays, presents to the sellers or their relatives, payment by the company of certain personal expenditures, etc.

Table 11.1   *Basic sales force compensation systems, sectors and the cultural values involved.*

Objectives/type of goods	Compensation plans	Values involved
Long-term sales efforts; equipment goods, turnkey sales	Fixed salary and promotions	Lifetime employment; co-operation within the sales team; collective performance
Reach precise sales quotas; consumer goods	Pure (or quasi-pure) commissions	Each has their own business; no loyalty to the company; individualistic and competitive. System orientated towards 'survival'
Achieve more precise goals (sales of certain products, new territories or segments)	Fixed salary, plus monetary and non-monetary incentives	Mixed values: contract and long-term orientation; loyalty but not unlimited commitment

Models 1 and 2 depict extreme characteristics, but real-world compensation systems combine intrinsic and extrinsic, individual and collective rewards. Rewards such as promotion and salary increases combine recognition (intrinsic) and money (extrinsic). A large range of possibilities for compensation exists which can be used to design a sales force compensation system adapted to the local culture.

11.4   Sales promotion: other customs, other manners[9]

Sales promotion targets some basic marketing objectives which are cross-culturally valid. It aims to engage the consumer in the following:

1. A first trial.
2. A first purchase.
3. An immediate purchase.
4. Re-buying or buying more frequently.
5. Entering a point of sale.

Sales promotion may also address the store personnel by encouraging them to stock the product or to display it in a favourable position, or to promote the product directly.

Sales promotion regulations differ cross-nationally according to various assumptions about what is moral or immoral and what is fair or unfair in the relationship between a merchandiser/sales promoter and a customer/shopper.

There is also some fear, as with advertising, that sales promotion costs would result in excessive overpricing of products. Czinkota and Ronkainen (1990) cite the example of AC Nielsen, which tried to introduce money coupons in Chile which had to be sent to the manufacturer for reimbursement. The supermarket union opposed the promotion on the grounds that it would raise costs unnecessarily and recommended its members not to accept the coupons.

Below are some areas where differences are most visible:

- Competitions. Generally speaking, Anglo-Saxon countries are more liberal than other countries, especially concerning competitions: most kinds of lotteries, free draws and sweepstakes are legally permitted. In most Anglo-Saxon countries, private organizations for betting are permitted (bookmakers). In most countries, betting (horse races, lotteries) is state-controlled, since it is seen as immoral for private individuals to profit from organizing lotteries. Italy authorizes lotteries and sweepstakes where prizes are not in cash but in kind. Prizes in competitions are often limited to small amounts: the Netherlands limits prizes to 250 guilders, which severely restricts the attractiveness of sales promotion competitions. Box 11.3 describes Switzerland's regulation of sales promotion by competition.
- Gifts. Many national regulations prohibit gifts or limit their value. In France, the value of a promotional gift cannot be higher than 4 per cent of the retail price and must not exceed ten francs (a little less than two dollars). The idea behind this prohibition is that consumers should buy products, *not* gifts. If the value of the gift is too high in comparison to the total price of the item, this could result in the consumers being fooled by the merchandiser. Collectors' items are subject to the same kind of regulatory ceiling as gifts: the value of the collector's item associated with the purchase is often legally limited.
- Sales promotions encouraging a first trial, such as cross-product offers, purchase with purchase offers or in-pack gifts, are often controlled by national legislation because when consumers pay for two products at the same time they cannot clearly assess the one for which they actually pay.

Table 11.2 (Boddewyn, 1988) reviews regulations regarding premiums, gifts and competitions in selected countries.

Some sales promotion techniques are fairly resistant cross-culturally, since they appear less questionable: free samples as a way to induce people to try the product; money off the next purchase as a way to induce consumers to repeat their purchase; point-of-purchase materials, product tasting or demonstration as a way to increase consumer knowledge of the product, etc.

Some countries object to sales promotion techniques in general because of the risk of consumers being misled. Whereas some countries believe in the personal responsibility and ability to seek and evaluate information (Great Britain, the United States), others have less confidence in the capacities of individual consumers to make free and responsible choices (Latin-European and northern European countries). In Scandinavian countries, the greatest difficulties are met when implementing sales promotion, since every promotion has to be approved by an official body.

Box 11.3 *Sales promotion through competitions in Switzerland (Geneva)*

Competitions for sales promotion are governed by the law on lotteries. The basic principle is fairly simple: *chance cannot be linked with an obligation to purchase*. On this basis there are three situations where a competition is considered lawful:

1. There is no purchase obligation *and* the right answers are not to be found by chance.
2. There is a purchase obligation *and* the right answers are not to be found by chance.
3. There is no purchase obligation *and* the right answers are to be found by chance.

Consequently, it is necessary to define the two expressions 'purchase obligations' and 'chance'.

Definition of 'purchase obligation'

- A label, a cap, or any part of a packaging has to be sent by post.
- The entry form for the competition is printed on the reverse of a label.
- The entry form is inside the packaging.
- There is a participation fee for the competition.
- The competition is announced in a place where people are attending a paying performance.
- Where the competition is organized by a newspaper and is publicly advertised, and the newspaper or magazine has to be bought in order to cut out the entry form.
- A piece of information is required which is on the label or packaging, and it cannot be found by simply looking at the product on the shelves.
- If, to obtain such information, people are compelled to enter a sales room where they cannot 'escape' the salesperson, the judge may consider that there is a 'moral constraint' on the purchase.

Definition of 'chance'

- Random drawing.
- Random drawing in the event of tied entries.
- A question which cannot be answered by skill, science, calculus or knowledge, for instance: time duration of the winner covering the distance of a race; flight-time of a plane; number of cigarettes or matches which have to be put end to end in order to cover the distance between two cities; to be the tenth visitor to an exhibition, the twentieth buyer of a product, and so on.

(Adapted from Chantal Gambiez, Hélène Lelièvre and Véronique Surget, 1988, *La Publicité et la promotion des ventes en Suisse*, Research paper for the International Marketing Seminar, Ecole Supérieure des Affaires, Université de Grenoble II, pp. 12–13.)

Table 11.2   *Regulations regarding premiums, gifts and competitions in selected countries.*
(Source: Boddewyn, 1988. Reproduced with permission.)

Country	Category	No restrictions or minor ones	Authorized with major restrictions	General ban with important exceptions	Almost total prohibition
Australia	Premiums	x			
	Gifts	x			
	Competitions		x		
Austria	Premiums				x
	Gifts		x		
	Competitions		x		
Canada	Premiums	x			
	Gifts	x			
	Competitions		x		
Denmark	Premiums			x	
	Gifts		x		
	Competitions			x	
France	Premiums	x			
	Gifts	x			
	Competitions	x			
Germany	Premiums				x
	Gifts		x		
	Competitions		x		
Hong Kong	Premiums	x			
	Gifts	x			
	Competitions	x			
Japan	Premiums		x		
	Gifts		x		
	Competitions		x		
Korea	Premiums		x		
	Gifts		x		
	Competitions		x		
United Kingdom	Premiums				
	Gifts	x			
	Competitions	x	x		
United States	Premiums	x			
	Gifts	x			
	Competition	x			
Venezuela	Premiums		x		
	Gifts		x		
	Competitions		x		

Teaching materials

A11.1 Case: ComputerLand in Japan

ComputerLand recognized that they would need a Japanese partner in order to enter the Japanese market. Because of government regulations and attitude, it probably would not have been possible to obtain permission to establish a wholly owned subsidiary. Additionally, the complexities of the Japanese market would have made development of franchises there very difficult. (Both McDonald's and Kentucky Fried Chicken entered the market with Japanese partners.)

ComputerLand wanted a partner who had experience in both procurement and distribution of computer products. Though they talked with a number of companies, Kanematsu-Gosho Ltd emerged as the top candidate. Kanematsu-Gosho was a major trading company, had experience in the desired areas, and already had business dealings with IBM.

Computerland entered into negotiations with the Japanese company in order to try to develop a joint venture. The discussions, which lasted for nine months, were detailed and difficult. The Chairman of ComputerLand was concerned that if his vice-president went to Japan to negotiate, he would be at a disadvantage trying to operate in the different culture. He therefore insisted that the negotiations be done in the United States by telephone from Japan.

This made it difficult for the Japanese to negotiate. The Japanese decision-making process requires much more consultation and agreement with the company than would normally be necessary in European and American firms. There were long delays and a lot that had to be done through telex correspondence. Among other things, the Japanese government had to be persuaded to allow the American partner to have a 50% ownership rather than the customary (at the time) minority position.

The agreement was finally concluded with ComputerLand contributing knowledge, trademark, and technology and Kanematsu-Gosho contributing cash to start the joint venture, ComputerLand Japan Ltd.

The Vice-President of ComputerLand then went to Japan to head the operation as Vice-President and Resident Director. A number of policy and operational problems had to be solved.

In the United States, franchisees were required to pay cash before merchandise would be shipped to them. An attempt was made to follow this policy in Japan. Retailers in Japan, however, are used to receiving credit from wholesalers – often for 30 to 90 days or even longer. A cash-in-advance policy proved to be impossible in Japan, so the company eventually went to a 10-day-open-credit policy.

In the United States, franchises were given only to individuals, not to corporations or other businesses. This was done so that the stores would be personally managed by the owners. ComputerLand Japan was not able to find a sufficient number of individuals who had or could obtain the necessary cash. Eventually the policy was changed to allow a company to own a minority interest.

As in Europe, store locations and format were also a problem. Within the United States, ComputerLand insisted on a minimum size for a store of 2000 square feet, a location with a large amount of traffic going by, and a parking lot in the rear. This was simply not possible in most locations in Japan.

It was also difficult to attract top-quality people as employees to work for a foreign company in Japan. Finally, there were simple problems of coordination between proprietor-owned ComputerLand and large, publicly owned Kanematsu-Gosho.

In spite of these difficulties, ComputerLand Japan was very successful, growing to 50 franchises with annual sales of US$50 million. It was assisted greatly by the fact that, for the first two years of operation, ComputerLand had the exclusive distribution rights in Japan for the IBM PC.

Over the years, Kanematsu-Gosho found it increasingly difficult to continue to accept some of ComputerLand's policy. Additionally, they felt that the American partner was simply exercising too much control. When ComputerLand offered to buy them out, Kanematsu-Gosho agreed. The operation then became a wholly owned subsidiary of the United States corporation. Eventually, this subsidiary was sold to one of the franchisees who continues to operate it under a license agreement with ComputerLand.

Questions

1. Was it wise for ComputerLand to insist on holding the negotiations in the United States? What were the advantages and disadvantages to each of the parties? Why did Kanematsu-Gosho agree to the location?
2. When exporting to another country or setting up a joint venture there, how can you decide which of the local customs and business practices you should accept, and which of your home country practices you should introduce?
3. Analyze the differences between the Japanese and American distribution systems as they appear in this case. Which elements of the 'ComputerLand model' are transferable to Japan?

(Written by John T. Sakai, Director, AZCA Inc., former Vice-President of ComputerLand. Reproduced with the kind permission of the author.)

A11.2 Case: Aunt Sarah's Fried Chicken

Early in March 1986, Jean Michel, president of Aunt Sarah's Fried Chicken-Europe, was faced with the problem of maintaining quality control among franchisees in Germany. He had received reports that several of the franchisees in Germany were serving potato pancakes instead of french fries. Also, there were reports of inconsistency in the size of the servings of chicken. Aunt Sarah's had built its reputation on its ability to offer a completely standardized product of high quality in every retail outlet.

Aunt Sarah's Fried Chicken was started by Sarah Browning in a little shop in Dallas, Texas, in 1958. The great popularity of her home-style fried chicken led to expansion to other locations in Dallas and in neighboring cities. Because of limitations of capital, expansion to other American markets was accomplished through franchises. By 1970, Aunt Sarah's had 760 franchise outlets in the United States. From the time she opened her second location in Dallas, Ms. Browning had found that her most difficult continuing problem was in maintaining consistent standards of quality in all retail outlets. When she launched into franchising, she recognized that this problem of quality control would become even more serious, since the many individual franchisees lacked the same experience and commitment to a standardized product as did members of the Aunt Sarah's organization. Franchisee visitation and quality control were placed under the direction of a separate division headed by Ms. Browning's daughter, Cynthia. In 1986, the American market was divided into nine regions, each with its own Sales, Site Selection and Construction, and Operations and Quality Control divisions.

In 1971, an entrepreneur in Paris, France, sought and received the first franchise outside of the United States. As requests began to be received for other foreign franchises, it became necessary in 1973 to establish Aunt Sarah's Export Company, a wholly owned subsidiary. Aunt Sarah's chicken fitted into European eating preferences well as a popular foreign novelty item. It soon became evident that the European market was potentially large and should be actively cultivated. In 1976, the European division was set up with Jean Michel, a Belgian advertising executive, as the new director, with the headquarters office in Brussels. Michel was successful in establishing new franchise outlets at the rate of about 10 per year. By 1980 there were 61 outlets in Europe, more than Michel could personally supervise. Since the Aunt Sarah reputation was just as dependent on high-quality food preparation and absolute consistency in Europe as in the United States, it was necessary to improve the system for maintaining careful supervision over the franchise outlets. Consequently, in 1981, Mr. Michel divided the European division into four regions – England, Benelux, Germany, and Italy – each headed by a regional manager (see Figure 11.1).

From the start, the regional division managers had difficulty enforcing company operating procedures among the international franchisees. Mr. Schmidt was having particular difficulty with the 15 franchises in Germany. The franchisees had little confidence in Mr. Schmidt and resented his attempts to control their activities. Most of the franchisees had been with the firm longer than he had. Each had gone through a company training program, either in Dallas or in Brussels, and had subsequently operated his business without the help or advice of a German regional manager. During the period of minimal supervision, many had modified their product to fit what they felt were the unique needs of the local market. For example, three franchisees had decided that potato pancakes would be more popular than french fries in their parts of Germany. Two others had modified the carefully developed mixture of spices used in the chicken batter. Although these modifications had been accepted in the local markets where they were made (the franchisees involved had excellent sales performance), these aberrant outlets failed to present the standardized product and atmosphere expected by Aunt Sarah customers throughout the world.

Mr. Schmidt was a graduate of the INSEAD graduate program in business in

Fontainebleau, France, in 1978. Before joining Aunt Sarah's in 1985, he worked for a large department store in Bonn. He was bright, well trained, and 26 years of age. The typical franchisee in Germany was in his forties and had worked in the restaurant or food business for a minimum of 10 years. These entrepreneurs were reluctant to accept suggestions about how to run their business from Mr. Schmidt.

Questions

1. Evaluate the organizational structure of the international marketing subsidiary of Aunt Sarah's. Could it be reorganized for greater efficiency?
2. What are the pros and cons of integrating the international operations into the domestic marketing organization?
3. How can Jean Michel help Mr. Schmidt in his relations with the German franchisees?
4. Evaluate Aunt Sarah's policy of standardizing operations and recipes according to the American pattern in different culture such as Germany and France.

(Cundiff and Hilger, 1988, pp. 295–7. Reproduced with permission.)

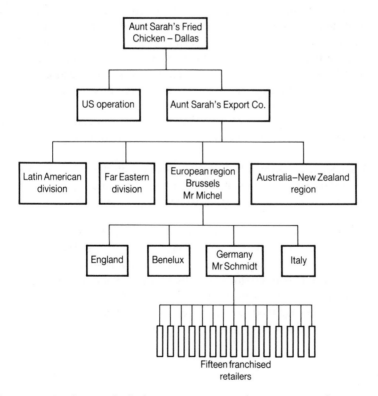

Figure 11.1 Aunt Sarah's Fried Chicken – Europe, partial organization chart, January 1983. (Source: Cundiff and Hilger, 1988. Reproduced with permission.)

A11.3 Case: Sunbeam in Italy

The history of two subsidiaries of the Sunbeam Corporation in Italy in the late 1970s and early 1980s provides important insights into the critical factors for success in international business. The experiences of these two companies highlight the need for a company to have an overall system for their business dealing with the composite of the critical factors for success, and subsystems for each of those critical success factors.

This case begins in Italy in 1977. The Sunbeam Corporation had a policy of keeping the brand names of the companies it acquired. For that reason, Sunbeam Italiana, the company's consumer products branch in Italy, marketed products under several brand names. In addition to the Sunbeam name, known in Italy primarily for electric shavers, the branch marketed products under the names of Rowenta, Oster, Cadillac, Aircap and Stewart.

Rowenta was a strong German appliance company acquired by Sunbeam partially in 1960, then fully in 1971. Oster, a well-known appliance company in the US, was acquired by Sunbeam, in 1960. Cadillac was a French company, acquired in the 1970s, which produced vacuum cleaners and rotisseries. Aircap, a US company acquired in the 1970s, produced lawnmowers. Stewart, a brand name adopted early in Sunbeam's history, was the name for sheep-shearing products.

By 1977, with help from the parent subsidiary in Germany, the Rowenta brand sales had increased sufficiently to equal the combined sales of the other brand names. The top executive of Rowenta convinced the chairman of Sunbeam that Rowenta should have its own subsidiary in Italy, and that it should not continue as part of the Sunbeam subsidiary. As a result of Rowenta's strength in the Sunbeam Corporation and close ties between Sunbeam's chairman and Rowenta's top executive, permission was granted. A new subsidiary, Rowenta Italia, was created in 1977; it reported to the Rowenta headquarters in Germany and, in turn, through the European vice-president for Sunbeam to the corporate headquarters. Sunbeam Italiana continued to report through the European vice-president.

Because Sunbeam's chairman had worked closely with the top executive of Rowenta during the period of the acquisition, there was a special relationship between the two men. Rowenta was given freedom to pursue strategies not established for other corporate subsidiaries.

At the time of the separation of Rowenta's business from the Sunbeam subsidiary, sales of the Rowenta brand were slightly higher than $2 million. Sales of the other brands combined were also slightly higher than $2 million. By 1980 annual sales of Rowenta Italia had increased five times to $10 million, while Sunbeam Italiana went out of business. There are several reasons for the strikingly different achievement of these two companies. By examining their performance critical factors necessary for international success will be highlighted.

Management

The general manager of the Sunbeam subsidiary was Swiss. He had been hired into the company in that position. Although he had no background in the small appliance business, he had some experience in consumer and industrial products in several countries. He had been hired in Switzerland, and continued to live there; he did not want to move to Italy. He flew to Milan each Monday morning arriving at the office at 10.00 a.m., then returned to Geneva each Friday afternoon at 2 p.m. He had no experience of working in Italy. He did not know the channels of distribution for small appliances in Italy. The key people in the trade did not know him and he did not have a network of business contacts in Italy.

The general manager for Rowenta Italia, on the other hand, was Italian and had lived in Milan for most of his life. He knew the appliance business from his 20-year experience as a marketing director in Italy. He had spent his entire business career in Italy and had a wide network of business friends and associates there.

Logistical differences

Rowenta had several factories in Germany; its principal plant was near Frankfurt. That subsidiary had invested heavily in the warehousing and shipping aspects of its business. The company also had an inventory management system that kept the inventories of all its subsidiaries at very good rates of turnover. Because Frankfurt is about a day's drive from Milan, shipments could arrive from Germany within 48 hours. Rowenta's German factories produced 220-volt products, the same voltage as required in Italy.

The Sunbeam subsidiaries in Europe were not part of a forecasting and feedback system. Sunbeam Italiana bought products from nine factories in the US and from several in Europe. Additional products were supplied from non-company producers in other countries. The lead time for orders on the various factories was four to six months.

The Sunbeam subsidiary factories in America produced 110-volt products, primarily for the US market. Changeover from the 110-volt to the 220-volt products usually caused the loss of three or four days production for the domestic business. The US marketing manager for Sunbeam brand products usually needed every unit he could get. He convinced the production managers of the various Sunbeam factories to delay the production of 220-volt products until he got enough products to meet his needs. Sometimes production of European orders was delayed four to six weeks by the demands of the US marketing manager.

In the meantime, Sunbeam Italiana, not notified of the delay on production, initiated advertising and sales promotions. As those promotions went into effect, there were no products to meet the demand. To the European subsidiary managers, this was 'fighting a war where you have guns but no bullets to put in them because the bullets were on a ship somewhere'. The European subsidiaries could not rely on receiving their order until the ship arrived in their harbour.

In the late 1970s, a forecasting and feedback system was developed for the Sunbeam brand products. The system required a rolling 12-month forecast of sales, the first four months representing firm orders. In addition, the US factories confirmed the orders, and there was a status report on all orders. Although these new systems helped the European subsidiaries, the Italian subsidiary of Sunbeam did not have the same kind of logistical support provided by Rowenta Germany to Rowenta Italia. The 48-hour delivery from

Germany to Rowenta Italia was far better than the long shipment times from the US to Sunbeam Italiana. Sunbeam Italiana was at the end of a 5,000 mile supply line, while Rowenta Italia was at the end of one of several hundred miles. From a logistics viewpoint, Sunbeam Italiana was in an uncompetitive situation.

Brand names

Rowenta had only one brand name. Advertising and sales promotion were easily translated from one language or culture to another. There was no confusion in the minds of the people in the company nor in the minds of consumers. The name of the company and the name of the products were the same. Rowenta built a very clear image, inside and outside the company.

Sunbeam Italiana was unable to concentrate on one brand name; it stretched its advertising and promotions over five brand names. Using five brand names may have satisfied the presidents of those subsidiaries in the far reaches of the world, but it caused confusion within the Italian subsidiary of Sunbeam and in the marketplace of Italy.

Corporate strategy

The Sunbeam Corporation management, in reviewing budgets for ensuing years, required that Sunbeam Italiana either make a profit in the next year or break even. When the budget for Sunbeam Italiana was prepared every October or November it provided for advertising. Corporate headquarters usually approved this budget, with some modifications, in late December or early January.

In February or March, at the time when Sunbeam Italiana was about to spend its first advertising money of the year, the profit results from the previous year were available. Sunbeam Italiana predictably would not have achieved its budget (because the budgeted profits for the previous year were always unrealistically high). The current year would look bleak. The corporate management would then decide to cut the expense budget so the subsidiary could break even for the year. Therefore, corporate management told Sunbeam Italiana to cut its advertising budget significantly.

Meanwhile, the local management was telling the trade in Italy that it would be supported by advertising. That advertising never materialised. The standard joke in the trade was that Sunbeam Italiana would provide some television advertising that year. The fact that Sunbeam seldom supported its dealers with significant advertising, after having announced its intentions to do so, gave the Sunbeam Italiana management credibility problems.

Rowenta, on the other hand, decided that to become a viable organisation in Italy it would have to make longer term investments in people, new products and advertising and sustain some losses for several years before making a profit. Rowenta developed a five-year market entry plan in which it would accept losses for several years to achieve a 20 per cent market share in the Italian market. By achieving a 20 per cent market share, they would then reap the rewards of very high profits in the years after breaking even.

For example, Rowenta knew from establishing subsidiaries in other countries that the minimum number of people needed in a country was 16 – the 'critical mass' of the organisation. The first year of operations was dedicated to the managers and sales personnel calling on the trade to build personal relationships and establishing the name Rowenta. The first two years were spent selecting the best products for the market and penetrating the market in four 'core' product areas – steam irons, toasters, coffee makers and dry irons.

Having developed the best product offerings for the market and having established the name Rowenta with the key people in the trade, Rowenta invested heavily in advertising during the third and fourth years. They aimed to achieve a 10 per cent market share by the third year, higher in the fourth year, then 20 per cent in the fifth year. In the fifth year, Rowenta usually made enough profit to offset most of the losses in the previous years. From the fifth year on, Rowenta made excellent profits in its subsidiaries, far more than if it had not made those earlier investments. Even though its profits were good, the Rowenta subsidiaries continued to plough money back into market growth, not content with their 20 per cent market share.

Rowenta aimed for 12 per cent return on investment for its subsidiary. The Sunbeam corporate target was a 20 per cent return, a rate not being achieved by any small appliance companies in Europe. Rowenta sold its target of 12 per cent to the chairman of Sunbeam by making the case for lower returns to allow for investment in the growth of Rowenta. Rowenta was allowed to pursue a sound strategy for Italy (and for all of Europe) because its profit targets were achieved. Meanwhile, Sunbeam Italiana was forced to pursue a short-term strategy, which emphasised current year profitability, but in fact resulted in yearly losses.

Sales management

Rowenta had systematic plans for its salespeople. Its sales personnel planned their sales calls a month in advance; their sales quotes were very quantifiable. For example, a salesman made three or four calls each day, with an objective for each sales call. He had a target for a customer, for example, 144 dry irons, 288 steam irons, 1,440 toasters and 720 coffee makers. The report following his call compared sales achieved against those targets. Planned sales calls, targeted sales-by-product, and call reports were part of the effective discipline of Rowenta Italia.

The sales management policy for Sunbeam Italiana, on the other hand, was essentially, 'call on as many people as you can next month'.

Sales promotion

Rowenta Italia used sales promotions proved successful in other Rowenta subsidiaries. They stimulated sales, but did not reduce sales in future weeks or months. Their sales promotions took sales from the competition, not from the normal sales of Rowenta.

Sunbeam's promotions trapped the subsidiary. One year a sales contest provided the winning dealers and salespeople with a free one-week vacation in Bangkok. This promotion was so successful that Sunbeam Italiana repeated it twice a year. Each time a trip was arranged to some exotic part of the world. Winners of the contest were based on the dealers' *purchases* for that season. Dealers, therefore, purchased only twice a year to qualify for the trip (and to take advantage of reduced prices offered during the contest). The company was starved for sales during the rest of the year. Even when these results became obvious, the contests continued.

Inventory management

Rowenta Italia used the inventory management system of the Rowenta group of companies which was tightly controlled both by the Rowenta headquarters and its subsidiary management. With the principal source of supply only hours away, inventory levels at Rowenta Italia would be kept to a minimum.

The inventory of Sunbeam Italiana was given little management attention. In addition to the long supply lines, which meant that the company either had no inventory or six months supply, the company often bought in larger quantities than it needed to obtain lower prices and to assure itself of the availability of products. Because it could not count on regular deliveries, it tended to over-order.

Sunbeam corporate management imposed strict regulations on capital expenditures: local managers could spend no more than $25,000 without higher levels of approval. The same was not true of product purchases. The general manager of Sunbeam Italiana could order several hundred thousand dollars worth of products without higher levels of approval. Late in 1977, the general manager ordered over $200,000 worth of floor polishers from a company in Spain. He had received what he considered a favourable price, and had a 'hunch' that these floor polishers would sell very well. He bought a 30-year supply.

The inventory on hand was not measured against standards. The local management looked only at the absolute dollar value of inventory. It seemed somewhat high to them, but the local management was not alarmed. I looked at that situation for corporate management. I found that in product after product, there was from 18-months to 30-years of supply. All levels of management, from the local management to the top management of the corporation, were dismayed.

The exit

By 1979 Sunbeam Italiana was in deep trouble. Corporate management replaced the general manager, but that was not enough to fix the problem. The inventory was in a desperate situation; receivables were equally bad. The company was giving terms of 6 to 12 months when the maximum should have been 60 days. Terms given during the special promotions caused much of that problem. To make matters worse, customers were not paying. Sunbeam Italiana had to liquidate the inventory at distressed prices. It wrote off many of the bad receivables. In effect, it went into an 'exit plan'.

Companies cannot leave a country without meeting certain obligations. Termination pay, amounting to many months, and even years, must be granted to severed employees. Sunbeam Italiana faced the classic exit problems as it departed the country.

Questions

1. Contrast the marketing strategies of Sunbeam Italiana and Rowenta Italia: brand names, sales management, logistics, etc.; which factors may explain why one company succeeded where the other one failed?
2. To what extent does national culture influence and 'explain' marketing performance in this case? What are the limitations of this influence?

(Myron M. Miller, 1990, 'Sunbeam in Italy: One success and one failure', *International Marketing Review*, vol. 7, no. 1, pp. 68–73. Reproduced with the kind permission of the publisher.)

A11.4 Critical incident: Setco of Spain

Planning target sales for the sales force is a universal practice. Nobody questions it. So it was when Mr Gonzales, a Spaniard, was recruited by Setco of Spain, the Spanish subsidiary of a large US multinational company. Soon after his job began, he was assigned a product line, of which he had some experience, in a new sales territory. The sales manager of Setco of Spain did not know precisely the market potential of this new area. Until then, potential customers in this area had never been regularly visited. Moreover few indicators were available in order to estimate the market potential of this new area in a quantified and precise manner.

When he first met the sales manager for Spain, Gonzales was amazed by his friendly tone; dialogue within the sales team and horizontal communication were the rules. Instead of being set an objective, he was invited to give his opinion on the matter. In fact, he could set his quarterly sales target himself, after visiting the area and making some preliminary contacts with prospects. Because of the newness of this area, the sales manager made no comment. Gonzales was confronted with a new freedom: in his previous positions as sales representative, he had never fixed his own sales targets by himself. He had always been given targets by his boss. His reaction was therefore to reduce significantly the objective relative to the sales he was reasonably expecting, in order to retain some leeway…

After four months, actual sales per area were released. Gonzales was surprised to see that he received a detailed report on his sales figures (he was used to this, since it was basic data for computing possible bonuses) and also his target sales, and the difference between actual and target sales. It looked flattering. The individual achievements of the other members of the sales team were mentioned in this memo as well. They did not match that of Gonzales.

At the meeting of the sales force, quarterly sales were examined, as well as the targets for the next quarter and the marketing programme. Gonzales was surprised to see how embarrassing his 'performance' appeared to the other sales representatives. Never had any sales rep at Setco of Spain so largely overshot the mark. He was teased by his colleagues, who made some bittersweet remarks and jokes. He felt bad about it, especially because he had been trying hard. He had used all his skills as a salesman, which were considerable and had been proved in his previous positions.

During the discussions, he acknowledged that his area's market potential had been largely underestimated. His sales target was therefore revised and increased by a large amount. This was done in full agreement with all the members (including him) of the sales team, who democratically discussed targets and achievements together during the quarterly sales meetings.

In the companies for which he had worked before, sales objectives were settled in a somewhat hierarchic way. The objectives were, fortunately, too high to be achieved. Being out of reach, the objectives worked as a sort of line of sight, an ideal level. It worked as a way of forcing lazy people to do more and of motivating the achievers to surpass themselves. Logically enough, actual sales were not carefully monitored, nor were individual achievements calculated by comparisons of target sales and actual sales.

At the end of the third quarter, Gonzales began to think that he had been set too high an objective. He had been working extremely hard for almost six months, pushed by enthusiasm for his new job. Moreover an unusually large order from a company in his sales area had swollen his first quarterly sales. This did not happen during the second and third quarters.

When the quarterly sales meeting took place, Gonzales once again appeared as the 'star' of the meeting: he had a record shortfall. No sales rep at Setco of Spain had ever experienced such a wide negative gap between target and actual sales. His colleagues made fun of him. They were slightly relieved to see him bite the dust. Some days later he received a personal memo from the marketing director, who made it clear that he had to adapt quickly or leave the company. 'You should know that in our company a salesman has to be able to settle his own objectives in a precise, realistic and dynamic way. Targets are the result of negotiations with the sales manager: they are based on market data. Individual sales targets are summed up, at every level in the corporation. They are the basis for the quarterly corporate sales figure forecast. The stocks of our company are registered on the New York Stock Exchange. Operators on the Stock Exchange are extremely sensitive to this kind of data. If every salesman in this company performed like you, our forecasts at the corporate level would be meaningless. Our headquarters simply cannot accept this.'

What should Gonzales do?

Notes

1. In order to put into perspective what is written in this chapter, readers may refer to some specialized books on distribution channels and retailing, for instance (a non-exhaustive list): Louis W. Stern and Adel I. El Ansary (1992), *Marketing Channels*, 4th edn, Prentice Hall: Englewood Cliffs, NJ; Erdener Kaynak (ed.) (1988), *Transnational Retailing*, De Gruyter: Berlin; André Tordjmann (1988), *Le Commerce de détail américain*, Editions d'Organisation: Paris.

2. Among the books that emphasize cross-cultural/intercultural management approaches are the following: Nancy J. Adler (1991), *International Dimensions of Organizational Behavior*, 2nd edn, Kent Publishing: Boston, MA; Philip R. Harris and Robert T. Moran (1987), *Managing Cultural Differences*, Gulf Publishing: Houston, TX. Other books deal with national styles of management. Several books deal with the Japanese style of management, for instance: Pascale and Athos (1981), see note 10 in chapter 14. An interesting approach of the French style of management has been proposed by Philippe d'Iribarne (1989), *La Logique de l'honneur*, Editions du Seuil: Paris. D'Iribarne studied work organization and labour relations in three plants of a large French industrial group, located in three different countries (Canada, France and the Netherlands). The Italian management style (flexible, family-oriented, valuing engineers) is portrayed by Florence Vidal (1990), *Le Management à l'italienne*, Interéditions: Paris. On the Korean style of management, with a comparative perspective on Japan and the United States, see Dong Ki Kim and Linsu Kim (eds) (1989), *Management Behind Industrialization*, Korea University Press: Seoul. On the Swiss style of management, see Alexander Bergmann, François Hainard and Laurent Thévoz (1990), *La Culture d'entreprise suisse, élément constitutif et reflet de la culture nationale*, CEAT-HEC: Lausanne.
3. See, for instance, John A. Quelch (1989), *Sales Promotion Management*, Prentice Hall: Englewood Cliffs, NJ (mostly case studies); or Terence A. Shimp (1989), *Promotion Management and Marketing Communications*, Dryden Press: Hinsdale, IL (textbook).
4. Kuribayashi (1991) and Montgomery (1991) note a change in the growth trend of retail stores: whereas it grew at 1–2 per cent p.a. until 1982, it is now declining at about the same annual rate (1 per cent). However, this process was largely slowed down by the 1974 large-scale retail store law, which was revised and in fact strengthened in 1979: the law limits the size of stores and requires the approval of smaller-scale retail stores, before a new large store (500 square metres or more) may open.
5. I was about to describe (in the French way which favours hierarchy) the next operator as 'inferior', but the relationship between two successive layers in this vertical distribution network would be better described as 'protected/obliged'.
6. According to Dominique Turpin, Japanese persistence is instilled into Japanese people by their mothers from early childhood. A survey based on a representative sample of 3,600 Japanese (over 16 years old) has shown that, among the ten preferred words of the Japanese, *doryoku* (effort) ranks first, *nintai* (persistence) second, and *kanjo* (tenacity) ranks fifth (Yoshihiko Inagaki, quoted by Dominique Turpin (1990), *World Competitiveness Report*, IMD/World Economic Forum: Lausanne, p. 85).
7. It corresponds to the problem raised by the National Office Machines case (Cateora, 1983, pp. 545–50), in which an American firm took over a Japanese company and tried to impose its own incentive systems on the sales force.
8. For a description of sales force compensation systems, see Chonko *et al.* (1992). See also sections A11.3 and A11.4.
9. A complete description of the rules of the main countries concerning sales promotion (regularly updated) may be found in Boddewyn (1988).

References

Adler, Nancy J. (1986), *International Dimensions of Organizational Behavior*, Kent: Boston.
Ali, Abbas and Paul M. Schwiercz (1985), 'The relationship between managerial decision styles and work satisfaction in Saudi Arabia', in Erdener Kaynak (ed.), *International Business in the Middle East*, De Gruyter: Berlin, pp. 138–49.

Anderson, Erin T. and Anne T. Coughlan (1987), 'International market entry and expansion via independent or integrated channels of distribution', *Journal of Marketing*, vol. 51, January, pp. 71–82.

Anderson, Paul F. and Terry M. Chambers (1985), 'A reward/measurement model of organizational buying behavior', *Journal of Marketing*, vol. 49 (Spring), pp. 7–23.

Boddewyn, J.J. (1988), *Premiums, Gifts and Competitions*, International Advertising Association: New York.

Cateora, Philip R. (1983), *International Marketing*, 5th edn, Richard D. Irwin: Homewood, IL.

Chonko, Lawrence B., Ben M. Enis and John F. Tanner (1992), *Managing Sales People*, Allyn and Bacon: Boston, MA.

Cundiff, Edward W. and Marye Tharp Hilger (1988), *Marketing in the International Environment*, 2nd edn, Prentice Hall: Englewood Cliffs, NJ.

Czinkota, Michael, R. and Illka A. Ronkainen (1990), *International Marketing*, 2nd edn, Dryden Press: Hinsdale, IL.

Czinkota, Michael R. and Jon Woronoff (1991), *Unlocking Japan's Markets*, Probus Publishing: Chicago, IL.

Dupuis, Marc and Renaud de Maricourt (1989), 'France/Etats-Unis/Japon, trois mondes, trois distributions', Cahier ESCP no. 89–91, Ecole Supérieure de Commerce de Paris.

Fournis, Yves (1968), 'La Politique et les méthodes de rémunération des vendeurs', *Revue Française du Marketing*, no. 26, 1st quarter, pp. 11–30.

Glazer, Herbert (1968), *The International Business in Japan: The Japanese image*, Sophia University: Tokyo.

Haley, John O. (1983), introduction to Ishida, 1983.

Hall, Edward T. (1960), 'The silent language in overseas business', *Harvard Business Review*, May–June, pp. 87–96.

Hall, Edward T. (1976), *Beyond Culture*, Doubleday: New York.

Hill, John S., Richard R. Still and Ünal O. Boya (1991), 'Managing the multinational sales force', *International Marketing Review*, vol. 8, no. 1, pp. 19–31.

Hofstede, Geert (1980), *Culture's Consequences: International differences in work-related values*, Sage: Beverly Hills, CA.

Ishida, Hideto (1983), 'Anticompetitive practices in the distribution of goods and services in Japan: The problem of distribution keiretsu', *Journal of Japanese Studies*, vol. 9, no. 2, pp. 319–34.

Keegan, Warren J. (1989), *Global Marketing Management*, 4th edn, Prentice Hall: Englewood Cliffs, NJ.

Kuribayashi, S. (1991), 'Present situation and future prospects of Japan's distribution system', *Japan and the World Economy*, vol. 3, no. 1, pp. 39–60.

Montgomery, David B. (1991), 'Understanding the Japanese as customers, competitors and collaborators', *Japan and the World Economy*, vol. 3, no. 1, pp. 61–91.

Nakane, Chie (1973), *Japanese Society*, University of California Press, Berkeley.

Ohmae, Kenichi (1985), *La Triade: Émergence d'une Stratégie mondiale de l'entreprise*, Flammarion: Paris.

Pascale, Richard T. and Anthony G. Athos (1981), *The Art of Japanese Management*, Simon and Schuster: New York.

Redding, S.G. (1982), 'Cultural effects of the marketing process in Southeast Asia', *Journal of the Market Research Society*, vol. 24, no. 2, pp. 98–114.

Ross, Randolph (1983), 'Understanding the Japanese distribution system', *European Journal of Marketing*, vol. 17 (Winter), pp. 5–15.

Shimaguchi, Mitsuaki (1978), *Marketing Channels in Japan*, Ann Arbor: Michigan.

Shimaguchi, Mitsuaki and Larry J. Rosenberg (1979), 'Demystifying Japanese distribution', *Columbia Journal of World Business* (Spring), pp. 38–41.

Still, Richard R. (1981), 'Cross-cultural aspects of sales force management', *Journal of Personal Selling and Sales Force Management*, vol. 1, no. 2, pp. 6–9.

Turcq, Dominique and Jean-Claude Usunier (1985), 'Les Services au Japon: l'efficacité ... par la non-productivité', *Revue Française de Gestion*, May–June, pp. 12–15.

Weigand, Robert E. (1970), 'Aspects of retail pricing in Japan', *MSU Business Topics*, vol. 18 (Winter), pp. 23–30.

Yoshino, Michael Y. (1971), *Marketing in Japan: A management guide*, Praeger: New York.

12
───── ◆◆◆ ─────

International promotion and advertising

This chapter could be subtitled 'national cultures, technological advances and the globalization of marketing communications'. Indeed it attempts to show, as Chapters 6 and 7 did, that globalization is not the very simple process that it is often believed to be. The first section of this chapter describes cultural differences as they pertain to various aspects of advertising: what are the general attitudes *vis-à-vis* advertising? How are creative standards affected by local culture? How is media selection affected by differences in media availability and style?

Since advertising is largely based on language and images, it is influenced by culture. Cross-national differences continue to exist, for the simple reason that we have not yet ceased to have different languages (see section 4.1 on the Whorfian hypothesis). Moreover language, be it through words or images, is the strongest link between advertisers and their potential audiences in marketing communications.

The management process for marketing communication *per se* does not depend on the particular country where the advertising campaign is launched. It is composed of six steps (see Figure 12.1).[1] Logically, these steps should be taken in order, although feedback at any step is possible and often necessary, especially after testing the campaign. The six basic steps are as follows:[2]

1. Isolate the communication problem to be solved: increase brand awareness, change the brand image, increase sales, differentiate from rival brands, take points of market share from the competition, etc.
2. Identify the relevant target population: which consumer segments? What are their sociodemographic characteristics, consumption habits, psychographic characteristics (consumer life-styles and values), etc.?
3. Define the marketing communication objective in terms of influencing the target population, either at the attitudinal or the behavioural level. Communication objectives may be, for instance, to convince consumers that they like the product (to improve product acceptance), to let people retry (to increase sales by building consumer loyalty), to let people act, or to educate the consumer, etc.
4. Select the advertising themes and a creative strategy: how will the brand name be emphasized? Which copy strategy should be used?

5. Design a media plan: which media to use, how to optimize the best media to reach the target audience, etc.
6. Implement and monitor the advertising campaign: pre- and post-tests of the advertisement effectiveness; research of different aspects (message recall, brand recall, aided brand recognition, actual influence on sales); etc.

The international dimension naturally has an influence on the implementation of each of these steps, but not an equal influence on each step. Let us take an example: to advertise life insurance in Tunisia, it should be taken into account that the life insurance market is a new one, where consumers have little knowledge of this kind of financial service. For this reason, the message shows a man and a woman watering a tree which grows by leaps and bounds. Finally, a large pine tree protects them with its branches, under whose shade they are sitting happily. Certainly culture will influence the objective: the education of the consumer would be a basic objective in a country where life insurance is almost unknown. But the changes caused by cultural differences are the most obvious with respect to the creative strategy (step 4). One should acknowledge and respect the values of Tunisian consumers who belong to an Arab–Muslim culture which is nevertheless strongly linked to two European cultures (Italy and France). The complex mix of Muslim and Western culture has to be considered, since values that involve important matters (life and death, protecting one's family, betting on the future) are at stake.

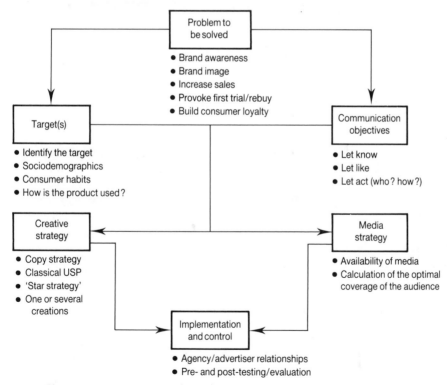

Figure 12.1 Main steps in the management of advertising communication.

The media plan will also be strongly influenced by local idiosyncrasies: media availability, viewing habits and media regulations still differ a great deal across countries. The topic of how culture influences creative strategy and media planning will be dealt with in the first section.

Conversely, the other steps in Figure 12.1 are not strongly affected by local factors: defining a communication problem or a communication objective, or testing the effectiveness of a campaign, calls for a similar approach in each country although the solution may be different. Although the first section of this chapter favours customization of advertising, the second section may appear to be in contrast to this. Technological advances that are now in progress world-wide, such as satellite television and the global reach of the media, have an undeniable impact on local attitudes and purchasing behaviour. In all probability, the emergence of world-wide advertising media will partly break down cultural resistance. In fact, they will open different lines of communication between cultures that previously were geographically and culturally separated, such as Western and Eastern Europe, or southern Europe and North Africa. Furthermore they will open the way to new marketing communications in areas of the world which are culturally fragmented, for ethnic, linguistic or political reasons: Europe, Southeast Asia, Central and Latin America. In this new style of international marketing communication, strictly national segments and audiences will be differentiated from cross-border regional segments and audiences. The choice of the appropriate media as well as the choice of the language in which to advertise will therefore be key factors for success.

12.1   Marketing communications are strongly culture-based

General attitudes towards the role and functions of advertising

Advertising, which is a large part of marketing communications,[3] is a field which is constantly changing. On the one hand it is closely dependent on the cultural and linguistic attitudes of the local target population. On the other hand, in so far as social representations are not fixed (Moscovici, 1961; Jodelet, 1988), advertising is a privileged method of cultural borrowing; advertising mirrors changing social behaviour. The relative freedom of advertising creation and the need to capture the audience mean that advertising is sometimes challenging and often innovative. It is therefore the ground for societal debates. This is illustrated below by several advertising-related issues, e.g. 'publiphobia' (rejection of advertising), attitudes towards comparative advertising and attitudes towards its informative content.

General attitudes towards publicity and 'publiphobia'

A view which has always existed (and still exists today among part of the population) is that advertising is nothing more than wasted money. This negative view of advertising is vaguely rooted in the ideas of the Saint-Simonist doctrine,[4] in which anything that does not involve the production of material goods is considered to be socially unproductive.

Retail sales and the service industry, including advertising, are considered to be parasitic activities. This view is often reinforced by the (misleading) argument that consumers pay for advertising costs which are included in the price of the product they buy.

This social representation was a part of the Marxist doctrine, and its influence on real socialism often produced disastrous consequences, such as shortages of basic staple items. This was largely caused by the absence of any effective distribution system through which products would have been made available to consumers. The shortage was further reinforced by the absence of a marketing communication system to inform people which goods and services were available to them, when, where and at what price (traditional and useful functions!).

In many European countries, especially in northern Europe and in France, there are still some traces of 'publiphobia'. The advertising profession in France was even forced to launch a huge poster and billboard campaign about fifteen years ago, against those known as 'publiphobes'. In certain countries such as Kuwait, advertisements for pharmaceutical products are strictly controlled or even forbidden. It is often considered immoral to spend too much on advertisements and sales promotions for ethical drugs, assuming that it unduly increases the final price of a drug and thereby reduces the chances of the poorest people to buy essential medical supplies and recover their health. As a consequence, many countries put a ceiling on pharmaceutical advertising, or subject it to a special tax.

At the international level, more attention is now being given to the idea that advertising, though undeniably useful to society, can also have negative results such as the encouragement of conspicuous consumption, the creation of needs that cannot be satisfied or deceptive advertising. Therefore the economic and social committee of the UN (United Nations) has proposed a resolution that would protect consumers in developing nations. Wills and Ryans (1982) have looked at how consumerists, students, academicians and managers differ in their attitudes towards advertising, across fourteen countries. They show that, across all the countries, the views held by consumerists and managers are quite different: managers often find advertising to be quite factual (75 per cent), providing important information about products or services (71 per cent), and both entertaining and informative (78 per cent), whereas consumerists rate it at a lower level on these dimensions (61, 48 and 50 per cent respectively). On the other hand, the attitudes of consumerists and managers do not differ significantly on various aspects of advertising: whether the ads are humorous, aesthetically pleasing or informative about prices. In all these aspects consumerists have a slightly less positive opinion. More than 50 per cent of the consumerists, on average (across the fourteen countries), tend to have a very negative opinion about the information content of advertising.

Attitudes towards comparative advertising

Attitudes basically depend on the responses which are given in a particular society to the following questions:

◆ What is the social function of comparative advertising?
◆ What are the prevailing arguments concerning the legitimacy of comparative advertising?

- How should competition between brands be facilitated?
- Does not comparative advertising result in fooling the consumer by using disputable information to praise one's own brand and put down others?

Socially dominant responses to these questions directly influence comparative advertising regulations in a given country. In some countries, comparative advertising is held in low esteem. This is the case in France, where it is considered a denigration of competing brands. It is therefore forbidden under Article 1382 of the Civil Code. In order for the advertisement to be considered comparative, there need only be a comparison of two competing products, even if the terms are neither inaccurate, nor tendentious, nor antagonistic. For instance, about twenty years ago Lip, the top French watch maker, was forced to pay heavy penalties to Timex, the top company in the American watch industry. The main feature of Timex's Kelton brand was its distribution through tobacconists, while Lip was confined to the more traditional channel of watch and jewellery stores. Lip was under attack from Kelton which, through the tobacconists, caused Lip huge sales losses. With the purpose of counterattacking in order to regain market share, Lip began an advertising campaign that showed a broken watch in an ashtray surrounded by a thick cloud of smoke, with a slogan that read: 'The watches sold in tobacconists are like cigarettes: they go up in smoke.'

Belgium, Italy and Germany are some other European countries that forbid comparative advertising (*Communication et Business*, 1988). It is sometimes argued that some countries forbid comparative advertising as an indirect way of protecting their national products from unfavourable comparisons with imported goods. According to Boddewyn (1984) the French authorities, which were about to legalize comparative advertising, took a step backwards, fearing that Japanese car manufacturers would use comparative advertising to communicate aggressively the advantages of their cars, thereby increasing their share of the French market where competition with other European producers is already active.

However, in the United States comparative advertising is legally permitted. The basic arguments in favour of comparative advertising seem to make sense: it facilitates consumer information, choice and competition between brands. Hence automobile advertising frequently gives performance statistics of competing models, such as fuel consumption, speed and comfort. Opponents of comparative advertising take the argument further and cast doubt on the possibility of using truly objective measures, which would be handled by completely independent testing organizations. As a consequence, comparative advertising would often end up giving either no information at all or partly misleading information to the consumer. Opponents of comparative advertising also implicitly support the idea that it is necessary to moralize business relationships between competitors. The role of marketing communications, by means of advertising, is to praise the virtues of their own product, not to put down (however indirectly) the virtues of competing products. The issue of comparative advertising is in a process of change at the European level. Already permitted in seven countries of the EC, comparative advertising is now the subject of a proposed common European directive by the European Commission in Brussels (*Communication et Business*, 1988). The issue of comparative advertising is in fact closely related to the question of consumer demand regarding the informative content of advertising messages.

Attitudes towards the informative content of advertising

The basic function of an advertisement is to communicate a message to an audience. Advertising style in communicating with the audiences of viewers, readers or listeners, can be roughly divided into three basic categories:

1. Persuasive.
2. Informative.
3. Oneiric (i.e. dream-orientated).

Thus, when comparing advertising practices in Turkey, Canada and Sweden, Kaynak and Ghauri (1986, p. 127) state:

> In developed countries, such as Canada and Sweden, advertising copy in general contains more writing and technical information, because most consumers have a high level of literacy and education.... Comparative shopping practices are limited in Turkey, and the general level of education is not high. Unlike Canada and Sweden, most of the advertising copy used by the Turkish agencies is persuasive in nature rather than informative.

The Turkish word for advertising is *reklam*: this corresponds to a more traditional vision of advertising, where persuasion and slogans are the key issues.[5]

In comparing the information content of American and Swedish advertising, by using a systematic analysis of the content of television commercials, Rita Martenson (1987) shows that Swedish ads have less information elements than American ads. She attributes this fact to the atmosphere of intense competition for the attention of television viewers that exist in the United States. The consumers change channels to avoid commercials, use commercial breaks to look at the programmes on other channels, etc. 'This means that [in the US] any commercial that does not have a very clear and simple message will strongly reduce its chances of getting the slightest amount of attention' (Martenson, 1987, p. 141).

Assuming that consumers are rational information seekers (which is not true in most cultural contexts), advertising content should be related to information sought by consumers in order to improve the relevance of their choices. If for any reason consumers are not 'good' (motivated and educated) information seekers, they will be less sensitive to the information content of an ad. This is the case if they do not directly use advertising information in their brand evaluations in order to reduce perceived risks when purchasing. Hoover *et al* (1978) compared Mexican consumers to their American neighbours: they found that Mexicans generally displayed a much lower level of perceived risk related to their purchases. Hoover *et al*. argue that the lower level of perceived risk is related to a somewhat fatalistic tradition which exists in Mexican society. Conversely, in the United States a more 'master-of-destiny' orientation implies a greater perceived risk of being disappointed by any purchase. Thus Mexican consumers and, more generally, consumers belonging to fatalistically orientated societies react more easily to persuasive messages (the brand name repeated numerous times) and also oneiric messages (a dream which allows one to escape from a daily life which is not always bright).

Relying on the dream-orientated part of the advertising audience is typical of the 'Seguela' doctrine. The dream-like dimension that surrounds the product is favoured at any price. Italian and French ads often appear as very dream-orientated: viewers and readers are supposedly willing to escape from the real world.[6] The oneiric style of advertisement enhances the fantasy of the consumer and emphasizes the imagination of satisfaction and enjoyment. It does so in a rather holistic way (the product and its benefits tend to be implied rather than actually shown). The oneiric style does not really concentrate on actual buying and consumption experiences. Germans, unlike the French or the Italians, are known to have a taste for highly informative advertising. A young German advertising specialist, Konstantin Jacoby (quoted in *Communication et Business*, 1988, p. 18) criticizes French advertising as follows:

> Certainly it [French advertising] is better than German advertising, but the French should take care not to sink in art for art's sake or in seguelomania.[7] The message of the Citroen advertising campaign is horrible. What is the link between the Great Wall of China and Citroen? Are Citroen cars manufactured there now?

The creative part of advertising

Language: the slogan

Language differences are one of the main barriers to effective communication. Advertising uses colloquial language, very subtle yet precise. Although not always apparent, colloquial language is very precise as far as meaning is concerned. Furthermore it is often based on almost slangy wordings, which are particular to local people. One rarely finds vernacular language in 'official' dictionaries. The viewer or the listener understands (and feels at ease) all the more readily when a great deal of work has been required to put the message into colloquial speech. The messages on greeting cards (such as those in the case of Eliot Greeting Card, section A5.1) show how difficult it is to put into words the delicate messages of daily life – sentiments, sensations, family relations, friendships, love affairs – that are reflected in creative advertising. Translating colloquial speech is especially difficult: there is little literal equivalence; colloquial language uses idiomatic expressions, which change from one language to another.

The slogan 'Put a tiger in your tank', for instance, is not as standardized as it might seem. It has been argued that it is standardized because at first reading, it looks as if it is fully equivalent across countries. However, in some countries the power is located in the tank (northern Europeans: 'Pack den Tiger in den Tank' in Germany; 'Stop'n Tiger in uw Tank' in Holland). In other countries, the powerful tiger is located in the engine (in French 'Mettez un tigre dans votre moteur'; in Italian 'Metti un tigre nel motore'). The interpretation differs as to where the power source is located. Examples of translation and conceptual equivalence problems abound, especially for advertising campaigns in which message standardization has been attempted (for examples see Ricks, Arpan and Fu, 1979). A full rewrite is usually needed to transpose slogans from one language to another. This implies a thorough search for words which have the same intended meaning, provided that this can be found in the target language as well as the source language (see Chapter 5 on the problems of translation and cross-cultural equivalence).

For advertisements that are required to be easily internationalized, one should avoid at all costs any problems related to language. This is entirely possible if the visual element of the message is emphasized, to the detriment of the textual component. As a consequence, television commercials aimed at a European audience often use a script where the characters speak neither to the audience nor to each other. Then a voice-over message on a sound track can be added to the image track. This avoids the drawbacks associated with dubbing. Most people lip-read unconsciously, at least in part. When watching a dubbed commercial, many people feel uneasy about the lag between lip movements and sounds. Written communication should also be avoided in messages targeted at a multilingual audience. For instance, a commercial or a detergent where a housewife is handed a packet of *Waschpulver* will be identified by British, Italian or French viewers as foreign or German. A few years ago, IBM used the character of Charlie Chaplin and the mode of a silent film in a multinational campaign, the goal of which was to foster corporate image. This allowed the advertisement to be used in any country of the world. The same can be applied to magazine advertisements where the text can be reduced or even virtually deleted. It may sometimes be kept in its original language in advertisements for ethnic products. The text must then be short and must strongly support an ethnic image (French for perfume, English for a large international newspaper, Italian for luxury leather shoes, etc.). The text must be universally understood, although not necessarily in full detail; the message should at least make sense with respect to the halo of meanings around the product proposal.

Roles represented in advertising creation

When depicting characters, advertising must be extremely careful. Whether it is the age, dress or situation of a character which is represented, nothing should be left to chance in advertising messages. An important issue is the representation of women: as consumers, domestic workers, housewives or as professional women, they are an influential consumer group within most societies. Advertising is often accused of condoning traditional societal sex roles, sometimes even acting as a vehicle for outdated ideas. The real situation is much more ambiguous: in most countries advertising acts as an agent of both social change and social maintenance. Advertising creation sometimes acts as an agent of change because social challenge is a method of capturing the attention of the audience, and because social innovators are also opinion leaders for new products and new ways of life. Advertising also reinforces traditional and sometimes old-fashioned social patterns: it is the mirror of society as a whole.

In a comparative study (Australia, Mexico, United States) of the advertising industry's attitude towards sex roles, Mary Gilly (1988) analyzed, for each country, twelve hours of programmes: 275 American, 204 Mexican and 138 Australian commercials were viewed. In neither the United States nor Mexico (as opposed to Australia) were women pictured in professional or executive positions. In these two countries men, more often than women, were shown in roles of authority or expertise with respect to the product, whereas women were more often shown in the role of the consumer. Finally, the only country where there is a difference in the situations in which men and women appear is the United States, where a woman is more likely to be shown at home.

One would have expected a more traditional image in Mexico, and a more modern image in the United States, with Australia somewhere in between. These results show that our basic intuitions as to which country gives the most 'modern' image of women are not necessarily backed up by facts.

As a consequence, one should study a representative sample of local advertising messages, whether commercials or magazine advertisements. This will give a good idea of the sex roles, age roles, typical everyday situations and social relations in a particular country. It can be achieved in a systematic way by a content analysis of newspaper, magazine and television advertisements, at least several dozen of each type.

Traditional roles that are not present in the source culture may unintentionally appear when they are used in the target culture. A 'spurious' meaning may appear in the target culture which was not intended by the advertiser in the source culture. Douglas and Dubois (1980) give the example of a brandy advertisement which was targeted at the South African Bantu market. It showed a couple seated at a table with a bottle superimposed over them. Many Bantus thought that the woman was carrying the bottle on her head, as many traditional African women do. This created an unintended and confusing contrast between the traditional, local aspect of the characters and situation and the modern, imported aspect of the product. It therefore prevented clear and effective marketing communication.

This, logically, brings us to the following statement: an advertisement should be created in co-operation with a native of the target culture, who would act as a test audience; or, in the case of internationally standardized ads, messages in the various linguistic/cultural contexts should be reviewed by natives of each target culture.

In order to avoid creating spurious associations, the advertising script may go so far as not to present any characters at all. For instance, certain Renault models were shown moving without a driver in French advertisements. This avoided having to choose a specific character, whose age, sex or appearance would influence the product's positioning unfavourably. When the target audience is not clearly defined, or is very large, the choice of characters is a difficult one. The car in the Renault ad drove around the middle of a scale-model scene, with no driver. This may be negatively interpreted in countries where such a situation is associated with a safety problem (runaway car) or a distortion of reality (how can a car drive without a driver?). This may inhibit a positive response to the message.

The influence of mores and religion

As suggested by McCracken (1991, p. 5), 'We may see consumer goods as the vehicles of cultural meanings ... consumers themselves as more or less sophisticated choosers and users of these cultural meanings.' From this perspective it is crucial to choose the appropriate symbolic elements by which cultural meanings may be communicated to the audience. The influence of mores and religion changes information components (a nude woman washing her hair in her bathroom, for example) into elements of culture-based meaning (it incites people to sexual debauchery). If one concentrates on information rather than meaning, it is difficult to become aware of the influence of mores and religions on advertising messages. This point is illustrated by examples from Saudi Arabia (see Box 12.1).

advertisements show people walking under ladders, unless, for the sake of humour,

Many of us have some superstitions, even though we may deny it. Rarely will advertisements show people walking under ladders, unless, for the sake of humour,

Box. 12.1   *The influence of religion on advertising in Saudi Arabia*

The Saudi legal system is unique in the sense that it identifies law with the personal command of the 'one and only god, the Almighty'. The Islamic laws known as *Sharia* are the master framework to which all legislation, existing and proposed, is referred and with which it must be compatible. The *Sharia* is a comprehensive code governing the duties, morals and behaviour of all Muslims, individually and collectively in all areas of life, including commerce. *Sharia* is derived from two basic sources, the Quran or Holy Book, and the *Hadith*, based on the life, sayings, and practices of the Prophet Muhammed. ... At the very minimum, an understanding of fundamental *Sharia* laws as contained in Quranic injunctions is necessary in order to gain insights into advertising regulation and content....

Three sets of Quranic messages have special significance for advertising regulation. First there are strict taboos (*haraam*), such as alcohol, gambling, cheating, idol worship, usury, adultery and 'immodest' exposure.... For example, alcoholic products are banned. There are no local ads, and foreign print media are only allowed into the country after all advertisements of alcoholic beverages have been censored. Promotions involving games of chance are illegal....

Other dangers for advertisers include messages which may be considered as deceptive by religious standards. According to Islam, fraud may occur if the seller fails to delivery everything promised, and advertisers may need to use factual appeal, based on real rather than perceived product benefits. Statuary should not appear in advertising, since it may be perceived as a symbol of idol worship. Since religious norms require women to be covered, international print ads may have to be modified by superimposing long dresses on models or by shading their legs with black. Advertisers of cosmetics in Saudi Arabia refrain from picturing sensuous females; instead, in typical ads a pleasant-looking woman appears in a robe and headdress, with only her face showing....

A second set of Quranic injunctions governs the duties a Muslim must perform, such as praying five times daily, fasting during the month of Ramadhan, giving *zakaat* (charity) to the poor, and respecting and caring for parents and the disadvantaged. Advertisers have to ensure that they do not hinder the performance of these obligations. For example, during the five prayer times, which last from 10 to 20 minutes, products cannot be promoted on radio or TV, retail shops close, and no commercial or official transactions are permitted. Ads should not depict, even humorously, children being disrespectful to parents and elders, whereas the image of a product could be enhanced by ads that stress parental advice or approval....

A third set of Quranic injunctions remind the faithful of God's bounties and enjoins them to thank Him for such blessings as good health, peace of mind, food, water and children. It is legal and sometimes recommended practice for advertisers to introduce their messages with Quranic words: 'In the Name of Allah, the Most Gracious, the Most Merciful'; 'By the Grace of God'; 'God is Great (Allah-o-Akbar)'; Al-Rabiah and Nasser, a manufacturer of water pumps, uses a Quranic verse: 'We made from water every living thing.' Such verses may also be used to legitimise operations or to assure that services are in accord with Islamic principles.

(Luqmani *et al.*, 1988, pp. 61–4. Reproduced with permission.)

customs of daily life also play a role, particularly those that are related to what is (locally) considered polite, courteous or hospitable. In this way, a well-known brand of tea alienated the Saudi public when it showed a Saudi host using his left hand to serve tea to one of his guests. Moreover, the guest was wearing shoes, which is considered in Saudi Arabia to be the height of rudeness.

Attitudes towards nudity can change from one country to another. French advertising is considered to have more nudity than nearly any other country. It is well accepted in French society, since the meaning conveyed by nudity there is very much related to beauty, excellence and nature. At opposite ends of the spectrum one can cite the example of the advertisements for the Guy Laroche perfume Drakkar Noir in France and Saudi Arabia (Czinkota and Ronkainen, 1990, p. 616). The original French advertisement showed a man's nude forearm, held at the wrist by a woman's hand, with the man's hand holding a bottle of cologne. The Saudi advertisement showed the man's forearm covered by a suit jacket, with only the cuff of the shirt showing, while the woman lightly touched his hand with one of her fingers. Respect for the existing social conventions in the target society will long remain a prerequisite to the localization of advertising messages. Furthermore, the role of advertising has never been (at least officially) to change a society's mores, but rather to sell a product.

Media

World-wide differences in advertising expenditures

One cannot help but be struck by the difference in advertising expenses across countries, even though these countries may have comparable levels of economic development. This can be partially attributed to media availability (radio, television, newspapers, magazines, film, billboards). Where some media are non-existent or their availability is limited, expenses are automatically restricted by the lack of space for advertising. In 1987, the world average per capita advertising expenditure was $52. Switzerland had the leading edge ($458), followed closely by the United States ($451). Many industrialized nations are clustered around the figure of $200 per capita p.a.: Japan $223, the Netherlands $219, Canada $212, Australia $188, Norway and Great Britain $181, Sweden $170, New Zealand $165 and West Germany $164, etc.

Obviously advertising expenditure is much less in developing nations. In most of the African countries, the figure of annual per capita advertising expenditure barely surpasses $1 per capita. The percentage of total GNP spent on advertising is small in developing nations. The figure in Turkey in 1981 was 0.31 per cent, as compared to 1.13 per cent in Sweden and 1.27 per cent in Canada (Kaynak and Ghauri, 1986). Since the population of developing countries is large with respect to their GNP, the per capita expenditure is very low: barely more than $4 in Turkey in 1981, compared to $127 in Canada and $138 in Sweden.

Availability of the media

The availability of advertising media is influenced by a country's level of economic development. Advertising is largely based on news and entertainment media. The communication support systems (television stations, transmitters, audiovisual equipment, printing presses, photographic equipment, etc.) are costly, in an area where financial support is not easy to find. Financial support in countries where banks have limited lending capacities is often based on political influence (which may prove unstable). In many countries the press is even more dependent on politics than on advertisers. The opportunity for advertising media remains limited in most developing nations.

Independent of purely economic factors, the availability of the media is also influenced by two social representations which relate to the relationship between the media and its audience:

1. What will be accepted by the viewer, listener or reader as a ratio between advertising time and entertainment time, such as (for television) talk shows, soap operas, news or informative content in general? What is considered adequate as far as the sequence between advertising and entertainment is concerned – should television movies, for instance, be interrupted by advertising, and how frequently?
2. Is advertising an entertainment in itself? Are people entertained by television commercials as such (i.e. waiting for television commercials, just because they like them)? The broader issue is: does the viewer/listener/reader expect to be compensated (entertained) for paying attention to the advertisement?

Many countries have instituted rules which place limits on television advertising. Sweden has no advertising on its national channels. West Germany limits advertising to twenty minutes per day over three to five time periods. France controls all its channels, public and private, with regulations (*cahier des charges*) that limit television commercials to about half an hour per day.

Conversely, where little or even no advertising regulation exists, there can sometimes be such an invasion by advertising that viewing programmes becomes nothing more than watching advertisements.[8] In Mexico City for instance, there are no less than 57 radio stations, and there are 775 radio stations for the whole country. On most of these stations there are 24 minutes of commercials per hour, and 2 minutes of news during each break, with 11 breaks per hour. This hectic schedule is extremely unpleasant for listeners, who are therefore constantly changing stations and cannot listen to one station, one programme or one speaker for any length of time. For this reason many advertisers buy a large quantity of media space for the same time block across several stations (Engels-Levine, 1982).

The question of finding the acceptable advertising dose is an important one. Studies have shown that in the United States an increasing number of consumers consider that television advertising is sometimes stupid and tends to be less intelligent than previously. US television viewers are therefore dissatisfied (Martenson, 1987). The situation is fairly paradoxical: as the media are increasingly available, it becomes more difficult to reach a target audience since viewers' saturation with ads can lead, first, to the scrambling of the consumer's ability to listen to advertising and, second, to reactions such as 'zapping' which can render audience monitoring quite difficult.[9]

This leads to another important question: is it necessary to reward the audience (viewer/ reader/listener) for having seen the advertisement? In other words: is entertaining the target *per se* a necessary condition for capturing the attention and interest of the viewer?

Consequently, is the additional creative effort at the risk of reducing the marketing effectiveness of the ad? The spectator who is attracted by the creative side of the message may end up forgetting the product that is being presented.

Responses to these questions probably differ between the United States and Europe. The aim of this book is not to answer questions as complex as these, but only to emphasize that the answers which are implicitly given to these questions in a specific country directly explain how entertainment and advertising are interrelated, television programmes being 'sliced up' by advertisements.

The emergence of global media

The previous section placed much emphasis upon differences in advertising across

Box 12.2   *The internationalization of the* Reader's Digest

'Since the formula of the *Digest* is so effective in the United States, why not attempt to repeat it elsewhere?' thought DeWitt Wallace. But exporting the formula of a magazine requires that the obstacle of language be overcome. The simplest solution was to begin in England, which could serve as a gateway into Europe. Accordingly, the first foreign edition of the *Reader's Digest* appeared in Great Britain in 1937. The second foreign edition, however, did not appear in Europe. In 1940, in the midst of the Second World War, the first issue of *Selecciones del Reader's Digest*, the Spanish-American edition, came out in Cuba. Why Cuba? The long-term objective was to attack the South American market, even if sales had to be made at a loss (as indeed occurred for many years). But for the time being, DeWitt Wallace's objective was more of a missionary one, for he sought to combat the Nazi advance. In 1942, a Portuguese edition in Brazil followed. This edition reached a print run of 300,000 copies. In 1943, there was a return to Europe with the publication of a Swedish edition. The war was not yet over, but DeWitt Wallace was already contemplating market entry into Europe. He offered cut-price subscriptions of the *Digest* to families of young Americans who had been called up. Along with chewing gum and nylon stockings, the *Reader's Digest* was to arouse the interest of young Europeans. After the war, in 1947, *Sélection du Reader's Digest* finally appeared in France under the management of General Thompson. There was an initial print run of 275,397 copies, which almost doubled for the second issue. The global expansion of the *Reader's Digest* did not stop ... Germany, Italy, Switzerland and Belgium, as well as India, South Africa, Australia and New Zealand, were all in turn to have their edition of the magazine.

Today, thirty-nine editions of the *Reader's Digest* are published, including one for schoolchildren, another in large type for those with sight problems and an edition in Braille. It can justifiably claim the distinction inscribed on every cover of being the most widely read magazine in the world.

Adapted from 40th anniversary special edition, *Sélection du Reader's Digest*, 1987, pp. 10–11, and *Reader's Digest* news release 'Products and services', 6/1988.)

countries. These differences do not offset certain similarities and convergences. Diverse media combine into a 'media landscape' which is primarily shaped by the freedom of choice of the media consumer. Some media have achieved almost world-wide recognition and a truly global audience. Among the international advertising media that have achieved the most impressive world-wide reach, appears the monthly *Reader's Digest*. It is the world's most widely read magazine, with a circulation of 28.7 million in 15 languages and 169 countries. It was founded in 1920 by DeWitt Wallace and his wife Lila Acheson. The first issue came out in February 1922 (see Box 12.2).

There are now some 'global' newspapers such as the *International Herald Tribune*, the *Wall Street Journal* and the *National Geographic* magazine. Their circulation covers almost the entire world. *Time Magazine* publishes 133 different editions, which enables advertisers to reach precise target audiences in a large number of locations throughout the world. Many French magazines such as *L'Express*, *Le Point* and *Elle*, and German magazines such as *Der Spiegel* and *Burda Moden* also publish international editions. The advertising clientele of these world-wide publications (or those on the road to globalization) nevertheless remains fairly limited. It consists of 'global' advertisers who are themselves mostly targeting a global clientele, namely a segment of well-off consumers who travel internationally. Industries that use media with global reach are basically airlines, banks and financial services, consumer electronics and telecommunications, cars, tobacco and alcohol, perfumes and luxury products.

As noted earlier, the picture has two facets: along with the preservation of culture-based differences in consumer behaviour and marketing communication practices (Chapter 6), a globalized supply of media is emerging. With regard to advertising media, technological breakthrough in international telecommunications will greatly serve the globalization of advertising. In turn, this will inevitably conflict with some national idiosyncrasies.

12.2　Technological advances will partially break down cultural resistance

The influence of television satellites

In the years to come, the television satellites which now reach all over the world will change the availability of media with regional or global coverage, particularly in Europe. The United States is a pioneer in this field – no less than thirty satellites were in service in the United States in 1990 (Mariet, 1990). They serve an impressive number of television stations. This section focuses on Europe, which, until now, has remained nationally fragmented.[10] Television channels were purely national ones, mostly state-owned, with some development of private hertzian and cable channels during recent years. Europe is now slowly following the United States.

Many satellites covering most of Europe are not available for transmission, such as Astra from Luxemburg, TDF1 and 2, TVSAT 1 and 2, which are French–German. Television is at the very centre of this technological change, but not the only beneficiary. Daily newspapers can also become globalized as a result of computerized typesetting, in which the core part of a newspaper (headlines and main articles, which are common to any local edition) is sent in the form of numerical (digitalized) information by telephone to automated printing workshops. The various editions can be 'localized' by adding local articles and advertising to a core text which is the same world-wide.

There are different possibilities for the use of television satellites:

• The transmission of images that will be used to make up a programme (primarily news and sports). Images transmitted by the satellite will ultimately be re-broadcast in a traditional form, e.g. hertzian ground television.

• The broadcasting of satellite images to viewers via a cable network. An infrastructure of ground receiving stations is then needed, before the images are sent to viewers through the cable. Ground stations can receive signals of minimal strength, amplify them and redirect them to private homes. The satellite does not need to emit very powerful signals, therefore it can broadcast over a broader range of channels than in the previous case. Thus the channels can be scrambled and paid for with the purchase of a decoder, or received, unscrambled and paid for by subscription to a cable channel or an hourly toll.

• A broadcast which is directly received by the viewer with a parabolic antenna (dish). In this case the satellite must broadcast much stronger signals so that they can be picked up on the ground. Because of this, the number of channels of a DBS (Direct Broadcast Satellite) will be reduced.[11]

Europeans lagging behind

The problem of satellite and cable network infrastructure is just as complex as the creation of new programmes which can fill the screens of the new television channels. For the European television industry the problem is acute. These stations cannot show only news from international news agencies and cheap talk shows, for the overall purpose of reducing the hourly cost of programmes. Television stations must set up some really entertaining programmes in order to attract viewers, so that they are given a reason to watch the shows and ... the commercials. The failure of the Europeans to keep up with these advances in the creation and international sales of television programmes is especially evident when compared to America (Sarathy, 1991). It is estimated, for instance, that the sudden changes in the European televisual industry will necessitate over 50,000 hours of new programmes per year. In 1987 the rights to one hour of the *Dallas* series cost $32,000, compared to $400,000 for the production of one episode of the series *Chateauvallon* by a European consortium led by the French state-owned station Antenne 2. In 1989, the re-broadcast rights to an American television film cost $70,000, compared to almost a million dollars for the production of a comparable European film (*Business Week*, 1987, 1989).

We can therefore expect the following three-part evolution in Europe:

1. The advent of media giants in Europe. Those who are likely to take control of large parts of the European televisual industry are Berlusconi from Italy, the German Springer Verlag and Bertelsmann, the French group Hachette, the Luxemburg television company, Jérôme Seydoux, the late Robert Maxwell's empire, and the Australian press magnate Rupert Murdoch (who has a strong European base). The bulk

of these groups are multimedia interests and are equally engaged in the development of the press media covering Europe as a whole.

2. Many European countries have invested in cable systems, which are competing with direct television (DBS). Some countries are already equipped with dense cable networks, such as Ireland, Belgium and West Germany, where more than half of all households are linked in. Other countries such as France are lagging behind and attempting to catch up. In general, there is much technology at stake and the standards for telecommunication technologies have not yet all been defined: high-definition television (HDTV),[12] fibreoptic networks, electronic transmission standards, etc. This all combines to make the scene rather confused. An effort is now being made at the European level to design new communication technologies in a co-ordinated way (Ungerer and Costello, 1988).[13] Technological, industrial, media, cultural and legal interests overlap in a realm of complex influences, where national state influence is still strong, as is the tradition in the European media and television industries.

3. Certain European regulations aim to protect the cultural identity of European audiovisual networks. The French, in particular, were somewhat disturbed by the invasion of American programmes,[14] to the detriment of European culture and creation. This implies an increasing influence of the English language, which the French and other Europeans fear could further damage the influence and reach of their own languages. In May 1989, the EC adopted a directive that required at least half of the programmes on European television to be produced in Europe. Nevertheless the text of this directive was fairly vague and allowed for loose interpretation by the member countries. The European Commission is also pushing, according to the 1985 EC White Paper on the completion of the internal market by January 1993, for common regulations in the field of advertising across the EC (see Box 12.3).

Enlargement and overlapping of media

The influence of media globalization and potential media overlap on marketing communications is quite significant, encompassing two major aspects:

1. A large increase in the available media space on television; new channels are all private, and must finance their operations either by advertising or by subscription (cable and/or scrambler/decoder).

2. Satellites have large overlap zones. This, combined with the extension of direct satellite television over the next few years, will produce greater overlap zones – not only in Europe – where viewers will be able to receive a large number of channels.

It is questionable whether media overlapping will be a problem in Europe, especially after 1993, when the physical borders between the twelve member-states of the EC will be abolished. Some people tend to underrate the importance of media overlapping:

> Much is made of overlapping media particularly in classroom situations. Yet the impact of imported overlapping media has only a marginal beneficial effect on audiences.... Evidence from Ireland, Austria and Switzerland indicates that where advertising is coming in from

adjacent countries it is largely ignored unless the product is also advertised locally, thus undermining the increased coverage potential. There is a need to harmonize creative presentation where overlaps occur to prevent confusion in the minds of potential customers. (Dudley, 1989, pp. 287 and 290).

Box 12.3   *Advertising regulations to globalize as well . . .*

Marlboro Man is headed for a showdown at the Brussels corral. The European Commission is trying to round up a posse to run the stetson-wearing hero of the cigarette industry's leading brand and the rest of its most potent symbols off the Community's advertising hoardings. It would also curb the use of brand names to market non-tobacco products such as lighters and fashion accessories. If the commission has its way, the directive on 'advertising of tobacco products in the press and by means of bills and posters' will be approved some time this year to take effect from January 1, 1992. From that date cigarette manufacturers would be expected to comply with standard Single Market rulings on the size and content of health warnings on cigarette packets, the presentation of tobacco products themselves and a ban on indirect advertising . . . .

As in many a Hollywood Western, the lawmakers are up against some powerful vested interests. . . . The market is divided between multinationals and state-owned companies. The multinationals led by the UK's BAT industries, Switzerland's Rothman's International, and US giants Philip Morris and RJ Reynolds, account for almost half the 560 billion cigarettes sold annually in the EC. Advertising is a vital weapon in their fight for market share. . . . State-owned companies, though, have little interest in siding with the multinationals. Public monopolies control the production, distribution and, in some cases, retail sales networks for cigarettes in four EC members: France, Spain, Portugal and Italy. . . . Cigarette advertising in all four countries is either banned (Italy, Portugal), soon to be abolished (France), or severely restricted (Spain). . . . Within the Commission only the UK, Germany and the Netherlands are opposed to the draft proposal, on the grounds that it encourages restrictive practices. Their votes are a blocking minority that present EC officials with a stark choice. Either they can withdraw the proposal and submit a new one supporting a total ban on tobacco advertising . . . or they can aim for a compromise that would meet the timetable and produce a partial ban.

But as the Commission tries to unite its forces it is coming under pressure from other interested parties . . . the sharpest shouting comes from advertising groups. 'For the first time, Community legislation is purporting to restrict indiscriminately the fundamental principle of freedom of speech,' declares European Advertising Tripartite (EAT), a Brussels-based group representing media, advertisers and agencies.

('Tobacco warning', *International Management*, February 1991, p. 56.)

One has to address the issue of whether media overlapping in Europe may lead to a compulsory standardization of brands and of the creative themes and presentation of advertisements. Sarathy (1991) illustrates this issue by citing Unilever's difficulties in creating advertising for its household cleanser which is called Vif in Switzerland, Viss in Germany, Jif in Great Britain and Greece and Cif in France. Mourier and Burgaud (1989) suggest that companies that adapt marketing plans to each European market risk being misunderstood by consumers. Indeed in switching channels, consumers would be disturbed if the same product were advertised under different brand names and had diversified packagings, and if different product uses and benefits were emphasized.

However, not all viewers will watch foreign channels, and not all products will be marketed throughout Europe. It seems more likely that there will be a combination of standardized marketing plans for European products that become regionally global, and local marketing plans for national or regional (within countries) target audiences.

12.3 Technological, economic and regulatory advances in progress open the door for more specific and segmented marketing

This section is strongly related to Chapter 7, which described the design of intercultural marketing strategies by the cross-over between zones and classes of cultural affinity. The concept of segmentation is crucial in appreciating the limits of the technological advances now in progress.[15] National, geographic and cultural variables will become a major factor in the process of market segmentation. Until now, domestic markets were considered to be the most likely units to be segmented. We will see the emergence of complex segments where country is not necessarily the segment*able* unit *par excellence*. The following examples illustrate this:

- Pan-European market segments, which account for a homogeneous population across countries – for example, age groups. This is the case when dealing with products for young people. Television stations such as MTV and Sky Channel are well prepared for this. The rock radio image, supported by the emergence of European rock, is carefully cultivated by MTV. As emphasized by Tom Freston, the president of MTV: 'Music crosses borders very easily, and the lingua franca of rock'n'roll is English. Rock is an Anglo-American form.' Freston further indicates what he considers to be the mission of MTV: 'We want to be the global rock and roll village, where we can talk to youth worldwide' (cited by Sarathy, 1991).
- Ethnicity may also work: pan-European market segments may be fairly effective when cultural and linguistic minorities are targeted. At the national level, these minorities do not reach critical numbers which could justify the creation of specific media, since they are scattered all over the countries of Europe. But minorities may be more significantly served at the European level. Mariet (1990) cites the case of the development of Hispanic television in the United States. There are two principal networks: Univision-SIN, started in 1961, now reaches 5.1 million households, that is, 85 per cent of Spanish-speaking Americans; the other large Hispanic network, Telemundo, covers 77 per cent of these households and is present in 35 states. In 1989, $305 million were invested in advertising on the Spanish-speaking media. It is predictable that such

initiatives will also flourish in Europe, in that they can fulfil the need for television communication of Arabic-speaking North African immigrants, Turks, Armenians or Jews.

♦ Segments which are based on classes of cultural affinity (see Chapter 7). In these groupings, consumers share similar buying habits or a common language; segments may be further divided on the basis of traditional criteria such as sociodemographics (age, sex, income, etc.). For example, a relevant segment may consist of beer drinkers in the zone of cultural affinity of Mediterranean Europe, identified by several common sociodemographic characteristics and/or by criteria linked to their consumption habits and psychographics.

♦ Market segments, the base of which will remain mostly a domestic one. As a consequence, they will be only slightly influenced by the regional market globalization in Europe. Car maintenance or ethnic food products such as the German *Knödel* would fall into this category.

♦ Finally, the possibility of targeting very precise and quite small populations. Regional and local marketing will develop alongside European global marketing. Local radio stations have emerged over the last ten years, but local television channels are almost non-existent in Europe. The marketing strategy of small segments of the service industry could be supported by emerging local media. Local cultural products have been relatively deprived of a true marketing strategy: local cultural products such as sports events, shows, private tutoring, etc., have been confined to direct marketing and door-to-door sales. When marketing at the local level, countries can be broken down instead of being treated as homogeneous segments. For example, a county in the north of France may be grouped with a county in French-speaking Belgium (Walloon) in a common segment for strategic marketing.

In the future there will undoubtedly be more standard brand names across Europe. Advertising and product offers could possibly be quasi-standard throughout Europe – Europe being divided into two principal zones, a Latin cultural-affinity zone and an Anglo-Saxon cultural-affinity zone. Among the industries that are potential candidates for regional marketing globalization in Europe are the following:

♦ Services, such as banks and financial services for private clients, European and transcontinental airlines.

♦ Products: almost all consumer goods distributed by hypermarkets and mass distribution, as well as many consumer durables such as cars, household appliances, stereo and video systems, and photographic equipment.

12.4   The globalization of advertising agencies

Agencies internationalize

Advertising agencies are nowadays largely internationalized. Saatchi and Saatchi, which ranks as one of the top agencies world-wide, is also one of the strongest proponents of ranks as one of the top agencies world-wide, is also one of the strongest proponents of global advertising; it has a total turnover of nearly US$13.5 billion. The largest Europe-based agencies are often smaller than American ones: the French advertising group, Eurocom, has a total turnover of about US$3.3 billion (*Advertising Age*, 1989). The largest American agencies (Young & Rubicam, McCann Erickson, FCB, Ogilvy & Mather, BBDO, J. Walter Tompson, Lintas, Grey, etc.) have built up a network of subsidiaries covering most countries in the world over the last twenty or thirty years.

The largest advertising agency in the world, Dentsu Inc.,[16] is Japanese. Japanese agencies are now present in a growing number of countries. The Japanese advertising market is a large one: it remains very attractive to Japanese agencies, which then target Southeast Asia and Australia in the first stages of their industrial expansion. Twelve Japanese agencies rank among the fifty largest advertising agencies world-wide (Dentsu, Hakuhodo, Dai-Ichi Kikaku, Daiko, Tokyu, Asatsu, Yomiko, Asahi, Chuo Senko, Nihon Keizaisha, Orikomi, Nan Nen Sha).

It is not always easy to launch 'triadic' agencies successfully. HDM, which was ranked seventeenth in the world (*Advertising Age*, 1989), appeared to be an attempt at merging European (**H**avas), Japanese (**D**entsu) and American assets (**M**arsteller, a large subsidiary of Young & Rubicam). It aimed to become a specialist in global marketing communication due to its clearly triadic position.[17]

Other agencies that are large but nationally based are compelled to follow this route to the internationalization of marketing communications, especially the internationalization of media and audiences. If they do not want to lose their customer base, they have to be able to organize cross-border campaigns for advertisers; but they must also remain knowledgeable experts on local idiosyncrasies in the implementation of marketing communication strategies. National agencies are trying to combine identity and knowledge of their national and cultural milieu on the one hand and the opportunities of the international market on the other. Because of their (sometimes) limited financial resources, they proceed by the acquisition of agencies in neighbouring foreign countries or by building an international network of national agencies by forming alliances or joint ventures in neighbouring countries.

The French Publicis group, for instance, has become associated with the American group FCB. The first French group for the purchase of media space, SGCMD, is now associated with the English group WCRS, ranking second in Europe and eighth world-wide (*Communication et Business*, 1988). There are many such examples.

Relationships between advertisers and agencies

As a consequence of the internationalization of advertisers, agencies have equally increased their operations in foreign countries. In the case of large multinational corporations with diversified product lines, this can lead to a complex advertiser/agency organization. The various levels (national, regional and world-wide) within both the multinational agency and the multinational advertiser must be in constant contact with each other. The usual communication problems related to large international organizations are more than doubled by adding the problem of the relationship between advertiser and advertising agency at each level.

Different approaches may be chosen for the organization of international marketing communication with respect to the agency/advertiser relationship. The Levi Strauss case, at the end of this chapter (section A12.1), offers several possible solutions:

- Using only one large international advertising agency, which allows for centralization of communication; this can be implemented for each product division separately, or for large brands, or for the purpose of managing the corporate image world-wide.
- Hiring local agencies that are well acquainted with local constraints with regard to media and consumers.
- Possible intermediate solutions between these two extremes which attempt to find an effective trade-off between world-wide co-ordination and local tailoring of ad campaigns.

One cannot underestimate the serious complexity of managing an international campaign (Clark, 1987), especially in the realm of agency/advertiser relations, which are often difficult to manage even when both agency and advertiser are excellent enterprises. For instance, Procter & Gamble has always been reputed to be a demanding advertiser for its agencies, but also very loyal to them. P & G, like many large companies, has always had very stable relationships (sometimes for forty years or more) with a group of agencies; some of them have world-wide responsibility for a product line and/or a major brand (*Advertising Age*, 1987). But the creative work is sometimes very conflictive between major advertisers and their agencies: their views concerning the strategy to be followed do not always correspond. Most advertisers then try to adopt a democratic style, by discussing opinions, facts, data and drafts of potential advertising campaigns. The final say always comes when campaigns are actually put into practice and their impact on various objectives may be monitored (brand awareness, brand image, sales increase, etc.).

The global campaign concept

The objective of a global advertising campaign has to be clearly defined: it does not seek to save on creative costs. It aims to promote a global brand name and image. Accordingly, the creative director for McCann Erickson world-wide, Marcio Moreira, emphasizes that an advertiser should not pursue a global advertising strategy as a way of saving money, trying to achieve in only one campaign what may in fact require twelve. The correct implementation of a global campaign requires a great deal of effort and creative time, and ultimately its cost may prove higher than the sum total of individual campaigns (Marcio Moreira, quoted by Hill and Winski, 1987).

Dean M. Peebles (1988), who was for many years the manager of international communications for Goodyear, the world's leading tyre manufacturer, recommends the following steps for the design and implementation of a global advertising campaign:

1. Choose a large advertising agency with subsidiaries all over the world; select in this agency an international account manager, who reports to the advertiser's headquarters.

2. Establish multinational planning meetings between the client and the agency, as well as a multinational creative team.
3. Brand managers at headquarters level should conduct and supervise consumer research and the pre-tests of the draft communication.
4. The resulting draft global campaign should be sufficiently finalized in order to facilitate discussion, but flexible enough to be transposed (rather than translated) into the various cultures and life-styles of the target audiences.

Figure 12.2 presents a flowchart of headquarters–subsidiary relations for the planning and co-ordination of world-wide advertising at Goodyear. This flowchart indicates the tasks to be performed and the (tight) time schedule imposed (Peebles and Ryans, 1984, p. 83).

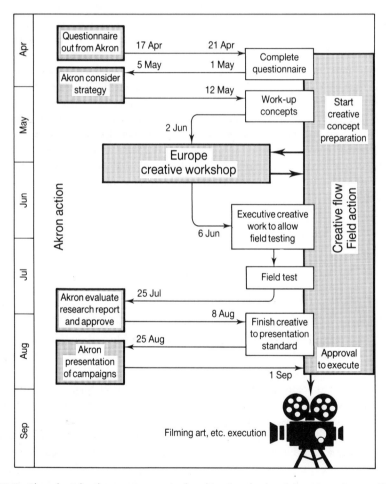

Figure 12.2 Flowchart for the management of multinational advertising campaigns at Goodyear. (Source: Peebles and Ryans, 1984, p. 83. Reproduced with the kind permission of the original publisher, the *Journal of Marketing*.)

Practical implementation of global advertising campaigns is not an easy task. The organization must be completely interactive, as emphasized by the American expression 'bottom-up top-down'. Communication between headquarters and subsidiaries should not be a 'sham' dialogue in which decisions already taken at the very top level would have to be accepted by local executives as if they were their own. This issue is all the more complex because interaction problems between various levels within the multinational advertiser (international headquarters, regional headquarters, country subsidiaries) are aggravated by problems of communication, co-ordination and agreement with the international agency (see the Levi-Strauss case at the end of this chapter, section A12.1).

Global communication is primarily intended to establish the corporate image of a company or foster recognition of one of its major brands across a large number of countries (e.g. McDonald's, Goodyear, Michelin, Nestlé, etc.). The next step is to advertise the products themselves, and at this point the creative input of local subsidiaries and regional headquarters, as well as their influence on the advertising strategy, is much more significant. But local campaigns, even if they advertise local products and local brand names, must be carefully co-ordinated so that they make a positive contribution to the global message. The core values which are conveyed by the company's corporate image should also be recognizable in its brand and product advertising at the local level (e.g. high technology, security, robustness, innovativeness, style, social responsibility, etc.). Finally, communication with market segments which remain specific to certain countries should be fully delegated to the local level. Not every piece of communication can be globalized. Accordingly, it is preferable to let local businesses develop on their own, even though they have only local coverage, as they may some day be extended to other countries.

APPENDIX 12

———— ◆◆◆ ————

Teaching materials

A12.1 Case: Levi Strauss Company: World-wide advertising strategy or localized campaigns?

The Levi Strauss Company, manufacturer of the famous LEVI'S jeans and other wearing apparel, markets its products in 70 countries. The company owns and operates plants in 25 countries and has licensees, distributors, and joint ventures in others.

The company is now in the process of evaluating its advertising policy to determine whether to apply a worldwide strategy to all advertising or settle on localized campaigns for each country in which it sells its products.

You have been asked to evaluate their present programs and to make recommendations that will assist management in deciding whether it is better (1) to create advertising campaigns locally or regionally but with a good deal of input and influence from headquarters as they presently do, (2) to allow campaigns to be created independently by local advertising companies or (3) to centralize at national headquarters all advertising and develop a consistent worldwide advertising campaign.

You are asked to do the following:

1. Prepare a report listing the pros and cons of each of the three approaches listed.
2. Make a recommendation as to the direction the company should take.
3. Support your recommendation and outline major objectives for whichever approach you recommend.

The following information should be of assistance in completing this assignment.

Company objectives

In a recent Annual Report, the following statement of objectives of Levi Strauss International was made:

> In addition to posting record sales, Levi Strauss International continued to advance toward two long-term objectives.
>
> The first is to develop a solid and continuing base of regular jeans business in markets throughout the world, thus proving a foundation for product diversification into women's-fit jeans, youthwear, menswear, and related tops.
>
> The second objective is to attain the greatest possible self-sufficiency in each of the major geographic areas where Levi Strauss International markets: Europe, Canada, Latin America, and Asia/Pacific. This requires the development of raw material resources and manufacturing in areas where the products are marketed thus reducing exposure to long supply lines and shipping products across national borders.
>
> Unlike some competitors, Levi Strauss International does not, in its normal markets, seek 'targets of opportunity,' that is, large one-time shipments to customers it may never serve again. Rather, the goal is to develop sustainable and growing shipment levels to long-term customers.

Organization

Western European group. The company's European operations began in 1959 with a small export business, and, in 1965, an office was opened in Brussels. The company now has 15 European manufacturing plants and marketing organizations in 12 countries. This group includes all Western Europe served by the Continental and Northern European divisions.

The Continental European Division is headquartered in Brussels and is responsible for operations in Germany, France, Switzerland, the Benelux countries, Spain and Italy. *The Northern European Division* is headquartered in London and is responsible for all marketing and production in the United Kingdom and the Scandinavian nations.

Other international group. The divisions in this group report directly to the president of Levi Strauss International. They are Canada, Latin America, and Asia/Pacific.

The Canadian Division consists of two separate operating units: Levi Strauss of Canada and GWG. Levi Strauss and Company is sole owner of GWG which manufactures and markets casual and work garments under the GWG brand.

The Latin American Division traces its origins to 1966 when operations began in Mexico. In the early 1970s, the business was expanded to Argentina, Brazil, and Puerto Rico. In addition to these countries, the division now serves Chile, Venezuela, Uruguay, Paraguay, Peru, Colombia, and Central America. Plans call for the division to explore new markets in Central America and the Andean Region.

The Asia/Pacific Division had its beginning in the 1940s when jeans reached this market through U.S. military exchanges. In 1965, a sales facility was established in Hong Kong. Markets now served include Australia and Japan, the two largest, as well as, Hong Kong, the Philippines, Singapore/Malaysia, and New Zealand. Business in Indonesia and Thailand is handled through licensees. The markets served by this division present opportunity for growth in jeanswear. However, diversification potential in Asia/Pacific is centered in Japan and Australia.

Other operating units. One other unit, EXIMCO, not aligned with either Levi Strauss USA or Levi Strauss International, reports directly to the president.

EXIMCO has two major responsibilities; market development and joint ventures in Eastern Europe, the USSR, and the People's Republic of China, and directing offshore contract production for the company's divisions.

Comments

The director of advertising and communications for International shares with you the following thoughts about advertising:

> The success of Levi Strauss International's advertising is derived principally from their judging it consistently against three criteria: (1) Is the proposition meaningful to the consumer? (2) Is the message believable? and (3) Is it exclusive to the brand?
>
> A set of core values underlies their advertising wherever it is produced and regardless of strategy: honesty/integrity, consistency/reliability, relevance, social responsibilty, credibility, excellence, and style. The question remains whether a centralized advertising campaign can be based on this core of values.
>
> Levi Strauss' marketing plans must include 70 countries and recognize the cultural and political differences affecting advertising appeals.
>
> Uniform advertising (i.e., standardized) could ignore local customs and unique product uses, while locally prepared advertising risks uneven creative work, is likely to waste time and money on preparation, and might blur the corporate image.
>
> Consistency in product image is a priority.
>
> International advertising now appears in 25 countries. Levi currently uses seven different agencies outside the United States, although one agency handles 80 percent of the business worldwide. In Latin America, they use four different agencies, and still a different agency in Hong Kong.

Levi is not satisfied with some of the creative work in parts of Latin America. The company wants consistency in Latin American strategy rather than appearing to be a different company in different countries. They are not satisfied with production costs and casting of commercials, and the fact that local agencies are often resistant to outside suggestions to change. They feel there is a knee-jerk reaction in Latin America that results in the attitude that everything must be developed locally.

The risks of too closely controlling a campaign result in uninteresting ads compared with decentralizing all marketing which produces uneven creative quality.

Competition

At the same time that Levi is looking at more centralized control of its advertising, another jeans maker is going in the opposite direction. Blue Bell International's Wrangler jeans company has just ended a six-month review of its international advertising and decided against coordinating its advertising more closely in Europe.

The concept of one idea which will work effectively in all markets is attractive to Wrangler. Yet the disadvantages are just as clear; the individual needs of each market cannot be met, resistance from local managers could be an obstacle, and the management of a centralized advertising campaign would require an organizational structure different from their present one.

To add to the confusion, a leading European jean manufacturer, the Spanish textile company Y Confecciones Europeas, makers of 'Louis' jeans, recently centralized its marketing through one single advertising agency. Louis, fourth largest jeans maker after Levi, Lee Cooper, and Wrangler, is intent on developing a worldwide international image for its Louis brand.

Review of current ads

A review of a selection of Levi advertisements from around the world provided the following notes:

European television commercials for Levi's were super-sexy in appeal, projecting, in the minds of some at headquarters, an objectionable personality for the brand. These commercials were the result of allowing complete autonomy to a sales region.

Levi's commercials prepared in Latin America projected a far different image than those in Europe. Latin American ads addressed a family oriented, Catholic market. However, the quality of the creative work was far below the standards set by the company.

Ads for the United Kingdom, emphasizing that Levi's are an American brand, star an all-American hero, the cowboy, in fantasy wild West settings. In Northern Europe, both Scandinavia and the U.K., they are buying a slice of America when they buy Levi's.

In Japan, where an attitude similar to that in the U.K. prevails, a problem confronted Levi's. Local jeans companies had already established themselves as very American. To overcome this, Levi's positioned themselves against these brands as legendary American jeans with commercials themed 'Heroes Wear Levi's,' featuring clips of cult figures like

James Dean. These commercials were very effective and carried Levi's from a 35 percent to a 95 percent awareness level in Japan.

In Brazil, unlike the United Kingdom, consumers are more strongly influenced by fashion trends emanating from the European Continent rather than from America. Thus, the Brazilian-made commercial filmed in Paris featured young people, cool amidst a wild traffic scene – very French. This commercial was intended to project the impression that Levi's are the favored brand among young, trend-setting Europeans.

Australian commercials showed that creating brand awareness is important in that market. The lines 'fit looks tight, doesn't feel tight, can feel comfortable all night' and 'a legend doesn't come apart at the seams' highlighted Levi's quality image, and 'since 1850 Levi jeans have handled everything from bucking broncos . . .' amplified Levi's unique positioning. This campaign resulted in a 99 percent brand awareness among Australians.

(Philip R. Cateora, 1983, *International Marketing*, 5th edn, Richard D. Irwin: Homewood, IL, pp. 525–9. Reproduced with permission.)

Questions

1. Based on the various copy strategies described in the case, analyze the possible themes which can be used to support Levi's image.
2. How should one operationalize the *set of core values*: across the various countries/cultures where Levi advertises its products, how can precise criteria be set which enable one to judge whether a commercial respects the core values?
3. Prepare a comparative table showing the pros and the cons of each of the three approaches listed at the beginning of the case.
4. Make a recommendation as to the choice which should be made by Levi's (one of the three approaches or a combination of them). Please argue your choice.

A12.2 Case: Agencia de Publicidad Aramburu SA (APA)

Mr. Aramburu was worried about the growing complexity of the operations of his advertising agency, from the point of view of both creativity and implementation of the advertising campaigns.

The agency not only created and implemented advertising campaigns for various Spanish products for the Spanish market but also had been creating and implementing since 1975 – at least in part – the advertising campaigns for Semo semolina, manufactured by Invesa, in various East African countries, in Morocco, and in the Middle East; subsequently, since 1983, it had agreed to create advertising campaigns for African or Arab customers to be aired in their respective countries.

On the one hand, it seemed worthwhile to put to use the body of knowledge acquired over the last ten years on how to advertise in Africa and the Middle East. On the other hand, he wondered if these markets really offered any opportunities in the medium term or if the good results obtained so far owed more to having ridden on the crest of a wave of favourable circumstances.

Previous international experience

Agencia de Publicidad Aramburu S.A. (APA), had its origin in 1940 as the advertising department of a food conglomerate (Vascalisa) and gradually developed into Publicom S.A., a wholly owned subsidiary of Vascalisa. In 1985, APA was founded as the result of a management buy-out. The buy-out came about because Vascalisa was an industrial group with only limited interest in advertising activities. Even as a separate entity APA continued to work with Vascalisa during a transitional period, on the basis of fees and other conditions stated in the purchasing contract.

Exporting advertising services

In 1975 Vascalisa set up an export department to sell semolina to countries in Africa and the Middle East. For this purpose, 'Semo' was developed in 1977, a semolina which could be defined as a tropicalized durum formula Semolín. In the same year, the Vascalisa subsidiary Internacional Vasca Export S.A. (Invesa) was created as the company within the group that would manufacture and market Semo. Invesa soon began to open markets in Central and East Africa, especially in the countries that made up the Horn of Africa.

Vascalisa decided to rename its export semolina, calling it Semo – which locally sounds something like 'semu' – which sounded better and was easier to pronounce than Semolín. The product itself was tropicalized too to make it more resistant in the environment of extreme climatic conditions, especially considering the length of time that passed between manufacture in Spain and consumption in countries such as Somalia, Tanzania, or Sudan. The product would be retailed in small individual bags, following local usage and to increase rotation, instead of boxes containing several bags, which was the format used to sell Semolín in Spain.

Right from the start, Vascalisa turned to Publicom S.A. for help in designing its marketing strategy in Africa. The product's name, the adaptation of the product's quality to the markets it would enter, its presentation (without box) were all minutely analyzed. From the business point of view, Publicom S.A. treated Vascalisa just like any other company, providing full service within the legal restrictions imposed by each African country. Vascalisa paid Publicom S.A. in Spain, using pesetas for the services provided.

In 1979, both Vascalisa and Publicom S.A. began to feel the need to evolve toward a more aggressive sales strategy; by 1980, this feeling had become a determination to gradually progress from push marketing to pull marketing.

As Mr. Aramburu explained: 'At first, we had to feel our way; it did not seem reasonable to us to invest in expensive advertising campaigns in markets whose possibilities we did not exactly know. Later on, we saw that the sales of Semo were growing, that we had a large potential market, and that it could be profitable to invest money in "pulling" the product from the point of sale. We also understood that any campaign we made had to be aimed at promoting a specific demand, and not just a purely generic demand, as some Italian brands had already been around over there for much longer than us.'

The first task was to decide *how to advertise*. It was obvious that the methods and ideas used in Spain could not be easily exported to the markets in East Africa. There was also the language problem: In Tanzania, for example, the only official language was Swahili,[18] a widely used native language that was written using the Latin alphabet, although English was fairly common at certain levels; there were also several major dialects that were spoken but not written. In view of the reduced level or even nonexistence of television and the low readership levels, especially among women, the media that seemed to be the most suitable was radio; in any case, there were no audience surveys and it also had to be borne in mind that the radio stations were usually run by the respective governments, with very little room for maneuver, and centered on news. The same could be said about television in those countries where it existed, to the extent that there were no censuses of the number of television sets.

'Advertising,' commented Mr. Aramburu, 'is just one more cultural phenomenon. Each advertisement must stimulate the consumer's preference toward the brand, and the advertisement's message cannot be dissociated either from the product that sponsors it or from the idiosyncrasies of the potential consumer it is directed toward. We avoided "advertising colonization" as much as possible because of our lack of knowledge concerning the region and because it seemed advisable to us from the point of view of working relationships with the government authorities. Thus, only an observant and open-minded person would realize that in those countries the housewife appearing in TV commercials would have to be a plump and well-fed woman; or that a dish must be tasted almost unavoidably with the fingers.

'In those countries where they existed, we reached agreements with local agencies. This was the case in Tanzania, Somalia, Ethiopia, and Kenya. In other countries where there were no established advertising agencies, we had to work directly with the advertising departments of the broadcasting stations.'

Publicom S.A. tried to generate ideas in the meetings held with the staff of the local agencies. Normally, these were young people who had studied in Europe or occasionally an English expatriate who had started up on his own. All their ideas, collected in the field and processed in Bilbao, were expressed in a video, in a radio spot, in a jingle, in an image, that Publicom S.A. then showed in Madrid to a group of contacts from the country concerned – mostly students – to ensure that the message was appropriate.

'In Kenya, in 1983, we ran a campaign consisting of a truck with a film projector that toured through the jungle and when it arrived at a village, showed a promotional film; the driver–operator then handed out free samples of Semo to the audience. In 1984, we launched the multimedia campaign "The Four Pleasures" in Tanzania, a country which has color television. It referred to the four pleasures of cooking: the purchase of the ingredients, the preparation of the dish by the housewife, the offering of the food to the head of the family (the father), without whose approval the meal cannot be served, and the tasting of the dish by him. The commercial was announced by a "kotch-barma," a mythical character, a king's witch doctor, a kind of oracle who – unlike other counselors who may indulge in intriguing – always tells the truth. This character combs his hair with two perpendicular partings so that it is divided into four parts, like a harlequin. In the commercial, the witch doctor shows his head with his hair dyed in the four colors of the Semo bags while he recommends its use for cooking to be able to enjoy the four pleasures it provides to the consumer. Before launching the message on the market, we wanted to be sure that the video would not be sacrilegious or scandalous and so we showed it to about a dozen Tanzanians we had contacted in Madrid who could read and write Swahili. This campaign was shown on television in two countries and broadcast on radio in a further five; produced in 14 different dialects, as well as Swahili, French, and English. At the time it was the basic advertising communication in those markets.

'In 1984, we also launched a jingle on the radio in Uganda with such intensity that many thought that it was the national anthem and stood up every time they heard it. In each case, we tried to get maximum advertising benefit from the media available to us and for this we had to know the particular features of each region and the coverage of the various media. Thus, we discovered that in some villages it was the custom for families to get together in large groups to watch television. On other occasions, it was impossible for us to get around the pressure we were subjected to by associated agencies or the media themselves to advertise through certain media, such as newspapers, which seemed ineffective to us.

'We also launched two blind-test commercials: in these, people tasted two different soups, one of which was made with Semo. Everybody delightedly guessed which was Semo after successively dipping their fingers in each and licking them.'

The trips to Africa

In line with his philosophy of adapting the advertising and marketing to the particular idiosyncrasies of each national market, Mr. Aramburu went to Africa for the first time in 1982. The purpose of the trip was to 'smell out' the market on the spot, to find out for himself what it was like. In Dar-es-Salaam, Carlos Aramburu had the opportunity to deal directly with the distributor of Semo, with some of his salesmen, and with retailers.

'One thing that stands out straight away is the vital importance of the point of sale for effectively marketing the product. In the markets of the large capitals, the stalls measure barely one meter square. They may be open-air or lightly covered and are usually attended by a mammy. [*Mammy* or, perhaps less frequently, *mummy* is used generically in Africa to refer to women who sell in the market.] These mammies are usually extraordinarily fat women who sit on a box and arrange the consumer products they sell on the ground in front of them. In the countryside, the retail outlets are shacks where no more than a dozen different brands are stacked.

'I have visited a large number of these bazaars and street markets, sticking stickers or offering posters showing the Semo squares, colors, and logo; this aspect of loyalty to an image is vital in those countries where the written transmission of slogans or even of the product's name is virtually useless. This direct contact with the mammies, with the salesmen, with the agents, even with the personnel of the media advertising departments, with the market, and with the country in general has been very useful. We have found out what the market is really like, it's given us idea, it's enabled us to gain the channel's trust. In fact, I don't think that any other manufacturer has made so much effort to get close to the market. The fact is that we are gaining market share and I suppose the other manufacturers are getting pretty worried.'

Diversification of APA's export business and its opening up to local advertisers

Little by little, on the basis of the reputation gained from the marketing of Semo, Publicom S.A. began to make a name for itself in some of the countries in which it operated. The distributors were pleasantly surprised by the success of Publicom S.A.'s campaigns; the personal contacts made during the visits helped to create an atmosphere of rapprochement and trust; the dinners held in the Carvajal family's house, to which the small but warm-hearted Spanish colony in Dar-es-Salaam was invited, were the scene of interminable conversations which gave Carlos Aramburu a clearer idea of life in those countries.

The importers and/or distributors of Semo were usually influential men of Indopakistani or Lebanese origin who had businesses in several industrial and commercial sectors. Mr. Aramburu spoke of them with a certain air of indecision. 'In my opinion, it is vital to deal directly with people. I think that everyone likes being treated on an equal footing in a natural and respectful manner; I have always tried to establish a climate of polite deference and I think that it has opened a lot of doors for me. In any case, not all Europeans agree with me and there are some who have had undoubted success in the area in spite of – or perhaps thanks to – their rather arrogant and scornful attitude.'

In the spring of 1983, the importer of Semo in Tanzania requested Publicom S.A. to design the advertising campaign for the umbrellas it manufactured and sold, bypassing Counterpoint, which was the local agency that Vascalisa, Publicom S.A., and the importer itself had worked with right from the first day Semo was marketed there. In another two countries, Publicom S.A. was given direct assignments from the respective importers. The importer of Semo in Zanzibar also sold a line of Italian detergents and it placed Publicom S.A. in charge of the advertising campaign for these detergents.

The main problems facing Publicom S.A. at that time were basically two-fold. First, the importers did not have or were simply not used to providing the type of information on the market, the channel, and the markups that was essential to organize a meaningful campaign. 'Over there,' said Mr. Aramburu, whose voice had recovered its forceful tone, 'you've got to be prepared to listen. If you hand the potential client your BID[19] the chances are he won't be able to fill it in because to do so, certain basic knowledge is required not of marketing but of the market, of what you really want to achieve. Also, in addition to the problem of the lack of a qualified sales manager, you've also got the lack of statistics on media audiences and, worse still, the lack of awareness of advertising techniques.'

There was also the problem of payment because until then Publicom S.A. had always been paid by Vascalisa in Spain, using pesetas. When it started to work directly for local companies, as the product that Publicom S.A. sold to its new companies was an intangible consisting of advertising ideas and action techniques, sometimes it was difficult to justify the origin of the dollars received in fees to the customs authorities at the airport when leaving the country.

Basic features of exporting advertising services to Africa

'In all these countries,' said Mr. Aramburu, 'the normal procedure is to start talking about money. When they decide to invest, it is because they feel it is advisable to do so but normally they don't know how much. It can even occur that they say to you, ''I've got so many million shillings. What can I do with them? Maybe I could put posters on buses, or print ads in the newspapers?'' They are at that point where a country or company is starting to feel interested in advertising. It happened in Spain 30 years ago and it's happening to them now.

'The advertiser has no information on the market in his own country and neither do we. So somehow we have to complement the ''empirical'' information available. Mr. Abdullah Bequer, for example, does not know for sure who is buying his products; he knows his customers are natives because he knows the points of sale. But he doesn't know their social class, their age, their background. Neither does he know to what extent his customers are loyal, that is, repeat buyers, or whether his sales are usually only occasional first purchases. You have to work a bit on trial and error to get an idea of the situation.

'Also, and as a result of the above, major changes may occur in the course of the campaign. For example, if it is seen that the campaign is successful, its budget may be considerably increased.'

In Spain, on the other hand, the process was usually started on the advertiser's initiative, who nearly always had a certain idea of the market situation. The advertiser selected an agency, who proposed his fees and method. Advertiser–agency 'marriages' were frequent, i.e., an advertiser may consistently use the same agency to advertise some or all of its products. After preparing the briefing, the agency was in a position to be able to define the campaign's total cost. After that, it started to develop the creativity, the idea, or concept to communicate and the way to communicate it most effectively. The next steps were media definition, budget distribution, contracting the media chosen, and putting the campaign into action and monitoring it.

In other cases, it was the agency that took the initiative, seeking out a client with whom to reach an initial agreement for the presentation of a tentative campaign based on an overall budget. From that mutual loose commitment, the agency developed the creativity to present it to the advertiser. If the advertiser was satisfied with the agency's ideas, it implemented the ensuing steps of defining the media, distributing the budget, contracting the media, and executing the campaign. On the other hand, if the ideas created by the agency were not to the budding client's liking, it could cancel the contract on the spot.

Carlos Aramburu commented on the differences between the situation in Africa and the normal working methods used in Spain: 'You cannot place all the local agencies under the same heading. For example, in Mogadishu, Vascalisa has its local agency, Oggi, which is very dependable. Oggi contracts the media and bills Vascalisa locally for them. Also, Oggi creates the idea, designs the storyboard, and films the commercial or records the spot and prepares the original graphics. Our function in this case is to closely supervise the operations and ensure that the standards desired by Vascalisa are met.

'In other cases, for example, the United Arab Emirates, APA does the complete creativity and the local agency buys the media, supervises the copy, determines the amount of posters to be printed, and gives information on local culture.

'Finally, in those countries where there are no local agencies, APA resorts to the managers of the advertising media for advice on local culture, review of the copy in the local language, hire actors and speakers.'

Carlos Aramburu's concerns in September 1986

Carlos Aramburu was aware of the prudence required to manage a company recently starting out on its own and with rather limited financial resources. He also liked to define himself as a businessman 'like they used to be,' concerned to get the most out of every peseta spent and unwilling to take on additional expenditure items if it was not clear that they were absolutely necessary.

As part of this line of thought, APA's prime goal was to consolidate a market in Spain. The image its team of professionals had created for themselves over the last 30 years, the successes achieved, and the enormous amount of creativity shown by campaigns as varied as those for a major Japanese photocopier manufacturer ('Japanese through a Tube'), a well-established Bilbao newspaper ('In Writing, Please'), a chain of supermarkets covering the entire Basque Country, Navarre, and Rioja ('We Sell Quality') or a cookie manufacturer ('Heaps Better'), among many others, provided a major business asset which had to be capitalized upon.

Furthermore, the team of professionals in APA had been working in the sector for many years, knew everybody in Spain, and were in a position to present themselves as a group experienced in working together, that had been enriched after the purchase of Publicom S.A. with new human and technical resources and was able to offer each advertiser a dual response of creativity and service adapted to each client's particular situation.

However, the general manager of APA did not want to give up the idea of strengthening his markets abroad and he was well aware that a significant part of the agency's billing for creativity – excluding therefore the buying of media – came from Vascalisa and the overseas clients.

Carlos Aramburu realized the enormous prospects that were opening up to him in the East African and Arab countries. The multinational agencies had yet to establish any significant presence in these quasi-virgin territories and Mr. Aramburu was afraid that, if he let time slip by, he would end up losing his lead to them. He had noticed that the sales office of an Italian agency in Mogadishu had been recently relaunched after years of inactivity. In this area, he considered that he had several possible alternatives: establish branches (wholly owned subsidiaries), continue as until now cooperating with the agencies existing in each country on the basis of agreed 'contractual' collaborations, or form associations with the local agencies, buying some of their shares and providing basically technical assistance, such as training personnel in Spain or dealing with certain aspects of the creativity. In any case, it seemed clear that each country would require individual treatment.

APA, both in Spain and in the other nine countries it had worked in, had developed a know-how and an image that it should not let go to waste. They had been four years of work well done by Publicom S.A. and APA in Tanzania, Somalia, Kenya, Uganda or

Morocco; four years of traveling, learning, contacting markets, agencies, and media, of winning the company's first clients. To wait two years, which was the least time required to ensure continuity in Spain, for pushing strongly abroad, was not without risk.

Mr. Aramburu did not forget Vascalisa, the temporarily captive customer he had gained with the agency buy-out, which for the time being guaranteed a certain minimum billing for the agency. In any case, the terms were not particularly generous and Mr. Aramburu was considering renegotiating – updating – some of the clauses because, in his opinion, the quality of the service given by APA was improving day by day and in some cases was significantly higher than that given when the contract for the management buy-out of Publicom S.A. was written.

In Mr. Aramburu's opinion, the policy of exporting services could be focused along two approaches: the European companies that exported to Africa and the Middle East and the local companies. APA had already made contacts with some Spanish companies that were looking for markets in those regions.

In addition to these general issues, Mr. Aramburu also pondered on a number of other more specific but no less important problems.

Among these was the question of the profitability of the foreign clients. Most of these were medium-sized companies and – especially in the case of the foreign clients – required traveling. This inevitably meant an increase in the cost of the service, should traveling expenses be charged direct to the clients, or a significant decrease in profitability should APA include such costs as one more item in its income statement. Mr. Aramburu wondered to what extent, in the medium term, these charges could be borne by him or by his customers and, looking at the problem from another viewpoint, what should APA's fees be for it to be worthwhile for him and his clients.

Mr. Aramburu was also aware that, in September 1986, APA had no export manager; there was the feeling in the agency that such a position would unnecessarily burden the overhead and the time for such a person was not yet ripe. As Mr. Aramburu explained: 'There's no doubt that an export manager – or foreign accounts manager as we would call him – would significantly lighten my workload and enable me to give greater attention to the Spanish market. In November, for instance, I should be going to three countries and the way things are, it looks that I won't be able to go. A trip abroad, in addition to totally absorbing your attention for a few days, always leaves a few loose ends to be tied up because when you get back you have to send a leaflet or agenda to the inquisitive government officer who asked for them, send an answer to this or that client, review the conclusions of this or that matter, write a letter of intent, report to the board. But I think that it's best to wait a while because to fill this position would cost money and it's got to be done properly. We would need someone who would fit in with the company's corporate philosophy, who was familiar with the bureaucratic problems existing over there, who knew the methods of payment and the systems of credit, and who could feel at ease in those countries.

'Then there's what I call advertising "colonization" and which we have consistently avoided: we sell creativity not preconceived ideas tailored to the European markets; also, you've got to bear in mind our own limitations, our lack of in-depth knowledge of the reality and idiosyncrasies of each country, of the need to know how to work with people over there.'

The conception of a business strategy: strengths and possibilities

Deep down, what worried Mr. Aramburu most was the doubt he constantly had as to the suitability of the present business strategy. Sometimes, he caught himself muttering, 'The idea of a medium-sized Basque agency going out and running campaigns in Africa is ridiculous! A thousand things could happen to convert it into instant disaster.'

In any case, Carlos Aramburu tried to look at the situation from another viewpoint. He was aware that the agency he owned and managed had not yet had time to attain large volumes but he knew that he had a wide range of possibilities before him and the decision he took – which under no circumstances should endanger the company's continuity – could differentiate the advertising product he offered and speed up the company's growth path. In short, APA seemed to be facing the following strategic options:

1. Stop all exporting of advertising services – giving up also Vascalisa with a billing volume of 23 million pesetas and a margin of 12 million pesetas a year – in view of the risk that in the medium-term, as local agencies appeared in the various countries, the local advertisers would leave APA, preferring to work with these native agencies. Mr. Aramburu could not quite get out of his mind the niggling sensation that all that had been achieved through Vascalisa was only a fly-by-night affair without any real substance.
2. Continue to let himself be carried along by Vascalisa without actively trying to gain new clients for campaigns outside Spain. This meant continuing to sell 'without pushing,' to carry on 'waiting for them to come'; in any case, even if this option was chosen, it seemed advisable to define the time when such a strategy would no longer be sufficient and the company should launch itself with more determination in the conquest of new markets.
3. Continue to think how to make best use of the know-how acquired but to preferably direct efforts toward Spanish companies with sales activities in those countries. Mr. Aramburu could not wait to find out who was exporting to the countries that APA knew so well; Mr. Aramburu would initiate contacts – first by letter/pamphlet and then by personal visit to each of these exporters – to offer them APA's services, backed by the successes achieved with Vascalisa. This offer could be made in at least two ways:

   • Directly approach the exporting agencies.
   • Approach these companies' advertising agencies. APA could act as a specialist consultant in these countries.

   Or, looking at things from another point of view:

   • Only approach those companies that were already exporting.
   • Try to find out (how? where?) which companies were potential exporters to the countries in the area and approach them.

4. Preferably direct efforts at the native companies in each African country, which to a certain extent was the path followed so far under Vascalisa's wing. In any case, it seemed clear that the BID to be used for these local clients would have to be refocused.

In addition to these four options related to client segments, at a more general level of the organization there existed the possibility of seeking associations with another larger advertising agency or even with some group that wished to create, develop, or cultivate markets in East Africa. This idea did not particularly appeal to Mr. Aramburu from a 'personal fulfilment' viewpoint but he was sure that any company who bought APA would be buying valuable know-how that would enable it to gain rapid penetration in certain countries. This know-how was an asset that increased the company's value and, in a services company – which is what an advertising agency is par excellence – this meant a great deal. After all, Mr. Aramburu said to himself with a slight smile of self-satisfaction, 'I don't know any other agency apart from APA that has in its files, for instance, the prices of market media in Kenya.'

(This case was prepared by Pere Gil, a second-year student at IESE, under the supervision of Francesco Parés, lecturer, and Professor Lluís G. Renart. Copyright 1987 IESE, Barcelona, Spain. Reproduced with kind permission.)

Questions

1. How would you identify APA competences, especially as far as cultural know-how is concerned?
2. What is the value of this know-how? For which advertisers, in which markets?
3. Which course of action would you recommend? Who should implement it?

A12.3 Case: Nove Ltd

Nove Ltd is a large concern located in Hong Kong which manufactures a line of household appliances in which sales expansion has been very rapid. For certain new articles this increase has been so fast that production capacity could not keep up with demand. For one of the new products – electric (dry) shavers – management foresaw and provided for more than normal commercial expansion. Production capacity for these articles has been enlarged to the extent that even in the face of a rapid sales growth, a sufficient number of dry shavers could be manufactured. In view of the enlarged production facilities, more effective sales efforts became necessary. Total 1988 sales amounted to three million shavers. The 1989 sales target was set at three and one-half million pieces.

In order to put the planning indicated above into effect, a more intensive marketing communication campaign was considered desirable. In countries A, B, and C (countries so designated for purposes of disguise) particularly favorable results were expected from a stepped-up advertising campaign. The approved advertising budget for these countries was therefore separated from the normal sales budget and determined individually. The company's advertising manager felt that for the most effective results, the advertising budget should at least be doubled. In view of the enormous amounts planned for advertising the management suggested a preliminary investigation in the countries concerned to ascertain why dry shavers in general, and the company's own brand, 'Nover,' in particular, were purchased. Nove intended to obtain arguments that might best be used in its advertising and get some tips for sales promotion.

Consumer investigation

Before the investigation, Nover enjoyed a strong market position in the three countries. Otex was its largest competitor while Porde accounted for an insignificant market share.

Shaving habits

From the answers about shaving habits it appeared that in Country A approximately 100% of the men shaved themselves, while in Country C an important number (23%) went to the barber shop for a shave. The portion of men who shaved themselves daily varied from 13% in Country C to 77% in Country A. The majority of dry shavers were found among the men who shaved themselves daily. To stimulate sales it might thus be useful to promote the habit of shaving daily.

Following a request to indicate the advantages of dry shaving, the most frequent reactions were: ease, speed, and absence of skin irritation. All wet shavers were asked why they had not yet switched to dry shaving. Between 40 and 50% replied that dry shavers were too expensive.

Characteristics of the dry shaver

Table 12.1 indicates, in percentages of total dry shavers, replies made to the question: 'Why do you shave electrically?'

How did users obtain their dry shavers?

It appeared from the market research that an important part of the dry shaver owners had received the shaver as a gift – in Country A, 52%; in Country B, 40%; and in Country C, 40%.

The greater part of those receiving gifts (approximately 65%) had expressed the desire for a shaver themselves. Usually the wife or the fiancee (in approximately 60% of the cases) made the gift. It was also important to determine the place of purchase. Most dry shavers (75 to 80%) were bought in radio shops and electrical appliance stores. An entirely different situation, however, appeared to exist in Country A. There, radio shops and electrical appliance stores accounted for only 30% of sales. Most dry shavers in this country were bought in barber shops and department stores.

Choice of brand

In the process of buying, it is important to know what portion of future buyers has gained information in advance about various brands. It appears that more than 50% of the buyers

Table 12.1

Arguments	Country A	Country B	Country C
Ease	52	84	80
Speed	38	52	50
Absence of skin irritation	24	52	30
Other arguments	76	64	30
Total	190	252	190

Table 12.2

Motive	Country A	Country B	Country C
Seen in shop and advertisement	28	22	18
Advice of acquaintances	23	26	20
Price of shaver	13	12	10
Advice from shopkeeper	11	11	10
Other reasons	25	29	42
Total	100	100	100

Table 12.3

Brands in use	Country A	Country B	Country C
Nover	24	64	50
Otex	33	8	30
Porde	1	1	2
Miscellaneous	42	27	18

Table 12.4

Brands known	Country A	Country B	Country C
Nover	67	88	79
Otex	80	33	60
Porde	4	2	15

had in fact formed an opinion in advance about the brand to be selected and intended to ask for additional information. Factors which favored the purchase of a certain brand are expressed in Table 12.2 in percentages of the total answers recorded.

Further investigation of brand choice was based on brand distribution among the shavers in use. The brands in use in each country are shown in Table 12.3.

Familiarity with three brands is shown in Table 12.4.

Table 12.5

Brands	Country A	Country B	Country C
Nover	14	55	44
Otex	57	22	34
Porde	1	1	11

Table 12.6

Advertising noticed by	Country A	Country B	Country C
Wet shavers	60	48	28
Dry shavers	67	58	39
Both groups	62	51	30

Replies to a question about the best brand generally favoured Otex, rather than Nover.

Results indicated that brand loyalty is very important. In the case of Otex, this loyalty seems to be somewhat stronger than for Nover. In Country C, however, a larger percentage of Nover users seem to be willing to switch brands than among Otex users. Relating the findings about brand switching to the results concerning the best brand (as expressed by wet and dry shavers), it can be concluded that there is a greater preference for Otex than for Nover by the wet shavers. This last observation could be an important aspect in attacking the potential market. Subsequently the question was raised: 'Which brand are you likely to buy?' Reactions are expressed in Table 12.5 in a percentage of those intending to buy and who at the same time mentioned a brand name.

Factors which favor the purchase of a certain brand

Seen in shop and advertisements   It is known that advertising and sales promotion are important influencing factors. The extent to which this has affected dry shavers, however, has not yet been determined. The number of men, both wet and dry shavers, who have noticed advertising for dry shavers, is expressed in percentages of the group in Table 12.6.

It thus seems that dry shavers are more quickly aware of dry shaving advertising than wet shavers. This could be explained by the concentration of shaver owners in the higher-income brackets. This group reads more, and consequently is confronted with more publicity and advertising matter than the lower-income classes. In view of the high percentage of shaver owners remembering publicity, it is probable that shaver owners in general have an active interest in dry shaving publicity. Of the replies to the question, 'Where, or in which media have you noticed dry shaving advertising?,' those favoring Nover were divided among publicity media as set forth in Table 12.7.

Table 12.7

Publicity medium	Country A	Country B	Country C
Newspaper	62	67	29
Weekly magazine	44	39	54
Shop	26	39	46
Posters	3	25	8
Movie	–	8	8
Folders, etc.	3	6	3

Price of shaver   Wet shavers generally regard price as an objection to buying a dry shaver. However, the influence of price in brand selection was not unfavorable for Nover, compared with other brands. In percentages of total Nover shaver owners, price was important in their selection of Nover to 12% in Country A, 17% in Country B, and 12% in Country C. The price of a shaver may be an important deterrent to a great segment of the population. This factor plays an important role in the gift market, where traditionally the cheaper brands are favored.

Question

Explain why Nove Ltd can or cannot standardize its advertising in countries A, B, and C.

(Gerald Albaum, Jesper Strandskov, Edwin Duerr and Laurence Dowd, 1989, *International Marketing and Export Management*, Addison-Wesley: Wokingham, pp. 350–3. Reproduced with permission.)

A12.4 Critical incident: Excel and the Italian advertising campaign[20]

Excel is a multinational company, based in northern Europe, which produces television sets, video recorders and other consumer electronics. It recently went through a phase of external growth by the take-over of the German and French subsidiaries of a large US-based company which had decided to divest itself of this industry. Within two years this Nordic company has tripled in size. It changed from having a mainly Scandinavian base to a complete European spread, with an 11 per cent share of the European market. The group, built in successive layers, inherited numerous local brands, namely those of the companies taken over. These brands are basically localized marketing assets, with only national coverage and brand recognition. Excel plans to have only one pan-European brand in the long run, with one local brand for each individual country.

European headquarters have been installed in Switzerland, near Lausanne. This location was chosen so that headquarters would be situated in Central Europe but not in a country where Excel already has a plant, as this might imply some sort of 'national preference'.

Besides, over the past two years an important reshaping of the industrial base has been undertaken, with massive lay-offs in some plants and industrial investment aimed to increase productivity.

Excel wants to minimize advertising expenses while simultaneously giving its brand a strong, similar image across Europe. In fact it has inherited some very diverse brand names, which were those of the companies recently acquired in their home markets. Excel is therefore willing to design a pan-European advertising campaign. The national subsidiaries were invited either to join this campaign or to design their own campaign. In the latter case, they would have to finance it with their own money. The campaign has been scheduled for autumn 1990.

Because of the World Cup taking place in Italy in June 1990, the Italian subsidiary decided that it could not wait until the autumn, as this type of sports event usually generates increased demand for television sets and video recorders. They managed to go ahead by themselves: they made an advertisement which proved to be a real hit and generated a significant sales increase. A television commercial was created and a poster also. The same advertising theme was used for sales promotion. The advertisement showed a superb television set with a video recorder as an integral part, encircled by a red ribbon which largely hid the screen. The slogan was '*Venite a vederlo; dal vero*' (come and see it; for real).

This campaign was a success soon after it started, and was presented to the subsidiary general managers, who met for a residential seminar in Switzerland with the people at European headquarters in Geneva. Reactions were very positive. They proposed the idea of using the same campaign, themes and creation in other European markets. At the beginning of March, Mr Mäkinen, in charge of marketing communications at European headquarters, decided to send a memo to the marketing/advertising managers of each subsidiary. A poster and a video presenting the Italian campaign were also enclosed. This memo was aimed at a concrete offer to the subsidiaries to adopt the themes and creation of this campaign. It asked them for feedback on their opinions. Mäkinen invited them to study the feasibility of using such a campaign in their home market and to send back their comments quickly, so that a pan-European campaign could possibly be launched in August. The Italian advertising manager, Signor Ragoli, was available if the European headquarters or national subsidiaries wanted any additional information.

'Responses' from the subsidiaries (that is, the answers plus the course of action finally adopted) were as follows. Answers were quite long in coming back, which could be explained by the overload of work experienced by people in the subsidiaries during this period of reorganization. Some countries never answered the proposal. Otherwise reactions were quite positive, except for that of France.

The Spanish answer came quickly. The advertising and public relations manager, Senor Gonzales, sent a copy of the letter to his Italian colleague at European headquarters. He wrote that Spain had decided to use the campaign created in Italy, in order to unify Excel marketing communication. The Spanish wanted to use five different television channels for a total of twenty-two slots. They supported this with a press campaign and sales promotion in distribution channels. They needed the original version of the Italian television commercial, with music on one track and speech on another (one image track plus two sound tracks). In Spain the final version of the Excel campaign was launched in

May 1990. The image track remained unchanged, but the music had been modified and there were several other minor changes. What seemed, at first sight, to be a straight copy of the Italian concept, finally turned out to be a largely modified version. Nevertheless Spain was the only country where the marketing team made the decision to use the experience of their Italian colleagues.

Sweden and Norway also responded quickly to the memo in similar terms. In neither of these two countries was advertising allowed on national television channels; furthermore, they traded under the Scandinavian brand name Scantel, rather than Excel. The Swedish response explained that the subsidiary did not advertise on television, since TV1 and TV2 did not offer any space; but with the growth of satellite television the Italian proposal might be interesting for the future. The Swedes thought that the Italian campaign was well designed and implemented. The model presented (Excel 7181) was usable with their brand name since they had the same make. The Norwegians' answer had also been very positive. They promised to keep in mind the concepts of the Italian campaign and further indicated that they would recommend its implementation for 1991.

In France the advertising and public relations manager, Monsieur Dubois, initially contacted by telephone, expressed a positive but rather cautious opinion. He said that he had first to discuss the themes and creation with his advertising agency. He called back to make it clear that even if he had any advertising funds left (in fact they were already entirely spent), he considered that the Italian campaign was not appropriate for Ariane (the brand name of the recently acquired French subsidiary). According to him, it did not fit in with the French criteria of what actually makes good advertising. In his opinion Ariane had a fairly traditional image in France, and French consumers would need more serious arguments to change their views. Consequently 'good' advertising for the Ariane brand had to emphasize, first of all, the high-technology image. Ultimately, he thought that the Italian campaign was not sophisticated enough, and that French people prefer more in-depth, sophisticated and detailed campaigns.

How can the failure of the European headquarters in having the Italian campaign adopted by the other European subsidiaries be explained? What is the right way to go about this in the future? What has to be changed?

A12.5 Critical incident: The Brenzy nouveau has arrived![21]

Legritte Company was founded just after the Second World War by a skilful engineer, Monsieur Legritte. Aided by the reconstruction boom which was followed by the rapid economic growth of the 1960s, the Legritte Company developed more by improving the quality of its products than by investing money in marketing and sales. The intrinsic quality of the products, namely electrical connections for industrial use, has been the strong point of the business from the very beginning.

The company is located near Lyons (France) and employs about 200 people, with an annual turnover of 80 million francs. Two years ago Legritte was taken over by a US-based multinational company, Brenzy. Monsieur Legritte, drawing near to retirement age and with no qualified successor, sold his property to Brenzy corporation, which now owns the full 100 per cent. Brenzy has progressively introduced more up-to-date management methods in this traditional family business. Inventory management, cost accounting and delivery systems have all been changed to fit with Brenzy's procedures.

Sales promotion in France and Europe is based on nicely printed catalogues, technical instructions and directions for use. The price list is degressive according to the size of orders. Products are promoted through small gifts given to the purchasers. Thus the launch of a new pre-insulated line of products, recently certified by EDF,[22] came with a free gift (electrical pincers) for any order higher than 10,000 francs. This offer was open for six months. In order to receive the gift, the buyer simply had to fill in the gift voucher and enclose it with the order, provided the amount was sufficient.

Brenzy-Legritte was a newcomer to advertising. Being a fairly traditional medium-size industrial company, they had not up to now invested a lot of money in advertisements. When they decided for the first time to advertise their products they did it by promoting their products along with what they called le Brenzy Nouveau.

An advertisement in a specialist journal showed a bottle of Beaujolais nouveau, with the following slogan above the image: 'The Brenzy nouveau has arrived!'[23] Text in bold characters at the bottom stated: 'You are thirsty and craving a new line of effective products! Brenzy-Legritte is happy to join you in ordering Beaujolais nouveau!' It was indicated that a minimum order of 3,500 francs entitled buyers to receive 3 free bottles and a minimum order of 5,000 francs entitled them to receive 6 free bottles. The expiry date for this offer was stipulated. The new line of Brenzy-Legritte products was shown on the label of the bottle of Beaujolais.

EDF, which is a large customer of Brenzy-Legritte, was not very happy about this humorous advertisement. It seems that EDF experienced problems amongst its personnel when the boxes of Beaujolais arrived at its offices....

Brenzy-Legritte is now undergoing drastic changes in its organization. Computers have been linked to the European headquarters in Brussels. Strictly defined management procedures have been imposed by headquarters. Brenzy has issued a professional code of conduct, the implementation of which is compulsory for the French subsidiary as well as for all the other subsidiaries around the world. It is a complete code of business ethics, comprising precise and detailed prescriptions. Below are some extracts.

Suffice it to say that this code of conduct is perceived by most people at Brenzy-Legritte, especially the salespeople, as largely inappropriate to the French context and a mere interference in their business. They prefer to disregard it.

Excerpts from the code of conduct at Brenzy-Legritte

Correct use of company funds

1. Company funds will not be used in order to make payments, or concealed loans, with the purpose of dishonestly influencing a supplier, a client or a civil servant. This prohibition applies not only to direct use of company money, but also to any kind of indirect payments, by the means of consultants/intermediaries, or by reimbursing to employees payments made by them.
2. No payment shall be made, for and in the name of the company or one of its

subsidiaries, with the intent or knowledge that part of such a payment will serve other purposes than those described in the documents related to this payment.

Gifts, favours and entertainment

Small gifts of symbolic value, minor favours and modest receptions may be offered at the company's expense only when they meet all of the following conditions:

1. They must be compatible with the rules of the company and current business practices.
2. Their monetary worth must be limited; they must be presented in such a form as not to appear as a bribe or remuneration; they must not give rise to suspicions about the impartiality of the beneficiary.
3. They must be approved by the general manager of the subsidiary or by a vice-president at Brenzy Corporation; they must be compatible with the instructions previously approved by the direct superior, the managing director and a senior vice-president at Brenzy Corporation.

Gifts and entertainment for civil servants

As indicated above, gifts, other than symbolic ones or gifts of a very modest value, whatever their nature, or a sumptuous reception, whatever its motives, are not allowed.

Issues related to these procedures and their violations

1. Any employees who want to ask questions about this code and its implementation shall discuss it with the head of the department. If it entails legal or accounting matters, they shall refer to qualified personnel from the legal services and the accounting department, who shall be consulted.
2. The discovery of a case which is fraudulent, illegal, or violates the rules of the company, shall immediately be reported to the legal counsellor. If such cases are identified, which imply senior executives in the corporation, this case shall be reported to the executive vice-president, for examination by the chairman of the board, the chief executive officer, and the chairman of the audit committee.
3. No derogation to this procedure will be accepted in these matters. There will probably be some 'business opportunities' in the future, when it would be necessary to make questionable payments in order to succeed against a competitor, for one reason or another. The duty of the employee, in this case, is to reject such 'opportunities'.
4. Any infringement to the above-mentioned principles will result in disciplinary sanctions, including dismissal, a suing of the employee and a detailed report to competent regulatory authorities.
5. Moreover disciplinary sanctions will be decided against any executive who initiates or approves such actions, or knows about them, or may have known about them, and did not quickly act to rectify them in accordance with this code. Adequate disciplinary sanctions will also be directed against any executives who neglect their hierarchical responsibilities, by not ensuring that their subordinates have been properly informed about the rules established in this code.

A12.6 Exercise: Borovets – a Bulgarian ski resort[24]

Compare the two short texts below (each dated the beginning of 1990). Both depict the Bulgarian ski resort Borovets. The first one is an extract from the magazine *Actuel* (no. 122), an article entitled 'Guide des bons plans à l'Est' (A guide to travelling in Eastern countries), p. 69. The other is an extract from the trade brochure of the Bulgarian state tourist corporation, *Balkanturist*, entitled 'Bulgaria welcomes you', p. 10.

Text 1: A charter flight to Bulgaria

The phenomenon already exists, it never stops swelling. Bulgaria is a hospitable place for exhausted proletarians in quest of cheap snow and sun. For the time being, most of the troop comes from Britain: 75 per cent of the tourists are English, 20 per cent are German, the remaining 5 per cent are Dutch, Swedish or French.

The Bulgarian government rubs its hands. The blaze of freedom which blasts through the East has already brought hordes of capitalist tourists. Bulgaria is in urgent need of foreign currencies. The country hopes to have its holiday resorts working at full capacity. Borovets is the most famous resort: in fact, it is a concrete boil encrusted on the mountains. The eight hotels, of luxurious appearance, offer limited comfort: water shortages, telephones out of order, ghost reception desks, bad-tempered staff and rooms where the cleanliness is somewhat dubious. Infrastructure, equipment and service do not meet minimum requirements.

Bulgarian tourism turns out dissatisfied customers. Like Franco's Spain of the 1970s, it is the same reinforced concrete everywhere. Varna and Burgas on the Black Sea coast look like Benidorm. The sea coast is built up with concrete rabbit hutches which swarm with Bulgarian city-dwellers, Greek spendthrifts or drunk Britons. Apocalypse! The rare nightclubs are inaccessible. Meals in the 300-place restaurants have all the style and allure of gymnasium banquets.

Text 2: Borovets

In Bulgarian, Borovets literally means 'beautiful place'.

Borovets during the winter has pure, ozone-rich air; it has 150 days of snow cover which provides exceptional ski slopes, from 1,300 to 2,500 meters high.

Each year Borovets is host to numerous international ski championships. Ingemar Stenmark, the Mahre brothers, Girardelli and many other famous skiers have spoken highly of this resort which welcomes everyone.

It is a very fashionable ski resort, with its numerous comfortable and cosy hotels, its enticing restaurants and various entertainment facilities for day and night. Borovets is located 50 miles from Sofia, and it has been enjoyed by children and adults since the end of the nineteenth century, when it was only a small holiday centre.

It is no exaggeration to say that Borovets can compete with the Swiss or the French ski resorts.

Now why wait any longer to visit us? We wish only to welcome you.

Questions

1. Why is there such a difference between these two pictures? Do these two articles refer to the same reality?
2. How can one get an idea of the level of service in this resort?
3. How should the state company for Bulgarian tourism (which manages the resort) communicate? What prevents them from doing so?

Notes

1. Figure 12.1 is a suggestion from my colleague Didier Lentrein, Maître de Conférences at the University of Grenoble (Graduate Business School). Reprinted with his kind permission.
2. Numerous books have been dedicated to advertising and marketing communications. See for instance: Dunn, Barban, Kruma and Reid (1989), *Advertising: Its role in modern marketing*, 7th edn, Dryden Press: Hindsale, IL; Patti and Frazer (1989), *Advertising: A decision making approach*, Dryden Press: Orlando, FL; William Wells, John Burnett and Sandra Moriarty (1989), *Advertising Principles and Practices*, Prentice Hall: Englewood Cliffs, NJ; David A. Aaker and John G. Myers (1987), *Advertising Management*, Prentice Hall: Englewood Cliffs, NJ; J. Thomas Russell and W. Ronald Lane (1990), *Kleppner's Advertising Procedure*, 11th edn, Prentice Hall: Englewood Cliffs, NJ.
3. In this chapter only international advertising is emphasized. However, there are other types of marketing communication with specific targets: public relations, sponsoring and, to a certain extent, sales promotion (on this last point, see section 11.4).
4. Saint Simon was a nineteenth-century social philosopher who advocated the view that distribution and services in general were economically unproductive activities.
5. Marcel Bleustein Blanchet, a publicist for more than sixty years, describes changes in the role of slogans in advertising:

   > Of course, things have changed in this field as well. The art of the slogan, as with advertising in general, changes in line with the public. Slogans have become simpler and more sophisticated at the same time. They are also less frequently used. Other techniques for increasing consumer brand recognition are taking over. But before the war, when the public was less demanding and less blasé, slogans were the best means of launching a brand. Especially when radio began to advertise. Actually, my pre-war slogans were a sort of *comptines* [little nursery rhymes]. They were *assonantal forms that the ear picked up instinctively*. Ultimately they became choruses and the public joined in. For example, when Berretrot, the announcer in the Vel d'Hiv (Paris cycling stadium), announced a prize during the 'Six Jours cyclistes' saying: 'Un meuble signé Levitan . . .', ten thousand voices shouted back '. . . est garanti pour longtemps.' (Marcel Bleustein Blanchet (1987), *La Rage de convaincre*, Robert Laffont: Paris, reproduced in *Sélection du Reader's Digest*, special edition, pp. 42–3, my emphasis).

6. This is directly related to section 3.2, about cognitive styles with regard to action.
7. Jacques Séguéla is a well-known French publicist, co-founder of the RSCG agency, reputed for oneiric, dream-orientated copy strategies.
8. This is the dominant view of Europeans concerning American television channels (United States, Canada, Mexico and Brazil).

9. It is surprising that the issue of whether the viewer/listener is entertained by advertising should be so rarely addressed, given its practical importance. 'Zapping' has been fairly widely studied, but most studies have only sought to demonstrate how an advertiser can avoid its unfortunate results. It is taken for granted that the audience has no saturation threshold, or at the very least an extremely high one. This assumption suggests the absolute legitimacy of mass advertising communication within a society that willingly portrays itself as being free-market orientated. On the other hand, many European countries started from the opposite assumption, and advertising therefore took a long time to assert itself on television.

10. The pace of change in European media and regional integration of marketing communications and marketing strategies could be speeded up by two important environmental changes: the EC 1992 programme, which is to abolish physical borders by 1 January 1993; and the Maastricht Treaty which was signed in February 1992. The Maastricht Treaty prepares for a common currency and central European bank by the end of the 1990s. It provides for a common European citizenship and political union (especially in the domain of foreign policy).

11. This description of satellite television technology is rather brief. For further explanation see: Watson S. 'Jay' James, 'The new electronic media: An overview', *Journal of Advertising Research*, vol. 23, no. 4, pp. 33–7.

12. There is now a common European standard for HDTV, which has been developed jointly by Philips of the Netherlands and Thomson of France, with German assent. But it seems that the Japanese HDTV standard is four to five years ahead: it is already operative whereas the European HDTV is still in the prototype phase.

13. The book by Ungerer and Costello, about telecommunications in Europe, describes the efforts which are being undertaken to harmonize standards and systems across EC countries. The book is based on an EC official report, the EC Green Paper on telecommunications in Europe, which has directly inspired EC policies in this field. It is advisable to monitor regularly the directives issued by the European Commission on telecommunications, media and advertising.

14. Once again, some people may be both faithful viewers of American television series and opponents of imported television programmes as a whole. Self-contradiction is possible.

15. See for instance the new chapter 'Differentiating and positioning the market offer' in Philip Kotler (1991), *Marketing Management*, 7th edn, Prentice Hall: Englewood Cliffs, NJ.

16. Dentsu publishes each year the *Dentsu Japan Marketing/Advertising Yearbook* which reports, with extensive figures and image data, the main trends of advertising in Japan (Dentsu Inc. 11–10, Tsukiji 1-chome, Chuo-ku, Tokyo 104, Japan).

17. At the beginning of 1991, the European part of HDM (Eurocom-Havas) withdrew from the alliance with Dentsu and Young & Rubicam/Marsteller, to form a joint venture with the British group WCRS.

18. Swahili is a Bantu language spoken in Tanzania (including Zanzibar) and Kenya, where it is the official language; in Uganda, where it is the official language with English, and in some areas of the Congo River basin. It is the most widely spoken Black African language and has been considerably influenced by Arabic and Persian. Although originally written in Arabic characters, in the nineteenth century Latin characters were introduced. Swahili is widely used as a written language in magazines and newspapers.

19. The BID – or Basic Information Document – was, in APA's terminology, what is usually known as a briefing or questionnaire often used by advertising agencies to gain information on the basic features of its client and the product to be marketed. This questionnaire is filled in by the potential client or by the agency itself after initial contact and will be used to draw the general lines of the advertising campaign.

20. Names of both people and brands have been disguised.

21. Company names have been disguised.

22. EDF (Electricité de France) is the state-owned public utility which distributes electricity throughout France.
23. There is a pun here: Beaujolais is a freshly harvested red wine and it is quite fashionable to drink 'Beaujolais nouveau'.
24. This short exercise is not meant to serve any other purpose than as a pedagogical exercise; it does not aim to describe any real situation and should not prejudice readers concerning holidays in Bulgaria.

References

Advertising Age (1987), 'The house that built ivory', 20 August, pp. 26–7.

Advertising Age (1989), 'Saatchi leads top 11 mega-groups' and 'No 1 Dentsu hits lofty $1.2 billion in gross income', 29 March.

Boddewyn, Jean J. (1984), 'The regulation of advertising around the world in the 1980s and beyond', in Gerald M. Hampton and Aart P. Van Gent (eds), *Marketing Aspects of International Business*, Kluwer-Nijhoff Publishing: Boston, MA, pp. 73–83.

Business Week (1987), 'The media barons battle to dominate Europe', 25 May.

Business Week (1989), 'Keeping up with the Murdochs', 20 March.

Clark, Harold F. Jr (1987), 'Consumer and corporate values: Yet another view on global marketing', *International Journal of Advertising*, vol. 6, pp. 29–42.

Communication et Business (1988), *Numéro 'Spécial Europe'*, no. 70, 14 March.

Czinkota, Michael R. and Illka A. Ronkainen (1990), *International Marketing*, 2nd edn, Dryden Press: Hinsdale, IL.

Douglas, Susan and Bernard Dubois (1980), 'Looking at the cultural environment for international marketing opportunities', in P. Kotler and K. Cox (eds), *Marketing Management and Strategy: A reader*, Prentice Hall: Englewood Cliffs, NJ.

Dudley, James W. (1989), *1992: Strategies for the Single Market*, Kogan Page: London.

Engels-Levine, Erika (1982), 'Commercial radio in Latin America', *International Advertiser*, January–February.

Gilly, Mary (1988), 'Sex roles in advertising: A comparison of television advertisements in Australia, Mexico, and the United States', *Journal of Marketing*, vol. 52, April, pp. 75–85.

Hill, J.S. and J.M. Winski (1987), 'Goodbye, global ads', *Advertising Age*, 16 November.

Hoover, Robert J., Robert T. Green and Joel Saegert (1978), 'A cross-national study of perceived risk', *Journal of Marketing*, July, pp. 102–8.

Jodelet, Denise (1988), 'Représentations sociales: phénomènes, concept et théorie', in Serge Moscovici (ed.), *Psychologie Sociale*, PUF Fondamental: Paris.

Kaynak, Erdener and Pervez N. Ghauri (1986), 'A comparative analysis of advertising practices in unlike environments: A study of agency–client relationships', *International Journal of Advertising*, vol. 5, pp. 121–46.

Luqmani, Mushtaq, Ugur Yavas and Zahir Quraeshi (1988), 'Advertising in Saudi Arabia: Content and regulation', *International Marketing Review*, vol 6, no. 1, pp. 59–71.

Mariet, François (1990), *La Télévision Américaine*, Editions Economica: Paris.

Martenson, Rita (1987), 'Advertising strategies and information content in American and Swedish advertising: A comparative content analysis in cross-cultural copy research', *International Journal of Advertising*, vol. 6, pp. 133–44.

McCracken, Grant (1991), 'Culture and consumer behaviour: an anthropological perspective', *Journal of the Market Research Society*, vol. 32, no. 1, pp. 3–11.

Moscovici, Serge (1961), *La Psychanalyse, son public et son image*, Presses Universitaires de France: Paris.

Mourier, Pascal and Didier Burgaud (1989), *Euromarketing*, Editions d'Organisation: Paris.

Peebles, Dean M. (1988), 'Don't write off global advertising: A commentary', *International Marketing Review*, vol. 6, no. 1, pp. 73–8.

Peebles, Dean M. and John K. Ryans (1984), *Management of International Advertising*, Allyn and Bacon: Boston, MA.

Ricks, David A., Jeffrey S. Arpan and Marilyn Y. Fu (1979), 'Pitfalls in overseas advertising', *Journal of Advertising Research*, reprinted in S. Watson Dunn and E.S. Lorimer (eds), *International Advertising and Marketing*, Grid: Columbus, OH, pp. 87–93.

Sarathy, Ravi (1991), 'European integration and global strategy in the media and entertainment industry', in Alan M. Rugman and Alain Verbeke (eds), *Global Competition and the European Community*, JAI Press: Greenwich, CT.

Ungerer, Herbert and Nicholas P. Costello (1988), *Telecommunications in Europe*, European Perspectives Series, Office for Official Publications of the European Communities: Luxemburg.

Wills, James R. and John K. Ryans Jr (1982), 'Attitudes toward advertising: A multinational study', *Journal of International Business Studies* (Winter), pp. 121–41.

PART IV

Intercultural marketing negotiations

13

——— ◆◆◆ ———

Intercultural marketing negotiations I

When marketing internationally, negotiation skills are needed. As emphasized in Chapter 4, many agreements have to be negotiated, drafted, signed and finally implemented: sales contracts, licensing agreements, joint ventures and various kinds of partnerships, agency and distribution agreements, turnkey contracts, etc.

There are various kinds of 'distances' between the potential partners: physical distance certainly, but also economic, educational and cultural distance. These cumulative distances tend to increase the costs of the transaction, which may be quite high. Negotiations for some contracts may take years, but fortunately not continuously. Any international deal incurs transaction costs, which are disproportionate to the costs related to a domestic deal for a similar amount. People in the domestic market (usually) share the same cultural background and language. Distances are much smaller: they minimize transaction costs. Culture, especially, acts as a knowledge base: it is much easier within the native cultural setting to know who will be a good payer, a reliable partner or a trustworthy supplier.

Thus it would be a mistake to go flitting about like a butterfly on the international market: always looking for new partners, new customers and new ventures, without following up. This results in a great deal of 'one-off' business. Business people and companies perform poorly if they do not understand the golden rule of international marketing negotiation,[1] which is: have few partners and conduct few negotiations, but make the stakes meaningful. This will enable both parties to build a durable partnership. In relational marketing one should marry well, not often (section 13.1).

This chapter seeks to develop two simple ideas. The first is that trust is a key variable when structuring and developing any relational exchange. The second is that trust between buyer and seller in an international sale or business venture is initiated and increases by using culturally coded signs. Trust may ultimately be withdrawn precisely because these cultural codes have been ignored. These difficulties in interacting, negotiating, planning common ventures, working them out and achieving them *together* are deeply rooted in the cultural background of business people. They are not related to a superficial variance of

This chapter is partly based on Usunier (1990). Reproduced with the kind permission of the review.

391

business customs. According to many international marketing texts, simple 'empathy' is required for the avoidance of misunderstandings. In fact, people with different cultural backgrounds often do not share the same basic assumptions.[2] This may undermine the process of building and maintaining trust between culturally uneven partners (section 13.2).

Subsequent sections deal with the various aspects of cultural differences which affect the trust-building process: misunderstandings about personal and institutional credibility (section 13.3); cultural predispositions to integrative negotiation, i.e. the preference for maximising the common cake before looking at one's own portion, or to a distributive orientation – maximizing one's own portion of the cake, rather than the cake itself (section 13.4); the existence of a common rationality between the parties (section 13.5). Section 13.6 is dedicated to oral versus written agreements as support for trust between the parties.

The following chapter complements this one: it examines the influence of cultural time patterns on the attitudes of people in international business negotiations, and depicts some elements of national negotiation styles.

13.1   The dynamics of trust in relational marketing

A marriage between buyer and seller

Many successful international marketing partnerships share the following characteristics: a long time span over which transactions occur, a large size as a unit sale (i.e. compared to total turnover) and a long-term relationship established between buyer and seller (Jackson, 1985). These characteristics all fit quite well with the concept of the 'domesticated market' (Arndt, 1979). In this type of market 'transactions are planned and administered, instead of being conducted on an ad hoc basis' (p. 70).

Marketing is viewed from this perspective as an ongoing exchange relationship (Bagozzi, 1975; Hunt, 1983). Exchange is no longer studied as if it were a time-series of independent, discrete transactions. Buyer/seller relationships are seen to extend far beyond the short time horizon of discrete, small-scale transactions. In turnkey operations for instance, this may even be seen as a continuous sales process when the owner is planning expansion or a new project, subject to the performance achieved by the contractor in the present project. Trust is an asset of prime importance in that it enables negotiation partners to overcome short-term conflicts of interest, personal confrontations or even communication misunderstandings. This holds true for the negotiation phase itself, that is before signing the contract(s), as well as for the negotiation process during the implementation phase.

The dimensions of relational marketing

In relational marketing switching from one supplier to another incurs high transaction costs. This may be contrasted with discrete transactions marketing, which is very similar to traditional marketing. It is applied mainly to consumer goods, with the following:

♦ Oligopolistic markets, where a few vendors face a multitude of buyers.
♦ Standardized obligations, which are often embedded in a unilateral contract where price cannot be challenged by the buyer.

Table 13.1, adapted from Macneil (1978, 1980) by Dwyer, Schurr and Oh (1987), compares discrete transactions and relational exchange, in terms of situation and process. It emphasizes the nature of the contractual links between buyer and seller.

Each of these transactions may be viewed as having its own history as well as encompassing its future, in as far as it may be anticipated by each partner (Macneil, 1978, 1980). Future collaboration (new orders, future common ventures, an extension or a revamping of the actual plant, etc.) as well as the conditions, atmosphere and end results of the actual co-operation, are dependent on the assumptions each partner makes about the *trustworthiness* of the other party.

In the field of consumer goods and mass markets, the unit transaction (a sale) only indirectly belongs to relational marketing; as such it belongs to the realm of discrete transactions. But negotiations for agency and distribution agreements with intermediaries (which are often on a buy-for-resale basis) belong to relational marketing. For instance, some of the relations between the Coca-Cola Company and its foreign dealers have been established for several decades. Discrete transaction marketing is not the only type of relationship with the individual consumer: one may form a more personalized relationship with individual consumers by establishing contact with them on a more personal basis through distributors and their employees, in order to build long-term consumer loyalty. This is largely the goal of the Japanese *Keiretsu* distribution system (see Chapter 11).

On the other hand, in industrial markets, relational exchange marketing is almost inevitable, especially at the international level. There is a large world-wide market for international turnkey projects and systems,[3] ranging from the turnkey brewery to the ready-made airport. These contracts are international by their very nature. The contractor (or companies which have jointly created a contracting consortium) and the owner belong to different nationalities. Different national/cultural backgrounds are then the source of communication problems and possible misunderstandings.

Credibility as an initial condition of trust-building in relational marketing

In order to develop the dynamics of exchange in relational marketing the role of the salesperson is primarily to establish personal credibility,[4] especially when dealing with competitive bidding sales situations (Slatter, 1987). In a survey about the salesperson's job in competitive bidding situations, Slatter shows that the sales visit consists of five main tasks:

1. Establishing the salesperson's personal credibility.
2. Undertaking market research.
3. Influencing design and specifications.
4. Establishing the firm's credibility.
5. Establishing a communication system.

Table 13.1   *A comparison of discrete transactions and relational exchange. (Source: Dwyer, Schurr and Oh, 1987, p. 13. Reproduced with the kind permission of the publisher.)*

Contractual elements	Discrete transactions	Relational exchange
Situational characteristics		
Timing of exchange (commencement, duration and termination of exchange)	Distinct beginning, short duration and sharp ending by performance	Commencement traces to previous agreements; exchange is longer in duration, reflecting an ongoing process
Number of parties (entities taking part in some aspect of the exchange process)	Two parties	Often more than two parties involved in the process and governance of exchange
Obligations (three aspects: sources of content, sources of obligation and specificity)	Content comes from offers and simple claims, obligations come from beliefs and customs (external enforcement), standardized obligations	Content and sources of obligations are promises made in the relation plus customs and laws; obligations are customized, detailed and administered within the relation
Expectations for relations (especially concerned with conflicts of interest, the prospects of unity and potential trouble)	Conflicts of interest (goals) and little unity are expected, but no future trouble is anticipated because cash payment upon instantaneous performance precludes future interdependence	Anticipated conflicts of interest and future trouble are counterbalanced by trust and efforts at unity
Process characteristics		
Primary personal relations (social interaction and communication)	Minimal personal relationships; ritual-like communications predominate	Important personal, non-economic satisfactions derived; both formal and informal communications are used
Contractual solidarity (regulation of exchange behavior to ensure performance)	Governed by social norms, rules, etiquette and prospects for self-gain	Increased emphasis on legal and self-regulation; psychological satisfactions cause internal adjustments
Transferability (the ability to transfer rights, obligations and satisfactions to other parties)	Complete transferability; it matters not who fulfills contractual obligation	Limited transferability; exchange is heavily dependent on the identity of the parties
Co-operation (especially joint efforts at performance and planning)	No joint efforts	Joint efforts related to both performance and planning over time; adjustment over time is endemic
Planning (the process and mechanisms for coping with change and conflicts)	Primary focus on the substance of exchange; no future is anticipated	Significant focus on the process of exchange; detailed planning for the future exchange within new environments and to satisfy changing goals; tacit and explicit assumptions abound

Table 13.1   *Continued*

Contractual elements	Discrete transactions	Relational exchange
Measurement and specificity (calculation and reckoning of exchange)	Little attention to measurement and specifications; performance is obvious	Significant attention to measuring, specifying, and quantifying all aspects of performance, including psychic and future benefits
Power (the ability to impose one's will on others)	Power may be exercised when promises are made until promises are executed	Increased interdependence increases the importance of judicious application of power in the exchange
Division of benefits and burdens (the extent of sharing of benefits and burdens)	Sharp division of benefits and burdens into parcels; exclusive allocation to parties	Likely to include some sharing of benefits and burdens and adjustments to both shared and parceled benefits and burdens over time

There are clearly two levels where credibility (which is a prerequisite to trustworthiness) has to be established: personal and organizational. The credibility of a particular person obeys cultural codes. People emit messages about their own credibility which are linked to physical, status and/or behavioural attributes.

The vendor will try to become personally acquainted with key decision-makers in potential target companies. There may be some problems in clearly identifying these key decision-makers, and establishing one's credibility with them. They may resent dealing with 'mere salespeople', because they are at a much higher organizational level. Hierarchical relationships *across organizations* are a very sensitive issue; all the more so because they supposedly exist only subjectively. Complex codes of interpersonal relationships govern the establishment of credibility: it is therefore often necessary to use sales assistants or market researchers as 'door-openers', who will quickly be succeeded by higher-ranking sales executives or sales managers (see Box 13.1).

Development stages in the process of relational exchange

One may distinguish several phrases in the development of a relational exchange (Scanzoni, 1979) which also corresponds with an intercultural setting:

1. Awareness.
2. Exploration.
3. Expansion.
4. Commitment.
5. Dissolution.

The practical interest of Scanzoni's model is its validity across cultures. It breaks down the exchange relationship into phases, where trust always appears as the 'central asset'.

Box 13.1   *The Japanese 'message-boy'*

During research into the key factors surrounding the success of Japanese engineering companies in world markets, I had the opportunity to interview several Japanese engineering specialists. One of them had worked for C. Itoh, a large Japanese trading company, on the sale and project follow-up of an oil refinery in Algeria. He explained by the use of a diagram (Figure 13.1) the Japanese 'method' for selling turnkey factories.

He stressed the central role of the *sogoshosha* (GTC: general trading company) as an *organizer*, a function that includes the responsibilities of information source, business intermediary and co-ordinator. An *organizer* is roughly equivalent to a 'sales prospection expert before, during and after the sale of a large and highly complex item'. In 1969 one of C. Itoh's small offices in Algiers, specializing in import–export, principally of textile products, learned of the existence of a new tender for an oil refinery which was shortly to be published. The Algiers office sent a fairly detailed telex to Tokyo – step (1) in Figure 13.1 – where the engineering company(ies) and the manufacturing companies (MFG) who would be in a position to tender for the project were sought out – step (2).

Even at this early stage, a project team will begin to assemble from among the different companies involved (3). The trading company contacts the official bodies: first, the foreign insurance division of the Ministry of International Trade and Industry (GOV) to determine whether the project has a chance of being covered for political and commercial risk (4). The Japanese Exim-Bank, the public export-finance body (BKG), will also be contacted for a preliminary study into financing options. These bodies will not make any firm commitment, but they will give a preliminary response: if the project risks not being covered by official guarantees, or only receiving limited cover, the project team instituted by the trading company may decide to abandon the tender. While all this is going on, and even before the bid documents are available, a preliminary team will be sent onto the site to examine the possibilities of water and energy supply, transport facilities, etc. Already the Japanese are gaining time (5). Once the bid documents are available to companies (6), the trading company's local representative will go to collect them personally from the future owner and dispatch the documents to Tokyo after having summarized the main points in a long and detailed telex. The representative will not hesitate to stay up most of the night to draft this telex. By this stage, the Japanese have already gained 15 days on their international competitors (7).

Once the detailed telex has been received, a larger team will go to examine the technical and economic conditions on site. The results of this survey and the consultation with various engineering partners, heavy equipment manufacturers (MFG) and carriers (TRP), will enable the formulation of a detailed bid, which very often has to be submitted within a fairly short time span (thirty days) after the publication of the tender. The bid will not be sent, but handed over by a young executive, who will be 25 to 30 years old: a 'message-boy' (8). His task is an important one: thanks to him, there is no risk of the documents being blocked by customs; he also has the job of 'sizing up' the people being dealt with and of discerning the people who will really make the final decision. Once more the Japanese have gained time; they are never late in submitting a tender, whereas a number of their foreign competitors submit theirs after the deadline. Although late delivery of a bid is usually accepted (bidding times are fairly short), it does not necessarily reflect favourably on the capacity to meet delivery dates.

Now the negotiation phase begins (9). This will easily last several months and in extreme cases will stretch, with long interruptions, over several years. Much shuttling back and forth between the various levels (10) will allow the finalizing of an offer. If successful, the offer will lead to the signature of the contract for a large-scale project (11), in which the trading company and the engineering company will generally be joint contractors. As a result, the trading company will adopt the role of co-ordinator between the various companies carrying out the project (12).

According to my Japanese informant, the 'message-boy' is typical of the Japanese way of doing business. He is even requested to scrutinize the face of the people to whom he submits the offer to determine their reaction to the Japanese bid. In the west, it is difficult to conceive of such care being taken to assess subjective reactions objectively.

(Adapted from Jean-Claude Usunier, 1985, 'Place de la recherche pratique et théorique dans l'enseignement de la gestion', *Enseignement et Gestion*, Winter 1984–5, p. 15. This case was reported by Mr Nobuhiko Suto, now a professor at Tokai University, who had been personally involved in the deal.)

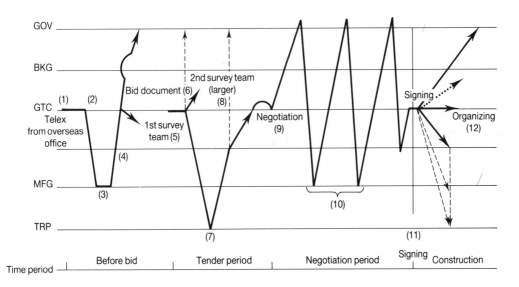

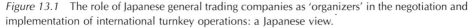

Figure 13.1　The role of Japanese general trading companies as 'organizers' in the negotiation and implementation of international turnkey operations: a Japanese view.

The first phase – awareness – deals with the recognition of the other party as a feasible partner for exchange. Short distances, whether cultural, geographic or linguistic, facilitate this process. It is easier to trade with 'local buyers' than with 'distant merchants'. The intercultural situation renders this phase more difficult.

In the second phase – exploration – the exchange relation begins. It remains a tenuous one. Partners are exploring the potential benefits and costs of an exchange. Several means are possible: trial purchase, installing a prototype plant, lending a machine or offering a technical visit to an existing plant.

Scanzoni (1979) distinguishes five subprocesses which are at work in exploration: attraction, communication and bargaining, power and justice, norm development and expectations development. Most of these subprocesses are subject to a certain cultural variance. For instance, bargaining attitudes, functions and rites vary according to cultures (see Chapter 10, section 1). Moreover the development of common norms is more easily attained if potential partners in the exchange belong to the same cultural background.

During the expansion phase partners reap the benefits of their relationship and simultaneously become increasingly interdependent. The subprocesses of the preceding phase are still at work during the expansion. If each party has a strong positive perception of the other party's performance, the motivation to maintain and increase the exchange relationship is strong. This in turn reduces the probability that one (or both) party(ies) is (are) looking for alternative partners, because of a lack of confidence in the future of the present exchange relationship ('unfaithfulness').

Signing one or more contracts is not a necessary step for the commitment phase. The parties exchange implicit or explicit signs (either written or oral) of their willingness to continue their exchange relationship. One of these signs may be the allocation by both partners of large resources to the joint venture. The credibility of commitment to the relationship can be further reinforced by the exchange of 'hostages', that is, a bilateral exchange of transaction-specific human or physical assets (Williamson, 1983). These signs of durability of the association are naturally subject to different culture-based interpretations.

Dissolution is a possibility at any moment of the exchange relationship. It rests on an internal evaluation made by each partner of the costs of discontinuing the exchange. If these costs outweigh the benefits, partners may negotiate the dissolution. These costs are difficult to estimate. The potential benefits of a new exchange relationship are also fairly uncertain and difficult to forecast. Breaking off is a complex process, often related to a crisis initiated by one of the partners. If the other party is willing to enter this separation ritual, dissolution becomes feasible. This 'divorce' is the counterpart of Levitt's (1983) relational marriage.

13.2   The influence of culture on some important aspects of marketing negotiations[5]

General influence of culture on marketing negotiations

Culture has an indirect influence on the outcome of negotiations. It works through two basic groups of mediating variables:

1. The situational aspects of the negotiation (i.e. time and time pressure, power and exercise of power, number of participants, location, etc.).
2. The characteristics of the negotiators (especially personality variables and cultural variables).

These two groups of factors in turn influence the negotiation process, which ultimately determines the outcome (Jolibert, 1988)

Most of the academic literature on the influence of culture on international business negotiations uses a comparative and cross-cultural setting (see for instance Graham, 1985). Generally, a laboratory experiment (the negotiation simulation of Kelley, 1966) helps in the comparison of negotiations between people of various nationalities.[6] Nationality is used as a proxy and summary variable for culture. A basic description is made of the cultural traits of a specific nationality in negotiations, which is then contrasted with one or more different national groups. It is the basis for some hypotheses on either the process or the outcome of these negotiations, where the membership of a specific national group is one of the main explanatory variables.

It is advisable to be prudent before directly transposing data, on the behaviour or negotiation strategies of people from a particular country, collected during negotiations with their compatriots.[7] Some traits may not be found when people are negotiating with partners of other nationalities. For instance, when Italians negotiate together, they do not adopt exactly the same behaviour and strategies as they do when negotiating with Americans.[8]

Below are examples and illustrations of how cultural traits affect negotiation (very generally, i.e. as ideal types in the Weberian sense). However, the correspondence between nationality and culture-based negotiation attitudes is not limitless. Cultural diversity within a country, cultural borrowing of values and individual diversity prohibit any simple country stereotyping.

An intercultural approach to trust-building in international business negotiations

Trust is a prime asset when negotiating in that it enables the parties to overcome conflicts of interest, personal conflicts and cultural and communication misunderstandings, which inevitably arise when discussing contracts and clauses. As stated by Sullivan and Peterson (1982, p. 30): 'where the parties have trust in one another, then there will be ways by which the two parties can work out difficulties such as power conflict, low profitability, and so forth.'

This chapter and the two following ones emphasize those aspects of cultural differences which most directly affect the process of the building and withdrawing of trust. Cultural misunderstandings undermine trust. Trust is conceived of as *the* mediating variable in the influence of culture on the process of international business negotiations. Relevant (but probably not exhaustive)[9] issues for building trust in international business negotiations are as follows:

• How do partners use their own cultural codes, as people and as representatives of organizations, to rate each other's credibility?

- Do the partners incline towards the adoption of a 'problem-solving' orientation (within an integrative strategy)?
- Do partners share a common approach to formulating problems, identifying relevant issues and alternative solutions, and finally choosing the best one? Partners must share, or at least try to share, a common rationality.
- What is the basic foundation of trust: is it an oral base ('my word is my bond') or a written base (only what has been laid down on paper and signed is binding)? What is the cultural attitude towards possible litigation? Some cultures are litigation-orientated as a result of the 'get-it-in-writing' mentality.
- How do people perceive and organize time? What is their cultural attitude when trying to comply with plans, schedules and deadlines? (See Chapter 14.)
- How do differences in business ethics affect international marketing negotiations, especially as far as illegal payments in international contracts are concerned? (See Chapter 15, on bribery and international marketing.)

13.3 Who is seen as a credible partner?

Cultural relativity of the encoding/decoding

Triandis (1983, p. 147) has emphasized three dimensions of the self-concept which may have a strong influence on the coding/decoding process of credibility:

- Self-esteem: the extent to which people think of themselves as very good or not too good.
- Perceived potency: the extent to which people view themselves as powerful, able to accomplish almost any task.
- Perceived activity: the person sees the self as a doer, an active shaper of the world.

Since people generally live in homogeneous cultural settings (i.e. countries or regions within countries with one language, a dominant religion and shared values) these messages are received by people who share the same cultural code. But when people do not share the same codes this may create problems for establishing credibility/ trustworthiness. For example, a credible person may be considered by the emitter (coder) to be somebody showing a low self-concept profile (modest, patiently listening to partners, speaking little and cautiously, etc.); if, conversely, the receiver (decoder) considers as a credible person somebody with a high self-concept profile (showing self-confidence, speaking arrogantly, not paying much attention to what the other is saying, etc.), there will be a credibility misunderstanding.

One of the main reasons for the seriousness of the Cuban missile crisis at the beginning of the 1960s was a misinterpretation by the Soviet leader Khrushchev of the credibility of the American president, John F. Kennedy. Kennedy and Khrushchev had held talks in Vienna, after the unsuccessful attack by US soldiers resulting in defeat at the Bay of Pigs. During their meeting, the young President Kennedy recognized that this attack had been a military and political mistake, which he regretted. Khrushchev saw this confession of error as a testimony of Kennedy's frank naivety and lack of character. He therefore inferred that it was possible to gain advantage by installing nuclear missiles in Cuba, which would have been targeted at the United States. This led the world to the brink of nuclear war between the superpowers. The events which followed showed that Khrushchev had been wrong in evaluating Kennedy's credibility. Ultimately, Kennedy showed great firmness and negotiation skill.

Khrushchev's mistake may be explained by differences in cultural coding of credibility. Whereas in the United States, reaching a high position while still young is positively perceived, Soviet people associate age with the ability to carry responsibilities. Moreover, the admission of a mistake or a misjudgement is also positively perceived in the United States. US ethics value frankness and honesty. It is further believed that individuals may improve their behaviour and decisions by taking into account the lessons of experience. On the other hand, in the Soviet Union, to admit errors was rare. It generally implied the very weak position of people subjected to the enforced confessions of the Stalinist trials. Naturally this does not mean that there is no cultural borrowing. In the climate of *perestroika*, the traditional situation in the former Soviet Union has changed. *Glasnost* ('openness' in Russian) indicates a provisional inversion of the symbolic values placed on frankness.

Signs of credibility

Personal credibility is decoded through the filter of numerous physical traits, which are not often considered as they seem to be only appearances or because we tend to use these reference points unconsciously (Lee, 1966). Being tall may, for instance, be perceived as a sign of strength and character. Stoutness may be considered a positive sign for a partner in societies where starvation is still a recent memory. Where malnutrition is a reality for a section of the population, it is better to be fat, that is, well nourished and therefore rich- and powerful-looking. Naturally these signs have a relative value. Weight, height, age and sex cannot be considered as adequate criteria for selecting negotiators. Furthermore people may in fact be partly aware of the cultural code of the partner.

Each of these basic signs plays a role in the initial building of a credibility profile: age, sex, height, stoutness, face, tone and strength of the voice, self-esteem, perceived potency, perceived activity, etc. This profile is a priori because it only influences credibility in early contacts, that is, in the phase of awareness and at the beginning of the exploration phase (Scanzoni, 1979). Moreover the credibility signs clearly bear a symbolic dimension:[10] the associative links between personal characteristics and credibility are, in part, fixed arbitrarily by culture.

Collective credibility: relating personal trustworthiness to institutional credentials

Collective (company and group) credibility is a complementary issue. Obviously, there are objective elements which permit assessment of the credibility of the firm, such as its balance sheet, annual reports, reference lists, technical specifications and all those elements which identify the financial and technical quality of a potential partner. Data and information increase the objectivity of the exchange relationship, but are not enough. For instance the Japanese, as well as many Europeans, do not emphasize financial perform-ance measured by profits or dividends as a sign of company credibility as strongly as Americans do. The Japanese and Europeans tend to place more emphasis on turnover, the company's connection with the government, its social reputation and its history.

Finding the appropriate level to establish contact may be an important issue. In decentralized decision-making societies, it may sometimes be better to contact those people who have the required authority for making decisions, even though they may be at intermediate hierarchical levels (small power distance). In more centralized societies, credibility on both sides is established by the meeting of top decision-makers. Where committee decision-making is the rule, the firm's credibility must be developed by contacts with many people, since it is often impossible to identify who is the ultimate individual decision-maker. There may be no such person. US or European companies often believe that they have lost a deal negotiated with the Japanese because they do not receive a 'yes' for weeks and sometimes months. During this time, the *ringi* has been at work in the Japanese company. Proposals are circulated among everyone involved in the deal, so that they can discuss it and ultimately affix their own seal of approval. Since (objective) credibility is based on power and decision-making, a capacity to understand the influence process in the other party's decision-making is therefore a key asset for effective negotiation.

As far as credibility is concerned, two issues have to be addressed:

1. Who is considered a legitimate representative of the firm: top-ranking executives only, all the employees as individuals or all the people collectively?[11]
2. To what extent is one prepared to meet and discuss with people whom one considers weakly credible, just because their firm is considered credible?

In any national environment there are always some institutions which enable potential partners in joint ventures to assess each other as credible (business schools, engineering schools or law schools, professional associations and meetings, clubs, etc.). Laton McCartney (1989), for instance, describes 'The Grove', an annual three-day encampment, organized by the Bohemian Club of San Francisco, which has played a significant role in the growth of the Bechtel empire, the world leader in turnkey operations for many years:

> But the real business of The Grove, where a favorite pastime was figuring out the corporate connections and interlocking directorates of incoming members, was just that: business. Not business by contract or by deal – both of which were barred on The Grove's grounds – but business by sheer association, by men spending time with, getting to know and like each other. 'Once you've spent three days with someone in an informal situation,' explained John D. Ehrlichman, who attended Grove encampments while a chief aide to Richard Nixon, 'you have a relationship – a relationship that opens doors and makes it easier to pick up the phone.' (McCartney, 1989, p. 14)

This type of meeting assembles potential partners, government decision-makers, top executives of large companies who buy plants (oil, chemicals, utilities, etc.) and the bankers who finance the dealers. By not speaking directly about business, they socialize and take the time to get to know each other. The simple fact of *being there* is the main credibility message. Collective credibility signs may range from education (English public schools, French *Grandes Ecoles*, *Herr Doktor*, etc.) to particular ways of speaking and writing a language, or even a particular way of dressing.

13.4 Culture-based dispositions for being integrative in negotiations

Integrative orientation versus distribution orientation

In business negotiations the purchaser (or team of purchasers) and the vendor (or group of vendors) are mutually interdependent, and their individual interests clash. The ability to choose effective negotiation largely explains the individual performance of each party on the one hand, and the joint outcome on the other. In pitting themselves against each other, the parties may develop opposing points of view towards the negotiation strategy which they intend to adopt: distributive or integrative.

In the *distributive* strategy (or orientation), the negotiation process is seen as leading to the division of a fixed 'cake' which the parties feel they cannot enlarge even if they were willing to do so. This orientation is also termed 'competitive negotiation' or 'zero sum game'. It leads to a perception of negotiation as a war of positions – territorial in essence. These are negotiations of the 'win–lose' type: 'anything that isn't yours is mine' and vice versa. The negotiators hold attitudes and objectives that are quasi-conflictive (Dupont, 1990). Interdependence is minimized whereas adverseness is emphasized.[12]

At the opposite end of the spectrum is the *integrative* orientation (Walton and McKersie, 1965). The central assumption is that the size of the 'cake' (the joint outcome of the negotiations) can be increased if the parties adopt a co-operative attitude. This idea is directly linked to problem-solving orientation (Pruitt, 1983). Negotiators may not be concerned purely with their own objectives, but may also be interested in the other party's aspirations and results, seeing them as almost equally important. Integrative orientation has been termed 'co-operative' or 'collaborative'. It results in negotiation being seen as an attempt to maximize the joint outcome. The division of this outcome is to a certain extent secondary or is at least perceived as an important but later issue. Here negotiation is a 'positive sum game' where the joint outcome is greater than zero.

Problem-solving orientation can be defined as an overall negotiating behaviour that is co-operative, integrative and orientated towards the exchange of information (Campbell *et al.*, 1988). Fair communication and the exchange of information between negotiators are important. 'Problem solvers' exchange representative information, that is, honest and objective data. There is no desire to manipulate the partner, as in instrumental communication (Angelmar and Stern, 1978). Exchanging representative information is considered a basic element in problem-solving orientation.[13] Empirical studies (experimental negotiation stimulation) have shown that this orientation positively influences the common results of negotiation (Pruitt, 1983).[14]

Factors favouring an integrative strategy

The adoption of an integrative strategy is facilitated by the following:

- A higher level of aspirations on both sides: the negotiators want to reach a better outcome or are under pressure from their principals who have defined increased outcome objectives while still allowing them explicit autonomy and room for manoeuvre (Pruitt and Lewis, 1975).
- The ability to envisage the future; this permits the discovery or 'invention' of new solutions, which enables both partners to overcome the problem of the fixed size of the 'territorial cake'. This size is strictly limited in the very short term.
- The existence of 'perceived common ground' (Pruitt, 1983); if sufficiently wide, this overlap between the interests of the two parties allows new solutions to be explored. This is termed 'flexibility' by the British and 'slack' by the Americans.

If one seeks to develop relational marketing, an integrative negotiating strategy is required. The nature of transactions imposes it. Business is fairly continuous and sometimes stretches over several years, and therefore implies a very strong buyer–seller interdependence. The performance level depends largely on the extent and the quality of the collaboration between the partners. In studying the styles of negotiation of industrial purchasers, Perdue, Day and Michaels (1986) have found, on the basis of a sample of 195 industrial purchasers, that the majority of them saw themselves as adopting an integrative strategy towards vendors.

Cultural dispositions to being integrative

Even though one may accept the increased effectiveness of integrative strategies, in as far as they aim to maximize the joint outcome, the problem of how this joint outcome is divided between the two sides remains unaddressed (Pruitt and Lewis, 1975; Pruitt, 1983). In integrating the dimension of nation–cultures, three questions merit consideration:

1. Do the parties tend to perceive negotiations as being easier, and do they tend to adopt an integrative orientation more readily, when they both share the same culture?
2. Do negotiators originating from particular cultures tend towards an integrative or distributive orientation? Furthermore, do negotiators originating from cultures which favour a problem-solving orientation risk seeing their personal results heavily diminished by a distributive partner who cynically exploits their 'goodwill'?
3. Do cultural differences and intercultural negotiation reduce the likelihood of integrative strategy?

Greater difficulties in being integrative in an intercultural negotiation situation than in an intracultural negotiation situation[15]

There is general agreement among the existing literature that the results of negotiation are less favourable when the negotiation is intercultural as opposed to intracultural, all other things being equal (Sawyer and Guetzkow, 1965). Van Zandt (1970) suggests that the negotiations between Americans and the Japanese are six times as long and three times as difficult as those purely between Americans. This increases the costs of the transaction for the American firms in Japan due to the relative inefficiency of communication. The subjective satisfaction of the negotiators (measured by a questionnaire) in their result tends to be inferior for intercultural negotiation compared to intracultural negotiation (Weitz, 1979; Graham, 1985).

Problem solving depends on a collaborative attitude which is easier with a partner from the same culture (Rubin and Brown, 1975). The similarity, according to Rubin and Brown, leads to more trust and an enhanced level of interpersonal attraction (Graham, 1985). As a result, each side considers communication from the other as more representative (in the sense of Angelmar and Stern, 1978): in other words, one party perceives that they transmit fairly objective information and do not try to influence the other party, as with instrumental communication.

The hypothesis that the similarity of the parties leads to a more favourable outcome was proposed by Evans (1963). Similarity facilitates awareness and exploration between parties. In fact it is more a question of *perceived* similarity which leads to more co-operative behaviour in negotiation (Matthews *et al.*, 1972). If this similarity is perceived, but not based on strictly objective indications (such as shared nationality, language or educational background), a dissymetric view of similarity may arise between the buyer and the seller. For instance many business people in the Middle East have a good command of either the English or French language and culture. Middle-Eastern business people are often perceived by their American or European counterparts as being similar, whereas they may perceive their Western counterparts as different. The role adopted in negotiation, buyer or seller, combines with perceived similarity: if sellers perceive a greater similarity, this can lead to a stronger problem-solving orientation on their part (Campbell *et al.*, 1988).[16]

In intercultural terms,[17] the possibility exists of a misunderstanding arising from a perception of similarity which is not shared by both parties. For example, one can imagine a situation where a seller (American, for instance) perceives the buyer as similar (an Arab buyer who is very westernized in appearance, who has a superficial but misleading cultural outlook because of his cultural borrowing). However, the reverse situation does not occur: the Arab buyer clearly recognizes that the American seller knows nothing about his culture. The seller will in this case have a tendency to take a problem-solving orientation whereas the buyer will exploit the seller without feeling obliged to reciprocate and will ultimately maximize his personal outcome by adopting a distributive strategy.

National orientations favouring the integrative strategy

The second question (p. 404) concerns the adoption of integrative strategies by some nationalities more than others. Studies tend to show that American business people show trust more willingly and more spontaneously than other cultural groups, and have a stronger tendency towards a problem-solving and integrative orientation (Druckman *et al.*, 1976; Harnett and Cummings, 1980; Campbell *et al.*, 1988). The level of their profits as sellers depends on the buyer responding positively by also adopting a problem-solving approach (Campbell *et al.*, 1988).

American negotiators have a stronger tendency to exchange representative communication, making clear and explicit messages a priority. This is in line with the American appreciation of frankness and directness (see Chapter 4, explicit communication according to Edward Hall). This is what Graham and Herberger (1983) call the 'John Wayne Style' (Box 13.2). They often meet certain difficulties with cultures who take more time in the preliminaries: getting to know each other, that is, talking generally and only actually getting down to business later. As a result, Americans may not foster feelings of trust in negotiators from other cultural groups who feel it necessary to get to know the person they are dealing with (Hall, 1976).

Graham and Meissner (1986) have shown in a study comparing five countries that the most integrative strategies are adopted by the Brazilians, followed by the Japanese. On the other hand the Americans, the Germans and the Koreans choose intermediate strategies that are more distributive. This is consistent in the case of the Germans who, according to Cateora (1983), use the hard-sell approach, where the seller is fairly pushy and adopts an instrumental communication and a distributive strategy (Campbell *et al.*, 1988).

There is no empirical study that has shown, for example, that the Arabs from the Middle East have a tendency to be more distributive than the Americans.[18] Americans tend to see the world as problems to be solved, whereas Arabs see it more as a creation of God. The concept of integrative strategy is strongly culturally influenced by the American tradition of experimental research in social psychology applied to commercial negotiation (see for example, Rubin and Brown, 1975; Pruitt and Lewis, 1975; Pruitt, 1983). It is based on a

---

Box 13.2   *The 'John Wayne Style': just call me John*

Americans, more than any other national group, value informality and equality in human relations. The emphasis on first names is only the beginning. We go out of our way to make our clients feel comfortable by playing down status distinctions such as clients and by eliminating 'unnecessary' formalities such as lengthy introductions. All too often, however, we succeed only in making ourselves feel comfortable while our clients become uneasy or even annoyed. For example, in Japanese society interpersonal relationships are vertical; in almost all two-person relationships a difference in status exists. The basis for such distinction may be one or several factors: age, sex, university attended, position in an organization, and even one's particular firm or company. ... Each Japanese is very much aware of his or her own position relative to others which whom he or she deals .... The roles of the higher status position and the lower status position are quite different, even to the extent that Japanese use different words to express the same idea depending on which person makes the statement. For example a buyer would say *otaku* (your company), while a seller would say *on sha* (your great company). Status relations dictate not only *what* is said but also *how* it is said.

(Graham and Herberger, 1983, p. 162. Reproduced with permission.)

'master of destiny' orientation which feeds attitudes of problem resolution. This presupposes a simultaneous concern for one's own outcome as well as for that of the negotiating partner (the 'dual concern model' of Pruitt, 1983).

Ability to envision the other party's interests: the concept of 'limited good'

Concern for the other party's outcome is not necessarily to be found equally across cultures. Cultures place a stronger or weaker emphasis on group membership (the other party is/is not a member of the 'in-group') as a prerequisite for being considered a trustworthy partner. In cultures where there is a clear-cut distinction between the 'in-group' and the 'out-group' (according to age, sex, race or kinship criteria), people tend to perceive the interests of both groups as diametrically opposed. This is related to what has been called the concept of 'limited good' (Foster, 1965).

According to the concept of 'limited good', if something positive happens in favour of the out-group, the wealth and well-being of the in-group will be threatened. Such reactions are largely based on culture-based collective subjectivity: they stem from the (very conservative) idea that 'good' and riches are by their very nature restricted. If one yields to the other party even the tiniest concession, this will directly reduce what is left for the members of the in-group. The concept of 'limited good' induces negotiators to adopt very territorial and distributive strategies. It is a view which clearly favours the idea of the zero sum game, where 'I will lose whatever you may win' and vice versa.

In Mediterranean and Middle Eastern societies where the in-group is highly valued (clan, tribe, extended family), the concept of 'limited good' is often to be found. It slows the adoption of a problem-solving orientation, since co-operative opportunities are simply difficult to envisage.

Ignorance of the other party's culture as an obstacle to the implementation of an integrative strategy in negotiation

One of the most important obstacles to effective international business negotiation is the ignorance of all or at least the basics of the other party's culture. This is intellectually obvious, but is often forgotten by international negotiators. It refers not only to the cognitive ignorance of the main traits of the other party's culture, but also to the unconscious prejudice that differences are minor (that is, ignorance *as absence of awareness*). This favours the natural tendency to refer implicitly to one's own cultural norms, especially for the coding/decoding process of communication (the self reference criterion of James A. Lee, 1966).

Lucian Pye (1986), in the case of business negotiations between American and Chinese people, and Rosalie Tung (1984) in US–Japanese business negotiations, note the lack of prior knowledge of the American negotiators about their partner's culture. Before coming to the negotiation table, Americans do not generally read books, nor do they train themselves for the foreign communication style, nor learn about the potential traps which could lead to misunderstandings. As Carlos Fuentes states (in a rather harsh aphorism):

'What the U.S. does best is understand itself. What it does worst is understand others' (Fuentes, 1986). French negotiators also tend to be underprepared in terms of cultural knowledge (see the following chapter on national negotiation styles), whereas the Japanese seemingly try to learn a lot more than the French or the Americans about the other party's culture before negotiation takes place.

The negotiation and implementation (which often means ongoing negotiations) of a joint venture may last for several years. In this case, national cultures tend to disappear as the two teams partly merge their values and behaviour in a common 'venture culture'. In order to improve intercultural negotiation effectiveness, it is advisable to build this common culture between the partners/adversaries right from the start of the negotiations. It means establishing common rules, communication codes, finding people on each side who will act as go-betweens and trying to agree on a common interpretation of issues, facts, solutions and decision-making. This must not be considered as a formal process; it is informal and built on implicit communications. Furthermore, it relies heavily on those individuals who have been involved in the joint venture over a long period of time and who get on well together.

13.5   Existence of a common rationality between the partners

If future partners do not share common 'mental schemes', it could be difficult for them to solve problems together. Buyer and seller should share some joint views of the world, especially on the following questions:

♦ What is the relevant information required for acting?
♦ How should this information be sought, evaluated and fed into the decision-making process?

An important distinction in the field of cross-cultural psychology opposes ideologism against pragmatism (Glenn, 1981; Triandis, 1983). As indicated by Triandis (1983, p. 148):

> Ideologism versus pragmatism, which corresponds to Glenn's universalism versus particularism, refers to the extent to which the information extracted from the environment is transmitted within a broad framework, such as a religion or a political ideology, or a relatively narrow framework. This dimension refers to a way of thinking.

Ideologists use a wide body of ideas that provides them with a formal and coherent description of the world: Marxism or liberalism, for instance. Every event is supposed to carry meaning when it is seen through this ideologist framework. On the other hand, the pragmatist attitude first considers the extreme diversity of real-world situations and then derives its principles inductively. Reality is seen as a series of independent and concrete problems to be solved ('issues'). These issues make complete sense when related to practical, precise and even down-to-earth decisions. Typically, ideologists *take* decisions, that is, pick a solution from a range of possible decisions (which are located outside the person who decides). Conversely, pragmatists *make* decisions, that is both decide and implement: decisions are enacted, not selected (see Box 13.3).

Triandis hypothesizes that complex traditional societies tend to be ideologist ones, whereas pluralistic societies or cultures experiencing rapid social change tend to be pragmatist. This distinction may also be traced back to the difference between the legal systems of *common law* (mainly English and American) and the legal system of *code law*. Whereas the former favours legal precedents set by the courts and past rulings (cases), the latter favours laws and general texts. They are intended to build an all-inclusive system of written rules of law (code). Codes aim to formulate general principles so as to embody the entire set of particular cases.

The ideologist orientation, which is to be found mostly in southern and Eastern Europe, leads the negotiators to try to set principles before any detailed discussion on specific clauses of the contract. Ideologists have a tendency to prefer and promote globalized negotiations in which all the issues are gathered in a 'package deal'. The pragmatist attitude corresponds more to northern Europe and the United States. It entails defining limited-scope problems, then solving them one after the other. Pragmatists concentrate their thinking on factual aspects (deeds, not words; evidence, not opinions; figures, not value judgements).

When negotiating a large contract (for a nuclear plant or a television satellite, for instance), ideologists see arguments in favour of their 'global way of thinking': it is a unitary production, it is a complex multi-partner business, it often involves government financing and also has far-reaching social, economic and political consequences. Pragmatists, on the other hand, also find many arguments in favour of their way of thinking: the technicalities of the plant and its desired performance require an achievement and deadline orientation (pragmatist values).

Box 13.3   *Cartesian logic in negotiation*

Rather imprecisely defined, the idea is that one reasons from a starting point based on what is known, and then pays careful attention to the logical way in which one points leads to the next, and finally reaches a conclusion regarding the issue at hand. The French also assign greater priority than Americans do to establishing the principles on which the reasoning process should be based. Once this reasoning process is underway, it becomes relatively difficult to introduce new evidence or facts, most especially during a negotiation. Hence the appearance of French inflexibility, and the need to introduce new information and considerations early in the game. All this reflects the tradition of French education and becomes the status mark of the educated person. In an earlier era observers made such sweeping generalizations as: 'The French always place a school of thought, a formula, convention, a priori arguments, abstraction, and artificiality above reality; they prefer clarity to truth, words to things, rhetoric to science...'*

(Fisher, 1980).
*Quotation from Théodore Zeldin (1977), *France 1848–1945*, vol. II, Oxford University Press, p. 205. Reproduced with the kind permission of the publisher.

Pragmatism is associated with a tendency to look at facts in detail, to measure, to validate empirically. Ideologists on the other hand have a liking for speech, words and ideas. They will be orientated more towards instrumental communication. In that they aim to manipulate other people, ideologists may be as effective (by means of instrumental communication – Angelmar and Stern, 1978) as the pragmatists.

Communication may be difficult when partners do not share the same mental scheme. The most unlikely situation for success is an ideologist-orientated contractor/supplier who tries to sell to a pragmatist-orientated owner/buyer. The ideologist will see the pragmatist as being too interested in trivial details, too practical, too down-to-earth and incapable of looking at issues from a higher standpoint. Pragmatists will resent ideologists for being too theoretical, lacking practical sense, concerned with issues that are too broad to lead to implementable decisions. In relational marketing, especially in the first two phases of the relational exchange, negotiation between ideologist and pragmatist may create mis-understandings which will be difficult to overcome during subsequent phases. Indeed, developing common norms will be fairly difficult, although it is necessary if partners want to be able to predict the other party's behaviour. A frequent comment in such situations will be: 'One never knows what these people have in mind; their behaviour is largely unpredictable.'

An American (pragmatist-orientated) describes negotiations with the French (more ideologist-orientated) in the following terms (Burt, 1984, p. 6): 'The French are extremely difficult to negotiate with. Often they will not accept facts, no matter how convincing they may be.'

13.6   Oral versus written agreements as a basis for trust between the parties

The hidden asymmetry in the perceived degree of agreement

Agreements are generally considered as being mostly written. They are achieved by negotiation and by the signing of written contracts, which are often considered 'the law of the parties'. This is unfortunately not always true. Keegan (1984) points out that for some cultures 'my word is my bond' and trust is a personal matter, which he contrasts to the 'get-it-in-writing' mentality where trust is more impersonal. The former is typical of the Middle East, whereas the latter is to be found in the United States where hundreds of thousands of lawyers help people negotiate written agreements and litigate within the framework of these written agreements.

This has to be interpreted: it does not mean that people rely *entirely* on either an oral base (oaths, confidence between people, membership of a common group where perjury is considered a crime) or a written base. Exploring, maintaining and checking the bases for trust is a more complex process (Usunier, 1989). It entails various possibilities:

1.   An agreement may be non-symmetrical. A agrees with B, but B does not agree with A. Various reasons may explain this situation: either B wishes to conceal the disagreement or there is some sort of misunderstanding, usually language-based.

2. People agree, but on different bases, and they do not perceive the divergence. They have, for instance, quite different interpretations of a clause or some kind of non-written agreement. Although much may be written down, some things will always remain unwritten. What is unwritten may, to one party, seem obviously in line with a written clause, but not to the other. Moreover, if there is no opportunity to confront their interpretations, they cannot be aware of their divergent nature.
3. The agreement is not understood by both parties as having the same degree of influence on:

   (a) the stability;
   (b) the precision and explicitness of the exchange relation.

Written documents as a basis for mutual trust between the parties

There is a fundamental *dialectic in written agreements between distrust and confidence*. At the beginning there is distrust. It is implicitly assumed that such distrust is natural. This has to be reduced in order to establish confidence. Trust is not achieved on a global and personal basis but only by breaking down potential distrust in concrete situations where it may hamper common action. Trust is built step by step, with a view towards the future. Therefore *real trust* is achieved only gradually. Trust is deprived of its personal aspects. Thanks to the written agreement, the parties may trust each other in business, although they do not trust each other as people. Trust is taken to its highest point when the parties sign a written agreement.

On the other hand, cultures that favour oral agreements tend not to hypothesize that trust is constructed by the negotiation process. They see trust more as a prerequisite to the negotiation of written agreements. Naturally they do not expect this prerequisite to be met in every case. Trust tends to be mostly personal. Establishing trust requires that people know each other. That is probably why many Far Eastern cultures (Chinese: Pye, 1982; Japanese: Graham and Sano, 1990; Tung, 1984; de Mente, 1987) need to make informal contact, discuss general topics and spend time together before they get to the point, even though all this may not appear task-related.

Subsequently, the negotiation process will be lengthy because another dialectic is at work. Since people are supposed to trust each other, the negotiation process should not damage or destroy the basic asset of their exchange relationship – trust. They will avoid direct confrontation on a specific clause, and therefore globalize the negotiation process. Global friends may be local foes, provided trust is not lost as the basic asset of the negotiation process.

The ambiguity of the cultural status of written materials as a basis for trust-building between the parties

That one should always 'get-it-in-writing' is not self-evident. The contrary idea may even impose itself ('if they want it written down, it means that they don't trust me'). Régina Traoré Sérié explains, for instance, the respective role of oral communication (spoken, transmitted through personal and concrete communication, passed through generations by storytellers) and written materials (read, industrially printed, impersonally transmitted, with no concrete communication) in the African culture.

> Reading is an individual act, which does not easily incorporate itself into African culture. Written documents are presented as either irrelevant to everyday social practices, or as an anti-social practice. This is because someone who reads, is also isolating himself, which is resented by the other members of the community. But at the same time, people find books attractive, because they are the symbol of access to a certain kind of power. By reading, people appropriate foreign culture, they get to know 'the paper of the whites'. As a consequence, reading is coded as a positive activity in the collective ideal of Ivory Coast society, since it is a synonym for social success. This contradiction between 'alien' and 'fetish' written documents encapsulates the ambiguity of the status of books in African society.[19]

Do written documents produce irreversible commitments?

In cultures where relationships are very personalized, confidence cannot be separated from the person in whom the confidence is placed. The basis for mutual trust is no longer the detailed written contractual documents, but my word which is my bond. It is not just any word, but a special kind of word which is heavily imbued with cultural codes (Hall, 1959, 1976). These 'words as bonds' cannot easily be transferred from one culture to another. Adler (1980) describes the case of an Egyptian executive who, after entertaining his Canadian guest, offered him joint partnership in a business venture. The Canadian was very keen to enter this venture with the Egyptian businessman. He therefore suggested that they meet again the next morning with their respective lawyers to fill in the details. The Egyptians never arrived. The Canadian businessman wondered whether the problem was caused by the lack of punctuality of the Egyptians, or by the Egyptian executive expecting a counteroffer, or even the absence of lawyers available in Cairo. 'None of these explanations was true, although the Canadian executive suggested all of them. At issue was the perceived meaning of inviting lawyers. The Canadian saw the lawyers' presence as facilitating the successful completion of the negotiation; the Egyptian interpreted it as signalling the Canadian's mistrust of his verbal commitment. Canadians often use the impersonal formality of a lawyer's services to finalize an agreement. Egyptians more frequently depend on a personal relationship developed between bargaining partners for the same purposes (Adler, 1980, p. 178).

If agreements are mostly personal, then their written base may be less important. Thus the demand for renegotiation of clauses by a Middle Eastern buyer in a contract already negotiated and signed should not be seen as astonishing. It should not necessarily lead to litigation. Behind the demand for renegotiation is the assumption that, if people really trust each other, they should go much further than simple and literal implementation of their written agreements. This leads to the following question: to what extent should the contract signature date be considered as a deadline which signals the end of the negotiation?

Written agreements as a deadline for negotiations

According to what has been explained above, there are two different ways to look at the influence and function of the written agreement on the time line of the exchange relationship. Those favouring written-based trust-building tend to see a written agreement as a very definite break in the exchange relationship. It completes a phase during which potential relations have been carefully discussed and explored. It establishes a strict contractual code, which has then to be implemented literally. Written words, sentences and formulas have to be strictly observed. If a party feels free to depart from what has been written down, the Damocles sword of litigation will hang over the parties. And nobody likes litigation, supposedly.

Those favouring oral-based, personal trust consider the signing of a written agreement as an important step, but only one of many in a continuous negotiation process. The negotiation process was active before signature and will be active afterwards. A continuous negotiation process, where the contract is only one step, is seen as the best basis for maintaining trust.

As stated by Edward Hall (1960, p. 94):

> Americans consider that negotiations have more or less ceased when the contract is signed. With the Greeks, on the other hand, the contract is seen as a sort of way station on the route to negotiation, that will cease only when the work is completed. The contract is nothing more than a charter for serious negotiations. In the Arab world, once a man's word is given in a particular kind of way, it is just as binding, if not more so, than most of our written contracts. The written contract therefore violates the Moslem's sensitivities and reflects on his honour. Unfortunately, the situation is now so hopelessly confused that neither system can be counted on to prevail consistently.

Different attitudes towards litigation

It is easy to understand that the function of litigation will be different for both sides. Recourse to litigation will be fairly easily made by those favouring written-based agreements as the ultimate means of resolving breaches of contract. The oral and personal tradition is less susceptible to recourse to litigation, because litigation has major drawbacks:

◆ It breaks the implicit assumption of trust.
◆ It breaches the required state of social harmony, especially in the Far Eastern countries, and may therefore be quite threatening for the community as a whole.

As David (1987, p. 89, my translation) states:

> ... in Far Eastern countries, as well as in Black Africa and Madagascar ... subject to the westernization process which has been attempted, one does not find, as in Hinduism or Islam, a body of legal rules whose influence may be weakened by the recognized influence of other factors; it is the very notion of legal rules which is challenged. Despite authorities having sometimes established legal codes, it is well known and seems obvious that the

prescriptions of these codes are not designed to be implemented literally. They should only be considered as simple patterns. The judge will be able to moderate their strictness and, moreover, it is hoped that this will not be necessary. The 'good judge', whether Chinese, Japanese or Vietnamese, is not concerned with making a good decision. The 'good judge' is the one who *succeeds in not making any award*, because he has been skilful enough to lead the opponents to reconciliation. Any dispute, as it is a threat to social harmony, has to be solved by a settlement through conciliation. The individual only has 'duties' towards the society. Recognition of 'subjective rights' in his favour is out of the question. Law as it is conceived in the West is seen as good for barbarians, and the occupation of lawyer, in the limited extent that it exists, is regarded with contempt by the society.'

These remarks by a specialist of comparative law give a good idea of the differences of litigation tradition between the Far East and the West. In the field of contracts, the Western saying 'the contract is the law of the parties' dominates the practices of international trade. But this is in part window-dressing. When marketing internationally, a set of written contracts is always signed. This is not to say that people choose either oral or written agreements as a basis for trust. The real question is rather: how should the mix of written and oral bases for trust, as they are perceived by the parties, be interpreted? People do not deal with the real world in the same way. Negotiating together requires changing one's views of reality. Not only differences in rationality and mental programmes, but also differences in time representations, may lead to a partner 'who thinks differently' being considered a partner 'who thinks wrongly'.

   The greatest caution is recommended when interpreting the bases of trust, whether written documents or oral and personal bonds. Even in the Anglo-Saxon world, where it is preferred to 'get-it-in-writing', a number of business deals, sometimes large ones – in the area of finance, for instance – are based on a simple telex or fax, or the simple agreement between two key decision-makers. It would be a mistake to believe that personal relationships do not exist in places where written contracts are generally required. Moreover, in cultures where 'my word is my bond', it should never be forgotten that it is difficult to trust somebody who is a member of the 'out-group', whether on a written or spoken basis. Trust has therefore to be established (and monitored) on both bases, while at the same time keeping in mind a clear awareness of the limits of each.

APPENDIX 13

——————— ◆◆◆ ———————

Teaching materials

A13.1 Case: McFarlane Instruments

An American firm, the McFarlane Instruments Company, had delivered approximately US$400,000 worth of instruments to a People's Republic of China government agency.

The agency refused to pay for the instruments, so the United States company contacted the American Embassy in Beijing for assistance. The American commercial attaché arranged a meeting between the PRC industrial ministry representatives, company representatives, and himself.

In the meeting, the government officials stated that they would not pay because the instruments did not conform to the guarantee of accuracy of plus or minus 0.2%. The United States firm found this to be very strange since they had not encountered accuracy problems with their instruments sold in other countries. They finally inquired as to the temperatures at which the tests had been conducted. The Chinese officials indicated that tests had been conducted at 10°C and at 50°C.

The American firm replied that international practice and standards called for such tests to be conducted at 25°C. The instruments were normally used at approximately room temperature. Because of differential expansion and contraction coefficients of the materials in the instruments, use under much lower or higher ambient temperatures resulted in different levels of precision and need for recalibration.

The Chinese officials then produced a copy of the company's brochure which stated the plus or minus 0.2% precision, but did not specify the test temperature. After approximately one hour of discussion, which consisted mainly of each side reiterating its position, the US firm attempted to break the deadlock. While avoiding any admission that the instruments failed to conform to international standards, they agreed to reduce the price by 30% 'in order to maintain good relations'. Their only other choice was to attempt to reclaim the machines, and then attempt to re-export them through potentially difficult Chinese customs administration to the United States or elsewhere. The Chinese officials requested that a written proposal be submitted. This was done and the offer was made valid for a period of 60 days.

Three months later the Chinese government organization rejected the proposal, restating that the instruments did not meet the promised precision. The US firm, after several more attempts at reconciliation, gave up and took back the machines. They now faced the difficult task of obtaining permission to re-export them, and the additional costs of doing that and paying for shipping costs.

Subsequent investigation indicated that the real problem had not had anything to do with the instruments themselves. Between the time the original contract had been signed and the instruments delivered, the currency of PRC had been devalued. While the contract was written in US dollars, the Chinese organization had been allocated a given amount of the PRC currency, the '*rem min bi*', to pay for it (through the appropriate foreign exchange agency). With the new exchange rate, the Chinese government organization did not have enough money to pay for the instruments. The discount offered by the American company had not been sufficient to make up for the difference in exchange rates. The Chinese found it easier to reject the instruments than to admit what had happened.

Questions

1. How can you determine the real problems which impeded the negotiations? What are they, in your opinion?

2. Would you expect it to be easy to get appointments with Chinese government officials? Why or why not?
3. Would you expect it to be easy to obtain information from Chinese officials? Why or why not?
4. What important lesson for negotiations does this case illustrate? How would you have approached this problem?

(Adapted from Gerald Albaum, Jesper Strandskov, Edwin Duerr and Laurence Dowd, 1989, *International Marketing and Export Management*, Addison-Wesley: Wokingham, pp. 388–9. Reproduced with the kind permission of the author, George Lee, San Francisco State University.)

A13.2 Negotiation game: Kumbele Power Plant

A consortium, BDH, has been established between a US-based engineering company, a French company belonging to the same sector and a German firm producing heavy industrial equipment. This consortium is in the final phase of negotiations to win a contract for building a turnkey electric power plant. The owner is the National Electricity Authority, a state-owned corporation which holds a monopoly on the transport and distribution of electricity in an English-speaking country in Africa. National Electricity Authority has issued the tender.

The tender procedure was initiated eighteen months ago. At first there were about twenty potentially qualified contractors which submitted bids. Most of them were engineering companies originating from the main industrial countries, and some came from newly industrialized countries such as South Korea, Brazil and Turkey. After a preselection phase, the number of potential contractors was reduced to a short list of five companies or consortia. The final selection process lasted for several months, as bids that were technologically incomparable had to be taken into account.

The consortium created by Brown Engineering Corp. (US), Duponval SA (French) and Horst BauTechnik AG (German) was chosen as the organization with which the final negotiations would take place. But a Japanese competitor has also made a very attractive offer and is equally in a position to supplant BDH, if BDH proves to be too demanding for National Electricity Authority. In fact BDH has a strong reference list, supported by similar plants it has built which are working effectively. Moreover, in addition to its offer, BDH provides a low-rate, long-term financing scheme for the buyer, which has been created by putting together export credits issued by public organizations from the countries of the three members of BDH: US Eximbank for Brown, BFCE (Banque Française du Commerce Extérieur) for Duponval and KfW (Kreditanstalt für Wieder-aufbau) for Horst BauTechnik.

The final price has not yet been settled, as there are still some important clauses to be discussed:

♦ The supply of basic materials by the consortium, during the start-up of the power plant.

♦ The possibility of signing a 'products in hand' contract.[20] In this case the consortium would agree to sign a management contract to run the operation until it reaches 100 per cent of its target capacity (400 megawatts).

The proposal which served as a starting base for the final bargaining process was priced at US$105 million. Each one of the partners-to-be has naturally retained its right to improve its position, either by obtaining a rebate (the buyer) or by increasing this base price level by astutely negotiating supplementary services (the consortium).

Since the inception of this tender, National Electricity Authority has made it known that the first power plant will be followed by the construction of two similar plants, all this being stated in the ten-year plan for the electrification of the country. It seems very likely that the contractor selected to build the first unit, if effective, will be well positioned for the next two orders which may possibly be placed by direct agreement between contractor and owner, that is, without a competitive bidding procedure.

At the negotiating table are three representatives of the buying organization and three representatives of the BDH consortium, each one an employee of one of the companies:

1. For the buyer:
   (a) Mr Ozuwu, who is in charge of project financing for industrial development at the Ministry of Finance. He might be a useful and even necessary go-between for many red-tape problems related to administrative and financial issues which could arise when completing the project: payments, clearing customs for imported equipment, fiscal and social problems of expatriates, etc.
   (b) Mr Kempele, who is the director in charge of energy at the Ministry of Industry. He is concerned with the co-ordination of this project with the other industrialization projects being undertaken in the country. There have been many negative experiences of this in recent years: two years ago, some ships with a full load of cement were stranded in the main sea port of the country because there was not enough unloading equipment such as docks and cranes. This caused severe delays on several projects.
   (c) Mr Bura, the third representative, is 38, much younger than both Ozuwu who is about 50 and Kempele who is 60. He has been trained in Britain and the United States and holds a Master of Science degree in Electrical Engineering. At National Electricity Authority he is in charge of new plants and investment projects. He is reputed to be ambitious but also capable and hard-headed. In the long run he is seen as a possible chief executive for National Electricity Authority. Bura has confidence in the country's development projects and in the capacities of local managers to run the new plants effectively.
2. For the consortium:
   (a) Mr Smith, a project manager aged 42, who has worked for many years at Brown, the US member of the consortium. Brown will take charge of the boiler part and the plant monitoring system. Brown is ranked among the leading US engineering companies. It has a high reputation for technical excellence as well as for cost control. Project managers at Brown are partly compensated with a bonus based on the margin generated by the project. A sophisticated cost accounting system

monitors actual and forecast costs and margins regularly during the project. When projects are completed after two to three years or more, final costs are calculated, with a minimal deviation from target costs.

(b) Mr Robin from Duponval SA, a French engineer who has worked for this company for the last ten years. Duponval has already formed several joint ventures with Brown, and Robin knows Smith because they have already worked together. Duponval SA is in charge of civil engineering and the total co-ordination of the work. This firm has established a good reputation world-wide for meeting delivery times.

(c) Mr Dietermeyer, a Doctor of Law, aged 55, has worked for the last twenty years for Horst BauTechnik. Although he has not been formally trained in engineering, he has built up a good knowledge of industrial engineering on the job. In addition to this he has attended many training sessions which have provided him with an in-depth knowledge of the technologies of a large variety of turnkey plants. He is considered in his company a skilful, experienced and effective business negotiator. His law background is very useful in discussing precise clauses, understanding what is at stake and the possible legal consequences of a specific clause. Horst is in charge of supplying and installing turbo-alternators and all the electrical parts in the plant.

BDH consortium has been chosen as the contractor with which National Electricity Authority is willing to negotiate the final agreement under the supervision of the Ministry of France and the Ministry of Industry. A sum of US$105 million is the starting point for the discussion; until now it has been considered a lump sum for a turnkey operation contract. But things have not yet been fully settled.

The African team wishes to negotiate either a rebate on this price level, arguing that there will be future projects which could be awarded to BDH, or complementary services or guarantees, which could be granted for free. These might possibly be the following:

◆ The free supply of materials required for production during the start-up phase, which will last one month.
◆ Free technical assistance for the industrial management of the power plant, in order to be able to serve consumers and manage the electricity distribution network properly.
◆ A commitment from BDH to subcontract part of the job locally, especially the less sophisticated part of the civil engineering work.

BDH naturally prefers to maintain its price, for which it had been selected from the harsh competition. In fact there were some cheaper competitors, sometimes $15 million less. But neither their reference lists nor their financing deals matched BDH's bid.

To tell the truth, BDH is somewhat worried about the delay penalty clause which National Electricity Authority wants to include. The fine is supposed to be 1 per cent of the total price for each construction month beyond the standard completion time. The consortium foresees that there could be some delay. It fears that it might be difficult to assign clear responsibilities to either the contractor or the owner (or the state authorities of the country,[21] or a large subcontractor, especially if it was a local business).

The parties have agreed to discuss the issue of transforming this pure turnkey operation, paid for by a lump sum, into a 'products in hand' contract. Under this scheme, part of the payment will be subject to a variable scale related to the level of capacity reached during the management contract period after the plant has been completed and started up. The possibility of a management contract has been discussed. It will probably be added to the turnkey contract (which includes the construction start-up phase, but no more). This management contract will encompass handling the industrial management procedures, the accounting system, setting salaries, customer service and providing training programmes for local executives. Progressively, local management is supposed to take over the management of the project. The basis on which the variable payment would be calculated has not been clearly settled up to now. This basis could be: the whole amount of the management contract, part of it, or the whole amount of the management contract plus part of the $105 million turnkey project.

The African proposal for this final negotiation includes the following elements:

1. The price of the management contract plus $10 million (on top of the turnkey price) to become a variable and conditional payment, subject to the capacity level reached within a certain time span. This scheme would extend throughout the total thirty-six months of the management contract period.
2. For this variable part the proposed payment scheme is as follows:
   (a) 15 per cent after six months if the output reaches at least 50 per cent of the target capacity;
   (b) 15 per cent after twelve months if the output reaches at least 60 per cent of the target capacity;
   (c) 15 per cent after eighteen months if the output reaches at least 70 per cent of the target capacity;
   (d) 15 per cent after twenty-four months if the output reaches at least 80 per cent of the target capacity;
   (e) 20 per cent after thirty months if the output reaches at least 90 per cent of the target capacity;
   (f) 20 per cent after thirty-six months if the output reaches 100 per cent of the target capacity.
3. The management contract may grant decision-making powers to the consortium in the following matters: recruiting personnel (workers, not the management), operating the plant and choosing supplies of appropriate quality and price. The selling price of the output as well as the operating costs are to remain the sole responsibility of National Electricity Authority.

The negotiation takes place at the headquarters of National Electricity Authority in Port Kumbele, where the power plant will be built. The talks simply aim at finalizing an agreement for beginning the construction as soon as possible. No detailed agenda has been prepared for the negotiations.

Discussion begins . . . .

Recommendations for playing Kumbele Power Plant negotiation game

The objective is to simulate business negotiations for international turnkey operations. It may be played in four half-days, preferably in half-day sessions, with some time between them. Participants should first discuss between themselves as a team in order to prepare their negotiation strategies and tactics. The discussion should be centred on business negotiation. Participants should not discuss technical matters related to the plant: first, the necessary information is not included in the text and, second, it is not meant to be an engineers' discussion.

The intercultural aspect may be adapted according to participants. The characters in the game may easily be changed to women.

This game may be played as a competitive game, where two teams compete for the contract with National Electricity Authority. One team representing BDH and one team representing the Japanese engineering company (let's call it Chikoda) will face the Kumbele team.

Participants should research some information about selling turnkey projects and management services internationally. See for instance: Michael Z. Brooke, 1985, *Selling Management Service Contracts in International Business*, Holt, Rhinehart and Winston: London, or (for those who read French) Jean-Claude Usunier, 1990, *Environnement International et Gestion de l'Exportation*, Presses Universitaires de France: Paris, ch. 6.

A detailed teaching note is available in the instructor's manual as well as personal and team role instructions, a standard contract form and an evaluation sheet for the negotiators.

A13.3 Note: Cases and teaching materials for intercultural negotiation simulations

Presented below are same negotiation games. Some of them feature the following:

♦ Person-to-person (dyadic) negotiation: buyer/seller. Other games present negotiations between teams of negotiators (three facing three, for instance).
♦ Simplified negotiation situations versus contextualized negotiation situations.
♦ Marketing negotiations (sales agreement) versus business negotiations (joint-venture or licensing agreements), some situations being in-between (a turnkey operation involving a set of different contracts: a sales contract as well as technical assistance and/or licensing of technologies).

As the training group has a variable composition (in terms of size, as well as nationalities) it is advisable, for the instructors and the participants, to have a fairly good degree of flexibility and a sense of democracy in the process of assigning groups for the simulations. Participants should play fair in following the rules set by the instructor. Participants should be offered a complete debriefing after the simulation and be allowed to comment as freely as possible, because they are themselves an important part of the teaching experience. Some participants should be allocated as neutral observers (that is, silent) of the 'players' so that they may provide the group and the instructor with a report on the process of the negotiation.

The ways and means to introduce the cultural dimension are always twofold:

1. Through the specific cultures and nationalities of the participants themselves; by

reflecting with them on the influence of culture, the outcome of the games, the report of the observers and their own subjective experience.

2. Through the situation depicted by the game; the context will then be more important. But culture cannot be imitated: if the game, for instance, describes a negotiation simulation between American and Japanese people and the participants are British and German, there is no reason for participants to imitate a nationality and a culture which is not theirs.

Simplified negotiation simulations

Kelley's negotiation game (1966) is widely used for research purposes in simulated negotiation settings, with the objective of measuring the influence of various personal and/ or situational variables and strategies on the process and/or outcome of negotiation. Kelley's game (in the instructor's manual) features a face-to-face negotiation between a buyer and a seller concerning three products (vacuum cleaners, typewriters and televisions). The profit sheets generally offer a good deal of 'common ground'; the instructor may change them in order to reduce the common ground, thereby making a positive outcome less likely and the strategies more distributive.

The advantage of this game is to distinguish very clearly the integrative strategy (where people see negotiation as problem-solving and try to maximize the joint profit) from the distributive strategy (where one or both of them is/are only preoccupied with their individual profit score). It is useful to study cross-national differences in problem-solving orientation, as well as negotiation processes and outcomes in intercultural pairs (versus intracultural pairs). Rules should be carefully followed by participants; since it is an American exercise, biases may be introduced by participants of other cultures:

◆ Cheating is less immoral in many cultures than it is in the US/Anglo-Saxon culture, especially when nothing 'real' is at stake; in some cultures, participants may exchange their private information sheets (even though it is prohibited by the instructions, which are reiterated by the instructor) and find the optimum solution without really negotiating.

◆ Carefully reading instructions and following them with accuracy is possible in cultures where emphasis is put on written communication; in cultures where spoken communication is emphasized, and in fact preferred, participants may have difficulties in following the rules, just because they are not used to reading and following written instructions.

Prisoner's Dilemma

Among what Dupont (1990) calls 'experimental abstract games', one of the most well known is the Prisoner's Dilemma. Two men have robbed a bank. The clerks have been able to alert the police. The two robbers escape and hide the stolen money. Shortly afterwards they are arrested by the police. They are suspected of the hold-up, but no clerk

Table 13.2   *Prisoner's Dilemma*

		Suspect B	
		Keep silent	Avow
Suspect A	Keep silent	(1) 1yr, 1yr	(3) 20 yrs, 0
	Avow	(2) 20 yrs, 0	(4) 10 yrs, 10 yrs

in the bank succeeds in identifying them. The only charge against them is their unlawful carrying of firearms. They are placed by the police in two different cells, where they cannot communicate with each other. Each suspect may either avow (confess) or keep silent. Each one knows perfectly well the potential consequences of his act. These consequences are as follows (cf. Table 13.2):

1. If one suspect avows and his 'partner' does not, he will testify against his accomplice in exchange for the promise of being forgiven. He will be released, whereas the other one will be sentenced to twenty years in jail (2 and 3).
2. If both suspects avow, they will both be sentenced to ten years.
3. If they both keep silent, they both will be jailed for one year only; a minimal charge is being held against them, that is, the illicit carrying of firearms (1).

We may assume that they only consider their own interests. What should each criminal (player) do?

This game features the paradox between co-operation and competition, while the exchange of information is impossible between the two criminals. The simulation may be played with mono-cultural pairs versus bi-cultural pairs: the objective is to examine if cultural similarity fosters trust-building in situations where communication is virtually impossible. It may also be played with culturally different mono-cultural pairs, to examine whether trust-building is easier for some cultures than for others (the debriefing needs to be cautious).

The practical setting and procedure of Prisoner's Dilemma is as follows. Two 'criminals' are placed in two different rooms; there are two 'police constables' in charge of questioning the prisoners (and possibly influencing them). The constables may leave their prisoners in order to discuss and co-ordinate their actions. After a short time span (quarter of an hour to half an hour) outcomes may be observed: avows, if there are any, should be written down. It is in fact a quasi-negotiation where the adversaries (the prisoners) are separated from each other, with no real communication. Negotiation is implicit and communication is very instrumental (as opposed to representative, in the sense of Angelmar and Stern, 1978). This archetypal situation occurs in international business when negotiation partners are located in physically and culturally remote places.

Prisoner's Dilemma with successive rounds

In order to simulate the influence of time duration on the trust-building process, Prisoner's

Dilemma may be played with successive rounds and a very simplified scenario. Both players face each other in the same room. In each round, the players face a simple dichotomous choice: they either trust the other one or not.

- If both players trust each other, they both win three points.
- If the first player trusts the second player but the second does not trust the first, then the one who has been trustful loses six points and the one who has been distrustful wins six points.
- If they are both distrustful, they both lose three points.

The rules of the game and the stakes are known by each player from the very start; they keep records of their successful individual outcomes. After a preset number of rounds (say ten) total scores are calculated for each player. The instructor may influence the situation by setting special objectives for the players: to maximize individual scores (with intra-pair competition), or to maximize an individual combination of the joint score and the individual score; the competition is then both a cross-pair one, for a maximum joint score, and an individual competition across all participants, for maximum individual score. The instructor may also adopt other numbers for the basic scores from those indicated above.

This game is easy to transpose to a marketing or business negotiation, where co-operation/competition mechanisms are always at work. To enhance the influence of the time dimension, one may repeat the exercise (rounds are independent and the outcome is written down each time) as follows:

- With additional stakes; for example, at the fourth round, the outcomes are multiplied by two; at the eight round, they are squared.
- With complementary communication and dialogue possibilities, such as total speech prohibition at some stages and dialogue at others; the possibility of using go-betweens, etc.
- After a specific number of rounds (ten or twenty, for instance), individual scores are calculated.

This game is very useful in demonstrating the dynamic of trust and its instability in the short term, especially where there is some apparent reward for betrayal. Basic scores may be changed, for instance, so that they correspond to a negative sum game, where distrust is basically favoured. The cultural setting may be based on mono-cultural pairs (comparison across cultures) or bi-cultural pairs (interaction between two players with different cultural backgrounds). Attitudes may be compared when the group is debriefed.

'Contextual' negotiation games and negotiation cases

Participants *play roles* in simulated situations which are richer in context, inspired by actual business negotiations. Teams represent the parties as described in the case. For instance, 'Bolter Turbine, Inc., Negotiation Simulation' by John L. Graham (1984, *Journal of Marketing Education*, Spring, pp. 28–36) presents a marketing negotiation for the sales contract of industrial equipment (a gas turbine purchase by a natural-gas producer). Both teams share some common information, and each team has its own private information. The parties negotiate not only the final price, but also a whole set of technical, sales and financial conditions (options, after-sales service, delivery date, trade credit, spare parts, etc.). Once again, this negotiation game may be played by teams belonging to different national/cultural contexts, and enables players to experience and compare the process and outcomes of various teams.

The classical negotiation textbook by Roy J. Lewicki and Joseph A. Litterer, *Negotiation: Readings, exercises and cases* (1985, Richard D. Irwin: Homewood, IL) presents numerous exercises (pp. 403–500) and cases (pp. 501–62) which may be used in cross-cultural or intercultural settings. In the *Catalogue of Teaching Material* of the Harvard Business School (1990, pp. 699–700), there are a number of contextual international business negotiation cases. Some present the negotiations of a multinational company with a host country, as for example Bougainville Copper which presents in four successive stages the negotiation for the installation of a copper mine and refining plant in Papua New Guinea.

It is necessary to avoid an oversimplified view of business negotiations, which is often given by simplified negotiation games. Some articles depict complex negotiation processes where the interplay of several layers of interests and actors make the whole process fairly difficult to analyze. See, for instance, on the negotiation of a joint car factory in California by General Motors and Toyota: Stephen E. Weiss, 1987, 'Creating the GM–Toyota Joint-venture: A case in complex negotiation', *Columbia Journal of World Business*, vol. xxii, no. 2, pp. 23–37.

Notes

1. This chapter and Part Four of the book in general *are not considered as a general approach to business negotiations*. They only emphasize the intercultural aspects. For a detailed view of negotiation in general (business, marketing and sales negotiation), see Herb Cohen (1980), *You Can Negotiate Anything*, Bantam Books: New York (a small book, which offers a dynamic and illustrated approach to negotiation); or the classic textbook by Roy J. Lewicki and Joseph A. Litterer (1985), *Negotiation: Readings, exercises and cases*, Irwin: Homewood, IL. Chapter 4 of *Going International* (1986) by Lennie Copeland and Lewis Griggs, Plume Books/New American Library: New York, entitled 'Negotiation: How to win in foreign negotiations', offers a series of twenty practical rules for international business negotiation, illustrated with examples. See also McCall and Warrington (1990) and Graham and Sano (1990).
2. See Chapter 3, where cultural differences are described and categorized.
3. For a description of international turnkey operations and contractual agreements for international co-operation, see: McCall and Warrington (1990); and Stephen Young, James Hamill, Colin Wheeler and J. Richard Davies (1989), *International Market Entry and Development*, Prentice Hall: Englewood-Cliffs, NJ; or (for those who read French) Jean-Claude Usunier (1990), 'Les Grands Projets Internationaux', ch. 6 of *Environnement International et Gestion de l'Exportation*, Presses Universitaires de France: Paris.
4. As emphasized in section 1.5, a salesperson is also a marketing negotiator. Although the salesperson may have limited authority for proposing alternative offers, this autonomy always exists. The sales role cannot be restricted to persuading the buyer of the attractiveness of a fixed offer.

5. This chapter covers both marketing and business negotiations.

6. As emphasized by Burt (1982), negotiation simulations using laboratory settings are reasonable 'replications' of the real world. However, they ignore many external influences and much of the complexity involved in actual international marketing negotiations. It is therefore advisable to be cautious, especially when using simulation exercises (such as those at the end of this chapter and Chapter 14) for training future negotiators and preparing them for actual negotiations.

7. In an article from the *Journal of International Business Studies* (vol. xx, no. 3, 1989, pp. 515–37) entitled 'Cross-cultural comparison: The international comparison fallacy?', Nancy J. Adler and John L. Graham address the issue of whether these simple international comparisons are fallacies, when and if researchers are trying to describe cross-cultural interaction accurately. They demonstrate that negotiators tend to adapt their behaviour in intercultural negotiations. They do not behave as predicted by what has been observed in intracultural negotiations. Therefore their behaviour as observed in intracultural negotiations can only serve as a partial basis for the prediction of their style and strategies when negotiating with people belonging to different cultures. Graham and Adler, for instance, show that French-speaking Canadians are more 'problem solving' orientated when negotiating with English-speaking Canadians than they normally are between themselves.

8. Hence the use of the word 'intercultural', which directly relates to the study of interaction between people with different cultural backgrounds. The word 'cross-cultural' relates to a research design that is generally comparative but may also be centred on the encounter/ interaction. The latter corresponds to the term 'intercultural', where cultural differences are studied *per se*, at a deeper level than in the cross-cultural/comparative/nationality-as-a-proxy view.

9. This chapter puts little or no emphasis on negotiation tactics; more elements can be found in Chapter 4, related to communication styles, and in section 14.2 which depicts some salient elements of national styles in marketing negotiations.

10. See Chapter 8 for a definition of a symbol, with regard to colours, shapes, odours and numbers.

11. This issue is closely related to the level of power distance in a society (see Chapter 3).

12. In practice, effective negotiation combines distributive and integrative orientations simultaneously, or at different stages in the negotiation process (Pruitt, 1981).

13. The 'dual concern model' (Pruitt, 1983) explains negotiation strategies according to two basic variables: concern for one's own outcome (horizontal axis) and concern for the other party's outcome (vertical axis). This leads to four possible strategies. According to this model, the ability to envisage the other party's outcome is a prerequisite for the adoption of an integrative strategy.

```
Concern for the other
party's outcomes

 Yielding                          Integrative strategy




 Inaction                          Contending
                  Concern for one's own outcomes
```

14. Rubin and Carter (1990) demonstrate the general superiority of co-operative negotiation by developing a model whereby a new, more co-operative contract provides both the buyer and the seller with cost reduction, compared to a previous adversarial contract. There are, however,

some conditions: the first is the availability of cost-related data, the second is the release of this data to the other party during negotiation. The sharing of data is obviously conditioned by culture, language and communication-related issues.

15. Generally speaking, it is more difficult to pursue an integrative strategy in an intercultural setting than in an intracultural setting. This is due to what might be termed 'subjective border'. The 'other' is perceived as occupying a different and rival territory. Everything you possess is on your side, therefore will not be on ours. This impression is further reinforced by the atmosphere of economic war (*guerre économique* in French, 'Japan bashing' for the United States in their relations with Japan). According to this view, a potential partner belonging to another country-culture would also be a global adversary. Yet a quite different view may be held: competition is sports-based, not war-based. Competition remains peaceful and aims for the highest satisfaction of customers, in the same way as sports aims for the satisfaction of players and viewers.

16. Although appealing, similarity-based hypotheses have been poorly validated by the empirical study carried out by Campbell *et al.* (1988). No significant relationship was found among American and British buyer/seller pairs: similarity did not favour problem-solving orientation. In the case of the French and the Germans, the perceived similarity only led to a stronger problem-solving orientation on the part of the seller.

17. And not cross-cultural, as in Campbell *et al.* (1988) where the dissimilarity was strongly reduced by the fact that all the simulated negotiations were intracultural.

18. As far as I know.

19. Extract from Régina Traoré Sérié (1986), 'La Promotion du livre en Côte d'Ivoire', Paper presented to the conference on 'Marketing and Development', Abidjan (Ivory Coast), December. Quoted in Alain Ollivier and Renaud de Maricourt (1990), *Pratique du marketing en Afrique*, Edicef/Aupelf: Paris. Reproduced with permission.

20. A 'products in hand' contract is a particular kind of turnkey operation, where part of the payment by the owner to the contractor is subject to the level of performance reached by the plant. After the start-up phase has been finished and individual pieces of equipment have been shown to work effectively, a phase begins where the contractor is assigned to operations. This means that a management contract has been signed. The variable fee may cover part or all of the turnkey operations as such and/or the management contract.

21. Usually turnkey contracts include a customs franchise for all the equipment imported in order to build the plant. But it is not that rare for customs officers not to apply these rules immediately, and it may delay the customs clearance of these components and equipment, thereby delaying the completion of the plant.

References

Adler, Nancy J. (1980), 'Cultural synergy: the management of cross-cultural organizations', in W. Warner Burke and Leonard D. Goodstein (eds), *Trends and Issues in OD: Current theory and practice*, University Associates: San Diego, CA, pp. 163–84.

Angelmar, Reinhardt and Louis W. Stern (1978), 'Development of a content analysis scheme for analysis of bargaining communication in marketing', *Journal of Marketing Research*, vol. 15, February, pp. 93–102.

Arndt, Johan (1979), 'Toward a concept of domesticated markets', *Journal of Marketing*, vol. 43 (Fall), pp. 69–75.

Bagozzi, Richard P. (1975), 'Marketing as exchange', *Journal of Marketing*, vol. 39, October, pp. 32–9.

Burt, David N. (1982), 'Simulated negotiations: An experiment', *Journal of Purchasing and Materials Management* (Spring), pp. 6–8.

Burt, David N. (1984), 'The nuances of negotiating overseas', *Journal of Purchasing and Materials Management* (Winter), pp. 2–8.

Campbell, Nigel C.G., John L. Graham, Alain Jolibert and Hans Günther Meissner (1988), 'Marketing negotiations in France, Germany, the United Kingdom and United States', *Journal of Marketing*, vol. 52, April, pp. 49–62.

Cateora, Philip R. (1983), *International Marketing*, 5th edn, Richard D. Irwin: Homewood, IL.

David, René (1987), *Le Droit du commerce international, réflexions d'un comparatiste sur le droit international privé*, Economica: Paris.

De Mente, Boye (1987), *How to do Business with the Japanese*, NTC Publishing: Chicago, IL.

Druckman, D., A.A. Benton, F. Ali and J.S. Bagur (1976), 'Culture differences in bargaining behavior', *Journal of Conflict Resolution*, vol. 20, pp. 413–49.

Dupont, Christophe (1990), *La Négociation: conduite, théorie, applications*, 3rd edn, Dalloz: Paris.

Dwyer, Robert F., Paul H. Schurr and Sejo Oh (1987), 'Developing buyer–seller relationships', *Journal of Marketing*, vol. 51, April, pp. 11–27.

Evans, Franklin B. (1963), 'Selling as a dyadic relationship: A new approach', *American Behavioral Scientist*, vol. 6, May, pp. 76–9.

Fisher, Glenn (1980), *International Negotiation: A cross-cultural perspective*, Intercultural Press: Yarmouth, ME, p. 50.

Foster, G.M. (1965), 'Peasant society and the image of limited good', *American Anthropologist*, vol. 67, pp. 293–315.

Fuentes, Carlos (1986), cited in 'To see ourselves as others see us', *Time Magazine*, 16 June, p. 52.

Glenn, E. (1981), *Man and Mankind: Conflict and communication between cultures*, Ablex: Horwood, NJ.

Graham, John L. (1985), 'Cross-cultural marketing negotiations: A laboratory experiment', *Marketing Science*, vol. 4, no. 2, pp. 130–46.

Graham, John L. and Roy A. Herberger Jr (1983), 'Negotiators abroad: Don't shoot from the hip', *Harvard Business Review*, vol. 61, no. 4, pp. 160–8.

Graham, John L. and Hans G. Meissner (1986), 'Content analysis of business negotiations in five countries', working paper, University of Southern California.

Graham, John L. and Yoshihiro Sano (1990), *Smart Bargaining: Doing business with the Japanese*, 2nd edn, Ballinger: Cambridge, MA.

Hall, Edward T. (1959), *The Silent Language*, Doubleday: Garden City, NY.

Hall, Edward T. (1960), 'The silent language in overseas business', *Harvard Business Review*, May–June, pp. 87–96.

Hall, Edward T. (1976), *Beyond Culture*, Anchor Press/Doubleday: Garden City, NY.

Hall, Edward T. (1983), *The Dance of Life*, Anchor Press/Doubleday: Garden City, NY.

Harnett, Donald L. and L.L. Cummings (1980), *Bargaining Behavior: An international study*, Dame Publications: Houston, TX.

Hunt, Shelby D. (1983), 'General theories and the fundamental explanation of marketing', *Journal of Marketing*, vol. 47 (Fall), pp. 9–17.

Jackson, Barbara B. (1985), *Winning and Keeping Industrial Customers: The Dynamics of customer relationships*, D.C. Heath and Company: Lexington, MA.

Jolibert, Alain (1988), 'Le Contexte culturel de la négociation commerciale', *Revue Française de Gestion*, November–December, pp. 15–24.

Keegan, Warren J. (1984), *Multinational Marketing Management*, Prentice Hall: Englewood Cliffs, NJ.

Kelley, Harold H. (1966), 'A classroom study of the dilemmas in interpersonal negotiations', in K. Archibald (ed.), *Strategic Interaction and Conflict*, Institute of International Studies, University of California: Berkeley, CA.

Lee, James A. (1966), 'Cultural analysis in overseas operations', *Harvard Business Review*, March–April, pp. 106–11.

Levitt, Theodore (1983), *The Marketing Imagination*, Free Press: New York.

McCall, J.B. and M.B. Warrington (1990), *Marketing By Agreement: A cross-cultural approach to business negotiations*, 2nd edn, John Wiley: Chichester.

McCartney, Laton (1989), *Friends in High Places: The Bechtel story*, Ballantine Books: New York.

Macneil, Ian R. (1978), 'Contracts: Adjustments of long term economic relations under classical, neoclassical and relational contract law', *Northwestern University Law Review*, vol. 72, pp. 854–902.

Macneil, Ian R. (1980), *The New Social Contract: An inquiry into modern contractual relations*, Yale University Press: New Haven, CT.

Matthews, H. Lee, David T. Wilson and John F. Monoky Jr (1972), 'Bargaining behavior in a Buyer–Seller Dyad', *Journal of Marketing Research*, vol. 9, February, pp. 103–5.

Perdue, B.C., R.L. Day and R.E. Michaels (1986), 'Negotiation styles of industrial buyers', *Industrial Marketing Management*, vol. 15.

Pruitt, Dean G. (1981), *Bargaining Behavior*, Academic Press: New York.

Pruitt, Dean G. (1983), 'Strategic choice in negotiation', *American Behavioral Scientist*, vol. 27, no. 2, pp. 167–94.

Pruitt, Dean G. and Steven A. Lewis (1975), 'Development of integrative solutions in bilateral negotiations', *Journal of Personality and Social Psychology*, vol. 31, no. 4, pp. 621–33.

Pye, Lucian (1982), *Chinese Commercial Negotiating Style*, Oelgeschlager, Gunn and Hain: Cambridge, MA.

Pye, Lucian (1986), 'The China trade: making the deal', *Harvard Business Review*, vol. 46, no. 4 (July–August), pp. 74–84.

Rubin, J.Z. and B.R. Brown (1975), *The Social Psychology of Bargaining and Negotiations*, Academic Press: New York.

Rubin, Paul A. and J.R. Carter (1990), 'Joint optimality in buyer–seller negotiations', *Journal of Purchasing and Materials Management* (Spring), pp. 20–6.

Sawyer, J. and H. Guetzkow (1965), 'Bargaining and negotiation in international relations', in H. Kelman (ed.), *International Behavior*, Holt, Rinehart and Winston: New York.

Scanzoni, J. (1979), 'Social exchange and behavioural interdependence', in R.L. Burgess and T.L. Huston (eds), *Social Exchange in Developing Relationships*, Academic Press: New York.

Slatter, Stuart St P. (1987), 'The salesman's job in competitive bidding situations', *Industrial Marketing Management*, vol. 16, pp. 201–5.

Sullivan, Jeremiah and Richard B. Peterson (1982), 'Factors associated with trust in Japanese–American joint-ventures', *Management International Review*, vol. 22, pp. 30–40.

Triandis, Harry G. (1983), 'Dimensions of cultural variation as parameters of organizational theories', *International Studies of Management and Organization*, vol. 12, no. 4, pp. 139–69.

Tung, Rosalie L. (1984), 'How to negotiate with the Japanese', *California Management Review*, vol. xxvi, no. 4, pp. 62–77.

Usunier, Jean-Claude (1989), 'Interculturel: La Parole et L'Action', *Harvard-L'Expansion*, no. 52, March, pp. 84–92.

Usunier, Jean-Claude (1990), 'Négociation commerciale des projets: une approache interculturelle', *Revue française du marketing*, no. 127–8, pp. 167–84.

Van Zandt, H.R. (1970), 'How to negotiate with the Japanese', *Harvard Business Review*, November–December.

Walton, Richard E. and Robert B. McKersie (1965), *A Behavioral Theory of Labor Negotiations*, McGraw-Hill: New York.

Weitz, B. (1979), 'A critical review of personal selling research: the need for contingency approaches', in G. Albaum and G.A. Churchill, Jr (eds), *Critical Issues in Sales Management: State of the art and future needs*, University of Oregon: Eugene.

Williamson, Oliver E. (1983), 'Credible commitments: using hostages to support exchanges', *American Economic Review*, no. 73 (September), pp. 519–40.

14

◆◆◆

Intercultural marketing negotiations II

This chapter complements the previous one. The first two sections describe differences in cultural time patterns which affect business negotiations. Contrary to a widely held implicit assumption, people do not necessarily share the same time concepts. They do not all, for instance, feel that 'time is money', so that some nationalities may be more pressurized by time in business negotiations. According to culture, people have distinct capacities for focusing towards the past or the future. This in turn will influence their attitudes and strategies in marketing and business negotiations.

The third section of this chapter is devoted to a summary description of some basic elements of national styles in negotiation. Taking the risk of what could be termed stereotyping, the salient traits of various nationalities are described: African, American, British, Chinese, German, French, Japanese and Middle Eastern.

14.1   The cultural relativity of business time[1]

The concept of time, and therefore of time-related behaviour, has been studied in numerous fields (Jacoby *et al.*, 1976; Feldman and Hornik, 1981). Contributions are to be found in such diverse disciplines as psychology, economics, sociology, theology, linguistics, mathematics, physics, literature and anthropology.

The case of management is a particular one and deserves some special attention. Most finance, marketing or management science concepts are time-based: actualization, product life cycle and critical path method, to name but a few. Management time is indisputable; its very nature is rarely questioned. It is perceived as linear, continuous and economic. It may be qualified as 'Anglo' time (Robert J. Graham, 1981) which is typified by North-American society.

This concept of time is hidden behind almost every piece of management literature. Theories (and therefore systems) of motivation and organization which have spread all over the world originated in the United States and did not really fit the cultural context of the countries into which they have been implemented (Hofstede, 1980a, 1980b).

According to Attali (1982), our relationship with time changes with respect to periods of history and the level of human development. Thus each vision of time (*Zeitanschauung*) corresponds to a vision of the real world, its origins and destiny (*Weltanschauung*). Time appears prominently through its social functions in that it allows people to have a common organization of activities and helps to synchronize individual human behaviour (Zerubavel, 1981; Attali, 1982; Hall, 1983).

Encyclopaedic approaches to the concept of time (Attali, 1982; Pomian, 1984) show that never has one time pattern eliminated another (previous) one. Each new time pattern superimposes itself on the one which previously prevailed. As a consequence, individual time perceptions may result from adding or mixing different basic patterns of time. Most of the literature in cultural anthropology considers time perceptions as cultural artifacts. As Gurevitch states (1976, p. 229): 'Time occupies a prominent place in the "model of the world" characterizing a given culture.' Numerous anthropological observations highlight that it is impossible to assume that humans are born with any type of innate 'temporal sense'. Our concept of time is always culture-based (Hallowell, 1955). Moreover, our perception of time is limited by the cultural milieu in which we are used to living (Metraux, 1967).

Dimensions of time perceptions

Two dimensions of time perceptions have been extensively described, especially by Edward Hall (1959, 1976, 1983) and Kluckhohn and Strodtbeck (1961):

- Economicity of time.
- Monochronic versus polychronic use of time.
- Temporal orientations: towards the past, the present and the future.

Economicity of time

The United States (and also many European countries) is quite emblematic of the 'time-is-money' cultures, where time is an economic good. Since time is a scarce resource, or at least perceived as such, people should try to reach its optimal allocation between competing ways of using it. Norms tend to be very strict regarding time schedules, appointments and the precise setting of dates and durations in a society where time is strongly felt as economic. This aspect of time is near to R. J. Graham's (1981, p. 335) concept of the 'European–American (Anglo) perception that allows time to have a past, present and future, and to be sliced into discrete units and then allocated for specific tasks.' From this view, time can be saved, spent, wasted or even bought, just like money.

Monochronic versus polychronic use of time

Of particular interest to business people are the patterns of use of time, essential for tasks and communication. Hall has described two extreme behaviours of task scheduling which he calls monochronism (M time) and polychronism (P time). Individuals, working under M time, do one thing at a time and tend to adhere to preset schedules. When confronted by a dilemma (e.g. a discussion with someone that lasts longer than planned), M-time people will politely stop the conversation, in order to keep to their schedule. In M-time societies, not only the start of a meeting but also its finish will be planned. P-time, on the other hand, stresses the involvement of people who do several things at the same moment, easily modify preset schedules and seldom experience time as 'wasted'. P-time may seem quite hectic to M-time people: 'There is no recognized order as to who is to be served next, no queue or numbers indicating who has been waiting the longest' (Hall, 1983, p. 47). P-time people are more committed to persons than to schedules. When confronted with a conflict such as the one described above, they prefer to go on talking or working after preset hours and break their schedule, if they have one.

PERT (programme evaluation and review technique) programming method is an example of a typical agenda-culture, M-time and economic-time device (Usunier, 1987). It explicitly aims to reduce a universe of polychronic tasks (they really take place simultaneously, which is part of the problem) to a monochronic solution (the critical path). Management methods, basically originated in the United States and Europe, favour pure monochronic organization. They clearly push aside polychronic attitudes, which tend to make plans and schedules rather hectic if they are M-time based. When it comes to delays and being 'on time', precise monochronic systems give priority to meeting dates and commitments to schedules.

To illustrate sources of tension between people who have internalized different time systems, Hall (1983, pp. 53–4) takes the example of a monochronic woman who has a polychronic hairdresser. The woman, who has a regular appointment at a specific time each week, feels frustrated and angry when she is kept waiting. At the same time, the hairdresser also feels frustrated. He inevitably feels compelled to 'squeeze people in', particularly his friends and acquaintances. The schedule is reserved for *impersonal* people such as this woman, but since he does not know them personally, keeping to the schedule is not important to him.

Temporal orientations: past, present, future

Time perceptions also tend to be related to temporal orientations *vis-à-vis* the arrow of time. As stated by Kluckhohn and Strodtbeck (1961, pp. 13–15):

> The possible cultural interpretations of temporal focus of human life break easily into the three point range of past, present and future. . . . Spanish-Americans, who have been described as taking the view that man is a victim of natural forces, are also a people who place the present time alternative in first position. . . . Many modern European countries . . . have strong leanings to a past orientation . . . Americans, more strongly than most people of the world, place an emphasis upon the future – a future which is anticipated to be 'bigger and better'.

R. J. Graham (1981) has tried to represent a synthesis of time perception dimensions, not only as a set of different perceptual dimensions, but also as complete temporal systems. He contrasts 'Anglo' time, which he describes as being 'linear–separable', with the 'circular–traditional' time of most Latin-American countries. This perception arises from traditional cultures where action and everyday life were not regulated by the clock, but rather by the natural cycles of the moon, sun and seasons. Graham proposes a third model, 'procedural–traditional', in which the amount of time spent on the activity is irrelevant, since activities are procedure-driven rather than time-driven. This system is typical of the American Indians, and to a large extent it also typifies Bantu time.[2] Graham's (1981) 'procedural–traditional' time is hardly a 'time', with the meaning that we Western people attribute to the word.

Naturally, some people may share different cultures and move from one time model to another, depending on the other people involved and the particular situation, using different types of 'operating cultures' (Goodenough, 1971). As Hall states (1983, p. 58): 'The Japanese are polychronic when looking and working inward, toward themselves. When dealing with the outside world ... they shift to the monochronic mode. ... The French are monochronic intellectually, but polychronic in behaviour.'[3]

14.2 Time-based misunderstandings in international business negotiations

Management cannot easily admit that there may be other models of time than those on which it implicitly stands. Naturally it would be naive to consider that, for example, nowadays Bantu people (see Box 4.1 and section A4.1), especially those who are involved in some form of international business, have purely traditional time patterns such as those that have been previously described.

In fact, complex patterns of time-related behaviours may be used by people sharing several cultural backgrounds, one of them being the original in-depth background, the other(s) being much more superficial. Furthermore the original cultural background may be undervalued for many reasons: its 'inefficiency', its 'bone-in-the-nose' look or the simple fact that it is unknown to foreigners. Accordingly, people of non-Western cultures often have a tendency simply to ape the cultural way of life that they tend to favour as the 'best' way. It might result in buying a superb watch as an item of jewellery or a diary because it is fashionable. But the functional behaviour which is in line with the watch or the diary will not be adopted. After these objects have been bought, they lose their cultural value as practical tools of the economic/monochronic/linear/separable time pattern. People involved in such ambiguous cultural borrowing might prove unable to take any appointment seriously. They will probably experience difficulties in following any preset schedule.

Even those with a genuinely double cultural background do not find it easy to merge two quite different time patterns. This is the problem of operating culture (Goodenough, 1971). People move from one cultural background to another depending on the other people involved and the particular situation. It does not dictate which situations are in line with which cultural behaviour and who must adapt. Shared prejudices of the relative ability of different cultures to deal with real-world problems have a definite influence on the choice of the common culture by business partners.

Ideal patterns and actual behaviour

The idea of possible discrepancies between ideal patterns and actual behaviour was expressed by Linton (1945, pp. 52–4):

> All cultures include a certain number of what may be called ideal patterns. ... They represent the consensus of opinion on the part of the society's members as to how should people behave in particular situations ... comparison of narratives usually reveals the presence of a real culture pattern with a recognizable mode of variation ... it [the ideal pattern] represents a desideratum, a value, which has always been more honoured in the breach than in the observance.'

In everyday management behaviour (appointments, scheduling, meetings) it is quite probable that we face a high level of cultural borrowing. Actual time behaviour of successful (from an economic and managerial point of view, in the long run) countries like the United States or countries of northern Europe might well have been imported by other nations as ideal patterns.[4]

It is, for instance, very clear that in France and other Latin-European countries (not to mention the Bantu countries, some of which we colonized) PERT technique, which is designed for the scheduling of interrelated tasks, has been implemented mostly for its intellectual appeal. PERT is based on graph theory, and has an appealing US 'management science' look. In France,[5] where many managers and top executives have been trained as engineers, there has been a great interest in this scientific management technique. Real project planning in France and Latin-European countries very often works with high discrepancies relative to PERT dates. As noted previously, French people tend to be intellectually monochronic but actually behave in a polychronic manner (Hall, 1983).

Sometimes people even use two completely different systems in parallel.[6] This somewhat schizophrenic situation is most easily recognized by looking at the construction of some turnkey projects in developing countries (CNUCED, 1978; Tiano, 1981). At the beginning, during the negotiation process and on signature of the contract, everybody seemingly (and also sincerely) agrees about using economic time/monochronic pattern. In fact the partners share the same belief, but as an ideal pattern on one side and as an actual behaviour on the other. There may not even be discussion about it: obviously it is the right way to proceed. But afterwards extreme confusion appears when the project is being implemented.

Some have an actual economic time pattern whereas others talk about ideal economic time and act in a polychronic/non-economic manner, which is much more their normal style. A high level of misunderstanding is usually generated by this very process. As Deutscher states (1973, p. 163):

> The peculiar relationship between what men say and how they otherwise behave is, or ought to be, a focal concern of the social sciences. ... There is no theoretical basis for assuming that what people say correlates with whatever else they may do. ... In fact sometimes they do as they say, sometimes they do not, and sometimes they do the exact opposite.

These discrepancies between words and deeds (Deutscher, 1966; Usunier, 1989) are more or less a universal phenomenon.[7] In fact not only is economic time borrowed as an ideal pattern, but non-economic/polychronic patterns also seem to be borrowed by those who are actually economic-time minded.[8]

The pressure of time as 'wasted time'

The expression 'to waste time' has little meaning for Bantus. One may lose something tangible, like a ring or a pencil. But in order to waste and lose time, time should be a thing or – at least – it would be necessary to be able to separate time from the events with which it is inextricably bound up. Indeed the Bantus find it difficult to equate abstract time with a monetary unit of measurement. As outlined previously, within their culture Bantu people know nothing comparable to a linear Newtonian time, where events take place. There are events, and each one of these events carries its own desire and its own time. Time cannot be wasted or lost, because time has simply to be lived or experienced, whatever may be the way to experience it. No one can steal time, not even death.

The same quietness in the face of time may be seen in the Orient, compared to the Occidental anguish and guilt about time that might be wasted or lost. Several authors in the field of international business negotiations note that time pressure is strongly felt by American negotiators, whether they negotiate with the Chinese (Pye, 1982) or with the Japanese (John L. Graham, 1981; Graham and Sano, 1990; Tung, 1984a, 1984b). American negotiators are eventually forced to yield by their representation of time, potentially wasted or lost if it is not optimally allocated. When this logic is pushed to its extreme it may result in total inefficiency. People spend their whole time thinking of possible alternative uses of their time and calculating which of these alternatives offers the best marginal return.

As noted by Adler (1986, p. 162):

> Americans' sense of urgency disadvantages them with respect to less hurried bargaining partners. Negotiators from other countries recognize Americans' time consciousness, achievement orientation, and impatience. They know that Americans will make concessions close to their deadline (time consciousness) in order to get a signed contract (achievement orientation).

14.3   Some elements of the national style of business negotiation

The interaction between cultures in negotiation triggers a specific situation where the image of the other negotiating party is very important: in other words, a collection of stereotypes, often meaningful, that form a portrait of the national culture of the other party. This exercise in mutual reflection is best illustrated by referral to what was observed by the negotiators in Burt (1984).[9]

It is unlikely that an Italian or a Spaniard, for example, would have an identical perception of the French negotiation style to Burt's (rather caricatured) perception. It is therefore necessary to use a matrix to effectively describe the negotiating style of any particular country as that style can only be defined through the perception of another country: for example, the Italian style can be defined in terms of how it is perceived by the Americans, by the French, etc. The complexity of this perception is demonstrated not in the abstract, but in its application in the interaction between cultures. Various notable elements of national styles of business negotiation are set out below (they are obviously inextricably linked to national mentality) but it is not claimed that the list is exhaustive.

Japanese style

Numerous books are devoted to consideration of the Japanese style of negotiation and more generally to the Japanese mentality and style of management.[10] Several major traits can be distinguished:

- The Japanese are well prepared, particularly from the point of view of familiarity with the culture of the people with whom they are dealing (Tung, 1984a). They are a highly ethnocentric people who are, paradoxically, at the same time very conscious of this ethnocentrism. They are also well prepared as far as definition of their basic interests is concerned and are willing to struggle quite bitterly to defend them.
- The purchaser's role is predominant. Vendors must be fully aware of this fact and adapt their behaviour accordingly (John L. Graham, 1981).
- Although at heart they are very sensitive and emotional, they seek to conceal their true emotions as far as possible (Burt, 1984; see also section 4.3). Like all Asiatics they must not be made to 'lose face': in practice (at the very least) their foreign counterparts should avoid a style of communication that would be resented by the Japanese as being too direct.
- Within a group of Japanese negotiators it is difficult to determine who really performs what function and who holds what power; it is always unwise to rely solely on 'who says what' as a clear indication of 'who holds power'.
- Japanese negotiators display quite a high level of tolerance of ambiguity. Whereas ambiguity may be perceived by Americans as a sign of weakness and a lack of masculinity and assertiveness, the Japanese do not see ambivalent behaviour as contradictory to masculinity (Hawrysh and Zaichkowsky, 1990).
- Japanese people are very long-term orientated. In large companies lifetime employment is the rule. These companies are often backed by large banks which, as the shareholders, do not strive for a quick return. They are both more concerned with the soundness of the long-term business strategy of the company to whom they lend. This partly explains why Japanese negotiators do not feel as strongly pressured by time lines as their Western counterparts.
- Like most Asians, the Japanese tend to prefer an agreement based on trust to a written contract. Even though this agreement may be loosely worded, in their view it is a better expression of the mutual trust that has developed between the parties (Oh, 1986).
- The empathy of Japanese people may be very high: the interpersonal sensitivity of Japanese people and their sincere interest in foreign cultures and people may make them

friendly hosts at business lunches or dinners. As emphasized by Hawrysh and Zaichkowsky (1990, p. 30): 'Before entering serious negotiations, Japanese business-men will spend considerable time and money entertaining foreign negotiating teams', in order to get to know their negotiating partners and establish with them a rapport built on friendship and trust. But it should never be forgotten that Japanese negotiators remain down-to-earth: they are strongly aware of what their basic interests are.[11] They are reputed to be tough negotiators.

French style[12]

* The French are said to be somewhat difficult to negotiate with. As noted earlier, the French tend to be ideologists and find it difficult to 'accept facts, no matter how convincing they may be. Although they may consider themselves to be experts at negotiating, at times they tend to be amateurish and inadequately prepared' (Burt, 1984, p. 6).
* The fact that the French are conflict-prone, do not mind confrontation and sometimes even enjoy it, is confirmed by Weiss and Stripp (1985) who describe the French negotiating style as competitive and inherently confrontational. They also tend to use emotional and theatrical ways of behaving in negotiation.
* In France (as in Britain) social class remains an important feature of society. Social-status consciousness is very strong in France, as is power distance (see Chapter 3). French negotiators are sensitive to the organizational status of their foreign counterparts, requiring equivalence.
* France is still one of the most centralized nations in the world, with a very long tradition of Paris-based decision-making (inaugurated by Hughes Capet, in 987!). High-ranking civil servants (*énarques* and *polytechniciens*) have a substantial say in business deals which involve large companies and their subsidiaries.
* At times, some French negotiators may be resented as arrogant and disdainful:[13] in a very high-power-distance society, which is at the same time individualistic, power display may be exacerbated, to the detriment of politeness and courtesy.
* Burt (1984, pp. 6–7) complements his view of the French negotiation style as follows:

> The French seem to enjoy negotiating for its own sake. When they are in the mood – sometimes for several days – very little progress is made. Sooner or later though, they tire of the game and want to reach closure. A careful count of the numbers of cigarettes consumed per hour serves as an indication of the restlessness and the willingness to make concessions in order to reach closure. Leisure time and the desire for the 'good life' are key motivators. An awareness of these motivators can be useful in reaching agreement, as is indicated in the following dialogue:
> American: 'We need to reach agreement, since I've booked us at (the Frenchman's favourite restaurant). But we can't go until we reach agreement on these remaining issues.'
> Frenchman: 'I agree. Let's go!'

Chinese style

One of the main experts in business negotiation with the Chinese, Lucian W. Pye (1982, 1986) lists the following factors, which combine to demonstrate that the Chinese are tactical, skilful and fairly tough negotiators:

◆ 'As hosts, the Chinese take advantage of their control over the pace of negotiations. First they set the agenda, then they suggest that the Americans start the discussions ... their proposals become the starting point from which all compromise follows.' (Pye, 1986, p. 77).

◆ The Chinese deliberately adopt a fairly passive attitude, taking care not to show enthusiasm, covering up any feeling of impatience, playing their game impassively so as to force their opponents to be the first to show their hand.

◆ They do not shy away from appearing very manipulative: with a view to disconcerting the other side and in the ultimate hope of obtaining further concessions, they will attribute an exaggerated importance to minor details, which in reality are of no consequence to them, or return to discussion of points where full agreement seemed to have previously been reached.

◆ The bureaucratic orientation is often noted:[14] socialism has imposed strong government control on industry. As a consequence, Chinese negotiators tend not to be capable of individual decision-making. Before any agreement is reached, official government approval must be sought by Chinese negotiators (Eiteman, 1990).

◆ Chinese business people tend to overrate the advantage offered by their large population in terms of market opportunities. However, per capita purchasing power remains quite low. The Chinese promote their country as being 'the last big market on the planet' but underestimate the opportunities offered to their foreign partners by other countries (Eiteman, 1990).

◆ Like the Japanese, the Chinese are less economic-time minded and less short-term orientated than Westerners. 'The Chinese use time shrewdly. If they sense that business people are in a hurry to leave China, they may slow down negotiations and turn the deadline to their advantage' (Pye, 1986, p. 78).

◆ Pye also notes the role played by differences of attitude relating to the concept of 'friendship'. Thus it seems that whereas the Americans view friendship in terms of a feeling which rests on a natural mutual exchange, in other words on a principle of reciprocity, the Chinese view friendship in terms of loyalty. The idea is that of a long-lasting obligation:

> What the Chinese neglect in terms of reciprocity they more than match in loyalty. They not only keep their commitments, but they also assume that any positive relationship can be permanent. A good example of this is the number of Chinese who have tried to establish pre 1949 ties with U.S. companies and individuals – as though nothing had happened in the intervening days.' (Pye, 1986, p. 79).

American style

The American style is orientated towards several major aspects which are linked to the US national character, namely: individualism, with the emphasis on ability, competence, decision-making and explicit communication. As a consequence American negotiators usually possess the following qualities: seriousness, pragmatism and accuracy in writing clauses. American negotiators have fairly well-defined autonomy and room for manoeuvre, but clear limits are also set, and they have to report to their principals. In the negotiation process, Americans often consider that decisions have to be made on the spot by the individual who has the most expertise or responsibility in a given area (Beliaev *et al.*, 1985).

- Professionalism is a quality that is very widely recognized in Americans. In business negotiation, it means careful selection of the negotiators and methodical preparation of files.
- In their failure to take sufficient account of the culture of other parties (Tung, 1984b), the Americans, like the French, are an 'ethnocentric–missionary' people. They are quite convinced (as are the French) that their system is the 'one best way', and that the other peoples of the world would do well to adopt their system of values and behaviour.
- A great deal of attention is (pragmatically) paid to precise issues to be debated, to facts and evidence, to an attitude orientated towards matter-of-fact discussions and to a tight negotiation time schedule. This renders them susceptible to becoming irritated by negotiating parties that are more interested in general principles or even logical reasoning (the French, for example; Burt, 1984). This may also lead to their interpretation of the attitudes of their negotiating counterparts who have a non-linear style as delaying tactics. They will resent global negotiation as a way of reconsidering what has already been decided and as a failure to respect preset agenda.
- A strong positive emphasis is placed on frankness and sincerity; Americans show willingness to make the first move by disclosing their position in the hope (sometimes unfulfilled) that their adversary will do likewise. They are also prepared to adopt the 'John Wayne Style' (Graham and Herberger, 1983; see Box 13.2), by pushing frankness to the bounds of arrogance. This can shock people from cultures where self-assertion must be contained within strict limits.
- A genuine naivety, ingenuousness and a 'retarded adolescent' style (noted by Margaret Mead, see Chapter 3) can sometimes lead Americans to choose positions that are very tough be cause they are – genuinely – disappointed. This occurs mainly when, having demonstrated their – genuine – sincerity, they then feel that they have been badly treated, by being taken advantage of their open-mindedness. However sincerity and frankness are by no means universal cultural values, contrary to what a good number of Americans may believe.
- Equality between purchaser and vendor, and 'let the best man win' (Adler, 1986). This can surprise people who deal with Americans, since Americans value personal assertiveness and can therefore appear tough: there is little sympathy for anyone who loses. In the US business mentality, no consolation prizes are won by 'losers'.
- The Americans are supposed to be informal in everyday life. In fact, compared to other peoples, they are formal in different areas. When it comes to negotiating agreements, they are quite formal and anxious about the preciseness and explicitness of written contracts which are therefore drawn up with care. These contracts, the law between the parties, are also the basis for attitudes which are readily orientated towards recourse to litigation and legal battles with the assistance of lawyers.

◆ As noted earlier, Americans tend to be short-term orientated. In the American–Vietnamese negotiations at the end of the Vietnam War, Americans booked hotel rooms for a week, whereas the Vietnamese rented a château for a year (Adler, 1986). The US time pressure in business may be easily explained by the quarterly reporting system to the shareholders and the Stock Exchange. US companies depend more strictly on the financial markets; labour mobility is high. Accordingly people must get quick results, and show a faster return than their foreign counterparts. This 'short-termism' tends to disadvantage them in negotiations.

German style

◆ The German love of formality is one of the first elements that stands out clearly. For example, the title of *Doktor*, even *Professor Doktor*, is a recognized sign of ability and will be employed. Formality and the presence of constraining rules (which are generally respected) in the decision-making process on the German side are characteristics of the German system which seeks to avoid uncertainty (as defined by Hofstede, 1980b). These rules are often the end result of a reasonably solid consensus. The respect for accepted rules is more interiorized by the Germans than forced upon them.

◆ Decisions in a German company are taken at a fairly slow pace. The machine is 'well-oiled', but it is also rather cumbersome. A fairly substantial number of signatures will be required for any final agreement.

◆ Great pride is taken in the technical quality of products manufactured in Germany; thus a reaction of disbelief is instinctively provoked when a German is faced with something that originates from abroad and which fails to conform, for example, to the DIN standards. As a result, readiness to participate in detailed discussions with technical experts is essential.

◆ German earnestness is no myth. The Germans are people who keep their word, and who will respect the agreement made, whether it takes a written or an oral form. They loathe anything that approaches flippancy, in particular negotiation for negotiation's sake, or indeed the failure to keep to appointments.[15] Germans, when they negotiate with the Italians or the French, often resent their Latin counterparts' unreliability in keeping to their commitments.

◆ Explicit communication, and a temporal style that is clearly monochronic (Hall, 1983).

◆ The role of emotions and friendship (in negotiations) is fairly limited: in the process of negotiations, Germans keep their distance. They feel that a personal relationship could interfere with the result of their work (Schmidt, 1979).

◆ There is a very ambiguous halo around the perception of Germans by other people: Germans are both admired and disliked. As stated by Barzini (1983, p. 94),[16] this 'has its roots not only in their less amiable traits – arrogance, tactlessness and obtuseness – but also in their great virtues, their excellence in almost al! fields.' Germans should be considered as individuals more than any nationality in the world. This is the best way to avoid negative bias when negotiating with Germans, who, after all, are not personally responsible for every event of German history.

British style

Together with the French,[17] the British are those who have been most affected by their tradition of diplomatic negotiation. The British Empire and the influence of the United Kingdom have affected the British style. It is characterized by the following:

- A 'soft-sell' approach (Cateora, 1983) which is essential. British coolness is not an empty phrase. An air of confidence, restraint and calm is essential for any negotiators in the position of seller. They must never be seen to be pushy in negotiation.
- The English have the reputation of being less motivated by money than the Americans; with the relative decline of Great Britain, they are more inclined towards their free time; companies are often full of administrative personnel. This situation has a tendency to slow down the decision-making process significantly (Burt, 1984).
- The study carried out by Campbell *et al.* (1988), using the vehicle of a simulated negotiation (Kelley, 1966), demonstrates that the factor that has the strongest influence on negotiation in Great Britain is the role of negotiator (purchaser or vendor). In the negotiation simulation, British purchasers obtained slightly superior results to vendors of the same nationality. This is consistent with the reputation of the British of having a 'soft-sell' type of approach, where the vendor must take care not to annoy the purchaser by being too pushy, turning up too often, making too many proposals or by adopting an attitude that is too action-orientated.
- Although seemingly closest to the Americans, the British are not necessarily those who resemble them the most in the field of business practice. They are usually more contextual in communication and indirect, hence a willingness to try to interpret the British position in business negotiation is essential.
- Language-related issues (the style of writing clauses, for instance) are treated very differently by the British and the Americans. Whereas US people easily accept a somewhat simplified 'international English' that will be used for drafting agreements, the British, like the French, take pride in correct language, and are sensitive to style for style's sake.

Middle Eastern style (Arab-Islamic world)

If a 'Middle Eastern style' truly exists, it would display some basic characteristics:

- The countries considered here are almost exclusively Arab-Islamic countries, except for Persia which is affected by Shi'ite Islam but which is not Arab, and Turkey which is Ottoman and Islamic but not Arab and has dominated the Arab world for centuries. Yet it would be a mistake to ignore the enormous diversity of the Middle East. Christian minorities (Lebanese Maronites, Egyptian Copts, Iraqi Nestorians, Armenians, members of the Orthodox churches, etc.) are present almost everywhere and influential in some countries.[18] These religions are in fact fully integrated in the Middle East. It is therefore essential to be fully aware of the fact that a world that is somewhat hastily classified as Arab-Islamic is also composed of Arabs that are not Muslims and Muslims that are not Arabs.

- The importance of 'concrete territorialities': knowledge of the subgroup to which the negotiator belongs is essential; the relationships between the parties must be explored with great care, to find out who is who and what relationship each negotiator has with the different groups.
- The role of intermediaries ('sponsors' in Saudi Arabia) is very important. As a result of European colonization over the last two centuries, the majority of 'Middle Eastern' business people speak French or English and understand European civilization; whereas the reverse is rarely true. Intermediaries must be employed for a simple reason: we (the Europeans and Americans) systematically underestimate the cultural divide.
- It must always be borne in mind that Middle Eastern civilizations were largely the founders of those in Europe. They have left many traces behind, and as far as art and culture are concerned, their influences were dominant for many centuries during the Middle Ages. The pride of the person with whom you are dealing must be – truly – respected.
- One must expect a great deal of emotion, theatricality and demonstrativeness, interspersed with true pragmatism. The mixture is often bewildering. Friendship is sought, relationships are personalized, and the idea of a cold 'business-like' relationship is difficult to envisage. Once a true friend has been made (which is far from straightforward), the sense of loyalty can be very strong.
- As has already been emphasized, Islamic values permeate daily life.[19] For example, if the negotiations lead to consideration of a loan and interest rate, although this problem is not insurmountable, a great deal of caution is essential. The question of *riba*, which is usually translated as 'interest', never fails to pose problems for Koranic law and the different legislative assemblies entrusted with its interpretation. These assemblies have been more or less strict in their interpretation of *riba*, which is mentioned several times in the Koran, as being forbidden. Thus specific financial operations, excluding the imposition of a method of repayment for loans which is fixed in advance, have been settled in accordance with Islamic law and on the basis of ancient practices: *mudaraba, musharaka, ijara, murabaha* and *qard hasan* (Naulleau, 1985).

Black African style

- Black Africans' love of talking is always amazing for those used to 'useful speech'. Africans simply do not have the same relationship to the universe as Europeans and Americans do. Differences relate to basic concepts such as time and space (see section 14.1 and Chapter 4). Poetry has a powerful meaning for Africans. The African is a very verbal person: language (Africans are almost all polyglots) is an instrument for the enjoyment of the pleasure of speaking. As a result, negotiations can sometimes seem to be rather ill-directed, not purely because Africans enjoy debating, but also because they enjoy speaking.
- There is an absence of a strictly economic individual motivation:

  > Money does not have the same value as in Europe. Westerners are accustomed to an age-old tradition of exchange based on money which has acquired a strong symbolic value as reward for work, as a means of saving, as a measure of personal success and as the fair

price of things ... [in Africa] attitudes towards money follow different rules. Money is only a means of obtaining enough for survival and projection of self-image, whereas its other attributes fade into the background ... this money is taken without remorse, and in good humour [the 'baksheesh' that is – see Chapter 15], and usually benefits not just the person who receives it but also the whole family. The African system of distribution functions in such a way that money goes to the one who needs it: the employee whose salary does not allow him to live decently, the high-ranking civil servant who supports a large family in the village for example. (Gruère and Morel, 1991, pp. 122–3).

- The reality of tribes and the group is never to be ignored: during the process of business negotiations, the influence of the family and ethnic background will inevitably make its presence felt, whether it be through the participants or the beneficiaries of its results.
- The concept of time is simply not the same. This has a direct influence on the progress of business negotiations.
- As Gruère and Morel (1991) emphasize, Black Africa is a mosaic, involving various characteristics of diversity: ethnic, religious (Christianity, Islam, animism) and linguistic. There too, as in the Middle East, a map of the 'human landscape' must be prepared in advance. In the West, we rarely consider people first as members of their tribe. People tend to be considered purely as individuals. The advantage has been the growth in tolerance and the reduction in violence between groups whose identity conflicts. The disadvantage has been the increase in individual isolation, since individuals are significantly less supported in their personal life by the in-group.

APPENDIX 14

◆◆◆

Teaching materials

A14.1 Negotiation stimulation: Lump Sum

Emergency meeting of representatives from (state assemblies on educational planning for Malaysia)

You have been called together in this special emergency meeting to represent the unique interests of your (constituencies) in making an extremely important decision. The future of our (country) may depend on your decision today and the unique opportunity presented to us.

A representative of the (United Nations' Special Fund) has today informed me that due to bureaucratic oversight there is (US$10,000,000) which has not been allocated in the budget for any specific project and which is available for the use (of Malaysia) *provided* that you can make a rapid decision on allocation of those funds and inform (the Secretary-General of the United Nations in New York) by this afternoon. We have an open telephone line to (the Secretary-General's office) to notify him as soon as a decision is made. The representative apologized for the urgency of this request but the fiscal year for the (United Nations) ends to night and all funds already appropriated but not allocated to specific projects by that time will revert to the (United Nations General Fund) and will not be available for (Special Fund).

For the sake of speed and the fair allocation of the money, special representatives (from the various state assemblies of Malaysia) have been called together today to draw up a specific allocation of the money. The (United Nations) does not care how the money is allocated but (for the sake of national unity and the good of the whole country) they stipulate *absolutely* that you *must* come to a unanimous agreement on your decision within the time limit or lose the money.

(The United Nations) agrees to abide by whatever allocations you *unanimously* decide on within the next (ninety minutes).

You are already divided into your (six State Assembly) groupings:

1. Sarawak-Sabah.
2. Perak-Penang-Province Wellesley.
3. Kelantan-Trengganu.
4. Pahang-Johore.
5. Negri Sembilan-Malacca.
6. Kedah-Perlis.

For the sake of a speedy decision, each group will select its own negotiator and the (six) negotiators will carry out the actual negotiations on allocation of the money.

Because only (two hours) can be allowed to reach a conclusion, we have established a timetable which *must* be rigidly adhered to. You will have adequate time to express the proposal of your delegation, to present your proposal to the group, and to negotiate privately as well as publicly with other delegations towards unanimous agreement. While the actual negotiations will take place through your elected negotiator, you may, if the majority of the delegation is dissatisfied with his performance, replace your representative with someone else selected by the majority of your delegation.

Your timetable is as follows:

1. (*Twenty minutes*): Each delegation will meet together and settle among themselves who will be the negotiator representing them in the negotiations, and draw up specific plans for how the entire ($10,000,000) ought to be divided and allocated according to the needs of the entire (country) and the special concerns of your own (constituency).
2. (*Eighteen minutes*): In the first Negotiation Session, each representative will be given three minutes to report on how his delegation proposes to allocate the money. There will be no discussion among the representatives but each representative will be given opportunity to explain the merits of his delegation's allocation of the money to the assembled company.
3. (*Ten minutes*): In the first consultation, representatives will go back to their own delegation for ten minutes to consult with them on strategy, presentation, any changes in their proposals they may want to make, and private consultation with members of other groups.

4. (*Ten minutes*): In the second Negotiation Session, representatives will present any modifications which may have been made on the basis of having heard the other representatives' proposals or on the basis of the consultations which have just taken place.
5. (*Ten minutes*): In the second consultation, further modifications in each group's proposals can be made. Also, this is the time to consult again with other groups on any private compromises which may be proposed to secure their co-operation.
6. (*Twenty minutes*): In the third Negotiation Session, representatives will discuss and present their final and presumably unanimously agree upon a proposal for the allocation of the ($10,000,000).

Instructions for the role-play of this simulated situation of conflict among competing interest groups are available in the instructor's manual.

Two alternative seating arrangements for Lump Sum

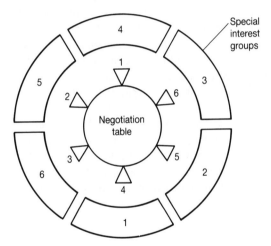

Figure 14.1   Lump Sum: first alternative seating arrangement.

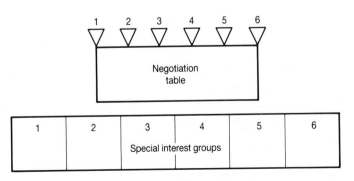

Figure 14.2   Lump Sum: second alternative seating arrangement.

(Adapted from 'Lump Sum: A bargaining simulation game design', by Professor Marshall R. Singer and Dr Paul B. Pedersen, 1970, Kuala Lumpur, Malaysia, in William H. Weeks, Paul B. Pedersen and Richard W. Brislin, 1987, *A Manual of Structured Experiences for Cross-Cultural Learning*, Intercultural Press: Yarmouth, ME. Reproduced with the kind permission of the publisher.)

A14.2 Case: Tremonti SpA

Tremonti SpA was a small company located in the suburbs of Milan. Like many small and medium enterprises in the northern part of Italy, it specialized in special machines and mechanical engineering. Tremonti SpA had developed a sophisticated knowledge in the production of machines for assembling electronic components.

The company had been founded by an *ingeniere*, Mr Stefanini, who owned the business and gave it its technological drive. Until now he had always made the choice to invest more money in research and development than in production operations. The company therefore cared more about prototypes than mass production (if that means anything in an industry where world-wide markets rarely exceed tens or hundreds of machines).

A large part of the production was in fact subcontracted. This made factory investments lighter and gave production flexibility in the face of unsteady demand. But subcontracting about 60–80 per cent of the parts and a large amount of the assembly work was not satisfactory in that it made it difficult to follow and monitor production schedules accurately.

The export manager, Mr Lesca, had considerably increased export sales during the last five years. Export sales at Tremonti SpA were 80 per cent of the total corporate sales figure. Clients were mostly located in the United States and in Europe, with a very small proportion in Japan. Lesca's team was composed of two export salesmen, who had a technical background and provided maintenance for machines located abroad, and two English-speaking secretaries who were in charge of export logistics and paperwork.

I

Lesca was worried by a problem with an American customer. The American had already bought one machine from Tremonti SpA and was very satisfied with it. It worked at full capacity, it had been delivered on time and it was reliable. Then he ordered a second machine, which was now in the production process.

Unfortunately, according to the manufacturing department, the production of this machine seemed to be delayed by four to six weeks from the agreed delivery date. Yet the American customer was willing to order a third machine, since the first one had been working satisfactorily for the last six months. He did not know about a possible delay for the second machine.

Lesca wondered what he should do:

1. Should he tell the American customer about the delivery delay of the second machine, during his next visit to negotiate the sale of the third machine? The agreed delivery date

of the second machine is six weeks after the next visit of Lesca to his American customer.

2. If yes, how should he announce it?

II

Finally, after the visit had taken place, Lesca was satisfied with the tactics he had adopted. He felt a need to extract some more stable principles out of this communication experience. When flying back from the United States, he wondered how he should have acted with people from the following national/cultural backgrounds: German, Japanese and Saudi Arabian.

III

Demand had been growing quickly. Since Tremonti SpA's machines were up-to-date and reliable, they were especially sought out. But delivery delays were increasing. A conversation with a German customer, Herr Weisslinger, gave him another opportunity to become aware of the high level of sensitivity of clients to their suppliers meeting delivery dates.

'You Italians,' began Weisslinger, 'you do not really know what a delivery date is. There are huge differences between the delivery date agreed upon when signing the contract and the actual delivery date. And you wait until the last minute to tell us that you won't be able to meet your delivery date. Sometimes you do not even report it and we have to send you a fax to try to find out when the machine will be delivered. Yet it should already have been delivered, and we are not even informed.'

'No, you carry it too far,' answered Lesca. 'I do not believe that we deliberately miss delivery dates. You have to understand: a delivery date is indicative. When ordering, a date is fixed that best suits the client. We indicate the delivery date that we think we are able to meet. Numerous hazards may then occur. Our suppliers and subcontractors do not adhere strictly to their delivery dates, and this causes a large part of our own delays.'

'If I understand you correctly, we have to take things as they are,' said Weisslinger.

'I am afraid so,' replied Lesca. 'I am the personal advocate of our clients within the company. But, you know, my authority is limited, and the Italian national character values deadlines and time precision far less than Anglo-Saxons do. Moreover it is an organizational problem: everybody has to feel committed if we want to achieve a greater respect for delivery dates.'

'Yes indeed,' said Weisslinger, 'I think your machines are of good quality and your maintenance and after-sales service are OK. But your competitors provide equal qualities and they meet their deadlines. We have to make rational choices. You do not meet your delivery dates.'

Mr Lesca is now wondering how he should allocate his efforts. Should he go on playing the role of a 'trade ambassador', trying diplomatically to make the foreign clients accept delays? Should he, on the contrary, spend more time in the company and undertake action to improve the organizational functioning for delivery dates? How should he tackle the issue with Stefanini? Which ways and means would be sufficient to improve the commitment to delivery dates?

IV

Some time after this conversation with Weisslinger, Lesca went to Japan for a business trip, where he had the opportunity to present Tremonti SpA's technical achievements. On his return from Japan, he went to Stefanini's office to discuss the potential of the Japanese market. 'We did place some orders there, but they are small compared to the total Japanese market, and particularly small when compared to the sales we achieved in the United States. I have had preliminary talks with a large electronics company called Nokan. We examined the possibility of a marketing joint-venture, which would be responsible for selling and servicing our machines on the Japanese market. It looks fine; but I know that Japanese people are not easy to deal with. They are extremely polite, courteous and gentle, but what are their real intentions? Frankly, I do not trust them. Besides, they have a reputation for ransacking technologies, and it is a fundamental that we protect our knowledge base.'

Stefanini wanted to prepare for the negotiation of this marketing joint-venture. He asked Lesca the following questions:

1. 'How can we get information about Japanese culture?'
2. 'Which aspects are relevant to our problem?'

Notes

1. The first section of this chapter partly derives from Usunier (1991).
2. Time representations are conveyed by the means of language, as a means of communication and therefore collective action. See Box 4.1.
3. Let me take a personal example (illustrating the intellectual monochronic/behaviourally polychronic French time style): I use a diary where I keep a record of my (future) appointments, meetings and commitments: but I rarely look at it. It is aimed more at memorization, than at actually managing my schedule. Therefore, sometimes, I may forget appointments.
4. In an attempt to capture empirically the differences in business time patterns, a psychometric scale which opposes non-economic/polychronic time against economic/monochronic time was developed (Usunier, 1991), following Hall's conceptions of time-related cultural patterns (Hall, 1973, 1983). One of the items of this questionnaire was 'Time is money'. People had to give their level of agreement/disagreement on a seven-point Likert scale. The setting was cross-cultural and 500 questionnaires were administered in 5 countries (Brazil, France, Mauritania, South Korea, West Germany). Surprisingly enough, the Mauritanians and the Brazilians were those with the highest scores of agreement on the fact that 'time is money'. They were followed by the Koreans; then came the French, and the last ones were the West Germans. The same results were found for the first factor of the scale, which summarized economic time. This draws our attention once again to the complex mechanisms of cultural borrowing and imitation, which may be a major source of misunderstandings especially when time (linear–separable), which is so fundamental to refined and reliable management, is concerned.

5. I apologize for, once again, taking a French example. As you may have noted throughout the book, I have tried not to be overly chauvinistic. *Qui bene amat bene castigat* (he who likes, chastises accordingly).

6. People can live with large discrepancies between their actual behaviour and the ideal standards of their society. Sicilian Mafia godfathers order murders and go to Mass. They do both sincerely, since ultimate forgiveness for any sin is possible in Catholic societies.

7. See Box 3.1 on Wishful Thinking.

8. I conducted some twenty non-directive, in-depth interviews, each lasting about three-quarters of an hour, with a theme list which featured the same constructs and emphasized the same situations as those in the questionnaire. Northern European (Swedish) students presented an ideal time pattern which was non-economic. They tended to develop some sort of 'ecological' idea of time not being money – not an economic good – and fully available to them. Other nationalities surveyed included Chinese, Brazilian and Moroccan. They tended to show an ideal economic time pattern, agreeing with the statement of 'time is money' introduced in the conversation. They also described their activities as quite organized, with a diary, precise appointments and so on (Usunier, 1991).

9. In this text the quotations about national negotiation styles are 'invitations' to refer to the original texts. Much relevant information may be obtained through universities and research centres which deal with area studies and oriental languages.

10. A number of books have been written either by Japanese authors or by non-Japanese observers of the Japanese society on the Japanese national character; for instance Chie Nakane (1973), Boye de Mente (1987), and Robert J. Ballon. Several books have been written on the Japanese style of management, including the following: R.T. Pascale and R. Athos (1981), *The Art of Japanese Management*, Simon & Schuster: New York; William Ouchi (1981), *Theory Z*, Addison-Wesley/Avon Books: New York; William Ouchi (1984), *The M Form Society*, Addison-Wesley/Avon Books: New York; Arthur M. Whitehill (1991), *Japanese Management: Tradition and transition*, Routledge: London; Dominique Turcq (1985), *L'Animal stratégique: l'Ambiguité du pouvoir chez les cadres japonais*, Editions de l'Ecole des Hautes Etudes en Sciences Sociales: Paris; Dominique Turcq (1992), *L'Inévitable Partenaire Japonais*, Fayard: Paris. On business negotiations with the Japanese see Van Zandt (1970), Graham and Sano (1990) and McCall and Warrington (1990), as well as many articles authored by John L. Graham (who has managed the IBEAR programme financed by Toyota at the University of Southern California) and Rosalie Tung.

11. See the Lestra Design case at the end of Chapter 8.

12. I am not necessarily the most objective observer of my compatriots' negotiation style, but, as you may note, I am not overly chauvinistic in the description.

13. Gruère and Morel (1991) propose stereotypes of the French as they are seen by various other nationalities and cultures (Box 4.4).

14. This is true for the People's Republic of China only, not for Taiwan, Hong Kong or diaspora (Malaysia, Singapore, etc.) Chinese.

15. The German–French relationship is an important one in intercultural communication research. Before being at the centre of European integration during the last forty years, France and Germany have been active foes for centuries. Several books are dedicated to communication problems between the French and the Germans: Edward Hall and Mildred Reed Hall have published a book about the hidden differences between the French and the Germans (published by *Stern Magazin*, Grüner & Jahr). See also: Jean-René Ladmiral and Edmond Marc Lipiansky (1989), *La Communication interculturelle*, Armand Colin: Paris, which deals with the communication problems and misunderstandings between the French and the Germans.

16. Luigi Barzini, a well-known Italian journalist and writer, has written one of the best books on

the national mentalities in Europe, *The Europeans*. The salient traits of the imperturbable British, the quarrelsome French, the careful Dutch, the mutable Germans, the flexible Italians and the baffling Americans (Barzini's adjectives) are portrayed in a well-documented and brilliant style.

17. The intercultural communication style (which permeates the negotiation style) of the British and the French, as well as the other three European colonial nations (the Dutch, the Portuguese and the Spanish), is heavily influenced by their former colonial ties. There is a mix of disappointed 'parental' feelings with a sense of superiority, which makes communication somewhat problematic with now fully independent peoples, who sometimes resent this attitude. However, apart from this shared trait, each ex-colonizer/ex-colonized relationship remains *sui generis*: for instance, the British-Indian cannot be really compared to the French-Tunisian or to the Portuguese-Brazilian relationships.

18. Saddam Hussein's foreign minister Tarek Aziz is a Christian, as is the new Secretary-General of the United Nations, the Egyptian Copt Boutros-Ghali.

19. Some books about Islamic law may be very useful when trying to undertand the Arab-Islamic world, especially J. Schacht (1950), *The Origins of Muhammadan Jurisprudence*, or *An Introduction to Islamic Law*, Clarendon Press: Oxford; A.A.A. Fyzee (1975), *Outlines of Mohammadan Law*, 4th edn. At a more general level, one way to prepare for business negotiations with partners belonging to a different culture is to try to learn about their legal and jurisdictional system. The study of comparative law is full of useful guides to understanding how people frame an agreement. Some useful references are: R. David and J.E.C. Brierley (1985), *Major Legal Systems Today*, 3rd edn; H.W. Ehrmann (1976), *Comparative Legal Cultures*; W.E. Butler (1985), *Comparative Approaches to International Law*, Nijhof: Dordrecht; R. Schlesinger (1980), *Comparative Law*.

References

Adler, Nancy J. (1986), *International Dimensions of Organizational Behavior*, Kent: Boston.

Attali, Jacques (1982), *Histoires du Temps*, Librairie Arthème Fayard: Paris.

Barzini, Luigi (1983), *The Europeans*, Penguin Books: London.

Beliaev, Edward, Thomas Mullen and Betty Jane Punnett (1985), 'Understanding the cultural environment: US–USSR trade negotiations', *California Management Review*, vol. xxvii, no. 2, pp. 100–12.

Burt, David N. (1984), 'The nuances of negotiating overseas', *Journal of Purchasing and Materials Management* (Winter), pp. 2–8.

Campbell, Nigel C.G., John L. Graham, Alain Jolibert and Hans Günther Meissner (1988), 'Marketing negotiations in France, Germany, the United Kingdom and United States', *Journal of Marketing*, vol. 52, April, pp. 49–62.

Cateora, Philip R. (1983), *International Marketing*, 5th edn, Richard D. Irwin: Homewood, IL.

CNUCED (1978), Monograph on the transfer of technology at Boccaro Plant, Geneva, *CNUCED/ UNCTAD* TD/B/C 6/27.

De Mente, Boye (1987), *How to do Business with the Japanese*, NTC Publishing: Chicago, IL.

Deutscher, I. (1966), 'Words and deeds: social science and social policy', *Social Problems*, vol. 13, no. 3 (Winter), pp. 235–54.

Deutscher, I. (1973), 'Asking questions cross-culturally: some problems of linguistic comparability', in D.P. Warwick and S. Osherson (eds), *Comparative Research Methods*, Prentice Hall: Englewood Cliffs, NJ.

Eiteman, David K. (1990), 'American executives' perceptions of negotiating joint ventures with the People's Republic of China: Lessons learned', *Columbia Journal of World Business* (Winter), pp. 59–67.

Feldman, Lawrence P. and Jacob Hornik (1981), 'The use of time: An integrated conceptual model', *Journal of Consumer Research*, vol. 7, March, pp. 407–19.

Goodenough, Ward H. (1971), *Culture, Language and Society*, Modular Publications, no. 7, Addison-Wesley, Reading, MA.

Graham, John L. (1981), 'A hidden cause of America's trade deficit with Japan', *Columbia Journal of World Business*, Fall, pp. 5–15.

Graham, John L. and Roy A. Herberger Jr (1983), 'Negotiators abroad: Don't shoot from the hip', *Harvard Business Review*, vol. 61, no. 4, pp. 160–8.

Graham, John L. and Yoshihiro Sano (1990), *Smart Bargaining: Doing business with the Japanese*, 2nd edn, Ballinger: Cambridge, MA.

Graham, Robert J. (1981), 'The role of perception of time in consumer research', *Journal of Consumer Research*, vol. 7, March, pp. 335–42.

Gruère, Jean-Pierre and Pierre Morel (1991), *Cadres Français et Communications Interculturelles*, Eyrolles: Paris.

Gurevitch, A.J. (1976), 'Time as a problem of cultural history', in L. Gardner *et al.* (eds), *Cultures and Time: At the crossroads of cultures*, Unesco Press: Paris.

Hall, Edward T. (1959), *The Silent Language*, Doubleday: Garden City, NY.

Hall, Edward T. (1973), *The Silent Language*, Anchor Books: New York.

Hall, Edward T. (1976), *Beyond Culture*, Anchor Press/Doubleday: Garden City, NY.

Hall, Edward T. (1983), *The Dance of Life*, Anchor Press/Doubleday: Garden City, NY.

Hallowell, I. (1955), *Culture and Experience*, University of Pennsylvania Press: Philadelphia.

Hawrysh, Bryan Mark and Judith Lynn Zaichkowsky (1990), 'Cultural approaches to negotiations: Understanding the Japanese', *International Marketing Review*, vol. 7, no. 2, pp. 28–42.

Hofstede, Geert (1980a), 'Motivation, leadership and organization: Do American theories apply abroad?', *Organizational Dynamics* (Summer), pp. 42–63.

Hofstede, Geert (1980b), *Culture's Consequences: International differences in work-related values*, Sage Publications: Beverly Hills, CA.

Jacoby, Jacob, George J. Szybillo and Carol K. Berning (1976), 'Time and consumer behavior: An interdisciplinary overview', *Journal of Consumer Research*, vol. 2, pp. 320–39.

Kelley, H.H. (1966), 'A classroom study of the dilemmas in interpersonal negotiations', in K. Archibald (ed.), *Strategic Interaction and Conflict*, Institute of International Studies, University of California: Berkeley, CA.

Kluckhohn, Florence R. and Frederick L. Strodtbeck (1961), *Variations in Value Orientations*, Row-Peterson: Evanston, IL.

Linton, Ralph (1945), *The Cultural Background of Personality*, D. Appleton-Century: New York.

McCall, J.B. and M.B. Warrington (1990), *Marketing by Agreement: A cross-cultural approach to business negotiations*, 2nd edn, John Wiley: London.

Metraux, R. (1967), panel discussion in 'Interdisciplinary perspective of time', in Edward M. Weyer (ed), *Annals of the New York Academy of Sciences*, vol. 138, article 2, pp. 207–8.

Nakane, Chie (1973), *Japanese Society*, University of California Press: Berkeley.

Naulleau, Gérard (1985), 'Le Développment du système financier islamique', in *Actes du colloque cultures et transferts de technologie*, Inalco-Musée Guimet: Paris, pp. 16–20.

Oh, T.K. (1986), 'Selling to the Japanese', *Nation's Business*, October, pp. 37–8.

Pomian, Krysztof (1984), *L'Ordre du temps*, Gallimard: Paris.

Pye, Lucian W. (1982), *Chinese Commercial Negotiating Style*, Oelgeschlager, Gunn & Hain: Cambridge, MA.

Pye, Lucian W. (1986), 'The China trade: Making the deal work', *Harvard Business Review*, vol. 46, no. 4, pp. 75–84.

Schmidt, Klaus D. (1979), *Doing Business in France, Germany and the United Kingdom*, pamphlets published by the Business Intelligence Program, SRI International: Menlo Park, CA.

Tiano, André (1981), *Transfert de technologie industrielle*, Editions Economica: Paris.

Tung, Rosalie L. (1984a), 'How to negotiate with the Japanese', *California Management Review*, vol. XXVI, no. 4, pp. 62–77.

Tung, Rosalie L. (1984b), *Business Negotiations with the Japanese*, Lexington Books: Lexington, MA.

Usunier, J.C. (1987), 'Négociation des délais et différences culturelles', Working paper no. 87-32, Centre for Research in Management (CERAG), Graduate School of Business, Grenoble.

Usunier, Jean-Claude (1989), 'Interculturel: la parole et l'action', *Harvard-L'Expansion*, no. 52, March, pp. 84–92.

Usunier, J.C. (1991), 'Business time perceptions and national cultures: A comparative survey', *Management International Review*, vol. 31, no. 3, pp. 197–217.

Van Zandt, H.R. (1970), 'How to negotiate with the Japanese', *Harvard Business Review*, November–December.

Weiss, Stephen E. and William Stripp (1985), 'Negotiating with foreign businesspersons: An introduction for Americans with propositions for six cultures', Working paper no. 85–6, Graduate School of Business, New York University.

Zerubavel E. (1981), *Hidden Rhythms: Schedules and calendars in social life*, University of Chicago Press: Chicago.

15

◆◆◆

Bribery in intercultural marketing negotiations

Few months go by without some new affair of international corruption appearing in the news. These affairs are often linked to the sale of major international products (turnkey factories, nuclear plants, aircraft sales, etc.). In large international sales, the influence of secret payments cannot be ignored. Marketing large international sales involves a selling approach where the customer's decision-making process inevitably presupposes political influences, although these are not necessarily corrupt.

This issue is not addressed directly in terms of business ethics: instead, a more pragmatic view has been adopted, whereby the implicit economic justification for these illegal payments is assessed. In the face of legislation which punishes those who make illegal payments as well as the recipients of such 'baksheesh',[1] their persistence is amazing.

Bribery is considered by most business people as a key issue in international marketing ethics. According to Mayo *et al.* (1991), more than one-third of a sample of US executives ranked bribery as the top ethical concern out of ten possible ethical problems that may arise in international marketing operations. It is generally felt that ethical problems tarnish the firm's corporate image and have a negative impact on its ability to transact business overseas.

The first section of this chapter examines the facts in an area that, understandably, is clouded with secrecy. The second and third sections describe the methods by which such payments are effected. Research into this issue has been carried out mostly by academics specializing in international accounting, since the recording of illicit transactions is obviously a sensitive matter.

Various 'economic' explanations are then proposed (sections 15.4 and 15.5). These explanations are pushed to the limits of their usual assumptions:

1. The illegal payment corresponds to a fee for an implicit agency contract.

This chapter is largely based on Jean-Claude Usunier (1989), 'Marketing international et rémunérations occultes', *Economies et Sociétés, Sciences de Gestion* series, no. 14, pp. 221–42. Reproduced with the kind permission of the review.

2. The illegal payment is reward for an implicit property right on the signature of the deal.
3. The illegal payment is an implicit salary, compensating 'facilitators'.

Returning to a more ethical perspective, the responsibility of the briber is examined in section 15.6. It is not only examined as far as the briber's country is concerned, but also in terms of the individual risk taken by the sales executive who actually carries out active corruption. In view of the adverse consequences for the recipient country (section 15.7), achieving a reduction in these practices is socially desirable. Apart from increased penalties and more effective enforcement, there are two ways of reducing illegal payments: the first is an increase in awareness of the personal risks for the briber; the second is the introduction of national legislation which legalizes and restricts the scope for the payment and receipt of sales commissions, as is the case in Saudi Arabia (section 15.8). Examples in this chapter particularly concern international sales of heavy-duty equipment and turnkey operations.

15.1 Facts

Information and data on illegal payments are very sparse and often fragmentary. Such issues are sensitive and companies remain very secretive. Factual data have been collected, however, either through the investigations carried out by financial journalists (Beaudeux, 1980; Péan, 1988) and academic researchers (Walter, 1989),[2] or more systematically in the United States, as a consequence of prosecutions under the Foreign Corrupt Practices Act 1977 (e.g. Kaikati, 1977; Jacoby *et al.*, 1979; Kaikati and Label, 1980; Gillespie, 1987).

It must be recognized that the practice is too widespread to be ignored. It takes various forms:

• Small and large gifts. Beaudeux (1980) reports in the following way the remarks of the director of international operations of a large multinational company: 'It is common practice for a Permanent Secretary or a leading [foreign] politician to be offered two weeks at a hotel in Paris, and also lent a limousine for the duration of his stay, which ultimately he will always forget to give back.' Likewise the general manager of an engineering company states:

> These stopovers in Europe seem to be trivial affairs, but when you add in all the additional expenses: receptions, restaurants and, above all, pretty hostesses for an evening, you are talking about at least £500 or £600 a day! A Secretary of State has just announced his arrival. We gave a sigh of relief when he told us that he had come with his wife! A Nigerian official left us a bill for 120,000 francs for a twelve-day stay.

• 'Percentages' based on the contract value itself. Here the form of illegal payments results in much larger sums being paid because of the size of the contract (sale of a squadron of fighter planes or a turnkey plant, etc.). Indeed, in the United States, during the public disclosure of the illegal payments involving American multinationals in the 1970s, sums of up to $70 million were mentioned. The companies involved were, among others, Lockheed, United Brands and Gulf Oil. There were many other firms implicated, principally in the mining, aeronautic and engineering sectors (Cateora, 1987). The famous Lockheed scandal destabilized Japan's Prime Minister Tanaka, Prince Bernhardt in Holland, the Christian-Democrat Party in Germany and Italy, and even President Lopez of the Honduras.

Beaudeux quotes the official of an American multinational, who considers Venezuela and Mexico major centres in South America for 'baksheesh', with percentages tending to settle around the 10–15 per cent mark. At the time there also seemed to be widespread corruption in Uruguay and Paraguay since, according to the experts, even in deals of around 200 million francs, a third of the total would be laundered through a nominee company acting as a figurehead, keeping the money safe before its collection by high-ranking South American civil servants (Beaudeux, 1980).

15.2   Methods

The extent of these practices can only be assessed if certain realities are faced (Usunier, 1992a):

♦ Whether illegal payments are made and what sums are involved vary widely from one country and one industrial sector to another. They will be much more substantial, for example, in the construction industry or in Nigeria than in electronics or in Australia.
♦ The ways and means of bribing are many and varied.
♦ Not everyone is corrupt. There is nothing worse than attempting to bribe someone who strongly disapproves of such immoral behaviour. This last point is clearly illustrated by Agpar (1977) who quotes the case of the managing director of a large American multinational who offered 500 Saudi riyals in cash to a Saudi police officer (about $140) to ensure that a decision on a fairly minor offence against labour law would be favourable. In fury, the officer reported the attempted bribe to his superiors. After spending twenty days in prison, the businessman was sentenced to a fine of 25,000 riyals and was fortunate to escape a more serious penalty.

This case clearly demonstrates the danger and also the ineffectiveness of the direct method (passing cash from one hand to another). Accordingly, more indirect methods exist instead:

♦ Slush funds are set up to effect small payments by cheque, nominally as payment for services rendered. Lee Radebaugh (Daniels, Ogram and Radebaugh, 1982) mentions the case of Braniff Airlines, which sold 3,500 plane tickets in South America for a total of $900,000 without making any record of the transactions in their accounts. This money was used to set up a slush fund that in turn fed a secret bank account. This money was neither mentioned in the parent company accounts, nor in those of the subsidiary. This secret account was used to pay additional commissions to organizers and travel agents in clear breach of the Federal Aviation Act.
♦ The transfer of 'brown paper packets' is often made by an intermediate consultancy company. These companies often have their head office in Luxemburg or Liechtenstein,

or in some other tax haven. The consultancy company is often involved right from the tendering stage in the case of a factory or turnkey project. Consider the scenario where one of the key decision-makers for the final selection of the foreign contractor controls a local construction consultancy company. During a reception, this person whispers to the head of the negotiating team of a large engineering or construction company he is dealing with that it would be advantageous if his consultancy company were to be requested to carry out preliminary technical studies. These studies will in fact be largely fictitious. The fees paid for these studies will correspond to the commission. If these studies are further subcontracted to a nominee company in Luxemburg, the baksheesh money will be transferred to a 'safe place'.

♦ Nominee and local consultancy companies, to whom 'phoney' consulting contracts are given, may be used in different ways. For example, an approach may be made to an adviser of the Transport Minister for country X who is well placed to influence the decision on an underground railway project in town Y. It will be suggested that he be made a part-time employee of the Luxemburg-based nominee company. Without having to move an inch he will receive a salary each month which, for reasons of discretion and convenience, will be paid into an account in Switzerland. When going skiing with his family, the adviser/consultant will take the money out of his bank account in Geneva, then discreetly spend it in an exclusive ski resort. Money spent abroad is less compromising than money brought back home.

♦ Two other accounting solutions are frequently employed (Daniels *et al.*, 1982): the over-invoicing of certain transactions, expenditure or receipts, and the recording of fictitious transactions. For example, the American Hospital Supply company was obliged to pay a 10 per cent commission to obtain the contract for the construction of a hospital in Saudi Arabia. AHS artificially inflated the price of the contract, then recorded a commission for consultancy fees, even though no service of this type had been rendered. This allowed the ten per cent commission to become tax-deductible expenditure and made the payment apparently legitimate, whereas in fact it remained illegal.

15.3 The process of illegal payments

First, illegal payments in their various forms are examined, and then the ambiguous nature of communication between potential donor and recipient is considered in more detail. No moral perspective has been adopted, whereby the existence of illegal payments is assessed purely in terms of business ethics. Conversely, no strictly pragmatic perspective has been adopted either, which would involve a somewhat cynical analysis of the effectiveness of these practices in winning contracts. This approach avoids the risks of the simplistic attitudes whereby illegal payments are either roundly condemned or, alternatively, unequivocally accepted on the basis of merely being 'realistic'.

Illegal payments seen from different perspectives

When analyzing the process of secret payments, one may focus either on the individuals (briber/bribed), the way their relation is sealed, the authorities to whom they report, or even the messages and style of communication they use in this sensitive and precarious business. The following perspectives may be adopted:

* One view centres on the economics of the transaction. In business negotiations, the issue of implicit remuneration arises between the purchaser and the vendor. The basic question concerns what this remuneration is supposed to be buying. How should the service be defined, its price determined – in other words, what should be the level of the baksheesh?

* Another view centres on the individual, either the donor or the recipient of the illegal payment. These people are taking risks, even sometimes risking the death penalty. The donor is very poorly rewarded for these risks as he may be prosecuted and punished. Reward for the recipient of the payment depends on the ultimate allocation of the money. If it goes into his own pocket, the risk-taking can be viewed from the perspective of individual interest. If the money goes into a political party's funds, it is more difficult to assess the individual risks taken. In the latter case, personal risks are diminished by the power of political influence and the lack of strictly direct and personal benefit.

* Another view centres on the group. Bribers and the bribed are not isolated individuals. They work in negotiating teams and report to higher authorities. Whenever they personally request the bribe, they have to share it with other people. In turnkey contracts, both the contractor and the owner are often complex organizations which comprise hundreds of representatives of various companies, ministries, utilities and agencies, all of whom are involved in the decision-making. The methods of dividing up the illegal payment within the owner's group that acquires the project is a key issue in keeping it secret. A single individual rarely receives everything, for it would be difficult to avoid this fact becoming known because of jealousy. Anyone who could potentially exert blackmail, such as a secretary who types a compromising letter or a minister who has to sign the letter, must therefore be 'paid off'.

* Another view centres on communication. It is easy to imagine that the messages communicated between the purchaser and the vendor may often be complex, and that misunderstandings may frequently occur. The person offering the baksheesh must make his initial approach tentatively. When he has identified the person(s) whose influence could be bought, he will have to be very cautious in the preliminary signals that suggest the possibility of a mutually beneficial co-operation. If he is dealing with someone who is incorruptible or, even worse, someone who has an objective interest in playing this role, and/or (worse still) someone in whose interest it is to make this known, the situation then becomes extremely dangerous. The messages given out by the person offering the baksheesh must therefore remain largely implicit. They must be capable of being decoded by the person addressed, but will not be of such an explicit character as to give rise to any risk of prosecution for attempted bribery.

The implicit aspect of communication in illegal payments

Support here is derived from the conception of communication developed by the American anthropologist Edward Hall (1959, 1976). An explicit style of communication, where the context plays a weak role in message comprehension, is contrasted by Edward

Hall with an implicit style of communication. A rich contextual communication allows the decoding of messages that are otherwise complex, even imprecise and confused.

The means of communication that comes naturally to mind is language. We live, more or less, with the necessary fiction that words and sentences have precise meaning and that people receive clear messages. Yet communication involves several complementary elements outside the purely verbal aspect: non-verbal messages (e.g. gestures, postures), feedback mechanisms to check or improve the clarity of the message, and also the influence of context on the decoding of the communication.[3] Although Edward Hall does not define context precisely, the following components can be proposed: the place, the characters (age, sex, clothes, perceived social status, etc.), the subject of the communication, etc. In the case of illegal payments, explicit messages are by their very nature extremely limited since they increase considerably the risk taken by the two parties. Therefore only implicit messages are communicated.

The messages are never straightforward. At first, meta-communication between the corruptor and the corrupted will serve to establish the rules of the game and ensure that the relationships are fair. A potential bribe-receiver may discreetly signal his willingness to be bribed by casually mentioning, with a certain emphasis, his personal acquaintances, the influence he has over them and the information they can obtain. This is worded without once raising the subject of money. It is even explicitly stated that there is no question of any money. As a result, the offer of becoming a bribed 'business agent' is implicit. Other potential bribe-receivers may, for example, complain about the poor salary earned as a customs officer; they further evidence a missing document and, ultimately, mention their effectiveness at granting customs clearance for goods. All this constitutes an implicit appeal for remuneration to the business engineer who is seeking to obtain imported equipment for the factory he is constructing. Another example: somebody may state authoritatively and as a responsible civil servant, not motivated by money, that he is seeking to select the best supplier, and that the choice is ultimately his. This may be a concealed reminder to the foreign contractor of an implicit property right over the signing of the deal.

15.4 Implicit economic explanations for illegal payments

'Economic explanations' for bribery are nevertheless not excuses for unacceptable practices. The basic assumption is: there must be some strong economic reasons for bribery, although unlawful, remaining in existence. The important word is, of course, 'implicit'. It is not claimed that the attempted explanations can be expounded and defended explicitly, particularly in real-life situations. The arguments considered contend:[4]

1. Illegal payments constitute an implicit agency contract.
2. Illegal payments are related to an implicit property right: is the person who has the final say on a contract also entitled to waive this right in return for money?
3. Illegal payments are an implicit salary; that is, they are fringe benefits for poorly paid civil servants and managers, particularly in developing countries where some officials may go for months without receiving their salary. This situation is tolerated as long as bribes do not exceed a 'fair' level.

The implicit agency contract

Often in international tenders, the organizational links within the 'owner' consortium are poorly defined; a state-owned utility acquires a turnkey factory, under the supervision of various ministries and banks; various consultants also intervene.[5] The areas of responsibility of each body are in fact vaguely defined. As influences can be diverse and relational networks complex, someone may offer a chance to escape the labyrinth by identifying the relevant officials, assessing the extent of their influence and may ultimately influence them. The tasks for the potential recipient of the baksheesh may therefore include the following:

- Supplying the briber with confidential information on the client organization.
- Supplying the briber with information on the competitors (warning: the recipient – or the one who is tantalized by the prospect of a baksheesh – may be a double agent!).
- Manipulation: he can spread false information to the briber's benefit, so as to discredit a competitor. He may even seek to cloud the issue so that the imminent signature of the contract with a competing company can be avoided.
- Implementing baksheesh redistribution: by sharing out part of the illegal payment he can influence the necessary authorities or a particular decision.

The originators of agency theory, Jensen and Meckling (1976), define the agency relationship as a contract in which one (or more) person(s) make(s) use of the services of another person to accomplish some task. This involves a delegation of decision-making from the principal to the agent. Agency costs arise in every situation where principal–agent co-operation is involved, even if the principal–agent relationship is not clearly defined (Charreaux, 1987).

Originally, agency theory was applied to rather different relationships, mainly those between shareholders and the managerial teams that govern businesses they do not own. It rests on two behavioural hypotheses (Charreaux, 1987):

1. Everyone acts so as to maximize their own utility function (in our case this can realistically be assumed to be true).
2. Everyone is capable of rationally calculating the impact of agency relationships on the future value of their personal wealth.

Demonstrating the accuracy of this second hypothesis in our case is rather more difficult. Although the recipient of the baksheesh inevitably acts fairly rationally by balancing high risk against high return, the donor (e.g. the executive of an engineering company) has to offset high risk against low return. He may simply be fulfilling his role in the company hierarchy (obeying his superiors), or acting out of certain fears (that failure to win the contract will result in him losing his job). These attitudes are not always based on rational criteria.

Agency relationships can give rise to opportunistic behaviour. Each individual may seek to extract personal profit from any flaws in the contracts. These flaws will be very major in our case, since the 'contracts of bribery' are never written down. It is not unheard of for baksheesh to be given to intermediaries without the contract being ultimately won. The risks thereby incurred when hiring an agent necessitate that one of the principal areas of expenditure in agency costs will relate to control of the agent. There must be some incentive for him to succeed and some measures of retaliation against him, should he fail to achieve his set objectives. Such retaliation has sometimes extended in extreme cases as far as hiring a paid assassin and making the agent aware of this. Conversely, a bonus on the signature of the deal may dissuade the agent from opportunism.

This also means that the commission must be paid at the last possible moment, once the signature of the deal is imminent and the selection of the final contracting party is effectively decided and cannot be changed. Games akin to hide-and-seek are often played between the contractor and the agent in this final stage. As a result it may be worth considering an extension of the agency relationship. Providing for the continuation of the relationship after the signature of the deal ensures that the agent has an interest in carefully controlling his behaviour in the hope of future gains.

The implicit property right on the signature of the deal

It is not rare to see the ruler of a country (e.g. a dictator) appear almost astonished at being reproached in an interview for having accumulated huge sums of money as a result of illegal payments whilst in power. Some dictators have transferred to foreign bank accounts the equivalent of a large part, if not all, of a country's cumulative foreign debt (e.g. Marcos or Mobutu). Almost unconsciously the ruler is convinced that the state belongs to him personally and often also to his family. At the very least he implicitly holds the opinion that it is legitimate that someone in power should be entitled to use his influence for personal enrichment.

This situation can almost be compared to one of a property right. Demsetz (1967) suggests that property rights permit individuals to know a priori what they can reasonably expect in their dealings with the other members of the community. He claims that these expectations manifest themselves in the laws, customs and morals of a society. In the case of international bribery, the right, originally based on customary law and therefore unwritten and implicit, is to derive personal profit from a position of power over the signature of public deals. On the basis of this rather wide definition, Couret (1987) suggests different 'efficient characteristics' of property rights:

◆ Property rights should be both exclusive and transferable. An exclusive right occurs when one single individual receives all the profits, but also has to bear all the adverse consequences that may arise. These rights must be assignable and transferable since the individual must be able to proceed to effective arbitrage. He must be permanently in a position to exchange property rights on efficient markets on which these rights are quoted.

  Except for dictators who establish a veritable implicit personal ownership over their country, rights on the signature of deals are rarely exclusive. Moreover these rights are not transferable, or only in a very limited way, to an heir in dictatorship (e.g. the dictator Duvalier in Haiti was succeeded by his son, Jean-Claude).

◆ Transaction costs: in other words the costs that must be borne to ensure respect for one's rights by others (bodyguards, secret agents, repression of enemies, elimination of economic and political opponents, etc.).

◆ Costs of information: to improve the efficiency of one's property rights, each agent must personally bear a certain number of information costs. This may even extend to paying for a sophisticated information network (i.e. spies).

As far as these two characteristics occur in international bribery, these rights are only temporarily and partially exclusive. The property right on the signature of the deal can only really be considered as subjective and implicit.

This fact leads on to two real dangers incurred by making illegal payments:

1. Letting oneself be dragged along by the megalomaniac subjectivity of an authoritative ruler who, seeing the country as his personal property, sells the right to win business there. These rights are not transferable and no dictator rules for ever.
2. Property rights on the signature of deals have never been legally recognized:[6] most countries prohibit the use of any position of authority for personal enrichment. Even when it is clear that in reality the baksheesh is a widespread practice throughout a particular society, it must not be forgotten that it is forbidden by law, and accordingly the most stringent precautions must be taken.

Illegal payments as implicit salary

A work contract is not rewarded purely in explicit monetary terms. Financial remuneration may be the principal and essential reward, but there are other aspects of the contract that are termed 'implicit remuneration':

◆ A good quality of life at work (low level of stress, friendly atmosphere between colleagues, etc.).
◆ Flexibility in working hours.
◆ A job which is inherently self-satisfying.

If the employees are poorly paid, but hold authority and responsibility (e.g. a police officer, a customs officer or a tax inspector) it may be 'implicitly understood' that in exchange for carrying out poorly rewarded public duties, such officials may supplement their income. Thus when passing through customs, obtaining a tax form (for a mandatory declaration) may require the 'greasing of someone's palm'. That can be assimilated to an implicit salary, in that the authorities are perfectly well aware of the existence of such practices and consider this implicit salary as justified by the failure to increase the official basic salary.

The three implicit economic explanations for illegal payments that have just been described actually correspond to the three most common bribery scenarios:

1. The agent who penetrates relational networks, supplies information and exerts influence.
2. The 'dictator' in the wider sense, namely someone very important, who sells his right to award deals.

3. Small-scale everyday corruption of a poorly paid (if at all) public civil servant who supplements his income by exploiting his bureaucratic power.

Far from being mutually exclusive, these forms of remuneration combine to reduce social rivalries, in societies where everyone on his own level sells his personal level of influence.

15.5   The means of redistribution: an important aspect

There is often a tendency to oversimplify the issue of international corruption to one of a face-to-face meeting between two people, a donor and a recipient. In reality the donor of the baksheesh, even when it is large, is often faced with a group of recipients. The benefit of an illegal payment has a group aspect. It rarely benefits one single person. As a result, bribery is intermingled with a dense network of social relationships:

◆ Bonds of fraternity and complicity between people of the same ethnic background or tribe. These people are necessary intermediaries for ensuring that the influences, the information research and the handing over of the baksheesh may all be effectively implemented.

◆ Bonds of everyday co-operation, which call for redistribution of small parts of the bribe: the secretary who guesses the existence of the baksheesh, the customs officer who intercepts a 'brown paper parcel', etc.

◆ Bonds caused by potential retaliation; those who have not requested a baksheesh, but who have a strong suspicion as to its existence, may either inform the authorities or exert a sort of implicit blackmail by demanding their 'cut'. They may even take no action by simply closing their eyes to what is happening. They are guided by their rationality: they can either take the risk of participation in illegal remuneration and benefit personally; exert blackmail and thereby take the risk of offending those in power leading to ultimate punishment; or lastly, inform against the bribe-recipient and suffer any adverse consequences that may result.

Primitive civilization of hunter-gatherers that are described by ethnologists (Maquet, 1962) can be used as an archetype for the redistribution of a bribe considered as plunder. While the men hunt (symbolically: those who hold power and go 'hunting' for large sums), the women, children and the elderly devote their efforts instead to harvesting (symbolically: those who collaborate on menial levels, but are still aware of what is happening). Ultimately the bribe/plunder is divided up according to fairly precise rules. Redistributing plunder and crops among the members of one's tribe is basic moral behaviour in many countries (see Box 15.1).

Bribery only achieves the desired result (independently of ethical questions) if certain conditions are satisfied, namely that payments remain secret and are effectively targeted. Therefore the following are necessary:

◆ The parties to be influenced must be clearly identified (Usunier, 1992b, pp. 180–3) and accordingly relations between them must be monitored. Conflict between two rival groups can instigate a denunciation.

- The ways and means of redistribution of the baksheesh within the group must be sufficiently clearly defined, even if they are implicit, so that there is no conflict over the 'sharing out of the cake'. Public disclosure of baksheesh is often the result of personal frustrations.
- The individuals who, for ethical or other reasons, decline to receive part of the bribe must be identified. It may be wise to ensure their neutrality by acknowledging their honesty.

In all cases, that is, when even circumstances seem to demand that an illegal payment be made, it may in fact be wise not to make it, as it may backfire on the company when it has won the deal and therefore have a negative impact on its corporate image.

15.6 The responsibility of the payer

Only one country, the United States, has been brave enough to look into the problems of business ethics posed by illegal payments. In the mid-1970s the Attorney-General's enquiry into the Watergate affair revealed that suspect payments had been made to foreign politicians by large American companies. In 1977 the FCPA (Foreign Corrupt Practices Act) made it illegal for companies to influence foreign officials by personal payments or transfers of money to political groups. This law obliges firms to institute an internal

Box 15.1   *A good minister in Senegal*

For the man in the street, a good minister is a demagogue, someone who is adept at by-passing the law and its rulings to keep the voters from his region, his parents and his friends happy. If you try to behave like a minister acting objectively by treating your cousins, your allies, members of the branch of your party in the same way as all other citizens, even political opponents, the people will be totally confused. You will not be understood. You are not respecting the rules of the game. You will be the object of public contempt. You are not a minister for the purpose of serving the nation or carrying out the policies of a government which is in power for the good of all its citizens. You are first and foremost a minister for your own good, so that you may take advantage of your position, and enable your parents and allies, your friends and the members of your party to benefit too. No one will reproach you, everyone will understand. Those who are out of office are the only ones who will criticize this behaviour although if they were in office themselves they could not be sure of resisting the demands of their own tribe, family, or parents-in-law. There is nothing wrong in taking advantage of one's position to help out one's relatives; the ideal would be to consider all citizens as your own relatives.

(Cheikh Alioune Ndao, 1985, *Excellences, vos éspouses!*, Les Nouvelles Editions Africaines, pp. 34–5, quoted in Jean Ziegler,[7] 1988. Reproduced with the kind permission of the publisher.)

accounting control. The FCPA's definition of what constitutes bribery is very wide. It does, however, exclude small payments known as 'backhanders' and tips paid to minor civil servants to speed up customs clearance or any administrative formalities.

After the introduction of this legislation, over forty articles appeared in the management literature in the United States criticizing the FCPA on the basis that it was detrimental to American companies abroad (Gillespie, 1987). Among the arguments that derive from this business pragmatism are the following:

♦ Kaikati and Label (1980) claim that the FCPA placed American companies at a competitive disadvantage compared to European or Japanese competitors. Kaikati (1977) emphasizes the issue by pointing out that in West Germany, although illegal payments paid to German citizens are not tax-deductible, those paid to foreign officials are.

♦ Jacoby, Nehemkis and Eells (1979) point out that in response to the FCPA the majority of American multinationals substantially reduced or eliminated these practices. They either abandoned certain export businesses, or turned their former agents into separate companies, independent of themselves, who could buy and sell in their own right; sometimes they even abandoned their long-standing competency as a prime contractor and acted as simple subcontractor for French, German, Japanese or Korean companies.

♦ A further frequent criticism of the FCPA is that it destabilizes political regimes that are friendly to the United States. It is alleged that the leaders of these countries are sometimes forced into making compromising revelations.

Gillespie (1987), who has studied affairs of corruption in the Middle East for the last ten years, carried out an analysis of about sixty cases of corruption where foreign companies were involved. She concluded that arguments against the FCPA were not strictly borne out by the facts. Some regimes remained stable despite major scandals (e.g. Turkey, Egypt, Saudi Arabia), others fell (in the case of the Shah of Iran) for more deep-rooted reasons. Furthermore, Gillespie's study of the changes in the export market share of the United States (in comparison with its major international competitors) showed that US foreign trade with the Middle East had not been adversely affected by the FCPA. This had already been backed up by the study by Graham (1983).

The ethical attitudes within the major developed countries towards illegal payments are not uniform (Lee, 1981). US managers tend to adopt stronger ethical standpoints than their European and Japanese counterparts. In a recent study, Becker and Fritzsche (1987) suggest a scenario which poses a business ethics problem linked to an illegal payment. Three sample groups of business people were interviewed, one from the United States (124 respondents), one from West Germany (70 respondents) and one from France (72 respondents). The scenario is as follows:

> The Rollfast Bicycle company has been barred from entering the market in a large Asian country by collusive efforts of the local bicycle manufacturers. Rollfast could expect to net 5 million dollars per year from sales if it could penetrate the market. Last week a business man from the country contacted the management of Rollfast and stated that he could smooth the way for the company to sell in his country for a price of $500,000. If you were responsible, what are the chances you would pay the price? (Becker and Fritzsche, 1987, p. 89)

While the replies from the French and German managers differed little, those of the Americans indicated that they were, by and large, less prepared to pay the secret payment. While 47 per cent of the Americans (F, 15 per cent; G, 9 per cent) gave as an explanation that this was unethical, illegal and contrary to the corporate code of conduct, 38 per cent of Germans and 55 per cent of the French thought either that 'the competition would force us to accept' or that 'it's simply the price you have to pay for doing business'.

France and West Germany have legislation prohibiting the bribing of public civil servants, but these regulations do not apply extra-territorially. French and German business people cannot be prosecuted for bribes effected outside their national territory. Conversely, the FCPA as well as numerous other American regulations (anti-trust, fiscal, etc.) does have extra-territorial application. Despite the fact that the FCPA increases the probability of disclosure, the corruption scandals in the Middle East have by no means involved only the United States. Gillespie (1987) notes that the affairs of corruption in the Middle East involving European or Asiatic multinationals were revealed either locally or by newspapers in the countries making the payments. In not one of the scandals that she studied (for the period 1970–85: 42 involving American companies, 29 involving European or Asiatic countries) were Americans imprisoned, whereas Europeans or Asiatics were put in prison in seven instances.

The businessman who takes the risk of suggesting the possibility of an illegal payment, either through company loyalty or personal interest (sales commission or promotion) also involves his company in the risk of being implicated in a scandal, and himself risks being implicated, indicted, imprisoned and ultimately sentenced to a long term of imprisonment. Accordingly, the relations between the project negotiator and the engineering company or consortium of contractors who have given him responsibility for the negotiations are key ones. Unless he actually brings up these issues directly and openly, the exact extent of his power and authority to take risks will be insufficiently clarified. The business engineers who sell factories or turnkey equipment often 'go into battle' with little prior warning or protection. An illustration of this is given by Beaudeux (1980) who quotes the case of a British business engineer who negotiated a $50 million contract in Algeria.

> I knew that my competitor's offer was about $40 million and I battled for several weeks to convince the purchaser that I was overall the cheapest. So afterwards I was absolutely outraged, as well as scared to death (you know what they do to bribers in Algeria), when I learned on my return that my head office had negotiated over my head, and that the true price was $40 million. The other $10 million was the baksheesh that we had paid to win the order.

It is clear from other cases that the payment of a baksheesh always involves the individual responsibility of the donor, even if his company, or the consortium that he represents, also risks being drawn into the scandal. A pragmatic view for an individual requires reference to a behavioural norm, not a corporate one. Useful guidelines for those confronted with this issue is provided by the definition of a 'moral personality' proposed by John Rawls in his *Theory of Justice* (1971). A moral personality is characterized by two capacities, namely the capacity to conceive good and the capacity to develop a sense of justice. The first is realized through a rational project for one's life. The second implies a continuing desire to act in a way that one believes is just. Thus for Rawls, moral personalities have chosen their own goals, they prefer those conditions which enable them to fully express their nature of rational, free and equal beings. The unity of such people is then manifested by the coherence of their project. This unity is based on a higher-order aspiration to follow the principles of rational choice in a way which corresponds to their sense of justice.[8]

These words deserve to be reread several times. They oppose a certain cynicism that is growing even in the United States (Brenner and Molander, 1977). There is unfortunately no common international legal framework which can circumvent bribery. Moreover, national-based legal texts, since they simply prohibit or permit certain acts, do not explain how to behave in the real world. The only universal sources for guiding one's behaviour are, for instance, the guidelines which stem from United Nations codes and from some analyses which provide the basis for the identification of ethical issues (Haegg, 1983), based on case studies.[9] Ethical conflicts must therefore largely be documented on a moral rather than legal basis, keeping in mind that moral judgements are partly universal, partly culturally relative. Rawl's views suggest individual behaviour that is realistic and autonomous. If individuals were to consider objectively both their personal morality and the risks they take, the practice of illegal payments would decline.

15.7   Negative aspects of illegal payments in the recipient country

The big loser from the system of baksheesh is the recipient country. In the end it is always the recipient country that pays for the received bribes, since they are inevitably included in the full contract price. The practice provokes numerous adverse consequences (see Box 15.2):

* Idle factories. Tiano (1981) gives many examples of factories in Third World countries that are either idle or surplus to market needs. For instance, two identical truck factories were constructed in Venezuela, just outside Caracas (Beaudeux, 1980). Although they were far in excess of the real needs of the market, the amounts of the bribes were apparently so large that both 'had' to be built.
* Discouragement of the use of purely professional skills. The recipient countries often have skilled professionals: engineers, administrators, accountants, etc. They see their expertise poorly rewarded. When they compare their incomes to those who have the political decision power and use it to obtain baksheesh, they naturally lose motivation. They gradually lose the will to make effective use of their skills. As a consequence they spend most of their time trying to attain those political positions where illegal payments enable significant personal enrichment.
* The generation of a low level of commitment to technical quality and to respect for standards. Problems are encountered during the completion and operation of turnkey factories: delays, under-capacity, unsellable production, etc. This results partly from the practice of paying baksheesh, even though the necessary local expertise exists. Bribes may be actual motivators for underperformance: for example, a technical adviser to the government of the recipient country is bribed by being made a fictitious employee of a fake consultancy company situated in Luxemburg. His objective interest is that his

salary should be paid for as long as possible, therefore the factory should be constructed over as long a period of time as possible. He may be unconcerned with keeping to deadlines, because it would stop his bribe. As a consequence, he may even give poor data and advice so that trouble on site interrupts the progress of construction.

One of the most damaging consequences of these practices is to create, through strict necessity, a radical separation between words and deeds. A certain country, for example, forces international contracting parties to include a clause 'excluding intermediaries' which is very precise and detailed. The legislation governing corruption is very strict in that country, yet bribes are common practice there. Claimed honesty and actual corruption creates a sort of social schizophrenia due to the combination of regulations often inherited from colonization with conflicting local cultural patterns. Imported legal systems are impersonal and official and provide for a severe repression, whereas actual behaviour is based on a clan system and assumes that personal relations and group influences are essential. They override legal considerations and are to be obtained by money or other means. This distinction between words and deeds is sometimes very hard to accept for

Box 15.2   *'Article 15'*

On the banks of the large [Zaire] river, just as in the province of Shaba, no one in Zaire is surprised to see a civil servant demanding a 'matabiche' in return for a passport or some other official document. On the contrary, people would be worried if such a request was not made. No Zairean would take offence at having to pay for an official hearing, or to have a letter sent to a department head. Seals and headed notepaper are bought and are sometimes forged. In Zaire, civil servants are 'resourceful people' and know how to supplement their income. The police set up roadblocks when they need money: drivers never have the requisite paper and are therefore obliged to put their hands in their pockets.[10] At the main post office in 'Kin' [Kinshasa, the capital], letters and parcels may – like anywhere else in the world – be posted in a box, but it is less than certain that they will arrive at their destination. The 'citizen' (in Zaire, the 'Supreme Guide' has brought into fashion this revolutionary title) greatly increases the chances of this occurring if he greases the palm of the postman. Likewise, a citizen may make a telephone call to the other end of the planet for the price of a tip. All this comes under 'Article 15', a shameful way of designating the small-scale corruption practised by civil servants. This corruption is institutionalized and widespread; it also goes under the name of 'matabiche': bribe, backhander, a 'little something', brown paper packet.

The practice is so ingrained that President Mobutu did not shy away from encouraging it in a speech on 20 May 1976: 'If you are going to steal, steal a small amount and do it intelligently, in a nice way. If you are going to steal so much that you become rich in a single night, you will be arrested.'

(Péan, 1988, pp. 139–40. Reproduced with permission.)

Western minds; it makes corruption just as hard to recognize as honesty and gives no clear indication as to the means of establishing a fair business communication (Usunier, 1989).

15.8 Reducing illegal payments

As a response to various scandals, Saudi Arabia introduced legislation that sought to legitimize and control the payment of commissions. A 1978 royal decree has banned the use of influence to obtain government contracts and has fixed the conditions where agents (called 'sponsors') may be hired. They must be Saudi nationals. Their remuneration cannot exceed 5 per cent of the value of the contract, and they cannot represent more than ten companies. Even members of the royal family have to publish a list of their principals in official registers. Furthermore, military contracts as well as intergovernmental transactions may not give rise to an agent's commission.

The legal qualification of 'sponsor' which is given to these agents is in reality rather vague. It covers the notion of guarantor and can be combined with the function of commercial agent. The 'sponsor' is often the business agent and the local intermediary who is indispensable in sorting out any administrative problems (visas, import licences, etc.).

This legislation is a step in the right direction, although it does not prohibit illegal payments from the donor country, as the FCPA does. It does, however, recognize that someone who contributes to the winning of the contract and acts as an effective intermediary is entitled to receive remuneration for those efforts. Those who hold high-level positions may have a right to derive benefit from their position, but since they have a specific authority, they have to exercise that authority within a clearly defined framework.

In conclusion, it must be emphasized that any improvement in the actual situation, which is costly for many and from which only a few reap any benefit, can only result from a disclosure of the facts. An effort to codify the services rendered by those who receive bribes also seems necessary. But international co-ordination assumes cultural convergence on ethical issues. Finally the fixing of thresholds for these payments as well as formalities for public recording of certain transactions would be a better means of monitoring and controlling the practice of illegal payments.

APPENDIX 15

———— ♦♦♦ ————

Teaching materials

A15.1 Case: Houston Oil Supply

Fred Allman, director of marketing and sales for Houston Oil Supply, was faced with the difficult job of penetrating the Mexican oil market. The Mexican market consisted of a single firm, PEMEX, the government-owned oil production and marketing monopoly. Allman had had no previous experience with foreign buyers until last June, when he was approached by a representative of British Petroleum, who was interested in Houston's new service station pump for its Canadian stations. This started him thinking about the enormous potential for sales abroad, and he immediately focused his attention on the rich Mexican market south of the border.

Houston Oil Supply had operated in the oil-producing regions of the south-western United States since 1946. The company was founded by Jake Grashof, an unsuccessful wildcat oil producer, to supply the needs of oil producers in the field. The company prospered over the years, and by 1980 was one of the leading oil well supply firms in the industry. At that time, Grashof, who had surrendered active management of the company to his two sons, was approached by the inventor of a revolutionary new electronic gasoline pump for service stations. Recognizing a potential winner in the marketplace, Grashof obtained production and distribution rights to the pump and established a new division to produce and market it. It was at this time that Fred Allman was hired to sell the new product. By 1985, the new pump was being sold in all major markets in the United States, and sales for the division had climbed to $11 million.

Allman was attracted by the Mexican market because of the PEMEX monopoly. Although the Mexican market was large and growing rapidly, it was nowhere near as rich as the American or Canadian markets because of the lower percentage of ownership and usage of automobiles. However, it was still a large user of gasoline pumps, and its unique attraction lay in the fact that the entire market could be reached through a single buyer, PEMEX.

Fred Allman had no idea how PEMEX officials made their buying decisions, but he was aware that their methods of doing business were very different from those of American buyers from reading newspaper accounts of the U.S. Justice Department action against Gary Bateman and Crawford Enterprises (See Exhibit 1 for a description of *Bateman/Crawford Enterprises* case.) The parties involved apparently had obtained purchase orders from PEMEX through payoffs to officials of the government-owned company. While such action is not legal, he understood that Mexico's political and business infrastructures have permitted monetary 'subsidies' to influence and/or dictate transactional decision making. Known as the *mordida* or 'bite,' public corruption had permeated all socioeconomic levels, becoming a 'way of life' among Mexicans. Since bribes are effected in various forms, no country is immune to their existence. In Mexico, however, payoffs were conducted more openly – a catalyst for prompt, assured action.

◆◆◆

Exhibit 1   *U.S. v. Gary Bateman/Crawford Enterprises*

In October 1982 the U.S. Justice Department brought action against Crawford Enterprises and Gary Bateman, former marketing vice president of Crawford Enterprises, for bribery and corruption of two PEMEX officials. PEMEX is a petroleum production and distribution monopoly owned and operated by the Mexican government. The indictments charged that the parties involved had obtained purchase orders from PEMEX through payoffs to officials of the Mexican oil monopoly.

Late in 1981, Gary Bateman, former marketing vice president of Crawford Enterprises of Houston, Texas, pleaded guilty to making payoffs totaling $342,000 U.S. in bribes to Guillermo Cervera, administrative secretary to the chief of purchasing at PEMEX.

When fired from Crawford Enterprises on February 9, 1979, Bateman opened his own business – Applied Process Products Overseas, Inc. – with the idea of transacting business with PEMEX. Bateman had offered to pay Cervera 30 percent of Applied's gross profit in exchange for assistance in obtaining business. Cervera presumably agreed and became 'administrator and handler' of the money, which would be divided with other PEMEX officials. Bateman's company obtained approximately $5 million in purchase orders from PEMEX until March 1981, when Bateman signed a cooperating agreement with the U.S. government bribery investigation in return for minor offense charges.

However, the U.S. government stated that while marketing vice president at Crawford Enterprises, Gary Bateman handled company dealings with PEMEX and usually carried large amounts of currency from Houston to Mexico City. This led to further investigation, and in October of 1982, the U.S. Justice Department alleged that a bribery scheme was set up by Crawford Enterprises paying $10 million in bribes to two former PEMEX officials to secure orders for gas compression equipment totaling $225 million between June 1977 and March 1979. The U.S. government contended that Crawford Enterprises funneled cash to a Mexican intermediary company, Grupo Industrial Delta, to be passed on to the PEMEX officials.

Crawford Enterprises, Inc., had been accused of representing the additional interests (in submitting bids to PEMEX) of Solar Turbines International, a subsidiary of Caterpillar Tractor Co., and Ruston Gas Turbines, Inc., a subsidiary of General Electric England Ltd. Crawford Enterprises has denied any wrongdoing in connection with the allegations.

◆◆◆

While corruption had been overemphasized as the cause for Mexico's current state of the economy, the new administration of President de la Madrid, which took office in 1983, was striving for a 'moral renovation' that would include an attempt to reduce waste and political graft. To set an example, the Mexican government formally charged and subsequently dismissed three PEMEX officials for accepting over $342,000 in bribes from the U.S. firms in the Crawford Enterprises affair.

Allman found himself in somewhat of a quandary. The U.S. government had taken a consistent stand against the corruption and bribery of foreign buyers and particularly foreign government officials. And the Justice Department had followed an aggressive course of action against American offenders. Yet it seemed evident that despite current Mexican government opposition, the *mordida* was still a part of the Mexican culture and might be a necessary requirement for getting the attention of PEMEX buyers.

Questions

1. Why are there differences in business practices between the United States and Mexico? What are these differences?

2. Is bribery the same thing as corruption? A bribe is defined as 'money or favour given or promised to a person in a position of trust to influence his judgment or conduct; something that serves to induce or influence.' Corruption is defined as 'the impairment of integrity, virtue or moral principle; morally degenerate and perverted'.
3. How are ethics established and whose ethics prevail in a foreign environment? Must foreigners comply with local customs, or can traditional business practices be challenged? Should marketers behave as 'change agents' in foreign markets?
4. If you were Fred Allman, competing for foreign contracts worth millions of dollars in sales, what would your ethical parameters be? Which actions would you take?

(Adapted from Cundiff and Hilger, 1988, pp. 123–5. Adapted from a case prepared by Carol G. Spindola. Reproduced with permission.)

A15.2 Case: G. H. Mulford Pharmaceutical Company

Grace Mulford, president and chief executive officer of G. H. Mulford Pharmaceutical Company, asked Sam Gregory to review the political and legal ramifications of the Latin American market before the company embarked on a proposed major expansion in South and Central America later in 1986. In the past, the company had been strongly oriented toward the American market; it had stumbled into the Latin American market almost by chance. When Grace Mulford became president in mid-1985, she focused efforts on international markets as the most promising area for expansion. One of her first administrative changes was to establish an international division and to hire Sam Gregory to head it. Gregory was particularly familiar with the Latin American market, having worked for Coca-Cola in Brazil.

In 1943, George Mulford leased a portion of an abandoned textile mill in Fall River, Massachusetts, to manufacture aspirin. His aspirin, which was introduced under the brand name Blue Seal, was positioned to sell at a price one-third lower than that of Bayer, the industry leader. During the next 20 years, he added antacid tablets to the line and gradually expanded his market throughout northeastern United States. In 1960, his son Daren joined the firm. Concerned with the company's dependence on two mature products that might at any time become obsolete, Daren persuaded his father to develop a research division and to introduce antibiotics and other prescription drugs. By 1985, Mulford was marketing a line of 17 drugs. Although Blue Seal Aspirin still accounted for 39 percent of sales, sales of prescription drugs were steadily increasing as a share of company volume. In 1985, Mulford had a 1.7 percent share of the American pharmaceutical market.

In 1971, Bailey and Sons, a Boston export agent, suggested that Mulford could find a market for Blue Seal Aspirin in Argentina. The market proved to be profitable, and ultimately Mulford opened a sales office in Montevideo to service both Argentina and Uruguay and a second South American office in São Paulo, serving Brazil. In 1982 Daren Mulford investigated the possibility of launching the full line of prescription drugs in the Latin American market. He discovered that it would be necessary to learn a lot more about the political and legal hazards in new Latin American markets and to design new marketing strategy for each market. As a consequence, he delayed further action on this market.

Gregory wanted to concentrate his efforts on Latin America, first because Mulford already had a toehold in the area, but, more important because it was potentially rich. In a study by Sogen-Swiss Corporation in 1973, Mexico and Brazil were classified as the eighth and ninth largest pharmaceutical markets in the world with sales of $580 million and $550 million, respectively, representing 4.1 percent of the world market. Since that time, both countries had continued to experience explosive population growth. Although per capita consumption of pharmaceuticals was much lower than in the United States in all of Latin America, the market was still a huge one, and competition was less rigorous.

A logical starting point in evaluating the individual Latin American markets was the market potential as measured by population and wealth, but in Gregory's opinion a second factor of major importance was the political climate. Latin America had a reputation for political instability. The Mulford Company had experienced major problems early in their tenure in Argentina when the military regime was causing problems for all foreign companies and their employees. Mulford's expansion in the Brazilian market had been much more rapid because of a stable government. Despite the stereotype of instability, Latin American governments ranged from very stable as in Mexico, Venezuela, and Brazil to wildly unstable as in the case of Bolivia, where the government had changed at least 15 times in 15 years. Gregory found that methods had been developed to measure political risk in foreign markets, so he could compare the various promising Latin American countries. However, he wasn't sure that political instability was as dangerous for a firm selling products essential to health as for firms selling luxury products from abroad. In addition, he wasn't sure what level of risk would be acceptable in relation to potential profits. He didn't want to make the mistake made by a number of large international banks, who were so attracted by potential profits from loans to Latin America, that they badly underemphasized the risks of nonpayment.

Gregory found that a pharmaceutical firm faced a different legal and ethical environment in Latin America than in the United States. For example, in the United States, physicians obtain information about drugs from the *Physicians' Desk Reference*, a standard reference book providing information on all ethical drugs. The statements found in this reference book reflect the official attitudes of the FDA and its expert consultants. Each manufacturer must submit statements about its drugs to the U.S. Food and Drug Administration for approval: it is from these statements that the descriptions in the *Physicians' Desk Reference* are drawn and, also, all package inserts, medical journal advertisements, and all other labeling and promotion are drawn. The Food and Drug Adminstration requires full disclosure of unpleasant, dangerous, or potentially lethal side effects. In general, American manufacturers have welcomed these disclosure requirements as both clinically essential and socially desirable, but also as an important protection in product liability litigation.

The situation is very different in South America. Although the extent of government protection of drug consumers varies somewhat from country to country, the level of control is much lower. The standard reference books, commonly called PLM (*para los medicos*) by the doctors, allow much more extensive and unsupported statements about the drugs, and the listings of hazards are curtailed, glossed over, or totally omitted. The same is true of advertising, both to the physicians and to the patients. There is much more use of hyperbole and omission of undesirable facts.

The medical reference book for Brazil indicates that the information was provided by each manufacturer based on texts approved by the government's Servicio de Fiscalizacão de Medicina e Farmacia, but apparently Brazilian law does not require that the promotional material is subjected to government approval. The situation in Argentina is quite different. The texts of *Therapia Vademecum* were written by the staff from material contributed by the manufacturers, and the material was not submitted to laboratories for approval.

For the past three years, there had been a running battle between the advertising department in Fall River and the manager of the Montevideo office. The director of advertising wanted the promotional and informational copy prepared for the United States market to be translated into Spanish and Portuguese and used unchanged in the Latin American markets. He believed that such action was not only morally and ethically proper, but that it provided protection from litigation by injured customers. Lopez, in Montevideo, argued that Mulford products could not compete effectively in the local markets unless he was allowed to follow competitors' practices of overstating potential benefits and understating hazards or limitations, all of which was legal under local laws. Grace Mulford asked Gregory to propose a company policy on this matter.

Questions

1. How important is political risk for a foreign manufacturer of ethical drugs (e.g. sold under a physician's prescription)?
2. Product liability: examine the differences which are evidenced by this case between the United States and Latin America.
3. What are the cultural differences between US (and more generally Western European) people and Latin Americans which may explain differences in marketing communication practices (advertising claims, information content of instructions for use, and so on)?
4. What should Gregory's recommendation be with respect to advertising claims in the Latin American market? Which style and content should he give to directions for use of the drugs? Which instructions should he give to medical visitors?

(Adapted from Cundiff and Hilger, 1988, pp. 226–8. Reproduced with permission.)

Notes

1. The following words are used with the same meaning of illegal payment: baksheesh, envelope, brown paper packet, tip, secret payment, bribe, etc. Payments may vary in size or location (baksheesh has a 'foreign' connotation), but the basic principle is always the same: to obtain a favour unlawfully by the means of money.
2. The books by Walter (1989), *Secret Money*, and Péan (1988), *L'Argent Noir*, are among the very

few books which describe corruption practices in great detail. Ingo Walter, a professor of international finance at New York University and Insead, describes world underground financial mechanisms: money laundering, tax havens, mafia investments, and extends to insider trading (which often includes some bribery). Pierre Péan describes in detail the bribery affairs related to international arms sales and to large turnkey operations, when they are governed by governmental relations and covered by public foreign insurance and finance.

3. For a presentation of Edward Hall's theory of intercultural communication, see section 4.2.
4. Gérard Verna (1991) has developed a framework for the analysis of the relativity of ethical conceptions. He considers both a legal and regulatory point of view (*legality*) and acceptability in terms of social practices (*legitimacy*). In this way, he shows that there are four categories of activity:

   1. 'Normal activities' which are both legal and legitimate.
   2. 'Unofficial activities', at the margin of legality but often legitimate: underground economy and moonlighting in developed countries, parallel economy in developing countries.
   3. 'Criminal activities' which are those that are intentionally carried out in breach of the law, and are totally devoid of legitimacy.
   4. 'Legal violence' which designates those areas where an action is legal but not legitimate: forcing the population of a district to accept a hazardous factory, certain expropriations nominally in the public interest, the export of toxic waste to Third World countries, etc.

   For a deeper understanding of these concepts, see Verna (1991) and Lelart and Lespès (1991).

5. For illustration of turnkey operations see the negotiation simulation at the end of Chapter 13.
6. Except on the fringe: some national regulations provide that state civil engineers, who are instrumental in deciding which supplier is selected in public works auctioneering, are legally paid a fee. This legal fee is supposed to reduce the temptation and compensate them for the work overload which the review of submissions may sometimes create.
7. The different publications of the Swiss sociologist Jean Ziegler (who has not always been unanimously praised in his own country), offer a critical and informed view of the Third World:

   Each return from Africa or Brazil is painful: as soon as I leave the airport at Cointrin [Geneva airport], the shock hits me. But the human warmth, the conviviality, the beauty and the affinity of my hosts remain within me. I wander through the streets of Geneva for three or four days. I am unable to work, to sort out my notes. Days and nights are spent in confusion. Then I plunge once more, slowly, painfully into the world of commercial rationality, carefully timed meetings, fierce competition, struggle, perpetual failure of people to understand each other, and solitude. (Ziegler, 1988, p. 20)

8. Even though I personally like Rawls' definition of a 'moral personality', it nevertheless remains a rather Western one, in that rationality, individualism and equality with others are strongly emphasized. In many other cultural contexts, where moral personalities actually exist, these traits would not be emphasized in such a definition.
9. See for instance the *Journal of Business Ethics*.
10. To prevent this being slightly misinterpreted: whereas some form of minor tipping of civil servants may exist in developing countries, it is not only Africa that is implicated. Corruption exists everywhere and we have seen numerous examples in Europe, Japan and South America.

References

Agpar, M. (1977), 'Succeeding in Saudi Arabia', *Harvard Business Review*, January–February, pp. 14–33.

Beaudeux, Pierre (1980), 'L'Economie du backchich', *Harvard-L'Expansion*, 5 December.

Becker, Helmut and David H. Fritzsche (1987), 'A comparison of the ethical behavior of American, French and German managers', *Columbia Journal of World Business* (Winter), pp. 87–95.

Brenner, S.N. and E.A. Molander (1977), 'Is the ethics of business changing?', *Harvard Business Review*, January–February, pp. 57–71.

Cateora, P.R. (1987), *International Marketing*, 6th edn, Richard D. Irwin: Homewood, IL.

Charreaux, Gérard (1987), 'Le Théorie positive de l'agence: une synthèse de la littérature', in Gérard Charreaux, Alain Couret, Patrick Joffre, Gérard Koenig and Bernard de Montmorillon, *De Nouvelle Théories pour gérer l'entreprise*, Economica: Paris.

Couret, Alain (1987), 'La Théorie des droits de propriété', in Gérard Charreaux, Alain Couret, Patrick Joffre, Gérard Koenig and Bernard de Montmorillon, *De Nouvelle Théories pour gérer l'entreprise*, Economica: Paris.

Cundiff, Edward and Marye Tharp Hilger (1988), *Marketing in the International Environment*, 2nd edn, Prentice Hall: Englewood Cliffs, NJ.

Daniels, John D., Ernest W. Ogram and Lee H. Radebaugh (1982), *International Business: Environments and operations*, 3rd edn, Addison-Wesley: Reading, MA.

Demsetz, H. (1967), 'Toward a theory of property rights', *American Economic Review*, vol. 57, May, pp. 347–59.

Gillespie, Kate (1987), 'Middle East response to the US Foreign Corrupt Practices Act', *California Management Review*, vol. xxix, no. 4, pp. 9–30.

Graham, John L. (1983), 'Foreign Corrupt Practices Act: A manager's guide', *Columbia Journal of World Business*, vol. 18, no. 3.

Haegg, C. (1983), 'Sources of international business ethics', *Management International Review*, vol. 23, no. 4, pp. 73–8.

Hall, Edward T. (1959), *The Silent Language*, Doubleday: Garden City, NY.

Hall, Edward T. (1976), *Beyond Culture*, Anchor Press/Doubleday: Garden City, NY.

Jacoby, N.H., P. Nehemkis and R. Eells (1979), 'Naivete: Foreign payoffs law', *California Management Review*, vol. xxii, no. 1.

Jensen, M.C. and W.H. Meckling (1976), 'Theory of the firm: Managerial behavior, agency costs and ownership structure', *Journal of Financial Economics*, vol. 3, October, pp. 305–60.

Kaikati, J.G. (1977), 'The phenomenon of international bribery', *Business Horizons*, February, pp. 25–37.

Kaikati, J.G. and W.A. Label (1980), 'American bribery legislation: An obstacle to international marketing', *Journal of Marketing*, vol. 44 (Fall), pp. 38–43.

Lee, K.H. (1981), 'Ethical beliefs in marketing management: A cross-cultural study', *European Journal of Marketing*, vol. 15, no. 1, pp. 58–67.

Lelart, Michel and Jean-Louis Lespès (1991), *Pratiques informelles comparées: les fondements de la non-légalité*, proceedings of the Conference on Informal Economy, Nouakchott, December 1988, Presses Universitaires de France: Paris.

Maquet, Jacques (1962), *Les Civilisations noires*, Marabout-Université: Paris.

Mayo, Michel A., Lawrence J. Marks and John K. Ryans Jr (1991), 'Perceptions of ethical problems in international marketing', *International Marketing Review*, vol. 8, no. 3, pp. 61–75.

Péan, Pierre (1988), *L'Argent noir*, Librairie Arthème Fayard: Paris.

Rawls, John (1971), *A Theory of Justice*, Belknap Press of Harvard University: Cambridge, MA.

Tiano, André (1981), *Transfert de technologie industrielle*, Economica: Paris.

Usunier, Jean-Claude (1989), 'Interculturel: la parole et l'action', *Harvard-L'Expansion*, no. 52 (Spring), pp. 84–92.

Usunier, Jean-Claude (1992a), *Environnement International et Gestion de l'Exportation*, 5th edn, Presses Universitaires de France: Paris.

Usunier, Jean-Claude (1992b), *Management International*, 5th edn, Presses Universitaires de France: Paris.

Verna, Gérard (1991), 'Légalité ou légitimité: les pièges du Tiers Monde', in Franck Gauthey and Dominique Xardel (eds), *Management Interculturel: Modes et modèles*, Economica: Paris, pp. 75–93.

Walter, Ingo (1989), *Secret Money*, 2nd edn, Unwin Hyman: London.

Ziegler, Jean (1988), *La Victoire des Vaincus: Oppression et résistance culturelle*, Editions du Seuil: Paris.

Postscript

Globalization as 'modernism' brought to backward nations

As Ernest Dichter emphasized in an article entitled 'The World Customer', which is considered a seminal article in the field of international marketing, particularly as it was the first to picture the phenomenon of the globalization of world markets:[1]

> Only one Frenchman out of three brushes his teeth. Automobiles have become a must for the self-esteem of even the lowliest postal clerk in Naples or the Bantu street cleaner in Durban. ... Four out of five Germans change their shirts but once a week (p. 113).

The explanation is to be found further on: 'The fact that 64% of the Frenchmen don't brush their teeth is in part caused by the lack of running water in many communities' (p. 116). The Germans rank first for the 'self-illusions' a nation can have about itself. Dichter proposes the following illustration: 'Germans still refer to themselves as a nation of poets and thinkers; yet the largest selling newspaper, the *Bildzeitung*, has a circulation of $2\frac{1}{2}$ million based largely on sensationalism and tabloid treatment of news' (p. 117). According to Dichter (at the beginning of the 1960s) Dutch housewives would use instant coffee accompanied by the verbal protest that instant coffee is used only as an emergency. 'What happens, however, is that the number of emergencies has increased amazingly' (p. 117).

One might think that globalization emerged from the advances in modernity and cleanliness accomplished by these backward people, when they overcame their resistance to change. One may also wonder whether there is any real connection between Goethe, Schiller, Kant or Heidegger on the one hand and the *Bildzeitung* on the other, except the fact that they are all German. It is necessary to highlight the first paradox in this approach: many arguments in favour of the globalization of markets are totally ethnocentric; as such, they are in contradiction with the spirit of globalization, which is based on the rejection of ethnocentrism.

477

Some true reasons for the globalization of markets

Globalization is, first of all, based on technological advances, which in turn explain globalization on the supply side: economies of scale and experience effects, drastic changes over the last forty years in transportation and also new telecommunications technologies. The globalization of consumers and demand will certainly occur in the future, but it will happen much later than its early defenders imagined. Moreover the process of world-wide globalization of demand may be quite different to what they visualized: a steady extension of the 'American way of life' throughout the world which would contribute to the global happiness of humankind.

But cultural coherence should not be forgotten and marketers still have to be aware of it. Consumers buy meanings, not just products. Meaning is intersubjectively shared in the cultural community. The process of globalization of demand will be long term because of the local nature of culture and its contribution to collective identity. Moreover, this evolution can be achieved only by individuals who *learn*. Learning is a large part of the process of culture. Globalization implies that consumers throughout the world have to borrow foreign ways of life, experience new behaviours and construct shared meanings with people from other cultures. At present, a great many things are shared among the cultures of the world, but just as many remain culture-specific. *Amnesty International*, the practice of *judo*, playing or listening to *jazz*, the *Olympics* and many other cultural artifacts, even though they were born in particular cultures, are probably bearers of future universal values. Obviously each national culture has a specific contribution to make to the movement towards globalization. If there is any true (and sincere) way of being *global*, it is not by denying differences, but by being aware and responsive to them.

We face a second paradox, the two sides of which must be constantly kept in mind: on the one hand life-styles apparently tend to become global; on the other the claims for recovering cultural identity are stronger than ever. Numerous peoples who have been denied a sovereign state (Balts, Kurds, Armenians, Eritreans, etc.) are demanding their independence as nations, emphasizing the uniqueness of their culture. The concept of a nation-state, although a fairly recent one historically,[2] remains very strong for many individuals. While it is not the only way of protecting cultural identity, it is still the most elaborate and efficient one.

The law of comparative advantage is noted in the Introduction for it has almost completely eliminated the concept of culture from international trade theory. One may remark, as Galtung does, that: 'In short, this "law" [of comparative advantage] is a piece of cultural violence buried in the very core of economics.'[3] Ignoring cultural differences, the law of comparative advantage imposes a paradigm of international trade, which is excessively utilitarian: it assumes the *complete pre-eminence of utility over identity*. Yet real people do not live only with what is useful to them, they also live out of the maintenance and self-actualization of their identity, of which their cultural identity is a large part. This is why it is necessary to integrate the dimension of culture in marketing strategies and in their implementation, when they focus on international markets.

Designing tailored marketing strategies, and implementing them with respect for the local context

As this book (hopefully) shows: marketing strategies tailored to national/cultural markets are not in contradiction with the choice of a global business strategy. On the contrary, cultural tailoring is a basic element of a global business strategy. The reality of cultural exchanges world-wide is now so complex and so inextricable, that any oversimplification is dangerous. Let us take a concrete example: using instant coffee does not imply that one has, once and for all, adopted ready-made standardized consumer goods. Bean coffee and ground coffee have made a tremendous come-back against instant coffee, regaining lost market share in most coffee-drinking countries of the world. No evolution is fixed; consumers change from 'tradition' to 'modernism', but also back to (almost) traditional ways of consuming. Among the segments targeted for an intercultural marketing strategy there will be both transnational market segments and national market segments, to which specific offers will be made. National culture will continue to influence strongly the implementation of marketing strategies, under many aspects: choice of distribution channels and trade partners, setting of prices, sales and marketing negotiations, etc.

This is fortunate because, if cultural differences were to disappear, I suspect that we would become bored.

Notes

1. I am sorry for the unkind use of certain sentences of this article (Ernest Dichter, 1962, 'The World Customer', *Harvard Business Review*, vol. 40, no. 4, pp. 113–22). It is a superb example of sincere ethnocentrism, as well as of relative lack of long-term vision. The article does, however, comprise many insightful remarks.
2. The concept of a nation-state emerged clearly at the end of the seventeenth century and during the nineteenth century. Germany and Italy, for instance, were not united as nation-states before the end of the nineteenth century, under the auspices of Bismarck in Germany and Cavour in Italy. Decolonization was the heyday of the concept of the nation-state: many countries were formed which corresponded neither to a nation, nor to a shared culture among the various groups of citizens, nor even to a geographical unit.
3. Johan Galtung, in an article entitled 'Cultural violence' (1990, *Journal of Peace Research*, vol. 27, no. 3, pp. 291–305), thoroughly defines what the process of cultural violence encompasses. In particular, one section of his article (4.5) argues about the role of Ricardo's doctrine (developed further by Hecksher and Ohlin, and others) as justifying the world division of labour. 'The principle of comparative advantage sentences countries to stay where the production-factor profile has landed them, for geographical and historical reasons' (p. 300). However, marketers are not economists: their pragmatism may induce them to choose *culturally non-violent* marketing strategies, if they prove successful.

Author index

Aaker, David A., 385
Abbeglen, James, 23, 35, 267, 276
Adler, Keith, 35, 264–5, 279
Adler, Nancy J., 36, 73, 96–7, 133, 162, 320, 337, 412, 425–6, 435, 439–40, 450
Adler, Peter S., 111, 129
Advertising Age, 359–60, 387
Agpar, P., 455, 475
Albaum, Gerald, 118, 160–1, 164, 298, 379, 416, 429
Alberts, William L., 219–20
Ali, Abbas, 317, 337
Ali, F., 427
Allen, David Elliston, 12, 35, 285, 303
Allvine, F. E., 192
Alpay, Guvenc, 252, 280
Amine, Lyn S., 12, 35, 147, 162
Anderson, B., 259, 278
Anderson, Erin T., 316, 338
Anderson, Paul F., 321, 338
Anderson, W. T., 258, 276
Angelmar, Reinhard, 139–40, 164, 403–5, 410, 422, 426
Archibald, K., 428, 451
Arndt, Johan, 392, 426
Aronson, Elliot, 62, 165
Arpan, Jeffrey S., 346, 388
Arrow, Kenneth J., 219–20
Arthur, M. B., 96
Athos, Anthony G., 337–8, 449
Attali, Jacques, 431, 450
Avlonitis, G., 277

Bagozzi, Richard P., 4, 7, 20, 35, 293, 392, 426
Bagur, J. S., 427
Bahn, Kenneth D., 276–80
Bailly, A. M., 245
Ballon, Robert J., 449
Bamossy G. J., 260, 276–7
Bannister, J. P., 254, 276

Barabba, Vincent P., 220
Barkhai, Haim, 219–20
Bartlett, Christopher, 182, 191, 219
Barzini, Luigi, 440, 449–50
Bateson, Gregory, 113, 129
Baudrillard, Jean, 36
Baumgardner, S., 148, 162
Baumgartner, Gary, 254, 276
Beaudeux, P., 454–5, 465–6, 475
Becker, Gary, 288, 303
Becker, Helmut, 464, 475
Beliaev, Edward, 439, 450
Belk, Russell W., 16, 36, 176, 191
Benton, A. A., 427
Beracs, Joszef, 277–8
Berent, Paul Howard, 131, 162
Bergmann, Alexander, 60, 337
Berning, Carol K., 451
Berry, John W., 62, 97, 133, 162
Bhandari, Labdhi, 192
Bilkey, Warren J., 251, 275–6
Bitterli, Urs, 60
Blackman, S., 34
Blackwell R. D., 19, 36
Bleek, W., 115
Bleustein-Blanchet, Marcel, 385
Bliemel, F., 277
Boas, Franz, 52
Boddewyn, Jean J., 171, 180, 192–3, 198, 220, 323–5, 337–8, 344, 387
Bon, Jérôme, 36, 252–5, 276
Boston Consulting Group, 195
Boya, Ünal O., 338
Bradley, Frank, 219
Brenner, S. N., 466, 475
Brierley, J. E. C., 450
Brislin, Richard W., 62, 92, 97, 125–8, 133, 148, 162, 446
Brooke, Michael Z., 420
Brown, B. R., 405–6

Burgaud, Didier, 200, 221, 357, 388
Burgess, A. L., 428
Burke, W. Warner, 426
Burnett, John, 385
Burt, David N., 410, 425, 427, 435–41, 450
Business Week, 354, 387
Buske, Erwin, 170, 180, 192
Butler, W. E., 450
Buzzati, Dino, 22
Buzzell, Robert D., 180, 191

Cabat, Odilon, 264, 276
Cadix, Alain, 36
Calantone, Roger, 134, 162
Calori, Roland, 174
Campbell, Donald T., 110, 130, 137, 139, 142–3, 163
Campbell, J. B., 163
Campbell, Nigel C. G., 97, 403, 405–6, 426–7, 441, 450
Camphuis, Pierre-Arnold, 226
Carroll, John B., 41, 61, 100, 128–9, 171, 191
Carter, J. R., 425, 428
Cateora, Philip R., 23, 28, 36, 82, 94, 96, 311–17, 338, 366, 406, 427, 441, 450
Cattin, Philippe, 249, 254, 257, 276
Cavusgil, S. Tamer, 12, 35, 137, 147, 162–3, 257, 277
Cecchini, Paolo, 179, 191
Chambers, Terry M., 321, 338
Chandran, Rajan, 139, 165
Chantraine, Pierre, 93
Chao, Paul, 276
Charreaux, Gérard, 459, 475
Chen, Yan, 33, 36
Chéron, Emmanuel, 173, 193
Cherrie, Craig, 92, 127–8
Cheskin Masten, 171, 192
Chien, M., 17, 36
Child, John, 40, 61
Chonko, Lawrence B., 321, 337–8
Chun, K. T., 146, 163
Churchill, Gilbert A., 137, 163, 429
Clark, Harold F. Jr, 173, 177, 184, 191, 268, 276, 360, 387
CNUCED, 434, 450
Cohen, Herb, 424
Cohen, R. 163
Communication et Business, 344, 346, 359, 387
Condon, John C., 105, 129, 130
Contensou François, 267, 276
Copeland, Lennie, 232, 424
Costello, Nicholas P., 355, 388
Coughlan, Anne T., 316, 338
Couret, Alain, 460, 475
Craig, C. Samuel, 132–3, 141, 144–8, 163
Crawford, John C., 254, 258–9, 276–8
Cummings, L. L., 405, 427
Cundiff, Edward W., 156, 176, 191, 257, 261, 272–6, 279, 329, 338, 471–3

Cunningham, I. C. M., 164, 258, 276
Curry, David J., 289, 303
Cushner, Kenneth, 92, 127–8
Czinkota, Michael R., 96, 187, 191, 216, 266, 276, 302–3, 308, 312–6, 322, 338, 350, 387

D'Iribarne, Philippe, 337
Daniels, John D., 303, 455–6, 475
Darbelet, Michel, 96
Darling , John B., 83, 259, 276
Dasen, Pierre R., 62, 97
David, René, 413, 450
Davies, J. Richard, 35, 424
Davis, Harry L., 134, 163
Day, Ellen, 168,
Day, George S., 196, 220
Day, R. L., 404, 428
Dayan, Armand, 15, 36
De Bettignies, Henri, 179, 191
De Bodinat, Henri, 263, 276
De Chantérac, Véronique, 270, 276
De Leersnyder, Jean-Marc, 276
De Maricourt, Renaud, 36, 307, 311, 314, 338, 426
De Mente, Boye, 411, 427, 449–50
De Montmorillon, Bernard, 475
De Mooij, Marieke K., 220
Deher, Odile, 180–1, 192
Demsetz, H., 460, 475
Dentsu Inc., 35, 386
Derr, C. Brooklyn, 79, 96
Deutscher, Irving, 142, 163, 434, 450
Dholakia, Ruby Roy, 176, 192
Diaz Del Castillo, Bernal, 60
Dichter, Ernest, 169, 192, 477, 479
Dornoff, Ronald J., 258–9, 276
Douglas, Susan P., 132–3, 141, 144–8, 163, 165, 169, 171, 192, 200, 221, 277, 348, 387
Dowd, Lawrence, 118, 298, 379, 416
Doz, Yves, 219
Droit, Michel, 111, 129
Druckman, D., 405, 427
Dubois, Bernard, 18, 36, 169, 192, 348, 387
Dudley, James W., 356, 387
Duerr, Edwin, 118, 298, 379, 416
Dun and Bradstreet Corp., 121
Dupont, Christophe, 403, 421, 427
Dupuis, Marc, 307, 311, 314, 338
Dupuy, François, 267, 276
Durkheim, Emile, 53
Dwyer, Robert F., 393–4, 427

Eckensberger, Lutz H., 133, 163
Eells, R., 464, 475
Ehrmann, H. W., 450
Eiteman, David K., 438, 451
El Ansary, Adel I., 336
El Haddad, Awad B., 12, 36
Eliade, Mircéa, 45, 62
Engel, J. F., 19, 36
Engels-Levine, Erika, 351, 387

Enis, Ben M. 338
Erickson, Gary M., 62, 252, 261, 276
Erikson, Erik, 61, 112, 129
Eroglu, S. A., 256, 276
Eshghi, Abdolezra, 171–2, 192
Essad Bey, Mohammed, 68, 96
Etchegoyen, Alain, 269, 277
Ettenson, R., 255–8, 277
Etzel, Michael J., 251, 277
European Communities, 199–200
Evans, Franklin B., 405, 427

Farley, Lawrence, 191
Farr, Robert M., 53, 62
Fay, T., 142, 165
Fei, X. Y., 17, 36
Feldman, Lawrence P., 430, 451
Ferraro, Gary P., 91, 106, 128–30
Fisher, Glenn, 114, 130, 409, 427
Fiske, D., 137, 163
Foster, G. M., 407, 427
Fournis, Yves, 198, 200, 321, 338
Fox, Richard J., 172, 192
Francis, Dick, 302
Freud, Sigmund, 95
Freuhling, Royal, 125
Frijda, Nico, 133, 139, 163
Fritzsche, D. J., 464, 475
Fu, Marilyn Y., 346, 388
Fuat Firat, A., 36, 191–3
Fuentes, Carlos, 407–8, 427
Fyzee, A. A. A., 450

GATT, 177, 192
Gabel, H. Landis, 246
Gaedeke, Ralph, 254, 257, 277
Gaeth, Gary J., 255–8, 277, 290, 304
Galapakrishna, P., 258, 277
Galtung, Johan, 71, 97, 478–9
Gambiez, Chantal, 324
Gans, Herbert, 246
Garland, B. L., 277
Garreau, J., 134, 163
Gauthey, Franck, 110–13, 117, 130, 476
Geertz, Clifford, 94, 97, 136, 163
Gentry, J. W., 134, 163
Ghauri, Pervez N., 345, 350
Ghertman, Michel, 276
Ghoshal, Sumantra, 169, 180, 192, 219–20
Ghymn, Kyung-Il, 247
Gil, Pere, 375
Gillespie, Kate, 454, 464–5, 475
Gilly, Mary, 347, 387
Giordan, Alain Eric, 226, 264, 277
Glazer, Herbert, 308, 338
Glenn, Edmund S., 408, 427
Goldstein, K. M., 34
Goodenough, Ward H., 40, 47, 62, 433, 451
Goodstein, Leonard D., 426
Goodyear, Mary , 141, 145–7, 163

Graby, Françoise, 249, 254–5, 258, 277
Graham, John L., 36, 399, 405–6, 411, 423–7,
   435–6, 439, 449–51, 464, 475
Graham, Robert J., 29, 35, 100, 130, 430–3, 451
Green, Paul E., 160–2, 164
Green, Robert T., 132–3, 136, 139, 144, 147, 163–4,
   387
Griggs, Lewis, 232, 424
Gruère, Jean-Pierre, 112, 443, 449, 451
Guadagni, Peter, M., 34
Guetzkow, H., 405, 428
Gurevitch, A. J., 431, 451

Haegg, C., 466, 475
Hagen, A. J., 229, 247
Hainard, François, 60, 337
Haley, John O., 311, 328
Hall, D. T., 96
Hall, Edward T., 67, 97, 102–5, 109, 129–30,
   317–18, 338, 406, 413–14, 427, 431–4, 440,
   448–9, 451, 457–8, 474–5
Hallowell, I., 431, 451
Hamel, Gary, 180, 192, 219–20
Hamill, James, 35, 424
Hampton, Gerald M., 170, 180, 192, 253, 277, 387
Hansen, D. M., 183, 192
Hao, J., 163
Harnett, Donald L., 405, 422
Harris, Philip R., 106, 130, 337
Hawking, Stephen W., 46, 62
Hawrysh, Bryan Mark, 436–7, 451
Heckscher, Eli, 479
Helmick Beavin, Janet, 108, 130
Hempel, Donald J., 144, 164
Herberger, Roy A. Jr, 406, 427, 439, 451
Hernandez, Sigfredo L., 139, 165
Heslop, Louise A., 254, 277–8
Hilger, Marye Tharp, 156, 176, 191, 272–6, 329,
   338, 471–3
Hill, John S., 180, 183–4
Hoff, Edward J., 180, 193, 219–20
Hofstede, Geert, 3, 7, 67, 73–9, 97, 162, 164,
   317–21, 338, 430, 440, 451
Hollensen, Svend, 219
Hoover, Robert J., 345, 387
Hornik, Jacob, 430, 451
Houston, M. J., 193
Houston, T. L., 428
Hout, Thomas, 180, 192
Hovell, P. J., 171, 180, 192
Howard, J. 19, 36
Hsieh, Y. W.,17, 36
Hsu, F. L. K., 17, 36
Hughes, M. A., 134, 164
Hunt, H. Keith, 37, 165
Hunt, Shelby D., 392, 427
Huszagh, Sandra M., 172–3, 192

Inagaki, Yoshihiko, 337
Inkeles, Alex, 49, 50, 61–2

Ishida, Hideto, 311–3, 338
Ishihara, Shintaro, 86, 97

Jackson, Barbara B., 392, 427
Jackson, Don D., 108, 130
Jacobs, Laurence , 233, 247
Jacoby, Jacob R., 288, 303, 430, 451
Jacoby, N.H., 454, 464, 475
Jaffé Eugene D., 256–60, 277–8
Jahoda, Gustav, 133, 139, 163
Jain, A. K., 34
Jain, Subhash C., 174, 192–3
James, Watson S. 'Jay', 386
Jensen, M. C., 459, 475
Jodelet, Denise, 53, 62, 342, 387
Joffre, Patrick, 475
Johanson, J., 14, 36, 204, 220
Johansson, Johny K., 14, 36, 256–7, 261, 276–7
Johar, Jotindar, 162
John, J., 163
Jolibert, Alain, 27, 36, 254, 257, 261, 399, 427, 450–1

Kadima, K. , 115, 130
Kagame, Alexis, 115, 130
Kahle, Lyn R., 134, 164
Kaikati, J. G., 454, 464, 475
Kapferer, Jean-Noel, 34, 267, 276–7, 280
Karns, David, 259, 278
Kaynak, Erdener, 137, 163, 176–7, 192, 257, 336, 345, 350, 387
Keegan, Warren G., 4, 7, 180, 192, 220, 302–3, 410, 427
Kelley, Harold H., 399, 421, 427, 440, 451
Keown, Charles, 247, 303–4
Khanna, Sri Ram, 259, 278
Khera, Inder, 259, 278
Khuri, Fuad I., 285, 304
Kieser, A, 40, 61
Kim, C. Y., 259, 278
Kim, Dong Han, 173, 193
Kim, Dong Ki, 337
Kim, G., 254, 278
Kim, Linsu, 337
King, A. Y. C.,17, 36
Klein, Jean, 276
Kluckhohn Clyde, 39, 61–2
Kluckhohn, Florence R., 39, 62–3, 66, 70, 93, 97, 431–2, 451
Koenig, Gérard, 475
Kosaka Hiroshi, 13, 36, 97
Kotler, Philip, 12, 36, 386
Kracmar, J. Z., 145, 164
Kraft, F., 259, 276
Krisnakumar, Parameswar, 252, 278
Kroeber, Alfred L., 39, 62
Kumcu, E., 36, 192–3
Kuribayashi, S., 309–12, 337–8
Kushner, J. M., 16, 36, 145, 164

Label, W. A., 454, 464, 475
Ladmiral, Jean-René, 449
Lagerlöf, Selma, 63, 93
Lamb, Charles W. Jr, 251, 258–9, 276, 279
Lambin, Jean-Jacques, 266, 278
Lane, W. Ronald, 385
Langeard, Eric, 132–3, 164
Langenscheidt (Dictionary), 130
Laufer, Romain, 33, 36
Lauginié, Jean-Marcel, 83, 96
Laurent, André, 73, 79, 96–7
Laurent, Clint R., 36
Laurent, Gilles, 34
Lawrence, B. S., 96
Lawrence, Peter, 174
Lazarde, Michelle M., 275, 278
Lazer, William, 13, 21, 36, 69, 97
Le Clézio, J. M. G., 60
Lee Manzer, L., 163
Lee, George, 120
Lee, James A, 109–10, 130, 229, 247, 401, 407, 428
Lee, K. H., 464, 475
Lee, Y. Y., 37
Lehmann, Donald R., 260, 275, 278
Lelart, Michel, 474–5
Lelièvre, Hélène, 324
Lentrein, Didier, 385
Leonardi, Jean-Paul, 164
Lespès, Jean-Louis, 474–5
Lesser, J. A., 134, 164
Leung, K., 133, 164
Levhari, David, 219–20
Lévi-Strauss, Claude, 62
Levine, Robert A., 110, 130
Levinson, Daniel J., 49, 50, 61–2
Levitt, Theodore, 2, 7, 132, 164, 169–70, 192, 225, 247, 398, 428
Levy-Bruhl, Lucien, 52
Lewicki, Roy J., 424
Lewis, Steven A., 404–6, 428
Liebermann, M.B., 219–20
Lillis, Charles M., 254, 278
Lim, Jee-Su, 261, 279
Lindzey, Gardner, 62, 165
Linton, Ralph, 39, 50, 55, 62, 434, 451
Lipiansky, Edmond-Marc, 449
List, Friedrich, 2
Litterer, Joseph A., 424
Little, John D. C., 34
Littré, Emile, 39
Lohnes, Colleen, 276
Lonner, W. J., 162
Lorimer, E. S., 388
Louis, Ernst A., 171, 193
Ludlow, Peter W., 177, 192
Lumpkin, J. R, 153–4, 278
Lumwanu, F., 115, 130
Luostarinen, Reijo, 277–8
Luqmani, Mushtaq, 349, 387
Lynn, Robert A., 292, 304

Maalouf, Amine, 82, 84, 95–7
Machleit, K. A., 256, 276
McCall, J. B., 35, 303, 424, 428, 449, 451
McCarthy, E. Jerome, 211, 221
McCartney, Laton, 402, 428
McClelland, David, 75
McCornell, J. D., 171, 192
McCracken, Grant, 348, 387
McKersie Robert B., 403, 429
MacNeil, Ian R., 393–4, 428
Makridakis, Spyros, 221
Malhotra, N. K., 34
Malinowski, Bronislaw, 41–4, 59, 62
Malliaris, P., 277
Maquet, J., 463, 475
Marcel, Claude, 279
Marchetti, Renato, 142–3, 164
Mariet, François, 353, 357, 387
Marks, Lawrence J., 475
Marmet, Guy, 257, 278
Marois, Bernard, 276
Maronick, Thomas J., 275
Martenson, Rita, 345, 387
Maslow, Abraham H., 34, 36, 75
Mather, Anne, 217–18
Matthews, H. Lee, 405, 428
Mauviel, Maurice, 87, 97
Mayer, Charles S., 131, 142, 164
Mayo, Michel A., 453, 475
Mazze, E. M., 162
Mead, Margaret, 47, 51, 91
Meckling, W. H., 459, 475
Meissner, Hans Günther, 406, 427, 450–1
Metraux, R., 431, 451
Michaels, R. E., 404, 428
Michon, Christian, 36
Miller, Myron M., 335
Min Han, C., 256, 261, 278
Miner, Horace, 59, 62
Molander, E. A., 466, 475
Monoky, John. F. Jr, 428
Montesquieu, Charles de, 50–1, 62, 67, 85, 93, 97, 107, 130
Montgomery, David B., 196, 220, 309, 313, 337–8
Moore, C. A., 36
Moorman, Christine, 176, 193
Moran, Robert T., 106, 130, 337
Morel, Pierre, 112, 443, 449, 451
Morello, G., 252, 254, 278
Morganosky, Michelle A., 275, 278
Moriarty, Sandra, 385
Morris, Michael, 162
Morschbach, Helmut, 107, 130
Moscovici, Serge, 53, 62, 342, 387–8
Mourier, Pascal, 200, 221, 357, 388
Mullen, Thomas, 450
Murata Shoji, 16, 36, 97
Murdock, George P., 55, 59
Murray, J. A., 225, 247
Myers, John G., 385

Nagashima, Akira, 249, 254, 259, 278
Nakane, Chie, 312, 338
Napoléon-Biguma, Constantin, 116
Narayana, Chem L., 254, 278
Naroll, R., 163
Nath, Ragu, 162, 164
Naulleau, Gérard, 442, 451
Ndao, Cheikh Alioune, 463
Nebenzahl, Israel D., 256–60, 277–8
Nehemkis, P., 464, 475
Nes, Erik, 251, 275–6
Niffenegger, Phillip, 257–9, 278
Nonaka, Ikujiro, 14, 36, 277
Nugent, Thomas, 62

Obenga, Théophile, 130
Oberg, Kalvero, 111, 130
Ofir, Chezy, 260, 275, 278
Ogram, Ernest William, 455, 475
Oh, Sejo, 393–4, 427, 436, 451
Ohlin, Bertil, 479
Ohmae, Kenichi, 178, 192, 200, 221, 313, 338
Oliver, Lauren, 264–5, 279
Ollivier, Alain, 252–5, 276, 300, 426
Olson, Jerry C., 288, 303
Onkvisit, Sak, 266, 278
Oritt, P. L., 229, 247
Osherson, Samuel, 163, 450
Ottosen, Rune, 94
Ouchi, William G., 449

Palia, Aspy P., 303–4
Papadopoulos, N. G., 255, 260, 277–8
Paradeise, Catherine, 33, 36
Parameswaran, Ravi, 135, 164, 260, 278
Pares, Francesco, 375
Pascale, R.T., 337–8, 449
Péan, Pierre, 454, 467, 473, 475
Pearson, Emil, 116, 130
Pedersen, Paul B., 62, 97, 125–6, 446
Peebles, Dean M., 269, 279, 360–1, 388
Perdue, B. C., 404, 428
Perlmutter, Howard, 200, 221
Perrin, Michel, 257, 279
Peter, J. P., 137, 163
Peterson Blyth Cato Associates Inc., 171, 192
Peterson, Richard B., 399, 428
Peterson, Robert A., 62, 261, 279
Petit, Karl, 93
Philpot, J. W., 148, 165
Picard, Jacques, 183, 193
Pike, Kenneth, 135, 164
Pinson, Christian, 34
Plummer, Josef, 132, 164
Pomian, Krysztof, 431, 451
Poortinga, Ype H., 62, 97, 133, 164
Porter, Michael E., 170, 178, 193, 194, 219, 221
Porter, R. E., 130
Post, J. E., 176, 193
Prahalad, C. K., 180, 192, 219–20

Pras, Bernard, 139–40, 164
Prezworski, A., 133, 164
Pruitt, Dean G., 403–7, 425, 428
Prus, Robert C., 220, 283, 286, 304
Punnett, Betty Jane, 450
Pye, Lucian W., 407, 411, 428, 435, 438, 452

Quelch, John A., 180, 193, 219–20, 337
Quraeshi, Zahir, 387

Radebaugh, Lee H., 303, 455, 475
Ramuz, Charles Ferdinand, 60
Rapping, Léonard, 219, 221
Ratz, David G., 184, 193
Rawls, John, 465, 474–5
Reader's Digest, 352–3
Redding, S. G., 16, 36, 320, 338
Reed Hall, Mildred, 449
Reierson, Curtis, 251, 254, 261, 279
Reischauer, Edwin O., 81, 95, 97
Renart, Lluis G., 375
Ricardo, David, 1, 2, 7, 479
Richins, Marsha, 136, 161, 164
Ricks, David A., 180, 193, 346, 388
Riesz, Peter C., 289, 303
Rogers, E. M., 225, 247
Ronkainen, Illka A., 96, 187, 191, 216, 266, 276,
　　302–3, 315–16, 322, 338, 350, 387
Rosen, Barry-Nathan, 171, 193, 262, 279
Rosenberg, Larry J., 314, 339
Ross, Randolph, 311, 338
Roth, 176, 193
Rubin, J.Z., 405–6, 425, 428
Rudden, Eileen, 192
Rugman, Alan, 193, 388
Russel, J. Thomas, 385
Ryan, J. F., 225, 247
Ryans, John K., 184, 193, 343, 388, 475

Saegaert, Joel, 134, 156, 165, 387
Sahagun, Bernardino de, 60
Saito Duerr, Mitsuko, 118, 298
Saito, M., 130
Sakai, John T., 327
Salles, Robert, 279
Samovar, Larry, 130
Sano, Yoshihiro, 411, 427, 435, 449, 451
Sapir, Edward, 42, 98–101, 130, 135, 165
Saporito, William, 178, 183, 193
Sarathy, Ravi, 354, 357, 388
Saunders, J.A., 254, 276
Savitt, Ronald, 163
Sawyer, J., 405, 428
Scanzoni, J., 395, 398, 401, 428
Schacht, J., 450
Schein, Edgar H., 79, 97
Schieb, Pierre-Alain, 257–9, 279
Schlesinger, R., 450
Schmidt, Klaus D., 440, 452
Schooler, Robert D., 251, 258, 279

Schurr, Paul H., 393–4, 427
Schwiercz, Paul M., 317, 337
Sechrest, L., 133, 142, 165
Segall, Marshall H., 52, 61–2, 96–7
Sekaran, U., 133, 165
Sentell, G. D., 148, 165
Shalofsky, Ivor, 268, 279
Sharif, Mohammed, 192
Sharma, S., 255, 279
Shaw, John J., 266, 278
Sherry, John F., 176, 193
Sheth, Jagdish N., 19, 36, 171–2, 192
Shethi, S. Prakash, 176, 193
Shimaguchi, Mitsuaki, 307–14, 338
Shimp, Terence A., 255, 279, 337
Shoemaker, F. F., 225, 247
Shoemaker, Robert, 145, 163
Silk, Alvin J., 163
Singer, Marshall R., 446
Sirgy, M. Joseph, 276–80
Sissmann, Pierre, 169–70
Slatter, Stuart St P., 393, 428
Smith, Adam, 23
Soehl, Robin, 183, 193
Sood, James H., 172, 193
Spindola, Carol G., 471
Sproles, George B., 289, 304
Stalk, George Jr, 23, 35, 267, 276
Stanton, John L., 139, 144–5, 148, 165
Steele, Murray, 174
Stern, Louis W., 336, 403–5, 410, 422, 426
Stigler, George J., 302–4
Still, Richard R., 180, 183–4, 192, 317, 319, 338–9
Stobaugh, Robert B., 180, 193, 219, 221
Stoetzel, Jean, 198, 221
Strandskov, Jesper, 118, 298, 379, 416
Strauss, M. A., 133, 165
Strazzieri, Alain, 164
Stripp, William, 437, 452
Strodtbeck, Frederick L., 61–3, 66, 70, 93, 97,
　　431–2, 451
Suk, Jong, 261, 279
Sullivan, Jeremiah, 399, 428
Sumitomo Corporation, 178, 193
Sunmer, G. A., 109, 130
Sunoo, D. H., 251, 279
Surget, Véronique, 324
Suto, Nobuhiko, 397
Szybillo, George J., 451

Takashi, S., 146, 175
Tankersley, Clint B., 259, 276
Tanner, John F., 338
Tanouchi, Koichi, 21, 37
Tansujah, P., 163
Telesio, Piero, 180, 193
Tellis, Gerard J., 34, 290, 304
Terpstra, Vern, 256, 278
Teune, H., 133, 164
Thévoz, Laurent, 60, 337

Thoenig, Jean-Claude, 267, 276–7, 280
Thorelli, Hans B., 261, 279
Thorndike, R. M, 162
Tiano, André, 225, 247, 434, 452, 466, 475
Ting, W., 303
Tixier, Maud, 27, 36
Tongberg, R. C., 258, 279
Tordjmann, André, 336
Townsend, P. L., 219, 221
Traoré Sérié, Régina, 426
Triandis, Harry C., 61–2, 67, 97, 400, 408–9, 428
Tull, Donald S., 260–1
Tuncalp, Secil, 145, 148, 165
Tung, Rosalie L., 411, 428, 435–6, 439, 449, 452
Turcq, Dominique, 243, 307, 311, 339, 449
Turpin, Dominique, 243, 337
Tylor, Edward, 41, 62

Ueda Keiko, 104, 130
Ungerer, Herbert, 355, 388
Urban, Christine D., 171, 192
Usunier, Jean-Claude, 72, 95, 97, 116, 142–3, 164, 169–70, 177–9, 193, 199, 208–10, 221, 249, 256, 278–9, 289, 304, 307, 311, 339, 391, 397, 410, 420, 424, 428, 434, 452–3, 462, 468, 476

Vahlne, J. E., 204, 220
Valette-Florence, Pierre, 198–9, 221
Valla, Jean-Paul, 279
Van Gent, Aart P., 387
Van Raaij, W. F., 12, 19, 37, 133, 137, 148, 165, 175, 193
Van Zandt, H. R., 405, 428, 449, 452
Vandenbergh, Bruce, 264–5, 279
Verbeke, Alain, 193, 388
Verhage, Bronislaw, 136, 161, 164
Verma, Y. S., 229, 247
Verna, Gérard, 297, 303–4, 474–6
Vernon, Raymond P., 204, 221
Verzariu, P., 302
Vestergaard, Harald, 219
Vidal, Florence, 337
Von Stackelberg, H., 24, 37

Wadinambiaratchi, G., 229, 247
Wagner, J., 255–8, 277
Walker, Bruce J., 251, 277
Walsh, Len, 84
Walter, Ingo, 473–6
Walters, P. G. P., 171, 180, 192
Walton, Richard E., 403, 429
Wang, Chih-Kang, 251, 258, 279
Warrington, M. B., 35, 303, 424, 428, 449, 451
Warwick, Donald P., 163, 451
Watson Dunn, S., 388

Watzlawick, Paul, 108, 130
Wayne-Saegaert, M., 165
Weber, Max, 291, 304
Weeks, William H., 54–5, 62, 88, 97, 125–6, 446
Weigand, Robert E., 294, 304, 309–11, 339
Weiss, Stephen E., 424, 437, 452
Weitz, B., 405, 429
Wells, William, 385
Welt, L. G. B., 302
Werner, O., 139, 142–3, 163
Wesley, John, 291
Weyer, E. M., 451
Wheeler, Colin, 35, 424
White, Gregory P., 259, 276
White, John, 257, 278
White, Phillip D., 133, 136, 139, 147, 163, 257, 276, 279
Whitehill, Artur M., 449
Whitelock, J. M., 200, 221
Whiting, J. W. M., 133, 165
Whorf, Benjamin Lee, 41–2, 98–101
Wildt, A. R., 251, 279
Williamson, Oliver E., 398, 429
Wills, James R., 343, 388
Wilson, David T., 428
Wind, Yoram, 141, 144, 165, 169, 180, 193, 200, 221
Winski, J. M., 360, 387
Woods, Walter A., 173, 193
Woronoff, Jon, 308, 312–4, 338
Worthley, Reginald, 247

Xardel, Dominique, 111, 117, 130, 476

Yang, Chung-Fang, 16–17, 19, 37
Yang, K. S., 37
Yaprak, Attila, 135, 164, 252, 260, 278–80
Yau, Oliver H. M., 16, 37
Yavas, Ugur, 252, 280, 387
Yong, Mahealani, 92, 127–8
Yoshimori, Masaru, 266–7, 270, 280
Yoshino, Michael Y., 307, 312, 339
Young, Stephen, 35, 424
Youssef, Fahti, 105, 129

Zaharna, R. S., 111–12, 130
Zaichkowsky, Judith L., 172, 193, 436–7, 451
Zaidi, S. M., 142, 165
Zaltman, Gerald, 220
Zax, M., 146, 165
Zeithaml, Carl P., 212, 221
Zeithaml, Valarie, 212, 221, 288–9, 304
Zeldin, Theodore, 409
Zeller, Eric, 310
Zerubavel, E., 431, 452
Ziegler, Jean, 463, 474, 476

Subject index

Academic journals (in international marketing), 13, 34
Act of God, 102, 109
Adaptation to climate, 224–6, 228
Advertiser-agency relationships, 341, 359–60
Advertising agencies, 358–62
Advertising expenses per capita, 350
Advertising legislation, 25–6,
Advertising standardization, 184
Advertising textbooks, 385
Africa, advertising, 171, 348, 366–75
  consumer behaviour, 285
  culture, 61, 77, 411–14
  negotiation style, 442–3
Agency contract, 453, 458–60
Algeria, 253, 396
Amae, 312
American Way of Life, 478
Anglo-Saxon, 26, 72, 80, 95, 99–100, 106, 208, 232,
  323, 358, 421, 430–1,
Anti-trust legislation, 23
Arabs, 82, 92–4, 96, 103, 127–8, 138, 232, 341,
  358, 372, 405–6, 413, 441–2
Arbitrage, 294, 302
Argentina, 76, 471–3
Armenians, 86, 107, 358, 441, 478
Asia, 16–20, 189, 413–14, 436, 438
Attitude towards action, 67–73, 99–100
Australia, 76, 172, 258, 325, 345–6, 350, 366
Austria, 75–6, 104, 172, 260, 325, 355
Azerbaidjan, 86

Back-translation, 142–3
Backsheesh (size), 454–6
Bahrain, 252
Bali, 91
Bantu (People), 115–16, 348, 433, 435, 477
Barbados, 172
Bargaining, 283–6, 302
Belgium, 76, 80, 172, 299–300, 344
Body gestures, 105–7

Bolivia, 148
Brand image, 248–51, 270–2
Brand loyalty, 18–19, 34
Brand names, 332, 357, 376–8
Brand, *see also* trademark
  linguistic connotations of, 264–5
  functions of the, 266–7
  global, 269–70
  international, 262–3, 268–9, 270–2
Brazil, 76, 366, 448–9
  consumer behaviour, 171, 232, 471–3
  Made in Brazil, 254, 259
  negotiation style, 406
Bribery, 453–74
Brown paper packet, 473
  see also bribery
Bulgaria, 106, 203, 250, 384–5
Buy National campaigns, 255–6
Buyer–seller relationships, 27–9, 268–9, 270–2

Cameroon, 115, 226
Canada, advertising, 345, 350
  consumer behaviour, 134, 172–3
  culture, 104
  made in, 253
  management style, 76
  negotiation style, 412
  sales promotion, 325
Cartesian logic, 409
Cassis de Dijon ruling, 245
Catholic, 33, 86, 207, 220, 290–1, 449
Chile, 76, 172, 322
China, consumer behaviour, 16–17, 172, 231–3
  cognitive style, 20
  culture, 33, 449
  management style, 80
  Made in China, 254
  negotiation style, 406, 411, 414–15, 435, 438
Clan, *see* Group membership
Code Law, 409

Cognitive, processes, 96
    styles, 19–20, 34, 70–3
Collectivism, 16, 66, 69–70, 74–8, 94, 319–22
Colloquial speech, 160–1
Colombia, 76, 172
Colonization, 60–1, 96, 450
Colours (cultural meaning of), 230–3
Commerce, 4, 209–12
Commercial continuity, 316
Common Law, 409
Common sense, 94
Communication
    and context, 102–5, 129, 458
    instrumental, 403, 410, 422
    interpersonal, 78–9, 123–5
Comparative advantage (law of), 1–2, 478–9
Comparative advertising, 344
Comparative law, 450
Competencies (cultural relativity of), 52
Competition,
    avoidance, 23–4
    brand, 267–8
    international, 178, 365
    globalization of, 177–9
Competitions (sales promotion), 306, 323–5
Conceptual equivalence, 133, 136–8, 346
Constructs, 161
Consumer behaviour, 18–20, 261–2
Consumer
    cultural resistance of the, 175–7
    dissatisfaction, 26, 136–7, 161, 211–12
    ethnocentrism, 255
    involvement, 19
    world, 170,
Consumerism, 26, 343
Contextual equivalence, 133
Copts, 441
Copy strategy, 341, 355–6
Corn Laws, 2
Corporate culture, 74, 79–81
Corporate image, 362
Cost-volume relationships, 195–6
Costa Rica, 76
Costs, 292, 302
Counterfeiting, 96
Country of origin images, 250–62, 272–5
Courteousy bias, 145
Credibility
    of brands, 268
    collective, 398, 401–2
    personal, 393, 399–401
Critical incidents, 54–5, 88–92, 121–3, 301, 335–6,
    379–83
Cross-border cultures, 48
Cross-cultural, 35, 131–3, 425
Crusades, 82
Cuba, 259, 400
Cultural Affinity
    classes, 207, 209–10, 219
    zones, 207–9, 358

Cultural assumptions, 63–7, 79–81
Cultural borrowing, 12–15, 81–5, 101
Cultural consumption, 176, 205
Cultural hostility, 85–8
Cultural identification, 108, 206–7
Cultural identity , 2–5, 44, 111
Cultural resistance, 175–7, 353
Cultural violence, 479
Culture
    and consumer behaviour, 15–20
    and nationality, 40, 46–50
    and perceptions, 52, 61
    definitions of, 39–40
    elements of, 41–4
Culture Shock, 111–113
Culture-free, 170
Custom duties, 179, 296

Data collection, 133, 143–6
Decentring, 143
Decision-making process, 29–30, 68–9, 408, 419
Delivery dates, 72, 331, 446–8
Denmark, 76, 80, 205, 325
Developing countries, 136, 183–4, 350
Directeur commercial, 12–13
Distribution,
    channels, 210–1, 336
    choice of foreign distribution channels, 315–16
    exclusive distribution agreements, 295–6, 303
    Japanese, 306–15
    store and country images, 261, 275
Distributive orientation, 403–7, 425
DPP0 (*Direction participative par objectifs*), 77–8
Dual concern model, 425
Dumping, 292–4, 302

Eastern Europe, 409
Eating habits, 18, 246, 327–8
Economic development (marketing and), 176
Economicity of time, 431–5, 448–9
Economies of scale, 177, 197
Economies of scope, 196
Ecuador, 76
Educational practices, 51–2
EEC (European Economic Community), 179, 198–9,
    245, 303, 344, 355–6, 386
EFTA (European Free Trade Association), 7, 245
Egypt,
    business ethics, 464
    culture, 77, 105
    marketing management, 12
    negotiation style, 412
Emic, 135, 141
Empathy (international), 113
Equivalence,
    cross-cultural, 132–3, 160
    measurement, 139
    translation, 141–3, 346
Eritreans, 47, 478
Eskimos, 101

Ethiopia, 77, 368
Ethnocentrism, 108–10, 121, 200–1, 231, 255, 302, 477
Etic, 135, 141
Euro-Brands, 182
Europe,
    culture, 44, 108, 198–9, 205, 208, 430–2, 450
    internal market, 4, 7, 179
European audience, 347, 354–6
European consumer, 182, 198–200
European Economic Space, 7
European Patent, 275
Exchange rates, 139, 283
Expatriates, 11, 246
Experience curve, 219
Experience effects, 177, 195–6
Experiential equivalence, 133
Extended family, 16–17, 138
Extrinsic rewards, 321–2

Familism, 17
Fatalism, 49, 65, 91, 126–7
FCPA (Foreign Corrupt Practices Act), 463–5, 468
Feminity, 66, 74–7, 129, 320
Finland, 76, 172, 254
Food and Drug Administration (FDA), 175
Force Majeure, 102, 129
Foreign exchange controls, 296–7, 303
France,
    advertising, 343–8, 350–1, 356–9, 380–1
    business ethics, 381–3
    consumer behaviour, 171–2, 198, 228, 232, 244, 477
    culture, 75, 96, 103, 108, 112–13, 127, 320, 409, 448
    management style, 76–80, 91–2, 337
    market research, 139–40
    Made in France, 236–9, 242, 250–7, 260
    marketing management, 14–15, 121–3, 196, 267, 337
    negotiation style, 408–10, 426, 437
    sales promotion, 323, 325
Franchise, 326–9
Friendship, 95, 109, 285, 438, 440
Functional equivalence, 133, 139
Future orientation, 65, 138, 431–2

GATT (General Agreement on Tariffs and Trade), 177–9
Gaï-Jin, 308, 311
Geocentrism, 200–1, 302
Germany,
    advertising, 344–7, 350–1, 356–7
    business ethics, 455, 464–5
    competition, 23–4
    consumer behaviour, 172, 198, 232–3, 477
    culture, 83, 95, 103–4, 448
    Made in Germany, 239, 250–7
    management style, 76–9
    marketing management, 314, 320

negotiation style, 120–1, 426, 440
    sales promotion, 325
    selling style, 28
    technical standards, 224–5
Ghana, 77, 232
Gifts (promotional), 306, 323, 325
Glasnost, 401
Global advertising campaigns, 360–1
Global brands, 173–4
Global marketing, 187–8, 194
Global media, 352–3
Global strategy, 194, 200–5, 216, 479
Globalization, 169–88, 194–7, 477–8
    of demand, 170–7
Grammatical equivalence, 133
Great Britain,
    advertising, 350, 356–7, 359, 365
    consumer behaviour, 131, 172, 174, 198
    culture, 76, 96, 103–5
    Made in Britain, 252, 254, 256–7
    management style, 78–80
    marketing management, 299, 315
    negotiation style, 426, 441
    sales promotion, 323, 325
    selling style, 28
Greece, 76, 106, 198, 357
Greeting cards, 149–56, 161
Grey markets, 303

Hard Sell approach, 28,
Harvard Business School (Teaching materials), 424
HCCD (Highest Common Cultural Denominator), 205
Hierarchy of needs, 15–16, 34, 75
Hierarchy, 43–4, 73–80
Hinduism, 220
Hiragana, 85,
Hispanics, 151–6, 357–8
Home country rule, 245
Honduras, 455
Hong Kong, 16, 76, 220, 325, 375
    made in, 253–4
Hopi Indians, 100, 102,
Hungary, 255
Hypermarkets, 205, 244, 267, 310, 316, 358

Icon, 229
Ideologism, 65, 93, 408–10
Idiomatic equivalence, 133
Immigrants, 87, 426
Implicit messages, 102–5
Implicit salary, 461
Import license, 297
In-group, *see* group membership
Incentives, 317–18
India: consumer behaviour, 232, 252
    culture, 67–8, 109
    Made in India, 250, 254, 259
    management style, 76
Indians (American), 45, 100

Individualism, 16, 66, 69–70, 74–8, 94, 319–22
Individuals (acculturation of), 39–40
Indonesia, 76, 80, 298
Industrial products (images of), 257
Inflation, 133, 137, 139
Informative advertising, 345–6
Insh'Allah, 91, 126–7
Instructor's manual, 7
Integrative orientation, 403–8, 425
Intercultural communication, 108, 129
Intercultural marketing, 194–221, 479
Intercultural setting, 35, 425
International diffusion of innovations, 227
International trade, 1–2, 61, 128, 177–8
Interpreters, 114
Interviews, 145
Intracultural setting, 35
Intrinsic rewards, 321–2
Involvement (consumer), 19, 34
IQ tests, 86
Iran, 76, 252, 254, 464
Iraq, 77
Ireland, 76, 243, 355
Islam, 106, 138, 348–50, 441–3
Islamic law, 450
Israel, 76, 94, 257
Italy,
    advertising, 344, 346, 356, 380–1
    business ethics, 455
    consumer behaviour, 132, 182, 198, 228
    culture, 83, 87–88, 103
    Made in Italy, 250–1, 253, 257
    management style, 76, 80, 337, 446–8
    marketing management, 21–2, 330–5
    sales promotion, 323
    selling style, 28
Ivory Coast, 232, 426

Jamaica, 76
Japan bashing, 426
Japan,
    advertising, 35, 350, 359, 364–5, 386
    business ethics, 455
    competition, 23–4, 35, 178, 196, 203, 316
    consumer behaviour, 21, 171, 189, 232–3, 237
    culture, 81, 83, 86, 95, 106–7, 205, 246, 312,
        337, 449
    distribution, 306–14, 326–7, 337
    language and communication, 84–5, 103–4, 241
    Made in Japan, 239, 252–4, 257, 259
    management style, 76, 80, 91–2, 449
    market research, 14, 131
    marketing management, 13, 267, 320
    negotiation style, 117–18, 396–7, 405–8, 411,
        414, 435–7
    sales promotion, 325
    technical standards, 238–41
John Wayne Style, 406, 439
Joint ventures, 391–2, 424, 448

Kamei, 267
Kanban, 309
Kanji, 84–5, 246
Katagana, 85, 246
Keiretsu, 268, 305–13, 393
Kenya, 77, 106, 232, 386, 372
Kikuyus, 106
Knödel, 358
Koran, 68, 349
Kultur, 39
Kurds, 47, 478
Kuwait, 77, 343

Language, 41–2, 83–5, 93, 98–109, 114–16, 146,
    262–6, 346, 368–9, 441
Latin Americans, 103–4, 109, 365
Latin Europe, 291, 358
Latins, 26, 72, 93, 95, 105, 434
Law of one price, 283, 301
Learning, 204, 259, 478
Lebanon, 77, 95
Legal systems, 25–6, 409–10, 413–14, 474
Legal violence, 474
Lexical equivalence, 133
Libya, 77
Liechtenstein, 455
Life insurance, 138, 341
Life-styles, 220, 340
Litigation, 121, 410–14
Logistics (of international trade), 331–2
Logo, 264
Long-term orientation, 268, 436
Lotharingian Europe, 208
Lotteries, 306, 323
Loyalty, 18–19, 438
Luxemburg, 455–6

MBO (Management by Objectives), 77–8
Madagascar, 413
Made in label, 249–62
Madrid Agreement, 270
Malaysia, 54, 76, 106, 220, 443–6
Management of marketing communications, 340–1
Market research, 131
    cross-cultural, 131–62
Marketing mix, 215, 245
Maronites, 441
Masculinity, 66, 74–7, 129, 320
Mastery over nature, 65
Mauritania, 285, 449
Measurement reliability, 161
Media availability, 350–1
Media Planning, 341
Meiji Era, 81
Membership group, 64, 407, 414, 443, 462
Mercatique, 83
Meta-communication, 20, 107–8
Metalanguage, 20
Metaphysical world, 45–6, 60
Metempsychosis, 93

Methodism, 291
Mexico, 28, 45, 60, 76, 172, 232, 256, 259, 272–5, 345, 347, 351, 455, 468–70
Middle East,
    advertising, 366, 372
    business ethics, 464–5
    culture, 103–4, 109
    negotiation style, 285, 405–7, 410, 412, 441–3
Misunderstandings (cultural), 108, 113–14
MNCs (multinational companies), 80–1, 170, 182–3, 273
Modal personality, 49–50
Monochronism, 64, 431–4, 448
Monopoly, 24, 26
Monopsony, 26
Morocco, 366, 372, 449
Motivation, 73–5, 317–22
Multidomestic, 178, 185, 197
Multilingual persons, 101, 128–9
Muslims, 82, 96, 105, 138, 220, 341–2, 349, 413

Nation-state, 46, 479
National character, 49–51
Nationality (and culture), 46–50
Navajos Indians, 102.
Negotiation games, 399, 416–24, 443–6
Negotiation styles, 435–43
Negotiation textbooks, 424
Nestorians, 441
Netherlands,
    advertising, 346, 350, 356
    business ethics, 455
    consumer behaviour, 136, 172, 182, 477
    culture, 96
    management style, 76, 80
    sales promotion, 323
New Zealand, 76, 258, 350
Nigeria, 77, 85, 455
Non-tariff barriers, 177–9, 241, 296
Non-verbal communication, 105–7, 129
Northern Europe, 290–1, 320, 343, 409, 449
Norway, 75–6, 350, 381

OEM (Original Equipment Manufacturer), 270
Objectives of communication, 340–1
Oligopoly, 24
Oneiric style of advertising, 345–6
Oral agreement, 410–4
Oral behaviour, 95
Organizational structure, 78–9, 360–6
Organization of international advertising, 360–6
Out-group, *see* Group membership
Over- and under-invoicing, 296–8
Overlapping of media, 355–6

Packaging, 233
Pakistan, 76

Pan-European market segments, 357
Panama, 76
Paraguay, 455
Parallel imports, 294–6, 299–300
Paris Union, 269
Past orientation, 64, 431–2
Peace research, 94
Perceived potency, 400,
Perceived risk, 19, 253–4, 345,
Perestroïka, 401
Personalization, 64
Peru, 76
Philippines, 76, 220, 232, 253, 256
Pizza relativity, 246
Poetry, 68
Political risk, 472–3
Polycentrism, 200–1, 302
Polychronism, 64, 431–5, 448
Portugal, 1–2, 76, 129, 198, 356
Potential reality, 70–1, 94
Power distance, 74–8, 425
Pragmatism, 65, 93, 408–10, 442
Premiums, 323, 325
Present orientation, 65, 431–2
Price,
    declaring prices, 286–7
    manipulating prices, 292
Price-quality relationships, 288–90, 299
Problem solving, 80, 404–6
Procedural traditional time, 100, 433
Product adaptation, 222–7
Product life cycle (international), 204
Product standardization policy, 180–3, 214, 222–33
Production flexibility, 180–1
Protestants, 86, 207, 220, 290–1
Proxemics, 129
Psychographic variables, 132, 134, 210
Public relations, 385
Publiphobia, 343

Quality, 237–43, 288–90
Québecois, 134, 173
Questionnaire, 73, 80, 156–60

Racism, 85–7
Rationales for A3.3–5, 96
Rationality, 408, 414
Record industry, 206–8, 219
Regiocentrism, 200–1
Regional differences, 48, 134
Relational exchange, 301
Relational marketing, 392–5
Reliability (of a research instrument), 161
Representative communication, 403, 410, 422
Resale Price Maintenance, 303
Respondents, 144–6, 157–60
Response style, 145–6
Riba, 442

Ringi, 30
Rituals, 45, 55–9, 94, 285–6
Russia, 106

SRC (Self Reference Criterion), 110, 121, 231
Saint-Simonism, 342, 385
Sales calls, 333
Sales force, 305
  compensation systems, 321–2, 337
Sales objectives, 28, 318–19, 335–6
Sales promotion, 26, 214–15, 244, 306, 322–5,
    333–4, 337, 381–2
Salespeople, 27–9, 317–22, 424
Salvador (El), 76, 259
Samoa, 89
Sample,
  representativeness of, 146–8
  size, 148
Sampling equivalence, 133
Sampling unit, 144
Satellite television, 199, 208, 353–5
Saudi Arabia,
  advertising, 349–350
  business ethics, 454–6, 464, 468
  culture, 77, 92–4, 126–8, 348–50
  marketing management, 252, 317
  regulations, 138, 148
Scale (psychometry), 139–40, 260
Scale effects, 196
Scandinavia, 103, 323
Secrecy bias, 144
Segmentation of markets, 134, 205–9, 357–8
Self-concept, 66, 400
Selling styles, 27–8
Semantic differential, 139
Senegal, 463
Service attributes, 224, 227–9
Sex cultures, 47, 95, 206
Sex roles, 347
Sexual bias, 145
Sharia, 349
Shipping charges, 197
Sierra Leone, 77
Similarity hypothesis, 405
Singapore, 16, 76, 220, 232
Ski resorts
  competition, 197–8
  image of, 260, 275, 384–5
Slogans, 160–1, 346, 385
Social representations, 53–4, 283, 342
Socio-demographic variables, 209–10, 340–1
Soft sell approach, 27–8
Sogo-shosha (general trading company), 234, 236,
    314, 326
Somalia, 367–8, 372
Sophism, 33
South Africa, 76, 115
South Korea,
  consumer behaviour, 173, 233
  culture, 448

Made in South Korea, 159–60, 252, 254, 256–7
  management style, 76, 337
  marketing management, 270–2
  sales promotion, 325
South East Asia, 320
Soviet Union, 254, 400–1
Space (cultural language of), 66, 115–16, 129
Spain, 45, 60, 76, 103, 198, 228, 244, 301, 334–6,
    356, 366–75, 380–1
Sponsoring, 385
Sponsors, 442, 468
Standardized advertsing, 346, 362–6, 379–81
Standards
  international, 226
  technical, 224–5, 245–6, 302
Stereotypes, 28, 31–2, 83, 108–13
Strategy,
  international marketing, 179–84, 213–16
Sudan, 367
Sweden,
  advertising, 345, 350–1, 381
  culture, 75, 77, 121–3, 320, 449
  Made in Sweden, 254, 257
  marketing management, 213–16
Switzerland,
  advertising, 350, 355
  culture, 60, 103–4, 129
  Made in Switzerland, 250, 260
  management style, 60, 77, 337
  sales promotion, 324
  selling style, 28
Symbolic aspects of,
  colours, 230–3
  money, 442–3
Symbolic thinking, 31
Symbols, 45–6, 59, 230, 269
  definition of, 222, 229, 246

Taïwan, 77, 120, 220, 252, 259–60, 271
Tamil, 47
Tanzania, 77, 376–72, 386
Temporal equivalence, 133
Temporal orientations, 43, 65
Tender, 396–7
Territoriality, 43
Thailand, 77, 93, 148, 220, 319
Theory of climates, 50–1
Third World consumer, 176
Time (cultural patterns of), 64–5, 92–3, 95, 100,
    115–16, 128, 430–7, 446–9
Tokugawa era, 81
Trademark, 235, 264, 275
Trading company, *see Sogo–shosha*
Transaction costs, 302, 391–3
Translation, 141–3, 346
Transliteration, 266
Transportability, 197
Treaty of Rome, 303
Triad, 202, 359
Tribe, *see* Membership group

Trust, 393, 399–400, 410–14
Tunisia, 341
Turkey,
  advertising, 345, 350
  business ethics, 464
  consumer behaviour, 135
  culture, 77
  Made in Turkey, 253
Turnkey operations, 391–3, 396–7, 424, 426, 434, 454
TV programmes, 351, 354

Uganda, 369, 372, 386
Uncertainty avoidance, 65, 74, 129, 319–20, 440
United Arab Emirates, 77, 371
United States,
  advertising, 345–7, 350–4, 359
  brands, 171
  business ethics, 381–3, 453–5, 464–6, 468–73
  consumer behaviour, 134–6, 171–3, 175, 228, 232–3, 244
  culture, 75, 88, 93, 109, 126, 128, 246, 316, 319, 421, 430–2
  Made in the USA, 252–7, 259
  management style, 76–80, 92–3
  market research, 139–40, 149–56
  marketing management, 12–13, 83, 267, 326, 362–6
  negotiation style, 117–21, 405–9, 415, 426, 435, 438–40

  parallel imports, 294–5
  sales promotion, 323, 325
  technical standards, 226
Uruguay, 77, 455, 471

Validity, 137, 161
Value orientations, 93
Values, 61, 209,
  cultural, 63–70, 340–2
Veblen effect, 29
Venezuela, 77, 325, 455, 466,
Vietnam, 88
Visual illusions, 52

Walloon, 86
Weltanschauung, 431
Whorfian hypothesis, 42, 98–101, 128–9
Wishful thinking, 72, 95
World Intellectual Property Organization (WIPO), 270
World market share, 203
World production (growth of), 177
Written agreements, 410–14

Yea-saying, 144–5
Yugoslavia, 77, 172

Zaibatsus, 23, 314
Zaïre, 467
Zanzibar, 370, 386
Zapping, 351, 386